Mr. Republican

a biography of

Robert A. Taft

Portrait of Senator Robert A. Taft by Peter Phillippse
of Shelton, Connecticut, commissioned by the law firm
of Taft, Stettinius, and Hollister of Cincinnati.

Mr. Republican

a biography of

Robert A. Taft

JAMES T. PATTERSON

Illustrated with Photographs

HOUGHTON MIFFLIN COMPANY BOSTON

Third Printing

Copyright © 1972 by James T. Patterson.
ISBN: 0-395-13938-4
Library of Congress Catalog Card Number: 72-516
Printed in the United States of America

To Nancy

Preface

NOT LONG after William Howard Taft died in 1930, his son Robert Alphonso began looking seriously for a biographer. With other members of his family he considered many eminent historians before settling on Henry Pringle, the biographer of Theodore Roosevelt. It was in some ways a risky choice, for Pringle was a political liberal sympathetic to the New Deal. But the family had decided, and Bob Taft set about making the writer's task as easy as possible. Pringle got complete and sole access to the voluminous Taft papers, full cooperation from the family, and financial support. When he turned over his manuscript to the Tafts to read, many, Bob Taft included, often disagreed forcefully with it. But they stopped there, for they understood that Pringle's book had to be his own.

It is a mark of the sense of tradition within the family that when Robert Taft died in 1953, the next generation followed the same procedures. The family made sure that his papers, like his father's, were organized and deposited in the Library of Congress; it preserved trunks full of personal material in his home; it began seeking a biographer. This search moved slowly, however, and in 1967 the family had still settled on no one. At this point I approached the Tafts — they had never heard of me — and expressed my interest in doing the book. Perhaps because the Tafts were happy to find someone at last, they agreed, and I became an "authorized" biographer with the same indispensable cooperation (except for financial aid, which I did not want) that Pringle had enjoyed. When I finished the manuscript, I showed it to Robert, Jr., by then a United States senator. Like his father, he offered many suggestions, and like Pringle, I was free to accept some and reject others. It is possible that the family's intelligent attitude led me to see in Robert A. Taft admirable qualities which I might otherwise have missed. But if so, that is my doing, not the family's; the Tafts did not demand the change of a word in my manuscript.

After embarking on the research early in 1968, I had to decide what kind of biography to write. I rejected first the idea of trying to be "definitive." Such books are too often fact-ridden, unventuresome, and dull; and they tell most readers more than they want to know. Because Taft left behind him some 1400 boxes of papers, a "definitive" work would have run to two or three lengthy volumes. And because he has been dead less than twenty years, it is early to pretend to define his place in history.

Yet this book is presumptuous in two other ways. First, it tries to probe Taft's character as well as his career; it is therefore more ambitious than the genre known as political biography. Second, it offers judgments and interpretations frequently and explicitly. Taft usually tried to state his views so that people knew where he stood; I feel it a historian's obligation, indeed necessity, to do the same. In these two regards this is at times an immodest biography.

I can hardly count all the people who helped me. Grants from the John Simon Guggenheim Foundation and the National Endowment for the Humanities gave me a year and a half to devote to research and writing. Mrs. Betty Neal and Mrs. Penny Archer were my excellent typists through many drafts. Robert Miller, librarian of Indiana University, provided me with essential office space for a year, and Mrs. Nancy Cridland, history liaison librarian at Indiana, frequently helped me find scarce materials. Robert Smith, a graduate student at Indiana, proved an able research assistant. Mrs. Elizabeth Mason of the oral history research office at Columbia University was enormously helpful, as were Harry Jeffrey, Jr., and John T. Mason, Jr., who did much of the interviewing for the Robert Taft oral history collection there. Drs. Johnson McGuire and Charles M. Barrett of Cincinnati and Frank Glenn of New York took time to talk to me concerning Taft's medical history and to read the relevant portions of my drafts. And the following archivists were especially gracious: Kermit Pike of the Western Reserve Historical Society; Philip Lagerquist and Philip

Brooks of the Harry Truman Library; John Wickman of the Eisenhower Library; Robert Wood of the Herbert Hoover Library in West Branch, Iowa; Mrs. Erika Chadbourn of the Harvard University Law School Library; Judith Schiff of the Yale University Archives; Henry Stearns, archivist at Taft School; Conrad Weitzel of the Ohio Historical Society; Elfrieda Lang of the Lilly Library at Indiana University; Ben Bowman and Robert Volz of the University of Rochester Library; and John Broderick and Paul Heffron of the manuscripts division of the Library of Congress.

Many of Taft's friends or their descendants were kind enough to let me look at personal papers. These included Blanche O'Berg, his personal secretary; Mrs. I. Jack Martin, widow of his key senate aide; Gordon Grayson, stepson of George Harrison, his college friend and best man; Mrs. Lillian Dykstra, one of Mrs. Robert Taft's close friends; Mr. and Mrs. Stanley Rowe, personal friends of the Tafts from Cincinnati; L. Richard Guylay, his public relations director; John Hollister, Taft's law partner; and the late Thomas E. Dewey. Reed Coleman of Madison, Wisconsin, granted me special access to the papers of his father, Thomas Coleman, one of Taft's major advisers in 1952. I am especially indebted to Mrs. Darrah Wunder of Cincinnati, who became Mrs. Taft's companion in 1950 and after 1952, and to Paul Walter, a long-time Taft aide from Cleveland. Each spent many hours talking with me, sending me materials, and letting me have access to personal papers. And of course I thank the following Tafts: Robert's sons, William (and his wife Barbara), Robert, Jr., Lloyd, and Horace; his brother Charles; and his sister Helen Taft Manning.

Students who read parts or all of the drafts included Indiana undergraduates Richard Sanders, Robert Schuckman, and Edward Kleckley, and graduates Brian Cass, Robert Smith, and especially Peter Curtis, a very perceptive critic. Charles Brown, a graduate student at the University of Missouri, proved a rigorous critic of sections on housing and education. Professors Elmus Wicker and Fred Witney of the Indiana University economics department graciously read portions on international monetary matters and the Taft-Hartley Act, respectively. Professor Alton Lee of the University of South Dakota, and Thomas Shroyer, a Washington, D.C., attorney who was one of the draftsmen for the Taft-Hartley

Act, also read the sections on labor policy, as did J. Mack Swigert of Cincinnati, one of Taft's advisers for the law. Professors Frank Freidel of Harvard University, William Leuchtenburg of Columbia, Richard Kirkendall of Missouri, Justus Doenecke of New College, Gary Reichard of Ohio State, and William Baughin of the University of Cincinnati ably criticized portions of the manuscript. Professor Don Bennett of the Indiana University geography department and his wife Joan assisted me with my section on the Philippines. My friends Townsend Ludington, professor of English at the University of North Carolina, Chapel Hill, and his wife Jane offered very useful criticisms of the early chapters, as did Dr. Alexander Martin, a psychiatrist from New York and Old Lyme, Connecticut; Professor Leon Levy of the psychology department at Indiana; and Gates Agnew, professor of English at Indiana. My parents, J. Tyler and Sarah Patterson of Old Lyme, read the entire manuscript for me.

History department colleagues at Indiana also criticized portions of my drafts. These included David Pletcher; Chase Mooney; Philip West; Gerald Strauss; Alexander Rabinowitch; John Thompson; Irene Neu; John Wiltz; and George Flynn, who is now at the University of Miami. The following historians who criticized the entire manuscript deserve special thanks: George Juergens of Indiana; Thomas Buckley, now at the University of Tulsa; Richard Davies of Northern Arizona; Barton Bernstein of Stanford; David Burner of the State University of New York at Stony Brook; and William Miller, professor of religion and political science at Indiana. My editors at Houghton Mifflin, Richard McAdoo and Craig Wylie, gave me thorough criticism which greatly improved the book.

Among the scholars who led me to useful sources or who shared their ideas with me are Selig Adler of the State University of New York at Buffalo; Henry W. Berger of Washington University; James MacGregor Burns of Williams College; Wayne Cole of the University of Maryland; Harl Dalstrom of the University of Nebraska at Omaha; Richard Fried of Fairmont State College; Robert Griffith of the University of Massachusetts; James Jones, a graduate student in history at Indiana University; Ronald Lora of the University of Toledo; Donald McCoy of the University of

Kansas; Justus Paul of the University of Wisconsin at Stevens Point; Stanley Solvick of Wayne State University; and Athan Theoharis of Marquette University. W. C. Mullendore, author of the official history of the United States Food Administration, kindly sent me photographs, and L. D. Warren, cartoonist for the Cincinnati *Enquirer,* provided me with cartoons.

My wife, Nancy, was the indispensable one. She read my drafts, criticized them, accompanied me on some of my travels, took care of Steve and Marnie, and lived cheerfully under the strain of helping me write a book like this one. Thanks to her, the five years of doing this book have been the most satisfying of my life.

J.T.P.

Bloomington, Indiana
March 1972

Contents

Illustrations

Frontispiece: Portrait of Senator Robert A. Taft by Peter Phillippse of Shelton, Connecticut, commissioned by the law firm of Taft, Stettinius, and Hollister of Cincinnati

following page 496

Robert A. Taft. *Robert Taft Papers, Library of Congress*

Robert Taft's birthplace, East McMillan Street, Cincinnati. *Charles P. Taft, 2nd, Papers, Cincinnati*

Bobby, approximately one year old. *Robert Taft Papers, Library of Congress*

Helen Herron Taft, Bob's mother, c. 1905. *Charles P. Taft, 2nd, Papers, Cincinnati*

Charles P. Taft, Bob's uncle, and William Howard Taft, c. 1907. *Library of Congress*

The Taft Family, c. 1909. *Library of Congress*

Martha Bowers Taft, 1914. *Robert Taft Papers, Library of Congress*

Taft as Ohio legislator, 1923. *United Press International Photo*

Three generations. *Robert Taft Papers, Library of Congress*

Taft in Washington for his father's funeral, 1930. *United Press International Photo*

The Taft home, Sky Farm, Indian Hill, Ohio. *Robert Taft Papers, Library of Congress*

The Taft family, late 1940's. *Robert Taft Papers, Library of Congress*

*Several political cartoons
appear with the text*

PART I

The Search for Self

CHAPTER 1

A Striving Boy

THREE MILES before reaching the center of Cincinnati, the Ohio River, muddy and meandering, curves gracefully to the south before resuming its lengthy course into the Mississippi. Along the bend, steep bluffs spring up from the northern shore, offering the suburban citizens of Walnut Hills sweeping vistas of green Kentucky countryside. One of the loveliest views belonged to William Howard Taft, who moved his bride into a new house on East McMillan Street in 1886. The roomy Victorian structure rested on a hill, and the young couple prized the scrolled porches, colored-glass windows, gables, and turrets, fashionable in the 1880's. From one side of the house the Tafts looked out library windows at the dark green of a forest. Their world was quiet, sedate, and secure.

Twice since their marriage Will Taft and Helen — Nellie, everyone called her — had sailed to Europe to explore the cathedrals of England, the shops of Paris, the grandeur of Rome and Florence. But they stayed home in 1889, for Nellie was expecting her first child in September. On Sunday the eighth she awoke with warning symptoms, and Will called the doctor. A friend brought a nurse, and Nellie's mother hurried over to be on hand. Undeterred, Nellie went on with household duties, but after lunch labor began in earnest, and an eight-pound boy arrived before five in the afternoon. "It was of course a new experience for me," Will wrote his father the next day, "and I never before realized the excruciating agony which must be undergone to bring into the world a human being. It is awful . . . Nellie stood the pain bravely and the compensation came in the ecstatic joy she had when the pain was over and she knew that the boy had arrived in good shape." The baby, said the proud father, "is said to be a remarkable child. He has a large head, and Nellie rather thinks that his hands and feet are like those of his Uncle Horace. I am obliged to give my judgment for those, *nemine contradicente,* who contend that the boy is one of the most remarkable products of this century." [1] Will wanted to name the boy after his own father Alphonso, but Nellie thought otherwise. They compromised on Robert Alphonso Taft.

.

The Tafts were among the fortunate in 1889. As Nellie smiled at her first-born, a fight broke out in Wilmington, Delaware, between gangs of Italians, Poles, and Slovaks, and a man was pummeled to death. In St. Louis a mob overpowered a sheriff, seized a seventeen-year-old Negro boy accused of assaulting a white girl, and hanged him from the courthouse window. On the Plains and in the South impoverished farmers were cursing the capitalists. One of their spokesmen, William Jennings Bryan of Nebraska, was launching a spectacular political career that was to bring him three Democratic presidential nominations. He lost the elections each time to Ohioans: twice to William McKinley, the last time to William Howard Taft. And to the southwest of the home on McMillan Street lay Cincinnati proper — sooty, dirty, packed with almost 300,000 people. Patrolling the teeming neighborhoods of the West End were scores of noisy scissors grinders, ragmen, and street-corner vendors selling smut, pretzels, and patent medicines. The foreign born had thronged to Cincinnati, and north of downtown lay the most heavily German section — Over the Rhine, it was called. Here and elsewhere were the odor of sawdust and stale beer, the sound of music drifting from the saloons, the excitement of vaudeville and minstrel shows, and the temptations offered by prostitutes who plied their trade throughout the city. Disease lurked in the alleys, and officials plastered red and yellow posters of quarantine on dingy homes.[2] Presiding carelessly over these thousands was a tight Republican machine, which Will Taft alternately courted and snubbed during his odyssey to the presidency in 1909 and which his son supported loyally in his own career a generation later.

William Howard Taft knew something of this world — from a distance. In 1889 at thirty-two years of age, he was already a superior court judge. When Bob ("Bobbie," they called him then) was four months old, Taft had to decide a case involving a secondary boycott by local bricklayers. His decision against the workers attracted national attention and fastened to him an undeserved antilabor reputation. A month later, in February 1890, President Benjamin Harrison named him solicitor general, and the Taft family moved to Washington for two years. In March 1892 Taft became a judge of the United States Court of Appeals for the Sixth Circuit and returned to Cincinnati.

Labor strife again intruded on the court. In 1894 the American Railway Union threw terror into the hearts of men of property by striking against the Pullman Company. A court injunction forbade the stoppage, but violence exploded between federal troops, sent ostensibly to keep the mails moving, and the strikers. Chicago, scene of the bloodletting, seemed in the grip of revolution, and "respectable" people shuddered. "The Chicago situation is not much improved," Taft wrote. "They have only killed six of the mob as yet. This is hardly enough to make an impression." [3] Taft then presided at the trial of a union leader who had come to Cincinnati to direct the local strike and sentenced him to six months in jail for contempt. Thus was Cincinnati "saved" from anarchism, and the strikers filed sullenly back to work.

Judge Taft also knew something of the capitalists. And he did not offer them much sympathy. For years the Rockefellers, the Harrimans, and the Morgans had been amassing huge fortunes while transforming the nation in a fury of economic expansion and industrialization. Entrepreneurs in Cincinnati, the proud "Queen City of the West," had watched newer industrial centers — Pittsburgh, Chicago, Cleveland — spring past it in population and had seen the ever more gigantic corporations swallow up small businesses. In 1890 Congress passed the Sherman Act to halt the monopolies, but court decisions in the next few years destroyed its effectiveness. Dismayed, Judge Taft reversed this judicial trend in 1898 by ordering dissolution of a combination of six corporations engaged in the manufacture and sale of cast-iron pipe. [4] Taft's decision, upheld unanimously by the Supreme Court, breathed vigor

into the Sherman law and paved the way for a series of prose-
cutions that he was to demand as President eleven years later.
Walnut Hills was far removed from the soot of the Cincinnati riverfront, the circuit bench a distant haven from the fearless pecula-
tions of the boardroom and the sweat of the rail yards. Judge Taft,
nonetheless, had plunged into the maelstrom.

But not Bobbie. When his parents returned to Cincinnati from
Washington in 1892, they let out their Walnut Hills home and
rented a comfortable house on the northeast corner of Third and
Lawrence streets, only two blocks from the river. Though their
new neighborhood lay but a few streets east of the downtown business district, it was the most fashionable of the city. It also placed
Will within walking distance of his office and Nellie close to her
parents' Pike Street house. On Pike Street, too, lived Will's half-
brother Charley in a gracious white mansion which later became
the Taft Museum, one of the city's most beautiful landmarks.[5]
Bobbie's was a small boy's world in which beaming aunts and dignified uncles — Nellie had seven brothers and sisters, Will four —
were always stopping by to call and to stay for dinner. It was also
an existence in which family ties always mattered above almost
everything else.

It was a world, too, of ceaseless activity. Bobbie and his playmates, sons and daughters of families like his own, marveled at the
well-groomed horses and shiny wagons in the firehouse across
the street from his home, and they raced to the sidewalk when the
clanging of bells announced that the horses would soon come clat-
tering out onto the street. The children thrilled to the sound of
the *Island Queen,* calliope screaming, as it churned to and from
Coney Island, the city's amusement park. Above all, they were attracted to the river. Sometimes after the thaws of early spring it
cascaded over its banks and destroyed tenements in the low-lying
areas of the city further west. Most of the time, however, it flowed
serenely on, and for Bobbie and his playmates it was the source of
endless fascination.

In 1898 when Bob was eight years old, his parents moved again,
this time to a large house which they rented on Madison Road east
of Annwood Avenue in East Walnut Hills. This was a quiet
neighborhood as fashionable as nearby McMillan Street, where

Bobbie had been born. Nearby was the imposing estate of M. E. Ingalls, president of the Chesapeake and Ohio and other railroads. His son Albert and daughter-in-law Jane Taft Ingalls, Charley's daughter, were to have a son, David Ingalls, who later served his cousin Bob Taft as a close adviser and friend. Nearby, too, was the home of Will's Yale classmate, Judge Howard C. Hollister, whose sons Howard and John became Bob's most frequent playmates. John was to help Bob found their law firm in 1924. The environs of Madison Road were more rural than those to which Bob had become accustomed in the East End, and the Hollisters even kept cattle grazing on their property. Bob had to forgo the pleasures of the river, for tough boys who lived in shacks along the bank threw rocks at the well-dressed children who descended the hill to invade their turf. But Bob still had plenty to do. He and his friends tramped along dirt roads and across the fields to school. They competed at kick-the-wicket, swung from wild grapevines in the nearby woods, and chased each other through the trees at games of cowboy-and-Indian and hide-and-seek. On rainy days they stayed warm in their rambling houses and played Parcheesi. It was simple, too, for Bob to accompany his mother on visits to friends and relatives on Pike Street, because electric streetcars now ran in the middle of Madison Road down the hills and into the city.[6]

Bob's two years in these suburban surroundings meant new friends but little change in his easy, comfortable style of life. Judge Taft's starting salary in 1892 was only $6000 a year, and he never grew rich. But his wealthy brother Charley often helped, and Nellie proved a frugal housewife. Always there were substantial furnishings, roasts of meat for dinner, abundant space permitting privacy. Always Bobbie had governesses, as did his sister Helen, born in 1891, and Charlie, who completed the family circle in 1897. Always there were maids and handymen because the Taft houses were large and because the father, traveling the circuit court from Michigan to Tennessee, was often far away. Occasionally there was Sunday school, and at night "Now I Lay Me Down to Sleep" and perhaps the Lord's Prayer. Little else, for Will was a Unitarian, Nellie an Episcopalian, and neither very devout. Children behaved respectfully, learned to say please and thank you, spoke when spoken to, held their tongues in the presence of adults. But Mamma was always there when needed, the rules reasonable, the tempo of life measured.

In the summers they went to Murray Bay. The Tafts first visited this small French Canadian town a hundred miles northeast of Quebec city in the summer of 1892. They were enchanted with its fresh, clean air — so crisp that one often needed blankets and a fire at night. And they were charmed by the majestic St. Lawrence River, fifteen miles wide at this point. Steep hills rose from the northern shore, and the summer homes spaced along them enjoyed magnificent views of the rolling green hills of Quebec. At first the Tafts rented cottages; then they bought a small frame house with gable windows jutting from a shingled roof. It was set quietly in a grove of fragrant pines. In the morning Will liked to sit on the porch, eat steak and drink cup after cup of coffee, and relax to the flow of the river. Over the years relatives arrived, for other Tafts also discovered Murray Bay. Eventually Will and Nellie had thirteen grandchildren, and the cottage became a rambling house of fifteen bedrooms and nine baths before it burned down in the spring of 1952.

In Bob's boyhood and through the years until his death, Murray Bay was the special haven. Here his mother moved for long, restful summers, and here his father, escaping the grind of the circuit, joined the family for weeks without interruption. Here Bob learned to play golf, whacking the ball around the crude local course with his father, uncles, and cousins. Here he discovered how to fish and explored the pleasures of the wild on camping trips far into the Laurentian wilderness. And here he joined the many relatives who, by congregating annually, maintained the primacy of family in his life. Always in later years he yearned to escape the soggy heat of Cincinnati and Washington for the invigorating air and unpretentious friendships of Murray Bay.[7]

·

It was, then, the good life — the carefree days of early childhood in a home full of love and affection, of easy circumstances, of security. Bob belonged; no one threatened him. But there was more to it, for the Tafts were special people, who were becoming as nearly a political dynasty as any American family save the Adamses or in later years the Roosevelts and the Kennedys. His mother, too, was a strong-minded, unusual woman. The result was an upbringing that was stable yet demanding, happy yet full of the tensions of childhood.

The first Taft known to be in America was also named Robert, a carpenter who settled at Braintree, Massachusetts, in 1678 and shortly moved to nearby Mendon. He became a selectman, acquired property, and died a man of substance in 1725. Originally, the name may have been Toft or Taffe, either a Scottish or an Irish name, and the first Robert probably migrated from England or Scotland during the Restoration. Perhaps, the guess is, he was a Puritan fleeing the easy virtue of Charles II.

It did not matter, for there was little that distinguished him and his descendants of the next few generations save their fecundity — Robert's five sons produced forty-five children of their own. They scattered over Massachusetts and Vermont, farmed and held local office, and died without fame or distinction. They were hard-working folk, perhaps a little stern, but life on the land was not easy in New England. They were Yankees and proud of it.[8]

The real founder of the dynasty was Alphonso, Will's father. Born in West Townshend, Vermont, in 1810, he was the only son of tough, pious parents who tended their land and remained solid citizens. But Alphonso, always earnest and ambitious, caught wider visions. He went to Yale University, was elected to Phi Beta Kappa, and graduated third in his class of 1833. He then had a restless time teaching school in Connecticut, attending Yale Law School, studying for bar examinations. In 1838 he set out to make his own way in the West. Stopping in New York City, he was appalled by the "notorious selfishness and dishonesty of the great mass of men you find . . . Money is the all in all, money without mind bears away the palm." [9] Most of the Tafts, like many other Midwesterners, were to share Alphonso's suspicions of New York, and his grandson Robert was to blame the influence of Wall Street, Times Square, and Madison Avenue for his political defeat in 1952.

Alphonso kept on moving west, stayed a while in Zanesville, and settled in Cincinnati in 1839. Slowly, cautiously, he established himself as a lawyer, and solemnly he picked a wife, like himself a Yankee from Vermont. Widowed after fathering Charley and another son, Peter, he returned to New England carefully to choose another wife, Louise Torrey. Though strong-minded and intelligent, Louise listened to her husband's admonitions to read good books, patiently accepted his homilies on the virtues of thrift and industry, and bore him Will in 1857, then two more sons, Henry and Horace, and a daughter, Frances ("Fannie").

Alphonso, meanwhile, was carefully climbing to distinction in law and politics: Whig city councilman, staunch Republican, delegate to national party conventions, superior court judge, honest secretary of war and attorney general in the scandal-stained administration of President Ulysses S. Grant, and Republican nominee for governor of Ohio, only to lose the election, family tradition emphasized, partly because of his court opinion against compulsory Bible reading in schools. Then he became minister to Austria-Hungary and Russia during his mellow old age in the 1880's. He died in 1891, leaving his Cincinnati house, an estate of only $482.80, and a solid lifetime of public service.

Bobbie, twenty months old at his grandfather's death, did not remember Alphonso, and it would be difficult to prove direct inheritance of personality traits across two generations. Yet Alphonso's shadow loomed large on all the Tafts. Kindly and affectionate within the home, Alphonso was otherwise austere, reserved, afraid to display emotion. "I will express my disgust at this wild and boisterous manner of receiving friends returned after long absence," he wrote his parents as a young man. "It is revolting to my feelings." [10] He also demanded much of his children, insisting that they exert themselves to the fullest. "Mediocrity will not do for Will," Alphonso complained when his son once stood fifth in a large class.[11] Not surprisingly, his sons listened. Will's half-brother Charley, the oldest, married Annie Sinton, daughter of a rich iron manufacturer, and became Cincinnati's leading philanthropist, owner of the influential Cincinnati *Times-Star,* and the indispensable contributor to Will's political campaigns; scholarly Henry became a leader of the New York bar and an author of numerous books; tall, lovable Horace founded Taft School in Connecticut and became a recognized leader of private school education in America. All five sons went to Yale and excelled; all, emulating their father, studied law; all except Horace and Peter ran for political or judicial office; all were staunch Republicans. Will's other half-brother, Peter Rawson Taft, was valedictorian of his Yale class, but broke down — too much striving, it was said — never recovered, and died of consumption in 1889.

What did it mean to be a Taft? No one phrased it better than Alphonso. Writing to his son Charley in 1854, he described a friend as a model young man: "He began poor . . . but accumulated. He was a man of talents, of great humanity . . . his sympathies were deep and strong and he was fearless in his expression of them. His character for sobriety and industry and integrity was without a blemish . . . He would stand firm against the most formidable opposition and never ceased to put forward his best." [12] Stern, outspoken, upright, unceasingly industrious, Alphonso was not flashy, profound, or even reflective. He lacked a broad philosophic bent, and his tastes ran to problem solving, not to ruminations on the sweep of history or to speculations about the future. He was open-minded without being imaginative, aware of the advantages of education and travel without cultivating a taste for literature or the fine arts. He cared very little for high society.[13] Alphonso left his mark on his sons. They in turn passed it on to theirs, and the children, sitting about the porch at Murray Bay, listened to their elders reminisce. Even Robert, seldom nostalgic or boastful of his ancestry, possessed an indelible sense of family, and in the 1930's he even found time to read the old family correspondence. When Uncle Horace sent him the letters of Grover Cleveland, Robert replied: "I must say that the early letters do not compare with the old Taft family letters. The whole background and the Cleveland family were very much less interesting." [14]

•

Will, it seemed, inherited his father's sweetness without being saddled with his austerity. "Big Lub," they called him as a boy, and he was always round, cherubic, good-natured, and in middle age immensely fat. People responded quickly to his infectious chuckle, his merry ways, his democratic manner, and readiness with a story. In his adult years he cultivated a bushy mustache, and when he laughed — which was often — his eyes twinkled, his mustache bristled, and his whole face seemed wreathed in joy. After he achieved national prominence, the republic chuckled with him when it read his famous exchange with Elihu Root, his friend and secretary of war. Taft cabled from the Philippines to say that he felt fine after a strenuous trip on horseback. Root, conjuring up the image of three hundred pounds of Taft on a horse at five thousand feet, flashed back, "Referring to your telegram . . . how is the horse?" [15] It was Taft who released the exchange for publication; he could laugh at himself.

Successes came easily to him. Leaving the security of the Court of Appeals in 1900, he accepted President William McKinley's charge to head the American commission to the Philippines. By 1904 he had replaced Root as secretary of war, and by 1909 he had succeeded his friend Theodore Roosevelt in the presidency — an office he had never much wanted and which provided the unhappiest four years of his life. Thanks to Roosevelt's efforts in his behalf, Will reached the White House with minimal effort; his son, struggling three times for the prize, would not even receive the nomination.

These things were true, yet the public image of a jolly fat man offered but one insight into a complex man. Will Taft was keenly intelligent and proud of it. Finishing second in his class at Yale, he had been elected to Phi Beta Kappa, and by his thirties he had become a respected judge. He was far from lazy; like Alphonso, he equated hard work with virtue, and as chief justice of the United States in his sixties he worked a twelve-hour day, arising at 5:15 for more than two hours of study before breakfast.[16] All his life he labored hard, and the picture of a carefree father spending long hours romping and picnicking with his family bears little resemblance to fact.

He worked purposefully, for Will Taft was highly ambitious. Even before the birth of Bob, he was thinking of securing an appointment to the Supreme Court, and throughout the 1890's he was frank to confess this dream. Although sociable and hearty, he was seldom careless or impulsive, and he gradually learned to keep a wary eye on the sycophants who sought his favor. Though some

people agreed with an enemy who called him a "large amiable
island surrounded entirely by persons who knew exactly what they
wanted," a shrewder judgment came from Archie Butt, who as
President Taft's military aide saw him every day. "Theodore Roosevelt," Butt confided, "once said that Mr. Taft was one of the best
haters he had ever known, and I have found this to be true." And
the journalist William Allen White, catching Taft off guard, noted
that behind the twinkle in his eye could be detected "almost the
hint of a serpentine glitter." Taft was gregarious and responsive.
But he also possessed the cautious, discerning, and well-honed
mind of an experienced federal judge.[17]

With his children Taft showed the same mixture of warmth and
cool observation. Bob, he wrote a week after his son's birth, "is
developing remarkable qualities and is in every way a phenomenon." In Washington as solicitor general, he was home a good
deal, and he enjoyed taking his wife and baby on leisurely drives to
the Cabin John Bridge or to the Old Soldiers Home. He kept his
parents posted on Bobbie's progress — the appearance of teeth
("he is rather irritable and peevish"), the first fumbling attempts
at speech ("He can say a number of things, but it requires the ear
of affection to detect what he means.").[18] "There is something
charming about Bobbie," he wrote Nellie, "that I don't see about
any other baby. Of course I look at every baby I see, but it is not
satisfactory. I need not argue with you to establish the fact that
our boy is different from other babies in many most desirable
ways." [19] When Taft's mother sent Bobbie a toy train, Taft wrote
appreciatively, "I wish you could see him when the train runs
swiftly around the track. He jumps up and down and claps his
hands with pleasure." [20]

Though his work on the circuit court was satisfying, he regretted
his frequent absences from home, and he sympathized with Nellie,
left alone to cope with two young children. "Kiss the babies," he
wrote. "Don't be discouraged because Robert seems stupid. He
will be catching on fast enough." Later, again away on the circuit,
he told Nellie to kiss his son. "Tell Robbie," he said, "that I send
him as many kisses as there are squares between Third and Lawrence and Freeman and Liberty." [21]

To say that Taft missed his son is not to suggest that he was indulgent or even particularly demonstrative. In fact, before the age of two Bobbie had to share parental affections with his sister Helen — "More Baby," he called her unhappily. And Charlie, eight years younger, later became his parents' favorite. Bright, bubbly, mischievous, Charlie reminded people of his jolly father, and he behaved so fetchingly that his parents could not force themselves to apply the same evenhanded discipline which they had dealt to his siblings. When Charlie, aged twenty, prepared to leave for Europe with the army, his father could not contain his feelings. "It is hard, my dear boy, to let you go. You are the apple of our eye . . . My loving son, good bye, till we meet again." [22] If Bob sensed favoritism on the part of his parents, he never expressed it, and he showed no resentment. But perhaps because he was given relatively little demonstrative affection, he was to return little of his own. Like Alphonso, he was self-contained, reticent, and slow to display his feelings.

Will Taft also expected much from his eldest son, he abhorred what he called "coddling," and he believed firmly in training his children for success. "We deny to our children," he wrote later, "the great and indispensable good that comes from discipline. Character is formed by the practice of self-restraint and self-sacrifice, by overcoming obstacles." Offspring of the wealthy required special instruction. "Of the sons of those who have luxurious homes and cherishing surroundings only the few who have force of character successfully to resist these enervating influences will be among the leaders of the next generation." [23] Mediocrity would not do, Alphonso had said. Will had listened, succeeded, agreed. While he showed more humor, less grimness than Alphonso, he let Bobbie know — first by force of example, later by letters and repeated admonitions — the necessity of strenuous effort, of overcoming competition. The world was harsh, and only the fittest could survive in it.

·

A French abbé once said of Jesus Christ, "God was his Father, but He also came of a very respectable family on his Mother's side."

Nellie Herron would have understood; she might even have smiled. For she was not only respectable — that mattered, though not too much — she was a truly unusual woman, and if she did not marry a god, she did find Will Taft, and she had ambitions to make him one. Cool, intelligent, extremely strong-willed, she encouraged — many said drove — her affectionate husband toward the presidency. It was she also who tended to Bobbie in his formative years between the ages of two and ten while her husband was off on the circuit. It was she, people said later, whom her eldest child resembled.

Four years younger than her husband, Nellie also grew up in Cincinnati in an atmosphere of law and politics. Her father, John Williamson Herron, was a Cincinnati lawyer, a friend of President Rutherford Hayes, and a Republican politician, who was to serve in the state senate from 1895 to 1897. Nellie, fourth of eleven children (eight survived), attended the christening of her youngest sister in the Hayes White House and stayed there for some weeks, a seventeen-year-old girl excited by the affairs of state. Possibly because she found her father tyrannical, possibly because eight children in the family forced her to fend for herself, she developed early a fierce independence and a restless ambition for herself and those she loved. As a girl she supported herself by teaching school; she shocked her friends by setting off unescorted to drink beer in a saloon; and she opened a literary salon. "We were bent on 'improving our minds,' " she recalled.[24]

As a girl she had been pretty and fascinating, and she had overwhelmed her husband-to-be. As a wife she proved an enthusiastic and often lavish hostess, an intrepid traveler who thought nothing of sweeping through the Orient with her children, a goad to Will's ambition, an active, intelligent woman who agreed with her husband on the fundamentals. Will always loved her, and their married life, especially in Bobbie's early years, was stable, happy, and full of understanding.

Still, Nellie sometimes distressed even her friends. She was too frank, opinionated, and outspoken. Some observers like Captain Butt came to appreciate this trait. "She is uncompromising in all matters of honesty and where principle is involved," he wrote, "and never deceives herself and in consequence never tries to deceive anyone else." Others, less kind than Butt, simply found her cold, for Nellie, eyes and mouth unsmiling, gazed at people with an unsettlingly calm and level look. Even her own family, Nellie commented, was amused at her "matter-of-factness." [25] To outsiders she never seemed agitated or responsive.

The family knew better. Nellie was in fact high-strung, emotional, inclined to be bossy. "I have cried myself to sleep half the time," she confided to her diary as a nineteen year old.[26] Later, married to Will, she refused to act the role of a simpering, dependent housewife, and she was quick to snap when displeased. Taft took her outbursts calmly. "I am so glad you don't flatter and sit at my feet with honey," he wrote. "You are my dearest and best critic." Later he quipped, "I consider obedience the first virtue of a husband." Repentant, Nellie would apologize. "I know that I am very cross to you," she wrote, "but I love you just the same." While these ripples of emotion hardly disrupted the calm of their married life, they suggested the inner tension which she resolutely kept hidden from outsiders. When a series of misfortunes descended in 1901–1902 — Will had three operations, and her mother died — she had what she later termed vaguely a nervous breakdown. Recovering, she rode triumphantly with Will to the White House on inauguration day in 1909, only to be struck two months later with what her husband at first called a "very severe nervous attack." [27] It was probably a cerebral hemorrhage, and though she fought back with typical resolution, it impaired her speech until her death in 1943.

Whether Bobbie sensed his mother's nervousness is unfortunately impossible to say. How easy it would be to ascribe his own coolness with strangers to a wariness developed in infancy from an uncertain mother! The truth was that Nellie, like most mothers, alternately adored and fussed about her first-born. Her letters to Will reveal no pattern:

[At nine months]   He is not himself, and is inclined to be cross and peevish.

[At eleven months]   Bobbie grows worse every day. I am beginning to think he has a very bad disposition.

[Six days later] He has been so cunning the last few days — smiles all over the whole time, and is, I assure you, very much admired.

[At twenty-one months] Every morning he comes creeping into my bed to wake me up and pats my face, or rolls his little curly head up close to mine. He is too cunning for anything.

[At two] He has grown very affectionate to me, and cries after me all the time which is a bad state of things . . . I am afraid he is getting spoiled . . .

[At two and a half] He is shy and not willing to be left alone with strangers . . . He is a very hard child to manage though so sweet when he wants to be. He certainly must be very backward . . . You know Robert can not repeat two lines of Mother Goose even . . . I fear he inherits my faculty for not paying attention.[28]

Many more such letters followed. They showed that Bobbie developed normally, contracted the usual childhood diseases, walked before he was one, talked before he was two, and wrote a letter (his first) to "Papa" when he was four. Much of this time he wore dresses and long blond curls. He was not always very lovable. But he was loved.

Soon Bob (by the time he was five, the diminutive had disappeared) became less dependent on his mother. She, in turn, channeled some of her inexhaustible energy into hospital work, the kindergarten board, the ladies musical club, especially the Cincinnati symphony orchestra. Bob attended kindergarten ("the kindergarten has been very good for him," his mother wrote, "in taking away that shyness he had so much of"), but he never acquired his mother's interest in music.[29] By age six he was in school, and he joined the Buckeye Cadets to drill in military garb with his friends. Soon he stopped clinging to mother and nurses.

School absorbed most of his time, and Bob plunged into the competition. He brought his problems home, and his mother, ambitious for her son, was glad to help. She read to him frequently — the romances of Sir Walter Scott, the novels of Charles Dickens, a few poems ("Horatius at the Bridge"). Soon Bob could read, and he sat for hours absorbed in the daring deeds of the characters of Henty and in the exciting battles of the Civil War. Inspired, he tried his hand at poetry: "General Pope, who washed his hands with Ivory soap." Before he was seven, he insisted that his mother teach him long division. Together they worked out math problems, sometimes past midnight while awaiting the last steamer from Murray Bay. Consistently at the head of his class, he once came home hurt because the teacher judged him in a tie with a schoolmate. "It was a real fraud," his mother complained. Leaving nothing to chance, Nellie offered a new enticement: Christmas money for doing well in examinations. Life was a contest. Bob Taft, his mother and father agreed, must always do his best.[30]

His mother watched him grow. She saw his blond hair turn brown, his curls disappear, and his hair grow unruly so that it had to be brushed back hard and flat on his large head. She noticed, too, that his gray eyes were ever alert, questioning, level, much as were her own. She saw him develop quickly into a sturdy boy, a little ungainly perhaps, but bigger and stronger than most of his playmates. And she observed that some of the shyness remained. Among those he knew well he played easily; with strangers he hung back, kept to himself, stayed in the house. He became fond of chess and other games he could work out by himself. The story goes that he began paying extended visits to the firehouse across the street from his house. Here, at age six, he quietly plotted the course of fire engines. Impressed, the firemen put him on a stool and let him make out station reports.[31] Playing with numbers, planning routes, compiling facts and figures — in general, the precision of mathematics — fascinated him. Perhaps they gave him a sense of certainty and self-assurance that his shyness prevented him from developing in human relationships. He was always to enjoy the solitary pleasure of thinking through problems, especially if they involved tables, statistics, or graphs.

To some, Bob seemed a little too shy, perhaps solemn and tense. Surely he lacked the gaiety which people were always to admire in his brother Charlie. Bob's enthusiasms, sympathies, and sensibilities were muted, and life seemed joyless at times — a constant struggle. But Nellie was pleased, for he was healthy and even a little precocious. Above all, she encouraged him to think for himself. She praised his remarkable ability to amuse himself, his industry, his powers of concentration on the task at hand. Admirers

MY DEAR PAPA
I LOVE YOU AND
I WILL SEND
&YOU·HELE·N·LOVE
AND MY OWN
AND WE ARE
ALL WELL.
I WROTE THIS
ALL BY MYSELF
ONLY AUNT
LUCY HELPED
ME WITH THE
SPELLING
ROBERT TAFT

MONDAY

Bobbie's earliest remaining letter, 1894

later extolled his independence of mind; enemies called him un-feeling, opinionated, and deaf to the ideas of others. Already the child was son of the mother and father of the man.

•

Psychologists and psychiatrists offer alluring, almost irresistible certitudes. Bob, they might conclude, lived in a home where both father and mother emphasized the joys of struggle, the virtues of hard work and self-discipline, the satisfactions of doing things on one's own. Bob listened, and he grew up making his own way. Naturally bashful (Was this the product of genes, of infancy, of being thrust on his own?), he found it difficult to make friends easily. So the wariness and the competitiveness reinforced each other, and Bob turned naturally to more solitary pursuits. There he could satisfy his drive for achievement without exposing him-self to the shattering cruelty of rejection by his peers. The ego, a fragile shuttlecock, survived.

So the reasoning goes. And one ventures further. Introverts tend to be anxious, nervous, insecure. So do first-born, for parents expect so much of them. So do children raised by strongwilled parents who set high standards in the already hostile world of childhood. Perhaps Bob Taft overcompensated, becoming not only competitive, but also self-assertive. Thus his apparent cold-ness, the forced harshness of his speaking voice, the stiffness of his public posture. Thus also the ambition to be President (How else does one match such a father?) and the ultimate disappointments of his life.

Perhaps. But the psyche, mysterious and labyrinthine, refuses to reveal itself entirely. Young Bob Taft was introverted; he did have to struggle against himself; and he was always reticent and self-contained. He did become ambitious and competitive, and so did his siblings. He did seem aggressive at times. Can these character-istics be traced largely to his mother, his father, to infancy, to early childhood, to family heritage? One guesses that they can be, but one cannot be sure.

Above all, there were the certitudes. Bobbie grew up in a secure world. His parents lived in the East End, in Walnut Hills, in Murray Bay. They loved each other and their children, agreed on the verities of life, concurred on how to raise their family, and by their self-assurance they presented Bob with little chance to doubt his place in society. They expected much, but they sometimes indulged, and they avoided ridicule or stern exhortation. Bob's childhood left marks, not scars, and if he felt any need to rebel, he never gave a sign of it. He was anxious about some things, but he was certain about many others. He always would be.

CHAPTER 2

The Struggle for Self-Control

IT WAS NOON April 17, 1900, in San Francisco. In the harbor lay the United States transport *Hancock*, its sides gleaming white in the sunlight. Nearby craft whistled salutes, gaily colored flags fluttered in the breeze, and the strains of "The Star-Spangled Banner" floated over the water from the deck of the battleship *Iowa*. At a minute after noon, William Howard Taft strode up the gangplank to the *Hancock*, and it cast off, bound for the Philippines 5000 miles to the West. Among the passengers were the Tafts, other members of the Philippine commission, and their families.[1]

The commissioners faced a trip of study and hard work, for stupendous problems lay ahead. Almost accidentally, America had suddenly acquired the Philippines in the aftermath of the Spanish-American War. The troops of General Arthur MacArthur were straining to keep order, but many Filipinos seemed less than enthralled with the prospect of American rule. As the *Hancock* steamed out of the harbor, the San Francisco newspaper appeared. "FILIPINOS SURPRISE AN OUTPOST," the headline read. "Three Americans Dead & Twelve Wounded. Rebel Force Driven off, Leaving Nearly Three Score on the Field."[2]

For ten-year-old Bob, however, the trip was an adventure, the beginning of a wider education and of a thirteen-year odyssey away from the familiar life of Cincinnati. The weather was balmy, the sea smooth, and flying fish skipped over the waves. Then, five days out, Bob saw the lovely green mass of Oahu rising sharply from its clean line of white beach. They stopped for four days, surfed on Waikiki, and relaxed. Away again, they steamed slowly toward the Orient. Two-year-old Charlie scampered about the ship and told people what to do. Bob, more sedate, played cards for hours, watched the sea, and spent long soft evenings with little to do. At last, late on May 10 they saw Fujiyama, snow capped and majestic, and then docked in Yokohama. There Bob contracted a mild case of diphtheria. The elder Taft went off to the Philippines, while Mrs. Taft and Maria, her sister, stayed behind to nurse Bob.

Recovering, Bob stayed in Yokohama with nurses while Nellie and Aunt Maria saw some of the sights of Japan. "Baby [Charlie] is very well and as cute as possible," he wrote his mother. Bob followed with childlike charm and characteristic precision: "Every morning I get up as soon as I wake up. The first morning it was at seven o'clock, the second at six, the third at half past six, the fourth at twenty-five minutes after six, and this morning at twenty minutes to seven. We are all learning to waltz." He began practicing the piano, learning "Arabesque." [3] Soon his mother returned and they traveled about Japan, then to Hong Kong. In August, more than four months out of San Francisco, their ship swung around the island of Corregidor, passed the hulks and spars of the sunken Spanish fleet, and came to rest in Manila. With interruptions it was to be Bob's home for the next three years. [4]

Manila lay under the heat — broiling, sticky, enervating. The sun beat down on the glassy bay, on the dirty Pasig River, and on the flat lowland that was Manila. The constant glare hurt the eyes and jangled the nerves. Lizards rustled in and out of doorways, and mosquitos, resting in the daytime, swarmed over nettings on the beds at night. The river hummed with color and activity — brightly painted cascos with fighting cocks tied to the decks, outrigger canoes darting about, women with naked babies thronging the banks to wash their clothes. In town, pony-drawn carts clogged the streets, and rows of shacks exposed a poverty that contrasted with the grand cathedrals and mansions of the old Spanish aristocracy. Sometimes typhoons rattled tin roofs and blew away the nipa huts perched on stilts. Disease struck ferociously: in 1902 more than 100,000 people were to die of cholera. Everywhere were throngs of brightly clothed people; everywhere were American soldiers. [5]

Amidst all this strangeness, Bob at first seemed anxious.

Though Taft had found his family a passably pleasant house on the bay, hired a force of servants, and secured a pair of handsome black stallions to pull his carriage, he did not know how to keep Bob occupied. "He stays at home and works intellectually all the time," Taft fretted. "He plays chess, and reads, and is too prone to stay in the house." If Bob could go to school, he might escape this solitary life. But Commissioner Taft dared not enroll his son in institutions run by the Jesuits, who were hated by the natives. Despairing, he even thought of sending Bob back across the Pacific to the school run by his brother Horace in Connecticut. Nellie, he sensed, "would not like it at all, but I feel that if we do not, this year will be wasted." [6]

Matters soon improved. For the first year Bob studied under an American tutor, the wife of one of Taft's party, and by November his father wrote proudly that Bob was "doing very well in his studies because Mrs. Le Roy is really keeping him up to the standard." Soon he was learning how to swim (though fearful at first after being badly stung by a jellyfish) and to ride a pony. Afternoons, he rode eagerly to the park by the bay, raced his pony, ran about with other children, and listened to the band, which played far into the cool of the evening. Some of the shyness was ebbing, and he was more at ease. [7]

There were other excitements. An American general (not MacArthur, who resented the civilian presence) invited him to visit northern Luzon, fitted him with horse and khaki garb, and took him on a pack trip with the soldiers. In the spring of 1901, Bob joined his parents on a leisurely voyage to the southern islands, stopping frequently and sailing a small boat in the innumerable bays and inlets which perforated the islands. A new school catering to children advanced in English opened in the autumn of 1901 and afforded Bob and his sister Helen new associations. By this time Taft had become civil governor and had moved the family into the rambling old Malacañan Palace on the river. He was working feverishly, trying to make America's unhappy colonial experiment worthwhile in the midst of continuing bloodshed and rebellion. [8]

Too feverishly. Returning from a tour of the provinces in late September 1901, Taft was attacked by dengue fever, a common tropical ailment. He took to his bed, then began suffering severe abdominal pains. Late in October a rectal abscess broke, and six people heaved him onto a stretcher for an immediate emergency operation. Mrs. Taft was touring China, and the children stood staring and crying in the hallway of the palace as their father was carried away to the hospital. Although the operation proved successful, he remained weak and underwent a second on Thanksgiving Day. Clearly, he had to return home for rest, and on Christmas eve of 1901 the Tafts sailed back across the Pacific.[9]

Hectic months followed. Arriving in America, the family hurried to reach Cincinnati, but their train encountered a blizzard on the plains. While the Tafts waited in Omaha for the weather to clear, word reached them that Nellie's mother had died. Shattered, Nellie began to break down, but they pressed on to Cincinnati. Here she recuperated while Bob stayed with the Hollisters. His father continued to Washington before returning home for a third operation. In late May 1902, the family prepared to set off together for Rome, where Taft had to conduct delicate negotiations with the Vatican over the disposition of church lands in the Philippines. But at the last minute Bob contracted scarlet fever, and Nellie again had to stay behind with him.[10] However, the delay was a short one.

Reaching Rome in June, Taft found the negotiations proceeding so poorly that he could not relax with his family. Bob saw aging Pope Leo XIII, who asked what the boy wished to be. Chief Justice, Bob replied, emulating his father's ambition. But Rome was hot, and Nellie remained on edge. She took the children to Vallombrosa, high above Florence, for lazy drives through the forests. They also visited the Florentine galleries. "There are three or four of Rafael's Madonnas there," Bob wrote a friend solemnly, "the finest of which is 'The Madonna of the Chair.'"[11] Taft managed to visit his family for a day, then set off again in late July for the Philippines. Nellie, accompanied by her mother-in-law, other relatives, and a series of French governesses, remained in Europe with the children.

At twelve years of age Bob had already taken on responsibilities beyond his years. Now, with his father far away, he indulged his skill in careful planning and figured out train schedules, fares, and timing for a grand tour of Europe. His grandmother was awed. Bob, she said, is "an improving companion, so intelligent and accurate. His locality is so infallible that he could even now be a guide or courier." His uncle, a professor of mathematics in Cincinnati, recalled his nephew's accomplishments and added, "Bob is the greatest man with figures I ever saw." When his father heard of Bob's talents, he beamed. "Who could have a finer boy than Robert?" he wrote. "I am proud of him down to the ground." [12] Nellie, as always, set a fast pace, trying to see as many cultural landmarks as possible. They saw St. Mark's in Venice, heard the music at Salzburg, absorbed the charm of Prague and the art of Dresden. Then to Leipzig, Weimar, the Thuringian forest and Nuremberg, and two weeks bathing and relaxing in Baden-Baden. Eventually they set sail for Suez and the Philippines on September 3, 1902, with more than two months of European travel behind them. Bob's plans had worked perfectly.

Back in Manila in October, Bob resumed the life he had left so hurriedly months earlier. He was "well and robust," his father reported happily in November. "Robert and Helen both ride a great deal and take much outdoor exercise and are enjoying their life here. They have a great deal of pleasure in their school." Soon Bob was leading his class again, and his father wrote happily that "Bob is a good student" who should have no trouble at Uncle Horace's school in the fall. [13]

So in August 1903 Bob, then almost fourteen, left his family behind to sail for Nagasaki, San Francisco, and finally overland for school in Connecticut. Lonely among tired returning soldiers, he kept a carefully detailed "Pilot Chart of the North Pacific Ocean," which showed the ship's daily position in solid, precise lettering. Almost a month later, on September 17, his ship crawled through high seas and thick fog into San Francisco harbor. It had been exactly three years and five months since the *Hancock* had steamed off in 1900. [14]

•

Bob's father thought these years abroad had quickened his son's curiosity. "Robert," he complained happily while in Rome, "can put more questions to me that I can't answer than ever before, and the number was always large." Bob's grandmother added that "Bob and Helen have gotten a great deal out of this experience that they will never forget. It is largely of course due to the wise guidance of Nellie, who includes them in her investigations and secures their sympathy in the study of Art and Architecture and History." [15]

His mother knew better. "The children," she wrote from Baden-Baden, "are as bad at picking up acquaintances as I am. There are several children in the hotel, but Bob and Helen are so absorbed in their books all the time that we are in the house that they have no eyes for anyone." Bob had seen the cultural wonders of Europe, shown more than ordinary interest in them for a young boy, and had applied himself, trying to pick up enough French and German from his governesses to get along. But the trip had been mainly an exercise in logistics — a routine of meeting trains, handling luggage, wandering about hotel lobbies, reading, taking care of the women folk. It also had been lonely, for his father was away, and his mother high-strung and emotional. He was to visit Europe often again as a young man, but he never learned to speak a European language (even in Murray Bay he seldom tried French) or to develop much interest in the fine arts. Like most American travelers, he met and knew few foreigners. These sojourns did not make him distrustful of Europeans — to a degree, distrust came with Versailles in 1919 — but they did leave him unimpressed, and he was never to join the interventionists of the 1930's and 1940's who sought to "save" western Europe from Hitler or Stalin.[16]

Even the Philippines seemed to have left little mark. Later, in the 1950's, he seemed more interested in protecting east Asia from the communists than he was in aiding western Europe, and it would be logical to root this perspective in boyhood. After all, his father had been an architect of American policy in the Orient. But Bob seldom was sentimental — about the Philippines or anything else — and like his father, he grew up with divided views about the virtues of American expansionism. When the Japanese seemed to threaten the Philippines in 1940, Bob Taft, although concerned, did not pay the islands the attention that he devoted to American policy in Europe; when Corregidor fell in 1942, he was sad but resigned. It was not until the days of Mao, of MacArthur, and of Syngman Rhee, that he became something of a zealot about Asia, and these were matters where nostalgia had no place.

After all, Bob was still but thirteen when he boarded ship for home in 1903. Too young to care much about foreign cultures or geopolitics, sheltered by the official position of his family, catered to by Aunt Maria and a household of servants, he was also too self-contained and solitary to venture far afield on his own. Indeed, his three and a half years must often have been unsettling, for they had bombarded him with new experiences — typhoons, strange languages and customs, lonely months without school or playmates save Helen and Charlie, diphtheria, jellyfish, a father who had undergone three operations, and a mother who had suffered a nervous breakdown.[17] The boy who had left America a quiet child of ten returned bigger but still reserved, wary, and tenser than he tried to let on to his parents. Because he had been encouraged to be independent and because he was dutiful, he managed his independence very well — at least on the surface. But his father realized that Bob remained very much a sensitive, competitive, and vulnerable boy struggling to grow up. "I do not think Robert has any bad habits," he told Horace,

at least I know of none, except that he keeps his mouth open and is not as particular in cleaning his nails as he ought to be. I hope you will find him readily amenable to discipline. He becomes intensely interested in games and discussions, and with a nature somewhat highly wrought his tears are pretty near to the surface . . . I hope that you will be able to prepare him in three years for college, for he would then enter in September of his seventeenth birthday, which is a good age for entrance, and would graduate in the class of 1910, which I prophesied on the day of his birth. Though he has more taste for mathematics than for languages, I am exceedingly anxious that his education should not be as defective as mine in the matter of linguistic knowledge, and that he should be able to speak French and German. He has quite a taste for history.[18]

Bob's native land had changed in his absence. President McKinley had been gone since September 14, 1901, a week after an assassin shot him down in the Temple of Music in Buffalo, and Theodore Roosevelt had already been President for two years. Magazines proclaimed the evils of corporate society, of corrupt urban bosses, of squalid lofts and tenements, and men like Roosevelt and William Howard Taft began looking for ways to bring order to a society run ragged by the excesses of unregulated capitalism. The old ways were passing, and a host of articulate reformers were beginning to proclaim the progressive era.

Bob was headed away from this excitement. Taft School, three and a half hours by train from New York City, rested in the lovely village of Watertown, Connecticut. His Uncle Horace had founded the school in Pelham Manor, New York, in 1890, had moved it to Watertown in 1893, and had developed it to an establishment of nine masters and eighty-six boys by 1903. Twenty were local boys, some on scholarship, but most came from eastern and midwestern families of wealth and position; Bob's move across the Pacific was more geographical than social. The hub of the school was the main building, an old, sprawling white frame structure that had been an inn. Here boys and masters lived, ate, and studied together. Porches surrounded the front of its two stories, giving a gingerbread effect. Tall trees shaded spacious lawns and fields in the spring and autumn. In winter the air was clean and bracing, the snow often lay thick for sliding, and the boys flooded the playground for skating and hockey.[19]

Dominating the scene was Uncle Horace, Bob's father's youngest brother. The "King," as the boys called him, presented a fine, imposing figure. He was tall (six feet four), lean, graceful, at the peak of his mental and physical powers. A few boys found him stern and chilly, but the majority loved him; he had no children of his own, and the school was his life. He knew how to bring out a boy, and he did it warmly and easily, for he had Will's easy manner and twinkling eyes. To Bob he was much more than a school master and more than an uncle; he was a source of warmth and strength, a figure almost as close to him for the next three years as his busy father had ever been able to be.

Yet Uncle Horace, like his own father and brothers, believed in rigor, discipline, and hard work, and Bob was expected to excel. The object of the school, said the catalogue, was to "give boys a thorough preparation for the best colleges, and to make them strong, healthy, and manly men." "Best colleges" meant Yale, where twenty-one of Bob's class of twenty-five went after graduation in 1906. It also meant long hours of study, for Yale had entrance examinations. And it meant no wasted hours, frills, or coddling. "There must be no child-centered school," Horace wrote later, "if by that is meant that the final decision as to courses and methods must be left to the child." [20] Horace Taft believed strongly in character building, in general education, in academic rather than utilitarian disciplines. Boys received very little exposure to art or music, much more to Latin and Greek and to English and American literature. One learned by rote, for memorization and recitation trained the mind.

Taft School also called for service — its motto was *non ut sibi ministretur, sed ut ministret* (not to be served oneself but to serve). Horace, like his brothers, expected boys to become useful citizens. He stressed debating, and he gladly judged the competitions himself. And he taught the seniors a course in Civil Government, to make each boy "feel such interest and sense of duty in regard to the subject as will lead him in college and elsewhere to prepare himself thoroughly to do his part in the State patriotically and intelligently." [21]

•

Bob arrived two weeks late, and Horace reported at first that "he has had a rather lonely, stupid time, as yet, because he has had to study by himself in catching up . . . He has done nothing since he came but study Greek." Yet even then Horace praised Bob's intelligence, adding that "I shall be very much surprised if he does not lead the class very soon." Two weeks later Horace wrote that Bob showed "no signs of homesickness," that he headed his class in Greek, and that his room was being fixed by Horace's wife "to make it attractive and homelike . . . to provide everything necessary for his comfort, such as other boys have." A week later Horace was pleased to say that "Robert is taking hold finely . . . He is quiet and it took him a little time to get acquainted, but he feels at home now with all the boys of his own age and is, I think, very well liked." Soon Bob acquired a roommate, plunged fiercely into third-team football, and got caught with other boys in an illegal "feed" after hours.[22] Placed as a sophomore, Bob was fourteen, more than a year younger than most of his classmates, but by Christmas he led his class.

So it went for the rest of the year. He learned to skate (they placed him at goal) and with characteristic precision he diagrammed the sport of hockey for his mother. In the spring he tried baseball, but he was young, growing rapidly, a little clumsy, and though he fought tenaciously in sports for three years, he never received his "T." In the spring, he played the role of Jolly, a traveling salesman, in the school play. "Taft made a good Jolly," the school paper reported. "His attitudes had a very un-drummer-like stiffness at times, but his broad smile, his full tones, and his general intelligence of what he was about, produced a first-class character." [23]

Bob's last two years at Taft followed the same seasonal rhythm, and in his junior year he made his first run for office, losing in races for class secretary and vice-president. He was not nominated again, and school politics did not seem to matter much to him anyway. He also sang in the glee club, acted in plays, belonged to the literary club, and served as president of the chess club. He joined a friend in starting the "Oracle," a literary paper, and contributed an article, lost to the historian, on the fierceness of college football. As a senior, he became one of five monitors who helped in the discipline of the younger students. More than most of his classmates Bob pursued a wide variety of activities; he was not a "grind." [24]

There were fun times, too. Vacations meant visits to school friends in Pittsburgh, playgoing in New York with Uncle Henry and Aunt Julia, rounds of parties with friends in Cincinnati. In the summer of 1904 he went to Murray Bay again, and in 1905 he sailed with Uncle Charley to Germany, Scandinavia, and England. "I now feel as if I had seen almost every part of the world," he wrote his father. Sometimes there were girls. At first his schoolmates had to apply "continued pressure," for Bob was busy with his work. But soon he was telling his mother about the school dance. "It was a splendid night, with a full moon which rather dulled the electric decorations and Japanese lanterns throughout the grounds . . . I didn't know anybody, but several I met were very nice. On the whole I had a splendid time and felt afterwards that it was also part of my education." A few months later, his father twitted him. "It was even intimated that you found pleasure in the company of a young lady, something which rather strained my credulity . . . I have observed your greater care with respect to your ties, finger nails and that sort of thing, which comes from attention to the young ladies, and which really is one of the great goods that comes from association with them." [25]

Bob also had a reunion with his father, who had returned to Washington to become secretary of war in January 1904, while Mrs. Taft rested in California during the winter. Too busy to see his son until March, seven months after Bob's departure from the Philippines, Secretary Taft then went to New York and was working on a speech when he heard a sound. "Who should come in," he wrote Nellie, "but a fine looking, modest, well dressed boy whom I had some difficulty in recognizing as Bob. He has grown much taller and stouter and he looks well kept. He is very quiet but very attentive." Later that month, Bob visited Washington, and his father could scarcely contain his pride. "Robert is a great joy to me," he wrote. "He looks like the Herrons and while not a beauty, he is a manly looking boy who attracts people." Writing Nellie again, he added, "I am very sure you would be proud of Robert. He looks so well in his long trousers and good clothes. He quite takes the cake when he puts on his tuxedo." And four days later he added, "Robert makes a good impression and people seem to like to have him. He is working diligently on his composition concerning the Panama Canal. He has the faculty for doing a little now, and a little then so that he saves time by using little intervals. I am sorry that I have not that gift." [26]

By this time Taft was close to the throne, and Bob met the court. He visited the Senate and the House for the first time ("I was very much interested," he wrote his mother dispassionately), toured the Library of Congress, and twice ate at the White House, where he met the Roosevelt children and TR himself. Bob was matter-of-fact about these White House visits, writing simply, "I met the whole family." The essay on the canal, even his role in the school play, evoked more enthusiasm. No clue suggests that future political ambitions blossomed in the Senate gallery or the White House dining room in March 1904. He enjoyed the sojourn, and he saw his father again. But there was work to be done.[27]

.

For at Taft, studies, debates, and essay contests came first. The competition was stern and endless. If Bob needed reminding, his father provided it, for he expected much of his son. "I do not need to tell you how anxious I am for you to study hard and do well in your classes," he wrote. "I have every confidence that your taste for study and your ambition to do well will show your Uncle Horace that you have got something in you." Soon he was worrying about Bob's enthusiasm for football and hockey. "Your Uncle Horace says that you are doing very well in your studies, and that you know, is the most gratifying thing that I can hear. I hope you will not allow your interest in athletics to interfere." To Horace, he expressed his values as William Graham Sumner, his mentor at Yale, had often preached them: "I am glad to know that Bob is getting along so well, though he says that there is somebody slightly ahead of him. 'Competition is the life of trade.' "[28]

Bob thrived on the struggle and because the simple examples of his father and grandfather were in themselves enough, he needed no pushing from afar. The boys received frequent and well-publicized numerical grades and always knew precisely where they stood. Leading his own class from the start, Bob never let up, and Horace was pleased to say that he "goes in with the determination to do his best in everything." Then, however, a boy named Camp, a class below, inched two-fifths of a point ahead. "I think his studies must be easier, and he takes almost no exercise," Bob complained. "I hope to be able to catch up with Camp, but if he gets 98 again, as he did last month, it is hopeless." Camp finished in front that year, but Bob need not have felt ashamed. He won the $10 scholarship prize for leading the top two classes, and a second prize in English composition. Taking nationwide entrance examinations at Yale a little later, he shared first prize in both Latin and Greek. His classmates, a bit awed, snickered.

He Greek and Latin speaks with greater ease
Than hogs eat acorns and tame pigeons peas.

"Tafto," they said, "at times shows almost human intelligence." [29]

While achieving these honors, Bob competed in an unrelenting series of essay contests. Never blessed with a flowing style, he failed to win. But he struggled manfully, and the contests gave him a chance to pursue a developing interest in political questions. He wrote on Tammany Hall, the fall of slavery, the Long Parliament, the Panama Canal. Spoofing again, his peers predicted a career for him as "Boss Taft." [30]

Above all, he learned to debate. In his assigned positions in these debates he opposed the municipal ownership of utilities (if utilities are dishonestly run, he argued, why not supervise them instead of taking them over), favored abolition of the jury system (jurymen tend to be inexperienced and easily influenced by lawyers), and upheld a tariff for revenue only. Speaking in prize competitions, he failed to win when he discoursed on "Colonialization." ("Colonialization was always good," he told his mother, "when it was carried on with the good of the colony in view, and I cited history, chiefly Rome, Spain, and England to show this.")[31] Though he won an honorable mention in debating at graduation, even Uncle Horace recognized his faults. "Debating is hard for him. He grasps arguments easily, but has no readiness of speech on his feet." Horace added, "He is considerably handicapped by his voice, which is not a pleasant one when he uses it with great force as he does when he speaks." [32] Still reticent, Bob showed characteristic determination, even courage, in forcing himself to speak in public, but it did not come easily, and it never would. He seemed too much the advocate, too dry and factual, and he spoke too quickly. For Bob, the boy trying to assert himself, debating offered compensations; for Taft, the future politician, it did nothing at all.

The years at Taft left their mark. Though only sixteen years old at graduation in 1906, he had shot up physically to nearly his mature height of six feet, and he weighed 170 pounds. Although strong, he remained a little awkward, and he tended to stand stiffly in the presence of adults. His large ears, wide mouth, and slightly protruding front teeth seemed a little too big for his head, and he had to begin wearing glasses occasionally to correct nearsightedness. Because he was so often preoccupied, he seldom laughed or grew animated, and he rarely let himself go. And though there is nothing to suggest that he was unhappy or unpopular, he emerged from his three years there with few lasting friends. Indeed, it is possible that his sojourn at Taft, like his years abroad, had been frightening at times, for he had arrived as the son of the commissioner of the Philippines and the secretary of war, and as the nephew of the "King." An athletic extrovert like his brother Charlie could easily have surmounted these "handicaps," but Bob, who could not excel at sports and for whom easy camaraderie was impossible, had to find rewards in more solitary activity and to mask his feelings with the coolness and dignity that many people discerned in his mother. A master recalled that schoolmates "smiled at his indifference to others." [33] Given the careless cruelty of young boys, it is possible that the master should have said "snickered" instead of "smiled."

Still, the school was appropriate in that it reinforced the boy who came there. Trained to be respectful, he easily accepted the discipline of boarding school and the rigor of rote learning. Raised to excel, he plunged eagerly into the endless competitions and appreciated instinctively the stress on training for good citizenship. If the school emphasized knowing instead of thinking, or winning in place of playing, that suited him all right, and it made life at college that much easier. Bob had beaten the best in competition, and he was beginning to know what he could do. The thought that he was finding his strengths and concealing his weaknesses must have been bracing as he prepared for life in New Haven.

CHAPTER 3

Avoiding the Limelight

TWO WEEKS after his inauguration as President, William Howard Taft, class of '78, returned to his alma mater to speak. "Whatever credit is due of a personal nature in the honors that came to me," he said fervently, "I believe is due to Yale." [1]

Bob, then a junior, may have been there to hear his father. Without thinking much about it, he may have agreed. But he did not have to think about it, because Yale '10 was his destiny from the day of his birth. Alphonso had started the tradition, excelling in his studies and helping found Skull and Bones, the senior secret society for the select few. Five sons followed, and Will, class orator and salutatorian, had also made Bones. Bob's father and grandfather had been members of the Yale Corporation, and both had received honorary degrees. Will had even been offered the university presidency. There was no other place a Taft could go.

Bob prepared carefully for his college years and looked for a room in New Haven a full year in advance. Take a quiet one, his father advised, "for I am anxious to have you succeed in college just as you have at your Uncle Horace's. I don't want you to get any foolish ideas from the boys with whom you associate that it is beneath you to study hard. Don't be afraid of being called a 'dig,' and to stand well . . . So engage your room, old boy, and believe that your mother and I follow you every minute of your time, and with the hopes of your great success." [2]

Bob listened and arrived in New Haven in September 1906. Had he explored, he would have discovered a fair-sized city of smoky factories, sprawling slums, and long undistinguished avenues. But Yale, like prep school, was secluded, a decorous enclave of elm-shaded streets and Gothic dormitories sitting quietly along-side the Green. Peaceful courtyards, sedate houses in Greek re-vival style, and occasional brick homes of colonial vintage offered a reassuring feeling to the young men from Lawrenceville, Andover, and Taft.

Some things, of course, were new. Yale was bigger, and Bob was one of 337 who started off in the class of 1910. There were strange customs such as elaborate battles with the sophomores and the mys-teries of fraternities and of Bones. Most of all there was freedom — gone were the constraints of family, the cloister of boarding school. And boys were supposed to become men. They trooped to Mory's to lift their steins of beer in song. Afterward, on dark spring evenings, they weaved happily across the Green, joyous, idealistic, irresponsible.

> What the hell do we care, what the people say
> We are, we are, we are the Yale YMCA.[3]

Bob took little part in such antics. He had come to learn, and he was bent on resuming the rhythm that had marked life in prep school. One of his roommates was a friend from Taft, and he joined old schoolmates in an eating group.[4] Being a prep school graduate — and a Taft — established him socially; being one of Uncle Horace's products made studies easy. From the beginning the familiar ruled, and Bob adjusted with no signs of strain.

As at Taft he plunged into a variety of activities, for competition reigned again. Dink Stover, the fictional hero of *Stover at Yale* (1911), properly explained that at Yale one had to *do* something to *be* someone. So Bob tried rowing, but though large and strong, he failed to excel and quit after two years. Casual about church, he served as treasurer of the YMCA. He joined his father's junior fraternity. He went to dances at nearby girls' schools, took time out for cards with classmates, cheered the football team against Harvard, and joined enthusiastically in the annual frosh-soph snowball fight.

These things one did because they were done. They did not ex-cite him, and a few years later he advised his brother Charlie not to get caught in such a routine. "Avoid all the little things which keep coming up, and which you are apt to drift into. It seems to me now that I wasted a lot of time on things which were excellent but in which my part did not amount to anything." [5]

The social scene, too, mattered little. Asked to join a fraternity with some friends, he told his mother he had decided to "throw it down" and go "where papa was": these friends were "rather fast." On the eve of all-important tap day in his junior year, the crowning glory of the select and the despair of the rest, he was unconcerned. "There is great excitement through our class especially," he wrote. "Some people take it terribly seriously, but I can't feel that it really decides very much." Like his father and Uncle Horace, Bob was tapped for "Bones," and his year in the society became a cherished interlude ("it is almost impossible to tell about adequately," he told his fiancée three years later). Bonesmen remained his closest friends in later years. But he rarely grew solemn about it, and he told his son, at Yale thirty years later, not to worry. "The effect in after life is negligible," he wrote. "The only danger is giving more importance to it than it deserves." [6]

Somewhat more absorbing was the City Government Club, over which he presided as a senior. Its purpose, he explained, was "not to reform politics, or take an active interest in politics, but to arouse such an interest as shall make the whole college feel their duty of participating actively in politics after graduation." Undeterred by the apathy of his classmates, he rode to New York City to watch the polls for the Republicans in the election of 1909. The experience prompted a characteristically cautious response. "We did not feel that we had been of any indispensable assistance," he remarked, "but perhaps we did something for the cause of cleaner politics." College students, he argued sensibly, "cannot accomplish very much" and "may even arouse the sort of opposition which always greets a tactless missionary." Leave politics, he often said later, to the regulars. [7]

Once again debating attracted him, and he threw himself into speaking competitions. As at Taft sheer energy brought modest results, and he won one of four second prizes in public speaking as a junior and presided over the debating association as a senior. Two of his major efforts, *Non Scholae sed Vitae Discimus* ("We learn through life, not through school") and "The Working out of

Volunteer Watching in New York.

I have been asked as a member of the Yale City Government Club to write a paper on my experience as a watcher last Autumn in New York City. I have undertaken the task most unwillingly because of the fact that many men in other colleges have had far wider experience in this field than I, and because in particular there are Columbia men who worked throuout the entire campaign in this city, and served as watchers on the four registration days as well as at the election. The Yale men who came down, about a dozen in number, were only here on the one day, and of course their lack of experience in the work prevented their offering any great assistance at the polls. But perhaps this paper may lead to a discussion of the advisability of taking part in active political work, and thus prove not entirely useless.

We came down on Monday evening at the invitation of Mr. E. S. Whitin. who had

Taft's handwriting, for a speech in 1910. His writing
changed little over the years

the Fifteenth Amendment," revealed his formative opinions about public service and contemporary politics. In the first speech he complained about the irrelevancy of college life. "There is too little thinking," he said. "The undergraduate never mentions or refers outside of the classroom to the subjects which he has listened to . . . The classroom is utterly apart from his actual college life." In the old days, he claimed, "the whole college was aroused by a political campaign. Today the surface is scarcely rippled. As a consequence, the incentive to public service, which used to be such a marked feature . . . is dying away." Already, the family tradition was working.[8]

His other speech typified contemporary northern thinking about the Reconstruction period in American history. He praised the Fifteenth Amendment, for it conferred on Negroes the right to vote, and he congratulated Negroes for their advances since the Civil War. Their gains, he said, "triumphantly refute the contention that color is a fair index of intelligence." But Bob then scored the so-called Radicals for their "fanaticism" and lamented the lack of educational tests for voting. The result, he complained, has been to create a "rule of ignorance" in the South. Worst of all, Radical Reconstruction had angered the South, turned it into a solid Democratic section, and forced "the naturally conservative south to vote with the most radical of the western states." Concluding, he called for a stronger Republican party in the South — "A party which shall exist to win and not to hold public office." The speech, given a month after his father entered the White House in March 1909, foreshadowed nineteen-year-old Bob's strong partisanship as well as his lifelong flirtation with southern Republicanism. One wonders if he remembered it forty-three years later at the Republican national convention of 1952, when a battle over southern delegates helped bring him defeat in his last bid for the presidency.[9]

For Bob, debating mattered, but not so much as studies. "Young Taft," the local paper paraphrased him, "will not go in for athletics but will devote himself to the task of leading his class." And he did, collecting a handful of prizes and finishing with a scholastic average of 357 — straight A was 350 — even though he took nine extra course hours. His professors marveled at his quickness, his thorough knowledge of their subjects; and his classmates voted him "brightest," "most scholarly," and fifth "most likely to succeed." He finished, of course, number one in his class, and his father rejoiced at the adding of a second Yale valedictorian to the family.[10]

Though he excelled, his courses failed to excite him. An occasional professor roused him to disgusted disagreement — "how fantastical! Tommy rot," he scribbled while listening to his philosophy professor expound on "no freedom of will in Spinoza" — and he listened carefully to Irving Fisher, a bright young economics professor who discoursed on child labor, sanitation, and the need for "national efficiency." But he usually sat passively, kept careful notes, and spun them back on examinations.[11]

The fault was partly Bob's. Nothing in his previous schooling had called for much more than rote learning, and little in his intellectual makeup demanded it. He lacked then and always that playfulness and tentativeness of mind which is often the mark of the intellectual. "Very bright but . . . too practical a mind," was the perceptive verdict of his unhappy philosophy professor.[12] Bob was diligent, quick, and thorough, and he possessed a striking capacity to retain all sorts of information. But he seldom let his mind roam freely, and as his philosophy professor had observed, he was impatient with abstractions. Thus Bob left Yale much as he had entered it — with little appreciation for literature, art, and the other humanities, and with few doubts about the essential justice or propriety of the American social system.

Yet the blame was also Yale's. Then emerging painfully from a nadir in its intellectual life, Yale claimed a few luminaries on its faculty and was beginning to offer a more exciting curriculum. But most courses still handled subject matter in dry, mechanical fashion. A basic English course stressed "vocal training," in which the student was expected "to acquire a correct and refined pronunciation of English and a distinct and natural utterance." History was primarily European history, with stress on the ancient world and constitutional formalities. Economics, except with Fisher, ignored Marx and Engels for Malthus and Adam Smith. Literature usually meant Shakespeare — or Scott, Parkman, and Irving — not Flaubert, Dostoyevsky, or Shaw. Professor William Lyon

("Billy") Phelps had recently succeeded in introducing a course on modern literature into the curriculum, but only after winning a battle against the faculty. Most professors, far from expecting intellectual excitement from their classes, worried about discipline and imposed rigidly formal methods to prevent disruption. It was a safe, conservative college with but a touch of intellectual excitement; for young men like Bob it confirmed existing beliefs without disturbing them.[13]

Yale, like Taft School, believed also in competition, in training the mind, in a general rather than a specialized education. This meant entrance examinations in Latin and in mathematics (77 per cent of Bob's Yale class also took them in Greek), few electives, and no chance to pursue subjects in depth. Bob took eleven hours each of English and German, nine of economics, and a smattering of eight other subjects, most of them at uninspiring elementary levels. As a Yale student of the time recalled, "I don't think educationally it was an exciting place. I had no difficulty being among the top scholars . . . It was reporting back what the professor had told you." Bob, advising his brother a few years after graduation, was harsher. "It seems to me," he said, "that I took elementary courses in so many things that I never got advanced in anything; now I believe that I would like to have something that I really knew about, preferably English literature . . . never touch a modern language, which are stupid and useless." He concluded, "I am now reading a good many things I ought to have read long ago." [14]

.

Long before finishing Yale, Bob knew that the next step was to be the same as that pursued by his grandfather, father, and uncles: law school. And for bright, ambitious sons of the upper classes in 1910, there was no place quite so highly regarded as Harvard Law School. Its dean after 1910, Ezra R. Thayer, was a friend of Bob's father, and most people agreed it represented the pinnacle of excellence. "If there be a more successful school in our country or in the world for any profession," President Charles W. Eliot of Harvard said, "I can only say that I do not know where it is. The School seems to have reached the climax of success in professional education." [15]

As always, Bob arrived ready to excel. "I'm here to study," he told reporters who interviewed him, now the President's son, in Cambridge. "I do not intend to go into athletics or to be a social lion or to do missionary work or" — tact was not his forte — "to be interviewed." He added:

I'm here to work hard. I didn't come to Harvard for the fun of it. A fellow may go to college to have a good time; but when he gets through he thinks of more serious things. I thought of law. I decided that the Harvard Law School was better than the Yale Law School, and I am here . . . I intend to practice, but probably not . . . in New York, but in some other state . . . I do not expect to have any spare moments here in the law school to fritter away.[16]

He judged correctly the lack of "spare moments," for Harvard Law deserved its fame. Giants such as Thayer, Roscoe Pound, and Edward H. ("Bull") Warren studded its faculty, and they gloried in their rigorous standards. Look at the person on each side of you, Warren liked to tell the first-year men. "One of you will not be back here next year." Competition was backbreaking. Everyone knew everyone else's grades, and nothing counted more. Bob's class began with 296; only 176 graduated three years later in 1913.[17]

As at Yale, Bob was careful not to seem only a striver for grades, and he occasionally took time out for the theater and cards with the many friends who had come up to Cambridge with him from Yale. Modest, quiet, extremely careful not to dwell on the fame of his father, he moved as unobtrusively as possible through the routine, and he impressed those who watched him. One such classmate, writing home, captured him honestly and accurately:

Have I mentioned anything of the Taft boy? He — Robert — you know is in my class. He is very quiet, appears not to be even the slightest swell-headed, yet seems not to care at all what people think or don't think, but does exactly as he pleases. He gives the appearance of a person with lofty ideals, and the courage of his convictions and to spare. He dresses in very plain and sober clothes, which strike me as being somewhat out of date. Finally,

he is a hard student, and an unusually intelligent one. I don't believe there is a brighter fellow . . . in our class . . . He is well
built, but not very good looking.[18]

Bob felt the competition, and he worked hard. "I could do
pretty well without banquets of any sort myself," he wrote. "I
would rather stay home and read." One classmate, perhaps exag-
gerating a little, recalled finding Bob in the law library on thirty
consecutive evenings, and Professor Pound, an early riser, used to
discover him standing in front of the library, waiting for it to open.
His notebooks reveal an extremely thorough, attentive student
who wrote in a flowing but neat hand, who took the trouble to set
himself "queries" in the back, and who compiled tables of contents
for easy reference during examinations. There was no wasting of
time, no sloppiness, no doodling.[19]

And so the pattern repeated itself. Number one at Taft, number one at Yale, number one at Harvard Law. He won the award
given to the most promising member of his class, and he presided
over the law review his senior year. Dean Thayer wrote Bob's father about the son's "faithfulness and severity . . . He is a demon-
stration that a legal mind is heritable." And Taft decided that his
son could rest: "Bob has taken the highest marks that have been
taken in Harvard for fifteen years, so we are going to let him take a
run to Europe before he settles down." [20]

At last the grind of law school was over, and again he had excelled. But again one doubts that the experience changed him
much. Proud of its pioneering case method through which students arrived at so-called general principles of the law, Harvard
Law School stressed knowledge of judicial precedents. Students
were to find out what the law was, not what it ought to be. And
the law in those times of rapid change had to be an agent of stability, not of social reform. It was, said a contributor to the law review in Bob's time, an "honest, and in the main adequate, system
of principles under which justice can be fairly administered between litigants without respect to class, or rank, or condition." [21]

The curriculum need not have been so absolute, for Harvard,
like the nation, was beginning to feel the winds of change. And
among the leading iconoclasts was Pound himself, who published

his famous three-part article on sociological jurisprudence in the *Harvard Law Review* in 1911 and 1912. Law, he said, was not static, but a "social institution which may be improved by intelligent human effort." Judges should always consider the practical social results of their decisions. Bob's classmate Zechariah Chafee, later a famous member of the Harvard law faculty, audited Pound's course his senior year, and was awakened. "It excited me," he said, "about possibilities of doing something to make the law better." Soon Pound, Chafee, Felix Frankfurter, and others were abandoning some of the old orthodoxies, and the law school entered a new era.[22]

More intriguing to Bob was another possibility: he was offered the chance to be law clerk for Justice Oliver Wendell Holmes of the Supreme Court. The image of Holmes, probing, immersed in the great socioeconomic issues of the day, sitting down daily to discourse with young Bob Taft, earnest, competitive, a little solemn, is irresistible. Would Bob have found time to reflect, to relax from the rounds of contests and competitions, to imbibe some of Holmes's own moderately pragmatic legal thought? One can only guess, for this was a path not taken. Instead, Bob was eager to get started in a firm, and he wrote his father for advice. Go to Cincinnati, his father replied, and begin your practice.[23]

For Bob Taft, the law school, like Taft and Yale before it, admirably suited his quick, retentive mind, his penchant for facts, his uneasiness with broad philosophical dimensions. All three schools appealed to his instinct for competition, and they intensified his passion for achievement. Probably they honed his already organized and systematic mind. Whether the schools could have molded a more curious and inquiring attitude in such a boy is one of the mysteries of pedagogy. But because he sometimes seemed abrupt and dogmatic — "so firm in his convictions that it made him somewhat adamant and autocratic," a law school classmate recalled — it is relevant to say that they did not.[24]

If schooling proved unexciting, what of the wider world? For while Bob was striving for excellence at Yale, his father was moving reluctantly toward his inauguration as President in 1909. As Bob toiled at Harvard, the great TR returned from the hunt in Africa to engage Bob's father in grimmer battles. Soon the old friends were fighting furiously over the future of the Progressive movement and the Republican presidential nomination of 1912. Roosevelt, irate at the Old Guard, confessed a wish to shoot his old friend Elihu Root, now allied with Taft. And Taft, shattered by the break, blurted, "even a rat in a corner will fight," and later retired to his Pullman car and cried. Too busy combatting congressional insurgents in 1910 even to attend his son's graduation, he confessed sadly, "Sometimes when I have been greatly distressed over my own shortcomings as President, I have found full consolation in Robert's achievements." [25]

Consolation, perhaps, but not inspiration, for President Taft proved an often inept politician at a time when the forces of change would have tried the skills of a genius. Clinging to the party machinery, he staved off Roosevelt's challenge at the 1912 convention, but the Rough Rider rode again. Accusing Taft unfairly of "stealing" southern delegates, TR broke from the party and ran on a Progressive ticket. The split destroyed Republican chances in November and permitted Woodrow Wilson to slip into the White House, where he remained for eight years. The hapless Taft, all but ignored in the campaign, finished a poor third with only two states and eight electoral votes.[26]

Taft, ever philosophical, had often complained about public life anyway — "politics," he told Nellie in 1906, "makes me sick" — and time killed the pain.[27] But what of the son? Did living amidst the pomp of the White House develop social graces in the young man who worked so unremittingly at Yale and Harvard? Did he gradually adopt his father's views on public issues? Did the bitterness of 1912 sour him on reformers and insurgents and turn him toward conservatism? Above all, what of the effect on his later ambitions? Did Bob, solemnly watching the inauguration of 1909, resolve to follow his father to the White House? Did the defeat in 1912 make him grim, revengeful, ambitious to regain the scepter that the enemy had snatched from his father's hand?

Social life on infrequent vacations in Washington did soften Bob — a little. Often he invited friends to extended house parties, first at the Taft home on K Street, then in the White House. His sister Helen, who was two years younger, did the same, and the party goers relaxed at cards, rode about Washington, attended the theater, dined with the social and political leaders of the city. Bob, enjoying absurd plays on words, especially liked charades, and he delighted in acting out ridiculous roles: wriggling through a maze of whiskey bottles to describe "Coming Through the Rye," and crawling about, nose to the ground, as a bloodhound in *Uncle Tom's Cabin*. Perhaps his most memorable role was the poisoned Hamlet, gasping, "I die, Horatio," just as a group of shocked visitors entered the White House. (He was acting out the word "dynasty" as "die nasty.") A college friend, who recalled boisterous games in the darkened White House, said that this was a "side of Robert Taft that m. ny people didn't have the chance to see. In other words, he was gay but restrained. He was a charming person, very thoughtful, rather full of fun, and turned out to be a very different person from the orator that I'd looked upon with such awe on the campus." [28]

Bob relaxed elsewhere too. He played golf with his father in Georgia during the winter before Taft assumed the burdens of the presidency. He attended debutante parties and weddings of friends. Summers he spent in Murray Bay or Beverly, Massachusetts, where the Tafts vacationed during the presidential years. Twice, in 1911 and 1913, Bob journeyed with classmates to Europe.[29] He also visited old friends in Cincinnati. "I hardly had time to turn around," he wrote his aunt after one such stay. "We had parties every day and all day, and I had a wonderful time." And he went to house parties, reporting to his mother that "there were four Brooklyn girls . . . and six fellows from here. It was a great success, and we all fell in love, but not seriously." His frugal mother worried that he was wasting money, but Will reminded her of the benefits of his presidential salary. "Let them have a good time while they can," he told her. "In four years we may all have to be pedestrians again . . . They are not children to be spoiled by a little luxury now." [30]

Bob had his fun, but there were uncertain and even unhappy times as well. While at Yale, he often did not know where his parents might go. "Could you dispose of yourself this summer?" his mother wrote hurriedly in June 1908, when she anticipated the campaign ahead.[31] After March 1909 he could always stay at the White House, but his mother's stroke in May 1909 temporarily incapacitated her, and political controversies plagued his father. For Bob, the White House served more as an occasional refuge than as a home, and he was seldom nostalgic about it. What roots he had — and even these did not sink deeply — were in Cincinnati, not at 1600 Pennsylvania Avenue.

His social life, such as it was, also failed to change him substantially, and though he developed more poise as he matured, he seemed as self-contained as ever. Even his friends smiled at his reserve. "You human safety valve of enthusiasm," a girl friend chided him gently. A classmate, urging Bob to go to Europe with him, worried only partly in jest that Bob found him too fun-loving. "I'm a reformed character," the friend insisted. When Bob returned from this trip, his sister laughed, "It seemed a good joke for such a serious minded and systematic person as yourself to be seeing Europe with such happy go lucky people as Kim and Jack." She pegged him well: the White House years left Bob as reserved as before. Save among his closest friends, he always would seem cool and preoccupied, and he seldom took the reins from his emotions. As a law school classmate phrased it, Bob was "distressingly undemonstrative, which made many people regard him as cold." [32]

Whether the White House years determined the course of Bob's political philosophy cannot be settled absolutely, for the making of a mind defies precise description. Yet those were the impressionable years, and the tribulations of the father did not go unnoticed by the son. To begin with, William Howard Taft occasionally found time to talk about public affairs with his children and even to read editorials aloud at the breakfast table. President Taft respected Bob's mind and in 1911 wrote him a detailed sixteen-page letter dealing with the intricacies of tariff legislation. The son followed his father's fortunes closely in the press, while working to interest his apathetic classmates in public affairs. [33]

Bob also observed politics firsthand. In 1908 he watched his father receive the presidential nomination in the broiling Chicago Coliseum, and though the press reported that the "glare of publicity has proved embarrassing to the youth," it also noted that he was "taking his visit seriously" and intently tallying the vote. Taking time off from Yale in March 1909, he braved the blizzard that ominously disrupted his father's inauguration and, "serious and solemn," watched the ceremonies from a seat in the Senate gallery. Sensibly avoiding the 1912 convention, he stayed with his father at the White House and eagerly followed the balloting. Bob was fully aware of his father's activities and intelligent enough to grasp the essentials of his thinking.[34]

The similarities in the mature thought of father and son, moreover, were striking. As a judge, William Howard Taft had thundered against the secondary boycott and quickly acquired a poor reputation among unions; the son, equally blunt, later wrote the Taft-Hartley Act, which banned the practice, and he fought labor spokesmen ever after. The father always insisted that tariffs could be set scientifically by determining costs of production at home and abroad; so, despite formidable evidence to the contrary, did his son. Both Tafts, like Alphonso, consistently criticized eastern monopolists and Wall Street speculators, and both believed firmly that the Sherman Antitrust Act could keep them under control. In their later years both men evolved social philosophies sanctioning limited governmental action to secure social justice for the lower classes.[35]

Their political ideas revealed other marked parallels. Both adhered unquestioningly to the Republican party and insisted on control of the party by regulars. Both inveighed against the excesses of party primaries and of the initiative and the referendum. They denounced "agitators" for overnight reforms and deplored the excessive volume of meddlesome legislation. Each cherished strict interpretations of the Constitution, especially the doctrines of separation of powers and of states' rights, while at the same time adopting a broad view of the commerce power of the national government. Both insisted on the preservation of individual freedom, so long as it did not infringe the liberties of others.

Above all, both stressed the absolute necessity of what they called government by law, as opposed to rule by decree, bureaucracy, or naked power. For William Howard Taft, pre-eminently the jurist, this was high dogma; for Bob, product of Harvard Law School, it was no less so. This trust in law profoundly shaped their views of world politics, for both cherished the faith that international law could resolve serious disputes between nations. On the domestic scene Bob always felt that the rule of law was his father's root faith. Reading a draft of Henry F. Pringle's biography of his father, Bob insisted in 1939 that Pringle had missed this point. "I do not think you distinguish clearly enough," he wrote, "between the attitude of mind which considers that the whole future of civilization depends on the rule of law in an ordered society, and one which sympathizes with the big bankers of Wall Street and the reactionary heads of small industrial concerns." [36] While chief justice in the 1920's, William Howard Taft ordered the motto, "Equal Justice Under Law" to be inscribed on the new Supreme Court Building. His son, two decades later, gave the same title to perhaps his most famous speech. It denounced arbitrary government in general and the ex post facto nature of the war crimes trials in Nuremberg in particular.

Bob not only sounded like his father, but also in later years prided himself on it. "I don't definitely remember my father giving me any direct political or philosophical advice," he wrote in 1945. "However, he did frequently state his own views on many subjects of current interest and undoubtedly I derived many of my political and philosophical ideas from these views." Two years later he went further: "I don't suppose anyone has a more sincere admiration for him than I have. Most of my political philosophy was derived from him, and I have never read any of his speeches that I do not wonder at his clear-sighted analysis of governmental problems." In 1952 he concluded that "my course, both in domestic and foreign affairs, would meet his entire approval." [37]

Naturally father and son did not always agree. President Taft, remembering his endless struggles with Congress, was often contemptuous of senators, while for Bob legislative work in general and the Senate in particular provided endless satisfactions.[38] Taft, judicious, hated to offend and tended to temporize; Bob, increasingly sure of himself in later years, was more forthright, though ready as a legislator to compromise — in a way that his less political father rarely could.

But these differences mattered relatively little. They reflected contrasts in personality more than in political thinking. Surely, Bob did not emerge from law school in 1913 with a coherent political credo, and his father did not try to force his views on his children. "I have really started to correspond with my father," Bob wrote in late 1913, "which pleases me a great deal . . . Before this I have always written regularly to my mother, but have felt doubtful, perhaps rather foolishly, about bothering my father, or taking his time." [39] But President Taft's example already loomed large, and his career seemed to Bob so upright, honest, and decent. Of the myriad instruments which modeled the mind of young Bob Taft, the ample image of his father impressed itself as deeply as any.

.

Bob's thinking may have resembled that of his father, but one wonders if his father's example also led to the subsequent choice of politics as a career. Many people later thought so. *Time* magazine, in one of its typical effusions, argued in 1953 that "more than anything else, Robert Taft wanted to follow the footsteps of his father, the huge mustachioed William Howard Taft, into the White House." And his sister Helen, writing in 1952, suggested tentatively that Bob was "tremendously excited" by his father's inauguration. "To this day Bob can relate step-by-step every detail of the ceremony. Perhaps, unconsciously, it was there that he acquired his first ambition to be President." [40]

Bob also showed considerable interest in the 1912 campaign. "We hope that TR will draw more from the Democrats where the latter are made up of labor and socialistically inclined," he wrote with characteristic precision. "Then we hope to get a good deal of the foreign and Catholic vote." When Wilson won, Bob consoled himself with the thought that "the Republicans will return just about the time we can begin to take a proper interest in politics." And in April 1913 he thought about his own future:

> I don't favor the state legislature. I don't see why you can't take part in politics, and in every campaign and convention and the like, and not hold office, at least until you have established enough of a law practice so that you can go back and make money enough to live on. I don't see why it should take very much time, and it really seems to me as if everybody *ought* to do that much. [41]

Bob's interest in politics at this stage — and especially his desire to serve once he had achieved financial independence and freedom from pressure — were incontestable.

But he had drawn no blueprint. Indeed, he was to begin his own career seven years later as a state legislator. Neither his father nor his mother ever encouraged him to think about the presidency, and Bob's friends, though jokingly calling him the "Crown Prince" at Yale, recalled that if he had latent presidential ambitions, he wisely kept them under his hat. Later, of course, he worked tirelessly for the presidency, but only after long years of service in state and local politics. Like his father and grandfather before him, Bob believed in moving up gradually.[42]

Even 1912 seemed to leave him unmoved. "The election," he wrote, "was a disappointment but not unexpected, of course. My chief disappointment is that TR polled so many votes, and promises lots of trouble in the future. Then I have a feeling that Wilson succeeded by means of a good deal of hypocrisy . . . Perhaps not, and I should rather like to see him turn out well if he really is sincere." Later he worried about the influence of William Jennings Bryan, and he came to find Wilson "intolerant," but he never lashed out, publicly or privately, against either TR or Wilson, and Roosevelt's daughter, Mrs. Alice Longworth, became a warm personal friend. Reverses, he seemed to imply, simply happen in politics, and one keeps on fighting in hopes of winning the next time around.[43]

Possibly, of course, Bob merely repressed his feelings and determined to avenge his father some day in the future. More probably the 1912 contest against TR reinforced his faith in party regularity. Certainly he respected his father's reluctance to play to the crowd, as he himself refused to try to do in his own career. But however instructive, the election of 1912 was not traumatic, and it left neither marks nor scars that had to heal. Molded by family tradition, Bob moved naturally into politics in 1920. Trained to achieve and to excel, he moved steadily ahead until in 1940 he grasped for the ultimate prize. Before then he had probably dreamed of reaching the White House — as a politician growing in stature, it would have been surprising if he had not. Besides, he had always been number one. But he kept his dreams to himself, and they looked to the future, not to gaining revenge for the political defeats of his father.

•

The years of adolescence and postadolescence, it is often said, may engulf or even overwhelm the fragile psyche. At least, they tyrannize it, molding a man out of discrete and impressionable parts. These frightening years do much to develop the adult personality, to shape a style of life, to establish an identity through which one comes to terms with himself and the wider world.

For Bob Taft, they were indeed bewildering and tense, because they thrust a sensitive, uncertain boy — "with a nature somewhat highly wrought," his father had warned Horace in 1903 — into new and difficult worlds. One by one, he conquered them the only way he knew how, by masking his feelings and by straining his powerful mind to excel in his studies. As he surmounted the hurdles, he began acquiring the sense of self-assurance and of belonging necessary in the world of adults.

But only gradually. Bob had long since stopped clinging to his mother, but his father still exercised a firm hold on everything he did. At thirteen Bob had crossed the Pacific alone to go to his uncle's school. Barely seventeen, he had moved on to Yale, his father's college, followed him into Skull and Bones, labored to surpass his father's academic record, doggedly entered the speaking prize competitions, and even joined his father's fraternity. Without questioning why, he had become a Republican and had taken the lead in trying to instill some sense of political consciousness into his fun-loving companions. Again automatically, he had followed the example of Alphonso, of his father, and of his uncles by going on to law school and by excelling once again. In all these activities Bob showed not the slightest sign of rebellion or resentment, and openly, at least, he never did. In some ways there was no good reason why he should have, for the path he pursued was neither unreasonable nor unusual for young men of his class and generation. His success in his studies also offered ample compensation for shortcomings in sports and in making friends. Yet Bob's unrelenting attempts to please his father suggested that he might have doubted, as adolescents are wont to do, the strength of the love his undemonstrative parents held for him. And his unquestioning obedience was proof indeed that he was yet far from being an adult by 1913.

His father's prominence affected Bob's personality as much if not more than it did his thinking. It pushed a boy already self-conscious ever more into the limelight. It made a competitive, striving boy all the more anxious to succeed on his own. "Be careful whom you pick as friends," Dink Stover's friend Le Baron advised when Stover arrived at Yale. "Remember, you're going to be watched from now on." Bob, the "Crown Prince," was watched closest of all, and he strove to prove himself. The Taft name helps, he said in 1910 to the ever inquiring reporters. "I know it's an asset. It supplies the impetus which gives a man his start, but this impetus does not last forever. After the start is made, it is only by his own efforts that a man can keep going, and one with a family name has a lot to live up to." Later he added, "I had a deathly fear that I would be accepted because of my father and not for myself." [44]

A competitive boy in the limelight. It meant unceasing effort to excel, and by the grace of intelligence and good health he shone in school, college, the law, and later in politics. It also meant increased knowledge, ever growing faith in his own wisdom, a sense of direction and purpose that was astonishingly intense, and ultimately a confident and unflinching courage rare among politicians. But success also required rigorous self-control and hours of solitary effort which, in turn, reinforced the shyness. He developed into something of a loner, he was vulnerable to the charge of being "cold," and he lacked the dubious virtue of suffering fools gladly.

A reticent boy in the limelight. It meant a refreshing modesty, a reluctance to capitalize on the fame of a name. While traveling abroad with his college friends, he refused to use his father's name to gain entrée to special occasions, and he flared angrily when one of his companions tried to do so. While he was in law school, a girl tried to place him. "Where are you from?" "My family's from Ohio." "Do you visit there on holidays?" "No, they're in Washington now." "What does your father do?" "He has a government job." "Where do they live?" "Pennsylvania Avenue." The girl gave up the inquiry, and Bob, who was not indulging in coquetry, preserved his privacy. Even in his years as a senator, veteran reporters marveled at the essential modesty underlying the apparent crust of certitude, and much more than many other sons of famous men, Bob Taft preserved his plain ways and sense of proportion.[45]

Ducking the spotlight meant tensions as well. Photos of him in adolescence invariably show a boy wary, withdrawn, obviously anxious to get away. Overaware of his inherited prominence, he grew more, not less self-conscious, and he shunned the company of strangers. Instead of developing an easy camaraderie, he held back, reluctant to expose himself. Later, choosing the most vulnerable of professions because he wanted to *do* something, he learned to live with the glare of publicity, but the man remained the boy, a democratic politician caught to his disadvantage in an age of mass politics and mass media.

As he prepared to leave his classmates at Harvard in 1913, Bob ruefully recognized how he seemed (and always would seem) to others. I am sorry to be leaving my classmates, he wrote. "I am afraid that I feel we are good friends perhaps more than they do. I must give the impression to people that I don't enjoy their company, when it is quite untrue. George [Harrison, a friend] once called it a quiet reserve. That sounds very well; but it ought to go by a harsher name, and perhaps it does." [46]

CHAPTER 4

Days of Drift and Deference

As soon as Woodrow Wilson took the oath of office in 1913, he electrified the nation by calling a special session of Congress and driving it, wrangling and rebellious, through the Washington summer. Attacking the trusts, cutting down the tariff that had bedeviled his predecessor, he brought to politics a moralistic fervor that thrilled his supporters. America stirred with the drama of high politics.

In saying "no" to Justice Oliver Wendell Holmes, Bob Taft spurned all this excitement. After traveling around Europe, he headed for the only place he could begin to call his home. Cincinnati, complacent and relatively unexciting, received him in September 1913. Except for a brief interlude during World War I, he was to remain there until entering the Senate more than twenty-five years later.

Taft made this decision a little reluctantly. "Washington," he wrote, "really seems the nicest place in the country to live, and I hate to think of going to live elsewhere." Cincinnati, on the other hand, seemed strange. "I shall have no friends, to begin with at least, and shall have to go almost without ever seeing a great many people whom I have come to know very well." Then he consoled himself; "if after a year or so I do not like Cincinnati, it would be practically no loss of time to go to another city." [1] Such were his initial ties to the city that always considered him its own.

Why this fateful decision? For one thing, he lacked deep roots anyplace else. Many people urged him toward New York, site of the great and important law firms, and Uncle Henry offered him a place there. Like Alphonso, Bob refused the rewards of the nation's financial center. "They are so aggressive," he complained of New Yorkers. "Perhaps it is seeing so much of New York and Eastern people. I have so long decided that New York was the last place, that I spend a great deal of time in argument, uselessly." And although he liked Washington best of all, his parents were moving to New Haven, where his father became professor of law at Yale in 1913. Bob would have no family in the capital.[2]

Not so in Cincinnati. His Uncle Charley and Aunt Annie, having no sons at home, beseeched him to stay with them. Most important, his father prodded his son toward the city of his birth. "He is very anxious," Bob wrote, "that I should make a success in Cincinnati, both at law and in politics." Indeed, his father had written a friend in 1910 as follows: "I expect to send him to Cincinnati; and there have him grow up in the place where I lived and where I think he ought to make his reputation."[3] Leaving nothing to chance, Taft even placed Bob with the firm of Maxwell and Ramsey. His letter to Lawrence Maxwell, an old acquaintance who had served with him on the University of Cincinnati law faculty in the 1890's, spoke volumes:

> I have the prejudice of a father, but I think you will find him a very earnest, quiet, hard worker, with courage to speak when it is needed, but without any disposition to exploit himself. Of course, I am quite aware that he is not able in his present condition to render service of value, and you can find out when he is of any assistance to you and compensate him accordingly. I should hope that in a year or two years he would acquire sufficient knowledge of the practice to start out for himself; or, that if you find him useful, you and he can agree upon terms without any intervention of mine.[4]

Maxwell, no fool, agreed to hire Harvard's top graduate for nothing. Then Taft informed Bob of what he had done. "I don't want you to be anxious about the compensation you are getting," he said. "You can count on me to give you enough to live on but not to splurge on." Bob knew he could earn a salary with Uncle Henry in New York. But Maxwell, who had been President Grover Cleveland's solicitor general from 1893 to 1895, enjoyed a nationwide reputation. And Bob honored his father. Still unsure of himself and willing in any event to try Cincinnati, he acceded without questioning his father's right to make such binding decisions. "I had a letter from my father yesterday," he wrote, "that he had made all the arrangements for my going into Mr. Maxwell's office next year. It was all news to me, but it is about the best office in Cincinnati to start in, and I suppose someone had to make the arrangements." [5]

Despite his misgivings, Bob soon found Cincinnati a pleasant place to be. His aunt and uncle doted on him and established him in their splendid and graceful house on Pike Street in downtown Cincinnati. Bob marveled at the Rembrandts, Corots, and other art treasures that decorated the interior. "It gives me more pleasure to sit and look at them," he wrote, "than at all the galleries in Europe." Aunt Annie, a pillar of the symphony, took him along regularly, and he met a variety of interesting people. Cincinnati, he said, "seems to be rather an enterprising place artistically . . . It is self reliant . . . And the people are more friendly and have more pride. I really like it very much." [6]

Soon he had settled in. He joined the University Club. He played bridge. Sundays he golfed. "If it would *only* snow," he joked, "I should certainly go to church." He danced Indian-style for a vaudeville benefit. He worried about losing his hair. "The barber," he wrote, "assures me that I will lose it . . . I have taken to using tonic and rubbing frantically every night." He read steadily: the novels of Anthony Trollope, George Trevelyan on the American Revolution, William James on psychology, his father's new *Popular Government,* and many books on economics and politics.[7] And he took part dutifully in the whirl of parties and dances that his many relatives arranged. "I succeeded in paying three calls," he wrote, "on people whom I did not want to see and who were all out." At one dinner he endured a boring girl: "the most uninteresting person in the city, and does not know it." And at another he grew careless: "I did a queer thing," he confessed. "I drank two cocktails whereas usually I only drink one; two is too many and I felt very dizzy and especially as we waited until 8:30 for dinner." [8] Bob, his intimates knew, had a quiet, wry sense of humor, but he was never to drink immoderately.

But there was nothing amusing about his job, and Bob soon regretted the decision to take it. At Harvard he had listened to great minds; he had been reared to think about important things; and he was truly and idealistically ready to serve. "I believe that I can start off in life with a better aim and purpose, and more definite ideals and beliefs than I could have done before," he wrote in September 1913. "I have made up my mind what course is right, and that I will follow it with all the energy and courage I can." Maxwell could perhaps have fulfilled these aspirations, for he was then engaged in an important case defending the National Cash Register Company of Dayton against antitrust proceedings brought by the Wilson administration. The firm also handled many other significant cases involving corporate and antitrust law, and Bob might at least have profited from observing the painstaking thoroughness and attention to detail for which Maxwell was famed. Instead, Maxwell, a remote, frugal Scot, proved too absorbed in his work to be concerned with the welfare of his new acquisition. Bob seldom got the chance to talk with him, and he received little attention from the other members of the firm. "The law," he complained, "really seems to be the most dilatory proceeding anyway. No one is ever in a hurry and everything can be and is postponed. If you have a tendency to procrastinate, this is the place to do it." [9] In place of challenging dialogue with Oliver Wendell Holmes and the bright law clerks of Washington, Bob — number one wherever he had gone — had a desk of his own (no stenographer), a decent view of the city, and time on his hands.

Restless, he turned elsewhere. He studied for his bar examinations and passed them in December with the highest marks in the state. He undertook legal-aid work. Defending a "nice looking darkey" charged with murder, Bob gradually found him to be a "cheerful kind of a coon," and worked successfully to reduce the charge to assault and battery. "It is a sort of charity that I can really take some interest in," he wrote. "In fact I seem to be engaged in free legal work most of the time, and it might as well be for the poor . . . I do feel rather sorry for the indigent criminal." [10] And he engaged in legal tasks for relatives, especially for Uncle Charley and Aunt Annie, whose far-flung financial enterprises included a 157,000-acre ranch in Texas, such companies as the Taft Packing House and Taft Crystal Shortening, and countless investments, the *Times-Star* among them, in Cincinnati. Later, these interests were to occupy much of Bob's time. Still, he fretted. Legal-aid work, however satisfying, did not absorb him, and the business for relatives was so routine it was laughable. "I am thinking of taking to glasses as a regular thing," he joked, and "practicing a deep, sonorous voice." He was — and he knew it — "a farce." [11]

One of Bob's fortunate attributes was a steadiness that was always to stop him from despair, and he tried hard to rationalize his menial status. After all, he reasoned, one has to begin somewhere, and working for Maxwell saved the expense of starting an office of his own. He forced himself to see the silver lining. "I do feel confident now," he wrote, "that I can make a success, that is, that I shall not make a failure. I am not very good at some things, but at one or two kinds of work I think I am pretty good, and there are so many stupid men apparently making a living easily that I feel encouraged." [12] But the months rolled by, and Maxwell still paid him nothing. Bob looked for "some man a little older than I" with whom to go into partnership, and he flirted with an offer to work with another lawyer, turning it down, again on his father's advice. Finally, he attacked Maxwell directly, tapping him for $70 a month starting in July 1914. He stayed with the firm three more years and gradually increased his monthly income to $150.[13] But he remained restless, underworked, and poorly paid. A more confident man might have abandoned the firm before then, but Bob liked Cincinnati and he still needed time to break familial bonds and to strike out for himself.[14]

·

Besides, he was courting. Martha Wheaton Bowers — brown-haired, dark-eyed, and vivacious — had captivated many young men, including young John Foster Dulles, who even proposed marriage to her on one occasion.[15] She had first met Bob at a dance in 1908 at Rosemary Hall, a girl's boarding school in Connecticut. Bob, a Yale sophomore, had not paid much attention to her then. But when her father, Lloyd Bowers, Yale valedictorian, classmate and friend of William Howard Taft, left his important job as counsel for the Chicago and Northwestern Railroad in Chicago to serve as Taft's solicitor general in 1909, she moved to Washington. Inevitably, she met Bob, home on vacation at Christmas, for she was then twenty, only three months younger than he, and her brother Tom was Bob's close friend at Yale and Harvard. Soon Bob became attentive, and by 1912 he was corresponding with her. They hiked together in Montana, duly chaperoned, that summer. Bob had never shown such interest in any girl before, and well before he arrived in Cincinnati in 1913 his heart belonged in Washington.[16]

Martha was a slim, graceful, pretty girl, who enjoyed the social whirl and who loved to travel; in 1913 she took a trip around the world. But she also appreciated intelligent conversation, and she was deeply interested in political questions. Her father had drawn up the injunction served on Eugene Debs during the Pullman strike of 1894, and well before his appointment as solicitor general he had been recognized as one of the most brilliant corporate lawyers of his generation. "I do not think that Yale has ever given her degree to a man with a finer mind," Charles Evans Hughes, the future chief justice, said of Bowers in 1915.[17] Because Bowers was widowed when Martha was seven, and because he did not remarry until she was sixteen, it was he who assumed the major role in her upbringing before he died suddenly in 1910. He took her to the opera, gave her lessons in Latin when she was eight, brought her along on trips, and introduced her early to the worlds of law and politics. A strong student, she impressed her schoolmates as the brightest girl in her class: "And still they gazed and still their wonder grew,/That one small head could carry all she knew," read the salutation given her in the school yearbook. She then taught Latin briefly at Rosemary Hall and attended the Sorbonne in Paris before settling in Washington. Because she was talkative and witty she seemed the opposite of her quiet, solemn suitor. Yet Bob and Martha enjoyed remarkably similar backgrounds, their fathers had long been close, and they had many friends in common. Bob, who appreciated intelligent girls, may have seen in Martha something of his own mother's interest in public affairs, and Martha may have found in Bob the qualities of quickness and dedication which had characterized her suddenly deceased father.[18] At any rate, Bob discovered at last someone with whom he could share the emotions that he kept resolutely hidden from others. Returning on board ship, after seeing her in Europe in 1913, Bob revealed his feelings. "I have never before been free from a strong sense of restraint with anyone, and a feeling that I did not want them to know all my thoughts. And I have never felt that I should be so comfortable as a confidant." [19]

In Cincinnati he missed her, and Martha longed to be with him. But George Harrison, Bob's close friend at Yale and Harvard, had taken the job with Holmes that Bob had rejected, and was lavishing attention on her. The situation was awkward because neither Bob nor Martha wished to hurt Harrison. Finally, George confessed his love. ("I could not help myself," he wrote to Bob. "She became everything on earth to me. My every thought and hope was centered in her.") Martha let him down gently, Bob was understanding, George became best man at the wedding, and the friendship between the rivals persisted through life. But the triangle had tried Bob's patience as he fretted, unpaid, unable to marry, in faraway Cincinnati.[20]

Christmas time 1913 arrived at last, and Bob hurried to Washington. There he proposed formally and was accepted. Returning to the empty hours at Maxwell and Ramsey, he poured forth his love. "You are the best, bravest, sweetest, prettiest, *and* most sensible girl in the world, and I would give *anything* to be with you for this evening and kiss you good night." Later: "When I sit down to write to you, the first thing I want to do is tell you how much I love you, and the moment a sentence is finished it is not enough, and I want to tell you how much more than that it is, and so probably my letters seem very foolish." And: "When we are married I am afraid you will have to sit with me a good many evenings before the fire, and listen to me talk, or read together. As I can think of nothing in the *world* I should like better (except for my talking), I am sorry for you." [21]

Bob, outwardly so manly and dignified, could mock himself and even turn giddy to Martha. "Do you think I ought to ask permission to marry you? And what would you do if they refused? Perhaps I ought to make a formal proposal to Tom for his sister's hand. That's what they would do in Trollope." He cherished the awkwardness of his proposal: "With all your experience can you tell when a man intends to propose? Did you know I was going to? Or were you really as surprised as you looked? If only it had not been so cold, and I hadn't stammered so, it would be a very much more poetic memory." He hid nothing. Hearing she was ill, he said, "I don't intend ever to let you be sick even if you have to gargle listerine. As proof of my *devotion,* I will tell you that I have put tonic on my hair regularly since I came back, and I do think my hair has stopped coming out." Compared with Martha's letters, which were decorous and reserved, Bob's revealed a tenderness and great depth of feeling.[22]

He grew lonely again. Determined at first to support Martha by himself, he despaired at his lack of progress with Maxwell. But Martha's father had left her an estate of $200,000, and Bob decided to swallow his pride and to use the income from that until he could make his own way. "I did not like the idea of living on your money," he told her. "I don't exactly now. But it would be a very long time before I could really earn enough to supply half our expenses . . . I don't believe having money easily will affect my work. I shall work just as hard, and I am quite sure that having you with me will be a good deal more of an inspiration than money will be a deterrent . . . So altogether I submit gracefully to being spoiled, and it will not be so very long before I will do my share at least." [23]

This settled, he gingerly approached his father. "As long as Martha has the money," Bob explained, "it seems that we might as well be married next fall and use it. We shall not be extravagant . . . In fact, I shall not be entirely comfortable living on it . . . You have always given me the best opportunities and the best ideals. I don't believe that in not waiting I am injuring either, and I will do my best to make as much of a success as I know you would like." William Howard Taft beamed and contributed $2000 to the cause. "Nellie and I are both happy about it," he wrote. "We are very fond of Martha. I loved her father. If there is anything in eugenics, it is a wise match — she has a wonderfully bright mind like that of her father." To Martha he confessed his ambitions for his eldest son. "What gives me special satisfaction is that you . . . will be so ambitious for him that it will be your happiness to help him overcome any possible temptation to abate the hardest kind of work to earn his way to the head of his profession and to all the positions of great public usefulness that he could fill so well." [24]

All the hurdles had fallen. They announced their engagement in March, and with the press reporting every detail, they married in October 1914. After a short honeymoon they returned to a rented home at 1812 Dexter Street in Walnut Hills, less than a mile from Bob's birthplace and even closer to the home on Madison Road where he had lived between 1898 and 1900. It was a quiet, tree-shaded neighborhood of large, three-storied homes, and in moving there Bob was truly bringing Martha back to the familiar associations of his childhood.[25]

Martha proved a wise choice — the most helpful in politics, *Time* reported later, since Jessie Benton aided John Frémont. She bore Bob four sons, raising them during his many absences. Poised and witty, she was as gracious and charming as Bob was reserved. They complemented each other well and soon enjoyed warm friendships in Cincinnati. With the passage of years she grew a little high-strung, and she sometimes snapped at Bob for his carelessness in dress and his apparent indifference to what others thought of him. But these things mattered little, because Bob tried to please — it was stupid to argue over trifles — because Martha never brooded, and because they enjoyed a rare intellectual compatibility. They seldom demonstrated open affection, and there were few whispered confidences, meaningful looks, or public embraces. But that was their way, and no one doubted the bonds that united them. When a stroke crippled her in 1950, Bob's genuine tenderness revealed the strength of their ties.

Above all, they agreed on the large things, where to live, whom to have as friends, how to raise their children, how to be *useful* in life. Bob was ambitious, often busy or away, but Martha was unlike Nellie, who criticized Will for arriving late to social engagements. On the contrary, Martha seldom complained, for she maintained interests of her own, she cared deeply about the issues as well as the glitter of politics, and she shared all Bob's aspirations. Too outspoken to keep silent, she felt free to disagree with her husband. But she rarely nagged or pushed to change his style, and Bob was used to intelligent women in his family. He was proud of her, pleased to test his wits against her, happy to have her seen and heard. And to the distress of some of his friends and occasionally even of his sons, it was she and she alone who provided the deep human companionship that he could not bring himself to share with others. It was one of those unusual partnerships of equals, of individuals liking, loving, and respecting each other.[26]

.

For some people, marriage spurs ambitions. Cutting ties with the past, it drives them to work harder, to worry about the future, and to develop a sense of independence.

With Bob this may have been true in some ultimate, gradual sense, because marriage forced him to make decisions without always listening to his father. But winning a belle like Martha over such clamorous competition as Harrison seemed at first to give him such self-confidence that he took time out from ceaseless striving to tarry and to enjoy his new marital status. Visiting the young couple early in 1915, Bob's father was pleased. "Bob and Martha," he wrote, "seem to be like two cooing doves in a nest. They are sympathetic in their tastes, they are quiet in their manner, philosophical in their temperament, considerate in their treatment of everybody, and effective for work in their methods." [27]

Though Bob's work annoyed him, he stayed with it because he was not yet ready to strike out on his own. Instead, he kept busy with a myriad of activities — legal-aid work, Boy Scouts, fund raising for Uncle Horace, writing the minutes as secretary of the Cincinnati Yale Club. At home he hung pictures, maintained the house, read a good deal. For exercise he gardened, and he golfed with old friends like John Hollister every Sunday. Martha owned an electric car, and they rattled over the surrounding country on weekends. For most of his life Bob tired easily of all such diversions except golf, fishing, and detective stories. But these were the easy years of early marriage, and if he grew restless, he gave little sign of it.[28]

From afar his father continued to remind him of the satisfactions of public service, but even civic affairs failed to move Bob in these happy years. "I do want to do some sort of political work, and will almost certainly have time," he had written Martha in 1913. But he delayed. Discovering that he could not vote in the elections that fall, he wrote, "I have not done anything about politics . . .

I want to find out something more about things before doing any thing." Once married and settled, he moved gingerly into politics by joining the local Republican club, doing some precinct work, and taking part in the City Club, a good-government group active in seeking a home rule charter for Cincinnati. He attended the 1916 national convention, and he joined other young Republicans in criticizing Wilson for what Bob regarded as insufficient courage in resisting the claims of organized labor. (Wilson, Bob said privately, was a "hypocrite and opportunist.")[29] But Bob was dabbling.

The local situation in part accounted for his relative unconcern. Solidly Republican, Cincinnati remained tightly controlled by the heirs of the political machine developed in the 1880's by George B. Cox. The journalist Lincoln Steffens in 1905 had called it America's worst-governed city, and it had not advanced in the next decade. The machine was unimaginative, inefficient, dependent for control on masses of politically apathetic slum-dwellers in the central city. The bosses did not need Bob Taft, and he, in turn, shunned their saloons and corner clubhouses. "The mayor," he had written Martha early in 1914, "is an old German about thirty years behind the times and nothing but a gangster anyway." Yet he also distrusted do-gooders. Encountering one, he told Martha "he is something of a reformer and like most of them a little queer." The machine, Bob admitted in a most revealing letter, was "about as crooked as possible." But what was one to do?

> I have always believed in going into a party and staying there unless there is some great change. The weakness of any reform movement is that though it succeeds once or twice, a machine which is continuous is such a powerful means of getting out the vote in a city that it is almost certain to prevail in the long run. People will not vote, or a large number won't, if there is nothing except the papers and civic welfare to urge them. In addition to that I think that bad as the machine may be it is bound to do negative good in preventing radical changes into which any reform movement is apt to slide.[30]

Thus it was characteristic of Bob that his one serious venture into politics in these years was to support the City Club's drive for a home rule charter. Such a change, he thought, would free the city from the clutches of rural state lawmakers in Columbus. Other reformers, eager to diminish the power of the machine, wished to go further and called for a city manager, a short ballot, nonpartisan elections, and election of city councilmen at large instead of by the ward system that helped to preserve the machine. Bob opposed these changes. Perhaps because he recalled the disastrous effects of insurgency on the Republicans in 1912, he preferred to try to influence the party from within rather than take aim at the principle of party government. When the home rule charter passed in 1917, as he and other moderates wanted, it gave the machine even more freedom from the state and reprieved it for another seven years. Pleased with this triumph over the reformers, Bob turned again to other pursuits.[31]

Chief among these was buying a home, and in 1917 he and Martha found what they had been looking for in an eight-room farmhouse in Indian Hill, twelve miles east of the downtown city. It needed repairs and lacked water or electricity. But it was surrounded by forty-six untouched acres, and it lay in lovely, largely unsettled woodlands high on a rim overlooking the Little Miami River. Taking out a mortgage, they bought it for $15,000 and spent considerably more in expanding and renovating it during the next six years. During this time they had a nearby tenant farmer cultivate the land and lived there themselves in the warm weather months.[32] They called it Sky Farm.

Summers, they also visited Murray Bay. Martha suffered from hay fever and was always quick to go. Left in sweltering Cincinnati, Bob was often lonely. He puttered in the garden, shopped, read novels, and wrote regularly. "I miss you every minute of the day," he sighed. "What do you need? For I can ship anything from rubber nipples to ice chests. Good night, dear, and may you be as happy as is possible (that is, as is possible without me)." A month later, he could hardly wait to escape the office. "The weather is warm today, but not at all bad; the birds are singing merrily outside, and the crickets are beginning; so I feel fairly happy, but somewhat lonely . . . I love you more than all the world." Soon he escaped Cincinnati to revive himself in the familiar associations of the North.[33]

Life grew more complicated when Billy (William Howard Taft III) was born in August 1915. The parents rejoiced, but Billy proved sickly at first. He failed to gain much weight, contracted pneumonia in 1916, and was slow in learning to walk and talk. Seriously frightened, Bob and Martha watched him carefully.[34] But good health developed gradually, and three more sons had arrived hale and hearty by 1925. Blessed with intelligence and easy circumstances, Bob and Martha were lucky parents as well. Until her stroke in 1950, they led fortunate lives, spared financial strain or personal tragedy. Bob was no Abraham Lincoln, mourning a lost son and brooding over human existence; no Franklin D. Roosevelt confined to a wheelchair. If the luck of the draw narrowed his perspective, it freed him from anxiety and preserved his talents for clear-eyed pursuit of his goals.

CHAPTER 5

Finding Himself

IN THE SUMMER of 1914 Europe stumbled into a war that was to leave a generation of its young men maimed or dead. Until early 1917 America stayed at peace, but then Germany determined to stop the flow of food that was aiding the Allies, and the word went out: Sink on sight. Woodrow Wilson, the triumphant days of 1913 far behind, agonized, hardened, finally asked for war.

For some, like young Harry S Truman of Missouri, war meant combat and the chance to test one's mettle under fire. For others, like General Douglas MacArthur, it meant heroism on the battlefield and rapid promotion. For America it meant victory in the war to end all wars, then rapid disillusion and a mood of noninvolvement that profoundly affected the world for decades. For Bob Taft it meant departure from Walnut Hills and the law, the end of the years of drift, the molding of a man of undeviating purpose and dedication.

Like his father and like Wilson, Bob had hoped to avoid war. It seemed none of America's business, and TR, who was striding about calling for intervention, appeared ridiculous. "Aren't the nations of Europe a queer lot, to go to war for nothing?" Bob wrote in 1915. "I can't help thinking that without any cause for war somebody can succeed in making peace." Unlike some of his German-American acquaintances in Cincinnati, he hoped for an Allied victory, and joined other young lawyers of Cincinnati in a preparedness day parade in the summer of 1916. But intervention in Europe's war still seemed foolish.[1]

The sinkings on the Atlantic in 1917 changed many minds, his own included. Bob agreed with his father and with Wilson that

Germany had broken the law, and that illegality must be punished. When Wilson severed diplomatic relations with Germany, Bob approved, and on March 10, 1917, he joined his friends in the Cincinnati Yale Club in urging Wilson to do anything necessary to "defend our national honor and the rights of our citizens upon the high seas." The resolution also called for a "highly increased standing Army" and a "permanent and democratic system of defense, based upon Universal Military Training and service under direct and exclusive federal control." For Bob these were strong words, and he may well have been pleased in 1940, when he was denouncing the draft and defending restrictions on traditional American rights on the seas, that no one resurrected his signature from the forgotten archives of the Cincinnati Yale Club.[2]

In early 1917 Bob was twenty-seven years old, six feet tall, 165 pounds, in vigorous health. He did not wish to fight, but he volunteered for camp, took his physical examination, and prepared to go. Then came the surprise — his eyes were poor, and the Army would not reconsider. Bob was surprised, for he wore glasses only irregularly. "I can see pretty well without glasses," he complained, "and with them as well as anybody." For a while he considered appealing to the surgeon general, but dropped the idea. There were only two reasons for appealing, he said laconically: "one that I am very anxious to be granted a favor which I am not; and the other that I will make such an exceptional officer that the rules ought to be waived, which I very much doubt." His father offered to try to get him into the judge advocate general's office, a haven for lawyers. But Bob rejected that as well. "It seems to me to be a pretty stupid job." Instead, he tried at the next call for officers — and was turned away again.[3]

At first, rejection did not bother him much. But he did wish to do something useful, and he had already heard of the relief work being carried out in Belgium by Herbert Hoover. When Wilson picked Hoover to head a Food Administration in Washington in May, Fred Chatfield, a Cincinnati friend who worked for Hoover, put forward Bob's name. Bob quickly offered his free services, and by June 1917, Hoover was urging him to come. By July, Bob had left Cincinnati for his first government job — with a Democratic administration. Only later, in the summer of 1918, did he chafe seriously enough under his civilian status to volunteer again. "Nearly all my friends are in the Army," he appealed to Hoover. "My failure to enter the Army requires and always will require explanation, and I shall always feel that those who have suffered in the war . . . are regarding me as one who failed to do his real duty." But the law required Hoover's permission, and he stalled, insisting that Bob must not leave his side. This was October. A month later the guns had stilled at last.[4]

.

In wartime Washington thousands of soldiers milled about, brawls broke out on the streets, and suffragettes demonstrated stridently before the city's temples of government. War workers arrived from all parts of the nation, and millionaires labored in cubbyholes for a dollar a year. The city's population, 350,000 in April 1917, leaped to 526,000 by the end of the war, and the slums, already endemic, grew crowded with thousands of blacks who migrated from the South in search of wartime jobs.

If Bob and Martha noticed this turmoil from their dwelling on K Street, they said nothing about it in their letters. She rejoiced at seeing old friends, at the excitement of Washington after the interlude in Cincinnati, and he found time to play golf and poker with Fred Chatfield, Tom Bowers, George Harrison, and other friends from college and law school. Bob also saw more of his father, who moved to Washington in 1918 to become joint chairman of the National War Labor Board. A second son, Bobby (Robert Taft, Jr.), had arrived in February 1917, and Billy, who was slowly learning to talk, seemed better. At first, they had worried about money, but Bob's father helped, and Martha's great aunt died, providentially leaving her $5000. Taking the job with Hoover involved a slight financial sacrifice, but the young Tafts did not suffer.[5]

Bob's job, especially after the tedium of Maxwell and Ramsey, proved stimulating. One of four assistant counsels for the Food Administration, he served in what eventually became a bureaucracy of three thousand salaried and eight thousand volunteer employees. Its task, to speed the production of food, to keep prices down, and to ship provisions rapidly to the soldiers abroad, crucially affected the war effort, and Hoover captivated the nation's imagination with slogans such as "Food Will Win the War" and "Wheatless days in America make sleepless nights in Germany." Relying on licensing agreements, on the power to buy and sell selected commodities, and above all on voluntary agreements to limit retail prices, the agency strove successfully to avoid federal dictation. "I do not believe in compulsory rationing for the American people," Hoover explained. "Americans are the most cooperative people in the world. They are the easiest to lead, the hardest to drive." The Food Administration gave every appearance of brilliant success, and Hoover emerged one of the few heroes of the war effort.[6]

Bob's task would have seemed unglamorous to most. Stuck in a makeshift, wallboard office in hot Foggy Bottom, he worked long hours, and he chafed at what he called the "red tape and delay and confusion" of bureaucratic life. He spent much of his time drafting and interpreting licensing agreements, and he had to master details of the complex American economy. Should Washington regulate tomato pulp, Honduras rice, sweet yeast? What concessions were due the makers of catsup, of green coffee, of evaporated apples? Could the Food Administration commandeer distilled spirits for redistribution? Bakers complaining of a lack of albumin for dried eggs demanded that Bob review the terms. And the radical Nonpartisan League of North Dakota, furious at regulations on the pricing and grading of wheat, forced Bob to take a trip to the Plains, where he engaged in negotiations with Attorney General William Langer of North Dakota, who was later to be one of his most aggressively independent Republican colleagues in the Senate. Bob fretted at the innumerable complaints, and in later years he was to insist that human selfishness made price control unworkable except in wartime.[7]

Still, his work offered some satisfactions. He liked the precision and the detail, and he enjoyed the feeling of being useful for a change. Hoover, who at first had paid Bob little attention, soon appreciated the work of his energetic counsel and asked him to sit on the executive board. By 1918 Bob was performing important work and was being judged by his immediate superiors to be giving "splendia service — very efficient." A cipher in Cincinnati, he was working at the hub in Washington and excelling.[8]

If Bob thought the return of peace would end his work, he was mistaken, for Hoover asked Bob to join him abroad as legal adviser for what was to become the American Relief Administration, handling postwar relief in Europe, and on the afternoon of November 16, 1918, Bob joined "the Chief," as his bright young men called Hoover, in New York. Amid tight security they boarded the British transport *Olympic,* still camouflaged in black and white, staircases boarded up, portholes painted to conceal lights. The sun shone brightly, the water was smooth, and the party rejoiced at the end of war and the prospects for everlasting peace. "We were certain," Hoover recalled, "that the purification of men and the triumph of freedom would herald a new Golden Age. We were indeed proud to play a part in the rebirth of mankind." [9]

A few days out, the warm weather blew away. It grew gray, rainy, rough, and many of the passengers disappeared below. But Bob assured Martha of his "insolent health." Also aboard were such friends as Fred Chatfield and Lewis L. Strauss, Hoover's young personal secretary who was to serve as chairman of the Atomic Energy Commission after World War II. Bob played bridge, relaxed, and enjoyed the comforts, such as they were, of the ship. Hoover occasionally called the party together, but Bob revealed no anxiety about the days ahead. On November 23 they arrived in London; three days later they reached Paris.[10]

Daily life for the Parisians was hard in the winter of 1918–1919. Thousands had lost relatives in the war, and those who had survived lived in a city that still bore some signs of the fighting. Big Berthas had ripped holes in the Luxembourg Gardens, shrapnel had scarred the bridges over the Seine, and children played on German tanks and trench mortars which had been captured and left in the Place de la Concorde. The thousands of dignitaries who streamed into the city for the forthcoming peace conference jammed the cafés and the metro, and American doughboys looking for a high time irritated the natives. The weather, normal for Paris that time of the year, was often dark, raw, and drizzly.

Still, Americans had been eagerly awaiting the peace conference,

and many bright young men like Bob had managed to find spots
on the American delegation or in many of the related agencies and
organizations that participated in the peace which was to end all
wars. John Foster Dulles and his brother Allen, nephews of Secretary of State Robert Lansing, were there. So were Perrin Galpin,
Yale 1910, later president of the Belgian-American Educational
Fund; Stephen Philbin, another of Bob's classmates at Yale who
had been a member of Skull and Bones; George van Santvoord and
Frederick Trubee Davison, who were later to serve with Bob on
the Yale Corporation; and Charles Seymour, a Yale history professor whom Bob and his colleagues on the corporation voted to make
president of Yale in 1937. Bob knew these men and many more
who were later to cross his path.[11]

The sojourn in Paris promised good times as well as peacemaking to these young Americans. Despite the scars of war, Parisian
night life offered endless gaiety, and the Folies Bergères enjoyed
sizable crowds of tourists. For others there was ample choice of
cafés and restaurants, many of which provided fine food and wine
to the Americans who could afford it. Bob occasionally partook of
the more harmless diversions, especially the light opera, which he
often attended with Strauss. Once he joined Philbin, Seymour,
and others for dinner and talked late into the night about such
heady topics as social conditions in eastern Europe, the fighting
ability of the Italians, and the blunders of the delegates at the
peace conference. Most of the time, however, Bob declined to join
the lighter spirits, even though some of them thought him unso-
ciable, even standoffish, as a result. No innocent abroad, Bob had
seen Paris often before, and he cared little for night life. And he
never forgot Martha and the two children at home. In the spring
of 1919, when Martha managed to find reliable nurses in Washington for the children, she sailed over to join him, and Bob rented a
flat for two. Then his associates saw even less of their preoccupied
colleague, for Martha was ever the center of his life.[12]

Besides, from the start Bob had ample work to do, for the relief
needs of the Europeans proved staggering. Placed in charge of arrangements, Bob secured office space for Hoover and his staff, and
before long, fifty rooms echoed to the chatter of typewriters, adding machines, and telegraph instruments. At first he lived with

Hoover and other staff members in a large house near the Troca-
dero, and the party worked harmoniously, often eating together,
entertaining dignitaries, enjoying good talk and the intrigue of
international politics. In addition to handling the administrative
duties of the Paris office, Bob drafted letters and memoranda for
Hoover. He coordinated the relief of a typhus epidemic in Serbia,
haggled with Rumanian officials over credits, and served on the
important Permanent Committee of the Supreme Council of Supply and Relief. This committee, later renamed the food section
of the Supreme Economic Council, met regularly, trying to reach
agreement on supplying foodstuffs to the nations of Europe. Bob
concentrated on Poland and in August accompanied Hoover there,
where Bob received a decoration from Paderewski and a warm
reception by thousands of flag-waving children. Like so many
other young men at Paris, he was a cog, not a vital wheel, in the
immense machinery of peacemaking. Woodrow Wilson never
sought his advice, and Colonel Edward House failed to call. But
Seymour among others deliberately asked him to dine on one occasion in order to get Hoover's perspective on the conference. Bob
also served a key mission which employed 350 people in the Paris
office alone. He was close to Hoover and to the dramatic events of
Paris and Versailles, and he savored the excitement.[13]

He was close enough, indeed, to flinch at what he saw. The Europe of 1919 seethed with misery and rumors of revolution. While
the statesmen struggled in Paris and Versailles, revolutionaries
battled police on the streets of Berlin, and children searched for
food in eastern Europe. Hardened by more than four years of the
deadliest war in history, the English re-elected David Lloyd George
prime minister to the accompaniment of the slogan "Hang the
Kaiser," and the French seemed to glory in the *Realpolitik* of
Georges Clemenceau, the aged premier aptly nicknamed the
"Tiger." In this atmosphere the peacemakers picked for small advantages and petty prizes. When they finally finished their labors
in the summer of 1919, they had written a series of treaties which
departed substantially from the prescriptions proposed by Wilson
and others during the war itself.

The diplomatic intrigue gradually soured Hoover, and through
him — for Hoover inspired enduring loyalties — it discouraged

Bob Taft and the other members of the relief mission. Arguing that more than 200,000,000 people lived in social disorder, Hoover worried about the threat of imminent starvation, especially in the chaotic east European lands once ruled by the Austro-Hungarian Empire. He fretted also about the threat of Bolshevik revolution. "Famine," he had said on leaving New York, "is the mother of anarchy." Distrusting the Allies from the beginning, he believed they were trying to gain control of relief administration so that they could advance their own selfish objectives.[14]

Fearing the worst, Hoover quickly found it. When he disembarked in London, he had discovered the Allies determined on joint authority — a "pool" of relief administration. To Hoover, however, control belonged to the nation supplying most of the food, the United States. Calling on Bob to draft a series of memos to that effect, he held out for American administration of relief. Wilson backed him, and the Allies eventually had no choice but to surrender. By 1919 Hoover and his American aides commanded without dispute, but the haggling had only begun. The Food Administration had encouraged American farmers to produce in mountainous quantities, and had loaded ships with goods for Europe even before the Armistice. The Allies, however, insisted on maintaining the blockade on shipments of food, not only to their former enemies, but also to the neutrals, to stop leaks to the enemy. Hoover's loud protests, coupled with threats to break the blockade of neutrals, restored the food contracts and propped up American farms, banks, and lending institutions. And foodstuffs that leaked from neutral nations helped avert mass starvation in eastern Europe and Germany. But the Allies waited until March 1919 to remove the ban on shipments to their former enemies. The long struggle left Hoover forever convinced of the gulf between what he considered the idealism of America and the *Realpolitik* of Europe, which he dismissed as a "storm of repression and revolution." America, he said, should "retire from Europe lock, stock, and barrel," for the United States was "the only great moral reserve in the world today." [15]

These struggles marked Bob Taft as well. Never starry-eyed about the "war to end wars," he had been so horrified to read of American losses on the battlefield that he feared even to pick up a newspaper, and he doubted the long-range impact of Wilson's rhet oric. "They have been following a kind of illusive hope," he wrote of the administration in March 1918, "that they can win the war by talk." Not sharing the grand expectations of so many Americans at the close of the war, his personal disillusion was slightly less complete.[16]

But it was none the less severe. In Europe only two weeks, he worried that the conference would be the "greatest field for intrigue and international politics since the Congress of Vienna, and I almost wish, considering our representation, that we had let them settle their own troubles when we had licked the Kaiser." Echoing Hoover, he insisted that food should be "administered and distributed by an American," for everyone else had selfish designs. "The Italians are already asking a hand in relief in Jugo-Slavia, and the French in Serbia and Bohemia — the old idea of spheres of influence, political and economic, is still very much alive." The British, he added, are "terrifically afraid that they will lose some part of their trade supremacy," and the French were selfish and tight-fisted. "The whole structure of international politics seems to have reappeared in very much its old form." [17]

Back home in America, Bob's father led the League to Enforce Peace, an influential group of citizens backing a League of Nations, and Bob, who shared this faith, kept him posted. "I am not convinced that an international police force or executive would work," he wrote, "but a League without an agreement to use force, military or economic, against anyone who makes an aggressive war, would be worse than useless." Yet Wilson's rhetoric continued to trouble him. "There is the greatest haziness about the League of Nations, because Wilson has never made clear what he has in mind . . . it seems to me that any League of Nations concerned with economic control would soon fall to pieces . . . it ought to be confined strictly to preventing war and defining what constitutes an aggressive war." In January he complained that "the President is filling in the time by trips to the various capitals of Europe, making felicitous speeches which mean nothing and do not fool the leaders certainly. His 14 points are so indefinite that he can take whatever he can get and say that it was the particular thing he intended." By March he was despondent. "It certainly looks more doubtful [that the conference will succeed] here in Europe with all the international jealousies going around." [18]

As the months of acrimony dragged into 1919, Bob began to despair. The French, he said, have "imperialistic notions" and run their finances "a good deal like a corner grocery." The Italians were impossible: "if they had food, ships, and money they would be worse than the Germans." The American Peace Mission was "hopeless, and the President is undoubtedly to blame first for appointing them, second for neglecting them . . . The result is they all work along in the dark, afraid to call their soul their own." Echoing Hoover ("his view of the whole situation is certainly the soundest," Bob wrote), he resented the Allied blockade, and he trembled at what he regarded as the great appeal of Bolshevism to starving peoples. Bob continued to support the League, but like his father he began to hedge, and he acquiesced eventually even in the reservations attached to it by Henry Cabot Lodge in the Senate.[19]

.

When Bob took time out late in 1919 to reflect, he shared Hoover's pride in the accomplishments of the relief mission. It brought to 200,000,000 people, he said, "not only life but some concrete example of the spirit in which America had fought the war . . . It was by far the greatest purely unselfish task ever undertaken by one people for other peoples, and is certain to leave in Central and Eastern Europe a permanent affection for America and Americans." [20]

Yet the bad taste lingered. America had fought the war, Bob believed, to promote international justice, but the diplomats had bungled the peace. Already Bolshevism was spreading, and people were fighting in the streets. How had this happened? Rejecting "radicals of the *New Republic* class," he refused to accept the thesis that greedy capitalists had written the peace. At fault was the unwillingness of the Allies to "spend another ounce of effort or money for the same ends for which, when they appeared more concrete, they had poured out lives and millions." He deplored other weaknesses as well — the secrecy imposed on the proceedings, the lack of a judicial commission to settle boundary disputes, the absence of any hearing for the enemy ("clear injustice," he called it), and domestic pressures that pulled out American troops too quickly. Above all, the blame lay with the Allies, and Bob again echoed Hoover in distinguishing between American idealism and European selfishness.[21]

His experiences in Paris did not suddenly transform him into an isolationist, a nationalist, or any of the other labels pasted on him in later years. He continued to support (with reservations) the League in 1920, the World Court later in the decade, and the United Nations, again with reservations, in 1945. Yet his approach to international organization, then and later, was legalistic. Following very closely the views of his father, he stressed the need for clearly defined international law, especially concerning aggression, and for a world court to interpret it. What distressed him most about Paris was the emphasis on settling questions by compromise or by force, instead of through judicial tribunals operating according to established principles.[22] The hope that such principles could predominate in 1919 was naive and idealistic. But he had been trained to appreciate the virtues of legal principles, and he clung to this faith through the interwar years. In 1945 he criticized the framers of the United Nations for paying so much attention to power and security, so little to what he called law and justice.

If his father proved one model for Bob, Hoover served as another. Principled, brilliantly efficient, Hoover inspired amazing loyalty among subordinates. Working close to him, eating and sleeping in the same house, deeply grateful for the confidence shown in him, Bob was impressed by Hoover's quick mastery of facts and statistics, and he tended to perceive issues through the eyes of the chief. He endorsed Hoover's voluntaristic approach to price control, his dislike of red tape, and his denunciations of state-imposed economic policies. ("One of the dangers of our work is that of allowing the people to lie down on us," Bob wrote.) He shared Hoover's fears about Bolshevism, and he emerged from the battles of Paris with most of the same doubts about Europeans. Somewhat distant, Hoover did not encourage intimacy, and because Bob had been trained to think for himself, he would never have echoed Hoover's beliefs had they not reflected his own general views in the first place. Even so, Bob Taft kept in touch with his chief, backed him three times for the presidency, called on him in his own battles with New Dealers, and corresponded sporadically with him for the rest of his life. Second only to the awesome figure of William Howard Taft, Hoover seemed a model of what a public figure should be.[23]

By the summer of 1919 the danger of famine seemed over. Bob's work was coming to an end, and he left the squabbles of the Old World for the joys of Murray Bay. Loose ends remained, and he jumped back and forth from Cincinnati to New York and Washington in the coming months, but these things were minor. By September 1919, after more than two years away, he was home in Cincinnati, this time for almost twenty years.

The two years left as strong a mark on Bob Taft as did any comparable period in his life. Well before joining the Food Administration in 1917, he had been interested in public problems, and he had absorbed naturally the Republican views of his father and his friends, but he had never had the chance to test his ideas in practice. The exciting events of 1917 to 1919, which contrasted so sharply with the aimlessness of work at Maxwell and Ramsey, offered him the experience in government that he needed to give his opinions some substance; and because he tended to adhere tenaciously to conclusions once personal experience had reinforced them, he never changed them. He was always to resist peacetime price control and other broad-ranging regulatory efforts by the federal government and to doubt the ability of the United States to settle the ancient animosities of Europe.

The two years had done more than mold his views. The Bob Taft who left Cincinnati in 1917 had been something of a boy, supported by his wife, dependent on his father and his uncle, plodding at menial work. He lacked enough self-assurance to strike out for himself. The Taft who returned had matured. Gone was most of the boyish uncertainty. Though still quiet and though still respecting his father, he was now more assertive than deferential, more confident than hesitant. He had left the humdrum and the familiar to mix with the mighty (three of his colleagues under

Hoover later became senators, four governors), and he had excelled. He had written his father (now, sometimes, it was "Dear
Father," not "Dear Papa") what *he* had seen, and William Howard Taft, as if aware of the change, had listened and had refrained
temporarily from delivering homilies on the importance of
achievement. Throwing the past aside on his return to Cincinnati,
Bob ignored Maxwell and Ramsey and opened his own office. Letting the spotlight rest at last, he plunged immediately into politics,
first to advance Hoover as a presidential nominee, then to run for
the legislature in Ohio.[24]

Taft had found himself. He knew now where he was going, and
he never stopped. The days of drifting and deference were fading
quickly into the past, and years of purposeful self-assurance were
already taking their place.

PART II

The Political Apprenticeship

CHAPTER 6

Neophyte Politician

IF TAFT had suspected the hatreds devouring America in late 1919, he might not have sailed so happily away from Europe. President Wilson, prostrated by a stroke, lay weak and isolated in the White House, too defiant to deal with his enemies, too sick to listen to friends, and the nation drifted, deprived of a captain of state. The war, it seemed, had been wasted. Inflation was wiping out small businessmen, infuriating veterans, and driving organized labor to strike. The new decade dawned on a divided, turbulent country.

Returning to this uncertain scene, Bob Taft might well have shunned public life. Although his Uncle Charley greeted him warmly and launched him with welcome legal work, Bob needed money. He had earned nothing for two years and next to nothing before that; he and Martha hoped for more children; and he was still trying to rehabilitate Sky Farm into a year-round home. Eager to make his own way financially, Taft labored long hours, and by 1921 he was already earning $10,000, a substantial sum for the times. Had he done nothing else but work, no one would have wondered why.[1]

But politics proved too alluring to resist. He rebelled at the idea of nominating the chief Republican presidential contenders, Senator Hiram Johnson of California (a "radical"), General Leonard Wood ("he would not be personally a strong candidate or a very intelligent president"), or dark horses such as Ohio's Senator Warren Harding. "It is necessary," he said, "to nominate a moderate progressive who will defend the existing system but work out such constructive changes as will keep the Republican party a party of progress." Such a candidate would "return to normal relations between government and private enterprise," and back a plank "denouncing socialism and nationalization, within reason." Most important, he would support the League of Nations with reservations.[2]

For Taft and for many others, such a man was Herbert Hoover. Indeed, even Franklin D. Roosevelt, who was to run as the Democratic vice-presidential nominee in 1920, wrote a friend in January that Hoover "certainly is a wonder, and I wish we could make him President of the United States. There could not be a better one." Taft concurred. "He would make a great Republican President," he wrote, "sharing the views of the moderate progressive Republicans while avoiding Socialism and Radicalism on one hand and reaction on the other." Taft began writing letters, making speeches, and raising funds to nominate the man he had served devotedly in the years before.[3]

Taft and his friends fought against heavy odds. First, Hoover had to declare himself available, then he had to announce as a Republican. In March Taft journeyed east to try to secure these commitments from the Chief, and while riding home on the train he put his points in writing. "Much more effective results can be accomplished through the party channels," he told Hoover, "than by independent action." Taft's argument typified his faith in party government, and it was one of many used by others to drive Hoover into action. Five days later the Chief announced his availability for the GOP nomination.[4]

Like his fellow amateurs for Hoover, Taft had much to learn about politics, and with Fred Chatfield, John Hollister, and other friends he blundered early in the campaign by issuing a press release from the Queen City Club, gathering place for Cincinnati's business and professional elite. But he carefully avoided subsequent errors. Anxious not to offend the Cincinnati party organization, which favored Wood, he counseled against running Hoover in the Ohio primary. He also traveled about the state and tried his hand at public speaking in Columbus, Akron, Toledo, Youngstown, Cleveland, and Canton.[5]

In the flush of enthusiasm in March and April he thought Hoover really had a chance. "If neither Wood nor Johnson has enough votes," he wrote, "I believe that their supporters will be more likely to combine on Mr. Hoover than anyone else." But by the time the Republican convention opened in mid-June, he recognized his man had little hope. Still, he secured convention tickets from his father (other seats were "grabbed up by the politicians," he complained), and joined his earnest young friends at Hoover headquarters. They stood by helplessly as the bosses met in the infamous smoke-filled rooms and turned over the prize to Harding. Hoover, the hope of many of the party's younger, more progressive members, never got more than nine and a half votes.[6]

Few conventions in American history have displayed such cold-blooded unconcern for quality, and Taft, who sensed Harding's lack of qualifications, might have left the scene disillusioned with politics. Instead, he accepted the outcome — one of many disappointments at Republican conventions — with the characteristic resilience and party loyalty that marked him in defeat. He had also learned much about his native Ohio, and he had met many of the politicos. Although he had not flashed like a comet onto the national scene, he returned to his legal work feeling that he had supported the most qualified Republican in the field. It was a satisfying start toward a career in politics.

•

"You may have seen," Taft wrote his father early in June 1920, "that I am going to run for the legislature this Fall . . . I thought it would be interesting and useful, and the only political job which would not interfere with practice. I have been endorsed by the County Committee." [7]

Taft did not elaborate, and several questions still call for definitive answers. First, who really secured the endorsement for him? Ultimate control over such matters belonged to Rudolph K. Hynicka and his friends, heirs to the still potent Republican organization founded by George B. Cox, and Hynicka, with the reticence characteristic of successful bosses, said nothing about Bob Taft. Second, what of his stated reasons for running? After the excitement of Paris and the national drama of the Hoover campaign, why did he turn to the politics of Columbus? Why did he not wait a while — until a Republican administration in Washing-

ton offered him a better post, or at least until his practice, less than
a year old, had become better established?

While Hynicka's role remains obscure, neither he nor his allies
objected to Taft. They had known him as a young precinct worker
before the war, and they could not help but notice his diligence
during the Hoover campaign. Though they were supporting
Wood for the nomination — ironically, Taft, an apostle of party
regularity, started by disagreeing with the local organization — they
were professionals, and Taft's little group of amateurs were lambs
who had politely refrained from forcing a primary in Ohio. Hamilton County, containing Cincinnati and its suburbs, was entitled
to send nine representatives to the lower house, and the machine
sometimes had to look hard for qualified men willing to spend five
or six months every odd year in Columbus for little pay ($1000)
or prestige. Indeed, only one of the county's nine incumbent Republican assemblymen wanted to try again in 1920, leaving eight
slots to be filled. Above all, the Taft name was widely known. Soon
Hynicka's men were sounding out Bob's friends, who reported that
he would take the job. Late in May the party chiefs gathered fes-
tively at Camp Hiawatha and without controversy named Taft as
one of the nine to face the voters. Despite the prominence of his
father, even the press paid little attention.[8]

Why Taft agreed to run defies simple explanation. Much later
he explained that the mayor had urged him to go to Columbus to
secure tax legislation helping Cincinnati. Because Taft recognized
the city's financial crisis, and because he specialized in revenue legislation while in Columbus, it is probable that he regarded tax reform as the most "useful" service he could perform. But he said
nothing about it at the time of his nomination and little during his
campaign; it was not his only reason for running.

His brother Charlie, who was preparing at Yale to become Bob's
law partner, offered a wider perspective. "Bob," he wrote a friend
in August, "isn't getting into politics permanently, but on papa's
advice somewhat. He thinks the experience in the legislature with
service perhaps in the judiciary committee, together with the
benefits of the wide acquaintance there, will be of great use to him
in his practice." Because a term or two in the state legislature was
often a young lawyer's path to recognition, Charlie's explanation

sounds plausible. But above all, Taft yearned to serve and to involve himself in politics, and in Ohio going to the state legislature was a normal way to begin. Now that he was thirty years old, it seemed only natural to accept the nomination.[9]

Endorsement by the machine meant victory at the primaries in August; Republican candidacy in Cincinnati, where Democrats were barely respectable, meant triumph in November. Campaigning decorously before civic groups and avoiding the rough and tumble of street-corner politics, Taft fretted only about a tenth entrant who challenged the organization slate. "He has been making quite a campaign among the radicals and labor elements so I may still be beaten," he worried on primary day. Taft need not have been concerned. In the primary he finished fourth among the nine and secured but fifty-five votes less than the winning tally of 19,440.[10]

Assured of election, Taft hardly mentioned the legislative race during his campaign in the fall. Instead, he talked straight Republican doctrine in support of the national ticket. He denounced "quack remedies" such as initiative, referendum, and direct primaries ("a complete failure"), censured radicals for fomenting class-consciousness, and ridiculed the notion that the government "can wave its finger and accomplish any object." On the contrary, he argued, there were too many "absolutely conflicting interests" which could "never be reconciled except under the pressure of a great war." Inflation, he admitted, was serious, but "prices are bound to go up and down in general following the law of supply and demand. So long as the government does not interfere with that law no class can blame the government." Above all, people should depend on themselves, not on Washington. "Government," he insisted, "has reached almost the limit of effective action . . . Every government in the world is the same and every government tends to become a bureaucracy . . . There are some things which simply have to be borne until they remedy themselves." [11] It was time, said Harding, to return to normalcy and to reverse the bureaucratic excesses of Wilson and the war. Taft, in appealing to this nostalgic mood, talked good politics. He also believed devoutly in every word.

November proved a Republican celebration. Harding overwhelmed his Democratic opponent, James M. Cox of Ohio, the GOP swept the state, and the nine-man Republican legislative slate from Hamilton County coasted into office. Taft seemed especially strong, leading the nine with 107,592 votes, almost 1000 more than the next man and more than 2000 ahead of the others. Trailing 30,000 votes behind him were the hapless Democrats. With a minimum of effort Taft had won. Henceforth the spotlight seldom strayed from his face.[12]

•

January 4, 1921, broke fair and mild in southern Ohio, and for Taft, riding the train as it rattled between rolling brown hills toward Columbus, the political prospects seemed equally fair. The voters had not only chosen a Republican governor, Harry L. Davis of Cleveland, but had seated overwhelming Republican majorities of 113 to 12 in the assembly and 37 to 1 in the senate.[13]

The legislative session, however, was to witness little harmony. Gripped by depression and tense with reports of crime, the people of Ohio were uncertain where they wanted to go. The legislators reflected these tensions and arrived with few positive improvments in mind. Of the 125 assemblymen, only 54 had had prior legislative experience, and most of the remaining 71 were to serve but one term, gain the recognition they needed at home, and return to their private pursuits. Sharp conflicts divided even the veteran lawmakers because city Republicans clashed with their rural colleagues, and a "Cornstalk Brigade" determined to halt spending for the mushrooming cities. Because Ohio law assured each of the state's eighty-eight counties, no matter how small in population, at least one representative in the House, the rural bloc controlled more than half the votes on crucial issues, and advocates of urban relief, like Taft, were often frustrated. "The spirit of the legislature," he remarked at the close of the session, "particularly those from the rural districts, toward the state government is one which can be criticized for niggardliness rather than extravagance." [14]

With his impressive background of public service on the national level, Taft was even as a freshman lawmaker well qualified to serve in such a chamber, and as events were to demonstrate, he showed little hesitation in making his presence felt on legislation.

But if he exhibited confidence in matters of state, he showed no disposition to captivate Columbus with his personality. "I must give
the impression to people that I don't enjoy their company," he had
written to Martha in 1913, and in 1921 he could have repeated
himself without provoking much dissension among his colleagues.
One observer found him shy, boyish looking, a quiet youth who
spoke with a soft touch of Harvard in his tongue. A colleague marveled that he seemed more like a modest country lawyer than a boy
who had lived in the White House. And a third was struck by
Taft's laudable but grim determination to make his way on his
own. It was not unusual, this colleague recalled, for sightseers to
corner Taft, to pump his hand or clap him on the back, and to tell
him how much they admired his father. But Taft, like many self-
contained people, winced at such physical intimacy from strangers,
and he grimaced when people drew attention to his family. When
one effusive lady squeezed his hand and giggled, "I am so happy to
meet the son of the father," Taft froze and turned away abruptly.
If being the son of a former President eased his path into politics,
it also left him sensitive to the charge that he was riding on the
fame of the name. To one raised to be self-reliant and independent, even the hint of such a charge was intolerable, and Taft lacked
the guile to pretend otherwise.[15]

Those colleagues who perceived this tension in Taft, however,
were rare. Most of them saw instead a tall, slim young man, neatly
dressed in eastern-cut clothes, whose hair had already thinned
enough at the temples to give his large head an elongated appearance, and who stared intent and large-eyed at people through rimless spectacles. They saw, too, that he did not laugh easily, and that
when he talked, his broad mouth displayed a row of large upper
teeth. Dignified, wary of sycophants, naturally reticent, he seemed
a little stiff and solemn. Above all, his colleagues found him
content to be by himself. The sessions ordinarily convened Monday evenings and continued steadily through Thursday night,
and Taft had to stay in a hotel. Even so, he ate his meals alone in
the hotel restaurant. Finally, the story goes, some colleagues asked
him to join them for supper. "Do you think it would be all right?"
Taft asked hesitatingly. They did, and as he came to know his
colleagues, he appeared to unbend. But only a little, for he lacked

the forwardness and conviviality of many successful politicians. As in school and college, he seemed to say, he would make his mark through intelligence, hard work, and accomplishment, not through the dubious virtue of charisma.[16]

Partly because of the many divisions within the legislature, the issues produced a series of battles between city and country, assembly and senate, governor and both houses. The tensions of January 1921 exploded in April over Governor Davis's plan to streamline state government. Passed with a so-called emergency clause enabling it to escape a referendum in November, the law infuriated the minority, which called it a "ripper bill" focusing all power in the governor. The legislators also clashed over Davis's proposal permitting prohibition-enforcement officers armed with warrants to enter private homes in search of liquor. They fought endlessly over taxes. By May the assembly and senate hardly communicated, and Davis disgustedly prorogued the legislature for the first time in Ohio history.

Under such conditions it proved practically impossible to follow a strict party line, and although Taft usually supported the Republican governor, he also tended to vote as he saw the issues. A strong advocate of governmental efficiency, he voted enthusiastically for the reorganization bill and for the disputed emergency clause. He introduced, with no success, a bill to elect judges on a nonpartisan ballot, and he voted (again in the minority) against censorship of movies. He joined a large bipartisan majority in favor of a minimum wage bill for women, which later died in the senate. (The assembly knew it would die, critics said.) He also backed a noncontroversial increase in mothers' pensions and a measure to grant workmen's compensation to laborers afflicted with occupational diseases. On the other hand, he displeased labor unions by voting to create a state police force; the unions, fearing the use of such an organization in strikes, exerted pressure that helped beat the bill in the House, 59 to 46. Opposing a rent control bill, he led a successful drive to kill it in committee. "The higher the rents," he declared, "the more incentive there is for a man to own his own home." And he was one of eight legislators, seven of whom hailed from Hamilton County, to oppose unsuccessfully Davis's prohibition enforcement bill. Taft, who took a drink himself occasionally, called it an unconstitutional violation of civil liberties. He might have added that Cincinnati was a hotbed of "wet" sentiment. The Germans of Cincinnati, to say nothing of the suburbanites from Walnut Hills, had no use for such a draconian proposal.[17]

If these bills provoked controversy, the question of taxes split the chamber and set the Cornstalk Brigade against city representatives in unending warfare. Veteran lawmakers expected such trouble, for the plight of the cities had long divided the legislature. The so-called Smith Act of 1910 had limited property tax rates to 1 per cent or 10 mills (15 mills if approved by referendum) of the full assessed valuation of each taxing district. In turn, each district allocated this revenue to schools, counties, and municipalities. Because political power in most districts rested with county officials, cities suffered by receiving only the leftovers after counties and schools received their shares. Denied the authority to impose higher taxes, Ohio cities had had to borrow, and their bonded indebtedness jumped from $188 million in 1910 to $608 million in 1921 — a method of city financing both costly and unpopular.

As if the Smith law did not create enough troubles, the so-called uniform rule of the Ohio constitution, approved in 1851, required that all kinds of wealth — tangible property such as real estate and intangibles such as stocks and bonds — be taxed at the same rate. For years reformers had called for an amendment to the constitution authorizing lower rates on intangibles — or classification, as they called it. Then, they argued, Ohio residents could report such holdings honestly, and property taxes would be reduced. The reformers had a strong case, but the economy bloc from rural districts had always countered that lower rates on intangibles would necessitate increased taxes on land. With the Smith law setting maximum tax rates and the uniform rule preventing classification, the farmers rested content. Let the cities cut extravagance instead of running to Columbus for relief.[18]

This situation had reached crisis proportions in Cincinnati. Distrusting the inefficient Republican machine, the people had voted consistently against bonding, and in November 1920 they did so again. Local officials foresaw a $7 million budget with but $2.2 million forthcoming from taxes, and they turned to Taft for help.[19]

Taft had recognized the crisis well before the session opened; it was impossible not to. Realizing his inexperience, he adopted a technique that was to characterize his approach to much important domestic legislation throughout his career: he checked tomes of statistics from the library and outlined the alternatives. One possibility was state personal and corporate income taxes. But he rejected these. Legislators would balk, and the federal government had pre-empted these fields anyway. Privately he favored some form of tax on gross sales, but he recognized that it would contain "many inequities." Yet the property tax, which was carrying the brunt of the burden, had to be augmented from some other source. There remained but one answer. "Unsound as the practice is," he concluded, "there seems to be no alternative to asking the Legislature to pass at once a bill authorizing the issue of deficiency bonds . . . This is our first step. But we must secure further legislation which will enable the city to avoid forever the issue of deficiency bonds and to pay its bills as it goes." [20]

Having investigated the issue and having reached his conclusions, Taft displayed four other lifelong traits: an unshakable faith in his own reasoning on a subject he had researched; a tendency to translate his findings into statements of principle; a willingness to take the lead in potentially unpopular causes; and a grim determination to persist, whatever the odds seemed at first, until sheer energy brought the goal in sight. Taft had studied taxes and had decided on three principles that he pronounced tirelessly for the rest of the decade. First, the need for urban services made higher costs inevitable. Second, classification, or the realistic taxation of intangibles, provided a potentially excellent source of revenue. Third, the Smith law had to be amended or repealed so that cities could pay current expenses through taxes instead of through deficiency bonds. For Taft in Ohio, as for Taft in Washington, the pay-as-you-go principle was basic.

Taft had determined on his course before the session opened, and he saw no point in deferring to the custom that freshmen be seen and not heard. On the second day of the session, even before committee assignments had been made, he offered the first of three key tax bills. It authorized subdivisions to report their deficits by the first of February and then to issue bonds to cover them. These bonds had to be covered by taxes *outside* the mill-rate limits of the Smith law. In theory Taft admitted such bond issues were "vicious," but he felt the crisis demanded them. The bill was also politically shrewd, for it affected only those areas, primarily cities, with deficits. Urban legislators would back it of necessity, and others would acquiesce. He was right, and his bill soon passed both houses by large majorities. On February 21, Governor Davis signed it into law.[21]

Taft then offered a long-range measure. It permitted the voters of each taxing district to suspend the Smith law. Cities in such districts might then levy an additional 5-mill tax without subsequent popular vote. Once again Taft had correctly gauged the political possibilities. Urban legislators were happy at any escape from the Smith law and quickly backed his bill. Rural members balked at first, but they recognized that the law would not affect them. When Taft agreed to a three-year limitation on such suspensions, they went along, and the bill passed both houses unanimously. By May it had become law, offering Cincinnati a three-year reprieve.[22]

Taft could take pride in his first term. If he had seemed cold on the subject of rent control, he had acquiesced in moderate labor legislation, compiled a creditable record on civil liberties, and gained the respect of colleagues for his intimate knowledge of tax problems. Well prepared, extremely hard-working, consistently aware of the possible, he also operated according to clearly stated principles. He deserved the major credit for passage of his two important bills, and he had served his constituents well. His chief limitation, aside from his awkwardness in making friends with his colleagues, remained his style as a speaker. "While I have no difficulty in talking," he confessed to his father, "I don't know how to do any of the eloquence business which makes for applause. It is more like a rather dull argument in court." [23]

In 1922 he determined to serve again. Well known by then, he led the organization's slate in the primary by polling 18, 458 votes — 1000 ahead of the next man. In November Democrat A. Victor ("Vic") Donahey captured the governorship, but Republicans still ruled Hamilton County, beating the Democrats by margins of approximately 20,000. Taft finished first again, his 86,100 votes

2000 more than his closest Republican running mate. Dullness on the stump, it appeared, made little difference.[24]

When the new session opened in 1923, Republicans still dominated both houses, 103 to 27 and 31 to 4. And Taft was now a leader, chairman of the taxation committee and member of a committee of Republicans from both houses charged with scheduling legislation. But standing squarely in the path was Governor Donahey. A former state auditor, "Honest Vic" was a tall, broad-shouldered, stogy-smoking man of the people who proved responsive enough to unions to secure the labor vote while offering taxpayers the rigid economy they desired. To Taft he was the "smallest kind of rural politician, and there is no chance of getting any taxation legislation to help the cities so long as he is in." For the next six years "Veto Vic," as he also came to be called, made little effort to accommodate his Republican foes, and GOP legislators fought back with the disciplined precision of an army. Long before Taft reached the Senate he was used to partisan warfare against a Democratic chief executive.[25]

On some things, of course, even Taft and Donahey could agree. Taft supported increased payments for workmen's compensation, favored establishing a commission to study minimum wages for women and children (unhappy social workers wanted an actual law; opponents wanted nothing), and voted against a bill providing for an eight-hour day on public work. Labor, crying government interference, also opposed it, and it lost by a narrow margin.[26]

Taft and Donahey could also agree on one of the most divisive issues of the session: the Ku Klux Klan. Then at the peak of its political influence, the Klan claimed to have elected mayors in Akron, Portsmouth, and Youngstown, to have more than 400,000 members in the state, and fourteen chapters in Hamilton County alone. Unlike the nineteenth-century Klan, it was as hostile to Catholics, Jews, and foreigners as to blacks, and legislators had to tread carefully lest they earn its disfavor.[27]

At first Taft seemed to buckle under Klan pressure by voting for a successful bill requiring the publication of the value of all property (including that of the Catholic Church) that was exempt from taxation. But he opposed the Klan a few days later by approving a hotly contested measure requiring secret organizations to file their membership lists with the state. Many lawmakers claimed the bill violated civil liberties. "What of the Elks?" they asked. Taft and others replied with the obvious: the bill was aimed specifically at the Klan. The hooded knights rode hard, and the bill went down to defeat, 81 to 26. But Taft could take pride in his stance against the Klan.[28]

Taxes, however, again formed the most controversial question, and here Taft and Donahey fought uncompromisingly. As before, Taft worried about Cincinnati, which faced a $2.4 million deficit for the coming year. So he proposed a bill authorizing a maximum tax rate of 17 mills for cities, as opposed to the 15-mill limit imposed by the Smith law. Appeasing rural interests, he called for a 14-mill limit elsewhere. Taxes to cover sinking fund and interest charges were not to be included in these limits as in the past. As a hedge against excessive bonding, Taft called for a popular vote of 60 per cent of those voting on bond issues, as opposed to 50 percent in the past. The package promised revenue for the cities, economy for the countryside, pay as you go for current expenses, and modest bond issues for long-term projects.[29]

His plans quickly encountered the unbudging opposition of Governor Donahey, who insisted that Taft's plan meant higher taxes. Lobbyists for better roads opposed the tougher provisions on bonds. Most alarming, the Cornstalk Brigade called together its forces. Although many rural members approved of the firm limits on taxation, they worried about any departure from the Smith law, and they countered with the claim that a 2 per cent income tax could bring all the revenue the cities needed. They also called for stiffer enforcement of laws prohibiting false tax returns and insisted on appointive tax assessors in wards and townships. On March 1 these groups coalesced, with all twenty-seven Democrats joining forty-four others to send the bill back to committee, 71 to 50.[30]

With characteristic persistence Taft began looking for a more fruitful strategy. Soon he discovered the price: he must agree to back the bills to enforce the prosecution of false returns and to create appointive tax assessors. He quickly agreed, for neither measure seemed at all crucial, and his bill soon returned to the floor. Twenty-four of the Democrats continued to resist, but most of the others changed sides, and a week after it had been recommitted the bill passed, 85 to 33. The neutral Cincinnati *Enquirer*, impressed with his legerdemain, headlined, "STRATEGY OF TAFT TOO SUBTLE FOR CORNSTALK CLUB," and praised his "dogged persistence and refusal to compromise on essential points." And William Howard Taft congratulated his son when the bill passed the state senate three weeks later. "I am very proud of you," he wrote. "The greatest thing in life is to be useful." [31]

Donahey then counterattacked by making the Taft bill one of a record seventy-six vetoes that session. The placing of interest charges outside the limitations of the Smith law, he said, would encourage extravagance and result in higher taxes. Any tax increases over 15 mills, he added, must come through vote of the people concerned. Taft retorted cogently that his bill would institute pay as you go for current expenses. The Smith law, he explained, tried to curb taxation unrealistically while setting no limits on deficit financing; the Taft approach, by contrast, controlled both.

The Republicans then plunged recklessly ahead by passing the bill over Donahey's veto, 88 to 24. Taxpayer lobbies, spokesmen for real estate interests, even school officials who worried about the provision calling for 60 per cent majorities on bond issues, initiated a referendum to be held in November 1923, and Donahey urged them on.[32] Beaming from afar, William Howard Taft thought his son would "derive the greatest benefit in the matter of public speaking and in the matter of winning a reputation for clear statement and high motive." For Bob, however, the campaign for his bill proved frustrating. He took most of October off, circled the state in support of his bill, and spoke earnestly to uninspired audiences. But the effort was "tiresome because I do not really expect to carry it." [33]

He was right, for he had placed himself in the position of opposing Donahey's appealing insistence on popular votes for all increases. Taft, it seemed, stood for extravagance, Donahey for economy, and voters killed the plan by a 2 to 1 margin in November. Taft had worked for more than a year in vain. Grimly he stood for re-election in 1924 and surpassed even his showing in 1922, running number one on the successful Republican slate in both the primary and the election and sweeping 636 of Hamilton County's 638 precincts in November. He would try once more to get his program through.[34]

.

The election again gave the GOP huge legislative majorities, of 110 to 20, and 22 to 2. Anticipating such a sweep, Taft had already been angling for a position of leadership, and he shuttled back and forth to Columbus in December to meet with colleagues. Harry D. Silver, a rural Republican, seemed assured of the speakership; so Taft announced for the number two post of majority leader. The Klan advanced its own man, and the powerful Anti-Saloon League, which was suspicious of his position on prohibition, also seemed ready to oppose his candidacy. But Taft had served two terms, and he had worked hard. When he let it be known that he would preserve the status quo on prohibition — he could have changed nothing important anyway — the Anti-Saloon League acquiesced, and Taft easily defeated the Klan candidate and a third aspirant, 66 to 28 to 12. His opponents then made it unanimous. Taft would carry the Republican burden in the coming session.[35]

Some legislative leaders are so saddled with petty chores that they lack the time to sponsor and carry through bills and resolutions. Not so Taft, who continued to press for his objectives despite his already heavy work load. Because he lamented the inefficiency that stemmed from the rapid turnover in state administration, he sponsored a constitutional amendment creating four-year terms for high elective officials. He also introduced a bill authorizing preprimary party conventions. Though unsuccessful in both attempts, he persisted in appealing in later years for such plans to promote orderly administration and party government.[36]

He also kept himself informed of trends in labor legislation. He antagonized union spokesmen by again supporting (though unsuccessfully) a bill setting up a state police force. But he otherwise gratified organized labor by backing bills calling for proper labeling of convict-made goods and for increases in workmen's compensation. Easily his most progressive stand — one which he recalled regularly in later campaigns — was his support of the federal constitutional amendment against the use of child labor. Unpopular with manufacturers and especially with organized farm groups, the amendment failed, 91 to 35; and because Ohio proved the thirteenth state to reject it (only two had approved), it died. In opposing the majority of his party on the issue, Taft was moved partly by humanitarian considerations but primarily on the practical grounds that it would help Cincinnati industries meet unfair competition from southern states. His was nonetheless a forward-looking position, and in taking it he even disregarded his father's argument that such questions should be handled by the states, not by the federal government.[37]

Taft also showed himself willing to resist pressure groups. When he refused to back a bill making Armistice Day a legal holiday, the state adjutant of the American Legion attacked him and even demanded publicly to know why he had not served with the armed forces during the war. Undeterred, Taft insisted there were enough holidays already; the bill did not pass.[38]

A tougher pressure group was once more the Klan, which still controlled as many as 45 of the 110 Republicans in the assembly and which succeeded, 82 to 11, in passing, over Taft's objections, a bill that outlawed dancing on Sunday. Then it fought for a bill requiring public school teachers to read ten verses of Scripture every day to their classes. The bill aroused heated emotions and reflected the nationwide controversy over the teaching of evolution by natural selection. In late February it came to a vote, and Taft had no choice but to state his position.[39]

Taft's own religious inclinations were weak. His father was a Unitarian faithful enough to set aside $2500 in his will for his Washington church. But Will Taft never imposed his church preference on his children, all of whom followed Nellie into the Episcopalian faith. Bob, however, still spent most of his Sunday mornings on the golf course, not at religious services, and the Bible bill seemed to him a flagrant violation of the individual liberty that he held essential to human development. He also shared the family's pride in grandfather Alphonso's judicial opinion against compulsory reading of the Bible in the schools. So he left his party, took the floor, and made such an impassioned speech against the measure that even the newspapers, whose coverage of legislative events in the 1920's left everything to be desired, gave it ample play. The Constitution, Taft said, guarantees freedom of speech. Religion can and should be taught only in the churches. The Bible is great literature, but "in it religion overshadows all else." Aware that he would lose, he then sponsored an amendment that would have made the policy optional with district boards of education. But the Klan held firm, defeated his amendment 66 to 54, and passed the bill, 80 to 40. Taft, joined by most of the urban representatives, voted against the Klan both times.[40]

Encouraged, the Klan pressed on, and the senate also passed the measure, which then went to Donahey for signature. The governor courageously vetoed it. Some observers chided Taft for his role, arguing that he had let the bill be voted on as part of a deal to secure rural votes for other legislation.[41] But there was no evidence of a deal, that rural members paid any quid pro quo, or that he could have sidetracked the popular measure if he had tried. Whatever the case, no one doubted his personal belief in religious liberty; and his open stand on the bill, while acceptable to his urban constituents, required courage for anyone thinking of running eventually for statewide office.

Even the Bible bill paled in importance compared with the issue of taxes, and Taft determined to secure his objectives. First on his agenda lay the perennial emergency of Cincinnati, whose voters in 1924 had again rejected a series of proposed bond issues and tax levies. Anxious to find common ground with Donahey at least until the emergency had been taken care of, he avoided partisan excesses early in the session. "We still have a chance of working successfully with the Governor," he wrote in rejecting the idea of a Republican gathering in January. The governor also proved cooperative, and the legislature quickly approved a bill permitting cities with emergencies to levy special taxes of up to 3 mills for the last half of 1925, providing a majority of the voters so petitioned.[42]

The long-range obstacles of the Smith law and the uniform rule remained to be challenged. Some legislators wished to defy the governor as they had in 1923. Taft, however, had learned from the resounding defeat of his plans in November 1923, and he opted to proceed cautiously. This, in turn, meant convincing the voters that Republicans stood for pay as you go and for limits on spending. It meant no talk of taxation up to 17 mills — or any other specific figure. It meant acceding to Donahey's insistence on popular referenda before subdivisions instituted new taxes. In 1925 Taft counseled for results, not for meaningless headlines and fruitless skirmishes with a popular governor in an economy-minded state.

Taft realized that an omnibus bill presented the governor too easy a target, and he persuaded Republicans to sponsor a series of proposals. One important bill authorized bond issues only if approved by 55 per cent of those voting on the question. A parallel bill permitted subdivisions to adopt taxes beyond the limits of the Smith law if a majority of those voting in a referendum approved. Donahey assented, and the measures proved to be important in fiscal machinery of subdivisions.[43]

Taft's other bills ventured farther afield. One attacked outdated and uneven assessments by calling for compulsory reappraisal of property every six years. Another countered deficit financing by setting up a uniform fiscal year, requiring budget systems, and holding clerks and auditors personally responsible for inaccurate estimates. A third, the most important for Cincinnati, sought to circumvent county control over urban regions by giving cities with charters the right to set their own levies.

These measures broke the interlude of harmony between Donahey and the Republicans. The split first occurred early in February when the governor objected publicly to the reappraisal bill. Taft, claiming that Donahey had privately agreed to it, announced that the Republicans would pass it anyway. The GOP then widened the breach by approving a gasoline tax that Donahey had already opposed. By early March the break was complete, and Donahey retaliated by vetoing Taft's three bills and adding the gasoline tax for good measure. Unconcerned, the Republicans passed them over his vetoes.[44]

In triumphing at last, Taft had not achieved all that he wanted. The provisions for popular votes denied urban officials the flexibility he had hoped for. Classification permitting realistic taxation of intangibles was not to be enacted until 1931. Recognizing the remaining inequities, Taft agreed to preside over a committee on economics and taxation that eventually reported in December 1926. Besides recommending greater taxation to support state services, it called vainly for repeal of the uniform rule, the reorganization of county government, the abolition of township government, the elimination of small school districts, and the establishment of more realistic debt limits for many localities. Yet Taft's willingness to compromise, his wisdom in cutting up the bills piecemeal, and his unmatched knowledge of the problem had kept his party smoothly in line. If Ohio's fiscal problems remained far from solved in 1926, they were less desperate than they had been five years earlier, and no one could take more credit for the result than Robert A. Taft.[45]

The tax battles over, he could afford to relax. Indulging in uncharacteristic clowning, he appeared at a breakfast of the Cornstalk Club as a check boy. A few days later, with the session drawing boisterously to a close, he smiled good-naturedly while colleagues dumped a wastepaper basket of junk over his head. He was still so far from being convivial that he developed no close personal friendships in his three terms of service. But he proved at least that he could take a joke.[46]

He had also demonstrated his competence as a majority leader. Though he had been in the minority on such issues as the state police force, the child labor amendment, and the Bible bill, he had kept his poise, consulted others on policy, and maintained a united party front that provided decent appropriations for state institutions, enacted a workable tax program, and supplied the funds to begin bringing Ohio's roads out of the mud. He had resisted pressure groups, while at the same time developing the art of compromise so necessary to the leader in legislative politics. When the legislature convened for a brief special session early in 1926, his colleagues, again outvoting the Klan, elected him to the speakership. It was the highest honor and the final satisfaction of his six years in Columbus.[47]

•

Sometime in 1926 Taft decided not to run again. Increasingly busy with legal work, he had accomplished part of his tax program, and he had reached the pinnacle of legislative leadership.

The experience had not done much to change his thinking. He had gone to Columbus in 1921 believing implacably in party government, and he left in 1926 marked as a regular, dependable worker willing to rise through the ranks. He had arrived stressing the importance of fiscal responsibility and departed still proclaiming the virtues of that position. Always a friend of individual freedom, he became known for his libertarian positions on prohibition and the Ku Klux Klan. Though moderately sympathetic to organized labor, he was far from a social reformer, and he offered no protest when his Republican colleagues sidetracked the bill for minimum wages for women and children or when they buried bills for state payments of old age pensions. Like most of his fellow legislators in the early 1920's, he worried little about the social and economic imbalances of American society. In his constant emphasis on economy, on care in public spending, on streamlining government, he reflected accurately the well-intentioned and efficiency-conscious temper of his times.

Neither progressive reformer nor one to stand pat. What was he? As much as anything else he was a regular Republican conscientiously serving his urban constituency. Boss Hynicka wisely left him alone, and Taft for his part checked with the organization only occasionally.[48] Free to vote as he wished, he did so, and his views on taxation, the Klan, prohibition, child labor — indeed, on all the key issues of his time — caused him no trouble at home. But his freedom was a mixed blessing, for it left his intellectual frontiers unchallenged. Unlike Robert Wagner, Sr., of New York, he did not have to recognize or even to understand the masses of his native city. Unlike Franklin D. Roosevelt, he had no need to pound the hustings or to cultivate the art of public relations. Given his training and temperament, Taft might have plowed his own path of principle anyway. In Cincinnati and Columbus in the early 1920's the question never arose.

Above all, he liked the work. Because the local organization was so potent, there were at campaign time no dirty, sweaty crowds, no tours of slums or sweatshops, no confrontations with street-corner hecklers or impoverished farmers. In Columbus he accepted the lonely weeks in hotel rooms, the small mindedness of the Cornstalk Brigade, and even the drafty train and auto rides through the cold of winter to and from Cincinnati. He reveled in the useful work — studying statistics, drafting legislation, being recognized as the expert on public finance. He was learning how to conduct hearings, to offer carefully constructed amendments, to match wits and parliamentary tactics with the opposition. Though many people, his father included, tried to interest him in the governorship in 1926, he had no intention of making such a race, for he had grown fond of legislative work, and he left it in 1926 largely because he thought he had done as much as possible. When he tried again for public office in 1930, it was once more for the legislature — this time the state senate — and when he turned his ambition to higher things, it was first to the United States Senate.[49]

CHAPTER 7

Life in Cincinnati

CINCINNATI IN the 1920's had changed considerably since Taft's childhood. Though it had grown more slowly than many newer American cities, its population had increased from 296,000 in 1890 to 400,000 in 1920. The city had annexed many surrounding towns, and impressive viaducts had bridged the hills to make it a major urban center. Yet suburbs stretching as far as fifteen miles from the center of the city had drawn many of the wealthier people out of the downtown area and left only a few hardy souls like Uncle Charley to contend with the grime and soot that had become hazards to health. The crowded and once colorful tenements of the West End had degenerated into slums, and the riverfront which had fascinated young Bob Taft and his friends had become ugly and shabby. In Cincinnati, as elsewhere in urban America by the 1920's, the gulf between the social classes was deep.[1]

In the course of trying to alleviate Cincinnati's fiscal plight, Taft was aware of some of these imbalances. But he spent most of his free time in Walnut Hills and on his farm in Indian Hill; he was busy supporting a growing family; and he was securely anchored in the upper class of his parents' city. He stayed active, succeeded, and prospered. For Taft and for people like him, the 1920's were easy, satisfying years.

His legal work consumed most of his time. No philosopher, Taft did not thrill to the niceties of his profession, and he did not worry much about the imperfections of the legal process. Unlike many politicians who rode to fame upon courtroom performance, he preferred the more painstaking work of negotiation to the studied eloquence of the advocate. Though his father, who became

Chief Justice of the United States in 1921, wrote him long, detailed letters about life on the court, Bob seldom took this opportunity to engage in extended discussions on the key constitutional issues of his time. Unlike his father, he showed no interest whatever in becoming a judge. To Taft the law was satisfying and absorbing, but it was also as much a useful occupation and a bridge to politics as a career in itself.[2]

Thanks to his Uncle Charley, he quickly had all he could do. Even before the war, he had helped his uncle organize the Dixie Terminal Company, which was formed to erect an important downtown office building, streetcar terminal, and railroad passenger office; and he continued this work until the building opened in the spring of 1921. Setting up his offices there, he wrote his brother Charlie, who was completing his training at the Yale Law School, that "they are very palatial and costly; and it is doubtful whether the business will support them." [3]

This was modesty, as Charlie easily discovered when he joined Bob to open the new firm of Taft and Taft early in 1922. Uncle Charley relied heavily upon them to handle his empire of interests. Bob hurried back and forth to New York, working on the affairs of the McAlpin Hotel, and to Texas, where his uncle still owned a ranch. In his free time he kept a hand in the affairs of the Legal Aid Society, becoming its vice-president. And he labored over the complicated estates and interests of the Herrons, his mother's relatives. Without his Uncle Charley, a small, white-bearded, amiable, and very powerful old man, Taft might have had to struggle. With him, he progressed rapidly.[4]

In so doing, Taft began to develop a reputation for coldness that he would never escape. Partly, it came from rivals who resented the power of the uncle and the easy road of the nephew. Mainly, it came from Taft's manner, which was as reserved and preoccupied in Cincinnati as it was among the lawmakers in Columbus. Busy, often in a hurry, he always seemed absorbed in thought, and even when he was wearing his glasses, he seldom bothered to look up as he walked along the street or to acknowledge a greeting when jolted from his thoughts. In 1924 he and his brother teamed with his old friend, John Hollister, and with a fourth lawyer, John Stettinius, to establish the partnership of Taft,

Stettinius, and Hollister; and Taft drove himself ever harder. Punctual, thorough, always well prepared, he proved dependable and competent. But he wasted little effort on pleasantries, and he sometimes did not bother to stand when clients arrived or even to thrust out his hand in greeting. Business done, he rose quickly; it was time for the visitor to go.[5]

Occasionally the stubbornness or stupidity of a client roused him to outbursts of irritated impatience, for as one of his personal friends recalled, Taft could change abruptly from "an easy-going pacific sort of manner, to a strongly combative one." But many acquaintances might have welcomed such a show of temper in a man who seemed to them distant and unemotional. To these clients, indeed, he possessed what one later critic called a "rectitude which succeeds in stopping just short of self-righteousness" and what another observer was more accurately to label a "glacial calm that overlies the inner sensitivity of one of the most self-disciplined public men of our time." [6]

Taft gradually softened over the years, and he learned to relax a little with casual acquaintances. But repeated intellectual success in school, in Washington and Paris, and finally in Columbus, had toughened his confidence, and the mixed blessing of being the son of William Howard Taft left him as determined as ever to show people he could advance, indeed excel, on his own. So he paid little heed to the complaints about his personality. As ever, he insisted on being himself.

If these qualities discouraged some clients, they reassured others. The 1920's were a time of rapid corporate growth, and the opportunities for young, dependable lawyers in the city were boundless. Local entrepreneurs who came to Taft's office knew they were dealing with a young man who was already handling his Uncle Charley's multimillion dollar affairs, who was earning the respect of taxation officials throughout the state, and who possessed the discretion to keep their intimate transactions to himself. They also recognized that he wasted neither their time nor his and that he would bluntly tell them the truth no matter how painful it might seem at first. As a perceptive journalist was later to phrase it, Taft was wholly without cant. "He is not a bunk shooter or a humbug artist." Above all, they knew he would conduct their affairs honestly and thoroughly. In matters of corporate finance it mattered little that he lacked charm or that he seldom seemed animated. On the contrary, his self-contained qualities gave him an air of gravity and responsibility which were assets in so young a man.[7]

For all these reasons the work mounted, and Stettinius's sudden death a few months after the opening of the new firm left a gap that only harder work could fill. From the start Taft and Hollister shunned criminal or marital cases and specialized in estates and in problems of business management. Soon Taft became counsel for many of the city's largest corporations, and by the end of the decade he was a director of such important concerns as the Gruen Watch Company, the Central Trust Company, and the Covington and Cincinnati Bridge Company. Some of Taft's friends thought Hollister overly concerned with earnings and position, but Will Taft and John's father had been college classmates and neighbors, Nellie and John's mother had been warm personal friends, and Bob and John had known each other in childhood, at Yale, and at Harvard Law School. Their partnership was amicable throughout the fifteen years Bob was actively involved in it, and Hollister was to serve him in all his later political campaigns.[8]

Taft was happiest working on corporate problems that pulled him into urban affairs. One of these concerned city transit. For more than two decades the Cincinnati Traction Company had used a lease from the parent Cincinnati Street Railway Company to operate streetcars in the city, and by the 1920's citizens complained bitterly about the 10-cent fare, poor service, faulty equipment, and the deteriorating financial condition of the company, which was unable even to pay its franchise taxes to an already hardpressed city. Taft had become involved in the problem through his uncle before the war and soon became counsel for the parent company. His duty was to buy out the operators and to arrange a new contract with the city.

The task involved endless negotiations, and Taft, middleman between the city and the operators, often fumed at the stubbornness of both groups. "We have been in the position," he complained, "of satisfying fifteen men each wanting something different . . . the mayor is very weak and is not able to understand the situation." After the city had rejected one agreement, he moaned, "the traction business seems to have gotten into a complete mess. It is a long story and one of very painful stupidity." But he persevered, and in late 1925 he finally succeeded. The agreement provided service at cost, established an 8½-cent ticket fare subject to renegotiation, and obliged the company to improve its equipment within three years. The railway company could distribute dividends to its stockholders according to returns on invested capital. Pleased with Taft's services, the company kept him as its general counsel and provided him with a major source of his business for the next decade. The city government, almost as pleased, benefited from the improved service that resulted.[9]

Taft then turned his attention to the even larger problem of rail transportation. For years seven railroads had serviced Cincinnati at three separate terminals. The terminals not only used much valuable space, but antagonized weary through-travelers who had to drag their luggage across the city. Civic leaders had long tried to negotiate a central terminal, but the railroad companies had seen little to gain by such a change. When Taft, again through his uncle, became involved in 1923 as one of many leading Cincinnatians working for a single terminal, a solution seemed as far away as ever.[10]

At first the negotiations went slowly, and Taft and his associates on the newly formed Cincinnati Railroad Development Company encountered apparently endless delays. He had to talk to city officials to find an acceptable site for a central terminal and to arrange to feed the tracks of the seven companies into it. He went to Washington for delicate negotiations with the Interstate Commerce Commission. He rode the sleeper to New York and visited the railroad leaders in their elegant offices.[11]

In November 1927, Taft and his associates finally announced an agreement. The contract created a Cincinnati Union Terminal Company that was to issue stock to finance construction of a central terminal expected to cost $25 million and to accommodate two hundred intercity trains a day. Taft became a director of the new company and set off again, this time to Wall Street to arrange the financing with his old friend Lewis Strauss of Kuhn Loeb and Company. Soon construction began in the west side of the city on a cavernous concrete structure that displayed colorful mosaics on its interior walls and that became one of America's most striking railroad terminals. But when the stock market crash struck in 1929, it dried up funds for investment, and it was 1933 before the terminal was finally ready for business. Because the railroads had already fallen into unprofitable days before the depression, the magnificent terminal in Cincinnati was, even on its completion, testimony to the well-meaning but grandiose vision of its promoters.[12]

The mixed ending to the terminal business symbolized the ambivalent legacy of Taft's legal activities in the 1920's. If one side of his work required skill in negotiation, the other called for a certain stridency as an advocate and for a willingness to see some complex questions in black-and-white terms.

As he developed ever greater self-confidence, he also tended to become critical of the intellectual weaknesses of his adversaries. Because he rarely appeared in court, this sense of intellectual superiority — or arrogance, as his enemies were later to describe it — was less obvious in the 1920's than it was to be later in the United States Senate. But some of his contemporaries noticed it even then, and later critics were also to ask the relevant question of whether experience as an advocate is always the best training for the open-minded and humane approach that they felt characterized gifted public officials.

Later critics also questioned whether Taft's legal work prepared him to understand the social issues that exploded into public consciousness during the depression. Taft's law practice, like his absorption in fiscal matters at Columbus, gave him little knowledge about the needs of the thousands of Cincinnatians who lived outside the world inhabited by the corporate leaders, bankers, and judges who joined him at lunch at the Queen City Club or at gatherings sponsored by the University Club. As the experience of the depression years proved, many men of his background and experience were to develop new perspectives on the American social order, and he eventually joined them on occasion. But for him the process was to be slower than it might have been had he had the exposure to a wider world earlier in his life.

Yet these long-range consequences of his legal work seemed trifling compared with the satisfactions that he was deriving at the time. Important matters such as the street railway and the terminal company gratified his desire to be useful and appealed to his passion for efficiency. They suited perfectly his talent for handling figures. And they helped attract clients to the firm. In Cincinnati as in Columbus, he had involved himself in some of the most complex financial issues of the decade. It was no wonder that law practice expanded his self-confidence, or that it was to be years before he made his first try for national office.

·

Taft's was the good life in other ways as well. For one thing, he was making money. Earning $10,000 as early as 1921, he received $75,000 from the street railway company alone between 1923 and 1924. By the late 1920's he was averaging nearly $70,000 per year after taxes, and Martha's investments were bringing in another $25,000 to $30,000. No plunger in the age of Babylon, he placed his earnings in safe investments, including the street railway company, Gruen Watch Co., and other solid local concerns. He never grew wealthy on the scale of his uncle, but he made his profession pay.[13]

He also enjoyed the satisfactions of good works. He tapped his classmates for contributions to Taft School. ("Personally," he wrote, "I feel there is nothing we can do more good in than in sending to a first class school boys who otherwise would not have the opportunity to go through.") He joined in establishing a non-profit store specializing in noncommercial books. He helped Aunt Annie raise funds for the symphony orchestra. And he spent much time toward the end of the decade helping his uncle organize a public endowment of more than $3 million to support the Cincinnati Institute of Fine Arts. The funds were to bolster the symphony, build up the art museum, and (after the death of his uncle in 1929 and of his aunt in 1931) turn the Charles Taft home into a museum. Uncle Charley's gift of a million dollars to the Institute, Taft wrote Uncle Horace in 1927, "is the greatest thing for Cincinnati which has ever happened." [14]

A particular pleasure for Bob and Martha was Sky Farm, to which they moved permanently in 1924. By then it was far more elaborate than the farmhouse that they had purchased seven years earlier. Extensive remodeling had created a stately sixteen-room white frame house graced with white pillars. Walnuts, oaks, and a large tulip tree standing in a circle at the front of the house provided ample shade and protection. The circle, in turn, marked the end of a dirt road that cut across part of their forty-six acres; the Tafts enjoyed complete privacy from all noise, traffic, and other distractions. At the other end of the dirt road lay a small house where Roy Finch, Taft's tenant farmer, lived with his wife and many small children. Otherwise, Taft and Martha saw only the countryside. To the north and east lay a broad expanse of lawn, flower gardens, and fields, and down the slopes that dropped off sharply to the south and west they could see the ribbon of the Little Miami River flowing toward the Ohio. On clear days they could see the skyline of Cincinnati twelve miles away, and the older boys recalled seeing at the top of the Central Trust tower the flashing of the green light which told the Tafts in 1924 that Calvin Coolidge had been elected President.[15]

Inside the house there was ample space for Bob and Martha, for Billy and Bobby, who turned nine and seven respectively in 1924, and for the two babies who finally arrived after many miscarriages — Lloyd Bowers, who came on New Year's Day 1923 while Bob was in Columbus, and Horace Dwight, who completed the family in April 1925. There was also room for an English nurse, who cared for the babies, and for the maid, cook, and chauffeur, who left Martha free to throw herself into work for the Cincinnati League of Women Voters and other civic activities. Because Martha displayed more interest in politics than in interior decoration, the home furnishings were heavy and Victorian, but she took an active interest in her garden, and she proudly displayed a large collection of etchings left her by her father. She also installed a grand piano in the living room and occasionally invited players in for concerts of chamber music. By the time the Tafts moved in permanently, the house was equipped with electricity and running water, and it was warm in the winter. The Tafts lived as graciously and comfortably as anyone could have asked.

Taft had little ear for music, and he seldom listened to the chamber concerts. But he sometimes joined Martha on her excursions to hear the Cincinnati Symphony Orchestra, and he kept busy at a variety of activities in the growing area of Indian Hill.

With the other young business and professional men who began
moving there, he helped establish a fire company, and he was one
of many boosters who organized the Cincinnati Country Day
School. With Fred Chatfield, John Hollister, and others he
founded the Camargo Country Club, where he played many rounds
of golf over the years. When developers late in the decade sensed
profit in the region and threatened to carve nearby land into
small lots, Taft and Stanley Rowe, a neighbor who was becoming
one of his closest friends, borrowed money to buy 230 acres.
They intended to get their investment back by selling the land
gradually in large lots. But the depression caught them, and they
had to sell some of the acreage at a loss to repay the loans; his investment earned only $21,800 over more than twenty years. But
the venture had preserved the character of the hill. For Taft, Sky
Farm always remained a haven from which he could drive slowly
down the hills into town and to which he could return and relax
after his exertions in Cincinnati or Columbus.[16]

All these activities kept him so busy that he always had to rush
out on Christmas Eve to do his shopping. They also left him with
rather little time for his family; he was not the sort of father who
regularly took his children to Coney Island, the city's amusement
park, or to Crosley Field, home of the Cincinnati Reds baseball
team. He exhibited no taste for the dubious joys of caring for in-
fants, and his reaction to the birth of his children was more wry and
detached than rhapsodic. "He is not handsome, but his looks are
improving," was his terse comment to his father concerning the
baby, Horace, in 1925. His letter to Aunt Maria about Billy, his
first-born, had been only a little less restrained. "I kissed the baby
for you," he wrote,

> and feel that he quite understood it was from his Auntie Mimi.
> He is growing rapidly, his last four days having gained three, two
> and a half, two and a half, and four ounces respectively, so that
> we expect a giant . . . He is a great sleeper and seldom cries. He
> is said to resemble his father altogether, but it seems to me that the
> resemblance is more or less fancied, based on the fact that he does
> not look at all like Martha.

The boys discovered that their father was reticent and undemonstrative. Indeed, he refrained from confiding in his sons, even

about the fatal illness which struck him in 1953. They realized, too, that he expected them to carry on the high standards of the family name. They went to the Cincinnati Country Day School, then to Taft and Yale — for the same purposes that earlier generations of Tafts had already pursued. All four boys performed well in school and college, all attended graduate schools, two — Bill and Horace — received Ph.D.'s (in English and physics respectively), and one, Bob, Jr., followed his father through the state legislature to the United States Senate. With Martha helping, Taft was successful in making sure that his boys used their social and intellectual advantages.

Yet Taft did manage to find some time for his boys. He always tried to save an hour or two on Sundays to take them on tours of the property, often with Finch, his farmer, and Finch's children in tow. In the evenings he often set up a card table in the living room. There he demonstrated his astonishing capacity for concentration by working on briefs, juggling figures, or even reading a detective story — and by looking up occasionally to take part in the family activities. When the boys grew older, he played golf with them, taught them to fish, and took time out to compete with them at chess. Still later, when they needed advice on graduate schools, money for social activities, or suggestions on careers, they found him tolerant and understanding. Because he believed strongly that they should gather the training necessary to be independent, he encouraged his sons to study economics and to go to law school. But he was less didactic about it than his father had been, for he cared less what they chose to do than how hard they worked at it, and only Bob, Jr., of his four sons actually followed in the family tradition by getting a law degree. Horace, indeed, discovered his parents sympathetic to his thoughts of pursuing a career in music. If Taft's sons occasionally wished for more time and affection, they were loath to admit it later, and they recognized that their father had usually been ready to help when they needed it.[17]

The farm also occupied much of Taft's spare time. Technically he was a gentleman farmer, for he never showed a profit. He had to pay Finch close to $3000 a year for his services, plus shares of the money from the sale of strawberries and other crops that the Tafts sold for cash. The care of forty-six acres also required hiring frequent help for heavy jobs. Taft had to provide feed for the horses, cows, pigs, and hundreds of chickens that proliferated about the place and to pay for the seeds and machinery necessary to plant and harvest crops of asparagus, hay, and potatoes. He lost $4002.58 in 1925, despite sales of eggs worth $1064.36 and of strawberries worth $648.50. The next year he lost $3790.06. So it went through the decade.

Taft took his farm seriously, and his ledgers, neat, precise, and detailed, show that he worked many evenings trying to cut expenses. He badgered the state department of agriculture for advice on crop rotation, the profitability of soybeans, and the pros and cons of different brands of fertilizer, and he delighted in his strawberry crop. "You will find us very rural indeed," he laughed to his brother early in the decade, "and I have almost given up golf for gardening. In fact, my principal interest in life is in fruit catalogues." When his sons grew up and went away to school in the 1930's, Taft, who kept the farm partly because of the pleasures it afforded them, spent less time and money on these agricultural pursuits. And by the end of the decade he was too engrossed in politics to have time for anything else. Yet he kept Finch on, continued to produce poultry, eggs, milk, and butter, and persisted in selling some crops for cash. He truly enjoyed not only the seclusion of his home but the business of farming.[18]

Not even the pleasures of Sky Farm were permitted to intrude on the annual exodus to Murray Bay. Some visits there included festive occasions, as in 1920 when Helen married Frederick Manning, an instructor in history at Yale, or as in 1927 when 150 guests celebrated the seventieth birthday of Chief Justice William Howard Taft. Most of the time there, however, Bob played golf, fished, and went camping with his sons. His mother, by then an eccentric and matriarchal figure, was always there for the summer, and frequent residents included Aunt Maria, Uncle Charley and Aunt Annie, Uncle Horace, and many other relations. Indeed, by the early 1930's the Tafts enjoyed something of a compound, for Helen and Fred Manning built a small house of their own, and Louise and Will Semple, daughter and son-in-law of Uncle Charley, had inherited another large home nearby. The focus of Taft's life in Murray Bay, however, remained the rambling house that his father was always expanding in order to accommodate the grandchildren. No matter how pressing the business at home, Taft always managed to stay there for three weeks to a month toward the end of the summer.[19]

As their children grew, Bob and Martha were able to take other excursions together. Sometimes they visited Washington to socialize with old friends and to pay their respects to Bob's parents, and sometimes they went to New York, where Martha saw her brother Tom, then a banker, and where Bob played poker, competed at golf, or reminisced with George Harrison, the Bowers, and other old friends. Once a year they also tried to get to New Haven to watch the Yale football team and, in the 1930's, to visit the sons and nephews who were students there. None of these trips lasted long, and for Bob they were always mixed with business, but they provided a change of scene.

With all these things to do, Bob and Martha had little time to engage in much social life, but that did not trouble them because neither cared for elaborate entertainment. They also took little part in club activities or in the Episcopal church, and they sent their sons to the convenient Methodist Sunday school if they desired to go. Instead of attending church services, Taft used every Sunday morning he could for golf, which he played doggedly but well enough to shoot in the low 80's. His regular companions on these rounds included George Warrington, a lawyer from an old Cincinnati family who had also served with the Food Administration; Clifford Shinkle, a bank president; and Tylor Field, a construction company executive who served on the Cincinnati city council in the late 1920's and early 1930's. When Martha was away at Murray Bay with the children, these rounds often went to 36 or 54 holes and culminated in a light supper at one of the others' homes. Otherwise, Taft returned home from the links in time for his tour of the farm and for a family dinner that often included various Tafts, Herrons, and Semples and that featured spirited talk about public affairs.[20]

The Tafts also developed close and lasting associations with others. Besides Bob's golfing friends, these included Stanley Rowe, a Yale graduate and business executive who became his partner in preserving the chastity of Indian Hill; Rowe's wife Dorothy, charming and high-spirited; John Hollister; Hulbert Taft, a cousin who was running the *Times-Star* for Uncle Charley; and John's and Hulbert's wives. And until political differences intervened in the 1930's, the Tafts' close friends included the Russell Wilsons. An editorial writer for the *Times-Star* in the 1920's, Wilson was a personable extrovert who became mayor of Cincinnati in 1930. In the 1920's he served for a while as the paper's drama critic, and he often took Bob and Martha along for relaxed evenings at the theater.

On rare occasions the Tafts joined these and other friends at large parties, where there was gaiety into the night. More often, however, they saw them in small groups for informal Sunday suppers or simply for extended conversation. Their friends were lively, intelligent, and public-spirited people who preferred informed talk to cards and who grew bored by acquaintances who could discourse only on their businesses or professions. Bob and Martha particularly enjoyed gathering with the Wilsons, Hollisters, Rowes, and others for meetings of what they laughingly called the Culture Club. At each meeting one of the members read a paper — Bob once reported in detail on Thomas Macaulay and another time, equally seriously, on Isaac Newton — and the group then paused for refreshments, conversation, or perhaps a few short rounds of charades. On these occasions Taft showed none of the reserve that he displayed to the rest of the world, and more than Martha, who at times seemed sharp and impatient, he accepted his friends exactly as they were. He relaxed, talked animatedly about politics, and gossiped about the little things of life on Indian Hill. He seemed tolerant, even sweet, and he frequently broke into a broad smile that charmed his friends.[21]

These close acquaintances also recognized that he was kind and thoughtful. When Tylor Field died in 1936 immediately after Taft had arrived in Murray Bay for his vacation, Taft turned around and endured the two-day train ride in order to be at Field's funeral. And Dorothy Rowe later grew so irate at accounts portraying Taft as cold that she sent a letter to *Newsweek*. "My gorge rises," she wrote, "to read such stories. Bob is plenty of fun. He has a particularly keen sense of humor, and even better, a sense of the ridiculous. Just because he doesn't go down the street with a wide, toothy, politician's grin doesn't mean he doesn't like people." She concluded by telling of a Christmas Eve when her child was recovering from spinal meningitis, her husband was coming down with mumps, and her cook had suddenly been carried off with appendicitis. With a blizzard blowing outside, she was about to despair. Then, however, arrived *Newsweek*'s " 'unglamorous, unengaging statistician,' Robert Alphonso Taft. Conversation: 'Gee, Dorothy, I'm sorry for you. What can I do to help?' Dorothy: 'Not much I guess. What I really need around here is a cook.' Bob: 'All right, I'll get you a cook,' and he did." Some *Newsweek* readers concluded that her story told more about the luxurious life style of his circle than it did about his personality, and scholars may wonder at the veracity of the dialogue. But Dorothy Rowe spoke for others who knew him well during his days on Indian Hill. It was one of the misfortunes of his political career that he could not bring himself to develop such rapport with strangers.[22]

Above all, Taft's life in these easy years revolved around Martha. By the end of the decade the burden of bringing four children into the world was beginning to take its toll. Her once slight and graceful figure grew heavy, and her dark hair showed a few streaks of gray. She was no longer the girl who had captivated suitors prior to 1914. She also remained as frank and forthright as her husband, never flattered him, and seldom hesitated to tell him he was wrong. Yet perhaps because Taft had developed such self-confidence, he did not need flattery, and Martha's intelligence and independence pleased rather than upset him. As he grew more involved in politics, he knew that he could count on her loyalty under any circumstance, and that she was as ambitious for him as he could ever have been for himself. Charming, vibrant, strong-minded, Martha continued to be the one person on whom Bob could always depend. She always would be.[23]

Taft could hardly have asked for more out of life than he received in the 1920's. He was content in his work, close to friends with whom he could be himself, wealthy enough to travel when and where he wanted, and head of a happy family that was protected from the seamier life of the city twelve miles away. Perhaps because of these satisfactions, he was also remarkably free of the small illnesses that sometimes plague people who are developing emotional tensions. Indeed, Martha remarked in 1932 that Bob had not spent a day in bed since 1917. His life style led one later observer to note that if he had possessed any cant, he would have been an appropriate character in a Sinclair Lewis novel, for he was

> industrious, prudent, monogamous, proper in speech and com-
> portment, law-abiding, . . . a good provider, a believer in educa-
> tion, a tree grower, and a good care-taker of the temple of the soul.
> He has all the virtues of his business-lawyer caste and his Cincin-
> nati class.[24]

This portrait was a little sketchy. Taft lacked not only Babbitt's cant but his shallow conviviality and mindlessness, and he remained bent on excellence. Yet the description captured much of the Taft of the 1920's, for there were many things he could be complacent about. After all, he had succeeded in everything he had tried, and his world seemed to present no obstacles to whatever ambitions he might develop in the future. Thus it made sense to adhere to the honorable, profitable, and ascending path that he was pursuing. If this path were to strike some of his later critics as rather narrow and unventuresome, it was admirably suited to the times, and it was at least as broad as the routes being followed by thousands of other aspiring young lawyer-politicians of the decade. It was not surprising that he moved with the current instead of struggling against it or forcing himself to reassess his way of life.

CHAPTER 8

The Gospel of Party Regularity

COMPARED TO George B. Cox and his gang of saloon keepers, Cincinnati Republican boss Rudolph K. Hynicka was suave, articulate, more inclined to offer token representation to the diverse elements in the city. But as the 1920's slid by, he grew careless, devoted much of his time to running his burlesque houses in New York, and handled party affairs in Cincinnati like an absentee landlord supervising his feudal estates. The city, the wise men said, was run not only on a shoestring, but on a G-string.

It was no joking matter, for Cincinnati's growth had greatly increased the need for services without providing the cash to pay for them. Police were laid off for lack of funds, fire stations abandoned, street lighting and cleaning severely curtailed. Streets deteriorated, and a contemporary cartoonist captured the disgust of Queen City residents by portraying a man trying frantically to scramble from a hole in the pavement and shouting, "Hey, don't just help me! Get ready to pull my horse out, too!" Though Cincinnatians proved remarkably long-suffering, by 1923 resentment was building up rapidly.[1]

On one thing critics and bosses agreed: the city desperately needed money. Late in 1923 the local GOP could no longer ignore popular criticism, and it named a committee to investigate city problems. The committee then employed Lent D. Upson, an expert in municipal affairs, whose report in July 1924 described vividly the crisis in municipal finances. As if echoing Taft's speeches in Columbus, it pointed to the unhappy effects of the Smith law banning new tax levies. Unable to raise the revenue for essential services, the city had resorted to bonds, which had given Cincinnati the highest gross and net per-capita bonded debt of the forty-three largest American cities. Again agreeing with Taft, it blamed the county budget commission for starving municipal programs and concluded: "No government, good or bad, can be administered without funds. Were the city of Cincinnati governed by the most high-minded and efficient administrators in existence, they could not possibly, with the funds now available, give the citizens the type of government to which they are entitled." [2]

Most concerned citizens also agreed that Republican rule was relatively honest. To be sure, bidding on public contracts was seldom open or competitive, vote fraud was extensive, and the same contractors seemed to handle city work with disturbing regularity. But graft was limited, covert, and inexpensive. What distressed people was the machine's gross inefficiency, wastefulness, and lack of expertise. It issued bonds for inordinately long terms, took on unreasonably expensive improvements, and proved inexcusably slow in responding to the simplest complaints about sewers and rapid transit. Though desperate for funds, it failed to keep its accounts accurately, and reformers later discovered $600,000 the old administration had overlooked. Taxpayers recognized these deficiencies, and by the 1920's they consistently defeated bond issues. Even the *Times-Star* demanded in 1920 that Hynicka be driven from power. The city was ever on the brink of crisis. [3]

The Upson Report then shook its Republican sponsors by going beyond financial matters to propose changes in the political system. Cincinnati, it said, needed a "strong, intelligent, critical minority." The report recommended a nonpartisan ballot, a nine-man city council elected at large in place of the existing thirty-two-man body with twenty-six elected by wards, proportional representation, and a city manager form of government. In the politest imaginable language, the report was attacking the practice of one-party rule that in 1924 resulted in a council with thirty-one Republicans and one Democrat. [4]

The Upson Report was important in prodding the uncommitted toward reform, but it was not the prime mover. That responsibility belonged to a handful of civic leaders who formed the Cincinnatus Association in 1920. Led by Murray Seasongood, an eloquent, stubborn, and idealistic lawyer, this group was far from radical. Most members were young professional people of high social and educational standing. Most were also Republicans. Yet the physical deterioration of the city appalled them, and many of them moved from studying conditions and issuing reports to criticizing the mayor and the machine, and finally to revolt.

Seasongood began his battle in October 1923. Disgusted with the condition of city streets, he appeared before the Cincinnatus Association to lambaste the machine and to urge the defeat of a proposed tax increase. Moderates among the association like John Hollister and Hulbert Taft countered that the group ought to debate the issues, not engage in politics, and that the levy was essential to cover the budgetary deficit. But the press reported the speech, the machine foolishly engaged Seasongood in debate, and soon the tax levy became the hottest issue of an otherwise dull campaign. Republicans, pleading poverty, blamed the county and said that only the tax levy would permit improvements. Seasongood replied that "the same bunch controls both city and county and could change this." The levy might help, he agreed, but the present gang would misuse it. What was needed — and here he moved beyond the immediate issue — was a new city charter and the abolition of the present mayor-council system. When the returns in 1923 were counted, the voters had not only defeated the levy but turned down five of six proposed new bond issues. Seasongood, it seemed, had touched a current of resentment among the people.[5]

Encouraged, another reformer, Henry Bentley, formed the so-called Birdless Ballot League to remove party symbols from the ballot. (At the time, voters found an eagle over the Republican column, a rooster over the Democrats — "vote for the bird with pants," Republican leaders told their uneducated constituents.) Bentley's league merged in June 1924 with supporters of Senator Robert La Follette's Progressive presidential campaign and became known as the City Charter Committee. It soon went even beyond the Upson Report and called for nonpartisan, alphabetically listed ballots, a nine-man council elected at large, a city manager, and a system of proportional representation guaranteeing the minority a voice on the council. Mobilizing quickly, it circulated a petition to get these changes on the ballot as an amendment to the existing charter of 1917.

The Republicans took no official position on the amendment. But they foolishly tried to confuse the voters by placing two extraneous amendments of their own on the ballot. The aroused reformers then secured the necessary 20,000 signatures on their petition, campaigned vigorously, positioned watchers at the polls, and carried their amendment in November, 92,000 to 41,000. A year later they won again by placing six Charterites, as they came to be called, on the nine-man council. These six named Seasongood mayor, appointed a city manager, and moved on to repeated triumphs with the voters. In a few years the reformers swept out one of the most solidly entrenched political organizations in America and attracted nationwide attention in the process.[6]

The conflict between machine and reformers caught Taft in a dilemma, for he had to decide between his instinctive faith in party regularity and his desire for orderly government. Long aware of the inefficiency of the local machine, he had helped found the Cincinnatus Association in 1920, served as one of its original vice-presidents, and drafted its constitution. Throughout the early 1920's he pressed the city to improve its handling of taxation, bond issues, and even of such mundane matters as garbage collection. Well acquainted with Seasongood, Taft recommended him early in 1923 as the most qualified man in Cincinnati for a vacant federal judgeship. When the reformers threatened to break with the machine later that year, Taft's brother Charlie and many of his personal friends such as Tylor Field and Russell Wilson joined them, as did almost all of Martha's friends in the League of Women Voters. To stay with Hynicka and the ward bosses, with whom he was not close personally, would mean breaking with many of the civic-minded professional people he knew much better.[7]

The machine also distressed Taft, for it seemed to him vulnerable on the worst of grounds: sheer stupidity. "Unless the Republican organization shows somewhat more intelligence in their selection of men and handling of affairs," he wrote in 1924, "they are likely to get a severe jolt in November." A few days before the vote on the charter amendment that year he added privately that the machine had done "everything possible to discredit the present system" and that unless the Republicans nominated able men for the municipal elections of 1925, he might join the Charterites. When the Republicans lost in 1925, Taft even wrote privately that he was "glad of the result." To Uncle Horace he added, "I have hopes that a new broom will sweep clean for a while at any rate." Because he had been consistently disappointed by the sloppiness of the organization, Taft had ample cause to reject it.[8]

But he never did. In 1923 he opposed Seasongood's war against the tax levy, and in 1924, when the Cincinnatus Association called almost unanimously for the ousting of two regular Republicans from city jobs, Taft stubbornly defended them. Soon he was debating Seasongood angrily and denouncing the charter amendment. He was the "only public opponent," his brother Charlie wrote, "that amounts to anything," and for the next fifteen years he continued to fight the independents who had insolently threatened party stability in Cincinnati.[9]

He had ample reasons for choosing as he did. He was still struggling at the time to work out the street railway arrangement with city officials. And having labored hard to secure changes in tax laws, he honestly believed that the organization simply needed money; hadn't the Upson Report said as much? Reformers, he argued, should work within the existing system and name better candidates for office.[10] Given the organization's stubborn refusal to consider even moderate changes, Taft's argument for reform from within was at best wishful thinking. But nothing suggests that he was insincere or disingenuous.

Did political ambition sustain his loyalty to the regulars? The question demands an answer, for Taft's decision to stay with the organization proved essential to his subsequent advancement in state politics. Had he cast his lot against it, the men who had placed him three times in Columbus would have despised him, and he would have earned an ineradicable reputation as an insurgent who could not be trusted. As his brother Charlie later discovered to his dismay, anyone who broke with the party could expect no backing at home for any political office. Taft would have been blind not to appreciate the wisdom of party regularity in the highly partisan politics of Ohio. Though he was never foolish enough to broadcast the fact, he had ambitions to move ahead in politics, and these aspirations must have played some part in his decision.

Yet Taft was moved by much more than ambition. When the charter agitation began, he was already beholden to the organization as its three-time nominee to the legislature, and he possessed a dogged sense of loyalty to those who had given him his start. Staying with the regulars might appall his social circle, and it might cool relations with Russell Wilson and many other intelligent, well-meaning friends. But if lost friendships brought twinges of regret, he gave no sign of them. Throughout his political career he was to display the same kind of unquestioning loyalty to political associates, and no one could capture his attention long enough to change his mind.

The basic cause for his reaction lay in the fact that he was simply not an insurgent by nature. He responded instinctively to the need for order, rules, and systems. At Taft, Yale, and Harvard he had accepted things as he found them, worked within them, and risen to the top. In politics he had witnessed the destruction of his father by insurgents in 1912, and he believed instinctively in two parties at the local as well as state and national levels. Reformers might argue that there was no Democratic or Republican way to repair the streets, but Bob agreed with his father's insistence that "two great parties are the greatest aids to the successful administration of popular government." [11] Bob Taft's instinctive regularity and his unrelenting partisanship were entirely in keeping with his temperament and upbringing, and his fateful decision to stay with the organization really required little soul-searching. Taft did not need ambition to drive him on. He was practicing what he believed.

.

Though he had made his choice, for the rest of the decade he refused to abandon hope for compromise. Hynicka, tired and discouraged by defeat, retired in 1926, to be replaced by a collective leadership under a veteran organizer, Fred Schneller, and as Taft's power grew within the organization, he used it to move toward rapprochement with the insurgents. As early as 1926 he agreed to

serve on a three-man Charter Revision Committee (Bentley represented the insurgents, a Democrat was the third) appointed by
Seasongood. The committee recommended giving Cincinnati
greater freedom from legislative authority. Its revisions, which
voters approved overwhelmingly in November 1926, allowed Cincinnati to take advantage of the home-rule-in-taxation law of the
1925 legislature and contributed materially to the city's ability to
handle its fiscal problems.[12]

Partly because he conceded privately the ability of the reformers
("we have undoubtedly had a great improvement in our city government," he wrote in 1927), Taft tried to secure coalition tickets
with them.[13] In 1926, however, the insurgents refused to coalesce,
formed their own so-called Citizens ticket for county offices, and
won partial victory in a bitter primary. In 1927 the Charterites rejected a deal with the Republicans and maintained their 6-to-3
representation on the city council. When the GOP finally defeated the insurgents in the August 1928 primary, it refused utterly to deal with them. "I am afraid that this set-back has weakened all of the more moderate forces in the organization," Taft
wrote, "and made it more difficult to secure permanent improvement." Thereafter the reformers fought all the harder — and with
marked success. In 1929 Taft lamented, "I would very much
prefer not to have a Republican ticket," but his friends in the
GOP ignored him and endorsed a full nine-man slate, only to lose
again, 6 to 3. In playing the role of conciliator Taft was doomed
to frustration, for the contestants were too evenly matched to retreat and too full of the passionate hatreds of parted brethren to
unite.[14]

But to Taft conciliation did not mean surrender, and each time
he lost his struggles for coalition, he joined with the regulars. Although he grudgingly came to support the city manager system and
even the nonpartisan ballot, he continued to believe that proportional representation encouraged government by racial and religious blocs instead of by party. Regularity continued to count
above all else.[15]

The campaign of 1927 revealed the depth of his feelings. One of
the insurgents to win in the Republican primary of 1926 had been
his brother Charlie, who thereby became the Citizens' nominee for

county prosecutor. Confronted with this fait accompli, Taft and his fellow Republicans had then supported the entire ticket against the Democrats in the fall, and it had won with ease. In 1927 Bob believed that Charlie and the rest of the insurgent officeholders ought to reciprocate by endorsing the machine slate in the city election. But Charlie refused, insisting that municipal politics ought to be nonpartisan. Inevitably, the two brothers collided in their law office. "We had quite an argument," Charlie reported to his distraught father, "as to the propriety of a Republican office-holder, endorsed by the Republican Organization to a county position last fall, taking a political position opposed to the Organization in the city fight this year. He [Bob] felt that it was inconsistent . . . The controlling point in my mind, however, is the company he is in. At any rate, we failed to convince each other and parted amicably." [16]

Amicably, but not without tensions. Charlie was eight years younger than his brother, and most unlike him. He was athletic, outgoing, and so enthusiastic that one observer later described him as "a faint suggestion of St. George and St. Paul, with a dash of Frank Merriwell," while others dismissed him as a Boy Scout. Already, the fraternal relationship had suffered from these differences in temperament. In working to develop the firm Bob — and especially John Hollister — were upset by Charlie's proclivity for time-consuming public speaking and by his devotion to the national YMCA movement. "If his name wasn't Taft," enemies grumbled, "he'd be a YMCA secretary" and no more.[17] Aware of the conflict, the father tried to hold his younger son to the single track ("these cheering tones of the YMCA people do not contribute to income or knowledge of the law," he confided to Bob), and Uncle Horace, while supporting the reformers from afar and conceding that Charlie was "as amiable as possible," lamented that "he shoots away and never seems to think what he is going to hit or how anything sounds." [18] Adding to the sense of difference was the complete lack of rapport between Martha, who was public-spirited and outspoken, and Charlie's wife, Eleanor, who had entirely different ideas and causes, who was busy raising a family that was to include seven children, and who struck Bob, Martha, and many of their friends as a little flighty and silly.[19] With political dispute added to such tensions, the brothers drifted further apart. Charlie's refusal to support the Republican slate in 1927 led the organization, with Bob silently acquiescing, to retaliate by successfully denying Charlie renomination in 1928. Bob was sorry but matter-of-fact: "It was unfortunate that Charlie was not renominated, but he ran as well as any of the Citizens except one . . . I think the result shows that the entire Citizens Republican movement in the county this year was a mistake, and I am afraid more harm has been done by it than good." [20] The brothers remained law partners for another decade. But their differences in temperament and in politics had strained the bonds, and probably only the ties of blood — and Bob's reluctance to disappoint his father — prevented a rupture of their partnership. Nothing revealed more clearly Bob's determined defense of the principle of two-party government.

·

Taft was correct in fearing the political appeal of the reformers. Charterites won election after election in the city until 1941. Few municipal reform movements in American history proved so enduring or so successful at the polls.

He was also accurate in arguing, as he did in later years, that he had himself contributed to the success of the reformers. He had negotiated an arrangement providing improved streetcar service, and his legislative accomplishments gave the new regime a flexibility in planning denied to the hard-pressed organization men earlier in the decade. Pointing to the financial sections of the Upson Report, he argued with only slight exaggeration that the problem of taxes alone had been enough to discredit municipal officials before 1925.

Otherwise, he proved a poor prophet. Contrary to his predictions, the triumphs of the Charterites did not harm the local organization in state or national contests. By bringing good government to the city, the charter movement may even have helped to delay the response of Cincinnati's ethnic minorities to the Democratic appeal of Franklin D. Roosevelt in the 1930's. But, except for 1932 and 1936, when Roosevelt carried Hamilton County, the GOP continued strong, and Cincinnati became the only large metropolitan center in America to vote Republican in the presidential election of 1940.[21]

Taft also badly overestimated the willingness or the capacity of the organization to improve itself. It had ruled too long and had grown lazy, arrogant, and extremely sloppy. The reformers, like Taft, were heavily Republican; unlike him, they placed results ahead of an abstract faith in party loyalty. In amending the charter in 1924, they encouraged the voters to approve bond issues and tax levies that had repeatedly been denied the machine earlier in the decade. Authorized a total of $30 million in new issues between 1925 and 1931, the Charterites received excellent direction from their new city managers and turned a floundering and demoralized city into one of the most effectively operated in the country. In 1931 even Hulbert Taft's *Times-Star* was moved to concede that the Charterites were providing "a good city administration," and in 1932 Upson returned to Cincinnati and was astonished at what he saw. Cincinnati, he said, had "gone forward to accomplishments which in 1924 appeared to be not only improbable but impossible." [22]

Taft's stubborn defense of the regulars also left some of the Charterites bitter. The Cincinnati *Post,* which carried the banner for the reformers, grumbled in 1940 that "Robert Taft turned his face to the dead past; his first love and first loyalty were given to party, and he did not swerve from that narrow allegiance to take up the people's cause even while an angered citizenry smashed the party machine to give Cincinnati a decent government and a place of honor instead of shame among American cities." And Seasongood, the most idealistic and puritanical of the reformers, still bristled in 1958 at the mention of Robert Taft. "He used to lose his temper in debates with me," Seasongood wrote a friend, "and finally refused to continue them, admitting frankly that it was because of that that he did not do himself justice. Having in mind how persistently he opposed good government in the city, I cannot go along with those who classify him as a hero and great statesman." [23]

Had Seasongood been more charitable, he might have conceded that Taft had at least remained loyal to the people who gave him his start, and that his legislative accomplishments had helped pave the way for urban improvements. He might have observed that Harry S Truman also refused to abandon his early political associates even when they were proved to be corrupt in the 1930's. But he was accurate in stressing Taft's loyalty to party and to political allies above all else.

Seasongood was also correct in pointing to Taft's refusal to concede that he was wrong. By the late 1930's Taft was willing to admit that at-large voting and the city manager system had brought some progress. But he still defended the machine. "The government of Cincinnati from 1913 to 1925," he wrote in 1939, "was also a very good government, honest and well run . . . and the improvement has been greatly exaggerated by the advocates of a charter form of government. It was, however, hampered by a lack of funds due to state law, and the result was that the City became very much run down from a physical standpoint." [24]

By instinct a regular, Taft had remained true to his nature.

CHAPTER 9

Years of Frustration, 1930–1937

WHEN TAFT TURNED FORTY in September 1929 he could reflect contentedly on his past. There had been struggles — to match his illustrious father, to prove himself in Cincinnati. There had been defeats by the Cornstalkers, by Donahey, and by the buoyant Charterites defiantly in control of his native town. But carefully and steadily he had competed, found himself, and grown in self-assurance. Though his brown hair was noticeably thinning and though his father now found him "a little aldermanic in his proportions," he still enjoyed robust health, and he remained as energetic as ever.[1]

He also seemed at peace with his world. Sky Farm continued to be a source of pleasure, and the two little boys — Lloyd, who was six, and Horace, who was four — enjoyed watching the cows, hogs, and chickens and playing with the children of Finch, the tenant farmer. Bill, at fourteen, was spending his last year at home before going to Taft School, and Bobby, twelve, was to follow a year later. Taft still liked to make the rounds of his farm, and he watched happily as old friends bought nearby land and settled in. He was expanding his law firm, and being recognized as a civic leader who was already compared favorably with his father.

The nation seemed to bask in unprecedented prosperity, the western world lay in peace, and apparently matchless Herbert Hoover ruled in Washington. The world still suited Bob Taft and men like him.

Within the month signs of trouble appeared on Wall Street. Stock prices slipped, staggered back, dropped again, then on October 23 and 24 plunged sickeningly. Exchange officials closed the visitors' gallery, and the bankers huddled to reassure the traders. But stock prices continued to fall, and the average for fifty leading stocks plummeted from a high of 311.90 on September 3 to 164.43 on November 13. The days of complacency were over, and America took more than ten years recovering. For Taft the depression years meant repeated unhappiness and frustration.

•

The first blows were personal. Uncle Charley, who had been failing for a few years, sank into a coma and died on December 31, 1929. Bob's father ignored the advice of doctors, insisted on riding the train to Cincinnati for the funeral, and returned to Washington so weak that he had to be hospitalized. Soon he was helpless with advanced arteriosclerosis, and Bob had to go to Washington on February 3, 1930, to announce his father's retirement from the Supreme Court. Less than a month later, William Howard Taft, the only American to serve both as President and as Chief Justice, lapsed into periods of unconsciousness, and on March 8 he passed away at his Wyoming Avenue home in Washington. Bob and Charlie hastened from Cincinnati to be there the next morning, as did their sister Helen Manning, who had received her Ph.D. in history from Yale in 1924 and was pursuing a distinguished academic career at Bryn Mawr College. They consoled Nellie; watched their father's caisson move solemnly to the Capitol, where thousands waited in the rain to see him lie in state; attended the simple Unitarian services in Washington; and saw him laid to rest in the graceful slope of the Arlington National Cemetery.

In rescuing Bob's father from pain, death offered consolation of a sort. Nellie was still strong and buoyant despite continued difficulty with her speech, and she recovered quickly from her loss. Because Will had left her with an estate of $475,000 including their Washington and Murray Bay homes, she lived comfortably and traveled widely until her death thirteen years later.[2] Bob managed her finances but received nothing from the will; his father expected his sons to make their own way.

Still, his father's death deprived him of the model he had tried to please for so long. When Aunt Annie died less than a year later, only Bob's mother, Aunt Maria, and Uncle Horace, who would not retire as "King" at Taft School until 1936, survived from the family he knew best in the older generation. In entering his forties Bob was moving into a new cycle of life as patriarch of the family, trustee of the Charles Tafts' multimillion dollar estate, and watchman over their gifts to the Institute of Fine Arts ($1 million), the University of Cincinnati ($2 million), and the Taft Museum ($2.7 million). He was exchanging young manhood for the responsibilities of middle age.

Political frustrations occurred in the arena of former triumphs, the Ohio legislature. In November 1929, Ohio voters had at last broken the constitutional impasse by abolishing the uniform rule on taxation and permitting the realistic classification of intangible property. Perceiving his opportunity to put tax reform into practice, Taft agreed to run for public office in 1930, this time for the state senate.

The depression was already releasing broad waves of discontent, and Taft's route to Columbus proved far rougher than in the days of normalcy. A labor slate calling for state payment of old age pensions challenged the organization in the August primaries. Though it lost, and though Taft led the three-man Republican ticket with 20,750 votes (800 ahead of his closest pursuer), the labor group polled some 10,000 votes, remarkably high for an August primary in Republican Cincinnati.[3]

The results in November proved how restless the voters had become. Taft again led the Republicans by polling 93,832 votes. But one Democrat finished almost 4000 ahead of him, and another took third place with 93,664. Hamilton County, long the bastion of Republicanism, had placed two Democrats in its three-man delegation to the senate. For the next six years Taft had to contend with Democratic resurgence at the polls.[4]

Columbus offered some consolations, for the GOP still ruled both houses, 71 to 58 and 18 to 14. But Taft quickly suffered disappointments. Persisting in his quest for administrative efficiency, he introduced a resolution for a constitutional amendment giving four-year terms to state officials, a bill to permit preprimary conventions, and a plan for the consolidation of county welfare departments. The first failed in the senate, the others in the house.

With Indian Hill in mind, he introduced a bill to create county zoning and planning commissions. The commissions, he said, would prevent "somebody who wants to start a fertilizer factory or creamery from locating themselves immediately next to high class residential property," and would curb billboards and "the shack type of construction." He succeeded in the senate, 23 to 1, only to watch the house ignore the measure. Taft's bills reflected his abiding interest in party government, in efficiency, and in planning; but in the midst of economic crisis they aroused little interest.[5]

Taft also proved as baffled as anyone by the depression, and on occasion he sounded hardhearted. He opposed state-sponsored unemployment insurance by arguing plausibly that there was insufficient revenue to pay for it, but then added: "my inclination is very much opposed to any system which provides for the payment of money to men for doing nothing. I have no reason to think that a further study will change my mind." [6] He called for rigid economy and helped force a cut of $6 million in the already stringent house budget of $74 million. He rejected state payment of old age pensions and advocated instead a committee to study the matter. And he pressed Democratic Governor George White to sign a bill that would have reduced from five and a half to four years the time in which the state could foreclose property for nonpayment of taxes. Such a measure, he said, would primarily affect subdividers and corporations, but it ought to be applied to the homeowner as well. "If he is unable to pay his taxes for four years, it is fairly certain that he is living beyond his means and will never be able to catch up . . . It is far better for him to recognize the situation, dispose of his house, and live on a scale more commensurate with his means." [7]

Such statements as these showed Taft in his least attractive guise: assertive, budget conscious, and callous to the human dimensions of the economic crisis. Yet he was not always so unfeeling. He spoke publicly for a controversial and eventually successful bill to outlaw yellow-dog contracts and supported Governor White's request for a bond issue to finance state institutions. When the depression exhausted the resources of many Ohio communities early in 1932, he approved the calling of a special session to "get the absolutely necessary money to prevent starvation" and proposed creating a state fund to which counties might sell relief bonds.[8] At this session in March he and fellow Republicans endorsed a temporary state relief commission, permitted the diversion of gasoline and motor vehicle taxes for welfare, increased taxes on utilities, and authorized county relief bonds. When subsequent special sessions became necessary in May and September, he again cooperated with White by voting to authorize banks to borrow from the newly created national Reconstruction Finance Corporation, and to slash salaries of state officials, though he successfully resisted sharp cuts in the higher brackets. He also joined a unanimous senate in approving a measure authorizing limited-dividend housing companies to secure federal funds for slum clearance.[9] When he left the legislature early in 1933, Ohio had offered little state aid to the needy. But like other states, it was paralyzed with confusion and anxious for things to right themselves naturally. Taft shared this sense of frustration. He would do what he could to avert starvation. But surely there was light at the end of the tunnel.

These antidepression measures occupied him occasionally, but because he was named to head a joint legislative committee on taxation, budgetary questions took most of his time. The committee faced a formidable task. The depression had diminished state revenues, and frightened observers prophesied a $10 to $15 million deficit. But where to find the money? All kinds of advice poured in to Taft and his fellow committeemen.[10] Some recommended an increase in taxes on utilities. But Taft thought these high enough already. Though willing to consider a sales tax, he doubted that it would raise enough money on its own, worried about its effect on Ohio business, and recognized that it was "primarily a consumption tax, reaching the taxpayers in proportion to their expenditures rather than in proportion to their income and property." Partial to an income tax, he nevertheless distinguished between "earned" income from work and "unearned" income from investments, and he shrank from the idea of penalizing honest labor too heavily. Besides, he knew a tax on earned incomes stood no chance of passage. When Governor White came out early against sales or income taxes, Taft gladly dropped serious consideration of them.[11]

He turned instead to a tax on income from intangible property, especially from stocks and bonds. The existing intangibles tax, he argued, hit such investments at 2 to 3 per cent of their value (not their income in dividends) and caused wealthy investors to move their legal residences out of state or to refuse to report their holdings at all. Of approximately $10 billion in intangible property held by Ohioans in 1929, he estimated, only $100 million was reported. With the uniform rule abolished, he argued, Ohio could lower the tax on intangibles far enough to persuade people to pay. "It is a matter of psychology to get people to declare their holdings," he said, "and I believe it can best be done by using the system of taxing incomes rather than general capital holdings. Too much machinery to enforce the law would be required otherwise." [12]

Having reached this decision, Taft had to persuade his committee as well. He found it willing to endorse a 5 per cent tax on the income from investments but also eager to tax the value of intangibles that did not bring dividends. At first he resisted, but he was outnumbered, and the committee endorsed a smaller, 2-mill tax on the value of such intangibles.

With this agreement the committee was ready, and it finally reported in May 1931. Its package called for increased fees on automobile license plates, a 10 per cent tobacco tax, and a $5 million bond issue to support welfare institutions. Crowning the committee's program was the tax on income from intangibles, which Taft estimated would collect $27 million annually, or approximately $5 million more than it had before.[13]

Managing his committee was one thing; getting approval from both houses was another. Taft had to steer the package on the floor for more than two weeks. Southern Ohio tobacco farmers objected to the tax on their product, bankers to the tax on their profits, and homeowners to the rates on income from intangibles, which they insisted would not bring in enough revenue to permit a reduction in property taxes. Taft struck back by arguing that anything higher than a rate of 5 per cent on intangibles — close to the national norm — would drive investors out of state. The intangibles tax, he insisted disarmingly, might develop loopholes, but let us try it and see.[14]

The press applauded his performance. "The finest mind of

the Ohio General Assembly," one columnist declared. "Anyone who attempts to upset the program finds himself up against the proposition of a man who can ask questions and usually knows the answer in advance," wrote another. "No generalities will throw him off the track. He has the facts marshalled and when he enunciates them, he bites them off with a finality that leaves no room for quibbling." By mid-June the entire tax package had passed both houses and had been signed into law by the governor. Taft had been patient, willing to compromise, and ready to admit potential dangers. He had worked for the possible and had succeeded.[15]

But it was characteristic of these years of frustration that even his greatest legislative triumph quickly soured. His estimates proved optimistic, and the tax in 1932 brought in but $17 millon instead of the anticipated $27 million. The reason was not tax avoidance, for the 5 per cent rate backed by the threat of federal inspection proved fair and collectible. It was the depression that destroyed investments and left the state desperate for new funds. His intangibles tax remained on the books, but in the early 1930's it brought him criticism from people who had expected more than it delivered.[16]

The intangibles tax also lived to haunt him seven years later, when he engaged in a primary campaign for the United States Senate. His opponent, Arthur Day, showed that a homeowner with a $10,000 house had to pay a property tax of 15 mills, or $150, whereas a wealthy investor owning $10,000 in intangibles that paid a 5 per cent return had to pay but 5 per cent of his dividends of $500, or $25. Furthermore, he charged, the Taft law granted people who had avoided taxes on intangibles between 1927 and 1931 immunity from prosecution if they reported their earnings in 1932. Taft, he said, had spared rich people an income tax and had forced the state to turn to a regressive sales tax in 1934. "Throughout his legislative career," Day concluded, "he devoted every effort to protect the huge Taft estate against being taxed in keeping with the real value of its far-flung holdings." Taft, he said, was "essentially a tax evader. You all know the type — a professional reactionary."[17]

These charges came at the last moment in a campaign of a desperate opponent, and they were filled with inaccuracies. Though Taft had not supported a state income tax in 1931, neither had the governor, for such a tax was as politically impossible then in Ohio as it was in most of the country at the time. Taft also had nothing to do (despite Day's implication) with the sales tax in 1934, and he had included the immunity provision, which was noncontroversial at the time (and which he did not need for himself), merely to encourage compliance. Had Day enjoyed access to tax returns, he would have discovered that Taft owned almost exclusively stocks of Ohio corporations, which had been exempt under the old system. After passage of the intangibles law, he and Martha had to pay between $1000 and $1600 per year on the $20,000 to $32,000 income from stocks that they received annually in the 1930's; and they would have paid much more than that if the depression had not reduced their dividends. Day would also have discovered that many of the income-producing investments of the estate of Uncle Charley and Aunt Annie were also in Ohio corporations; under the new law these required a payment in taxes of more than $5000 a year — or 5 per cent of the approximately $100,000 a year earned by these securities.[18] Though Day's charges lacked substance, it was ironic that a tax aimed at people such as the Tafts should have led opponents to question Robert's integrity.

The distributive features of the intangibles tax hurt Taft most severely. To secure rural votes, he had included a temporary provision that called for counties collecting more than their quotas (based on past collections) to turn over the surplus to counties with budgetary deficits. But neither he nor anyone else anticipated the size of Cincinnati's surplus, and by mid-1932 it was already clear that Hamilton County would have to surrender at least $750,000 (political opponents said $1.5 million) of the nearly $2 million it was collecting. The county prosecutor, a Democrat elected with insurgent support in 1930, then took legal action to void the distributive feature. Taft contested the suit while at the same time conceding the necessity of securing a formula more favorable to the cities. If re-elected to the state senate, he promised, he would work to do so.[19]

He never had the chance. He not only lost the suit, but in November 1932 absorbed the only electoral defeat of his career.

The overriding reason was the Democratic sweep, which gave the
county to Roosevelt by 4500 votes. Another cause was Taft's concentration on the national contest. "He is forgetting to do anything about his own campaign," Martha wrote to Bob, Jr., at Taft
School, "so he may not get back to the Senate, and may be at home
more this winter." [20] But the intangibles tax, clearly identified
with his name, probably cost him the election, for after leading the
Republican slate in the primaries before the battle in the courts,
he stumbled in November. He not only trailed all three Democratic candidates by margins ranging up to 4500 but fell behind
the leading Republican (who finished second in the six-man field)
by 3000 ballots. "The Democrats," he concluded, "were too strong
for us, and the tax proposition lost me a few thousand votes." His
brother Charlie was even more explicit. Bob lost, he wrote their
mother, because of hard feeling from Charterites and because of
the "effect among the well-to-do classes of the intangibles tax.
Most unfairly, they blamed him for having to pay more taxes, and
it was a feeling that was very widespread." [21]

Until the challenge to his program in 1932, Taft had not
planned to run again anyway, especially because Hollister's eleva-
tion to Congress in a special election in 1931 had increased the
burden of work in the firm. So the defeat left him with mixed
feelings. "I really did not have time to go to Columbus anyway,"
he wrote. "With the Democrats in full control, I would either
have to help Governor White or be disagreeable, and neither of
these courses would be very satisfactory." [22] Yet his loss hurt, and
he was always careful not to draw attention to it in future years.
Had he been more philosophical, he might have pondered sadly
that political defeat had sprung in part from the seeds of a tax reform planted in his mind more than ten years before. He might
also have reflected on the political consequences of becoming too
closely identified with controversial legislation.

·

The early 1930's did offer Taft a few satisfactions. One was the
comfortable feeling of being sought after. Ever more prominent
in Cincinnati, he dutifully lent his support to the symphony orchestra, and he joined a group of leading citizens calling for

American participation in the World Court. He was asked to speak at Phillips Brooks House in Cambridge, to serve as a member of the organizational committee of the American Child Health Association, as a board member of the National Committee on Prisons and Prison Labor, as a director of the American Judicature Society, and as a trustee of the Harvard Law Review Association. Senator Robert Wagner of New York asked him to mediate a strike of clothing workers. Taft declined to be a mediator because his firm represented the Amalgamated Clothing Workers Union, and he told the others he was too busy. But he did find time to serve as a trustee of Taft School, and in 1936 he followed his father and grandfather by being elected (over Dean Acheson) a member of the Yale Corporation. He also spent hours choosing Henry Pringle as his father's official biographer and then offering him both assistance and suggestions on the book.[23]

Helping Hoover provided special pleasures. As vice-chairman of the Ohio Hoover for President Committee in 1928, Taft had run in a hotly contested primary as a delegate-at-large, gone to the convention, and rejoiced when Hoover won the election in November. "I am looking forward to reading *Life, Time,* the *Nation,* and the *New Republic,*" he chortled, "and seeing how they take the result. The discomfiture of the Eastern intelligentsia gives me as much pleasure as that of the radical farm leaders." The new President gratified Bob and Martha by occasionally asking them to visit the White House and by listening to Taft's recommendations on appointments. In 1932 Taft served again as a Hoover delegate, and though he was unhappy when Franklin D. Roosevelt took the election, he admitted being thrilled during the campaign to stand on the back platform of a train as it carried Hoover through the little towns of southern Ohio.[24]

Still, the larger frustrations continued. He watched Ohio voters knock the maximum rate on real estate down to 10 mills in 1933, and he despaired at the continued instability of the state's revenue system. In election after election, he worked for Republican statewide candidates, only to see them lose. By 1937 Democrats controlled the governorship and the state legislature and had elected both United States senators and twenty-two of Ohio's twenty-four congressmen; even Congressman Hollister, who survived Democratic sweeps in 1932 and 1934, fell by the way in 1936. Ohio, once a Republican bastion, had fallen to the foe.[25]

The Democratic trend was especially discouraging to his own political ambitions. Well before the depression he had begun thinking of horizons beyond the practice of law, and his upbringing left him restless for the satisfactions of public life. Close friends encouraged these ambitions, and his brother Charlie wrote in 1928 that "if only Bob were not tied up with . . . Uncle Charley's affairs, we could elect him Governor, or even Senator." Pressed by a friend to run for the U.S. Senate in 1928, Taft demurred: "We are building up a law firm which I cannot very well leave for some years to come . . . apart from the fact that I am hardly old enough to start out for the Senate." [26] Busy with his uncle's estate, he rejected overtures to run for Congress in 1931 and served instead as the key man in getting Hollister the nomination. "My personal affairs," he wrote, "are such at the present time that I will have to stay in Cincinnati for several years to come." [27] For a while early in 1930 newspapers also speculated that Hoover would name him solicitor general, the same office once held by both his father and his father-in-law. But for reasons that remain obscure — perhaps Hoover feared to name Bob to the post so soon after Chief Justice Taft left office — the President selected Thomas Thacher, a graduate of Taft and of Yale who was then a judge in New York, and even this intriguing possibility failed to materialize.[28]

The pressure of work continued to provide good reason for not seeking higher office after 1932, and Hollister's absences from the firm until 1937 — to say nothing of the problem of two law partners running on the same ticket — provided still more cogent excuses for staying at home. Yet rumors persisted — congressman at large in 1932 ("I have given some consideration to the question and do not feel that I can run at this time. Besides, we seem to have so many candidates from Cincinnati"); the governorship in 1936 ("I did consider doing so, but decided that I could not give up my practice at this time, and also it would precipitate a serious primary contest, which I thought unwise from the standpoint of the Republican Party this year").[29] He contemplated running for the Senate in 1934, but rejected the idea finally when the Republican incumbent, Simeon Fess, tried again. "I certainly do not look forward to a primary fight," he explained, "in which the only issue is one of personalities." Taft was wise to bide his time, because no Ohio Republican stood much chance of winning a statewide election in the early 1930's. But he was clearly willing to seize the first opportunity, and if Fess had stood aside Taft might have made the mistake, often fatal to impatient political aspirants, of contesting and losing to the then stronger party.[30]

Instead, he threw himself deeper into local politics, only to find the Charterites still so defiant that in 1930 they formed a fusion ticket with the Democrats. When Seasongood described Taft as "an ornamental target to cover a rotten structure," he cut so deeply that Taft thereafter refused to engage him in debate.[31] And when the fusion ticket swept the county offices in 1930 and dragged down the Republican state ticket as well, Taft was infuriated. He continued to mediate between the old guard and the rebels, but he knew that the bitterness of the 1930 campaign angered both sides, and more often than not thereafter it was impossible for them even to meet without recriminations.[32] He repeated tirelessly that the "continued strength of the two-party system is essential to the maintenance of American democracy . . . The only substitution will be a government by groups and blocs, leading inevitably to an ultimate dictatorship." The Charterites, however, demanded nonpartisanship in municipal affairs, and the break widened. By 1939, when Taft left these animosities behind for Washington, the GOP was holding its own, but the reformers still clung to the reins in the city, and the impasse remained.[33]

As if fighting the Charterites were not frustrating enough, Taft also had to contend with factionalism among the regulars. By 1930 the succession of defeats had forced Fred Schneller and his fellow party leaders to refurbish their images, and that fall they let Taft assume command of a new county executive committee. The position offered him the opportunity of launching his long-anticipated reform from within, and he began bringing into party councils younger professional people who had previously shunned the German-American ward and precinct leaders. He dreamed of a remodeled party that would even seduce the Charterites from their stubborn adherence to nonpartisanship.[34]

The ward leaders restlessly watched these energetic efforts. They had always felt uneasy with this coolly efficient lawyer and had been happy to have him away in Columbus. Now he was bringing silk-stocking types into the party and threatening their power. When Taft left for a special legislative session in May 1932, they met suddenly, cut the executive committee from eighty-five to twenty-five members, and authorized Schneller to name them.[35]

Some politicians, so publicly humiliated, would have gathered their troops for warfare. Not Taft. He prized regularity and the Republican party, and he wished to avoid a rupture. He kept silent, returned home, and talked with the bosses. Because Schneller recognized the wisdom of compromise, Taft was soon reappointed head of the committee. The episode was smoothed over, but it exposed the continuing tension between Taft and the older regulars. It also showed that Taft, regardless of provocation, would stay loyal to the machine. And it revealed his characteristic calm in the midst of factionalism. He had long since learned that politics meant controversy, that within the party it called for unemotional responses, for accommodation and compromise, not for fist shaking and harangues.

When the Republicans lost in 1932, divisions again erupted, and Schneller stepped down in June 1933. Taft then seized the opportunity and drew up a new party constitution. It institutionalized his reforms by expanding the executive committee, reducing the influence of the ward and precinct leaders, and requiring the leadership to alternate every two years.[36] The constitution promised no miracles ("I cannot really see that it amounts to much," his brother wrote), and Taft refrained from trying to purge his adversaries from positions of influence, but it offered a start.[37] He headed the executive committee until 1934 and remained a power within the local party thereafter. By the end of the decade his allies had replaced some of the old machine leaders, and the factionalism of the earlier years had declined. If the main reason for this limited improvement was the need of meeting the fierce competition from uncompromising Charterites and rejuvenated Democrats, another was the work of Robert Taft. To a degree he had helped advance the reform from within that he had long insisted was possible.[38]

In his later years Taft was grateful to escape some of the pettiness of these state and local battles. But his long apprenticeship had toughened him and prepared him well for the more titanic struggles of the future. Indeed, in 1937 he summoned the nerve to endorse the entire GOP ticket in the municipal elections, even though his brother was running (successfully as it developed) for the city council as a Charterite. Bob Taft was already a seasoned professional, and he would never be otherwise. As always, he thrived on competition, and he never stopped pressing for his objectives. "The trouble with Bobby," he wrote, describing his son to Uncle Horace, "is that he is too easily discouraged about anything he is trying to do. He does not seem to realize that the only way to get ahead is to try hard and keep on trying." [39]

More than anything else, Taft was describing his own credo.

CHAPTER 10

A Philosophy for Hard Times

PROSPERITY, THE REPUBLICANS repeated, was just around the corner. But events kept proving them wrong. Hundreds of thousands, then millions of jobless walked the streets, and clouds of dust rolled off the plains, choking farmers and driving them from their land. In Washington, Herbert Hoover struggled, despaired, cried, "We are at the end of our string." Even in Cincinnati, with a more diversified economy than most American cities, poverty was widespread: by March 1932, 21,000 families needed help; by June an employment census showed 26 per cent of the city's working population, or 53,000 citizens, unemployed; and by the end of 1934, 140,000 people, one-fifth of Hamilton County, were on relief.[1]

The tenacity of the depression baffled Taft and forced him to ask what had gone wrong. And when Franklin D. Roosevelt, serene, unorthodox, unpredictable, introduced his New Deal, paralyzing the Republican party in the process, Taft grew more and more agitated. For some the depression proved an intellectual watershed; for many it was the searing emotional experience of a lifetime; for Taft it was more than anything else a confusing and disturbing interlude that did more to confirm his ideas than to push him in new directions.

Unlike some of his more conservative friends he refused simply to wait things out. A month after the crash he was in Washington to assist his old friend George Harrison, now the governor of the Federal Reserve Bank of New York, in trying to persuade the Federal Reserve Board to pursue a more active policy of buying securities. In the legislature he acquiesced in Governor White's mild antidepression measures. Believing that home building offered the best way to revive the sagging construction industry, he took special interest in the Federal Home Loan Bank, and he not only endorsed passage of the Reconstruction Finance Corporation Act of 1932 but applied to it for funds to help with construction of Cincinnati's Union Terminal.[2]

Like many Americans, however, he continued to hope that such gentle measures would suffice, and he delayed applying his own analysis of the trouble. Only when Roosevelt began expanding the scope of the national government after 1932, did Taft attempt any serious explanation of the crisis. The result was characteristic of much of his subsequent thinking about economic questions: heavily reliant on statistics, budget conscious, and partisan in its conclusions.

Part of his analysis sounded oriented toward the needs of wage earners. The root of the trouble, he said, was "a slowing down in the circulation of purchasing power, or the economic cycle . . . More money must go into directly consumable goods, and the only way to do that is to increase the share of the wage and salary earner." He also acquiesced in some early New Deal measures. Thus he conceded the need to control the price of oil and coal, favored the expenditure of $3 billion in federal funds for public works, and admitted that debtors had to get some kind of relief.

But Taft, the adamant defender of pay as you go, refused to accept large-scale public spending as the cure for hard times. Instead he offered his own two remedies to stop the decline of purchasing power. First, he reflected his father's animus toward monopolies by criticizing their "false maintenance of prices through combinations and cartels." Second, he echoed Hoover in blaming international economic conditions. The war, he said, had shattered the economic self-reliance of foreign nations that had continued to trade in the 1920's only through the largesse provided by American lenders. But this artificial prosperity was doomed eventually to collapse. The crash had come, he concluded, only partly because of fictitious security values; really to blame were foreigners who suddenly proved unable to repay their loans. American enterprise then had to contract, and the vicious cycle began.[3]

At this time in the summer of 1933 Taft was tentative in these conclusions, and in his more reflective moments he continued to be. "The cause of the depression is still obscure," he admitted in 1940. "I have my own view of it, but it probably isn't any better than that of anyone else." Yet he repeated his thesis with increasing regularity, especially after World War II, when he was trying to cut American foreign aid. It was a conservative view. Stop excessive lending abroad, he implied, and stable international finance would eventually return. Meanwhile, businessmen would have to spend on plant and equipment, and securities would fall so low that people would want to buy them. "Suddenly," he concluded, "appears a demand for capital," and the cycle would move upward again.[4]

This analysis was one-sided as an explanation of the depression and inadequate as a prescription for its cure. American loans had indeed assisted international trade in the years since 1919, and financial instability abroad had contributed to the depth of the crisis after 1929. But in ascribing so much of the blame to this cause he downplayed such crucial domestic weaknesses as pockets of severe depression in coal mining and agriculture, rampant speculation, the jerrybuilt nature of the American corporate structure, and gross inequities in personal incomes. He also underestimated the extent to which the complexity of modern economic life sometimes required unprecedentedly positive action from the government. By advocating economy and efficiency in the 1920's, he had seemed at home with his times; by adhering to this faith in the 1930's, he proved consistent but increasingly isolated from the political and economic exigencies of the new age.

Several considerations led Taft to adopt such an inflexible perspective on the key issue of this time. Like most Americans, he believed unquestioningly in the capacity of capitalism to right itself. Temperamentally cautious, he was suspicious of experimentation. Naturally frugal, he abhorred waste. And everything he had ever been taught at home, in college, and in law school had stressed the importance of adhering to established principles. Tinkering with capitalism and playing around with deficit spending violated his sense of proper economics as well as his understanding of the responsibility of statesmen.

Taft's view of the depression was also comforting to him, for it confirmed many of the suspicions about Europe that he and Hoover had developed in 1919. It also enabled him, as it enabled Hoover, to absolve small businessmen and political leaders at home of the blame and to place it instead on a handful of Eastern speculators and monopolists. Taft's interpretation of the depression was as personally reassuring as it was sincere.

Finally, the economic crisis had by-passed him and his friends on Indian Hill. In 1930 his uncle left him a thousand shares of stock in the *Times-Star* valued at approximately $200,000. Harried corporate leaders and investors flocked in ever greater numbers to his law firm, which in the early 1930's consistently showed a profit after taxes of between $110,000 and $140,000. Taft himself earned approximately $50,000 a year after taxes, and Martha's investments brought in $20,000 to $25,000 more. A prudent investor, Taft emerged from the depression as prosperous as before, and his four sons attended Cincinnati Country Day School, Taft School (where the tuition fluctuated between $1450 and $1600 annually), and Yale, never doubting the inexorable rhythm of their private schooling nor wanting for money.[5] Martha took the children to Europe three times between 1930 and 1936, and on one of these trips, in 1932, Bob joined them for a few weeks. When he returned, Charlie reported to Uncle Horace that Bob, heavier, was "showing some signs of Munich beer," only to be reminded by Horace that Bob "had made a very good start before he saw Munich." Martha also had ample time for the League of Women Voters, for which she became national treasurer by 1938. Here she grew especially close to Mrs. Darrah Wunder, who was to become her companion for the last years of her life, and to Mrs. Lillian Dykstra, whose husband Clarence moved from the city managership of Cincinnati to the presidency of the University of Wisconsin in 1937. Thereafter, Martha always tried to visit Madison at least once a year to maintain the friendship. Bob's letters, always addressed to "my dearest Martha" or "my darling Martha," show that he missed her but also that he was content playing golf, relaxing with friends like the Rowes and the Hollisters, trying to run his farm, and suffering not at all from the economic crisis.[6]

Taft also found time to spend three weeks or more at Murray Bay in the late summer. Here he and a few friends leased 143 square miles of unspoiled lake country in the nearby Laurentians and established a hunting and fishing club. Years of experience had made him a competent fisherman, and he looked forward to spending a week or so each summer in this wilderness location, fly-fishing much of the day with Martha or the boys, and settling quietly with a book after dinner. Though guides handled most of the manual labor, these outings were far from luxurious. Taft helped pack in some of the gear, paddled, ate meals cooked over outdoor fires, and went to bed in a sleeping bag under a rudimentary tent. After the late 1930's the pressure of work prevented him from taking these excursions very often, but his friends recognized that he enjoyed the retreat and informality of the woods. In the summer of 1952 after his greatest political disappointment, he was to seek them out again and to find there a renewal of spirit.[7]

Indian Hill; Taft, Stettinius, and Hollister; Europe; Murray Bay — these were comfortable parameters. Taft had been spared the slightest discomforts, and he seldom saw how the other half lived. The depression did not disturb the equanimity of his daily life or rob his family of accepted traditions.

From that perspective Taft watched the New Deal unfold. Sometimes it baffled him; "I am dubious, but very much at sea," he admitted to Harrison. And sometimes he grudgingly approved of it, urging Congressman Hollister and Senator Fess not to oppose relief and public works, accepting the establishment of minimum wages under the National Recovery Administration, supporting, as he had done in the 1920's, a national child-labor amendment, and cautiously endorsing federal unemployment insurance and old age pensions.[8] Though he criticized the bureaucracy of the Securities and Exchange Commission, ("whatever else the New Deal may have done," he wrote laconically, "it has certainly tremendously increased the number of legal problems with which our clients must struggle"), he applauded the SEC's effort to control the buying of stocks on margin and to regulate new issues. In public speeches he was careful always to support some New Deal measures, and he even commented, "I do not agree with the statement frequently made that we should postpone reform until we have secured recovery." [9]

But from the beginning Taft distrusted Roosevelt. "I should hate to see Roosevelt get in," he wrote his mother in 1932, "because he seems to me to be such an opportunist, with no regard for anything except the political effect of his utterances." Recognizing the President as a fellow product of the upper classes, he suspected the sincerity of his commitment to the common man, and he thought him a devious and demagogic showman playing with maddening success to the popular will.[10]

To Taft, Roosevelt was a symbol of economic heresy. Taft thought in principles, not personalities. As early as the Hundred Days of 1933, he worried about edicts emanating from Washington, and his letters echoed those of 1917–1918 when he had stressed the impossibility of long-range and meaningful federal regulations and had deplored the delegation of powers from the Congress to the President. "There is very little the Government can do to really modify the tremendous economic forces involved in a worldwide business depression," he said. He worried particularly about Roosevelt's unorthodox monetary policy, and in October 1933 he sold his mother's Liberty Bonds for blue chip stocks in order to take advantage of anticipated inflation. "Considering the radical and experimental nature of the Democratic National Administration," he wrote two days later, "it ought to interest every businessman to see that the Republican party is kept alive under conservative leadership." [11] From the beginning the experimental and regulatory sides of the New Deal distressed him.

He worried also about the GOP, for the New Deal left Republicans in an agonizing quandary. Runaway inflation, he believed, might bring "profit politically" to the Republicans, but at terrific cost to the nation. Yet if conditions improved without inflation, Roosevelt would get the credit. "I do not like to be in the position," Taft observed sadly, "where the returning prosperity, which I am most anxious to secure, is bound to benefit the opposite party." [12] Immersed in local, state, and national politics, Taft seldom viewed the New Deal objectively, and he embraced the comforting Republican notion that prosperity had been returning by early 1933, only to be delayed and discouraged by the crackpot schemes of the New Deal.

With the approach of the 1934 elections he sharpened his criticisms. "The measures undertaken by the Democratic Administration are alarming," he commented in February. "Whatever may

be said for them as emergency measures, their permanent incorporation into our system would practically abandon the whole theory
of American government, and inaugurate what is in fact socialism." The present course of the administration, he wrote to potential party contributors a week later, "will lead directly to a Government control of everything, and practical confiscation of property
to effect a redistribution of wealth." In April 1934 he lamented
that "the time will come when everyone looks back at the first year
of the Roosevelt Administration as a fantastic nightmare." [13]

These statements of standard Republican oratory were strong
enough, but when Roosevelt began to criticize the wealthy in
1935, Taft reacted sharply. The New Deal, he said, was "largely
revolutionary." It was "deliberately stirring up prejudice against
the rich" and encouraging the "general theory of a redistribution
of wealth which would soon lead to a socialistic control of all property and income." The Tennessee Valley Authority, he said, "is a
step in the direction of Revolution," relief spending was both "unduly expensive and unduly ineffective," and the "complete reck-
lessness with regard to governmental expenditure" would lead to
the "destruction of the system and probably a socialistic state." [14]

In this aggressive mood Taft thrust himself into the national
limelight for the first time. The occasion was the administration's
decision to abandon the international gold standard and the congressional repudiation in June 1933 of obligations to redeem contracts in gold. Many bankers and creditors considered the policy
necessary for domestic recovery, but others responded with outrage. Some of these creditors realized that payment of debts in gold
with the much appreciated dollars of the early 1930's would bring
great profits. Others contended that the abrogation of the gold
clause in contracts would lead to loss of confidence in all governmental activities, and they carried several suits to the Supreme
Court. The government countered that payment in full gold value
in 1934 dollars would cost $1.69 for every dollar on its face, in-
crease public debt alone by $10 billion, and destroy the power of
the government to manage its own affairs.

Amid great tension and financial uncertainty, the Supreme
Court in February 1935 finally ruled for the government. But the
decision was reached by a vote of five to four. Chief Justice Charles

Evans Hughes, speaking for the majority, in fact denied the right
of Congress to abrogate the gold clause in public contracts, and
rescued the government only by taking the narrow ground that the
plaintiffs had shown no actual loss. The court seemed to say it
would entertain future claims if bondholders could show harm.

In March 1935 Taft made such a claim. Acting on behalf of the
Dixie Terminal Company, he thrust a $50 government bond at a
window in the Treasury office and demanded payment of the principal according to the value in gold on the date of issue in 1918. As
he had expected, the Treasury refused, and he immediately filed
suit with the court of claims. He directed his case not at the refusal
to pay in gold, but at the Treasury's policy of terminating its obligations before the dates of maturity. If the government refused to
honor its obligations according to their value in gold, he argued, it
ought at least to agree to pay interest until the original date of
maturity, which in the Dixie Terminal case was 1938. Holding up
a $1 interest coupon on the bond (which the government had
called in on April 15, 1934), he demanded $1.07 in currency, the
coupon's face value on its date of maturity in October 1934. "Our
claim," he said, "is that the Treasury must either pay the principal
in gold, or to continue to pay interest at least until the final maturity as stated in the bond." Unless it did so, he emphasized, "the
credit of the United States cannot long survive."

The case posed a real threat to the administration, for the suit
could halt the calling of up to $14 billion in bonds, cost the gov-
ernment more than $1 billion in interest payments, and threaten
its control over monetary policy. But Taft was the advocate, and
he gave no indication that he cared about the government's alarm.
Instead, he embarked on a publicity campaign to encourage people
to hold on to their bonds, and he filed a series of suits for other
bondholders throughout 1935 and 1936.

In November 1936 the court of claims rejected these suits. Unbowed, he carried them to the Supreme Court. There, a year later,
he appeared for the first time before the court his father had presided over, and in December 1937 came the final blow. Justice
McReynolds agreed with Taft and asked if the Eighth Command-
ment, "Thou Shalt Not Steal," still existed. But Justice Stone
went so far as to uphold the congressional resolution against the

gold clauses, and Justice Cardozo delivered the majority opinion on the narrower contractual grounds that the original bonds in fact authorized the government to redeem them early and therefore cease interest payments on the date of call. Taft received a modest $2500 fee for his two and a half years' work and carried the crusade no further.[15]

He had changed no one's mind. Moreover, he had undertaken a petty case. As Cardozo stressed, the right to terminate (though not to pay in legal tender) was clearly stated in the bonds, and the Treasury had given ample notice of its intentions. Had the suit carried, speculators would have reaped a windfall in interest payments, and the government would have been denied the right to direct monetary policy. The episode provided Taft the advocate with his first nationwide publicity, but it also showed the length to which he was prepared to go to implement his feelings against the New Deal.

While conducting this skirmish, Taft carried on his campaign against the administration by running as Ohio's favorite son in the May 1936 presidential primary. His candidacy was promoted by regulars who wished Ohio to have a voice in the national convention and who shuddered at the thought of a divisive primary involving the major candidates. Taft, they agreed in February, could serve as a nominal favorite son. He had made no serious enemies, and his name was known to all.[16]

Taft knew he would have competition because Senator William Borah, the veteran antimonopolist from Idaho, refused to be talked out of entering the primary. But he ran willingly, for he relished the chance to attack the administration. "I do not take the candidacy too seriously," he wrote, "except for the opportunity which it has given me to tell the people of Ohio what any reasonable man ought to think of the New Deal." Above all, he welcomed the exposure the campaign would bring him. "It is a considerable honor," he noted to Uncle Horace, "and puts me in a much better position if I want to run for Governor or Senator in 1938. As one of the Ward chairmen here said, after congratulating me, 'anyway, the publicity won't do you any harm.' "[17]

Not all the publicity was flattering, and Taft's first statewide candidacy did not even charm some of the more irreverent members of his family. When Bob, Jr., then nineteen, saw his father's picture in *Time*, he urged his mother to find a "less nasty" photograph, for "the last needed numbers on the bottom." But the state organization had matters well in hand, and the favorite son slate triumphed easily, losing to Borah only in the heavily industrial areas of Akron, Youngstown, and Steubenville, and carrying forty-seven of the fifty-two delegates. "The result," he wrote happily, "was exceedingly satisfactory. I think it finished Borah for good and all." [18]

As time approached for the Republican convention in Cleveland three weeks later, some of Taft's backers pretended to fight to the finish. But by then Governor Alfred M. Landon of Kansas seemed certain of victory on the first ballot, and even the Ohio delegates were eager to jump on Landon's bandwagon. Taft made no attempt to stop them, withdrew his name before the convention opened, and seconded Landon's nomination, as a candidate who "will tell the people that they cannot enjoy fancy government improvements and socialistic experiments without paying for them in increased taxation" and as a future President who "believes that thrift, industry, and intelligence produce happiness today as they produced it in the horse and buggy days." Then the call of the roll began, and Landon captured the dubious honor.[19]

Another prize remained to be caught: the vice-presidency. For months a few supporters in Cincinnati had been bringing up Taft's name, and while he never thought he would win, he did not discourage his friends. By May, Martha believed he had a chance. "I do think," she wrote Bob, Jr., "there is a possible threat that your Father might be nominated for vice-president. What would you think of that?" At the convention Hollister and others continued the campaign, but Landon had first wished a conservative Democrat as his running mate, and he finally settled on publisher Frank Knox, who had withdrawn as a presidential possibility on the eve of the convention. Taft had never had much of a chance.[20]

Taft had not expected any reward from Landon, and he left Cleveland "more than satisfied with the job the Convention did." He also displayed the optimism that rose in him like a tide while campaigning. "I am glad the issue is made," he wrote Martha.

"That is the only way the Republicans can win. Everyone is as optimistic as they were pessimistic six weeks ago." And he immediately worked for the state and national ticket. On one such occasion early in July he spent the day in Columbus with John Bricker, who was to be the Republican candidate for governor of Ohio in the fall. "I received an unfavorable impression of Bricker," he confided to Martha. "He seems to have become very conceited . . . I hope I may be wrong." It was one of Taft's first extended contacts with the man whose prominent career in Ohio Republican politics was to parallel and often conflict with his own.[21]

A more interesting experience occurred a few days later at a meeting in Cleveland of the American Youth Congress, which Taft agreed to address at the request of the GOP National Committee. Again he wrote Martha his reactions. The group, he said, was "the most radical party I ever attended . . . mostly dark foreign-looking boys and girls but with a fair scattering of American types." Still, he was more fascinated than alarmed by the occasion, and he explained that he had "quite a pleasant conversation with Earl Browder, the Communist speaker and candidate for President, and with the Farmer-Labor man. They uttered the wildest sentiments in the most agreeable way and were both quite attractive."[22]

This letter showed a side of him that his intimate friends recognized: opinionated yet tolerant of others in an amused sort of way. But the public Taft, like the debater in school and college, often sounded harsh on the stump. As the campaign, one of the nastier in recent American history, progressed, he reiterated the Republican argument that Roosevelt had destroyed recovery in 1933, insisted that socialism was on its way, and argued that "if Roosevelt is not a Communist today, he is bound to become one." Irving Fisher, his old economics professor, wrote to defend the administration's monetary policy, only to be told with shattering bluntness, "I have always disagreed completely with your position." Taft admitted laughingly to an old friend that he was "just at present making some reactionary speeches," but the fact remained that he was indeed willing to make them and with a hyperbole which was striking.[23]

His addresses in 1936 revealed more than mere partisanship; they clarified and hardened his economic thought into a mold from which it never fully withdrew. Central were two fundamental faiths. The first stemmed from his literal approach to the law and the Constitution. The administration, he said in words that echoed his father's complaints about Theodore Roosevelt and Woodrow Wilson, substituted "an autocracy of men for a government of law," and it ignored precedent and principle. It was experimental and inconsistent, a rampant bureaucracy of extralegal agencies. Taft was always to distinguish between law by congressional statute and decree by quasi-judicial agencies established by the executive branch.

Second, he attacked the centralization of power that was placing the executive branch above Congress and the courts and placing the national government above the states. This process, once started, was hard to stop. Taft found the NRA (National Recovery Administration) and the AAA (Agricultural Adjustment Administration) especially obnoxious, for they had attempted to tinker with prices — an effort that World War I had convinced him was futile and dangerous. Regulate prices, he said, and you had to regulate wages, then everything else. This would "destroy the whole American system of business initiative, individual opportunity, and reward for ability, intelligence and industry, and would substitute the dead hand of a socialistic state for the progressive and liberal system under which the people has steadily improved." Taft believed implacably that America was too large and complex to be governed from Washington, and he insisted that power corrupts. Perhaps remembering the cyclical theory of government taught at Yale in his youth, he concluded:

> History shows that once power is granted it is impossible for the people to get it back. In Greece republics gave way to tyrannies. The Roman Republic became an Empire. Medieval republics became monarchies. If we extend Federal power indefinitely, if we concentrate power over the courts and congress in the executive, it will not be long before we have an American Fascism.[24]

In denouncing bureaucratic government and castigating the expansion of executive power, Taft offered little that was new in the American political tradition. Indeed, practically all his fellow Republicans emulated Hoover in adopting this form of the Jeffersonian creed without combining it with the free play of Jefferson's intellect or the humanitarian intent of his thought. But Taft's criticisms commanded attention because they stemmed from a passionate conviction that often went beyond mere partisanship, important though that was. He had been raised to work hard, to compete, to excel; and so he had done. So, too, had many of the people he had known in his world of Yale graduates, lawyers, corporate executives, bankers, and professional men. He believed deeply in the necessity of preserving individual initiative above all else, and unlike some Americans who changed their minds in the 1930's, he remained zealous in this faith. Well before then this emphasis had offered more consolation to businessmen fighting governmental regulation than to the "forgotten man" whom Roosevelt talked about, but Taft did not perceive himself as a spokesman for privilege. On the contrary, he reflected a pervasive midwestern suspicion of idle speculators and eastern financial interests, and he was almost as critical of monopoly as were Borah and some of the older American progressives. Though wealthy himself, he also shared his father's and grandfather's feeling that a man should aspire to more than riches alone. Resisting an increase of $100 in Taft School's tuition (from $1500 to $1600), he argued that "the number who can afford the change is very few, and if the school is made up of those boys only, it would be strictly a rich man's affair." Criticizing a draft of Pringle's manuscript on his father, he concluded that Pringle "represented my father as too conservative. He did not seem to me to distinguish between conservatism in the Wall Street sense of defending property and big business. Of course this is a common failing of journalists and of historians." [25] Taft adhered to his faith in self-help in the 1930's because he sincerely believed the creed could operate equally for all.

As the campaign developed, he began to worry a little about Landon's lack of "dramatic appeal to the people at large," and he thought the margin "so close . . . that there cannot be very much confidence." But he still anticipated victory. Cincinnati, he told Bob, Jr., ought to go for Landon "by about 5000 — it is very close and a hard fight; the workingmen, the negroes, and the Jews all have been for Roosevelt, but are wavering." [26] But the voters a few days later provided the ultimate blow in what for him had been a discouraging decade. Roosevelt not only carried Cincinnati by 44,000 votes, but the Democrats captured five of the nine county offices and elected two of Hamilton County's three state senators, both its congressmen, and all nine of its state representatives. Baffled, Taft blamed Roosevelt's skill with the radio, the WPA (Works Progress Administration), and federal patronage. He came closer to the mark in commenting that Roosevelt acted as "friend of the poor man and against the rich man," but he refused to grasp that the New Deal had helped to work a political revolution by wedding to the Democratic party millions of underprivileged voters — blacks, national minority groups, laborers, relief clients — who had either voted Republican in the past or failed to vote at all.[27] This electoral coalition cherished Roosevelt for trying to pull them from hard times, gladly accepted the innovations that Taft detested, and refused to return to the GOP. Taft was to spend the rest of his life trying to digest the indigestible fact that the Democrats had become the majority party.

The seven years since the happy days of 1929 had transformed the nation, weakened the ideology of self-help, and shattered the Republican party. Taft thrashed in a backwater, while Democrats, rich with the prizes of office, swam at high tide. After the triumphs of the 1920's, the 1930's had proved frustrating indeed, yet all the disappointments of the decade had not shaken his resolve or altered his perspectives on the issues. America was changing dramatically, but Bob Taft was not.

CHAPTER 11

The Path to the Senate

TAFT WAS FORTY-SEVEN years old in 1937, and he was restless. After almost two decades in politics he had yet to face the voters outside his home county, and he yearned to declare his ideas from a loftier stage. For a man who derived satisfaction from the legal niceties of legislative work, this meant the United States Senate.

Perhaps to give himself time to think, he and Martha left in February for a vacation in Mexico with Stanley and Dorothy Rowe. Once south of the border, he confided his ambitions to the Rowes. They protested that no one could breast the tide of the New Deal and that a popular state supreme court judge from Cleveland, Arthur Day, was being conceded the Republican nomination. The name "Day," they argued to clinch their case, was popular among Ohio voters.

"Do you think," he flashed back, "it is better than Taft?" [1]

The Rowes did not then need to be told that Taft was determined to run. Indeed, Richard Forster, a *Times-Star* reporter, was already traveling about the state to test sentiment for him, and friends had long suspected that 1938 might be the year Taft would finally seek the office which rumors had had him pursuing since the late 1920's. It was his first opportunity to run since Hollister's defeat for re-election to the House in 1936 and the first year since 1932 that he would not have to challenge an incumbent Republican senator in a primary. Taft had served his party steadily since 1920, he felt (although a little uneasily) that John Hollister had had his chance, and he knew he had a strong base in populous Hamilton County. Thus he dismissed the obvious preference of the state leaders for Arthur Day and worried only about the ordeal that a campaign for the Senate would involve. "The principal objection," he wrote his Uncle Horace, "is that it means a year of running around the State, making speeches and shaking hands, all of which may be wasted." [2] Taft ran because he had been trained to serve, because he was ambitious, and because he had waited long enough.

Though he made up his mind at least as early as February 1937, he delayed a public announcement. But in March, he permitted the press to say that he was thinking of running, and in May he told a friend he was "inclined to go ahead." He also encouraged reporters to speculate about Day's excellent chances for governor. But Day ignored such diversionary tactics, and Taft recognized that a contest was unavoidable. "I am going back to a year of strenuous political campaigning to which I do not look forward," he grumbled to his sister Helen Manning. "A primary campaign is essentially disagreeable to anyone, except a thoroughly conceited man, and a ready talker." On July 29 he formally announced his candidacy.[3]

From the start he enjoyed several important assets. His long career in state politics had made him well known, and he was able to call on the services of many faithful lieutenants. One was David S. Ingalls of Cleveland, grandson of Uncle Charley, aviation ace in World War I, and GOP gubernatorial candidate in 1932. Ingalls, who was handsome and genial, had the special advantage of being a millionaire, and he proved a useful fund raiser. Another loyal aide was Willis D. Gradison, a shrewd Cincinnati stockbroker and former legislative colleague who headed Taft's organization. Cousin Hulbert Taft of the *Times-Star* offered undeviating support in his paper and freed Forster to handle publicity. And Taft secured a bonus early in 1938 when Paul Walter, a dynamic young Cleveland lawyer-politician, agreed to run the campaign in the northern part of the state.[4]

These men did not form a brain trust of the kind that surrounded Franklin D. Roosevelt or that John F. Kennedy assembled for his 1960 presidential campaign, and only Walter, a former social worker who was highly suspicious of southern Ohio conservatives like Gradison, presumed to offer Taft much advice in matters of national policy. The others contented themselves largely with the professional tasks of fund raising, voter registration, and publicity. Indeed, Taft tended to discourage intellectual ferment among his advisers, not by silencing those who offered gratuitous advice but simply by displaying his habitual air of certitude and preoccupation. So Gradison, a staunch partisan, Ingalls, whose loyalty to his cousin overrode all else, and the party functionaries whom Taft gradually attracted in the long campaign to come, usually let him think for himself. This method of organization offered him little chance to hear new ideas, and because he discouraged informality (only a few close coworkers ever called him "Bob" to his face), it also prevented him from forming close personal relationships with rank-and-file supporters. Unlike many successful politicians, his course was never to depend on the cultivation of hundreds of friendships.

Yet Taft's approach to political organization worked well for him in statewide contests. It freed him — usually — from having to worry about disputes among his staff. It permitted him to escape the time-consuming business of maintaining a host of chummy personal relationships — a task for which he had little inclination anyway — and to do what he enjoyed, poring over statistics to rout the opposition. His method also allowed him to be himself. He had been raised to be independent, schooled to take the lead, and had always relied on his own hard work and study to direct his way. His campaign in 1937–1938, like much the course that he undertook in his life, was unmistakably his own.

This method also attracted to his side some workers who might not have stirred themselves to assist more personable men. Vera Norcross, his secretary for the campaign, explained that he was always "intent upon accomplishing the tasks at hand, which were multitudinous, giving himself completely, always having the courage of his convictions." Like others who worked for him, she did not always find Taft approachable, and she rarely saw his personal side, but she sensed his sincerity, honesty, and dedication to his beliefs. She knew also that he was a regular who would never desert his friends, that he meant what he said against the New Deal, and that he brought to politics a sense of service rare among office seekers. It behooved campaign workers, in turn, not to trouble him about the issues, for Bob Taft had studied them, and he knew best.[5]

Another campaign asset was money. Friends and neighbors contributed some, and Taft himself provided more — perhaps $5000 in all. Wealthy Cincinnatians, like Mary Hanna, who offered $9500, gave still more. But the large sums came to Taft, as they had to his father, from his relatives, especially Uncle Charley's daughter, Louise Taft Semple of Cincinnati, who gave him at least $41,000. In June 1938 he complained to Mrs. Rowe that "I expect to be broke, whatever happens — only the generosity of the Semples will carry me through." But in fact he did not lack for money, and only a week before writing Mrs. Rowe he told Ingalls, "I do not know why you should be worried about the financial situation here in Cincinnati. We will raise more than $50,000 here, including what I have put up myself." By the time the primary campaign ended in August 1938, Taft had spent slightly more than $100,000 — a sum so large for such a contest in those days that a Senate committee in Washington later demanded full accounting of the money. Though the Senate uncovered nothing illegal, it focused attention on Day's charge that he was "buying" his way into the Senate, an accusation which formed an argument for Taft's Democratic opponents in 1938, 1944, and 1950.[6]

A third advantage was the stance of the press. Besides his support in the *Times-Star*, he secured help from the Cincinnati *Enquirer*, the Toledo *Blade*, the Dayton *Journal*, the Akron *Beacon-Journal*, the Cleveland *News*, and a host of smaller papers. Taft's chief worry was the Columbus press, controlled by the ardently pro-Day Wolfe family. Taft fretted about the Wolfes, and when they proved obdurate, he even got Herbert Hoover to intercede. Hoover was unsuccessful, but Taft could still console himself in the knowledge that the predominantly Republican and conservative Ohio press was heavily on his side. After the primary, he thanked the editor of the *Blade* for his support, which he thought had been "more than anything else the determining factor in the race." [7]

Probably his strongest asset was Martha. By 1938 she was stout, her hair was gray, and she lacked the physical glamor deemed important in politics. But through the League of Women Voters she had developed considerable knowledge of the issues and wide experience in public speaking. She knew Bob's views intimately, believed passionately in his ideals, and herself yearned for the excitement of political life in Washington. With only Horace of her four sons still at home, she was at last free to ride the campaign trail herself.

Martha's performance amazed even those who knew her. Driving her own car and speaking as often as ten times a day, she eventually visited fifty-eight of Ohio's eighty-eight counties. Once she swerved her car to avoid a dog, spun off the road, and rolled over. Climbing out shaken but unhurt, she cracked, "Anyway, that probably got us the SPCA vote," and kept her schedule the rest of the day. She spoke forcefully, mocked the New Deal, and refused to pretend that her husband was a common man. He had received and capitalized on the best education that money could buy, she told voters. Isn't that what you want in the Senate? Taft best described her role to Bob, Jr., who at age twenty was serving his own political apprenticeship as a campaign worker for his father. "Your mother is a wonderful campaigner and could really have an easier time getting elected than I will. Wherever she goes the votes roll in, or start rolling until someone goes from the other side, and stops them." [8]

All these advantages seemed obvious after the primary was over. But throughout 1937 and 1938 Taft's liabilities appeared overwhelming. One of these was the widespread belief in Day's invincibility. Handsome and vigorous, Day had been a captain in the infantry in World War I and a frequent candidate for political office thereafter. He was affable, charming, a good handshaker and mixer. Twice a member of the state senate in the 1920's, he had been elected to the Cleveland municipal court in 1931, the county common pleas court in 1932, and the state supreme court in 1934 — as a Republican in the face of Democratic landslides. Raymond Clapper, an experienced syndicated columnist, reported that Day was "reliably suspected of having shaken the hand of every man, woman and child in Ohio during the last few years." His opponent? "Robert Taft," Clapper wrote, "son of the former president, also is running for the senatorial nomination but in such a respectable and dignified way that he will get only the exercise." [9]

A related liability was the attitude of Republican leaders and especially of state chairman Ed D. Schorr, an enigmatically self-contained party professional, who was close to the Wolfes in Columbus. Schorr was persuaded that Taft could not win, and he quietly lent the power of his position to Day. Many county chairmen, the key to the state's Balkanized politics, did likewise for the same reason: Day they believed could win, Taft could not. Taft grew impatient, then angry with the state organization in Columbus. "I think the standard of political morality there is lower than anywhere else in the State," he grumbled.[10] Though he proved careful enough not to damn his own party leaders, he remembered Schorr's position and tended then and in later campaigns to rely on Ingalls, Walter, and others in his own intensely loyal organization. It was ironic that Taft the regular began his career in national politics without the backing of the established machine and that he advanced himself thereafter despite an undercurrent of coolness from it.

Chief among the liabilities, many observers thought, was Taft himself. His close friends still found him modest and good-natured. With them he smiled warmly, talked easily, and rarely lost his temper or his good manners. But many observers seeing him for the first time thought him an uninspiring, forbidding figure. His receding hairline focused attention on a high forehead, and his rimless glasses angling upward toward his large ears gave him a studious expression that even the smile could not dispel. Conversing with small groups, he tended to stare, very much as his mother did, and his gray eyes looked leaden and bulging. Orating on the stump, he squinted, frowned, looked over his lenses, and seemed cold and distant. Everything about him — his mouth, his teeth, his hands, his feet — seemed huge, even menacing, and his large head seemed to balance precariously on his frame. With his conservative clothes, stiff collars, and glasses, he looked severe and elongated — and critics enjoyed describing him as a chemistry professor, a small-town bank president, possibly a Sunday school superintendent, or vestryman. He seemed unapproachable — a cartoonist's dream, a party leader's despair.[11]

If Taft failed to encourage voters, his manner distressed even some of his supporters. Early in the campaign Paul Walter herded the Cleveland ward bosses in to see his candidate. The first leader, from a poverty-stricken ward, emerged furious from Taft's office. Taft, he complained to Walter, had simply stared, said nothing, and scribbled down facts and figures about the economic situation. "That cold hearted son of a bitch!" he said, "I just couldn't sell him to my people." To these urban leaders Taft seemed distant, mathematical, an aristocrat of aristocrats. Walter tried to soften him, and a few observers sensed improvement. One newspaper even described him as "amateurishly congenial, but learning fast." But most of the time Taft remained himself, and he changed very little during the long campaign.[12]

Addressing crowds, he was even less impressive, for years of debating and speaking had failed to improve his oratory. Instead of modulating his pleasant if flat baritone voice, he tended to shout, to rasp, to throw out a torrent of words at the rate of 150 a minute or more, to charge impatiently through applause, to cling to his text. He jerked his arms about, yanked off his spectacles, waved them about in the air, even let them dangle from his ear. His accent, a mixture of cultivated Yankee precision and midwestern twang, grew more pronounced on the platform, and his broad, nasal "a" — "Democraaht," "praahspehrity," "caahmehrce," "aahgriculture" — struck a rather harsh note that his audiences were quick to detect.[13]

Taft's fact-filled speeches distressed his supporters most of all. Well before the primary campaign he had researched the economic problems of the day, but he refused to excise the statistics he had laboriously unearthed. Instead, he wrote out his remarks longhand on yellow legal paper, then dictated them. Such a method saved him the drudgery of rewriting and the fatigue of sessions with ghost writers, but it brought a loss of eloquence. The drafts revealed few attempts at metaphor or image and remarkably little effort to use the alliterative phrase, the clever analogy, the literary allusion, or the pounding climax — the staples of American political oratory. There was no humor and so much detail that his speeches sounded clumsy, dry, and disputatious. Often they lacked even logic, for he liked to plunge into the heart of his discourse, to repeat himself, and to state his opinions in whatever order he happened to write them down. Although his passionate sincerity succeeded in evoking applause from those who thought as he did, his aim was that of the schoolmaster: not to incite but to describe and explain. Effective political speeches, one observer noted, are like posters: bold, clear, and colorful. Taft's were like cluttered etchings: precise, detailed, and dull.[14]

Why these weaknesses? One explanation was simply that he lacked experience in statewide electoral politics, that his circumscribed world left him unprepared for the handshaking and baby kissing which the professionals suddenly expected of him. Such a view, however, failed to explain why other men of the upper classes, including many novices in politics, did not suffer from such handicaps; it overlooked his trial run in the quest for delegates in 1936; and it ignored his inability to change appreciably during the campaign.

A sounder explanation was that he knew he could impress voters only if he remained himself. Many of his admirers insisted on this answer, and one young Taft enthusiast recalled that Taft's "twangy voice, his blunt and unornamental sentences, his manner of not seeming to be quite at ease, and his shyness in acknowledging introductions were a far cry from anything that my Indiana boyhood . . . had prepared me to accept." Yet Taft's "solid purpose" and "honest character" soon overcame all doubts. "He really charmed one young snake that day," the admirer concluded.[15] This image of Taft as a "man of integrity" did indeed grow during the campaign, and because he deserved it more than many politicians, it was to remain his greatest political asset.

In some of his frank remarks to Uncle Horace may be found another explanation for his failure to evoke much response from his audiences. Thanking his uncle for a book of humorous stories, he added that he had "already used several of them with excellent effect. If you come across any more, I should be very glad to have your assistance. Nearly all of them are new to me, and I feel quite certain that the audiences in rural Ohio have never heard of them. I am surprised at the way in which some seem to succeed where others which appear to me more deserving do not." In the same letter, he also thanked Horace for a book by Winston Churchill. "I may be able to get a few political hints out of it, although my conclusion from recent experience is that politics in Ohio is sui generis, and that little light can be thrown upon it from other more enlightened sections of the world." Taft's attempt to drop these stories like eggs on the heads of "the audiences in rural Ohio" suggested his inability to inject any humor of his own into his public addresses. And his remark about Ohio politics revealed his far from high opinion of the intellectual capacity of the voters. Thus he treated them as would an earnest professor handling students who need to be lectured to again and again on the same subject. He reached a few of his listeners — sheer repetition usually does — but lost many others almost from the start. Such were the dubious virtues of applying an intellectual approach to democratic politics.[16]

Taft's dry public posture stemmed also from his heavily statistical approach to politics. He simply could not bring himself to enjoy the many absurd rituals that ambitious American politicians are supposed to endure. When the Loyal Order of Moose insisted on inducting him into their sacred bonds, he consented, and he even wrote Martha a wryly humorous account of the occasion. "The Supreme Dictator," he noted, "explained to me . . . the glories of the Loyal Order of Moose. It was a long way from the great north woods where moose are moose." But he also complained of sweating profusely in the heavy regalia, and it was clear that the episode had been distasteful. Throughout his campaign he avoided such indignities and concentrated on the issues, not only because he felt more at home in the world of ideas, but because he believed that rallies and receptions brought fewer votes than did careful precinct organization and voter registration. "I think you have a wrong idea of political meetings," he had written Fred Manning, his brother-in-law, in the 1936 campaign. "The object is to get as many Republicans together as possible, and cheer them up. You may make a favorable or unfavorable impression, but one never makes votes at political meetings." [17] This view of politics often distressed his friends, but it stemmed quite naturally from his long experience as a regular in Cincinnati, and it suited perfectly his way of contending with the world. The Taft of forty-seven who pored over economic statistics and voting patterns was peculiarly the Taft of seven who had quietly charted the routes of fire trucks at the station across from his home.

His view of principled statesmanship offered another clue to his behavior. One of his first tasks upon becoming a member of the Yale Corporation in 1936 was to help choose a new university president. By the end of the year the corporation was settling on Charles Seymour, the eminent American diplomatic historian he had known in 1919 at the peace conference. Taft was willing to go along, but he worried. "My principal doubt about him," he wrote, "would be whether he is sufficiently direct in his methods . . . he seems to approach questions from the point of view of the diplomat, and to spend a good deal of time in getting to the point. I am assured, however, that he has courage . . . even if his methods are somewhat round-about." [18] Taft's models of leadership remained his stern and principled grandfather, his honest and decent father, and forthright Herbert Hoover. Such statesmen were uneasy with the cheap handshake, the facile conversation, the hearty slap on the back. Better to be serious and respectable than to appeal, like the synthetic FDR, to the masses.

Statesmen also talked about the *issues*. For Taft, who had studied them, the issues were of paramount importance. Having developed serious doubts about the New Deal, he felt compelled to school his listeners. And for all his doubts about the intelligence of people "in the sticks," he believed to an extent rare among experienced politicians that issues mattered more than personalities, that the GOP would inevitably win if previous nonvoters could be made aware of the facts. Thus he lectured rather than talked to the voters. "Bob Taft," his nephew recalled, "was cool to people, but he never disliked people . . . they were just facts he was surrounded with. You don't dislike a fact, you just figure out how to get along with it." Martha, explaining her husband's intensity, phrased it differently. "Bob," she said, "is not severe. He's just departmentalized." [19]

Self-consciousness reinforced this reluctance to play to the crowds. Taft was far from contemptuous of popularity, he liked being recognized, and he was always elated after winning an election. But the spotlight still glared, and he shifted uneasily underneath it. During the campaign he was expected to go to the annual dinner of the Ohio Bar Association, a glittering affair attended by the state's political luminaries. Judge Day and other dignitaries marched through the guests, greeted by a standing ovation, to take their places at the head table. By contrast, Taft walked through a back door and sat down unnoticed at a table in the rear. At another banquet a reporter observed him nodding but not stirring to shake hands with acquaintances. Why not? the reporter asked. "I don't like to force myself on people," Taft replied. On a third occasion he and Day appeared together for a rally in Middletown. Advised by his aides to buy beer for a reception, Taft did so. But when the festivities started, Day appeared, shook hands, and stood by the keg passing out glasses. Taft surveyed the scene from the doorway, waved blushingly, mumbled a few words, and departed in a rush.[20]

Martha later attributed her husband's uneasiness to his boyhood years as the son of a President. "Every time he stepped out of a door," she explained to Esther Carman, who worked in all Taft's campaigns, "there would be cameras flashing. This bothered him tremendously and tended to cause shyness." Martha did not account for his inability to surmount this "shyness," but her analysis fitted the facts. Taft remained too private to expose himself willingly to others, too self-conscious to appear easy and assured on the platform. If he seemed cool and withdrawn, it was not because he wanted to be but because he could not be otherwise.[21]

•

The strategy of the campaign was simple enough. First Taft staked out his position on the issues. As he had in 1936, he defended parts of the New Deal like old age pensions, unemployment insurance, and regulation of stock exchanges. But he attacked "excessive" federal spending, excoriated Roosevelt's court-packing plan, and repeatedly criticized governmental interference with business activity. Day, he said, should devote less time to handshaking, more to outlining his position on the issues. "Roosevelt himself is coming to Ohio," a Taft flyer proclaimed. "The Repub-

lican nominee must know the national issues. He will have to debate them . . . Bob Taft *KNOWS* the issues."

Taft also showed no hesitation in using the family name. Posters
and handbills boldly pictured his father, grandfather, and even his
great-grandfather, Peter Rawson Taft — "justice of the peace for
twenty-two years" and "member of the Vermont legislature." Another campaign piece went further. "As the twig is bent," it
proclaimed, "so the tree inclines . . . Bob Taft is a remarkable
exception to the rule that sons of great men seldom display the elements of greatness." Taft was as quick to capitalize on his ances-
tors as he was self-conscious about promoting himself.[22]

Above all, he tried to disparage Day as a vote getter. When he
heard that a reporter planned a feature article in *Collier's* on the
campaign, Taft wrote him to claim that Day's sole asset was as a
"good handshaker . . . I hope you will not overemphasize this feature in your article, because it is really helping him in his campaign." Meanwhile, Walter and others were taking more direct
steps. They loaded literature into an old truck and distributed it
liberally along the route about to be followed by reporters conducting the widely read straw poll of the Scripps-Howard press.
Unaware of these tactics, the pollers discovered surprising margins for Taft that may have caused party regulars to think again
about supporting Day.[23]

As the months passed, Taft pushed his Plymouth harder over
bumpy rural roads: through the villages of southern Ohio, bloom-
ing in forsythia and redbud, to the industrial wards of Youngstown,
Canton, and Steubenville, across the fields and farms in the interior, north to meetings in Toledo, and over to important Cuyahoga County, site of Cleveland and the largest bloc of votes in the
state. Publicly he seemed almost incredibly fresh and unper-
turbed, but privately the routine annoyed him. "The most perpetual three-ring circus I have ever seen," he told Seymour about
the campaign in explaining his absence from Yale Corporation
meetings. "I will never get into anything like it again." "An interminable and perpetual job which leaves me no time either in
the evening or on Sundays," he complained to Henry Pringle. "I
have never been in anything which offered so little relaxation."
To Bob, Jr., he was more explicit:

We aren't paying the attention to our family just now which it deserves owing to constant travels. Last week I made ten speeches and your mother four and we travelled about 1500 miles. Horace [his son] is disgusted with us; and the worst of it is that it's going on until August 9 at least. On the whole the campaign is going very well, but it is a hard fight and no result is going to be certain before the count is over. However it goes I shall be glad to have tried the campaign once — I have learned a lot, more about politics than can be learned any other way in ten years, and a good deal about people. I have acquired a lot of friends all over the state. If I get beaten I shall go back to a quieter and more comfortable life with a great deal of pleasure, and if I win, the experience in the Senate will certainly make up in interest the general inconvenience of being in politics.[24]

The hard labor gradually brought confidence. "There are many signs that I am making good progress throughout the state," he wrote Walter in April 1938, "and I believe I can beat Day." [25] By early August he was so certain of victory that he refused to get excited when Day charged him with passing the intangibles tax in 1931 to favor the wealthy and with spending huge sums in the campaign. These last-minute (and therefore unanswerable) accusations caused Uncle Horace to crack to Martha, "I see by the papers that Bob is trying to buy the nomination. If I had known about that, I would have sent him a contribution." And Bob was equally cool. "My opponent," he wrote, "has been so scared by the rapid progress I have made that he has undertaken a campaign of personal slander. Nevertheless I think it will hurt him more than it will help him." [26]

Taft had grounds for his optimism. In the primary he lost to Day in Cleveland 36,000 to 25,000, but he picked up 5000 votes in the more wealthy suburbs to trail by only 44,000 to 38,000 in Cuyahoga County, Day's home. Day also won by 21,000 to 12,000 in Franklin County, site of Columbus and stronghold of the Wolfe press and of the party regulars. Taft also lost Canton and other industrial towns by lesser margins, and he trailed in twenty-three central counties surrounding Columbus. But he carried Toledo, Dayton, and most of the towns and the villages, and he closed with victories in fifty-five out of eighty-eight counties. He overwhelmed his opponent in Hamilton County, 43,000 to 6000; the Taft machine was indeed efficient at home. The totals of 322,270 for Taft, 245,949 for Day, marked a surprising show of strength for the man who had started as an underdog.[27]

Taft attributed his victory partly to Day's "mudslinging" which "apparently increased my vote in most parts of the State." Others agreed and praised Taft's focus on issues instead of personalities. Still others, citing Day's overconfidence early in the campaign, credited Taft's stubborn energy. For all his failings on the stump, voters obviously preferred him to his affable yet ultimately more abusive opponent.[28]

A different perspective came from a reporter who argued that "Republicans of Ohio showed themselves to be still essentially conservative." This hypothesis probably approached the truth. If Taft's campaign had done one thing, it had stamped him as much the sharper foe of the administration, and his victory in the election three months later confirmed that opposition to the New Deal in Ohio was a political asset in 1938. The primary returns also revealed that his strength lay in the traditionally Republican rural and suburban wards. Because the hotly contested Democratic gubernatorial primary on the same day attracted some 900,000 voters — 300,000 more than those voting for the GOP — it seems likely that he attracted the vote of anti-New Deal Republicans, while many independents who might have preferred a moderate like Day to Taft ignored the GOP to vote Democratic. It was in any event ironic that Taft, long critical of party primaries, probably could not have conquered the bosses in a convention but was able to outflank them at the polls.[29]

What of his name and reputation? Voters in Senate races, experts have hypothesized, prefer candidates who are not like themselves but who are what they would like to be. Whether this was true of voters for Taft in 1938 cannot be proved. But it was clear that neither his wealth nor his high social standing harmed his chances, and they may have stamped him as a high-minded aristocrat in politics. And his name may have been decisive. "The result showed," he wrote proudly, "that the name of Taft was still a better name for political purposes here than any other (except possibly Roosevelt)." Paul Walter, driving about northern Ohio

early in 1938 to test Taft's chances, agreed. He found people mis-
taking Day for (Martin) Davey, Ohio's controversial Democratic
governor. "Davey's a crook," they said.

"I said, 'Not Davey, Day.' "

" 'Who's Day?' "

" 'Well, Taft and Day will be running for the Senate.' "

" 'Whatever William Howard Taft wants, we want.' "

Walter rang doorbells unsystematically, but he was probably
correct in stressing the role of the Taft name. In Ohio the name
Taft was valuable, and the candidate had used it for all it was
worth.[30]

•

Taking the election in November still lay ahead. His opponent,
the incumbent Senator Robert Bulkley of Cleveland, had served
eight years, had easily won his primary, and was clearly strongest
where Taft was weakest: the urban wards, where heavy concentrations of blacks, unemployed, union members, and foreign born
and their descendants could deliver massive majorities for the
Democrats. Taft, though optimistic, anticipated Bulkley's strategy. "Our difficulty," he wrote, "is only in the industrial cities.
There I think the workman is dissatisfied with the New Deal, but
it will take a good deal of work to convince him that he ought to
vote for Republicans." [31]

Because Taft's organization was highly tuned and confident, he
had grounds for optimism. The primary victory unleashed new
sources of funds. In spending more than $50,000 in the next three
months, he ended by reporting $159,000 for the primary and the
election — more than any other senatorial candidate in the country. The predominantly Republican press boosted his candidacy,
and Martha traveled as widely as before. After but a week in Murray Bay early in September he was pushing his Plymouth about the
state once again and staying up into the morning.[32]

Taft recognized the importance of organized groups in politics
and concentrated on getting the support of as many of them as
possible. He told Walter White of the NAACP that he favored a
controversial federal bill against lynching and that he would support cloture to bring the measure to a vote. He approved the idea

of a homeland for the Jews. And though he seldom passed up an opportunity to denounce heavy federal spending, he equivocated on the popular Townsend Plan, which would have provided federal old age pensions under a scheme generally regarded as inflationary and unworkable. "I will work to bring the measure to the floor for proper debate," he hedged. "This will give the Townsend Organization and its proponents an opportunity to prove the merits claimed for their legislation, and if such merits can be proven I shall be glad to support the enactment of such legislation into law." [33]

In the process Taft came a little closer than before to accepting the New Deal. While insisting that financing for social security should be pay as you go, he called for broadening of the act to provide old age pensions and perhaps unemployment insurance for domestic and agricultural workers. Though he opposed the federal regulation of working hours, he backed the minimum wage act passed earlier in the year. He criticized the National Labor Relations Act (it should enumerate unfair labor practices, he said, and separate the prosecuting and judicial functions of the labor board) but endorsed the federal guarantee of collective bargaining and consistently defended the unabridged right of labor to strike. He continued to oppose compulsory crop reduction but favored a "reasonable subsidy" for soil conservation and agreed that the government ought to have the option of buying surpluses in times of agricultural depression, providing it disposed of the surplus in the same crop year, so that the carryover did not become too huge.[34]

Taft also had sense enough to support relief spending, and he urged Senator Arthur Vandenberg of Michigan to correct the impression that workers would be "left to starve" under GOP leadership. "There should be a long term public works program," he said in Keynesian words, "which could be carried out more intensively in hard times and less actively in times of prosperity." "Robert Taft," Raymond Clapper wrote, "is a changed man. Once he was an outspoken hard shell reactionary. Now he calls himself a liberal. Once he was a dull sour-puss who couldn't unbend. Now he is a lively, jolly handshaker, the soul of affability." [35]

Clapper exaggerated, for Taft knew that Ohio was two, perhaps three or four states. Moderation might appeal to urbanites, miners, and relief workers. But in the small towns and on the ragged little farms that dotted the rolling hills of southern Ohio lived tens of thousands of voters whom any successful Republican candidate must not antagonize. Taft acted accordingly by slashing at the administration. He told southern Ohioans that "if Santa Claus did what Senator Bulkley is doing he would land in jail because the whole spending program is a fraud upon the people of Ohio." The farm program, he told Cincinnatians, was "socialism with a vengeance." As always, he saved his most passionate remarks for a denunciation of New Deal economic policy. "I say that the regulation of wages, hours, and prices and practices in every industry is something which is, in effect, socialism; which is government regulation of the worst sort; which means a totalitarian state. You cannot regulate prices in one industry unless you go on to others . . . You can't carry it out without the arbitrary power of a dictatorship of some kind." [36]

The campaign drew to a close against the tragic backdrop of German pressure on Czechoslovakia, and Taft did not let Ohioans forget it. "If we extend Federal power indefinitely, if we concentrate power over the courts and congress in the executive, it will not be long before we have an American fascism." To the Slovenes of northeastern Ohio he raised still another specter: communism. "The New Dealers are proposing a totalitarian state which they have today in Russia. It is not strange that the Communists in Cleveland have abandoned their own candidate and are supporting my opponent, Senator Bulkley, because they have the same system in Russia that the New Dealers would like to have in this country." [37]

Because of his experiences in the Food Administration, Taft was sincere in claiming the futility of peacetime regulation of the economy. But he overemphasized the degree to which the New Deal, which was more opportunistic and humanitarian than radical, was dictating to the economy, and his near equation of the Democrats with communism, socialism, fascism, and totalitarianism was simply demagogic. Yet he not only continued his attack along this front but was ready if necessary to move further. "I enclose some personal stuff about Bulkley," he wrote Walter toward the end of the campaign. "I don't want to use any of it myself, but you can use your judgment." The "stuff," whatever it was, remained private. But his willingness to have it used suggested how competitive he became in the heat of battle. Campaigning was always to bring this side of him to the fore.[38]

Taft's aggressiveness, though extreme on these occasions, received less attention than his skill in a series of six debates with Bulkley during the last weeks of the campaign. These debates were attended by boisterous overflow crowds and were carried over the radio. They focused nationwide attention on the contest. Taft had pressed hard for the debates, and after some hesitation his opponent agreed.

It was Bulkley's greatest mistake. The debates not only gave Taft equal billing but provided him with a perfect opportunity to place the incumbent on the defensive. Bulkley, a graduate of the Harvard Law School, was a high-minded, responsible officeholder, but he seemed too tame for a rough campaign. Harold Ickes, Roosevelt's waspish Interior secretary, dismissed him as "an uninspiring person and . . . only half a New Dealer." The progressive *New Republic* denounced Taft as "didactic and stiff," but still found him quicker than the "lumbering" Bulkley. Taft, armed with statistics, could hold the offensive even with his own brand of fact-filled oratory.[39]

The first three debates, in Marietta, Dayton, and Cincinnati, took place in Taft country and attracted rude and partisan crowds. Taft attacked by branding the moderate Bulkley somewhat inaccurately as a rubber stamp, castigating federal regulation, and accusing the WPA of coercing workers into the Democratic party. Placed on the defensive, Bulkley recited his record, defended the New Deal, and accused Taft of raising a "huge slush fund." When hecklers interrupted Bulkley, he tried petulantly but unsuccessfully to reason with them. In Dayton, Taft had to step to the platform to silence the catcalls at his foe, and in Cincinnati the booing created such bedlam that Bulkley could hardly be heard.[40]

Gradually even the Democratic press admitted Taft's grasp of the issues, his readiness to answer any question or accusation. And a worried Democrat wrote the White House suggesting that Bulkley "become indisposed a couple of days prior to the next debate." Overjoyed after the Toledo debate, Martha wrote Bob, Jr.:

Your father cleaned up on Mr. Bulkley in the opinion of all disinterested as well as interested observers. In fact Bulkley got lost
and wandering in the middle of the speech until I thought he was
going to give up. He told reporters afterward that he had lum-
bago. He's had an alibi for every one so far — once a cousin of his
had died — once he was ill — once the crowd was so noisy he
couldn't be heard, and once a lot of them walked out on him. The
debates were certainly a good idea! [41]

On election day Bulkley won in Cuyahoga County by nearly
60,000 votes and in Mahoning County (Youngstown) and Summit
County (Akron), by 8000 each. But as the downstate tallies trick-
led in, they swelled to an irresistible Republican tide. Taft sat in
the *Times-Star* offices with pencil and legal paper in hand and intently followed the returns. Precise and mathematical, he knew
even more than his jubilant supporters how glorious the result
would be: Hamilton County by 30,000; Lucas County, home of
Toledo, by 10,000; Stark County, home of Canton, 6000; Montgomery County, home of Dayton, 7000; Franklin County, home of
Columbus, 12,000; the smaller counties by lesser margins but steadily Republican. Long before dawn it was clear that Taft had
won.[42]

When the tallies were completed, they revealed a striking Republican triumph. At the top of the ballot, gubernatorial candidate John Bricker swept to an impressive victory by a margin of
close to 120,000 votes in a turnout of 2,410,000. Taft fared even
better, beating Bulkley 1,257,412 to 1,086,815, for a plurality of
170,597, and taking nearly 54 per cent of the votes. "Sky Farm,"
one columnist was moved to say, "may yet be a summer White
House."

More cautious journalists knew better. Taft had campaigned
well and he had won impressively. Yet deep divisions within the
Ohio Democratic party assisted the Republican ticket, and his tri-
umph was also part of a Republican trend throughout the nation.
Even in Ohio he had to share top billing with Bricker, and in New
York young Thomas E. Dewey came so close to beating Governor
Herbert Lehman that the pundits placed him high among the

presidential possibilities. The path to the White House lay twisted, still treacherous for travelers starting out in 1938.

When Taft unfolded his aspirations to the Rowes in 1937, he also implied that the Senate was but a step to the top, occupied by his father years before. If he let himself think so in 1938, however, he told no one else. And though victory left him a possibility for the presidency, it did more than that. It took him forever from law practice; toughened him as a campaigner; shaped his economic philosophy; and persuaded him, unwisely, that a frontal assault would always bring the Democrats to their knees.

Above all, the victory achieved against initially difficult odds brought him intense personal satisfaction. It broke the string of frustrations and greatly strengthened his already considerable self-confidence. Robert Taft was to feel moments of doubt and uncertainty in the fifteen years remaining to him. But they were rare and unnoticed by all but his close friends. Henceforth he was to plow his own furrow. Sometimes it was narrow and sometimes it turned back on itself, but it was always unmistakably his own.

PART III

Rising in the Senate, 1939–1945

CHAPTER 12

The Young Senator

THE WASHINGTON to which Taft returned after twenty years in Cincinnati was a city grown huge, crowded, and tense. World War I, the mushrooming federal bureaucracy, and the endless migrations of southern blacks had swelled its population to 660,000 and had strained its institutions. Slums spread through the city, devoured old neighborhoods, and threatened racial strife. Surrounding Capitol Hill, the slums offered an ugly contrast to the classical grandeur of official Washington.[1]

Like many others, Taft saw little of this tacky side of the city. For a few days he stayed out on Wyoming Avenue in the home where his mother, still active and imperious, was living her last years. Then he and Martha rented a twelve-room house opposite the Japanese Embassy on sedate Massachusetts Avenue. Old Washington friends stopped by to call and to congratulate him; Alice Roosevelt Longworth took Martha under her wing; the boys came home from schools and college whenever they could; and at the end of the month Bob, Jr., became engaged to be married that summer to Blanca Noel, whom he had known at Murray Bay. A senator's salary was only $15,000 a year, but Bob's and Martha's investments were paying well, and he still received some income from the firm. Money was never to be a problem during his years in Washington.[2]

Early in January Taft told Dorothy Rowe of his sadness at breaking ties with the past. "It is exciting but it is a pretty fundamental change in our whole life," he wrote. "I was really homesick the night we left Cincinnati with three boys, six trunks, and 17 bags, and I haven't got over it even though I tell myself I will spend half the year in Cincinnati." Yet his mournful remarks to Mrs. Rowe did not stop him from impressing Washington reporters, who observed that he accepted life in the Senate calmly, as if destined for it all along. "He gives a direct answer to each question," one wrote, "takes his time when he feels like it, laughs easily when someone wisecracks, and seems to be quite unworried by the first revealing shaft of the limelight." Another reporter added that Taft seemed "perfectly content to be what he is and was born, without show or assertiveness." [3] Taft had been trained to compete and to excel, and with success he seemed to soften. He was where he belonged.

Perhaps he took his achievements too much for granted, for he displayed little hesitation in telling people what he thought of life in Washington. He wrote Mrs. Rowe that it was a "strange world here — interesting but as yet quite unreal." The President was "talking worse nonsense than usual, on his spending fallacies in particular. The fight will be much more real in the end, I suppose, but at present it seems more like grand opera, and a long way from the good people of Ohio." Taft grumbled also about the deluge of mail, the clamoring of pressure groups, and the bureaucracy that staggered the imagination. In place of the excessive economic planning that he had denounced during his campaign, he found a thicket of conflicting agencies. "Every little department," he complained publicly, "seems to operate in a water-tight compartment, interested in its own special and narrow task. Instead of one great machine, there seem to be about as many private departmental machines as there are automobiles in the City of Washington, each one operating under its own power, without any brakes." [4]

Soon Taft was repeatedly thrusting such opinions on all who listened. Besides trying to learn the peculiarities of Senate custom, he undertook a rugged speaking schedule, including a series of radio debates on national policy with an able Democratic congressman from Illinois, T. V. Smith. These speeches occupied 132 pages of a volume entitled *Foundations of Democracy,* which Alfred Knopf published later that year and which provided easily the best single summation of Taft's thinking to that time. Between January and April he also drafted and delivered twenty-two prepared speeches and statements outside the Senate itself. His capacity for hard work enabled him to maintain the pace, but some of his associates were already worried that such hyperactivity might cause him to stumble and fall.[5]

They were right, and Taft picked the worst occasion to do so: the annual Gridiron dinner of the Washington press corps. A highlight of the political and social season, the affair attracted an audience of more than four hundred people, including six judges of the Supreme Court, nine ambassadors, five Cabinet members, nineteen senators, important newsmen, and practically all the leading national politicians and kingmakers of both parties. Roosevelt himself was the featured Democratic speaker, and Taft — a potential opponent in 1940 — was asked to represent the Republicans. Raymond Clapper, head of the press corps, reminded his guests that thirty years earlier a Roosevelt had vacated the White House and a Taft had moved in. Would it happen again? The audience settled back anticipating a hilarious duel like those that had traditionally marked these occasions as the liveliest of the year.

FDR, ever the master, met these expectations with what Turner Catledge of the New York *Times* later called "a savage but beautiful performance," ridiculing Taft as a man whose ideas belonged in the horse-and-buggy days. But Taft had rushed to the affair from New Haven, where he had attended a meeting of the Yale Corporation, and he had characteristically let no one else prepare anything for him. On the train he had scribbled a few notes, but they were little more than repetitions of earlier complaints about official life in Washington. After berating the administration, he even had the temerity to demand that Washington reporters, his hosts, cover the states instead of pretending that everything of importance happened in the capital.[6]

According to the tradition on such occasions, the speeches remained off the record. But the mighty had heard, and they were not impressed. "Did you ever see anybody commit suicide as quick as that?" Roosevelt whispered happily to Clapper. "He's laborin'," drawled Vice-President John Garner of Texas. "Senator Taft was a pitiful spectacle," said another. "It was the general opinion that he demonstrated his incapacity and that as a presidential candidate he is a wash-out." And *Time* reported that he had made a "'sensationally poor speech." Thomas E. Dewey, it noticed, "applauded, grinned" when it was over. On his first exposure to such a national audience, Taft etched a caricature of himself among the image makers that he never entirely erased. He was unbowed, but chastened. "He [Roosevelt] really tore me apart, didn't he?" Taft reflected wistfully to Turner Catledge the next day.[7]

Fortunately for Taft, legislative work proved more satisfying. He grew used to the avalanche of mail, the lobbyists, the vapid oratory within the Senate chamber. He listened politely to the claims of constituents and endured the arrival of schoolboys, Rotarians, and visiting firemen. Still reserved, he was slow to make friends with his colleagues, and he was working too hard to bother much with society. But Martha was lively, and he tolerated the garish banquets and receptions that sometimes overwhelm careless legislators from the provinces.

He also attacked his work with zest. Partly because of his potential as a presidential nominee, his mail was staggering — some five hundred letters per day early in the session. Much of it — requests for appointments to the service academies, complaints from veterans, pleas for jobs, demands for postmasterships — was new to him, and he had to struggle at first to fathom the meandering channels of official Washington. But he learned gradually to shake much of the routine onto his chief aide, Mildred Reeves, a Washington lawyer who had previously served as secretary to House Speaker Nicholas Longworth of Ohio and briefly to Congressman John Hollister in 1931, and onto a staff of other specialists whom Reeves recruited. It was characteristic of his solitary way of doing things, however, that he did not surround himself either with well-known Ohio political operators or with idea men. Indeed, his willingness to let Reeves, whom he hardly knew, worry about personnel underlined his offhand approach to office administration.[8] His casual attitude also offended some workers, and turnover in his office during his first term became serious enough to interfere with service to constituents. Visitors also discovered him too absorbed in the issues to reflect on the impression he made. When they entered his inner office, they found it cluttered with documents and adorned only by a few plants and a bronze bust of his

father. Taft received his callers promptly, but as in his law office in
Cincinnati, he seldom lingered. He shuffled papers, twirled his
glasses, examined his nails, shifted in his seat, came directly to the
point. The Senate was serious, responsible work, and there was
simply no time for pleasantries with coworkers or for idle chatter
with constituents.

From the start he built a reputation as a senator concerned more
with national than state problems. But he had sense enough not to
overlook Ohio entirely. During the first session ending in July he
introduced the modest total of nineteen bills, thirteen of which
requested pensions for Ohioans. Most of the eight amendments
that he offered merely involved technicalities; but two aimed at
giving Ohio its cut of public works; and one, which he pushed aggressively, sought to provide funds for flood control in the Mus-
kingum Valley. And though most of his forty-four speeches on the
floor — a considerable quantity for a freshman — concerned fiscal
problems, he knew enough to respond to local complaints and to
have his outside speeches placed in the *Congressional Record* for
the voters to see. Because Democrats ruled the chamber, none of
his bills and only one of his amendments succeeded in 1939. Few
became law in 1940 or in subsequent years. Taft never tried to
rely heavily on the reputation of having "done more for Ohio"
than anyone else, but he avoided unnecessary offense.[9]

Taft also kept the needs of Cincinnati in mind. Through his
friend Stanley Rowe, who served as chairman of the Cincinnati
Housing Authority from 1933 to 1944, Taft had gradually become
sympathetic to measures providing public aid for home building
and slum clearance; and he had carefully refrained from attacking
the United States Housing Authority, established in 1937. His
first important effort as senator was to introduce an amendment to
the USHA to facilitate slum clearance and low-rent public housing
in Cincinnati and other cities. When his amendment received the
support of progressives, it passed the Senate. Though it failed in
the House and though later in the session he tried to cut housing
funds on the tenable grounds that existing USHA money remained to be spent, he ended by supporting the full appropriation
after his attempt failed. From the start of his senatorial career he

revealed a sympathy toward federal housing legislation that contrasted with his vigorous assaults on other administrative programs.[10]

For it was the New Deal, after all, which had so exercised him in the past, and it continued to do so in 1939 and thereafter. He had campaigned against arbitrary federal regulation, wasteful spending, and sloppy administration. He had meant what he said, and he determined to carry out his demands.

On the surface it seemed as if 1939 was a most inopportune time to hope for success in such an effort at demolition. Democrats still controlled both houses of Congress by such overwhelming margins — 69 to 23 in the Senate and 260 to 169 in the House — that they spilled across the aisle onto the Republican side. Some of these Democrats, like Majority Leader Alben Barkley of Kentucky, and Robert Wagner of New York, a pioneering force behind much New Deal social legislation, stalwartly defended the administration. So did newer Democrats such as Harry Truman of Missouri, elected to the Senate in 1934; Lister Hill, a liberal from Alabama; Sherman Minton of Indiana, and others. And a few fiery Democrats like Claude Pepper of Florida often joined third-party men such as George Norris of Nebraska and Robert La Follette, Jr., of Wisconsin in pushing for legislation more progressive than Roosevelt dared to request.

Yet the President had already suffered repeated defeats in 1937 and 1938 at the hands of antiadministration Senate Democrats who voted with Republicans against his measures. One of these Democrats was Taft's former adversary, "Honest Vic" Donahey, who had been elected to the Senate in 1934. Another was Walter George, a stately Georgian of immense prestige on fiscal matters. They were joined by Harry Byrd of Virginia, Josiah Bailey of North Carolina, Millard Tydings of Maryland, and other veteran southerners who ranked high on important committees. When Roosevelt gave his State of the Union Address in 1939, he was greeted openly by rude guffaws from the assembled legislators. Veiled criticism of the administration earlier in the decade had often meant political suicide; broadsides in 1939 seemed as safe as they were commonplace.[11]

An ambitious Republican senator in 1939 enjoyed an especially easy opportunity to establish a quick reputation. A few veterans had survived the Democratic tide of the 1930's, but they were old and too individualistic to bother leading a team. Charles McNary of Oregon, the genial minority leader, was capable, but too gentle to exert strong leadership, too moderate in his views to encourage an onslaught against the administration. Hiram Johnson of California, once a feared and forceful progressive, had grown querulous, even choleric. William Borah spoke dramatically to the galleries, but he was quixotic and unpredictable, and he was to die within a year. Even Arthur Vandenberg, though perhaps the most influential Republican senator in 1939, lacked the aggressiveness to become a forceful leader. And younger men like Styles Bridges of New Hampshire and Henry Cabot Lodge, Jr., of Massachusetts, both elected in 1936, had yet to make their mark on the chamber. The party was far from being controlled by an entrenched oligarchy of senior statesmen, and it cried out for new leadership.

Even one so highly touted as Taft could not grab the reins immediately, and he knew enough not to try. But he seized what opportunities he could. McNary had offered him his choice of committees, and Taft took three of the most important: Appropriations, Banking and Currency, and Education and Labor. Though he waited until February 20 to make his first speech on the floor — a vigorous, fact-filled assault against increased appropriations for the Tennessee Valley Authority — he impressed observers immediately with his sharpness in committee and his poise before the press.[12] Most of all, he struck his colleagues as intelligent and well prepared. This reputation stemmed partly from the fact that many of them were not; Taft was a new fish in a pond muddied by stale rhetoric and exaggeration. Partly his reputation resulted from the apparent political vulnerability of the New Deal, his chief target. And it rested heavily on his command of statistics, which he used to intimidate opponents daring enough to challenge him. The same fact-filled delivery that seemed tedious to voters on the hustings served him well in extemporaneous debate within the Senate chamber.

Taft also usually sounded responsible even though he sometimes seemed impelled to use rhetoric that was much more extreme than his voting record suggested. "Many of the New Dealers," he charged, "have no concern whatever for individual freedom. They are collectivists, like Marx and Lenin and Mussolini." [13] But he was usually more careful in his assaults. He recognized that *parts* of New Deal programs made sense and that he should offer alternatives to those aspects which did not. Unlike many of his colleagues, he had diligently formulated his own ideas, and he was able to defend them with facts and figures.

Consistency regarding spending seemed Taft's greatest virtue. As in earlier years he denounced long-term deficit financing — "the very heart of the New Deal today," he wrote Herbert Hoover in February. "No nation," he argued, "ever has continued indefinitely an unbalanced budget without ultimate collapse." [14] His first resolution, offered with three Republican colleagues in February, demanded the repeal of Roosevelt's authority to issue up to $3 billion in paper money. Later he voted regularly against additional appropriations for the WPA, tried to limit funds for the Export-Import Bank, and opposed increases in parity payments for farmers. After favoring increases in payments for maternal and child health, he opposed extending Social Security coverage. Failing in these attempts at economy, he backed an across-the-board income tax increase to raise more revenue — a course which many of his Republican colleagues dared not follow.[15] By July 1939 he was leading a successful coalition against Roosevelt's pump-priming bill, and by December the President mockingly offered him a "very handsome prize" if he would show how the government could balance its budget. The budget could be cut, Taft replied, to $7 billion (it was then more than $9 billion) by eliminating waste, abolishing conflicting agencies, slashing funds for relief and for farmers, and above all by *wanting* to reduce spending. If higher taxes were still necessary to balance the budget, so be it. For the benefit of newsreel photographers he then tore up the administration's fiscal proposals for 1940–1941. "I think I have been more consistent than anyone else," he bragged to Uncle Horace, "in voting against all increases over the President's budget." [16]

Taft's obsession with cutting government spending sometimes clashed with his own views of desirable public policies. But a campaign against excessive expenditures seemed the only way of restricting the New Deal. Many of his colleagues, especially those from the farm belt or silver-producing areas, often talked economy and voted the other way on spending programs involving their own states, but Taft held firm. Partly because diversified Ohio had no single pressure group with overwhelming power, he was freer to vote his convictions, and his bluntness in defying the claims of lobbyists earned him the respect of his less consistent colleagues.

The unity of his attitude on all these issues reflected the same philosophy of government he had proclaimed during his campaign. Taft did not believe in laissez faire, he recognized that the national government must play an important role, and like his father he called for a strong presidency. "No one can question the duty of the Executive to propose a definite program," he said. "The policy making power of the President has always been the most dynamic force in American progress." [17] Yet leaders must rule according to established principles of law. Taft objected to the operations of the National Labor Relations Board because he felt that it was prosecutor and judge all in one, to spending because it developed rule by pressure groups instead of government through statute, and to New Deal agencies because he insisted they brought arbitrary standards instead of established "principles" to their regulation of business. Like his father, Taft revered precedent and established principles, and he refused to let the economic crisis of the 1930's overthrow them.[18]

What principles? Taft wanted to preserve equality of opportunity, especially for the small businessman or entrepreneur, the man of initiative so celebrated by the American dream. At Howard University in March 1939, he praised the progress made by the Negroes. It had come, he said, through "their own initiative and their own efforts, assisted, but not controlled by the government." [19] Higher taxes on corporations, he insisted, "would absolutely destroy all the incentive and initiative through which our success has been created." He wrote a friend that "the small businessman is the key to progress in the United States. It is a constant feeding of new men into business, which can only occur if small businessmen are successful, which develops new industries and builds up more employment." Grandfather Alphonso, he recalled, had prospered without a National Youth Administration and had succeeded on his own.[20] Curb monopoly and arbitrary governmental regulation, Taft said, and you assured a measure of equality of opportunity for all.

Above all, Taft exalted individual liberty, which by his definition required diminishing government activity. "When I started out in politics," he said revealingly in 1939, "I was strong for centralization on the theory that it would produce greater efficiency. The longer I have been in politics the more I have come to doubt the premise of this conclusion." [21] Thus he proposed to turn back administration of relief to the states and localities and suggested a form of revenue-sharing — distributing federal tax funds to the states with few strings attached. The Declaration of Independence, he said, exalted the rights of life, liberty, and the pursuit of happiness. "It is somewhat significant," he concluded,

> that the right endowed is not one of happiness but merely of pursuit . . . The whole history of America reveals a system based on individual opportunity, individual initiative, individual freedom to earn one's living in one's own way, and to conduct manufacturing, commerce, agriculture, or other business; on rugged individualism, if you please, which it has become so fashionable to deride.[22]

Taft's adherence to these principles remained the essence of his philosophy. And because they led him naturally to a partisan assault on the New Deal, they also accounted for his rapid acceptance among Republican senators in 1939.

These principles also sustained him through a short special session in the fall and through the skirmishing of early 1940. He voted unsuccessfully against an excess profits tax, tried to cut appropriations for the Tennessee Valley Authority, opposed the government purchase of foreign silver, denounced free traders, and insisted that the Tariff Commission could set rates according to "scientific principles" that would bring the price of imports up to that of domestic products. He tried again to cut funds for the Export-Import Bank. And he supported a successful bill providing $50 million in aid to states for hospitals, but only after helping to block a much more generous national program. Federal assistance to states, he argued, would lead toward equality of opportunity in medical care; the broader plan involving national administration was wasteful.[23]

On labor issues in 1940 he continued to pursue a middle ground. He voted against increased appropriations for the National Labor Relations Board. But he showed the consistency of his belief in individual rights by supporting a civil liberties bill aimed against the activities of strikebreakers and labor spies. To Taft such activities were as dangerous to the right to strike and to the liberty of the worker as excessively zealous regulation was to the businessman. Though twenty of his colleagues voted against it, Taft was among the forty-seven who pushed the bill through the Senate.[24]

Sometimes decisions were hard. Especially while he was being talked of as a potential presidential nominee, it seemed foolish to antagonize pressure groups. Yet he sometimes took the difficult path. After opposing an authorization of $200 million for a proposed seaway in the St. Lawrence River, he admitted he might be wrong but explained that he had to fight such expenditures. Besides, he explained to Ohio farmers, the seaway would bring cheap foreign food into their markets. Faced with a bill providing an additional $212 million in parity payments to farmers, he eventually joined a minority of nineteen against it. Some subsidies were necessary, he admitted, but $212 million was too much, and most of it went to states like Iowa that produced large quantities of staple crops. Ohio, on the other hand, received but $5.5 million (compared with Iowa's $18 million). Taft's stand did little to endear him to the farm lobby, but he had been consistent against spending, and he had at least offered an argument that Ohio constituents could understand.[25]

While usually voting in the minority, Taft did not think of trimming his sails. Instead, he revealed his deep antipathy toward the New Deal even in private matters. When Pringle's biography of his father appeared in 1939, Taft had sense enough not to interfere with it, but complained nevertheless that Pringle was "too much of a New Dealer for me." To the Yale Corporation he recommended Charles McNary, Hiram Johnson, and the ultraconservative Harry Byrd of Virginia for honorary degrees, and he sharply criticized the sociological orientation of a few of the professors in the law school. "I certainly do not object to constant changes in legal thought," he wrote, "but I do object to a point of view which is really opposed to the basic principles of American constitutional law and free enterprise as we have understood it." [26] Taft slightly exaggerated Pringle's bias, and he refused to listen to many people who regarded the law school as among the most imaginative in the nation. His watchfulness on all fronts, however, revealed the depth of his concern. By early 1940 Taft was already becoming the most consistent and forthright exponent of anti-New Deal Republicanism in the Senate.

CHAPTER 13

Foreign Policy Intrudes

SMASH THE COMMUNISTS, overwhelm the Slavs, liquidate the Jews — Adolf Hitler, courageous corporal, would-be architect, dictator of all the Germans, vowed his people's revenge on Versailles and clung to his satanic vision.

In East Asia, the Japanese were also restless and unhappy. Seventy million of them were crowded onto their rocky isles. *Lebensraum* for the Japanese in the Pacific meant the Greater East Asia Co-Prosperity Sphere, freer access to the atolls, to Manchuria and China, and to colonial possessions. It meant tension with the United States, possessor of the Philippines and self-appointed champion of the integrity (the "open door," Americans called it) of China.

Few Americans praised the Japanese militarists in 1939, and fewer still admired Hitler. Most people probably sympathized — public opinion polls were in their infancy — with the Austrians, the Czechs, and the Chinese. But sympathy was cheap, and the majority of Americans seemed cautious. They remembered the "war to end all wars" in 1917, they wanted no commitments, and they hated the idea of American bloodshed to save peoples abroad.

Prior to 1940, Franklin D. Roosevelt also moved cautiously. In October 1937 he had called enigmatically for a "quarantine" on the aggressors, in 1938 he had demanded and received new funds for the Navy, and in January 1939 he had requested dramatic increases in defense spending. Yet Roosevelt, too, hesitated to brandish the big stick. Possibly he worried about the so-called isolationists in Congress; probably he then shared the passion for non-involvement that had captured many of his constituents. Late in

1938, Hitler took over the Sudetenland of Czechoslovakia, and early in 1939 he struck again, devouring the remainder of Czechoslovakia in March, applying pressure on Poland, and sneering at the democracies ("worms," he called them) who protested his activities. Still the Roosevelt administration hesitated. America remained passive as Europe moved toward war.[1]

Like most of his senatorial colleagues, Taft sensed his country's unreadiness, and he backed the President's repeated calls for military appropriations in the early months of 1939. Defense spending seemed urgent, and it was popular. Because it involved no commitments to foreign nations and might even frighten the aggressors, Taft was happy to vote for it, and in March he supported more rapid production of planes than the administration requested.[2]

But he read the papers every morning over breakfast, again in the evening. He picked up stray copies of the *New Republic* and the *Saturday Review*. He heard rumors of the President's determination to aid Britain and France in case of war, and he grew suspicious. Though devoting relatively little attention to foreign policy during his senatorial campaign, he had even then opposed American involvement in a European war. "The basic foreign policy of the United States," he said in words he would repeat endlessly, "should be to preserve peace with other nations, and enter into no treaties which may obligate us to go to war. Our army and navy should be designed to provide an adequate defense against attack." [3]

On his arrival in Washington, he immediately criticized the President's intentions. Roosevelt's attitude would involve the nation in war, he pronounced on his second day in the Senate. A month later he tried to cut funds for the Export-Import Bank because the bank could "finance a European war without Congress knowing anything about it." [4] With the administration rumored in April to be considering changes in existing neutrality laws, he accused Roosevelt of "ballyhooing the foreign situation," and of "trying to stir up prejudice against this country or that, and at all costs take the minds of the people off their troubles at home." Taft's blunt accusations drew a sharp retort from the columnist Walter Lippmann. But Taft was unmoved. Lippmann, he wrote characteristically, "has a very limited influence among the intellectuals . . . I cannot avoid taking a position on foreign policy, and that position will be very critical of the President. The idea that he ought not to be attacked on foreign policy is pure bunk." [5]

Many impulses moved Taft to criticize the administration. One was his profound distrust of the President, whom he believed to be as devious in conducting foreign policy as he was opportunistic in domestic matters. Roosevelt, Taft wrote privately, was "the greatest menace to peace in this country." [6] This opinion also stemmed from his constitutionalism. Congress, Taft insisted, must be consulted on foreign policy questions, and senators must speak out. "If in time of peace any citizen feels that the President's handling of foreign policy is wrong or likely to lead to a war which he thinks unnecessary," he said in April, "it seems to me his right and duty to state that fact clearly, and to do whatever he can to change a policy which he thinks likely to result in war." In September he added, "there are some who say that politics should stop at the water's edge . . . I do not at all agree . . . There is no principle of subjection to the Executive in foreign policy. Only Hitler or Stalin would assert that." [7] This distrust of executive encroachment of course served partisan purposes perfectly. But it was nonetheless fundamental to his thinking.

Taft was almost as suspicious of the European nations as he was of Roosevelt, and his speeches came perilously close to sounding xenophobic. One critic later concluded that to Taft "other countries seem merely odd places, full of uncertain plumbing, funny-colored money, and people talking languages one can't understand." Such a criticism was exaggerated, but it did suggest Taft's total lack of sentimentality regarding European culture. The critic might indeed have proceeded by stressing Taft's instinctive revulsion against European politics. "European quarrels," Taft repeated, "are everlasting. There is a welter of races there so confused that boundaries cannot be drawn without leaving minorities which are a perpetual source of friction." [8] This emotional reaction stemmed partly from his experiences in Europe after World War I, and it never left him. Like many Americans, he shrank from intervention in European affairs in 1939 out of disillusion with the experiences of 1918–1919.

These views of Europe fitted neatly with his sense of America's strategic necessities. The United States, he said in January, "need not and shall not be involved [in a European war]. We have an isolated location, and it is still isolated in spite of all the improvements in air transportation." [9] America had a duty to defend herself and the Caribbean area, and by building up her own air power, she could easily deter Hitler or anyone else who was foolish enough — as he thought Hitler was not — to attack the Western Hemisphere. Taft's faith in air power may have been reinforced by his cousin David Ingalls, a pilot and a zealous advocate of a strong air force. But he did not need Ingalls or anyone else to persuade him, and he actually devoted little study to such military matters. To Taft, as to many others who cherished the idea that America's isolated location was defense enough, air power mattered, not because it would help win a war but because it would deter others from attacking the Western Hemisphere in the first place. Frequently citing George Washington's Farewell Address ("Europe has a set of primary interests which to us have none or a very remote relation"), Taft insisted, in 1941 as in 1939, that Europe's problems were its own.[10]

Skepticism regarding the capacity of central governments reinforced this faith in "America first." If the New Dealers could not manage things efficiently at home, how could they or any set of officials pretend to better the world? "We should be prepared to defend our own shores," he said in April, "but we should not undertake to defend the ideals of democracy in foreign countries." He added that "no one has ever suggested before that a single nation should range over the world, like a knight-errant, protect democracy and ideals of good faith, and tilt, like Don Quixote, against the windmills of fascism . . . Such a policy is not only vain, but bound to lead to war." [11] To a pronounced degree he lacked the messianic strain in American thinking that often led his countrymen to worry about the rest of the globe.

Taft also carried his fight against overseas involvement to the economic sphere. Some people, he said, insisted that a Hitlerized Europe would discriminate against American traders and damage the American economy. Taft ridiculed such a notion. "It is said that our foreign trade will be destroyed," he remarked. "I don't understand why, if peace is once restored, we could not trade as well with Germany as with England. A supposed hostility to Japan, a totalitarian nation, does not prevent Japan from being one of our best customers." Taft explained repeatedly that American foreign trade accounted for but 5 per cent of the national income, that the probable maximum loss of $500 million in commerce would "make very little difference to the United States," and that new markets, perhaps not quite so profitable as the old, could replace those which America might lose in Europe.[12] This unconcern for American commercial interests abroad reflected in part the animus which Alphonso and other Tafts held against foreign investors and overseas traders. It was also politically popular among many Midwesterners who shared his distrust of Eastern financiers. Taft, however, was not talking politics but adopting the perspective of many noninterventionists in 1939 who placed economic entanglements high among the causes that had led to war in 1917. Like other Americans, he was determined to prevent economic commitments from leading the nation into bloodshed.

Taft also utterly lacked the martial spirit. Even in the wilderness about Murray Bay he had never hunted, and he thought military life ridiculous and regimenting. "Modern war," he said, "has none of the glamour which we were taught to associate with war in our childhood. It is nothing but horror and mechanical destruction. It leaves the victor as exhausted as the vanquished, and a train of economic distress in its wake." [13] His call for peace made political sense: What responsible statesman wanted war? But again his stand had deeper roots than partisanship. Taft always thought war not only horrible but stupid, wasteful, and pointless.

If he had wavered from his stance, he would have had to contend with Martha, long an ardent advocate of peace. In 1944 the Chicago *Tribune* reported admiringly that she had opposed war ever since she had inspected Belgian towns with Bob in 1919 and watched workers "picking up men in pieces." This intriguing piece of journalism was exaggerated, for Martha had arrived in Europe too late to see anything as bloodstained as that. But she did display pacifist sentiments in the 1920's by joining the Woman's International League for Peace and Freedom and in the mid-1930's by serving as chairman of the Cincinnati Committee in

Support of the Senate Munitions Investigation, an inquiry directed by Senator Gerald P. Nye of North Dakota, which gave support to the notion that bankers and munitions makers had dragged America into World War I. Passionate in her convictions, she wrote her friend Lillian Dykstra in 1938, "I'll never bless any war either, and I still intend to get myself arrested if the government tries to take us into one!" In 1941 she was to speak widely for America First, the vehement organization against American intervention, and as late as 1943 she remained a vice-chairman of the pacifist National Council for Prevention of War.[14] Having four sons of or near fighting age must have strengthened Martha's pacifism in 1939, but she had worked against war long before it threatened her family. With her at his side, there was little likelihood that Taft would equivocate.

Yet neither Martha nor any other person in 1939 determined Taft's thinking. Indeed, his emotional distrust of American messianic tendencies resembled that of his father, the reluctant colonialist in the Philippines. America, William Howard Taft had said in 1917, is "not a knight-errant country going about to independent people and saying, 'we do not like your form of government, we have tried our form of government . . . and you have got to take it,'" and Bob even lifted the phrase "knight-errant" to make his case in 1939.[15] With this seed planted in his mind, it was not surprising that a more thoroughgoing disillusion with the rest of the world sprouted from his experiences in Paris. One of the reasons why Bob Taft was always to seem unbending in his opposition to extensive American involvement in Europe was that he had developed strong opinions early in life.

Above all, Taft approached foreign problems from the standpoint of their effects at home. Again remembering early experiences, he believed war would expand the role of the federal government, pyramid its spending, and lead to abuses of individual constitutional rights. It would "almost certainly destroy democracy in the United States.

We have moved far toward totalitarian government already. The additional powers sought by the President in case of war, the nationalization of all industry and all capital and all labor, already

proposed in bills before Congress, would create a Socialist dictatorship which it would be impossible to dissolve once the war is
over.[16]

Taft offered these remarks in January 1939, less than a month
after reaching Washington. As always, he drafted them himself
in longhand, then dictated them for delivery, and they resounded
with the hyperbole that he often displayed in his speeches. It was
symbolic of his strong feelings on the subject of intervening in Europe — and of his refusal to reconsider his position — that he
jumped so quickly into the fray and that he repeated such remarks
almost verbatim for the next two years. For Taft the national interest meant the preservation of liberty in the United States, not
the protection of democracy abroad. "My whole idea of foreign
policy," he wrote, "is based largely on the position that America
can successfully defend itself against the rest of the world." [17]

·

So long as peace ruled uneasily in Europe, Americans could
hope for the best. But in August 1939 Hitler and Stalin joined in
a pact of nonaggression; and in the early dawn of September 1,
German tanks churned into Poland. Two days later Britain and
France declared war.

Even before the outbreak of fighting, Roosevelt had determined
to press for repeal of the ban on American shipments of arms and
ammunition to all warring nations. But congressmen, like many
Americans, yearned for noninvolvement. They cherished a "neutrality" that kept Americans off belligerent ships, denied credits to
nations at war, and refused munitions to either side, aggressor or
victim. When war erupted in September, the neutrality acts
forced America to withhold munitions not only from Germany,
which did not need them, but from England and France.
Alarmed, Roosevelt called Congress back to Washington and once
again sounded the cry for revision of the embargo.

Taft backed Roosevelt's request for revision, for as early as April
he had stressed the absurdity of banning shipments of munitions
while simultaneously permitting belligerents to buy crucial strategic materials such as iron, oil, and rubber. Revision, he argued

with much more candor than the administration dared to muster, was necessary to aid England and France, and he joined seven Republicans and forty-seven Democrats in defeating, 55 to 27, a key amendment designed to maintain the embargo. Twelve of his Republican colleagues voted the other way. In his first crucial test over foreign policy, Taft had departed from the majority of his party to vote with the administration.[18]

But only with reservations. Like the President, Taft insisted that revision, far from moving America toward war, would strengthen Hitler's opponents and enable America to stay out. Like the majority of his colleagues, he demanded that both arms and strategic materials be sold on a "cash and carry" basis, so that American investors would have no loans to recover abroad and so that American vessels would not be exposed to German submarines. He also introduced an amendment preventing government agencies and private corporations from extending credits to belligerents. Still distrusting the President, Taft joined a Senate majority in refusing to give FDR discretion to apply the provisions of the law to one side and not the other. Taft believed America had entered World War I to protect her shipping against German submarines, and he was willing to accept stringent restrictions on traditional American maritime rights, to strike a blow at the American merchant marine in the process, and indeed to depart from his usual stance as a defender of American business enterprise against federal restraints.[19]

The battle had forced him reluctantly into the area of foreign policy. But it did not shake him from the suppositions he had carried with him to Washington. He had reached his opinion and had laboriously written his basic speech. With the battle for revision of the embargo far from over in October, he was already longing to turn to other issues that exercised him. "I am hopeful," he wrote, "that the whole matter will be settled soon, so that we can try to center public attention again on domestic issues." [20]

•

Senators, Woodrow Wilson once complained, do not grow. They swell.

By 1940 some people thought that of Taft. Washington reporters found him cool, and veteran Democratic senators resented his bluntness. "A quiet-looking person but friendly and agreeable," Interior Secretary Harold Ickes thought, on meeting him for the first time. "I doubt whether he has many human emotions." [21]

Particularly in debate, Taft sounded cutting. In his maiden speech he attracted eighty-eight senators curious to see what he could do, and his opponents quickly began questioning, interrupting, heckling. Taking on the venerable Kenneth McKellar of Tennessee, Taft impatiently accused him of "claiming the whole world." Not so, McKellar retorted hotly. "However, after twenty-two years of fighting in the Senate, I do claim to know something about the subject, and I believe I know more than the junior Senator from Ohio." Later Alben Barkley of Kentucky, the majority leader, shot a question at Taft. "I got all the figures I could on this question," Taft snapped characteristically. "It is purely a matter of mathematics," he continued, "if the Senator can understand mathematics." [22] Twenty years of state and national politics had taught the young student who once fled from the limelight to arm himself against the enemy. He was more confident now, and there was little time for fools.

Many found Taft aggressively wrong-headed and reactionary. His preoccupation with economy alienated government officials and pressure groups, and his attacks on the President infuriated numerous Democrats. His attitude toward England and France struck many as callous and defeatist. And his gloomy predictions about the long-range effects of government planning appeared wildly exaggerated.[23] Already some people were murmuring that Taft had the best mind in the Senate — until he made it up.

These critics were hitting some chinks in his armor. Publicly Taft was often impatient, testy, coldly partisan, hyperbolic. But in human relations he had not swelled into arrogant self-certainty or changed his ways. He still dressed plainly, drove his own car, traveled in day coaches, and held sycophants at arm's length. Kept waiting in the anteroom of a friend's office, he sat down patiently. After a long delay his friend appeared, discovered Taft, and apologized profusely. "Oh, this is fine." Taft smiled. "I had a chance to collect my thoughts." Explaining his failure to speak against increased parity payments, he admitted his lack of expertise. "There are twenty-five or thirty Senators," he said, "who could out-debate me on the subject." [24] Taft, apparently so self-assured, was still able to admit candidly to surprised reporters his lack of knowledge on a host of problems. If his irritation with colleagues sometimes offended, his gravity and seriousness of purpose proved ample compensation. From the start Taft was one of those comparatively few Senators who was listened to.

He was also less reactionary than his critics liked to maintain. Though occasionally extreme in his rhetoric, he proved temperate on questions involving labor and Social Security and constructive on housing. His attitude toward administration foreign policy, while suspicious, was more moderate than that of many of his Republican colleagues. Taft was usually partisan, sometimes shrill, but he was actually closer to the center of his party than to its fringes. As a friend explained privately, Taft offered a "rare and paradoxical combination of (1) a great internal self-assurance (which is necessary to support convictions), coupled with (2) a real humility (of the kind that begets understanding and tolerance)." [25]

Above all, Taft pushed himself. The Senate placed him at the hub where he had long wanted to be, and it sustained and satisfied him. More than most men, he felt secure, useful, at ease with himself and with the world into which he had climbed. But he had always demanded excellence of himself, and the Senate called for more. He sometimes seemed cold and strident because he still made no effort to be other than himself and because his sense of duty, his obligations to himself, and his ambition gave him so little pause.

CHAPTER 14

Seeking the Top

"I HAVE the greatest respect for the White House and the Presidency," Taft said in 1948. "This was instilled in me in my youth, perhaps to a greater degree than in most of my countrymen because my address was once 1600 Pennsylvania Avenue. I like the old homestead."

The occasion was yet another Gridiron dinner, and Taft, a wiser man than he had been nine years before, was needling Harry Truman.[1] Actually, the White House years had pained his parents, and his most uncharacteristic reminiscence of those unhappy years concealed much and answered little about his presidential ambitions. Safely ensconced in the Senate until 1944, aware of the tribulations his parents had endured, Taft had every reason to stay contentedly where he was.

He did not see it that way. "I'm going to go out for the Senate, and I'm not going to stop there," the Rowes recalled his saying in 1937. "I'm not counting myself out," he told reporters in December 1938. Hardly sworn into the Senate, he let his friends promote his presidential candidacy, and he undertook a strenuous schedule of public appearances. Worried about an article in *Time,* he grumbled about the "Dewey propaganda" and asked a newsman to see whether he could reach Henry Luce, "who takes a shot at me whenever he gets a chance." By June 1939, Taft was calling meetings to plan campaign strategy.[2] He had bolted from the starting gate. Why?

Given the circumstances, his friends replied, why not? He had waged a courageous race in a pivotal state. He had a famous name (was it fate for a Taft to succeed a Roosevelt?), and Republicans desperately needed new faces. Taft, they argued, was a historical necessity to the party, and he could not refuse to pull the crown from the hated Roosevelt's head. Indeed, to staunchly anti-New Deal Republicans, Taft seemed the only man courageous and forthright enough to return the nation to sound administration.

Taft felt a becoming loyalty to these anxious supporters, but personal drives also impelled him. Though his parents had suffered in the White House, they had also talked ceaselessly of excelling and of public service. The Senate indeed offered satisfactions, but Republicans would have to struggle in the minority for some time. Taft thought the nation was straying off course, and he had developed confidence enough to believe he could restore it. And to shun the battle would be to fail to compete. "I am not an active presidential candidate," he protested to reporters in December 1938.

"That doesn't mean that you would not accept the nomination, does it?"

"Of course not," he snapped. "What man wouldn't?" [3]

.

First, however, there was the problem of Ohio, source of fifty-two of the thousand delegate votes at the 1940 convention. Controlling Ohio meant disposing of Governor John Bricker, which would not be easy because the new governor was a highly popular leader with shrewd political instincts. Clearly, Bricker lacked Taft's intelligence, he paid little attention to national issues, and he seemed further to the right than Taft himself. But Bricker was handsome, affable, and folksy. Having headed the state ticket in 1938, he, too, had attracted national attention, and he saw no reason to step aside.

Taft could have met Bricker head on, but such a contest would have bruised both men, to say nothing of the party, and Taft steadfastly pursued the path of delicate negotiation instead. He started to raise money ($25,000 would do for six months, he thought). He reminded his rival of the two-year gubernatorial term in Ohio: a vain race for the presidency could cost Bricker the State House. And he arranged a quiet exploratory meeting in May 1939 with his opponent. Still sparring, both men agreed to the status quo.[4]

By June 1939, Taft was getting restless, and he increased his pressure on State Chairman Ed Schorr and on the county leaders. Taft had friendly journalists plant stories about his popularity, and he even toyed with the idea of running a publicity campaign against Bricker. When a Gallup poll showed Taft the favorite in Ohio, 62 to 38 per cent, he gave it the widest publicity. Yet Bricker still refused to withdraw, and Taft wrote angrily to Martha that "John seems to antagonize someone every day — he is making headway backwards with the county chairmen . . . I am only afraid he will make it hard for the Republicans to carry Ohio if he goes on making mistakes." [5]

Three days later, however, Bricker surprised Ohioans by renouncing his presidential ambitions for 1940. His announcement immediately inspired speculation that Taft had concluded a deal. Some accounts reported that he had agreed to support Bricker in 1940 if his own aspirations seemed hopeless by convention time. A more widespread opinion was that Bricker had pulled out in 1940 only after his rival agreed not to run in 1944. Such a deal may have occurred, because the two camps were then holding a variety of unpublicized meetings and because Taft did support Bricker for the presidential nomination in 1944. If so, however, none of Taft's aides were ever informed, and both aspirants steadfastly denied the stories thereafter. It was more likely that the poll had shown Bricker, who lacked Taft's contacts outside of Ohio, the futility of fighting further.[6]

Evidence suggesting that a deal, if concluded, was informal at best was Bricker's almost immediate change of heart. Instead of conceding Taft the delegates, Bricker's aides maintained their activity, and Taft again grew suspicious. The governor, he wrote, "can't make up his mind and keep it made up." Taft then seized the initiative by publicly announcing his own candidacy on August 3, 1939. When Bricker called, Taft grumbled confidentially that the governor "did not seem to me very cordial." But he then dictated a warm letter to his adversary. "I am most anxious that nothing be done by any of my friends which meets your disapproval," he told Bricker. "If you get the slightest rumor of anything of the kind . . . I will see that it is stopped . . . Your administration has reflected the greatest credit on the Republican Party in Ohio." [7]

Until the very eve of the convention a year later, Taft worried about Bricker's loyalty. ("Extremely annoying," he complained of his rival's activities as late as May 1940.) But with the Ohio delegation behind him by the end of August 1939, he worked hard to promote harmony, even inviting the governor and his wife for Sunday dinner and a World Series game in Cincinnati. [8] Taft, aggressive against Democrats in Washington, proved a careful, supple, and resourceful negotiator in the behind-the-scenes struggles of his native state.

.

With Ohio assured, Taft relaxed for a while. Indeed, he even dared hope to win the nomination without a fight. "We are trying to hold the situation until next fall or winter," he wrote, "when we can judge better whether it will be wise to make an extensive campaign or simply await the decision of the Convention." [9]

But he took few chances. Soon he was sending his speeches to national party leaders and dispatching David Ingalls and others on fund-raising explorations. He traveled to the West Coast, delivering speeches and conferring with GOP bosses en route. And he surrounded himself with an able team. Headed by Ingalls, who flew his own plane on his extensive political errands, it had a strong Ohio cast, including Charlie Taft, Paul Walter, and John Hollister. But it also included non-Ohioans. In New York City, Taft leaned heavily on his brother-in-law Tom Bowers, a gregarious lawyer and bank vice-president. In the South he counted on Colonel R. B. Creager, the hard-headed Republican boss of Texas; on Perry Howard, the black leader of Mississippi Republicans; on John Marshall, a shrewd West Virginia lawyer-politician, who had been an assistant attorney general under President Calvin Coolidge; and on other veteran state leaders who vehemently opposed the New Deal, fondly recalled William Howard Taft, regarded Bob as the most determined foe of Roosevelt, and who existed largely in the hope of passing out federal jobs under a Republican administration. Taft relied also on Richard Scandrett, an experienced politician from New York who offered his services out of admiration for Taft's stand for neutrality revision in 1939; he was to bombard Taft with advice on foreign policy for the next twelve years. Completing the team were two advance men; Mildred Reeves and other office workers in Washington; and in early 1940 Forrest Davis, an able and experienced journalist, who served as a part-time publicity man. Most of these aides were Taft's old friends, and most enjoyed close contacts with important political leaders and potential contributors. Taft seldom met with all of his aides at once, rarely argued with them, and never let them tell him how to stand on the issues. But they were professionals who knew their territories and their assignments, and, as in 1938, he rarely intervened in their organizational activities. In his first quest for the presidency, Taft did not make a full-scale effort in every state, he did not have a huge organization of volunteers, and he still rejected speech writers or a retinue. But he succeeded in drawing together an able, loyal, and professional organization.[10]

With the close of the special session of 1939, Taft stepped up his pace by touring the southwest, then Massachusetts and Maine in December. A break for Christmas followed, and then he took off for New York, Illinois, Delaware, North Carolina, Illinois again, Florida, Pennsylvania, Baltimore, Cleveland, Louisville, Pennsylvania again, and Virginia. By mid-February he had made forty major speeches, visited twenty-eight states, and traveled more than thirty thousand miles. It was a frantic pace, hardly approached by most of his rivals.[11]

His strategy was sound and precedented. He worked first to heal minor divisions within Ohio. When Bricker refused to permit the selection of Congressman Clarence Brown, a Taft supporter, as a delegate at large, Taft tried at first to avoid the bitter dispute, then sought to engineer a compromise — unsuccessfully as it turned out — making Brown a district delegate. When State Chairman Schorr balked at Taft's plan to have Ingalls selected as national committeeman, Taft had his aides quietly line up the delegates — successfully this time — before Schorr could get to them. And when one of the frequent feuds broke out between Paul Walter and the abrasive Congressman George Bender of Cleveland, Taft told his friend to back down. "I don't like the situation in Cleveland any more perhaps than you do," he wrote Walter, "but I do feel it is absolutely essential to have the enthusiastic support of George Bender, and my whole course has been based on that theory." [12] Taft's attitude toward politics had not changed since his struggles with the Charterites in Cincinnati: Work within the existing system and deal with the powers that be. Keep the organization strong.

Taft angled also for the backing of pressure groups, particularly of the blacks. "We ought to get Joe Louis on our side," he wrote Walter. "Your colored friends in Cleveland could perhaps do so." He never tired of stressing his past support for black office holding. "I personally always insisted on a negro nominee for the Legislature . . . and for city council," he wrote one concerned voter. "We have in Ohio and many northern states an influential colored vote which is really entitled to recognition," he told another. "The Republican Party came to take this vote for granted, and it was easy for Roosevelt to push it over with the WPA . . . We have to fight hard to hang on to what we have." [13]

Avoiding primaries was central to his planning. These cost money, took precious time, and polarized local factions. Instead, his advance men concentrated on persuading the leaders and influence makers. Taft wasted little time handshaking, but traveled from city to city, meeting quietly with the publishers and party leaders. He carefully kept lines open to Herbert Hoover and to other potential candidates. It was a traditional method, and it worried some of his advisers, who thought he should prove his popularity at least once. But it was also a politics that had worked for Warren Harding and for Alfred Landon. Doubting the odds in such primaries as West Virginia, New Jersey, and Maryland, and recalling the exhausting schedule of 1938, Taft shied away from the politics of personal popularity.[14]

Besides, Martha was helping him in that department. "Taft is regarded as a good man," a Washington insider reported, "but his wife is regarded as a better one." The veteran journalist William Allen White commented that "in her will lies the family's resilience, the ability to light on its feet — the understanding heart." Traveling tirelessly and jotting down phrases for her own extemporaneous speeches, she swung widely through the East and Midwest, and even to California. Like her husband, she denounced excessive spending and warned of Roosevelt's intentions abroad. Unlike him, she did so pithily, humorously, and so outspokenly that the columnist Drew Pearson claimed that some of Taft's friends wanted to muzzle her. But Taft knew enough not to do that, for she proved as much an asset on the national scene as she had been in Ohio two years earlier.[15]

As in past campaigns, Taft devoted his speeches to earnest comments on the issues. Sometimes he defended the humanitarian side of the New Deal, and occasionally, as in industrial Cleveland, he sounded almost like Roosevelt himself. "Millions," he said, "are merely unfortunate. Anyone who goes up and down the streets of our great municipalities will find family after family whose members would be eager and industrious workers if jobs could be found for them." Sometimes, too, he was bold. He upbraided a convention of advertising men for making false appeals and told Iowans that farm loans were wasteful. But he appeared most often at conventions of businessmen, insurance agents, bankers, and lawyers, and he told them what they expected to hear. "We will make more headway," he wrote a friend, "by attacking the New Deal and then listing the good features of it, which we intend to continue, rather than approving the New Deal objectives and criticizing a few methods. This was tried in 1936, and was certainly a disastrous failure." Well before the convention Taft was known for his staunch opposition to the administration, respected for his consistency, and criticized for his foolhardiness.[16]

Above all, the strategy was to stop Thomas E. Dewey from amassing too large a lead. Only thirty-eight years old, Dewey had yet to hold office higher than district attorney in New York City. Some mocked his youth — "Buster" Dewey, they said, was casting his diaper into the ring — and others thought him brusque, cold, and inquisitorial. But he was ambitious, orderly, and intelligent, and he was sweeping the primaries that Taft avoided. Early in his campaign, Dewey seemed assured of at least 300 votes, perhaps as many as 400, of the 501 necessary for the nomination. So Taft had aides compile charts trying to prove Dewey's weakness as a vote getter, and he urged on Arthur Vandenberg, a potential contender who might sap his rival's strength. ("You might write me from time to time," Taft told a friend, "so that I can stir him [Vandenberg] up to a little more activity.") He refused to have anything to do with talk of a Dewey-Taft ticket. And some of his aides started a letter-writing campaign labeling Dewey but another of the many favorite sons.[17]

By March the strategy seemed to be paying off. Money, already abundant through the largesse of his relatives, flowed in from outside contributors. So, too, did promises of support from party leaders. The Southern bosses secured a majority for him in Arkansas, Mississippi, Virginia, possibly in Louisiana, and a solid delegation of twenty-six in Texas. Alabama would give five or six, as would North Carolina, Colorado, California, Indiana, Kentucky. Illinois would begin with Dewey, but might later swing much of its fifty-eight-man delegation to Taft. So, too, might California, Wisconsin, and Pennsylvania. "The insiders," the reporter Raymond Clapper complained privately, "may throw it to him. He can produce plenty of money for them, and at heart he is right down the alley of the most reactionary people in the party." [18]

Clapper's remarks sounded a little harsh, but they represented considerable truth. Taft indeed had the support of the party's right wing, most of whom were more vitriolic than he was. One avid Taftite from Indiana wrote David Ingalls that "the New Deal is nothing more or less than socialism or disguised communism being propagated and practiced." Another complained to John Hollister that "the country is very tired of city slickers, political opportunists, and smart politicians. They are longing for a Calvin Coolidge, an Abraham Lincoln, a man who is smart enough to cope with the politicians and yet who is honest and straightforward." [19] Zealots such as these either failed to see the flexible side of Taft, or perceiving it, discounted it. Taft was occasionally to squirm privately at having such admirers, but he rarely said so publicly, and his sharp assaults on the administration always roused them to new heights of affection.

The media, perhaps sensing a winner, proved cooperative on occasion. The New York *Times* gave his campaign thorough coverage and called him "industrious and painstaking." *Time* placed him on its cover in January and approvingly quoted Alice Roose-

velt Longworth, who cracked that choosing Taft to replace Roosevelt "would be like drinking a glass of milk after taking a slug of
benzedrine." Syndicated columnist Paul Mallon described Taft as
"sincere . . . a thoroughly modern and social-minded conservative . . . A man with a flit gun and a broom intent on using both
in a quiet and orderly manner." And Walter Lippmann called
Taft "conventional and often narrow" but stressed his "saving
grace of intellectual humility . . . He is not opinionated . . .
He is not intoxicated with his own rhetoric or in love with himself as a public personage . . . He will never be a die-hard or a
foolish reactionary . . . Given a little more time to develop his
qualities, Mr. Taft, who has gone so far in one year of public life,
would then be as promising a candidate as the Republicans have
had for some decades." [20]

.

But Taft had two handicaps that pulled him back. One was his
image. The other was the state of the world at the time.

The image troubled professionals from the beginning. "In
small groups he made an excellent impression," a Massachusetts
leader wrote Hollister. But his formal speech was "nothing to be
wildly enthusiastic about. Everyone was impressed with his honesty, sincerity of purpose, courage, and knowledge of his subject,
but he left the audience fairly cold . . . he didn't really strike any
spark." An Indiana supporter agreed. When greeting and handshaking, he wrote, Taft was "charming and the people liked him.
His smile is the thing." But his speech was "a shade above the
heads of the average listener. He should conclude his paragraphs
and clinch his points with some homely clichés which the crowd
will applaud and carry away." Taft, a third observer commented
bluntly, had the ability but lacked the "oomph." [21]

Even his most loyal advisers worried. "Taft," his publicity director, Forrest Davis, admitted privately, "speaks as if he were submitting a brief in a probate case rather than addressing an audience
which might number several million fellow citizens." Hollister
urged Ingalls to get Taft to add personal comments to his letters.
"It is something on which we have to keep prodding him," Hol-

lister said, "for he lacks the 'feel' of this kind of thing, and does not understand how much people like to be patted on the back and think that there is a personal interest of the 'big shot' in them." Even Ingalls, one of Taft's most unquestioning aides, blanched occasionally. After setting up a breakfast meeting of important leaders, Ingalls listened behind a door while his candidate expertly answered questions. Suddenly hearing nothing, he looked in. Taft had pushed back his chair and was engrossed in reading the morning paper, oblivious to the angry looks of the surrounding company. "Please don't do that to me again,'" Ingalls pleaded later. "But I had learned all I could," replied Taft wistfully.[22]

Davis tried to humanize his man. He told reporters that Taft had a new telephone number: "ME[tropolitan]-1940." He prepared new copy about Martha, the family tradition, and grandfather Alphonso, who "trudged" to Yale to study. He urged Grove Patterson, the publisher of the Toledo *Blade,* who was preparing a nominating speech, to refute the notion that Taft was a "stuffed shirt, or at least a coldly mathematical human being . . . I am wondering if it might not be as well to get as much of a folksy, human color to the speech as the dignity of the occasion permits." [23]

Taft's unflattering image incensed Uncle Horace, who wrote Martha that "these reporters make me tired when they talk about Bob's lack of color. They seem to think he ought to be standing on his head or turning somersaults." It also annoyed Taft himself. "Who was the man who claimed I 'highhatted' him?" he demanded of a friend. "Undoubtedly I did not recognize him. I have met 50,000 people in the last two years, and they all expect me to know them." Unlike some politicians, he did not require the constant adulation of the crowd. But he wanted to be liked, and he wanted very much to win. So he tried to smile, and he sometimes captured the affection of smaller groups. Still, the people saw the big-domed intellectual with the rimless glasses, and they heard the metallic voice and the pedantic statistics. He is a "good, able, safe man," Congressman Bruce Barton of New York explained to Scandrett. But "if he ran in my district, he wouldn't get a single vote beyond the regular Republican members." [24]

Part of Taft's stiffness stemmed from a reserve so deep that his twenty-fifth wedding anniversary in October 1939 passed unreported to the columnists. "His passion for privacy is almost morbid," one syndicated reporter complained. Another interviewer kept probing, only to give up in the end. "I'm afraid you won't find much color in me," Taft told him. "I'm too darn normal." Too honest to manufacture amusing anecdotes and too absorbed to see how much the reporters needed them, he received the press genially, truthfully answered their questions, and sent them away with little that was new.[25]

Taft's unflattering image came also from his attempt early in the campaign to accommodate the many well-wishers who pleaded with him to humanize himself. He posed for news photographers in a business suit holding a limp and long-dead turkey, which readers were supposed to believe he had shot. Worse, he allowed himself to be pictured deep-sea fishing from a boat obviously tethered to a wharf and to be shown landing a conspicuously deceased sailfish. Though Taft's aides claimed later that he had been joshing for the cameramen, only to be double-crossed, the truth was that he had foolishly tried to pose as a sportsman. Forrest Davis called a halt to such patently ridiculous publicity, but not before a stereotype had been confirmed.[26]

If the media had played down his personality, he might have obscured this image. But some influential magazines gave his blunders the widest circulation. Henry Luce's *Time* not only printed the turkey picture but described him as a "tortoise" who had "piled one ineptitude on another." Instead of praising his courage in criticizing the size of loans to corn farmers in Iowa, it called him politically "inept." It talked of his "reassuring lack of charm," then described him tearing up Roosevelt's budget while "baring an artificial smile, evidently in response to a command." In its cover story *Time* avoided such language, but filled its account with trivia that added little to the creation of a favorable personal image. Luce's other mass magazine, *Life,* then opened up on Taft in February with a two-page pictorial spread on "What Really Happened" while Taft was fishing. Exposing his deep-sea adventures, it chortled about the "very dead" and "putrescent" fish that sailors had tied to his line. And *Time* completed the fusillade in April. His campaign, it said, ought to be labeled

"The Adventures of Robert in Bumbledom." Taft, it concluded, was the "Dagwood Bumstead of American Politics." [27]

The press, most experts agree, is more likely to confirm than to make men's minds. Moreover, singling out the Luce magazines overlooks the more balanced treatment Taft received from newspapers and neglects the public opinion polls, which, after consistently showing him trailing Dewey — and sometimes Vandenberg or Hoover — revealed no significant changes following the unflattering accounts of early 1940.[28] Still, such exposure in the mass-circulation magazines did not help his chances, and if it taught him the dangers of false publicity, it also left him more suspicious of photographers in the future. Pose with an Indian chief, they asked him, and Taft coldly refused. Smile, they insisted, and he threw them a look of frozen fury while their shutters clicked. Far from learning through experience, Taft emerged from the campaign of 1940 with much the same image as before and with a barely concealed contempt for some of the eastern journalists who spread it.[29]

•

Other politicians have suffered from stereotypes and still captured presidential nominations. But the revolution in the world balance of power disrupted the race and left Taft struggling for running room.

In the early months of 1940, he remained as suspicious as before about Roosevelt's intentions in foreign policy. "He is much more likely to get us involved in war than anyone else in the United States," Taft said privately.

> While I certainly do not consider myself an isolationist, I feel it would be a great mistake for us to participate in the European war. I do not believe we could materially affect the outcome and I do not believe we have shown any ability to make a peace after the war is over. In the meantime, we would certainly destroy democracy in this country.[30]

But he moderated his tone in public. He supported a loan to Finland, which was then fighting desperately against the Soviet

Union. Worried about provoking a Japanese assault on the Philippines, he refused to criticize the administration for not imposing an embargo on shipments to Japan. Though he sniped at Roosevelt's intentions, he minimized foreign policy issues. The central battle, he insisted shrewdly to a nation disposed to stay out of war, was the domestic New Deal.[31]

Hitler then began to make this neat strategy untenable. In April he seized Denmark and began an assault on Norway. And on May 10 he shocked the world by sweeping through Belgium and racing around the Maginot Line. His tanks churned into France, cut off the British armies, and drove them toward the channel. Hitler was toppling the balance of power in Europe and forcing Americans to decide. Either the United States backed England with all measures short of war, or it risked letting the Nazis dominate Europe.

Taft tried to hold his tongue, but his emotions gave him little rest. On May 16 when he set out on a trip to Kansas, he wrote Martha wryly that "as nobody seems to have any sense I may not be nominated which will be just as well," but assured her that he remained "calm, antihysterical and anti-war." With the British about to be trapped on the channel coast, he arrived in Topeka for a speech on May 18 and was informed by local leaders, including Alfred Landon, of widespread sympathy in the region for the Allies. Taft ignored the advice to equivocate. "This is no time for the people to be wholly absorbed in foreign battles," he told his audience. Instead, Americans should worry about domestic policy. "It is the New Deal which may leave us weak and unprepared for attack." [32]

In St. Louis two days later he burst out with the speech that proved most damaging to his campaign. First he dismissed the notion that the Nazis posed a threat to the United States. "There is a good deal more danger of the infiltration of totalitarian ideas from the New Deal circle in Washington," he said, "than there will ever be from any activities of the communists or the Nazi bund." Then he accused Roosevelt of trying to "stir up the emotions of the people." American entrance into the war, he proclaimed, would be "more likely to destroy American democracy than to destroy German dictatorship." Germany might beat England and create a world "where ruthless force had been triumphant over every principle of justice," yet "even that alternative seems preferable to present participation in the European war." [33] In the time of England's greatest peril and in the midst of a wave of sentiment toward aid for the Allies, Taft had demanded a policy of hands off, unequivocally, deliberately, and unashamedly.

Had he turned to friends for advice, he would have found them profoundly worried about his position on foreign policy. His brother Charlie was already talking of aiding Britain. Bob's views on foreign policy, Uncle Horace added in March, "don't suit me at all. I don't think they would have suited his father." John Hollister urged David Ingalls to stop Taft from seeming "entirely oblivious to European happenings," and John Marshall wrote that Taft was "too honest in this crisis . . . better promises would gain advantage." Forrest Davis and Richard Scandrett, both opposing Taft's position, exchanged anxious letters about what Davis called his "apparent callousness toward the Allied cause." [34]

But most of his aides kept their doubts to themselves, or they grumbled to each other in letters that their leader never saw. Some, like Davis, did not feel close enough to intrude, and others, like Marshall, properly regarded themselves as technicians, not idea men. All were reluctant to challenge one who seemed so assured and knowledgeable. Indeed, he did not encourage argument. He still rejected speechwriters, traveled alone or without policy advisers, and trusted the professionals to handle their assignments without presuming to worry about the issues. Reserved, reluctant to expose himself, Taft had been trained to think for himself and to compete on his own. Because he sought no confidants in this difficult time, he found none.

He probably would have ignored them anyway. Landon had warned him to soften his tone, as had practically every major Republican leader in Kansas and Missouri during his tour. Taft paid no attention for the simple reason that he believed unshakably in his position. Accustomed to addressing antiadministration audiences and trusting in his powers of persuasion, he hoped he could breast the popular tide of the moment. But he knew that he might destroy his chances for the nomination. In Kansas the *Times* newsman Turner Catledge happened upon him in a Pullman car. "His glasses had slipped down, halfway off his face," Catledge recalled, "and he kept repeating, in a distant voice, 'I'm just not going to do it.' " Taft, Catledge concluded, "couldn't shift his views for political expedience, and that was one reason he never captured the Republican nomination." [35]

.

Hitler's tanks ground on, pushed the British from the Continent, and in mid-June rolled into Paris. By the time of the Republican convention on June 24, Germany had forced France to its knees, and its planes were blasting English cities. Roosevelt looked for ways to help the British; the majority of Americans, so the polls indicated, were searching with him. Confronted with these revolutionary circumstances, Taft too might have looked and have entered the convention with a more moderate and accommodating line.

By focusing more directly than earlier on the most frightening possibilities, he seemed at times to be doing so. America should fight the Germans, he said on May 22, if Hitler sought a foothold in the Western Hemisphere. The United States ought also to be prepared to defend Canada, Central America, and the northern part of South America. He reminded listeners of his stand against the arms embargo, and he charged repeatedly that domestic expenditures were sapping national defense. "There is no recognition," he proclaimed, "of the fact that preparedness is a deadly serious business which can only be accompanied by sacrifice." [36]

Hitler's amazing triumphs also distressed Taft privately. "No one can be certain," he wrote a friend, "whether Roosevelt is right or not . . . the prospect of seeing England and France overwhelmed by Germany is one which I look forward to with the greatest misgiving." A few days later, again privately, he confessed "great uncertainty. I certainly would not like to commit myself or the Republican Party to any particular course in foreign policy, because it might have to be changed." By June 13 he sounded despondent. "I am very much encouraged with regard to the nomination," he wrote, "but the war in Europe is so depressing that it does not seem so attractive a goal as it once did." [37]

These were doubts, not changes of heart, for he still worried more about excessive spending at home than about dangers to the Allies. Indeed, his denunciations of unpreparedness overlooked his own repeated demands for economy. On June 19, with France on the verge of collapse and with the convention days away, he was one of five senators to oppose an excess profits tax aimed at increasing revenue for defense. Uncertain of Hitler's intentions, Taft never meant to oppose defense spending, and he always ended by supporting increased military appropriations. But he did insist on cutting domestic costs first.

The most dramatic manifestation of his stubborn courage occurred June 2 during a dinner party at the home of Ogden Reid, publisher of the internationalist New York *Herald Tribune*. Why he took time out from his schedule to attend this affair was unclear, but on arriving, he and Martha discovered that the guests included Lord Lothian, the British ambassador; Thomas Lamont, chairman of the board of J. P. Morgan and Co.; Dorothy Thompson, the influential New York *Times* columnist; and many other Anglophiles, including Wendell Willkie, an Indiana-raised New York utilities executive who had been rocketing ahead in recent weeks as a potential Republican presidential nominee. "The only other really human people besides ourselves," Martha wrote her friend Lillian Dykstra, were "Mr. and Mrs. John Pillsbury of Minneapolis."

In such company Bob and Martha determined to be noncommittal, but Mrs. Reid gave them little choice. After dinner she rose and, in Martha's account, toasted the "brave men in Flanders who are fighting our battle." Then she turned to Lord Lothian and to others, who echoed her sentiments. Taft held his tongue, but then Willkie declared that he would vote for Roosevelt before supporting any Republican who did not favor aiding the Allies. "At that point," Martha continued, "Bob exploded with a loud pop. Said he:

> I had not intended to take any part in this discussion but I feel that I cannot sit here and let my silence be interpreted as agreement.

"Then the fat was in the fire," Martha wrote. "Everybody began to scream at once, with Dorothy Thompson screaming more at once than anybody else. Bob got into the most violent argument with her. I thought I was going to have to throw pepper on them! But really it was horrifying.

"After a while," Martha concluded, "everybody's lungs gave out and we went home." [38] But the dinner had hurt her husband, because the guests enjoyed wide influence among eastern financial and journalistic circles, which did not forget his outburst. Taft, Dorothy Thompson remarked to a friend a few days later, "fails to comprehend the kind of world in which we are living." Stories about the dinner immediately began appearing in the newspapers, and eastern editorialists threw Taft on the defensive. The episode alone did not cost him the nomination, for many of these people were leaning toward Willkie anyway. But it probably confirmed them in their views, and it propelled Willkie still faster on his course.[39]

The dinner also cast a revealing beam of light on Taft. It showed that for all his self-possession he had a hot, quick temper which he could not always control. And it revealed his forthrightness. As Scandrett mused later, Taft "didn't do much in the way of proclaiming his own 'integrity' and 'aversion to expediency.' I found as my acquaintance with him grew that his advisers didn't get very far when they argued 'political expediency.' " [40] And Turner Catledge recalled that between Dewey, Willkie, and Taft, "the one I cared for the most, personally, was Taft." Catledge wrote:

He was not a warm or genial man — he was cold, and could be extremely hard and righteous — but there was a tremendous honesty about him that commanded respect, and beneath his frigid exterior he was a shy, pleasant sort of man. Sometimes his stubborn honesty made him seem awkward in the context of the Senate — it was the very opposite of the "to get along, go along" philosophy that prevails in Congress. Bob Taft would not "go along" with anything he was not convinced of after his long and tortuous process of reasoning.[41]

No one ever explained better why Taft sometimes failed to develop the intuitive grasp of popular moods that characterizes the most successful democratic politicians, or why, however wrong-headed, he still evoked abiding trust and loyalty among many Americans for the next thirteen years.

CHAPTER 15

A Certain Grace in Defeat

THE 1940 REPUBLICAN presidential convention opened on June 24 in unairconditioned Philadelphia. The atmosphere was thick, filthy, and sweat producing. Excited politicians, yearning for a Republican year, poured into the pit of Convention Hall, a battleground that turned into an arena of sealed-in heat. France was collapsing and waiting helplessly for terms from the enemy. It was a wide-open convention in a war-torn world.[1]

An impartial expert might have written Taft off. Everyone conceded Thomas E. Dewey the lead at the start, and in the wings pressed Wendell Willkie, already a whirlwind sweeping in uncertain delegates. Most neutral observers gave Dewey at least 350 delegates, Taft no more than 200, Willkie a maximum of 100 on the first ballot but with unlimited potential. Other possibilities such as Herbert Hoover; House Minority Leader Joseph Martin, Jr., of Massachusetts; publisher Frank Gannett of New York; and favorite sons Arthur Capper of Kansas; Harlan Bushfield of South Dakota; Hanford MacNider of Iowa; Styles Bridges of New Hampshire; Charles L. McNary of Oregon; Arthur Vandenberg of Michigan; and Governor Arthur James of Pennsylvania controlled the rest. To win, Taft needed 501 votes, and at least 300 of these would have to come from delegates committed at the start to others.[2]

Finding 300 delegates was obstacle enough, but the rush of events had strengthened an even more formidable hurdle: the feeling that he could not win the election if nominated. The American Institute of Public Opinion had asked Republican voters, "whom would you like to see elected President?" and had consistently discovered Dewey in the lead with more than 50 per cent and Taft and Vandenberg trailing with between 12 and 19 per cent. Willkie, ignored by the experts, appeared for the first time in late April with a paltry 3 per cent, but by late May he had attracted 17 per cent to move past Taft into second place. By early June it was Dewey 47 per cent, Willkie 29, Taft 8, and by convention time Willkie had stormed into the lead with 44 per cent. Dewey held second with 29, and Taft trailed with 13. Reflecting the uneasiness of many Americans, Walter Lippmann reversed the favorable opinion of Taft that he had held in February. Taft, he said on June 25, "has all the limitations of Neville Chamberlain, the same complacency, the same incapacity to foresee, the same apathy in action . . . to nominate him now would be to invite for the nation a disaster of preparedness, for Mr. Taft a tragic ordeal." [3] Few delegates assumed the polls to be precise, and fewer still relied on Walter Lippmann for their opinions. But no one wanted to pick a loser, and the trend seemed overwhelming.

Taft stayed confident amid these disheartening developments. He dismissed Willkie as a "Wall Street and public utility candidate" and as a "demagogue," feigned indifference to the polls, and predicted a lead on the first ballot. With his organization operating professionally, with his sons around to run errands, and with 102 hotel rooms reserved for his staff — by far the largest allotted to any candidate — he seemed so strong that even such seasoned observers as Democratic National Chairman James Farley and Roosevelt himself expected him to be the nominee. Taft had ample reason to be cool despite the heat of Philadelphia.[4]

.

Months earlier he had conceived a convention strategy, and he adhered to it as the carnival began on June 24. It was simple: hold on to the 52 delegates from Ohio, the 26 from Texas, the 40-odd from other southern states, the smattering from the Plains, the West Coast, and the heartland regions. These provided a solid, dependable core of 200. Then wait for Dewey, who was throwing all his strength into the first ballot, to begin to fade on the second. Then on the key third ballot, collect 120 Dewey delegates looking for a place to go, plus another 60 previously committed to Herbert

Hoover, Hanford MacNider, a noninterventionist favorite son from Iowa, and others. These would give him nearly 400. Doomed to defeat, Dewey would formally withdraw, and the magic tally of 501 would be in hand on the fourth ballot.[5]

Nothing in the preliminaries the first three days seemed likely to upset these plans; and as the balloting began on the afternoon of June 27 Taft, comfortably ensconced in his hotel with Martha, calmly maintained phone contact with Bob, Jr., on the convention floor. But signs of danger immediately appeared. Noisy Willkie-ites jammed the streets outside the hall. Pro-Willkie petitions and telegrams inundated the delegates. And in the gallery five thou-sand Willkie enthusiasts waved, whistled, and screamed above the bedlam already unleashed by the fifteen thousand regular ticket holders crammed into the hall. The galleryites had been admitted from the crowds in the street by Samuel Pryor of Connecticut, a Willkie supporter who was chairman of the committee on ar-rangements, and they kept up a steady, deafening chant: *"We Want Willkie, We Want Willkie, We Want Willkie."* Delegates complained they could not hear; Joseph Martin, presiding at the rostrum, appealed vainly for quiet; and Colonel R. B. Creager of Texas, Taft's floor leader, angrily threatened to bring the question of tickets before the convention. When Martin prom-ised to do something about it the next day, Creager relented. But the next day, as it turned out, was too late. The packing of the galleries with exuberant Willkieites may have changed few votes, but it charged the air with excitement, shook the delegates, and caught the Taft managers by surprise.[6]

Then followed the first two ballots. As expected, Dewey jumped into the lead with 360 on the first ballot, then sank to 338 on the second. The favorite sons also showed as anticipated, and Vanden-berg with 73 and James with 66 on the second ballot held the des-tiny of the convention in their hands. But Willkie had bolted for-ward with 105 on the first ballot and 171 on the second. Taft with 189 on the first ballot and 203 on the next still held second place, but by an uncomfortably narrow margin. As the delegates took a break for dinner, it was clear that he would have to summon all his reserves.[7]

During the recess he tried to do so, but failed. Joseph Pew, a power in the crucial 72-man Pennsylvania delegation, refused to talk with the Taft managers, and Herbert Hoover, who had forlorn hopes of winning, remained stubbornly in the race. So did MacNider of Iowa with his 34 votes. And Dewey also declined to pull out. At 8:30 the third ballot began amidst pandemonium and tempers flaring in the heat. *"We Want Willkie. We Want Willkie. We Want Willkie."* When it was over, Martin, Bridges, and Capper had lost 52 of their 53 delegates, and Dewey had slipped another 23 to 315. But Taft had picked up only 9 of these votes, for a disappointing total of 212. Willkie, by contrast, had attracted another 88 delegates and had swept into second place with 259 votes. The Taft strategy was crumbling in the face of the Willkie onslaught.

Still the balloting continued. So did the screaming, the shoving, and the shouts of triumph from the gallery. On the fourth ballot Dewey lost another 65 to drop to 250. Delegates started to leave the outsiders, and Willkie gained another 47 to forge into the lead for the first time with 306. But Taft rallied at last and began to capture stray votes here and there. When Dewey recognized his fate toward the end of the ballot and freed his followers, Taft gained still more. When the tally was complete, Taft had picked up 42 votes for a total of 254 — less than Willkie's 306, but ahead of Dewey's 250 and with hopes for more. It was becoming a two-man race.[8]

By then it was almost midnight, and the delegates had been struggling since 10 AM. They were tired, hoarse, uncertain, and angry. Creager simply refused to poll his increasingly rebellious Texas followers; thus they held firm for Taft. Alfred M. Landon, who headed the key Kansas delegation that had given 11 of its 18 votes to Dewey on the two preceding ballots, was beseeched by Taft and Willkie managers. So were James of Pennsylvania and Vandenberg of Michigan. John Hollister asked Taft if he wished to press for adjournment. "You people are on the floor," said Taft from his hotel room. "You decide." Taft's advisers concluded wisely that Willkie might be even stronger the next day, and the agony continued. Ballot number five.[9]

Dewey then collapsed. Losing 193 votes, he closed with but 57. Even James, stable at 59, surpassed him, and Vandenberg with 42 was not far away. Hoover also began to slip and lost 10 of his 31 delegates, and MacNider ended with only 4 of the 26 votes he had secured on the previous ballot. Landon, who preferred Willkie's views on foreign policy, swung from Dewey, and with him went the entire Kansas delegation of 18. An avalanche of cheers tumbled from the galleries. But Taft captured the whole of Kentucky's 22-man delegation, gained steadily in the West and South, and closed with 123 new votes for a total of 377. Though Willkie, too, had gained 123 new votes, 40 from Dewey's New York, for a total of 429, Taft was surging at last. With Pennsylvania and Michigan still undecided, the battle was not lost.[10]

"Thereupon," said the official proceedings of the convention, "many delegates, and more particularly the galleries, created a furore with their cheers and cries of 'We Want Willkie!' 'We Want Willkie!' 'We Want Willkie!' " John Bricker hurried to the platform to plead with Martin for a recess, but Martin secretly favored Willkie and refused. The ordeal went on into the morning.[11]

As the sixth ballot droned on, both candidates held their own by picking up a Dewey delegate here, a Hoover or Gannett delegate there. Then came Michigan and the ultimate blow. By voting steadily for favorite son Vandenberg from the start, the delegation had avoided a choice. Vandenberg, a staunch anti-interventionist, had earlier leaned to Taft, but he did not control his delegates, and he doubted Taft's potential as a vote getter. After the fifth ballot the delegates huddled on the floor, polled themselves, and determined to give Willkie 35 votes, Taft 2, and Hoover 1. Why they did so was unclear. Some Taft men later attributed the decision to pressure from eastern bankers on the delegation's small businessmen and auto dealers. Others maintained, probably correctly, that Michigan National Committeeman Frank D. McKay informed his fellow delegates that Willkie would favor Michigan in dispensing federal judgeships. But Vandenberg was most accurate in saying that the delegates leaned toward Willkie, a potential winner, from the beginning.[12]

Whatever their reasons, Michigan's announcement shook the convention, for the remaining delegations sensed Willkie's imminent victory and began to crack. Minnesota gave him an extra vote, Mississippi 2, Missouri 5, New Jersey 6, Oklahoma 13. Oregon left McNary at last and put Willkie within 15 of the magic 501, and Virginia gave him 16 for 502. Pennsylvania then belatedly threw Willkie its 72 votes, but it did not matter. The battle was already over.[13]

•

Taft, a reporter recalled, leaned heavily against a pillar in the lobby of his hotel after the struggle. "Never again! Never again!" he lamented to an aide.[14]

The story was plausible, for the defeat hurt. Yet publicly Taft was magnanimous. After a few hours' sleep he greeted his red-eyed staff the next morning. "I had a lot of plans and ideas I was going to tell you about," he said ruefully. "But I guess we will just forget about it now." He promised to "work just as hard for Willkie as I would for myself." Rejecting vague overtures to become vice-president ("I have a real job in the Senate," he explained privately, "whereas the Vice-President has nothing to do for four years except sit around and inquire about the President's health"), he joined the convention in approving the anomalous selection of McNary, a noninterventionist, as Willkie's running mate. By Monday July 1, Taft was back at work in the Senate.[15]

Martha, however, was a little bitter at first. Joe Pew, she agreed, was "a much maligned man. He isn't very smart, and he hasn't enough decision of character, but he has real ideals for his country and his party." But Sam Pryor, who had helped pack the galleries, was "the most despicable worm I ever saw," and the selection of Willkie confounded the imagination. "Don't blame this recent convention on the two-party system," she wrote Mrs. Dykstra. "If the party hadn't been jittery it couldn't have happened. And the whole thing was unbelievable."[16]

In much the same spirit Taft's allies also speculated on the might-have-beens. If Taft had held his tongue at the dinner with the Reids. If Pryor had been stopped from packing the galleries. If Hoover, Taft's alleged friend, had not been so selfish. If Dewey had been willing early to accept the vice-presidency under Taft. If the press had only been forthright enough to reveal the synthetic character of the telegrams and petitions for Willkie manufactured by what Richard Scandrett acidly called the "down-trodden rich" from Wall Street.[17]

Compelled to answer the unhappy letters of his friends, Taft tried not to second-guess. He praised the work of his aides and of Bricker, stoically recognized the inability of Vandenberg to have done anything about Michigan, dismissed without comment rumors of indiscriminate promises by Willkie's aides. Dewey, he recognized, could not have accepted a deal for the vice-presidency without dismaying his supporters. "He wanted," Taft wrote, "to avoid any suspicion of a deal." To Alice Roosevelt Longworth, Taft concluded: "We were very close to a different result, but I still haven't figured out any way that we could have changed it except by knocking some people down, and exercising fraud or duress." [18]

Yet he too could not resist some might-have-beens. "If Dewey had made up his mind one ballot sooner that he was through," Taft told Scandrett, "I think I should have won." Taft also berated Pew and the Pennsylvania bosses. "If Pennsylvania had come on the fourth ballot as it should have done," he wrote, "and added Michigan to it, I believe that I would have been nominated." Like his advisers, he grumbled about Willkie's propaganda campaign "engineered from Wall Street . . . and by the employment of every advertising agency in the United States." Above all, he bitterly assailed the press. The basic problem, he wrote, "was the public sentiment of the day, fostered and promoted by the newspapers, magazines and columnists, to regard politics as a show in which only an actor can be promoted. That state of mind affected all of the leaders who really should have been for me." [19]

Taft was right in assigning some of the blame to a synthetic propaganda campaign. The Willkie backers used so many phony names in their letters and telegrams to the delegates that Landon, returning to Topeka after the convention, found eighteen mail sacks of his responses to the telegrams marked "Address Unknown." [20] Taft was also correct in insisting that the so-called bosses eventually supported Willkie. Martin, Landon, McKay, Governor Harold Stassen of Minnesota, National Chairman John D. M. Hamilton, and many others had cast their lot with the winner before the decisive ballot. In the end Taft had to rely only on a handful of Southern oligarchs like Creager of Texas, the regulars in Ohio, and a smattering of delegates from the less populous plains and western states.

But he exaggerated the influence of people like Hoover, Dewey, and Pew. Hoover's support, however useful, would not have moved many uncommitted delegates. If Dewey had pulled out earlier, Taft would have gained, but so would Willkie, who in fact proved the ultimate beneficiary of Dewey's strength in the East.[21] And even had Pew wanted to help, which was far from certain, he lacked the power to deliver the delegation as a bloc to anyone. In fact, only the stubbornness of Arthur James prevented an earlier break of the Pennsylvanians for Willkie: 15 favored the winner on the third ballot, 19 on the fourth, and 21 on the fifth. Had Pennsylvania delegates voted their hearts, it is probable that Willkie would have won sooner than he did.

Taft also failed to give proper emphasis to the strong internationalist feelings of the eastern delegates. New Englanders voted 73 to 11 for Willkie on the fifth, the closest ballot, and New York, New Jersey, Maryland, and Delaware supported him 121 to 12. Willkie's margin of 194 to 23 in these states by itself surpassed the advantage of 103 to 58 that Taft held in the South and of 114 to 53 that he enjoyed in his stronghold, the Midwest. What Pew or Dewey or Hoover might have done at particular moments paled in importance in contrast to the rigid sectional alignments that worked to Willkie's favor, and these, in turn, stemmed in part from the revulsion of easterners to events abroad. Had the convention occurred in April, Taft would have had a considerably better chance.

He also refused to concede the damaging effect of his own image. His strategy was so free from technical errors that it proved the only one of his three attempts for the presidency that the second-guessers treated kindly. But he remained himself — sincere, forthright, and lusterless. In reporting his personal qualities, the press could have paid more attention to his courage and to his views on the issues than it did, and in revealing his lack of popularity, the polls may have been imprecise. But probably not very. If his attitude toward the situation in Europe damaged him with easterners, the feeling that he could not beat FDR worried delegates from around the nation. Under such circumstances he had come amazingly close to winning — as close in fact as he ever did.

The Taft who emerged from the ordeal of campaign and convention had changed a little. More than ever he suspected Wall Street financiers, syndicated columnists, mass circulation magazines, and eastern internationalist politicians. These people, in turn, were never to warm to him, for the 1940 convention symbolized the presence of deep sectional fissures within the party, which grew in the campaign, expanded throughout the 1940's, and plagued Taft for the rest of his life.[22]

But he bore no grudges, and he looked forward not back. "The convention," he wrote his aunt, "was a disappointment, but personally Martha and I are better off, and likely to live a longer and happier life." Because his sudden defeat at the hands of Willkie, dark horse and one-time Democrat, was more than a "disappointment," Taft was understating the blow that had struck him. But his self-control in this time of stress astounded observers, and one reporter, who had visited his suite during the final ballot, wrote Martha his impressions. "Quite aside from his great personal charm, which amazed me, and his kindliness," he told her:

I sat there in that final ten minutes while the world went tumultuously mad for a dollar bill and a wisecrack, thinking, "At last I have seen a great man, a great, a gentle, and a gallant man. I slunk away quite sick at heart, to pry into someone else's privacy.[23]

Had this reporter known Taft a long time, he might have recognized that his poise in times of stress was characteristic. He might also have begun to understand that it stemmed more from the iron hold that Taft clamped on his emotions than from some instinctive chivalry. But if Taft acted to preserve his privacy, he still deserved the plaudits that this reporter and others heaped upon him. His grace in defeat, together with the forthrightness he had displayed throughout his futile campaign, represented some of the finer hours of his life.

CHAPTER 16

The Road to Pearl Harbor

A MORE CONVIVIAL MAN than Taft might easily have found ample compensation for other disappointments in the social life of Washington in 1940 and 1941. Since 1939 he and Martha had been sought after by the political elite of the city, and by 1940 they had begun to form some friendships among his colleagues. Taft saw much of Arthur Vandenberg, with whom he often ate lunch in the Senate dining room and who collaborated frequently in sallies against administration foreign policy. Better friends were the Robert La Follette, Jrs. A Progressive from Wisconsin, La Follette stood well to Taft's left on most domestic issues, but the two men served together on the finance and education and labor committees, and they agreed wholeheartedly over foreign policy. The Tafts knew they were accepted; and with all of their children now away, they were free to go out as often as they wished.[1]

Martha particularly welcomed the excitement of Washington, and with characteristic wit she kept her friend Lillian Dykstra informed of her manifold activities. Early in 1940 she described the new house that they rented for the year on Massachusetts Avenue next to the place they had occupied in 1939. "Our house is not so attractive," she confessed. It was cluttered with marble statues:

> They seem to affect Bob so depressingly that I have hidden all that are too large. But I have told him that he will just have to accustom himself to a gory oil painting of "Sunset with Stag" complete in the living room, and a life size adolescent boy in marble selling something (I think it is Ivory soap) on the stair landing.

Martha's friends, who knew she cared little for domestic matters, must have enjoyed picturing the son and daughter-in-law of a President living amid such bizarre furnishings. They knew also that Martha's wit had a sharp point that could poke holes in others. When Mrs. Dykstra wrote for advice on how to dress for an engagement at the White House, Martha used the chance to laugh at the Roosevelts. "About the dress," she advised,

I think you always look darling, and that is more than I will say about Mrs. R., so don't worry. I think unless things are greatly changed for the better since I was last *to* the White House, that you will need long white gloves, and by the time you have bought them you probably won't have enough money left to worry about how the rest of your anatomy is covered.

Getting home isn't so difficult from the White House as from other places, for the President and Mrs. R. will walk out on you, not you on them . . . Don't . . . try to go anywhere ahead of Mrs. R., even to the john, and you will be alright. At least I think you will! [2]

But Taft cared little for the Washington social whirl. He dutifully attended the functions to which he felt he had to go, but the brisk pace that he and Martha set in 1939 and 1940 left him few opportunities to entertain or to let others intrude on his privacy or on the privacy of his family. Though Bob and Martha socialized with the La Follettes, they saw more of older friends like Alice Roosevelt Longworth and the Stanley Rowes and others from Cincinnati than they did of the politicos and their wives. Taft was to serve as a senator for fifteen years, but he died having kept a certain distance from his colleagues.

When Martha left for Murray Bay shortly after the 1940 convention, he grew lonely in Washington. Determined not to live alone in the mausoleum on Massachusetts Avenue, he moved in with Wallace White, a gentle and self-effacing Republican senator from Maine, who was to become the nominal minority leader in 1944. Taft found White's simple mode of life congenial, and he enjoyed hurrying off in the late afternoons to play golf with Charles McNary or with anyone who would join him on the first tee. But he still wrote Martha ("my darling Martha") every two or three days and confessed to her that "I do miss you terribly and feel as I were in prison." [3] The summer of 1940, like many thereafter when

Taft was trapped by senatorial duties in Washington, was often hot, grim, and lonely, and because of the political confrontations of the time it left him unhappy when it was over. The fierce struggles that followed in 1941 left him no respite either. For Taft, the eighteen months between the convention at Philadelphia and the Japanese attack on Pearl Harbor in December 1941 offered little save disappointment.

•

The first struggle, to elect Wendell Willkie in 1940, caught Taft with divided mind. Taft not only resented the methods of Willkie and his managers, but wondered privately whether the nominee were qualified. Willkie, he told Uncle Horace, was a "'very able man," but "he is of the salesman type, anxious to make a good impression on those who are immediately in front of him. Whether he will really stand up against pressure I have some doubt." To Thomas E. Dewey he added:

> I feel that the campaign has demonstrated one thing so far — that is that no convention should nominate a candidate who has never been engaged in a political campaign before. I am sure that Mr. Willkie has made a good many minor mistakes which we would not have made. I don't have much confidence in my judgment as to public opinion, and it may be that wise-cracking which keeps the nominee on the front page every day really gets results, but I rather doubt it.[4]

Still, Willkie had won the Republican nomination, and Taft knew his duty. "I am afraid you do Mr. Willkie an injustice," he wrote a constituent. "'I believe he can present the case against the New Deal better than anyone else, and will do a good job in cleaning out the chair-warmers when he is elected." To Harold Burton, who was running as Ohio's Republican Senate nominee, Taft added: "I don't think Willkie is the strongest possible Republican candidate in Ohio, but I do feel he will put on the kind of campaign which will be successful here, and assist the rest of you on the ticket." [5] Taft was careful not to tell casual acquaintances of his doubts about Willkie, and both he and Martha stumped actively for him during most of October.[6]

But Franklin D. Roosevelt won again, 27,300,000 to 22,300,000, and even took Ohio. Genuinely surprised, Taft groped for an explanation. Relief spending, he said, helped the Democrats, as did Willkie's failure to work with the Republican organization. The labor vote, which Taft reckoned as 100 per cent Democratic, struck him as most damaging of all. But throughout his letters Taft also implied that Willkie's refusal to confront New Deal domestic policy drove him to defeat. Taft emerged from the campaign more at odds than ever with the eastern wing of the party.[7]

Taft had permitted his personal view of the issues to cloud his perspective. Willkie had blundered on occasion and had offended some of the organization Republicans. But Roosevelt, who led the public opinion polls from the start, probably would have beaten anyone. If Willkie, whose 1940 score ran 5.6 million votes and 8 per cent ahead of that of Alfred Landon in 1936, had pursued the line which Taft suggested, he might have done better among non-interventionists, farmers in the Plains, and German-Americans. But he probably would have suffered even heavier losses elsewhere. Given Taft's lack of support in the East and his poor showing in the public opinion polls before the convention, it was unlikely that he would have received as many votes as Willkie — and probable that he would have fared considerably worse.[8] But at least Taft did not have to take the blame. He was free to fight again another day.

.

Taft continued his battle against Roosevelt's domestic program in Congress, for he still regarded domestic policy as the major front. Again he backed amendments to the National Labor Relations Act, introduced bills to repeal Roosevelt's authority to issue greenbacks and devalue the currency, criticized confusion in the federal bureaucracy, and demanded the return of relief administration to the states. Maximum-hour legislation, he said, should permit more exemptions. The government should provide "medical aid to the needy," but through grants to states instead of through a grandiose federal plan of health insurance. And Congress ought to study federal housing programs in order to eliminate bureaucratic overlapping.[9]

He also opposed federal aid for education, an issue which by

1941 was beginning to divide the Congress. It was true, he said, that states provided widely differing amounts of money per pupil, but it was not the job of the federal government to equalize standards. "If that government is going to guarantee equality in education," he said, "why not guarantee equality in wealth and economic condition? . . . the right to govern one's self badly is just as much an essential of freedom in a democracy as the right to govern one's self well." Taft deeply doubted the wisdom of letting the federal government try to remedy social problems throughout the United States.[10]

As always, Taft focused on the budget. In the two years before Pearl Harbor, the government spent billions for defense and began at last to drag the nation out of the depression, but in the process it incurred what Taft regarded as intolerably large deficits. Alarmed, he opposed government loans abroad, voted with eight others against increased appropriations for parity payments to farmers, and insisted on cuts of at least $1.5 billion in domestic welfare programs. Roosevelt, he wrote Martha, "is so much for defense and so anxious to keep the newspapers on his side that something might be done." [11]

Economy was not enough; taxes must be increased by at least $5 billion. Consistently speaking for the needs of small business, Taft denounced Treasury Secretary Henry Morgenthau, Jr.'s plan to limit corporate profits to 6 per cent, and he opposed more progressive income taxes. Instead, he demanded a reduction in personal exemptions and a 10 per cent across-the-board increase in personal income taxes. By early 1941 he was even leaning toward a federal sales tax with essential items exempted. When the Senate at last approved a tax increase of $3.5 billion in the fall of 1941, the largest single revenue bill in American history to that time, Taft voted for it, but complained that it did not raise enough.[12]

By April 1941 inflationary pressures led the administration to consider the more extreme move of price control, and it placed Leon Henderson, an economist, in charge of an Office of Price Administration and Civilian Supply. Far from applauding the move, Taft erupted in protest. Price fixing, he said, must not be left to the "whim of an economic theorist" like Henderson. Roosevelt should seek statutory authority, and Congress, in turn, should carefully define the powers of such an agency, limit them to "basic commodities and to those closely related to defense," and place the agency in the hands of a five-man board instead of a single administrator. Roosevelt's plan of regulating prices through executive fiat, Taft said with characteristic and calculated hyperbole, was "the most outrageous power grab which this country has ever seen." [13]

Yet Taft stopped short of opposing all controls, and in so doing he was closer to the administration than to many senatorial colleagues. When Congress finally began to consider controls in the fall of 1941, he called for a five-man board that would be required to hold hearings before imposing anything more stringent than sixty-day controls and demanded a statutory termination of price control in January 1943. But he joined administration spokesmen in opposing special concessions to farmers, and he courageously joined a minority of thirty-seven, who tried to impose meaningful controls on farm commodities. After failing in his attempts to amend the bill, he voted for it a month after Pearl Harbor, but he agreed with its critics that the special status given farm products would intensify inflationary pressure. In his concern he proved correct.[14]

Taft's views on domestic policy had changed little in late 1940 and 1941, and except on the subject of price control, he fought the President as consistently as before. But in opposing inflation, he was more determined than many of his colleagues. When the attack on Pearl Harbor forced America into the war, he was ready to assume the lead in carrying on his struggle.

•

Given a choice, Taft would have paid as little attention as possible to foreign policy. But Hitler was stepping up his attacks on Britain, and the world teetered on the brink of catastrophe. He had no choice.

Indeed, Taft had barely recovered from the disappointment of the 1940 convention when he plunged again into his personal war against war. Roosevelt had enraged many Republicans by nominating Henry L. Stimson and Frank Knox as secretaries of war and navy respectively. Taft approved of Knox, the Republican vice-presidential nominee in 1936, but Stimson had called for universal military training, repeal of the neutrality act, convoying by American naval vessels of merchant ships carrying supplies to England, and even for American assumption of British bases so they would not fall to the enemy. Determined to play a personal role, Taft secured special permission to question Stimson before the Senate Military Affairs Committee. Amid high drama and tension, the committee came together July 2, 1940.

Stimson, a widely respected elder statesman, had been secretary of war once before — under William Howard Taft, whom he had loyally backed in the 1912 campaign. Stimson had then served three other Republican Presidents, most recently Herbert Hoover as secretary of state. When Taft's turn to interrogate arrived, Stimson looked up at the son of his former chief and joked: "Have you got Wendell Willkie somewhere around?" The audience laughed. But not Taft. "I do not know that I have ever seen such a difficult problem for me to decide as this one," he responded gravely. "It is not any laughing matter to me." He then pursued a line of questioning that left no doubt of his seriousness.

Taft first tried to corner his adversary by asking if he really believed a cabinet member could "immunize" himself from administration foreign policies. Stimson agreed that one could not, then said how happy he was to answer such questions — "for not only personal but reasons of heredity." Furthermore, Stimson added placatingly, he was no longer sure America would have to take over British bases. Ignoring the allusion to his father, Taft tried to get Stimson to confess a desire to intervene on Britain's behalf. "As I understand you," Taft broke in:

> You are in favor of joining in the war just as soon as you figure that the British have no longer a chance, but you think that they are not as far gone as you then thought, and because of that . . . you think it is not necessary.

Stimson was fighting his temper. "That is not quite a fair way of putting it," he responded. He then insisted that he had said nothing about American intervention in the war.

Taft then demanded to know if Stimson still favored repeal of the neutrality acts that kept American ships from carrying goods to belligerents. When Stimson replied in effect that he did, Taft followed with a series of "what if" questions. What if a German plane sank an American ship carrying supplies to the Allies? Would that "almost inevitably lead us into war?" No, replied Stimson, it depended on the situation. What if the British needed credits? Would you favor granting them? Stimson grew heated. "That is not fair cross examination . . . It is not fair, Senator Taft; it is not fair for you to try to make me say now what the manifold conditions are which would govern such a decision."

Taft pressed on. Wasn't it true, he asked rhetorically, that Stimson favored American entrance into the war to "prevent the defeat of England and the destruction of the British fleet?" Again, Stimson balked. It depended, he said, on the state of American defenses at the time. He complained:

> I am rather saddened by the fact that you, of all people, should try to make such an unfair deduction. I have said so many times —

> Taft: But, Mr. Secretary, you have repeatedly stated it and it is no unfair deduction. I think upon examination of your own mind you will find in your own mind that you have repeatedly stated that our interests involve the preservation of the British fleet, and earlier in your statement you made that statement.

> Stimson: At present it does. At present it does. Three years from now it may not.

> Taft: Well, that may be true; anything may happen in three years from now.

> Stimson: Until you know; until you put in all of those conditions, you have got to refrain from asking dogmatic questions and I have to refrain from answering such questions.[15]

Other senators then interrupted, and Taft soon gave up trying to pin Stimson down. The battle of words had changed no one's mind. But the exchange revealed Taft at his best — and at his most infuriating. He had come well prepared and had forced his adversary to have "pangs," as Stimson confessed later, about some of his evasive answers. He had also adroitly used the dramatic occasion to show that Stimson's plan would inevitably tempt Germany to attack American shipping. But his depth of feeling also caused him to display a sharpness in questioning that was to become characteristic of him on other issues in the future and that led many opponents to regard him as rude, cold, unchivalrous, and as Stimson put it "dogmatic." Stimson, dismayed, thought Taft's questioning not "worthy of a son of William Taft," and another partisan observer, Supreme Court Justice Felix Frankfurter, recalled the episode distastefully twelve years later. Frankfurter wrote:

A man may have a fine reasoning machine and yet have disastrous premises. That's true of Bob — plus a total want of what I call the poetic sensibilities, sensitiveness to the feelings and needs of other people. He is not the only high standard product of our school [Harvard Law] of first-rate reasoning capacity, but without insight into the nature of man and the great current of society . . . his cross-examination of Mr. Stimson (imputing all sorts of motives to Stimson) . . . finished me with him on other than intellectual social grounds.[16]

If Taft was cowed by such hostility, he gave little sign of it. Instead, he cast a futile vote against Stimson a week later and took the occasion to accuse the administration of conspiring to go to war. German victory, he admitted, would "mean a world in which force had triumphed and international good faith had vanished." But better to live in such a world than fight. War, he said, would mean the "death and wounding of our boys, the terrible destruction of life and property, the practical establishment of a dictatorship in this country through arbitrary powers granted to the President, and financial and economic collapse. Nor do I think that our intervention in Europe can permanently solve the European problems any more than it did in 1919." America, he responded to criticisms from his sister Helen, is a land of 130,000,000 people. "It is not selfish in putting the interests of those people ahead of any prejudices or sympathies with other peoples." [17]

These beliefs motivated his most ardent stand on foreign policy in 1940: opposition to the draft bill that reached the Senate floor in August. The newsman William S. White, who later knew him well, observed that Taft's own failure to fight in the trenches in

World War I caused him to shrink from conscripting others in time of peace. Such feelings may have mattered, but at the root of his thinking lay his faith in individual liberty and in equality of opportunity. The avenues to success, he said revealingly, are "persistence and thoroughness." But the draft is like roulette. It cruelly cuts into a young man's career, deprives him of his freedom of choice, leaves him behind in the competitive struggle with his fellows, and turns society into a garrison state.[18]

Taft did not stop there. American defense, he said, ought to rely on a strong air force and a two-ocean navy, and the army should be composed of volunteers, not conscripts. If the pay for soldiers were increased to $1000 per year and if a $40 per month food and clothing allowance were added, the army could easily attract 750,000 men. The government could set up inexpensive summer training facilities for high school or college graduates, thus creating an additional reserve force of 200,000 per year. Such an army, Taft believed, would be large enough because its job should be defense, not warfare abroad. Germany, Italy, and Japan, he admitted, have "at least a temporary alignment." But "I do not think that any of these nations will attack the United States, and I believe that even if they do our present forces can defend us against an attack across 3,000 miles of water."

In the frightening late summer of 1940 the Senate rejected, 55 to 32, Taft's amendment limiting the peacetime army to 500,000 volunteers and 1,500,000 reservists, and the final bill then passed the next day, 58 to 31. It placed 12,000,000 Americans in the draft pool and made them subject to one year of service. Taft had struggled in vain against a peacetime draft, and he despaired to Martha that "I am very pessimistic about the future of the country — we are certainly being dragged towards war and bankruptcy and socialism all at once. Let's hope I'm wrong." [19]

His stand had offended many Republicans and old friends, who wondered at what they considered his callousness to England's plight. Uncle Horace complained that he could no longer talk with Bob and Martha on the subject. Others, more bold, presumed to write, and one old classmate dared to accuse the senator of playing politics. Taft shot back that "it would be a good deal easier to be for the conscription bill than against it. I suggest that

the next time you write me you do so a little more politely or perhaps you will never get an answer." The friend then apologized,
and Taft cooled off. "After being called the tool of Hitler and a
fifth columnist," he wrote candidly, "I have become a little too
sensitive." But he refused to change his mind. "The real purpose
of the draft bill," he wrote during his campaign for re-election in
1944, "was to make the country war-conscious and more inclined to
enter the European war." [20]

•

In the fall of 1940, Taft kept up his attack. He tried unsuccessfully to limit funds for foreign loans, criticized the "destroyer
deal" that provided England with American warships in exchange
for British bases, and demanded that Roosevelt create a War Resources Administration to coordinate defense planning. By December Taft was quietly encouraging, though declining to speak
for, the staunchly anti-interventionist America First Committee.[21]

At the same time England was pleading for more help, and Roosevelt was responding warmly. The answer, the President declared, was lend-lease. Like a friendly neighbor extending an old
garden hose to put out a fire, the United States would lease used
equipment to Britain. America would help quench the fire before
it spread — and later get the hose (maybe a new one) back.

It was an appealing simile, and Americans told the pollers they
approved. But the anti-interventionists in Congress predicted disaster from the lend-lease bill. "The wickedest piece of legislation
that has ever been presented to the American Congress," the venerable Hiram Johnson stormed. A bill to "plow under every
fourth American boy," Senator Burton K. Wheeler of Montana
declared. Lend-lease, they recognized, might lead to American
naval escort of convoys across the Atlantic and provoke attacks
from German planes and submarines. As in 1917, America would
have to fight to protect expensive supplies.[22]

Sensing Roosevelt's intentions, Taft came out for cash loans to
Canada and England (providing they offered collateral) as early as
December 11. "I should not like to stand on a complete refusal of
aid," he explained privately. "I am afraid it puts us in the indefen-
sible position, in which we will be accused of putting dollars ahead

of patriotism." [23] This position marked him as more moderate than colleagues who disapproved of all signs of favoritism in the European war.

But he still was a pole apart from the President. Failing to understand the passions of total war, Taft hoped the cash loans — $1.55 billion the first year and more later if needed — would enable the British to hold out long enough to reach terms with the Germans. Meanwhile, he envisioned that the devious, unpredictable Roosevelt would be denied the excuse to escort convoys across the ocean. Taft occasionally confessed his dismay at the rhetoric of some of his noninterventionist colleagues, and he conceded privately that they had "overdone" the charge that the bill gave Roosevelt dictatorial powers. But he dismissed other objections to their arguments. The bill "certainly authorizes him to take us into the midst of the war," he insisted, "and once we are there his powers will be unlimited . . . before we get through with that war the rights of private property in the United States will be to a large extent destroyed." [24]

Taft was not only deeply opposed to lend-lease but willing to speak publicly for peace at almost any price. "I detest every utterance of Mr. Hitler and every action of the German government in the last eight years," he told the Senate in February. "I do not contend that German victory would make no difference to the United States." But "if we enter the war today in order to save the British Empire, we will be involved in war for the rest of our lives. If the English Channel is our frontier, and this is our war, then we will have to defend it for years to come . . . War is a vain policy, except a war fought at home to establish or preserve the freedom of a nation." To a friend he added wistfully, "I don't see why the world isn't big enough to contain all kinds of different ways of life." And in the Senate he went further. "War," he concluded with painful clarity, "is worse even than a German victory." [25]

Taft spoke boldly and fought resourcefully. Relying on Herbert Hoover, still a mentor on matters of war and peace, he helped devise amendments to the lend-lease bill. He scored Roosevelt: "The words of his mouth," he said, "were smoother than butter, but war was in his heart." He tried to force his foes, as he had tried to force Stimson, to state their real intentions. And he even resorted to sarcasm, an approach rare in his exhortations. "Are we to send American guns to Europe stamped, like a refrigerator sold on credit, 'This is the property of the United States Government' . . . lending war equipment is much like lending chewing gum. We certainly do not want the same gum back. [Laughter] . . . The very title of the bill is a fraud." [26]

But Taft knew he was beaten. His opponents denied any intention of becoming involved in the war, labeled the bill number 1776, and simply evaded answering whether it would lead to the naval escort of convoys. After defeating, 51 to 38, his key amendment, which said that no clause should be construed as giving the President additional power to send forces abroad, they passed the bill with minor changes. Taft joined sixteen other Republicans, thirteen Democrats, and one Independent against the bill. But forty-nine Democrats, ten Republicans, and one Independent pushed it across, 60 to 31. On March 11 Roosevelt signed it, and on March 12 he called for $7 billion to implement it. The battle was over. [27]

As Roosevelt had hoped, lend-lease became England's right arm. But it was also the decisive step toward the escort of convoys and then to shooting between Germans and Americans. Martha was so irate when the League of Women Voters backed the President that she resigned her membership in April, and Taft began working behind the scenes to oust interventionist Republicans from power on the national committee. Seldom one to change his mind, he still insisted three years later on the wisdom of his position. [28]

·

After the passage of lend-lease in March, the United States seemed to slide unavoidably toward war. In April American naval vessels intensified their patrolling of shipping lanes and began warning British warships of Axis vessels. In July American forces occupied Iceland. In August the draft was extended an additional year and a half, and Roosevelt, after sailing to a secret rendezvous off Newfoundland, cosigned with Prime Minister Winston Churchill of Britain the idealistic principles of the Atlantic Charter. By September American naval vessels were escorting Allied merchant convoys on the Atlantic, tracking submarines, and radioing their positions to British warships. On September 4, a German submarine fired two torpedoes at the American destroyer *Greer*, provoking depth bombs in retaliation. Roosevelt concealed the tracking activities of the *Greer* from the public, righteously assailed the Germans, and called, in effect, for a shoot-on-sight policy on the Atlantic. The President then demanded permission to arm merchant ships and to send them into previously forbidden war zones off the European coast. Well before the attack on Pearl Harbor December 7, American blood had been shed on the Atlantic.

For Taft these were profoundly discouraging months, yet he refused to give up. Indeed, in May he was stressing more than ever that America was becoming imperialistic. Suppose, he said, that the United States did help to crush Hitler. What then? Taft's unhappy answer was that a new age of American "imperialism" promoted by Henry Luce, Henry Stimson, and their kind would follow. These people, he charged, "seem to contemplate an Anglo-American alliance perpetually ruling the world . . . Such imperialism is wholly foreign to our ideals of democracy and freedom. It is not our manifest destiny or our natural destiny." [29] Taft's argument was to appear often in his speeches during and after the war. Still later, by one of those ironies of history, it was to appeal strongly to critics of American expansionism in the 1960's and 1970's.

Taft also attacked each new move of the administration. When rumors circulated of a decision to escort British convoys, he assailed Roosevelt for deceiving the public about the consequences of lend-lease. When America occupied Iceland, he branded the action as unconstitutional. "The people," he grumbled to John Hollister, "seem to regard Iceland as an island off the coast of Maine. What concerns me is that if the President can do that in Iceland, he can certainly do it with Ireland, and England itself." [30]

In June, Germany invaded the Soviet Union, and Taft dared again to hope that England could negotiate a peace. The attack also gave him a chance to display his feelings about the Soviets. The Soviet Union, he said, was "as much of an aggressor as Germany." Stalin was "the most ruthless dictator in the world," and "the victory of communism in the world would be far more dan-

gerous to the United States than the victory of fascism." Taft qualified this statement by arguing that "from the point of view of
ideology there is no choice" [between communism and fascism],
and his primary purpose was to ridicule the notion that aiding the
Allies, who were now joined with the Soviets, would assist the
cause of democracy. But his remarks also revealed a deep antipathy to communism that stemmed directly from his faith in individual liberty and free enterprise. This antipathy was to color his
view of world affairs for the rest of his life.[31]

Taft was working too hard in Washington to go to Murray Bay
in the summer of 1941. He tried unsuccessfully to undercut the
draft extension with an alternative plan to extend it six months
and assailed the President for meeting with Churchill. Their
agreement, he said, seemed a "declaration that the United States
and England propose to run the world . . . I am inclined to think
that historians will regard it as a British-American alliance."
Profoundly upset by Roosevelt's misleading account of the *Greer*
incident ("grossly misstated," he called it), he joined a Senate
minority against a supplementary appropriation for lend-lease in
October and against the arming of merchant ships and abolition of
forbidden combat zones in November. The President, he wrote to
a friend in late November, probably opposes the sending of American troops abroad, but "he is like a boy playing with tin
soldiers." [32]

The attack on Pearl Harbor two weeks later surprised Taft as
much as anyone else. Like most Americans, he had regarded Europe as the more likely theater of war, and he had said little about
Asian policy save to question the wisdom of strong economic sanctions that might force the Japanese to exert pressure on the Philippines. Pleading ignorance of the facts, he had not even demanded
congressional direction of Asian policy, but had left it to the executive branch.[33] Once the attack was made, however, he had to respond. With a heavy heart Taft supported war against Japan and
Germany.

·

"One of the best fellows in the world," Uncle Horace had described his nephew privately in September 1941. But "dead wrong
on our foreign policy." [34]

Many Americans agreed with Uncle Horace. Taft, they sensed, simply found foreign affairs irritating. "I may make a foreign policy broadcast about August 29," he wrote to Martha in Murray Bay in 1941. "But I am more concerned at the moment about taxes and inflation." Late in November he still felt the same way. "Nine years out of ten," he wrote, "the fundamental issue is one of domestic policy, and we ought not to permit the breaking up of a party on any question of foreign policy." [35] He had involved himself in foreign problems, but only because events gave him no choice, and he maintained the point of view of a man who cared much more deeply about what was happening at home. As a consequence, he had consistently underestimated German power and overestimated the potential for a truce in Europe.

His unemotional attitude toward Great Britain shocked even his admirers. "I feel very strongly that Hitler's defeat is not vital to us," he wrote Scandrett in January 1941. "Even the collapse of England is to be preferred to participation for the rest of our lives in European wars." Americans, he added in September, "ought to determine their course entirely on what they believe to be best for the United States, whether foreign nations like it or disapprove of it." And speaking in Ohio the same month, he talked of the epithet "isolationist" that critics were hurling at him. "If isolationism means isolation from European wars," he announced proudly, "I am an isolationist." [36] At least since 1919, Taft had wasted little emotion on European civilization, and Hitler's depredations failed to change his mind. Until the Axis powers moved toward the Western Hemisphere, he insisted, America should keep herself free from involvement abroad.

His friends found him deaf to suggestion. A mutual friend asked Scandrett whether Taft was acting on poor counsel from advisers. No, Scandrett replied sadly, he thinks "under his own steam . . . I have argued with him by the hour, but have not yet been able to make a dent on him." Taft's friends had always admired his certitude and his courage. On foreign policy, however, some of them were finding him opinionated rather than informed, dogmatic rather than thoughtful, stubborn rather than open-minded.[37]

Even Pearl Harbor failed to change his mind. Addressing a

group of business executives in Chicago two weeks afterward, he still held out dim hopes for a negotiated peace that would save America the anguish of sending troops abroad. Four months later he told a friend that "we need not have become involved in the present war." Any nation with a strong army and navy, he proclaimed over the radio in July 1942, can and should stay at peace. The attack on Pearl Harbor, he admitted, forced America to fight in Asia, but could it be that Roosevelt's "policy of bluff" had driven Japan to desperation? In 1951, Taft looked at a divided world and still concluded he had been right. The New York *Herald Tribune,* he wrote, has "never forgiven me for the position which I then took that we should maintain a policy of neutrality in the war between England and Germany. It is almost impossible to guess what would have happened if we had pursued that policy. I don't see how we could be any worse off than we are today." [38]

Taft and his fellow noninterventionists deserved a better hearing than their critics, or later historians, tried to give them. He had at least been forthright and unafraid to fight in an increasingly unpopular cause. Forced by 1941 to choose between war and possible German victory over England, he did not evade the question by claiming England would win or by maintaining that lend-lease would keep America out, but openly opted for peace. Given the evidence of growing support for intervention, he showed political courage — enough that his statements lived to frustrate his presidential ambitions for the rest of his life. In raising questions about Roosevelt's expansive interpretation of the powers of the commander in chief and in calling attention to the administration's repeated evasions, Taft and his allies also focused on basic issues that Roosevelt's fondest admirers later found difficult to ignore. Taft demanded that Congress play a major role in formulating foreign policy and that the United States avoid moral crusades. And though his charges failed to deter the President, it was not because they raised bogus issues but because the Nazi scourge led the American people to settle for a pragmatic approach instead of adhering to the niceties of constitutional processes.

Taft may have been correct in the long run in some of his assumptions about the European war. Because Germany sapped itself on the icy plains of the Soviet Union, he could always argue plausibly that England would have survived without American intervention. And because a more neutral American policy on the Atlantic might have appeased the Nazis (who in 1941 did not want war with the United States), he could also maintain that Hitler might have pursued a policy of peaceful coexistence with America until the difficulties of holding onto extensive territorial acquisitions overwhelmed his successors and restored the old balance of power. Meanwhile the United States could have remained safely at peace.[39]

Yet Taft's critics also had a strong case. Because he was fixed on preserving liberty at home, he made little effort to inform himself of facts abroad. He refused to consult others, and his speeches, which merely elaborated on those of 1939, showed little of the research that he often brought to domestic matters. The same opponents who thought twice before challenging the facts and figures that adorned his remarks on fiscal matters did not have to take him seriously concerning foreign policy. Some dismissed him as a mindless isolationist, and many others ignored his exaggerated talk about the coming of socialism and the destruction of private property. They always would.

Taft also appeared inconsistent. Why, his critics asked, did he favor loans to help the Finns fight the Soviets in 1940, yet oppose the destroyer deal, the Atlantic Charter, and lend-lease? His answer was, of course, that aid to the Finns was cheap, and that it would not lead America to war. But in 1940 and 1941 the Nazis posed a much more frightening threat to the balance of power, indeed to Western civilization, than did the Soviets. Taft's instinctive anticommunism showed that he was more of a moralist about international relations than his cool objections to messianism suggested. He was always to distress people who called for an approach to foreign policy based on rational considerations of the balance of power.

Indeed, this very reluctance to think in terms of power made his position vulnerable by 1941. His defense of neutrality appeared reasonable to constituents in 1939. But after Germany overran France and the Low Countries, increasing numbers of Americans came to regard Hitler as an insatiable tyrant who thrived on appeasement. Under such frightening circumstances Americans grew alarmed and anxious, they refused to rest easy with the thought of a Nazi-dominated Europe, and they rejected what they considered to be the callous nationalism of Taft and his noninterventionist allies. So his appeals for restraint, for peace, and for a policy of continental defense, however sensible in the 1920's or early 1930's, failed utterly to counteract the fear and the revulsion that captured Americans amid the awesome Nazi advances between 1939 and 1941.

CHAPTER 17

Advancing in the Senate,

1942–1944

For millions of soldiers, World War II meant combat in faraway places such as Corregidor, Guadalcanal, and Saipan, Normandy, Bastogne, and Okinawa. At home the war meant economic recovery at last. Factories reopened their doors, and great scientific and industrial complexes developed such advances as the use of penicillin and blood plasma and such new products as B-17's, radar, and Victory ships. A mysterious complex of wizardry arose at Oak Ridge, Tennessee; Los Alamos, New Mexico; and other shrouded installations. War also meant a host of irritating minor sacrifices: margarine instead of butter, fish instead of beef, high prices, travel restrictions, whiskey and cigarette shortages, and ration books. It meant anxiety about sons and husbands abroad, the dread of the telegram, the grief when it came.[1]

Taft had to suffer many of these uncertainties of war. Two of his sons, Bob, Jr., and Lloyd, served as naval officers in the Pacific, Mediterranean, and Atlantic; and Horace, who was only sixteen years old at the time of Pearl Harbor, joined the army in 1943, rose to the rank of sergeant, and joined his brothers in the Pacific theater in 1945. (Bill, rejected by the services, served with Intelligence in the Pentagon.) None was injured, but Bob and Martha shared the worries of thousands of parents, and Bob may have found compensation for his anxieties by waging repeated attacks on the way the army and navy assigned personnel. In the spring and summer of 1945, when American fire bombs were devastating Japan, Taft urged the administration to offer concessions (including letting Japan keep Formosa) that would give the enemy the face he needed to come to terms. His revulsion against war could alone have prompted this attitude, but the thought of losing one or more of his sons in an invasion of the Japanese home islands may also have counted.

The war years brought death and sickness to various members of his family. In January 1943, Uncle Horace died peacefully at the age of eighty-one. Two months later Martha had to have an operation to correct thrombosis in the veins of her leg. And in May 1943, Taft's mother, who had suffered from circulatory ailments for more than a year, died and was buried beside her husband in Arlington National Cemetery. Taft had to worry about the health of his Aunt Frances ("Fannie") Edwards, his father's only sister. She had long lived in California and had seen little of the Tafts. But by 1943 she was widowed and suffering from arteriosclerosis, and it fell to Taft to arrange for her care and to handle her finances. Until her death in 1950, he performed these familial tasks.[2]

Taft did not allow himself to be distressed for long by these misfortunes. Besides, other events in the family brought satisfaction. In January 1942, Blanca Noel Taft, Bob, Jr.'s wife, provided assurance that the family name would endure by giving birth to Robert Alphonso Taft, II, and in 1943 she had a daughter, Sarah. Later in 1943 Barbara Bradfield, a Michigan girl whom Bill had married in 1942, made Taft a grandfather for the third time. Taft enjoyed both his daughters-in-law, especially Barbara. She and Bill lived with the Tafts for some months after their marriage. He also saw more of his brother Charlie, who had taken a wartime post with the State Department and who lived with him for a time in 1943. And he rejoiced at the accomplishments of his son Horace, who was graduated from Taft School in 1943. "Besides playing the piano, singing in the glee club, and acting in the play," he wrote Aunt Fannie, "Horace was second in a large class, delivered the valedictory address, and took the first prize in the essay contest and in the debating contest."[3] Bob, like his father, had encouraged his sons to do their best, and Horace had obviously listened.

The war years also gave Taft the satisfaction of watching new senators strengthen the antiadministration coalition on domestic policy. Two of these, Republicans Ralph O. Brewster of Maine and Wayland D. ("Curly") Brooks of Illinois, had arrived even before the war, and a more influential Republican, Eugene D. Millikin of Colorado, was sworn in two weeks after Pearl Harbor. Within three years the contemplative Millikin was to be Taft's most reliable comrade in struggles against New Deal fiscal policies. After 1942, Taft could rely on two other Republicans, Homer Ferguson of Michigan and Kenneth S. Wherry of Nebraska (who unseated the venerable George Norris), and on newly elected conservative Democrats like James O. Eastland of Mississippi and John L. McClellan of Arkansas. Taft also grew closer to La Follette and to Burton K. Wheeler, a veteran Democrat from Montana, who had joined in the crusade against intervention. It was ironic that Taft, who was known for his focus on domestic matters and for his denunciations of the New Deal, became friendly with these two men — veteran senators who were not even Republicans. But La Follette and Wheeler resembled him in having the courage of their convictions, in fighting Roosevelt's foreign policy, and in denouncing the power of Wall Street and eastern monopolists. These personal ties showed the depth of his feelings in the war against war before 1941. They suggested also that in developing friendships in the Senate he was moved neither by cronyism — for he remained cool and unconvivial — nor even by partisanship, but by cautiously discovering who among his colleagues could be trusted to fight for the causes he held dear.

Bob and Martha also felt more settled in Washington than they had earlier. In 1941 they had rented again — this time an unfurnished house at 1688 Thirty-first Street in Georgetown. Built in the heavy Victorian style of the 1880's, it showed the wear of time, and its dark red brick exterior, faded green shutters, and steep mansard roof were uninviting. Inside, guests encountered a dark dining room, an appallingly steep staircase to the second and third floors, and a large kitchen with an unsightly hot water heater and an old coal stove, which no one had bothered to remove. In the basement an ornery coal furnace — often stoked by Taft himself — strained against drafts that swept through the high-ceilinged rooms and hallways. Though gas heaters and fireplaces (one in each of the fifteen rooms) managed to keep the place comfortable in winter, and though the high ceilings were a boon during the sweltering summers, the house lacked the grace and amenities of Sky Farm.

Forced to find furnishings, Martha made a few basic purchases and supplemented these with heterogeneous pieces begged and borrowed from friends and relatives. Nothing was fashionable, but the chairs and sofas were comfortable, and Martha and her seamstress did their best to cover them with cheerful chintzes, and to place good reading lights everywhere to counter the darkness of some of the rooms. Martha also decorated the walls with magnificent prints — primarily landscapes — collected by her father, and brightened the hall with a striking Japanese tapestry portraying Columbus and Isabella. A portrait of Martha's great-grandfather graced the drawing room, and an unremarkable painting of Bob's father looked down on guests in the dining room. In the evenings, candlelight revealed a benign chief justice while concealing the deficiencies of the painter.

Financially, the Tafts had no worries, and they could easily have afforded more palatial accommodations. But Sky Farm was always their real home, they placed little emphasis on style, and "1688" offered many advantages. Less than a block from Dumbarton Oaks and Rock Creek Park, the neighborhood was quiet and attractive, and they were near many friends and colleagues. The dining room easily accommodated the large black-tie dinner parties they liked to give occasionally, and candle-lit old damask and silver, fresh flowers, shining brass, and blazing log fires provided a pleasing background for parties in the winter. Day-to-day living was also practical. A couple, Rheba and Frank, cooked, served, and looked after the downstairs; "Nurse," who had remained with the family since Bill and Bob, Jr., had been babies, took care of the upstairs. The second floor had an attractive sitting room, where Taft worked or talked with Martha and close friends in the evening, and several bedrooms were usually available for traveling family or friends who passed through town. The Tafts were at ease in this house. In 1945 they bought it, and it remained their Washington home until Bob's death eight years later.[4]

With so much to be thankful for in his personal and political life, Taft might have slackened the fearsome pace he had maintained since coming to the Senate in 1939. To a very limited degree, he did. He and Martha found more time to entertain the La Follettes, Wheelers, Millikins, and others, and he occasionally set his briefcase aside in the evenings to read a detective story. He also missed few opportunities to escape for golf, which he still played with the dogged determination that marked all his activities, and at which even then, in his early fifties, he sometimes scored in the 80's. Indeed, the regimen of golf, plus brief sojourns at Murray Bay, enabled him to retain the perfect health he had always enjoyed and to arrive at the Senate each day with a zest and vigor that never seemed to flag.

Yet Taft could not relax for long. He refused to see the war as a time for political peace at home, and he insisted that the duty of the opposition was to oppose. "Criticism in time of war," he said two weeks after Pearl Harbor, "is essential to the maintenance of any kind of democratic government." Foreseeing a war of "five to six years" and a national debt of $150 billion (it grew, in fact, to $258 billion by July 1945), he demanded the end in 1942 of the WPA, the National Youth Administration, and the Civilian Conservation Corps. He also called for an investigation of the Pearl Harbor attack. When his cousin Hulbert called in the *Times-Star* for a moratorium on politics, Taft dispatched an angry letter. "To stifle criticism of the administration," he insisted, "is very bad, because I see no other way in which the conduct of the war may be improved, and if it isn't improved, I don't know what may happen." [5]

Taft also argued that New Dealers were surreptitiously advancing their theories under the cover of war. "The administration," he complained to Herbert Hoover, "is still busy asking for every power they can think of, whether they need it or not, and I am making myself unpopular by objecting." When his cousin William Semple asked for financial advice, Taft told him to invest in real estate. "Liquidity," he said, is "greatly exaggerated. The truth is that today there is no real capital market . . . With the present attitude of the government toward business, and the long war which we face, I am not at all sure that [corporations] are necessarily going to survive, at least with anything like the financial structure they now have." [6]

In this frame of mind he set out in 1942 to amend domestic legislation on as many fronts as possible. In April he protested a bill
giving the war department authority to renegotiate contracts, calling instead for a fixed tax on excess profits and for a five-man
profits control board that would operate according to "definite
principles determining what excessive profits are" and that would
preserve the "incentive motive" among smaller businessmen. To
no avail; on April 24 the Senate thwarted Taft once again.[7]

Undaunted, he kept up his fire. In June he moved unsuccessfully to trim the budget by cutting funds for work relief, and in
August he assailed the administration's indictment of twenty-eight
citizens charged with conspiracy to undermine the loyalty of the
armed forces. Many of those indicted, Taft admitted, were "men
of known German connections," and some were "no doubt un-
American," but the Justice Department could show no evidence of
a conspiracy among them. The government, he said, in carrying
on his defense of the accused in 1943, should exercise the "greatest
care . . . in weeding out the innocent parties from the dragnets
which it is often necessary to spread in time of war." Taft's pleas
for the defendants, who included such noted anti-Semites as Gerald
B. Winrod and William Dudley Pelley, head of a pseudofascist organization called the Silver Shirts (SS), earned him little admiration, but when the government finally dropped its charges late in
1944, it conceded, in effect, the flimsy nature of its case and vindi-
cated Taft, who had been a lonely voice for justice amid the passions of war.[8]

As in the eighteen months before Pearl Harbor, Taft also
mapped his chief campaign against inflation. This meant, first of
all, increased taxation. He continued to oppose higher corporate
taxes and hotly denounced Roosevelt's proposal to limit individual
incomes after taxes to $25,000. "Income remaining," he said,
"should have . . . some relation to the return on the money that
he earns . . . The rate might be 90 per cent, but it should never
be 100 per cent." But he also insisted that the rich pay more than
in the past. "I am all in favor of taxing the rich up to the limit," he
wrote. "I believe that those with incomes in the past of $100,000
or more must look forward to living on not more than half
the amount they have formerly enjoyed," he added publicly.

Above all, he joined a growing chorus calling for a national sales tax of 5 per cent. Such a tax would exempt food, exist only during the war, and "supplement a heavily graduated income tax." He confessed that it would hurt lower-income groups, but in wartime everyone must sacrifice. "I don't see why," Taft said with typical bluntness, "every person should not pay at least 10 per cent of his income." [9]

Having staked out his position, he worked hard to secure it. Indeed, to get more revenue he soon backed a sales tax of 10 per cent. He questioned Treasury Secretary Henry Morgenthau closely, found him defiantly opposed to a sales tax, and complained privately that he was "the poorest and stupidest witness that anyone ever saw." (Morgenthau, irritated, grumbled to his diary that Taft was "not worthy of my mettle . . . I don't think you could change that man anyway.") Taft also objected to Morgenthau's call for increased corporate levies. "Within the New Deal," he wrote Hoover, "there is a deliberate attempt to reduce corporations to a point where after the war they will be dependent on the government for their very existence." Despairing as the summer wore on, he sent a check to his farmer on Indian Hill and concluded, "I don't know what I am going to do next year if we pass the tax bill the way it is." [10]

Taft probably exaggerated the yield to be expected from a sales tax; he left himself open to the charge of favoring the rich; and he even failed in his purpose of achieving a dramatic tax increase. When Congress finally passed a law in October 1942, it approved a 90 per cent excess profits tax, ignored Roosevelt's plea for a limit on incomes after taxes, and placed more moderate levies on corporations than Morgenthau had wished. The final bill also left the government reliant on bonds as a means of covering its deficits. For Taft the battle for higher taxes had ended in stalemate.[11]

Struggles with the administration over price control also engaged him, and by early 1942 he had fastened on five guidelines that sustained him year after year. First, he insisted on a minimum of bureaucratic regulation; for him, this meant selective instead of general controls. Second, he drew on his concern for small businessmen, particularly Cincinnati meat packers, to call for controls on commodities and raw materials instead of on retail prices. Third, he demanded a review board to hear protests by businessmen. Fourth, Taft objected to using prewar profits as the basis for setting maximum prices in an industry. Such a policy, he contended, unfairly used the small profit margins of the depression years as a guide and meant using as a standard the average profit across an entire industry, thus discriminating against smaller producers and retailers. Finally, he protested against the concept of a general "freeze." Wages and prices, he said, inevitably rise in wartime and create all sorts of pressures and inequities. The government should therefore permit gradual price increases. It should stabilize prices, but not "freeze" them.[12]

OPA chief Leon Henderson, whom Taft branded a "stubborn theorist," did not agree and established general controls on most non-farm prices, imposed them at the retail level, and used prewar profits as his primary guide. Still, Henderson lacked the power to control wages or farm commodities, and as these increased steadily, they pushed prices upward until Roosevelt finally announced in September 1942 that he would assume authority to curb price increases himself unless Congress acted within a month.

The President's demand outraged many congressmen. "The message," Taft said, "seems to be based on a doctrine so revolutionary and so dangerous to the existence of democratic government in the United States that I cannot let a single day go by without recording my own vigorous protest against the soundness of this doctrine." Yet he, too, had no use for the farm lobby that was paralyzing the will of his colleagues. (Besides, he explained to Martha, Republicans "have all the farmers anyway and we can't lose them.") When it came time to vote, he sided with senators from urban states against a formula that would have granted farmers 112 per cent of parity, and he later joined a unanimous Senate in giving the President the powers he had demanded.[13]

Because Taft's guidelines for price control were never tried, it is difficult to say whether he was right. But one may speculate. As he and others had warned, basing controls according to industrywide standards discriminated against some small businessmen. He was also correct in assailing the selfishness of the farm lobby. But his adamant defense of small business distorted his vision. He exaggerated the capriciousness of the OPA, which did provide fair hearings; he refused to concede the formidable administrative difficulties of treating different-sized companies according to different standards; and he failed to admit that controls on retail prices were essential to prevent unjustifiably large corporate profits. Given the potentially serious inflation — some 25 per cent by early 1943 — he was also wrong-headed in being content with selective controls, which, later OPA Administrator Chester Bowles said, tried to stop a stream by building a dam halfway across it. Not until Roosevelt, himself reluctant to act, imposed a rigid "hold the line" order on wages and prices in April 1943 did the administration succeed in restraining wartime inflation.[14]

•

As America entered its second year of war in 1943, Taft occasionally sounded mellow, even progressive. After a congressional tour of Puerto Rico in February, he expressed shock at poverty there and confessed that the Puerto Ricans were "adopting a number of socialistic measures, some of which are necessary." And in the spring he began to outline his postwar domestic program. As always, he opposed excessive government regulation, demanded "freer capital markets," and urged postwar abolition of the capital gains tax. But he also called for more public housing, federal aid to health and medical care, extension of unemployment compensation and old age pensions, and public works "when private activity falls off." Concluding in a tone characteristic of many postwar speeches, he said:

> I believe in the principle of insurance to everyone unless he refuses to work, a minimum standard of living, but it must be held within a reasonable cost, without setting up a vast Federal bureaucracy, without destroying local self government, and without removing the incentive to work which is the very keystone to adequate production.[15]

Yet the 1942 elections had also renewed his will to stymie the New Deal. Scoring impressively throughout the nation, Republicans came within ten votes of controlling the House and gained nine seats in the Senate. Though they remained a minority in the Senate, 58 to 37, they could often rely on influential Democrats like Walter George and Richard Russell of Georgia, Harry Byrd of Virginia, and ten to fifteen other foes of the administration. For the first time since Taft had come to Washington, he could hope to repeal parts of the New Deal, and in 1943 he often succeeded. The conservative coalition abolished the NYA, made a skeleton of the progressively oriented National Resources Planning Board, and ended Roosevelt's authority to devalue the currency.

During this time, Taft also developed useful relationships with the Southern Democrats like George, Russell, and Byrd. His progress was slow, for these were cautious and independent men who did not encourage intimacy with Republicans. But Taft's sincerity appealed to them, and they came to recognize that his word was all but sacred. They saw, too, the wide common ground which they shared with him: states' rights, fiscal conservatism, limited government, and the abolition of agencies that might disrupt social relations in their states. Thus, by 1944, Taft had earned the respect of George, a courteous veteran who chaired the finance committee and whose judgment on fiscal matters carried immense weight with his colleagues, and he had secured the personal friendship of Byrd, a courtly and cherubic gentleman, whose determination to cut the budget ranked second to none. Through them Taft edged closer to Russell, a vigorous and able man, who in a few years was to become the most powerful southerner of them all. This network of personal relationships was never so solid or Machiavellian as liberal critics maintained, but it helped prevent little misunderstandings and underlay some successes of the conservative coalition.[16]

With such allies gathering behind him early in 1943, Taft moved more assuredly than before. He demanded (again unsuccessfully) a 10 per cent sales tax and skirmished repeatedly over price controls. And he participated in a protracted controversy over Roosevelt's use of funds to buy commodities and then sell them to consumers at lower prices. The consumer subsidy program, as it came to be called, helped hold the line on commodity prices. Moreover, because it used funds earmarked for the Commodity Credit Corporation (CCC), a popular agency that loaned money to farmers, congressional opponents of subsidies faced a difficult choice. If they wished to stop the subsidy program, they

had to specify so in CCC extension bills, thus risking a presidential
veto killing the CCC at the same time. On the other hand, the
consumer subsidy program infuriated the farm lobby, which demanded higher market prices, and it angered fiscal conservatives,
who observed that the government was dispensing some $400 mil-
lion in support of consumers at a time when many wage earners
were prospering. With the CCC due to expire at the end of June
1943 unless extended, the stage was set for a battle.

It was the kind of issue — technical, statistical, grounded on the
principle of congressional prerogative — that appealed strongly to
Taft, and he plunged eagerly into the fray. Determined to control
public spending, he opposed Roosevelt's use of subsidies to "roll
back" prices to September 1942 levels. On the other hand, he favored modest subsidies to hold the line and to encourage production of key commodities, and he wished to continue the CCC. So
when the time came to vote in late June, he took a middle course.
Displeasing subsidy advocates by favoring limits on funds, he
nevertheless incurred the wrath of the farm lobby — and the dismay of almost all his Republican colleagues — by refusing to call
for the outlawing of all subsidies. Indeed, toward the end of the
protracted struggle, he even assumed unofficial leadership of administration forces and twice supplied the one-vote margin of victory for his unaccustomed allies.

At first the trend went against the administration. Farm-state
senators and fiscal conservatives succeeded in passing an amendment specifically outlawing the use of funds for subsidies. But
Roosevelt quickly vetoed the bill and killed the CCC in the process. The House, unable to override the veto, grew alarmed at the
loss of funds for price supports and reversed itself. The Senate resisted at first, but Taft helped persuade it of the futility of fighting,
and on July 8 it went along with the House by a one-vote margin.
Roosevelt had carried the day, but Taft was not depressed, for he
took heart at the repeated self-assertiveness of the Senate. "On the
whole," he wrote, "the record of Congress is very good, and it has
finally regained its independence for the first time in ten years." [17]

Taft's greatest success in 1943 was in leading the forces against a
bill calling for $300 million in federal aid to states for elementary
and secondary education. After studying statistics he conceded

that some pupils, especially Negroes in the South, were getting inferior schooling. But the so-called Thomas bill of 1943 struck him as a "revolutionary proposal, one of the most revolutionary ever presented this Congress." Instead of trying to help students in need, he maintained, the bill gave $200 million for teachers' salaries, and only $100 million in matching grants to start the task of equalizing standards within and among the states. "Education," he said characteristically, "is not and never has been a federal function. The only justification for asking federal money would be the poverty of the states. Figures presented show that the states have never been so prosperous and have today a surplus of a billion dollars . . . How ridiculous for the states to be asking aid from the Federal government."

Taft also argued that the bill would do little to rectify imbalances between black and white schools in the South. The "only real lack of educational equality in this country today," he said with some exaggeration, "relates to negro children. There is no reason why . . . we should be asked to pay three hundred million dollars for white children out of a Federal Treasury which threatens to be bankrupt." Produce a plan, he said, which raises Negro schools in the South to a minimum national standard, and he would favor it. But the Thomas bill, he said, failed to do that. Taking the lead, he encouraged Republicans to vote for an amendment barring racial discrimination in the use of federal money for schools. Northern progressives felt they had to back the amendment, and it passed, 40 to 37. But the provision offended southerners who previously supported the bill. They joined the Republicans, lined up against the final bill, and recommitted it to committee.[18] Taft's later views concerning aid to education suggested that he was groping sincerely for a way to use federal funds to help impoverished black (and white) schools, but in 1943 he had characteristically placed fiscal considerations ahead of all else and had resorted to parliamentary tactics to cement the conservative coalition. However, he had won. For Taft, it was the high point in a year of heartening victories.

•

Relations between the President and Capitol Hill deteriorated still further in 1944. Again shying away from imposing heavy taxes, Congress approved a modest bill providing but $2 billion — less than one-fifth of the $10.5 billion recommended by the Treasury — and Roosevelt vetoed it with a blast that it was "relief not for the needy but for the greedy." Stung by the veto, Majority Leader Alben Barkley resigned in protest, and applauding Senate Democrats immediately re-elected him to his post. Congress then overruled the veto by sweeping majorities. The administration, said the usually friendly writer Bernard DeVoto a few months later, was "tired, cynical, shifty, strained by its inner contradictions, grown as doubtful of its original ends as it is confused about its means." [19]

Sensing his opportunity, Taft advanced to the attack. He criticized administration price control policy, contradicted his demands for increased revenue by voting to override Roosevelt's veto of the tax bill, and stepped up his running criticism of inefficiency in the War Department. Within three or four years after the end of the war, he said repeatedly, the national budget must be reduced from its present $95 billion to between $17 and $20 billion, and taxes must be cut sharply in order to encourage business incentive. "We cannot solve the problem by government spending and relief," he proclaimed. "We must have an administration that wants to let go." [20]

Taft reserved much of his energy in early 1944 to engage in the controversy surrounding the ballot for soldiers in the 1944 elections. In late 1943 the Senate had approved a bill that required soldiers to send postcards to their states in order to get absentee ballots. But the administration fought back. Realizing that soldiers would be likely to vote for Roosevelt, their commander in chief, the administration was anxious to get as many to vote as possible, and it argued accordingly that they should receive ballots without special application. Such "federal ballots" would list the offices of President, vice-president, senator, representative, and representative at large, and soldiers would merely have to fill in the name — or just the party — of their choice for each office.

The federal ballot plan infuriated Taft, who had to run for re-

election in 1944. The federal ballot, he argued, would deprive soldiers of the vote for state offices, take away the constitutional right
of states to run their own elections, and enable ambitious commanders at the front to line up their men and tell them how to
vote. Dismissing warnings to avoid a partisan stance, Taft reminded friends of the consequences of a federal ballot in November. "Even if the President makes an issue of Republican opposition to the federal ballot," he said, "the votes to be lost on that
issue are negligible compared to the number of real votes the President will get if the federal ballot is adopted." [21]

It was a partisan issue of the sort Taft liked best, and he dropped
everything to assume command of a coalition of Republicans and
Southern Democrats. He bestrode the floor, heckled the opposition at every turn, and tried to stop the administration plan from
being considered. Failing in that attempt, he carried about a
printed roll of senators, cornered colleagues in corridors and cloakrooms, and tried to enlist a majority behind his amendment requiring soldiers to apply for federal ballots if they wanted them.
Impressed, reporters praised his parliamentary agility, his energy,
and his willingness to be branded a partisan. "He posseses more
downright intestinal fortitude than any other of the outstanding
figures in American life," one commented. "An amazing performance," another noted approvingly. [22]

When the measure finally reached the Senate floor early in February 1944, the administration had the votes. It defeated his
amendment, 46 to 42, then approved a modified federal ballot, 47
to 38. But the antiadministration coalition in the House had already passed a state ballot plan, and in conference it was not to be
denied. The final version prescribed federal ballots only if a soldier had first applied for and been refused a state ballot and if his
state chose to certify the federal ballot. Roosevelt disgustedly let
the bill become law without his signature, and in November it was
estimated that only 111,000 soldiers used federal ballots compared
with more than 4 million who used ballots sent out by the states.

Taft then jumped immediately into another issue: the still
controversial question of consumer subsidies. Late in 1943 the
Senate had enacted temporary legislation carrying on the subsidy
program until February 17. But by then the administration was

buying commodities at the rate of more than $1 billion per year, and the Senate voted to continue the CCC without subsidies. Another veto from Roosevelt then forced it to back down and authorize subsidies until June 30, 1945. Undaunted, Taft moved quietly to separate subsidies from the popular CCC and to tie them instead to the extension of price control. Lining up a majority on the banking and currency committee, he succeeded in having it report a bill that continued price control until the end of 1945 but also required the President to get specific authorization after June 30, 1945, for funds used as consumer subsidies. Roosevelt was afraid to destroy price control in the midst of the war and accepted the package in June 1944. By midsummer 1944 the anti-administration coalition seemed to have the White House on the ropes.[23]

•

The journalist Allen Drury, starting his job as a Senate correspondent in late 1943, was fascinated by the powerful solons he had to cover. Almost from his first day he was captivated by Taft, influential, complex, enigmatic. He wrote in his diary in December that Taft

> continues to impress me as one of the strongest and ablest members here, one of the men who acts consistently as though they think what is being done here really matters to the welfare of the country . . . Taft, perhaps more than any other, is the leader of the powerful coalition of Republicans and southern Democrats . . . one of the three or four most powerful men in the United States Senate at the present time.

Three weeks later Drury still pondered the contradictions of Ohio's senior senator:

> Taft is curiously quiet, at least on first acquaintance. Where is the dynamic fighter of the floor, I wondered, where the indomitable tilter at windmills and rattler of scabbards? Is all that fire banked in this quiet, silent, uncommunicative man? I know it is, but it is still rather a surprise at first to see the contrast between Taft the Man on the Floor and Taft the Man behind the Desk. I came to the conclusion finally that the silence which I took at first to be

calculated politics is simply the shy nature of a man who takes a while to warm up and a certain amount of knowing before he will speak out.[24]

Drury, whose gift for characterization later made him a best-selling political novelist, came as close as anyone to understanding the improbable mixture of reticence and ferocity, of humility and self-assurance that baffled so many commentators trying to pierce the rugged surface of Taft's personality. Taft, he recognized, was nasal, blunt, occasionally rigid. He held back business with irritating disquisitions on the excesses of bureaucracy and tirelessly offered obstructive amendments. ("That 'A' in his name stands for amendment," another reporter remarked.) He was a lunging, probing interrogator who tolerated no nonsense in committee, a debater whose hyperbolic predictions of doom left opponents speechless, a rigorous expounder of law who was shy except when provoked to combat, a man of so much presence that his behavior on the floor, as Drury put it, came "dangerously close to the line that separates the man of argument from the man of arrogance." He was also an impatient man who thought nothing of snapping at slow-witted colleagues or of rising in disgust from his second-row seat and stalking from the chamber, and he irritated even Republicans who anxiously sought a sign of affection, a moment of conviviality, or the gratuitous compliment that tempered the political animosities of the Senate. "Every time he stood up to speak," his colleague George Aiken of Vermont recalled, "'I wanted to fight him." Taft remained a man driven to work, to serve, and to excel on his own. A man apart from his colleagues.[25]

Yet, as Drury saw clearly, these weaknesses did not prevent Taft from becoming a man of influence by early 1944. Colleagues, sensing his seriousness of purpose and his willingness to work, knew also that he always kept his word. If he sometimes seemed cool and unfeeling, he also retained a quintessential decency. "Can I come up and see you?" a junior senator would ask. "No, I'll come down by you," Taft would respond. He never acted too busy to help a colleague, to explain his reasoning to anyone who seemed willing to make the intellectual effort, or to emerge from long hours of studying statistical reports, scholarly articles, and presidential speeches with a position that, if sometimes wrong, usually seemed researched beyond question. His Republican colleagues, wondering at his willingness to tackle such technical issues as soldier voting and consumer subsidies, let him take the lead. "Let Bob do it," they gladly told one another. Above all, Taft seemed prepared to follow his principles to whatever end might lie ahead. As Drury noticed immediately, he really *cared* about everything the Senate did. "On all sides," an impartial journalist noted as early as August 1943, Taft "came out of the recent hectic session of Congress as an outstanding figure on the counts of ability, energy, courage, and skill as a legislator. This was conceded even by those who often disagree with him." [26]

When Minority Leader Charles L. McNary died early in 1944, Taft might have maneuvered to succeed him. But the job involved hours on the floor listening to the inanities of Senate debate. Instead, Taft pressed to establish a steering committee to formulate Republican policy, and his colleagues gladly made him chairman of it. Wasting no time, he hired George H. E. Smith, an experienced writer and scholar who had collaborated with the historian Charles Beard on a number of books, as full-time executive secretary of the committee. He also asked fellow Republicans to submit study topics, and he began immediately to shape a party image far more aggressive than it had been under the mild-mannered McNary.[27] Bob Taft, after almost six years in the Senate, had arrived.

CHAPTER 18

Almost Defeated, 1944

BUILDING UP PRESTIGE in the Senate was satisfying and absorbing. But for what? Taft realized that unless Republicans won in 1944, the New Dealers would ignore him again. And unless he triumphed himself, all the hours over statistics, all the night sessions in the Senate would be wasted. By 1944 electoral politics were beginning to absorb some of Taft's time.

High on the agenda was beating Roosevelt, and this in turn involved a series of choices. Should Taft try to run again himself? If not, should he endorse someone else? Thomas E. Dewey? John Bricker? Arthur Vandenberg? General Douglas MacArthur? Whatever he decided would affect the party as well as himself.

Most politicians prefer to bide their time, to make sure the ground is firm before planting their feet. But as early as December 1941, Taft was questioning his chances of winning the presidential nomination, and by early 1942, with President Roosevelt assuming his new role of commander in chief, Taft wondered about Republican chances in 1944. Bricker, he recognized, would probably win a third term as governor in 1942 and use the Ohio organization to advance his own presidential candidacy. Above all, Taft thought beyond 1944. If he tried for the presidency and failed, he might have to surrender his seat in the Senate.[1]

The elections of November 1942 confirmed these thoughts. Bricker won again in Ohio, and Dewey swept to victory in New York. With Wendell Willkie also a likely candidate in 1944, the odds against Taft's nomination for the presidency seemed overwhelming. Taft arranged to see Bricker, told him he would not run, and offered to endorse him. "I think I will support Bricker," he wrote a friend at the end of November 1942. "He is very anxious to run and he gave me very good support in 1940." Four days later Taft surprised the politicos by endorsing Bricker as "exceptionally qualified to be the Republican candidate and the president." The first big decision had been made.[2]

As a regular Ohio Republican unwilling to precipitate a fight, Taft probably could have done little else. But neither loyalty nor gratitude played the major role in his thinking. He wanted above all to support a man who thought as he did. Willkie, internationalist and unpredictable, had by then moved so close to Roosevelt that he had split the GOP into two irreconcilable factions. Clearly, he would not do. And Dewey seemed to vacillate. "Tom Dewey," Taft wrote a friend, "has no real courage to stand up against the crowd that wants to smear any Republican who takes a forthright position against the New Deal." This left Bricker, untested in national politics, but clearly in the Taft wing of the party. Bricker, Taft wrote, is "all against Willkie. There is only one way to beat the New Deal, and that is head on. You can't outdeal them." [3]

Early in 1943, Taft remained pleased with his decision to stay out of the race. "I am swamped with work here in the Senate," he wrote David Ingalls, "and if I had to run a campaign besides, I would be crazy before the end of the year." "You have no idea how uncomfortable it is," he added to a friend, "to be a candidate and have to watch every word that you say." But he had never thought very highly of Bricker's intellectual capacity, and he grew distressed with his candidate's actions. "He needs an organization," Taft complained privately in May 1943, "and also one or two men to help him write speeches . . . his speeches don't amount to anything." In July he added that Bricker "is largely to blame himself, because he has not put on a more aggressive campaign." By November Taft still hoped for the best, but despaired. "I am hardly in a position to do anything with the Governor," he complained to Paul Walter. "I can't see any inclination on his part to ask my advice or to take it." [4]

By early 1944, Taft was alternating uncertainly between confidence and pessimism. On the one hand, Willkie finished last in the Wisconsin primary in April and withdrew from the presidential race. Taft also dared to dream of Republican victory in November. "The majority against Roosevelt seems to be pronounced wherever I go," he wrote John Hollister in March. Most encouraging, Bricker seemed willing to listen to suggestions and lavished compliments on his erstwhile rival. "Bob," he wrote in June, "I do want to say to you that if at any time it becomes apparent that you are the man to be the candidate for President, you have my support as you have had in the past." [5]

On the other hand, despite his optimism, Taft still maintained a grudging respect for Roosevelt's magic at the polls. "Hardly a move is made by the Administration today," he complained in January, "which is not political and aimed directly at promoting a fourth term. They have a tremendous publicity organization." Roosevelt was also too slippery to pin down on foreign affairs. "If we make an attack on any particular feature of the policy," Taft grumbled, "he can make some announcement that will cut the ground out from under our feet." [6] Even in his most optimistic moments, Taft was more cautious about predicting Republican victory in 1944 than he had ever been or ever was to be in his entire career.

Taft complained most of all about the growing Republican support for Dewey. Outwardly the two Republican powers had remained friendly since the conflicts during the 1940 convention. Indeed, Taft regarded Dewey as a foil against Willkie, the common enemy. "Some time," he wrote Dewey cozily in July 1942, "I should like to talk over with you the general Republican policy. The chief stumbling block to a united policy is your friend in New York." Dewey, equally smooth, wrote Taft after a large Republican conference at Mackinac, Michigan, a year later that "you and I were on the same side in practically every argument." Taft replied in kind. "Our differences," he agreed, "related almost entirely to phraseology . . . on the larger issues of domestic policy we are almost exactly in the same position." [7]

Taft sensed correctly that he was closer in 1944 to Dewey than either man was to Willkie. But well before 1944, he thought a good deal less of Dewey than he told him. He had counted on Dewey to back Werner Schroeder of Illinois for GOP national chairman in December 1942, only to feel that Dewey then reversed himself under pressure. Dewey, he complained privately, "promptly ran out and issued a statement against Schroeder himself to please the New York *Herald Tribune*." Far from finding Dewey easy to work with at Mackinac, Taft resented Dewey's call for a military alliance with England and recoiled at his personality. "Tom Dewey," he complained — again privately — "arrived in a private car with a bodyguard, and then was so arrogant that he made all the Republicans mad." By late 1943, Taft reluctantly had to concede that Dewey had the lead for the nomination. But the prospect irritated him. "I think I can get along with him," he wrote his son Bob, "although he is very arrogant and bossy." To his cousin Hulbert, Taft added his other objection: Dewey's excessive deference to the eastern establishment. "The real danger," he wrote, "is that [his advisers] will talk Dewey into too much internationalism . . . he comes from New York and sees the group opinions there as a lot more important than they are." In 1944, as in 1940, Taft's instinctive distrust of Eastern Republicans like Willkie and Dewey was rising uncontrollably to the surface.[8]

By the time of the convention in late June, Dewey had forged an insurmountable lead. He easily captured the nomination, accepted Bricker as his running mate, and set out to unseat the "champ." As in 1940, a New Yorker representing the Eastern wing of the party had triumphed over the stalwarts from Ohio.[9]

Dewey tried to mend his fences after the convention by congratulating Taft for the "grand job you did in harmonizing the widely conflicting views at the Convention concerning the platform." Three weeks later Dewey wrote again to compliment Taft on another "grand job" — this time referring to Taft's leadership in the Senate against Roosevelt's plans for postwar reconversion. Not to be outdone, Taft maintained the charade. "I should like to do anything possible which you think would be of assistance in the campaign," he wrote early in July. Your acceptance speech, he wrote Dewey three weeks later, "could not have handled the situation better." [10]

In fact, however, Taft remained uneasy. On the one hand he admitted that Dewey was "more likely [than Bricker] to "set up an effective organization, and less likely to make mistakes . . . he is a very able fellow, even if difficult to get on with." But on the other hand Taft joined many GOP regulars, Bricker included, in resenting Dewey's cavalier treatment of the more conservative Midwestern wing of the party. "The whole headquarters is run by New Yorkers," he wrote, "and Tom Dewey takes no advice from anyone. He will be hard to get on with if he wins." To Bricker, Taft was even franker. The delegates, he said, were influenced by the "conviction that Dewey was more popular with the Republican voters, as shown by the polls and by all the primaries . . . I ran up against the same thing in 1940. I think it must be the glamour attaching to a gang buster." [11] As he turned his attention to his senatorial race, there was not much on the national scene to encourage him.

·

A cardinal rule of politics holds that a candidate should take nothing for granted. Taft knew this in a general way. Aware of the possibility of defeat in his bid for a second term in the Senate in 1944, he had arranged to remain as counsel for his law firm through 1944, when he might return as a partner if necessary. He postponed buying a home in Washington until 1945. Declining an invitation to speak in Iowa in November 1943, he explained that he still might have an opponent in the primary in 1944, "so I am spending as much time in Ohio as possible." [12]

But senatorial duties gave him little rest. First came battles over foreign policy, then soldier voting and consumer subsidies. Weeks passed during which he rarely escaped to Ohio. Worse, his office workers grew discontented, for he remained too intent on legislative issues to pay much attention to them and demanded from them the same hard labor that he performed himself. "He expected everyone to do his duty without praise or medals," an associate recalled. Overworked, offended by his brusqueness, some of his staff had been quitting during the war years, and routine services to constituents had suffered. Early in 1944, Taft hired a personable young Cincinnati lawyer, I. Jack Martin, as his new administrative assistant. Taft was never to call much on Martin for advice on the issues — this was always his personal preserve — but he relied heavily on him for the next nine years to handle the relentless pressures of office work. Even the efficient Martin, however, did not take charge soon enough to solve all Taft's problems in the campaign of 1944.[13]

The weeks stretched into months, and when no one put him to the test of a primary, Taft grew casual about the race in November. He followed the Democratic senatorial primary between William G. Pickrel of Dayton and Marvin Harrison of Cleveland, but he worried less about the strength they might bring to bear against him than about the methods he would have to employ. "Pickerel," he wrote (misspelling the name) "will win which is all well and good because Harrison would be a much more disagreeable opponent. He is practically a communist." When Pickrel triumphed in May, Taft rested even easier than before.[14]

By the end of July, Taft had grown cautious enough to tell Allen Drury, "I think I'll win but — I'm not going to be sure until I have. You never know." A month later he told his son Horace, "Everyone says I shall have an easy time, but I am not so sure, and certainly can take no chances. The CIO will put on a nasty fight, and don't mind telling lies galore." Still, he remained confident. The Republican ticket will win by 200,000 votes in Ohio, he said both publicly and privately. "Everything seems in good shape politically," he wrote Martha, who was at Murray Bay, "more Republican than ever, less FDR popularity, and all right for me personally." [15]

Democrats thought differently, as did their influential allies in the CIO and the Farm Bureau Federation. Roosevelt, they believed, would lead the way, and Frank Lausche, the exceptionally popular mayor of Cleveland who was heading their ticket as the gubernatorial nominee, would overwhelm his Republican opponent, James Stewart of Cincinnati, and sweep the entire Democratic slate into office. Taft, seven places down on the ballot, would be buried in the avalanche.

The CIO, which was actively aiding many liberal candidates throughout the country, left little to chance in Ohio. Though lukewarm about Pickrel, a competent though uninspiring moderate who had served as lieutenant governor in the 1920's and 1930's, it placed Taft high on its list of enemies and concentrated on retir-

ing him to Indian Hill. Throughout the campaign which followed, the CIO set the tone, wrote many of the pamphlets, and
raised much of the funds for Pickrel in his campaign.

The Democratic-labor strategy against Taft was simple enough:
brand him again and again as isolationist, antilabor, procorpora-
tion, muddle-headed, reactionary, filthy rich. And Pickrel willingly pursued it. Taft, he charged in an early effort in July, "is the
Number One Tory conservative. He is the Number One opponent of the President. Senator Taft will never help the cause of
peace." "Taft comes from one of Ohio's wealthiest families," he
added. "He represents wealth and large corporations. Approximately $168,000 was spent in making him Senator. Why? He op-
posed the law limiting political contributions to $5000 per person.
Why?" Taft, he charged, "favored disbanding the Army a few
weeks before Pearl Harbor," he did not want soldiers to vote, and
he opposed public housing, Social Security, lend-lease, and rationing. He favored a sales tax to help the rich, and he was "quite
willing to stir the race prejudice of Senators from southern states."
Who else but Taft, Pickrel demanded, could have said in February 1941, "It is simply fantastic to think Japan would attack us"?
Taft, he concluded typically, was a "blind partisan, an obstruction-
ist, an isolationist, the worst reactionary Ohio ever had in the
Senate." [16]

As if Pickrel were not harsh enough, national figures chimed in.
Luther Patrick, a Democratic congressman from Alabama, toured
the state to describe Taft as the man "who has said more about less
than any man who ever served in Congress." Vice-President Henry
Wallace went to Cincinnati to call Taft the "smartest reactionary I
know." And Senator Harry Truman, Roosevelt's running mate,
made five sharp speeches in Ohio on one day. "Senator Taft,"
Truman said, "is one of those unfortunate cases where the son is
elected because the people remember the outstanding character of
the father." [17]

Easily the most extreme assaults came from two Ohio sources.
One, a widely distributed pamphlet written by Marvin Harrison,
Pickrel's foe in the primary, featured the title of "Robert A. Taft:
Our Illustrious Dunderhead." It devoted sixty-four detailed pages
to Taft's career from his early days in Cincinnati through his years

in the Senate and concluded that "he has a positive genius for being wrong. He is an authentic living representative of the old Bourbons of whom it was said that they 'learned nothing and forgot nothing.' " He "exemplified and embodied the viewpoint of the Conservative, the Tory, the Reactionary." [18]

The other attack, a pamphlet from the Ohio CIO Council, did not bother with facts to make its point. It was entitled, "HE WANTED TO DO BUSINESS WITH HITLER AND HIROHITO — THE AMAZING STORY OF SENATOR TAFT." Taft, said the CIO, was a "shrewd calculating Tory." His record "shows a systematic campaign to force America back into the 'Robber Baron' days when a few big business kings ran both the economy and the government of the country from a few offices in Wall Street." When Taft opposed war in 1940 and 1941, he "brought joy to the hearts of fascists and despair to thousands suffering in the dungeons of Europe." As a result "a fiend named Shickelgruber [sic] rubbed his hands with anticipation and speeded mobilization." [19]

Taft tried to ignore such attacks by speaking for Dewey, Bricker, and Stewart, and by outlining carefully his position on domestic issues. As in the past he turned over organizational work to personal friends like Paul Walter, John Hollister, and to Ben E. Tate, a conservative Cincinnati businessman who had become a neighbor on Indian Hill. And Bob called Martha down from Murray Bay. She minced few words about New Dealers ("parlor pinks," "ex-professors," "fellow-travelers," she called them) and made the most of the war service of her sons. "Would you be interested in hearing about my boys?" she asked audiences. "Three volunteered very early. One [Bob, Jr.] has been in landings on Guadalcanal — Sicily — Salerno — Normandy. One [Lloyd] started as a gob — now is an ensign in the Pacific. One [Bill] tried three times to get in the Army and Navy. He got a special physical — finally [went into] intelligence. Our youngest had to wait a while to be eighteen — now a sergeant in the Army." [20]

Taft also dwelt heavily on foreign policy. "Our course in France," he said in reference to Roosevelt's treatment of General Charles de Gaulle, "has apparently succeeded in alienating the friendship of the people and establishing in power a man whom we have consistently and foolishly antagonized." The so-called Morgenthau Plan to deindustrialize Germany, he added, "has prolonged the war and made the Germans fight more bitterly." Stalin, Taft admitted, was "one of the greatest military commanders in the world," but he had designs on Lithuania, Latvia, and Poland; did he really deserve $4 billion a year in lend-lease? Above all, the administration had shown "inexcusable neglect" and "criminal negligence" concerning the Japanese attack at Pearl Harbor. It was time to open up the documents and let the people know what had happened.[21]

These were the politics of attack, the politics he had always tried to pursue. But as election day approached, they did not seem to be enough. For one thing the newspapers seemed uninterested in such old material, and as early as September he lamented to Martha, "I wish I could think of new things to say and new ways to say them." [22] Although most of the key Republican papers eventually endorsed him over Pickrel, many also backed Lausche, the Democratic gubernatorial candidate whose name headed the ballot; and all the major dailies tended to focus on the more newsworthy presidential race. Taft was discovering that a candidate must say something new if he expects front-page attention.

If he had cultivated Ohio reporters during his six years in Washington, he might have secured slightly wider coverage. But he had treated them with the same cool efficiency he had shown visitors to his law office in the 1930's. "Taft made little or no effort to seek support," J. B. Mullaney of the Cleveland *News* recalled. "The press could take him or leave him. It was not altogether arrogance; he was not one to fawn on editors — or anyone else. Also, as Ohio's claim to fame, he had them anyhow." Mullaney recalled also an experience common to many Ohio reporters. After interviewing Taft in Cleveland, he discovered on seeing him two days later that the candidate "gave no indication that he had ever seen me before. As was his habit, he had his mind on something else. With most people I would have been annoyed; with Taft I was amused." [23] Mullaney was kinder than most in attributing Taft's behavior to preoccupation; other reporters merely found him remote.

Taft, however, worried more about combating the Democratic-labor charges than he did about currying favor with the press. Indeed, their accusations quickly forced him to the defensive. He had not opposed voting by soldiers, he said — only the administration's federal ballot plan. He emphasized that he favored increased Social Security benefits, public housing, price control, and (once America entered the war) lend-lease. His stand on federal aid to education, he explained in a statement to the black press of Ohio, stemmed from his opposition to racial discrimination in the schools. He explained that he had opposed yellow-dog contracts for labor in 1931 and had voted for the civil liberties bill against company espionage in 1940. And never, he explained, had he presumed to predict Japan's intentions in 1941 as dogmatically as Pickrel claimed.[24]

Taft was especially concerned about the vulnerability of his record on foreign policy, and he tried to shift attention away from his prewar positions. When a questioner bore down on him after a debate in Cleveland, he even confessed his fallibility. "As to whether as a matter of long policy we should have gone to war," he conceded, "I think I am willing to admit maybe I was wrong." At the same Cleveland debate, he favored an "association of sovereign nations — that is, nations which will maintain their own freedom and their own armed forces. I believe that the members, including ourselves, should covenant to use armed forces if necessary to prevent aggression by any measure." [25] Taft was doing his best to assure voters that he was willing to reconsider his prewar insistence on a policy of the "free hand."

Taft also decided to counterattack. Those responsible for the CIO pamphlet, he demanded, should be prosecuted by the Justice Department. Pickrel, he charged, was a "rubber stamp . . . about a third of his charges are wholly false, about a third are grossly distorted, and the other third represent differences of opinion." The CIO-PAC [Political Action Committee], he said, was "unable to tell the truth," and was dominated by Communist party leader Earl Browder and labor leader Sidney Hillman, whom Taft unfairly branded a dupe of the communists. "The New Deal," he said, "is enthusiastically supported by Mr. Browder and all the communists. There can be no doubt of the direction the New Deal is moving." In occasionally resorting to such tactics,

Taft was merely emulating Dewey, who charged recklessly that "the Communists are seizing control of the New Deal." [26] He was also throwing a finer grade of mud than that used by his opponents. But the fact that he threw it at all revealed his anger at the CIO, and it showed him once again in his familiar posture of aggressive campaigner. If the race did nothing else, it left him grimly resolved to curb the power of organized labor in the future.

.

On election night Taft workers went to his headquarters in the *Times-Star* building prepared to celebrate. Though a few observers sensed a sudden tide toward the Democrats, practically everyone thought he would swamp the unimpressive Pickrel.

The returns showed differently. As expected, Taft was winning the rural counties, but his margins were smaller than anticipated; and as Lausche amassed enormous support in the cities, it looked as if Pickrel might win. Taft sat, pencil in hand, grimly following the returns, predicting victory if the pattern maintained itself. But by 1 AM he trailed by 50,000. The workers wondered, and Martha was in tears. [27]

When the returns were fairly complete the next day, they proved Taft's guarded optimism to have been well founded. As in 1938, he lost many of the large urban counties. Cuyahoga (Cleveland) went for Pickrel by 96,000, Mahoning (Youngstown) by 25,000, Montgomery (Pickrel's home town of Dayton) by 21,000, Stark (Canton) by 9000, Summit (Akron) by 19,000, for a combined margin of 170,000. More surprising, Taft won by only 4000 in Lucas County (Toledo), by 5000 in Franklin County (Columbus), and by 12,000 in Hamilton County, which he had swept by 25,000 over Bulkley in 1938. But the rural regions saved him — barely. Carrying seventy-one of the state's eighty-eight counties, he polled 1,500,809 votes to Pickrel's 1,483,069. His margin of victory was 17,740 — a percentage of 50.3. [28]

The pundits, who were taken aback by the closeness of the contest, offered all kinds of explanations for Pickrel's startling showing. Taft, they said, had offended unions, internationalists, farmers, teachers — indeed practically all the powerful pressure groups. The Republican state organization had badly weakened

the ticket in the north by insisting on Stewart, another Cincinnatian, as the gubernatorial candidate, then by wasting its efforts on
Stewart's behalf during the campaign. If Lausche had shown more
enthusiasm for the rest of his ticket; if Pickrel had commanded
more support among party workers; above all, if the disorganized
state Democratic party had worked as purposefully as the CIO, the
race might well have gone the other way.[29]

The pundits were probably right — the returns provided no
proof of such intangibles. But as they realized, other factors had
much to do with Taft's near defeat. One of these was Taft's failure
to mend his fences before September. "You take a state like
Ohio," he confessed to a Senate committee seven years later. "If
you do not go back there — and you cannot when Congress is
meeting all the time — you must somehow keep in touch with the
people. In 1944 I did not do it and almost got beat." Another
reason was the strength of Lausche, an extraordinarily effective
politician, who won by 107,000. "The closeness of my election,"
Taft wrote Ingalls, "was due principally to Stewart's weakness, because, as you know, my name was about seventh on the state ballot,
and there was a tremendous amount of straight-ballot voting."
After a recount of ballots in Cuyahoga County seemed to confirm
these suspicions, Taft began to call for the so-called Massachusetts
ballot, which discouraged straight tickets by requiring people to
vote separately for each office. "With the Massachusetts ballot," he
said with some exaggeration, "I would have nearly broken even in
Cleveland." [30]

Taft also recognized a third major element in the closeness of his
election: the remarkable success of the unions in getting voters to
the polls in urban industrial areas. Though the turnout in the
senatorial race fell 76,000 votes short of the record-breaking total
in 1940, it actually increased by 4000 in the seven largest urban
counties, which produced 52 per cent of the vote. This development was partly the result of the rapid urbanization of Ohio during these war years. Moreover, it was possible that the political
activity of the CIO confirmed many rural voters in their Republicanism. But it also seemed undeniable that the unions contributed
to the size of Pickrel's margins in the industrial regions. The CIO,
Taft complained after the election, mobilized the "heavy radical

and ignorant vote in the cities. I doubt it changed many people's opinions, but they stirred up enough bitterness and excitement to bring out all their supporters." [31]

Taft might have mentioned three factors that perhaps tipped the scales in his favor. One of these he was loath to admit: Except for Stewart and the state ticket it was a Republican year in Ohio. Dewey, perhaps because he had the popular Bricker as his running mate, won by 11,000, and George Bender, the Republican candidate for congressman at large, won by 180,000 votes. The completed returns, while subject to endless interpretations, suggested that Taft had added little strength to the ticket, and Roosevelt, who had always found Taft irritating, even concluded that he could have changed the result by stopping off in Cleveland in the last week of his campaign. Roosevelt may have exaggerated, but he correctly sensed Taft's electoral vulnerability. The 1944 election was ever to confound Taft's insistence that he was a potent vote getter. [32]

The second factor was his open and persistent cosponsorship since early in the year, with Senator Robert Wagner of New York, of a resolution calling for unrestricted Jewish immigration to Palestine, leading to the creation there of a Jewish commonwealth. Taft never fully explained his motivation for such a stand, which was most uncharacteristic of his opposition to American meddling abroad. Indeed Taft, while generally free of religious intolerance, was enough a man of his time and class to acquiesce in Taft School's flexible and unofficial quota concerning Jews and other groups. "I know that you must enforce the quota, and must do so," he had written Paul Cruikshank, Uncle Horace's successor as head of Taft School in 1937. His defense of Zionism, which distressed some of his conservative Republican colleagues, did not stem primarily from some vague and paternalistic Judeophilism. [33]

Whence then did it come? In the narrow sense it depended heavily on the influence of Abba Hillel Silver, a rabbi from Cleveland who was among the most militant of leading American Zionists. Seeking bipartisan congressional support for his cause, Silver was advised by friends in late 1943 to sound out Taft. On doing so, however, Silver found him cautious. Send me the facts, Taft said. Silver wondered if the candidate was politely evading the issue,

but did as he was told. Characteristically, Taft immersed himself
in the literature, then summoned the rabbi for questioning. After
this careful process, he emerged early in 1944 as an ardent champion of Zionism. In February he cosponsored his resolution with
Wagner, in June he worked closely with Silver to include a Zionist
plank in the national Republican platform, and throughout the
summer and fall he badgered the administration, which was afraid
of alienating the Arabs, to support his resolution.[34]

This explanation of Taft's attitude embodied his solitary, intellectual method of reaching decisions. Had Silver been presumptuous enough to try to lecture him on the subject, he might have met
a chilly reception. Yet Taft's willingness to study the literature at
all suggested that he was ready to be persuaded. In fact, during his
senatorial campaign of 1938 he had complained about Britain's reluctance to grant the Jews a homeland in Palestine, and by 1944 he
needed only to study the facts carefully before taking the lead.

Taft would have been blind not to be aware of the political implications of such a position. Cincinnati, a center of Reform Juda-
ism, contained many Jews who were cool to the idea of Zionism.
But in Cuyahoga County, where Silver exercised great influence,
lived thousands of Jews. Perhaps most important, Americans of all
faiths had begun to be aware of the plight of European Jews — a
fact that the politicians of both parties observed in including Zionist planks in their platforms. If Taft had actively opposed Zionism
in 1944, he would not have helped his chances for re-election.

Yet political explanations probably had little if any effect on his
thinking. Indeed, Taft had often proved deaf to the pleas of other
more powerful pressure groups and in doing so had shown a courage which was rare among officeholders. Politics also failed to account for his remarkable zeal, which long survived the campaign of
1944 and kept him in the leadership of American Zionists until
Israel was born in 1948. Indeed, he could simply have temporized
on the issue, which was precisely what the Roosevelt administration was trying to do.

Uppermost in Taft's mind was what he considered to be the
simple merits of the case. Like his father, who had actively be-
friended Jewish causes, Taft felt that the Balfour Declaration of
1917 committed England to giving the Jews a national homeland.

Yet in 1944 both the British and the Roosevelt administration appeared ready to scuttle that declaration at a time when Jews were
desperate. Taft's position gave greater substance to the Balfour
Declaration — a statement of intent — than it merited. He also
overlooked the frightful animosities which Zionism exacerbated
in the Middle East. But in 1944 he was not alone in failing
to emphasize these long-range consequences. He also seemed to
believe the problem was one that Britain, not the United States,
would have to worry about; in this sense his stand was more consistent with his opposition to American "meddling" than it
seemed. In essence, Taft had become persuaded that justice demanded a Jewish homeland and that Palestine was the only place
Jews wished to establish it. When he placed issues on the plane of
justice, there was no changing his mind.[35]

In any event, he made excellent use of Zionism in the closing
days of his campaign. When Paul Walter told him that straight-
ticket voting might leave him far behind in Cuyahoga County, Taft
turned to Silver for help, and the rabbi invited him to his temple
to address a meeting on October 22. When Taft arrived, he discovered that Silver had brought in a huge crowd to listen. The
rabbi then praised Taft's services to the Jews in terms which
amounted almost to a political endorsement. Aware of Silver's
help, Taft sent him a letter of thanks the next day and added, "I
shall always be deeply grateful." [36] He then instructed his staff to
release Silver's remarks to the press.

On election day Taft lost Cuyahoga County by only 96,000
votes, while Stewart was losing it by 192,000 and Dewey by
112,000. When Pickrel demanded a recount in the county, Taft
workers discovered that many Democratic voters who had de-
viated to vote for Taft came from the heavily Jewish precincts
and that these same ballots also showed votes for Jewish Republicans on the ticket. Taft's standing among the Jews in Cuyahoga
County may well have saved him from defeat.

The third factor in Taft's success may have been his name and
national reputation. If voters still found him dull on the stump,
cool to people he did not know, occasionally inefficient in serving
constituents, they at least knew his name. They may also have
sensed his devotion to duty, his courage, his absence of cant, and

the distinction he brought to Ohio. So at least it appeared to his friends. So, too, it seemed to many of the reporters who noticed that other incumbent isolationist senators like Gerald P. Nye of North Dakota and Bennett Clark of Missouri were retired to obscurity by the voters.

.

The experiences of 1944 left Taft a wiser politician. Intelligent enough to suspect where he had gone wrong, he resolved never again to depend on the state organization. "If I ever have to run again," he wrote Paul Walter, "I shall set up my own committee the first of January and raise enough money to do a real job." And he wasted no time in encouraging his friends to press for a Massachusetts ballot. As it happened, Walter and others succeeded in getting one voted into the state constitution in 1949, just in time to protect Taft from another Lausche avalanche in 1950.[37]

But the politics of 1944 also left him unhappy with prospects for the future. Dewey had lost, and Roosevelt again enjoyed Democratic majorities in both houses. "If we could have had control of Congress and the Presidency," Taft wrote, "we would have had the framing of constructive measures to cover the problem." To David Ingalls he sounded almost despairing. "I do not have the slightest pleasure in looking forward to the next four years," he wrote. "Every few minutes I think of some man I had not thought of before who will continue his nefarious activities during that period. Perhaps Morgenthau can do more harm than anyone else." [38]

Taft, who always showed a remarkable ability to surmount disappointment, emerged from his struggles with an uncharacteristic trace of bitterness. Surprisingly, he absolved the Deweyites. No Republican, he believed, could have beaten the commander in chief in the midst of the war. But the taunts of the CIO had hurt, and Pickrel's demand for a recount in Cleveland stung still more. "The CIO," he wrote, "seem to hate me more than anyone in sight and could not bear to leave any stone unturned." His opponents gained nothing in the recount and quickly dropped it. But it cost Taft $1000 to secure faithful ballot-box watchers, caused him a few anxious moments, and appeared to reflect on the integrity of his campaign. Coming across a proxy statement of the Dayton Rubber

Company two months later, he discovered that the company had paid Pickrel's law firm $36,000 for services rendered in 1943 and 1944, and he responded with strong emotions which belied his image as a mathematical machine. "This is only one small company," he wrote a friendly reporter for the Cleveland *News*, "and Mr. Pickrel is corporation counsel for a good many other larger concerns in Dayton. He is hardly the barefoot boy represented in the campaign!

"I thought you might use this in your column." [39]

CHAPTER 19

Planning for the Postwar World

LIKE MOST Americans in the months after the assault on Pearl Harbor, Taft cautiously watched the course of the war before taking positions on foreign policy. He was also wise enough not to claim expertise in military strategy, and he publicly supported most of Roosevelt's actions as commander in chief. From the beginning, however, he worried about Roosevelt's intentions, and by the end of 1945 he had offered sufficient elaboration of his views to accentuate the nationalistic, noninterventionist position that he had held in 1941.

Early in 1942 he kept most of his feelings to himself. After finishing Herbert Hoover's book, *America's First Crusade,* in January 1942, he told his former chief how it "brings back vividly those days in Paris, and the complete shamelessness with which the Allies went after our money. Perhaps . . . the working out of our idealism may sink in on the American people before we finally have to send 10 million men to Europe." He also fumed at the grandiose postwar expectations of what he privately called the "war crowd." Already foreseeing in January 1942 a "real battle on the character of the peace to be sought," he told his cousin Hulbert Taft that he hoped "we can put it off for a number of months until the war enthusiasm of all but the zealots has worn itself out." [1]

He also worked to destroy the influence of Wendell Willkie and his internationalist allies within the Republican party. In May 1942, Taft traveled to Chicago to stop the national committee from endorsing Willkie's resolution calling for America to assure future international cooperation and free institutions throughout the world. But the committee went along with Willkie, and Taft again vented his feelings to Hulbert. "We are heading for a direct fight for control of the party machinery," he wrote. "I believe it would be fatal to the future of the Party if Willkie and Luce . . . together with the wealthy crowd in the East, succeed in their aim." [2]

Taft adhered to this basic position for the rest of 1942. While assuring correspondents that he favored some kind of a postwar league of nations, he opposed specific commitments, and he grumbled that the administration appeared more interested in "foreign peoples than in the welfare of our own." "I certainly am willing to undertake some obligations," Taft concluded. "But I do not want to police Europe, or become involved in every little boundary dispute that there may be among the bitterly prejudiced and badly mixed races of Central Europe." [3]

Taft also publicly attacked the idealists. Establishing what Roosevelt called "freedom from want" in the world, he snorted, overlooked America's failure to do so in Puerto Rico or even at home. America should help war-torn countries but should not set up an "international WPA." Calling for what he termed "practical" internationalism, he ridiculed such plans as "Union Now, freedom from want on the part of all nations, and a policing of the entire world by the Anglo-Saxon race." And he refused to admit that the Willkieites talked good politics. "We can't out-intervention Roosevelt," he wrote confidently, "any more than we could out-New Deal the New Deal." [4]

By early 1943 internationalist congressmen, anxious to commit the United States to postwar responsibilities, began introducing resolutions; and Taft had to state his views more precisely. His response was characteristic. He sat down to compose his thoughts, drafted them sketchily on long pads of yellow legal paper, and by March 1943 had the basis for a series of speeches and public statements regarding postwar foreign policy. It was typical of him that he did so without seeking advice from friends or colleagues and without trying to secure any inside information from the State Department. Thus his ideas reflected much of his earlier thinking, and with variations appropriate to the occasion he repeated them again and again not only during the war but for several years thereafter.

He opened his offensive in March with several speeches on the Ball-Burton-Hatch-Hill (B_2H_2) resolution in the Senate for American participation in a strong international organization after the war. Some kind of league would be advisable, Taft said, but it ought not to be given the power to grant relief. "We may wish to use the giving of such assistance," he said, "as a weapon to secure compliance in peace plans." Related proposals for an international bank, he said, sounded like "devices to get American money into the hands of foreign countries." Taft also complained that the resolution failed to specify how such a league would settle disputes. "The Senate," he argued, "cannot be asked to grant any blank check for the President to fill in." Above all, he worried about the recommendation in B_2H_2 for an international police force. Such a force, he said, would leave the world at the mercy of the generals in charge. Adhering to his faith in international law, he argued instead for covenants outlawing aggression.[5]

In the next few weeks Taft elaborated his position and in so doing made clear five of his fundamental assumptions. First, he agreed with Roosevelt that the midst of a war was no time to seek hard agreements regarding boundaries or other matters. These questions should be deferred until after military victory. Second, America should avoid joining a league until territorial and economic disputes had been resolved fairly. In the interim between the end of the war and the settling of such matters — a period that Taft believed might last five years — England, the Soviet Union, and the United States would take charge. Third, each region of the world should have primary responsibility for policing itself. Adopting Churchill's suggestion of regional councils, Taft said that America "should only be a secondary guarantor of the peace of Europe, to be called in only when the problem seems to be beyond the resources of the European council." Fourth, he ridiculed world federalism or a "one-world" state. The United States, he said, was already too big to rule herself effectively from Washington. How much more absurd it would be to govern the world from one place! And fifth, America must never repeat the fatal error of 1917: trying to "crusade" for idealistic ends. "I do not believe," he insisted, "that any war can be justified as a crusade." If you do so, he said, "you must admit that the Soviets have a right to crusade to impose Communism on the rest of the world . . . a crusade by its very nature is an aggressive act." Instead of imposing herself on the world, America should keep her own house in order. "The only effective way in which we can spread the four freedoms throughout the world," he concluded, "is by the force of our own example." [6]

At Grove City, Pennsylvania, in May Taft ranged in still more general fashion by taking as his foil Henry Luce's concept of an "American Century." Luce, he said, wished America to police the world in the twentieth century as Great Britain had done in the nineteenth. But such a policy would be "completely contrary to the ideals of the American people and the theory that we are fighting for liberty as well as security":

> It is based on the theory that we know better what is good for the world than the world itself. It assumes that we are always right and that anyone who disagrees with us is wrong. It reminds me of the idealism of the bureaucrats in Washington who want to regulate the lives of every American along the lines that the bureaucrats think best for them . . . Other people simply do not like to be dominated, and we would be in the same position of suppressing rebellions by force in which the British found themselves during the nineteenth century.[7]

By August 1943 Taft was certain of the course America should follow, and he drew his remarks together for a major speech before the American Bar Association in Chicago. Again he called for regional councils of defense, demanded fair territorial and economic settlements before creating a league of nations, and mocked world federalism as "fantastic, dangerous, and impractical." The problems of holding together such a "Tower of Babel," he said, "would be insuperable." No leaders would ever let an "international bureaucrat" run them. "If you can see Winston Churchill liquidating the British fleet, or Joe Stalin dismissing the Russian army, or either of them turning their forces over to President Whoozis of Worlditania, you are more clairvoyant than I."

If world federalism was impractical, a postwar military alliance as advocated by Walter Lippmann and others was frightening. The idea of an Anglo-American agreement to police the world, he said, "may appeal to the nationalistic sentiment of those Americans who picture America dominating the alliance and the world. It may appeal to the do-gooders who regard it as the manifest destiny of America to confer the benefits of the New Deal on every Hottentot." But such an alliance would have to rely on armed force. "It can only lead to vast national armaments in all parts of the world; every nation or at any rate every alliance of nations must be able to control the seas, which means control the world . . . They create a profession of militarists." Taft concluded that military alliances mean imperialism:

> Our fingers will be in every pie. Our military forces will work with our commercial forces to obtain as much of the world trade as we can lay our hands on. We will occupy all the strategic points in the world and try to maintain a force so preponderant that none shall dare attack us. How long can nations restrain themselves from using such force with just a little of the aggressiveness of Germany and Japan . . . Potential power over other nations, however benevolent its purpose, leads inevitably to imperialism.

What, then, was the answer? To Taft, as to his father, it was the law. The Allies, he said, should develop a code of international law, make an "affirmative statement of the principles on which the nations of the world may live together in peace," and set up a world court to interpret these principles in practice. Collective military sanctions, he conceded, might ultimately be necessary to uphold the court's decisions, but only after the court had identified the aggressors. No league of nations could succeed, he concluded, "unless there exists in the greater part of the world a public opinion educated to peace and to the principles of law on which it is founded." Many spokesmen for internationalism called first for a strong league of nations, then for the gradual evolution of legal principles to support it. Taft demanded agreement first on the principles, then and only then sanctions and collective security.[8]

Warming to his theme, he sharpened his language in subsequent speeches. When Thomas E. Dewey in September 1943 called for a postwar alliance with Great Britain and perhaps with China and the Soviet Union, Taft snorted that Dewey had "swallowed whole" the balance-of-power theories espoused by Walter Lippmann.

When Republicans the same month at Mackinac Island in Michigan approved "responsible participation by the United States in postwar cooperative organization among sovereign nations to prevent military aggression and to attain permanent peace with organized justice," it was Taft among others who insisted on the adjective "sovereign" and who called for the words "peace" and "justice" in place of references to collective security. The resolution, he wrote happily, "excludes by implication any international state, as well as extreme isolation." [9]

By November 1943, when the Senate finally approved, 90 to 6, the mild Connally resolution for American participation in a league of "free and sovereign nations," Taft was missing few opportunities to state his mind. The Connally resolution, he said in voting for it, was satisfactory, but it ought to have referred to the importance of the "rule of law." America should join such a league, but it ought also to adhere to the policy of the "free hand." "We do not wish to be a meddlesome Mattie, interfering in every trouble throughout the world," he said. On the contrary, "we should only be called in on a three-alarm fire." [10]

Taft did not spell out the emotional roots of his thinking. But these were no mystery, for they stemmed logically from his views between 1939 and 1941, which in turn owed their force to memories of Paris in 1919. Indeed, Taft's stress on regionalism, his insistence that territorial and economic rivalries be settled before the nation joined a league, and his demand that a league rest on law instead of on force reflected to an astounding degree the views which Hoover, his old mentor, was setting forth in a series of writings in 1942 and 1943. Having objected from the beginning to American participation in World War II, Taft also shrank from imparting broad humanitarian motives to American war aims. And he remained pre-eminently a nationalist whose attitude toward Europe bordered on xenophobia. "I believe all of us want to cooperate in the post-war world," he wrote a friend. "But on the whole I would rather give the country back to the Indians than give it to the Europeans and the South Americans and the Chinese." [11] Unlike many Americans swept up in the war, Taft remained cool to the idealistic "one world" of Wendell Willkie, the power politics of Walter Lippmann, the American Century of Henry Luce.

To many critics he seemed narrowly nationalistic, unduly pessimistic about Europe, blind to the necessary role of America in a contracted world. His extensive preconditions to a league and his stress on international law in the crazy world of the 1940's also seemed disingenuous. Either he was naive — which is what he criticized in others — or he was advancing the ideal of a world of law and justice in order to block short-run proposals for collective action against aggressors. Either way, he appeared less a realist than a wishful thinker, and internationalists argued that he glided over one important point: No league of nations could control aggression without possessing some powers to impose military and economic sanctions.

On the other hand, Taft by early 1944 had not let his ideal world prevent him from moving as far toward an internationalist position as Arthur Vandenberg of Michigan, who was to emerge in 1945 as the party's leading spokesman for internationalism. Taft supported the Mackinac declaration and the Connally resolution, and if he seemed reluctant to endorse wide-ranging proposals such as world federalism or binding military alliances in the postwar period, so did most Americans at the time. Indeed, Roosevelt himself told Stalin at the Teheran Conference in November 1943 that America would not even supply land armies to police Europe after the war.[12] And Taft had shown courage, indeed foolhardiness, in daring to suggest the danger of crusading, the possibility of American imperialism, the existence of a complex of militarists and industrialists who could thrust an unwanted Pax Americana on the rest of the world. Few Americans, let alone politicians in the midst of a patriotic war, ventured such a long-range view or adopted publicly such an unpopular perspective, and they continued to refrain from doing so until critics of the Viet Nam war in the late 1960's offered a remarkably parallel perspective.

.

The Senate did not get around to establishing American postwar policy until mid-1945. But this postponement did not lead Taft to depart from the views he had developed by mid-1944, and on the two key issues, international economic policy and the United Nations, he voted as he had been talking for more than a year.

The controversy over economic policy stemmed from a plan developed at a conference of experts at Bretton Woods, New Hampshire, in 1944. The conferees called for two new creations, an international monetary fund and an international bank. The fund, to consist of $8.8 billion in contributions from member nations, aimed at preventing discriminatory exchange controls, helping nations avoid currency devaluation, and facilitating the flow of world trade. Ideally, it would prevent currency wars and ruinous rounds of devaluation. The bank, with an initial capital of $9.1 billion, was to make direct loans for reconstruction and long-term development and to guarantee similar loans by private investors or public authorities. Its advocates maintained that the bank would undercut the appeal of communism and help the United States find markets for its investments and exports. The Bretton Woods plan was to be a keystone in assuring American participation in postwar international cooperation.[13]

Taft heartily disagreed. For more than a year he had joined such groups as the American Bankers Association and the United States Chamber of Commerce in criticizing the plan, and when it came to the Senate floor in July 1945, he was ready with even more statistics and documents than usual. Focusing his attack on the bank, he insisted that it threatened to usurp congressional control over lending, that it offered a "subsidy to the business of investment bankers," that it was foolishly generous with American money, and that it offered the United States no concessions in return. The American dollar, he proclaimed, is a "weapon, and I hope it will be used as a weapon." He also objected to the proposed American contribution of $3.1 billion to the bank. Together with dollars already earmarked for the Export-Import Bank, lend-lease, and the United Nations Relief and Rehabilitation Administration (UNRRA), he said, America would be dispensing more than $20 billion. Such a policy, he contended, would sap foreign nations of their incentive and promote inflation at home. Above all, he insisted that neither the fund nor the bank provided sufficient guarantees against use of American dollars to underwrite unsound loans. Foreign nations, he said, would eventually default, and a depression would follow as it had — for the same reason — in 1929. The whole program, he concluded scornfully, was like "pouring dollars down a rat-hole." [14]

As usual, Taft had readied an alternative. The postwar world, he agreed, needed stable exchanges, but these must be achieved through an agreement that set a satisfactory relationship between the dollar and the pound instead of trying multilaterally to stabilize all currencies. The world would also require American assistance, but it was better to give it unilaterally — such a procedure would be less wasteful and much easier to control. The bank, he said cagily, was not needed yet and should be deferred for a year or so. In the meantime, Congress should increase from $700 million to $3.5 billion the capital of the Export-Import Bank, a purely American institution that Congress could control and that ordinarily provided loans at interest rates high enough not to compete with private lenders. His proposal, like his call for direct loans as an alternative to lend-lease in 1941, stemmed from his antipathy toward long-range American commitments in the realm of international economics. It also represented his realization that blind opposition was foolish; had he been given a choice, Taft, who had frequently tried to limit the activities of the Export-Import Bank before the war, would have done as little as possible.

The debate stretched on into mid-July, and Taft held the floor for hours, cited reams of statistics from memory, and offered numerous amendments. Journalists marveled at his ability to stand for hours without sitting down and at his willingness to debate all colleagues who presumed to challenge his facts and figures. But the administration refused to back down on the essentials, and on July 19 the Senate approved both the bank and the fund, 61 to 16. Only a hard core of senators, most of whom had opposed internationalist ventures for years, stayed with him until the end.

Losing the battle discouraged him. The bankers, he complained, had withered under fire from the Treasury. "They had barely started the fight," he wrote, "when they began to compromise and compromise for a few crumbs." He also foresaw dire consequences. The bank, he wrote, might be "limited to a reasonable foreign investment, but the fund is cockeyed from the beginning

and is certain to be a waste of money." Still, he consoled himself
with the unduly optimistic assumption that he had rallied Americans to his cause. "Our fight," he wrote, "will definitely discourage
the Administration from lending many more billions around the
world."

In his long struggle against the plan, Taft had occasionally
scored relevant points. His repeated questioning in committee
hearings forced administration witnesses to concede that the success
of the bank and the fund did indeed depend on America's willingness to correct the disequilibrium in the world balance of payments. And his characteristic fear of wide-ranging American presence abroad led him to reach perceptive conclusions concerning
economic exploitation. American overseas investments, he
charged, led foreigners to view the United States as "absentee land-
lords," and had already provoked widespread anti-Americanism in
Cuba. Like many of his remarks, these sounded prophetic in the
1960's.[15]

But his arguments revealed that he really offered no consistent
alternative to Bretton Woods save carefully limited injections of
dollars through the Export-Import Bank and that he was still adhering strongly to a policy of America first. Moreover, his opposition to economic imperialism was directed not so much at private
lending, with which the Export-Import Bank would not compete,
but at the use of public funds for such purposes. His characteristic
habit of viewing foreign policies from the perspective of balancing
the domestic budget also caused him to adopt a nationalistic view
much like that which America had pursued in the 1920's. Far
from throwing away American money, the fund required borrowers of dollars to return equal amounts of their own currencies.
The fund also set voting rights according to the size of contributions, and because the United States supplied a third of the capital,
it was to have a dominant role in the operation. The bank not
only guaranteed the safety of American loans abroad but in practice proved so cautious that underdeveloped nations often complained. Undersecretary of State Dean Acheson, Taft's colleague
on the Yale Corporation, reacted angrily to Taft's close questioning in committee and accused him of "utterly unscrupulous

misrepresentation." [16] Failing to recognize the depth of Taft's instinctive dislike of heavy public spending abroad, Acheson was unfair. But he was correct in finding Taft wholly hostile to the administration's plans. Taft's response to Bretton Woods showed that in matters of foreign economic policy he was too budget-conscious and too nationalistic to listen to new ideas.

Even while standing against the Bretton Woods proposals, he had to consider the question of joining the United Nations. The UN Charter as developed at Dumbarton Oaks in 1944 and at San Francisco in May 1945 relied heavily on an eleven-nation Security Council with five permanent members — the United States, the Soviet Union, Great Britain, France, and China. Each of these five was to possess a veto. Though the framers also provided for a General Assembly and an International Court of Justice, they clearly relied on harmony among the great powers to keep the peace. The proposed charter was indeed far removed from the millennial aspirations of the "one worlders," world federalists, and the many other critics of the nation-state system.

Taft was willing to endorse the plan. "I am inclined to go along with any international organization that is set up, after presenting the objections for the record," he confided to Dewey in February 1945. The UN Charter, he repeated often in the spring, was better than a military alliance or an international state, and it wisely left to the member nations domestic matters such as control over immigration and minorities. He also recognized that the development of air power forced America to undertake new international obligations. "The policy of the free hand," he said in remarks that suggested he had departed somewhat from his prewar position, "is no longer the best method of preventing aggression against the United States." [17] A league of sovereign nations — the essence of the Mackinac declaration and the Connally resolution — could be a useful contribution to world peace.

Nonetheless, Taft had no illusions about the UN Charter. In the first place, he complained, the veto made the UN dependent on good will among the great powers. He predicted that it would prevent sanctions against the big five and their satellites and that it would provoke weaker nations to rearm. Still strongly anticommunist, he accepted the veto power as a way of keeping America from being forced by majority vote into projects that might aid the Soviet Union. But even so, he complained. Ideally, he thought, the veto ought not to be necessary.

Taft had an ideal — precisely the same as his father had advocated in 1918. It was a league of sovereign nations relying not on force but on law and justice. The nations of the world, he said, should establish an international law and then create a strong international court to enforce it. Whenever a dispute arose, it should be submitted to the court — and not, as planned under the UN Charter, to the Security Council. If the court decreed the dispute "justiciable," the same phrase used by his father, it should hear the case. Any nation that refused to submit disputes to the court, that refused to abide by a covenant providing for arms limitation and inspection, or that defied the court's decrees would clearly be an aggressor. In this case the member nations should — without option of a veto — adopt economic sanctions and ultimately force, if necessary, to halt the aggressor. Ideally, however, America would seldom have to involve herself in such collective sanctions, but would provide troops only after regional councils had failed to control the conflagration. Ultimately public opinion would require only the rarest resort to force. "If we can establish an international law and a Court to apply it," he said, "the moral force of those decisions may well dominate in time public opinion of the world, so that no nation dare defy it." [18]

He also objected strenuously to one more feature of the package presented to the Senate in July 1945: the absence of any congressional controls on the American delegate to the Security Council. In a league based on law such a question, like the veto power, would not matter. But in a league reliant on force, Congress ought at least to lay down the "general principles" on which the American delegate would vote — principles, predictably, promoting results "in accordance with international justice as well as international peace and security." This question was not settled in July, and he joined a majority of 89 to 2 in favor of the charter. But when the issue arose in December, he offered amendments to curb the delegate's discretion. When they failed, he joined six others in a futile vote against the administration.[19] Five years later, when the North Koreans swept south across the Thirty-Eighth Parallel, President Truman alone had the power to direct the American delegates at the UN.

Taft was realistic in arguing that the world was not ready to support collective security and that the "policeman" emphasis of the UN was little more than what one critic later called a "self-appointed lynch gang." He also dared to raise the unpopular but critical question of the right of the executive to wage war without congressional authorization. And his call for regional defense agreements, while motivated by his desire to free America from European entanglements, sounded curiously like the argument of "realists" in the 1950's and 1960's who advocated a spheres-of-influence approach to foreign policy. But whether a league such as Taft envisioned, heavily dependent on a world court, would have worked in the atomic age is extremely doubtful, especially since he would have endowed it with no police force to implement its decisions. And because he fully recognized the Soviet Union's opposition to a strong court, it is questionable whether he seriously expected his recommendations to be adopted. Indeed, the Soviets called such arguments for law and "justice" nothing but a cover that would enable a noncommunist league to deprive them of a buffer zone in Eastern Europe. In 1944 Taft had already sounded the alarm about Soviet designs — Roosevelt's actions at the Teheran conference, he complained, seemed "based on the delightful theory that Mr. Stalin in the end will turn out to have an angelic nature" — and all Taft's statements in 1945 merely echoed this refrain of distrust.[20]

Thus in calling for a strong court — and for a real surrender of sovereignty — Taft was seeking what he must have known the great powers would never accept amid the antagonisms of 1945. Far from having become an enthusiast for collective security, he remained cautious, nationalistic, anticommunist — and faithful to the visions of men like his father who had optimistically advanced international law as a solution to the world's problems before 1930. In so doing he saved himself from the delusion that the UN would reform the world. With Vandenberg and others Taft also managed to offer GOP modifications for the record. But he left himself in the position of calling for an impossible agreement on what international law ought to be and for an illusory covenant binding nations to it. He was in the short run more of a dreamer than the idealists he criticized.[21]

PART IV

Sources and Uses of Power

CHAPTER 20

The Partisan Dimension, 1945–1946

IN WARM SPRINGS, GEORGIA, President Roosevelt relaxed in the sun. But a few minutes after 1 PM on April 12, 1945, he clutched his head. "I have a terrible headache," he groaned. He slumped in his chair, fainted, and was carried to bed. By four o'clock he was dead, mercifully spared the travails of pulling the nation from the sacrifices of war into the pettiness of peace. After twelve years an era had ended.

At least Taft thought so. Distrusting Roosevelt, he had had practically no personal contact with him, and he showed little feeling of loss.[1] But Harry S Truman might be another matter. True, he was the product of the odorous Pendergast machine in Kansas City, and he associated with friends and sycophants whom Taft would have scorned. He had served Roosevelt for ten years in the Senate and criticized Taft sharply in the 1944 campaign. Yet Taft at first hoped for the best and decided to call on the new President and offer Republican assistance. "This is a pretty hard thing to do for a long time," he admitted privately, "but until he gets his feet on the ground I think we should go a long way in trying to help." On April 18, along with others who were paying their respects, he made his visit — his first to the White House executive offices since the days of Hoover — and the next day he went back, alone, primarily to urge the new President to reconsider the unconditional surrender demanded of Japan. With three sons in the Pacific, Taft, like many others in early 1945, hoped to avoid a land invasion of Japan, and he was willing even to permit Japan to retain Formosa if such terms would bring peace. To reporters, however, he was vague about his visit. "There were a lot of other people there yesterday," Taft told them. "I couldn't really talk to him. I just had some general suggestions to make, things I thought ought to be done." [2]

The honeymoon, many people predicted, could not last long. But for three weeks Taft tried to help. He sympathized with Truman, who had been thrust rudely into an office that had victimized William Howard Taft. Taft also liked Truman — "a straightforward man and much franker than Roosevelt," he confided to a friend. "He has the quality of decision which is a good thing in an executive." Perhaps, too, Taft was mildly flattered at being granted a presidential audience. "For the first time in many years," he wrote, "there is a chance that the Republicans may be consulted and given some part in the formulation of policy." Though he worried (like almost everyone else) about Truman's lack of "education or background to analyze soundly the large problems which are before him," he was charitable. "He will make every effort to hold the party together," Taft concluded, "and will go along with all the New Deal measures up to a point. If the party divides, however, I think he will go with the conservative side. Altogether I think it is a marked improvement, largely because the whole government is more inclined to follow the law instead of breaking it." [3]

Taft was right about Truman's frankness and capacity for decision, but he was mistaken in thinking the new President would rely on conservatives for advice. Indeed, on April 19 Truman endorsed the existing price control procedures and the international monetary fund. Discarding his cautious optimism of April, Taft resumed his attacks on the "super propaganda" of the State Department and carried on a running battle with the administration in May and June over price control. Truman, Taft wrote unhappily on May 25, "will be as much a New Dealer as Roosevelt. I cannot discover any tendency to turn to a conservative policy, and there are going to be a good many violent controversies here during the next twelve months. Especially, he seems to be embracing the spending policies of the New Deal and the making of huge loans abroad to keep up our employment in this country. I can only hope that he does not acquire the popularity of Roosevelt for election purposes." [4]

By June, Taft was openly attacking the administration. Worried about a flood of cheap postwar imports, he backed unsuccessfully a series of amendments to curb Truman's tariff-making authority. Tariffs, Taft conceded, must not be subjected to the logrolling temptations of Congress, but they must also be kept from the capricious bureaucrats who had been negotiating reciprocal trade agreements since 1934. Echoing his father, Taft argued that the Tariff Commission could equalize the difference between the cost of production at home and abroad. This approach underestimated the formidable practical difficulties involved in such a procedure, but he had long adhered to it, and he never changed his mind on the subject. It was characteristic of his insistence on guiding principles as opposed to executive discretion in the formulation of policy.[5]

By mid-August 1945, after the protracted struggle over Bretton Woods in June and July, Truman's honeymoon had ended, and Taft did not pause in his assault on the administration.[6] When the French showed signs of resenting American soldiers, Taft reasserted his opposition to the stationing of large contingents of American troops abroad. "The best we can do," he wrote, "is to get our men entirely out of France at the earliest possible moment . . . It is rather discouraging to find that we have made ourselves apparently very unpopular in the world in spite of everything we have done and all the money we have spent." When Truman at the Potsdam conference in July in effect confirmed the cession of part of eastern Germany to Poland, Taft insisted that the seeds of another war had been sown. Truman, he told David Ingalls, has made his "first mistake in the Potsdam Report. He really is a very limited and superficial statesman but up to date his moves have been popular, largely, I think, because he is such a contrast to Roosevelt." [7]

With war over at last in September, Americans stirred more restlessly than ever under governmental restrictions, and Taft and his allies began to score limited victories. The Senate abolished the excess profits tax as of January 1946, slashed the rates on corporations, and cut income taxes even more sharply than Taft wanted to do at the time.[8] It also hedged the so-called full employment bill by eliminating favorable references to deficit spending as the approved means of counteracting unemployment. Taft upset right-wing businessmen by agreeing that the federal government must play an important role in stabilizing the business cycle and by admitting the need for compensatory spending under certain adverse conditions. But he adhered otherwise to his faith in balanced budgets and insisted, as he had done years earlier in the Ohio legislature, that increases in spending must be accompanied by comparable increases in taxation.[9]

As 1946 approached, Taft despaired of Truman's policies. "He hasn't got the background or education to analyze complex economic problems for himself," Taft complained, "and so he takes what is handed to him by the bureaus which are full of New Dealers." Already, Taft was becoming one of Truman's arch foes in the Senate, and as the off-year elections approached, Taft developed a partisan stance as unyielding as he had ever displayed against Roosevelt.

The new year began with a confrontation over civil rights. Taft had long favored abolition of the poll tax and had supported federal bills against lynching. He also knew there was "real discrimination" in employment "so that negroes generally are laid off first in hard times and put on last in good times." But he complained of Northern Democrats, who he said were hypocritically calling for federal legislation. "I doubt if we can outbid Mrs. Roosevelt," he grumbled. He also concluded characteristically that federal laws by themselves could not root out injustices. "It is just about as difficult to prevent discrimination against negroes as it is to prevent discrimination against Republicans," he wrote. "We know the latter is impossible." And he therefore opposed vehemently the administration's wish for a permanent Fair Employment Practices Commission to prohibit discrimination in employment. Granting that the bill creating the committee should come to a vote, he joined Northern Democrats in favoring cloture against a Southern filibuster, then offered his own fair employment practices bill calling for a commission with powers of persuasion only.[10] If the administration exaggerated the potential for its compulsory bill, it faced the moral issue more clearly than Taft and argued the necessity of federal sanctions. Taft, like most white Americans in 1946, simply failed to appreciate the plight of the black man in American society, for little in his own experience had exposed him to it. For that reason and because of his revulsion against federal direction, he was never to accept a permanent and powerful FEPC.[11]

With the coming of spring, Taft began to focus his attention on the two key issues of the time: labor and price control. The labor problem was already severe. Union leaders, though cooperative during the war, had even then grumbled about inflation, and in late 1945 they began demanding wage increases. When management resisted, an unprecedented series of nationwide strikes in such essential industries as coal, steel, automobiles, and transportation gripped the country in the winter of 1946. In February alone strikes cost 23 million man-days. This militance led many people to talk of sharp new curbs on unions.

Responsive to this mood, Taft worked to revise the National Labor Relations Act of 1935. In February 1946 the House passed the so-called Case bill, which tried revision. This measure outlawed secondary boycotts and violent picketing, permitted antistrike injunctions, and provided for a thirty-day cooling-off period before strikes could be called. But in late March, Democrats on the Senate Education and Labor Committee reported a mild bill. Taft, assisted by Joseph Ball of Minnesota, an energetic Republican who strongly favored restrictions on unions, resolved to toughen the committee bill. The National Labor Relations Act of 1935, Taft argued, had been "reasonable," but pro-union implementation of it had "practically tied the hands and closed the mouths of every employer." The answer, he insisted, was to "redress somewhat the excessive power given to the labor unions in collective bargaining, so that unreasonable men may not be tempted to abuse that excessive power." [12]

With the nation in the grip of a rail strike in May, he succeeded. Republicans voted almost unanimously for the Taft-Ball amendments, and enough Democrats went along to carry the day by comfortable margins of almost 2 to 1. This form of the Case bill, which finally passed the Senate by a vote of 49 to 29 on May 25, set up a strong Federal Mediation Board largely independent of the Labor Department, provided for a sixty-day cooling-off period before strikes could be initiated, required unions to let employers coadminister their welfare funds, and outlawed secondary boycotts. It also made unions liable to prosecution for violation of their contracts and defined foremen as part of management, thus depriving them of the rights of employees under the NLRA. Though the bill fell short of the demands of many antiunion congressmen, it reflected the growing fear of the expanded power of organized labor.

Truman vetoed the Case bill in mid-June. The so-called cooling-off period, he said, might encourage rather than prevent strikes; the mediation board would undercut the authority of the secretary of labor; union welfare funds should remain a subject for collective bargaining; and the clauses concerning foremen and secondary boycotts were discriminatory. The House then failed, 255 to 135, to secure the two-thirds vote necessary to override the veto. Taft had lost, but he was encouraged by the clear congressional mandate for action. In 1947, with Republicans in control of both houses, he was to try again.

Thus far he had seemed merely one of many congressmen anxious to place restrictions on the unions. But another crisis on May 25 showed him in a more neutral light. On that afternoon, only a few hours before the Senate passed the Case bill, Truman appeared before Congress to ring the alarm against unions that disrupted the national safety and in particular against the rail workers, who were finishing their second day of a walkout. As he spoke, word reached him that the rail strike had been settled, and Congress erupted in applause when he told them the news. But Truman pressed grimly on. He requested authority to declare a state of emergency in case of strikes in vital industries or mines — authority permitting the government to operate the industries involved, to penalize defiant union leaders, and to draft strikers into the armed services.

It was a mark of the almost hysterical hostility toward unions that the House approved this sweeping request within two hours by a vote of 306 to 13. Everyone expected the Senate to follow suit that evening. But at this point Taft coolly objected to immediate consideration of the bill. He then entered into a most improbable alliance with Senator Claude Pepper, an enthusiastic New Deal Democrat from Florida, who had been resisting the Case bill all day. Truman's request, said Taft, "violates every principle of American jurisprudence"; there was no excuse for the President's "most extreme" and "unconstitutional" demands. Successfully preventing precipitate Senate approval, Taft then persuaded the GOP steering committee to recommend six amendments to Truman's request. In removing the authority to draft strikers, these would have cut the heart out of his program. By May 28, three days after the crisis, even administration Democrats were beginning to recognize the dangers of the President's blatant assault on unions, and they squirmed to delay a record vote. But Taft demanded a roll call, marshaled his forces, and succeeded in defeating the draft proposal, 70 to 13. Two days later the Senate passed, 61 to 20, a much modified bill, which made strikers in vital industries potentially subject to the loss of protection under the National Labor Relations Act. Distressed by even this infringement on the civil liberties of workers, Taft left his party to join a handful of progressive Democrats against it. As surprised observers were beginning to notice, he insisted on protecting the right to strike and refused to abandon this principle even in the face of nationwide alarm.[13]

They should not have been surprised. Taft's stand was not only characteristic of his determination to think for himself but consistent with everything he had said on the subject since the 1920's. Government interference with strikes, he said, was unfair to the worker and required a most undesirable expansion of federal power. "A democratic government cannot prohibit strikes and remain," he said. America, he explained to his cousin Hulbert Taft, "must protect itself against action threatening the health or safety of the people," but "it is a very difficult thing to write a law on the statute books authorizing the President to intervene in any labor dispute, seize the property, and put the workers in jail." [14] As ever, he shrank from the idea of federal intervention, whether to regulate business or organized labor. And if action must ultimately be taken, let Congress, not the President, set the ground rules. However sympathetic he was to the problems of businessmen, Taft had shown himself to be fair-minded, devoted to the principle of free collective bargaining, and far removed from the antilabor monster some of his Democratic critics liked to make him out to be.

Taft threw himself into labor questions partly because events left him no choice. On the question of price control, however, he took the lead against the administration from the beginning. When the struggle had ended in August 1946, he had succeeded in whittling away controls. But in the process he displayed a partisan zeal that outraged the administration. Few issues of his long career did more to stamp him in the eyes of his critics as a friend of business and an enemy of the poor man.

He began his assault as early as December 1945. Controls over scarce commodities, he admitted, were necessary, but the OPA was still too inflexible, too concerned with curbing profits instead of prices, too callous toward the needs of small businessmen. Wage increases, he argued, were forcing entrepreneurs out of business, discouraging production, and pushing up prices in the process. Director of Economic Stabilization Chester Bowles must permit processors and retailers profit margins that would reflect cost-of-living increases since October 1941, and he must remove controls completely on many abundant commodities. With these incentives, Taft concluded, manufacturers would rapidly increase production, which, by satisfying the increased postwar demand for goods, would automatically stabilize prices.

As postwar tensions mounted early in 1946, Taft found such a receptive audience among his colleagues that he never had to worry about retaining the support of Richard Russell, Harry Byrd, Walter George, or even that of Democrats ordinarily loyal to the administration. Truman, they argued, was permitting unions to demand higher wages, while employers were being denied increases in prices. Indeed, angry producers of such abundant commodities as meat and lumber were withholding their products in anticipation of forcing the administration to remove controls, and many Americans were already finding the black market the only source of meat. With the administration demanding continuation of strong controls after June 30, Taft and his colleagues girded for action.[15]

From the start the battle was bitter and personal. Bowles, Taft charged, was "like King Canute bidding the tide to stand still." When Bowles then appeared before the banking and currency committee in April, Taft immediately embarked on the aggressively hostile tactics which so infuriated New Dealers. He repeatedly interrupted the testimony, asked leading questions, and flung obscure statistics at Bowles, who had encountered such tactics from Taft before and tried to keep his temper. But Taft pressed on, and Bowles shot back. "Before you attack my point of view," he flared, "why don't you listen to it? I think that's the courteous way." Undeterred, Taft charged Bowles with "false statements." Taft's behavior typified his frequent sharpness in committee, and it widened the chasm developing between him and the administration.[16]

However, Taft's tactics merely gratified the committee, which overwhelmingly approved a host of amendments designed to curb the OPA. In June the Senate followed suit. Among these amendments, two in particular upset the administration. One, sponsored by aggressive, volatile Kenneth Wherry of Nebraska, granted to wholesalers, distributors, and retailers prices equal to their current costs plus the markup since 1941. The other, Taft's, banned price ceilings that did not give producers profit margins equal to those of October 1941, a time of sizable profits in most industries. The Senate then ignored all objections and passed the bill with these amendments by a vote of 53 to 11. The size of the majority proclaimed the extent of congressional hostility to the price control guidelines of 1946.

What followed pleased practically no one. Two weeks later the House approved a slightly more moderate bill, and after a show of resistance, Taft and the other Senate conferees backed down on some minor amendments. Democratic congressional leaders, aware that the bill was the most the administration could hope for, reluctantly voted for the conference report and urged Truman to approve it. But Bowles felt otherwise. Resigning as director of economic stabilization, he pressed Truman to veto the bill, and on June 29, one day before expiration of existing controls, Truman singled out the Taft amendment for criticism and leveled a sharp veto message against the bill. His action astonished his congressional leaders, infuriated Republicans, and left the country without any controls at all.[17]

Prices skyrocketed immediately, and by mid-July angry housewives and union members were already staging boycotts and demonstrations against retailers. Just as quickly, Taft and Truman exchanged recriminations. By the time Truman accepted a slightly revised bill on July 25, the cost-of-living index had increased by 6 per cent, double the rise under the OPA in the three years since 1943; and the new version proved so ineffective that the index increased another 9 per cent by November. The long struggle on Capitol Hill had culminated in hardship for the American consumer.

Many people blamed Congress in general and Taft in particular for this debacle. Profits, they conceded, tended to be small per item in 1946, but adequate overall because of increased sales. Controls, these critics agreed, eventually had to be relaxed, but not during the inflationary pressures of June 1946. Taft, they claimed, had forced passage of a bill that even he admitted would have resulted in price increases of as much as 10 per cent, and Truman had no choice but to take a stand against it.

Taft tried to refute these claims. Truman, he said, had fed inflation by surrendering to the demands of unions and by promoting policies that led to market shortages of abundant commodities. Taft conceded that some larger companies were prospering but insisted that smaller entrepreneurs were suffering. The President, he claimed, had tried to obscure months of bungling by a politically inspired veto. The result was price increases far beyond what the congressional bill would have created.

Because the original bill never had a chance to operate, it is difficult to evaluate these charges and countercharges. But some facts seem clear in retrospect. In the first place Taft had not been quite the reactionary defender of business that Fair Dealers maintained. On the contrary, from the beginning he had agreed on the necessity for some controls, and he was correct in pointing out the squeeze confronting some small businessmen. He had also dared to part company with irreconcilable opponents of price control by voting against the original Wherry amendment and against another amendment that would have removed all controls on farm commodities. He accepted the conference report over Wherry's vociferous objections and voted reluctantly for the revised bill in July — a bill that excised the "Taft amendment" and that Wherry angrily called a "manifest prostitution" of the will of the Senate. Taft pursued his own path even if it occasionally meant conflict with more antiadministration Republicans.

He was also more honest about his intentions than some of his allies. Unlike such pressure groups as the National Association of Manufacturers, he refused to claim that a relaxation of controls would have no effect. On the contrary, he admitted his own amendment might lead to temporary price increases of 10 per cent before increased production drove them down again. It was characteristic of him that he worried less about the impact of his amendment on the short-run buying power of consumers than about the individual rights of entrepreneurs and small businessmen, and that he was willing to say so.

Finally, Taft was probably right in accusing Truman of political motives in vetoing the bill and surely correct in pointing to his ineptitude. Had Truman stood firmly behind wage-price guidelines earlier in the year, some of the inflationary pressures could have been avoided. Had he stopped the War Production Board from removing restrictions on the making of items not covered by price control, he could have prevented manufacturers from concentrating on such items and from adding to pressures on prices of other, scarcer goods. And had he defended Bowles from the start, he might have secured a slightly more palatable bill in June. Instead, he implied to his congressional leaders that he would accept what he had to. When he rejected the original measure, he abandoned his congressional aides, left the nation without controls, and ended by accepting a bill in July close to that which he had vetoed in June. If Truman had listened to Congress in the first place, American consumers might have faced increases of 10 per cent or more under the bill forced on them by Taft and the Congress. Thanks to his belated veto, they probably fared a little worse.

On the other hand, OPA officials had ample grounds for objecting to Taft's amendment. They pointed out correctly that basing margins according to those of 1941 gave producers perhaps the highest unit profits on record. His amendment would also have removed brakes on wage increases, since manufacturers, assured of profits, would not have had to worry so much about labor costs. And the OPA complained most cogently about the administrative ramifications of his amendment, which would have forced the agency to replace dollars-and-cents price ceilings with complicated formulas based on five-year-old records. But Taft possessed an unconcealed contempt for OPA bureaucrats, whom he regarded as New Dealers prospering at the public trough, and he dismissed such administrative technicalities. What mattered was the principle of protecting businessmen against the hand of arbitrary federal regulation, and if the clerks and pencil pushers could not do that, let them find another job.

Taft's dislike of extensive federal regulation had also led him to a faulty analysis of the economic situation in 1946. Underpinning his amendment was his belief that guaranteed profit margins would give manufacturers the incentive to increase production until it matched demand.[18] But this assumption failed to recognize that manufacturers were already producing close to capacity. More important, it underestimated the demand. Americans had been unable to purchase many consumer goods during four and one-half years of war, and in 1945 and 1946 they demanded much more than producers could supply. Recognizing these pressures, Bowles argued that controls must remain at least until the end of 1946; and the price increases which followed the dismantling of controls in July 1946 proved that he had been correct. Had Taft possessed less hostility to the OPA, he might have listened to the many economists who supported Bowles's analysis.

•

The struggle over price control had been fought in frightfully hot and humid weather, and Taft had often labored on the Hill far into the night. With adjournment at the end of July 1946, he gladly escaped to Murray Bay for the first real rest he had enjoyed since before the war.[19]

For a change he could do so with satisfaction. To many Americans, Truman seemed inept, uncertain, vulnerable at the polls, a sad successor to Roosevelt. And the press was even beginning to give Taft some attention. *U.S. News & World Report* placed him on its cover in May, *Time* featured him in June, and *Newsweek* gave him a cover study in July. Even Joseph and Stewart Alsop, syndicated columnists who had often criticized him, recognized his skills as a parliamentarian. To his Republican colleagues, Taft's courage and sheer hard work were making him their undisputed, indeed towering leader. And to thousands of

Americans he was becoming the most solid bastion of opposition to the New Deal-Fair Deal philosophy.[20]

Meanwhile, Truman's political fortunes plummeted still further. Henry Wallace, his secretary of commerce, grew so critical of the administration's unyielding policy toward the Soviet Union that Truman fired him in September. Meat became so scarce that controls on it had to be removed in October. "To err is Truman," Martha reportedly quipped, and Republicans gleefully picked up her turn of phrase as they prepared for their first great victory since 1928. Their slogan, "Had Enough?" captured the mood of the nation.

Taft responded happily to the opportunity. "If Truman wanted to elect a Republican Congress," he wrote Dewey, "he could not be doing a better job." Envisioning large Republican gains, he cut short his vacation and took to the campaign trail. Knoxville, Denver, Utah, Philadelphia, Indiana, Ohio, Chicago. Back and forth across the East and Midwest. With Soviet-American relations deteriorating, he also permitted himself excesses that infuriated his opponents. The Democrats, he proclaimed, "at Tehran, at Yalta, at Potsdam, and at Moscow pursued a policy of appeasing Russia, a policy which has sacrificed throughout Eastern Europe and Asia the freedom of many nations and millions of people." Truman, he added, coveted the "support of . . . the Communists in the November election," and sought a Congress "dominated by a policy of appeasing the Russians abroad and of fostering Communism at home." The Democratic party, he concluded, "is so divided between Communism and Americanism that its foreign policy can only be futile and contradictory and make the United States the laughing stock of the world." [21] Few people noticed such speeches, but Taft, like many other Republicans in 1946, was anticipating the strategy of a man who was himself to be elected as a freshman senator that fall: Joseph McCarthy of Wisconsin.

In November Republicans swept to victories throughout the nation and emerged with majorities in the House of 245 to 188 and in the Senate of 51 to 45. For the first time since 1930, Republicans would control the Congress. And Truman, it appeared, was doomed to defeat in 1948. Pleased, Taft departed with Martha for a leisurely vacation in Central America.[22]

But these months since Truman's accession to the White House in April 1945 were a mixed blessing to Taft. Repeatedly he had battled the administration — over Bretton Woods, full employment, civil rights, unions, and price control — and he had won as often as he had lost. Yet his partisanship, his combative nature, his rhetorical excesses, his zealously sincere desire to dismantle the New Deal — and above all his power — made him an object of fear and of criticism by his opponents. These traits also made him the chief target of many commentators and journalists, and Walter Lippmann, dean of them all, was moved in 1945 to conclude that Taft

> has never acquired sufficient wisdom and understanding . . . He is probably more responsible than any other single man for leading the Republican party into blind alleys of dumb obstruction on the vital issues of our time.[23]

This appraisal neglected to mention Taft's courage, sincerity, and moderation on some issues. But Lippmann reflected a not uncommon opinion. When Taft later turned his head toward replacing Truman in the White House, he was to discover the price to be paid for leading the crusade against the Fair Deal.

CHAPTER 21

The Taft Philosophy

PERHAPS BECAUSE of the din set loose by the partisan controversies of 1945 and 1946, few people stopped to scrutinize the convictions underlying Taft's attitudes at the time. Yet during this period he showed that beneath the partisanship of his rhetoric lay a mind capable of change. It was during this time, too, that his domestic philosophy revealed him as one of the more consistent thinkers among the politicians of his generation.

He expressed this philosophy most cogently on three issues, housing, aid to education, and the trials of German leaders for war crimes. Of the three, housing seemed the most urgent in 1945. Ten years of hard times in the 1930's had sharply curtailed residential building, and the ensuing years of war had forced contractors to turn their attention to higher priorities. By 1946 an acute housing shortage of nearly five million units had developed. People crowded into chicken coops, attics, basements, and boxcars, and it was estimated that between 20 and 30 per cent of all Americans lived in substandard housing. With returning veterans already complaining bitterly and with the baby boom pyramiding the problem, it was clear that the federal government would have to step in to alleviate the shortage.[1]

The question was how. Practically all congressmen favored expansion of the Federal Housing Administration and of the home loan banks — programs that provided government aid and guarantees to private builders and home buyers. Many congressmen also favored federal loans for rural housing and for urban renewal. But these programs would have done little to assist the millions of poor people who could not afford down payments for homes. Progres-

sives argued that only public housing projects would provide the
poor with the shelter they needed. It was over this question of
public housing that the battle had to be waged in Congress.

Through Stanley Rowe, his Indian Hill neighbor who had
chaired the Cincinnati Housing Authority between 1933 and
1944, Taft had long been familiar with the arguments for public
housing. Indeed in 1937, Rowe persuaded him to tour the slums
of Cincinnati, and in 1938 Taft also visited public housing projects
in Cincinnati and Cleveland, where he came to know Ernest J.
Bohn, head of the Cleveland Housing Authority and later founder
of the National Association of Housing and Redevelopment Officials. More tours followed — in and out of fetid alleyways, up dark
staircases, and through filthy overcrowded dwellings. These experiences left him all but convinced that public authorities must
somehow take a hand. The housing movement, he wrote, "is one
of those things that appeals to the people as a whole as progressive,
and I think it can be done without the dangers that a general socialistic housing plan might bring about." [2]

Still, Taft refrained before 1945 from heading a movement for
public housing. While voting for modest appropriations to carry
on the United States Housing Authority, he seemed as interested
in abolishing bureaucratic overlap in federal housing agencies as
he was in pouring large amounts of money into public housing.
Above all, he felt the need of facts and figures to corroborate what
his eyes had suggested to him. Until he had the statistics, he declined to go further.

Taft's opportunity for study had come in 1943 when he took
charge of a subcommittee on housing and urban redevelopment
under the Special Committee on Postwar Economic Policy and
Planning. His willingness to assume this responsibility suggested
the extent of his interest, and the time he devoted to it proved it,
for he quickly began work by sending questionnaires to national
housing bodies and to private organizations. His purpose, he explained cautiously, was to consider and evaluate public housing
and its alternatives. Meanwhile some of his colleagues on the subcommittee, especially Democrats Robert Wagner of New York and
Allen Ellender of Louisiana, felt no need for such study: they already favored rapid extension of public housing. By early 1945,

when his subcommittee completed exhaustive hearings that eventually filled a thousand pages of testimony, Taft was inclined to agree. While still uncertain about some things — the number of units to be subsidized, who would be eligible to live in them, whether the poor should be helped to buy such units — he was ready to take a stand with his Democratic colleagues.[3]

In August he did so by issuing his subcommittee's report. It called for a broad housing policy featuring grants for slum clearance, easier FHA loans for home buyers, and the organization of housing operations into a permanent National Housing Agency. It set a goal of 1.25 million new living units per year for the next ten years. Most controversial, the report recommended that the government finance 500,000 public housing units within the next four years. "Every family," the report stated, "must have a decent home in which to live. The character of that home determines more than anything else the character of family life, the conditions in which children grow up and the attitude of people toward the community and government." [4] For Taft, these were strong words indeed.

It remained to translate these words into legislation. Wagner, long a champion of public housing, had chafed throughout the spring at Taft's painstaking study. But because Wagner was anxious to secure his Republican colleague as a cosponsor of a public housing bill, he awaited Taft's report, submitted legislative drafts for his approval, and treated him deferentially during hearings of the Banking and Currency Committee. But Taft still held back from agreeing to cosponsor a bill. The real estate lobby, he recognized, adamantly opposed public housing, as did the majority of the House of Representatives. Precisely because he was convinced of the need for public housing, he wished to move quietly lest the enemy rouse itself to action. Wagner, he complained in June, was "hurting the cause by stirring up the opposition." [5]

By August, Wagner had tired of waiting. "I don't think housing needs more investigation," he snapped. "I think it needs action." When Taft still refrained from cosponsorship, Wagner and Ellender went ahead on their own August 2 with a bill calling for 1.2 million housing units to be built per year for the next five years. The bill differed only in minor respects from Taft's subcommittee report, and Taft told reporters he would work to bridge the gap. Privately, however, he was annoyed. "Wagner," he complained to Stanley Rowe, "went ahead with his bill without showing it to me. It contains many of the proposals recommended in the report, but there is a lot in it that I do not approve of, and I am sure that the private housing people will regard it as a public housing bill . . . all of the talk has a patronizing tone of the public houser." [6] Taft's differences with the Democrats revealed the tensions involved in introducing bipartisan legislation. They also showed him in characteristic pose: precise, cautious, ever aware of the foes of public housing. Government aid for housing, he had come to believe, was necessary because there was no other way. And because it was necessary, Congress must approve it, quickly if possible, but above all carefully and soundly.

With these goals in mind, he refused to let Wagner's impatience disturb him and spent much of a late summer recess working for compromise. In November they finally settled their differences and cosponsored the so-called Wagner-Ellender-Taft housing bill, which set a goal of 1.25 million new housing units per year for the next ten years. The bill recommended federal grants for slum clearance, easier FHA loans for would-be homeowners, long-term low-interest government loans for the construction of 500,000 public housing units within the next four years, and government subsidies for their maintenance. Tenants in these public units would pay a fifth of their incomes in rent, which in turn was to be at least 20 per cent less than the prevailing rent for standard housing in the neighborhood. Cost of the controversial public housing section was expected to approximate $90 million over the next four years.[7]

This bill, while modified slightly in ensuing congressional sessions, formed the substance of Taft's convictions on housing, and he missed few opportunities to proclaim its virtues. The free enterprise system, he bluntly told Cleveland home builders in December, "has certain definite faults. We have not learned to eliminate ups and downs, booms and depressions, and so there is unemployment at times and hardship . . . in short, while the average is high, the necessary inequality of the system leaves millions poor." Socialism, he continued, would not work in the United States, but

neither would " 'let the devil take the hindmost.' If the free enterprise system does not do its best to prevent hardship and poverty, it
will find itself superseded by a less progressive system which does."
Congress must "undertake to put a floor under essential things to
give all a minimum standard of living, and all children an opportunity to get a start in life." [8] His speech shocked his reactionary
admirers. But it became characteristic of his philosophy of social
welfare for the rest of his life.

Though Taft had expected opposition to the bill, even he was
taken aback by the abuse hurled in his direction. Progressives, on
the one hand, distrusted his prominence in their cause. Taft, the
New Republic sneered, was "jumping on the housing bandwagon." *The Nation* called the bill "mild and watered down."
But the real estate lobby, led by the National Association of Real
Estate Boards (NAREB), spearheaded the assault. It claimed that
public housing would subsidize lazy and immoral people, waste
government money, and confront builders with ruinous competition. It reserved its greatest outrage for Taft, the spokesman for
business turned traitor, who "does not any longer believe in the
American private enterprise system. He is at heart a socialist." [9]

Taft gave no sign of retreat under such criticism. Instead, he
engaged Herbert U. Nelson, head of the NAREB, in debate in
Cincinnati. Public housing, Taft said, was not socialism, and it
would be available only to low-income people who would otherwise live in slums. Indeed, as some of the more progressive advocates of public housing pointed out, the W-E-T bill did nothing
for a million families earning less than $750 a year, and offered
most to middle-income families who could take advantage of those
sections of the bill liberalizing FHA mortgages. The bill also
offered no competition to builders. As Taft pointed out, they had
more than enough to do constructing houses for home buyers, and
they had always shunned low-income housing as unprofitable. He
also argued that public housing might ultimately save money.
Relatively small outlays, he said, could stop whole neighborhoods
from turning into slums, encourage private builders to invest in
such areas, and thereby limit the number of public housing units
needed to a million over the next ten years. Taft had accepted the
need for public housing, and he was prepared to authorize more

than a million units if necessary. But he saw it as a means of entic-
ing builders into urban redevelopment, not necessarily as a permanent government program of supporting the poor.[10]

To Taft, as to many other converts to the cause, public housing
was not a radical or socialistic plan but a practical means toward
one of the most honorable of conservative aspirations: preservation
of the family by ensuring it a decent environment. He was on
solid ground in dismissing the claims of the real estate lobby, and
was abreast of his times in attempting to attack one of the symptoms of the decay that was threatening to engulf American cities.

Taft's cosponsorship of the measure surprised some of his right-
wing Republican friends. "I hear that the Socialists have gotten to
Bob Taft," John Bricker was reported as saying in 1946. But most
of his Republican colleagues reacted more temperately. Surely
Taft was no radical, and if he thought the bill was necessary, perhaps it was worth studying. Given the serious housing shortage,
they felt obliged to back the portions of the bill assisting middle-
income housing, and rather than prolong the fight, they acquiesced
in the public housing section as well. With Taft carrying the
brunt of debate on the floor, the bill passed the Senate on April 15,
1946 without even a roll call.[11]

But the House rebelled. A conservative coalition in the Banking and Currency Committee not only refused to hold hearings on
the bill but twice denied Taft himself the courtesy of testifying. In
July the committee voted against reporting the plan to the floor,
and the measure died. Taft was to try again in 1948 and to succeed
in 1949. But the defeat in 1946 showed how little influence he
possessed over the deliberately independent House Republicans,
who left him helpless with frustration and enabled President Truman to make a plausible case against what he called the reactionary
thrust of Republican congressional leadership.

•

Taft's position on housing reinforced earlier predilections. His
statements on federal aid to education, by contrast, represented a
sharp break with his recent past. Indeed, his conversion to the
cause in 1945 and 1946 marked a shift in his thinking as profound
as any of his lifetime.

During much of 1944 he had seen little reason to depart from the hostile stance that had defeated the federal aid to education bill in 1943. Indeed, he held to his position, a precarious one for a senator seeking re-election, throughout his 1944 campaign. He favored higher teachers' salaries, but as a conscious alternative to federal aid. "The increase to teachers," he wrote in August 1944, "is a matter of justice. If that increase is not fairly general in the United States, we are almost certain to have a bill passed providing federal aid to education. I believe this would be a substantial step toward federal control of schools and the subordination of State government to Washington." In January 1945 he still defended his position of 1943. "I opposed the bill," he said, "because I don't want the Federal government running our schools and trying to indoctrinate our children." [12]

Even in 1943, however, he had begun to wonder. His visit to Puerto Rico had shocked him, and he began to recognize that poverty and inferior schooling were related. In poring over statistics, he was struck by the evidence of gross inequities in per-pupil spending for schools and by the low expenditures, especially in black districts, in the South. He also grew alarmed by figures showing that poor educational backgrounds had caused more than a million Americans to fail selective service examinations. When the Education and Labor Committee again studied federal aid in January 1945, he was already moving toward providing poorer school districts some sort of assistance. But as always he had to be sure. He continued to plow through statistics, study reports, ask questions, and hold witnesses to the facts and figures; and he became increasingly distressed by the disparities in educational opportunity. In comparing per-pupil expenditures with data on per-capita wealth he also discovered that many Southern states were spending larger percentages of their citizens' income on education than were Northern states: low expenditures per pupil in the South stemmed from simple poverty, not — as he had assumed earlier — from neglect by state officials. The conclusion was inescapable: Only federal aid could promote equality of educational opportunity. And only such opportunity could assure each American a proper start in the quest for success that lay at the core of Taft's philosophy of life.

Characteristically, Taft did not become a convert overnight, and he shrank from issuing headline-catching reminders of his growing concern. Besides, there was much negotiation to be done — with Democratic Senators Elbert Thomas of Utah and Lister Hill of Alabama, earlier sponsors of federal aid; with the National Education Association, which still stressed the need of direct subsidies for teachers' salaries; with committee staff experienced in devising formulas for grants. But by early 1945 he was already working on a bill aimed at encouraging states to spend a certain minimum percentage of their income for education. All states that did so and yet failed to reach a stated minimum in expenditures per pupil would qualify for federal money. The long-range goal of the bill would be to establish what he was fond of calling a national "floor" under spending for schools.[13]

Other questions still held Taft back. Catholic spokesmen demanded that aid go to parochial as well as to public schools, while others just as heatedly argued that such a provision violated the separation of church and state. Taft, like many other advocates of federal aid, was caught in a dilemma. His grandfather Alphonso, he believed, had lost a chance to become governor of Ohio by opposing compulsory Bible readings in the schools, and he felt the same way. On the other hand, he had spent a lifetime opposing federal dictation, and he shrank from telling the states how to spend their money. It was best, he concluded, to let the states do as they wished. Taft's willingness to compromise on this sensitive issue earned him no friends among Catholic prelates. But it revealed his consistency on the subject of states' rights and underscored his essential practicality. The key, after all, was getting a useful bill through.[14]

By early 1946 Taft had determined on his course, and with Thomas and Hill he introduced a bill that authorized federal aid to states making the required effort and that aimed at a minimum expenditure per pupil of $40 in state and federal aid. The states, in turn, were free to spend the money as they wished. For Taft, who had favored a lower minimum expenditure, $40 represented a concession, for it enabled thirty-three states to qualify for aid. But the bill still satisfied his goal of benefiting poorer states more than others, and it authorized the suitably modest sums of $150 million the first year, $200 million the second, and $250 million thereafter. Critics, indeed, noted that $40 per pupil was well below the national average. It was a moderate bill that he could readily endorse, and he did so repeatedly in the ensuing months. The federal government, he said in words that upset his right-wing admirers, has a "secondary interest to see that there is a basic floor . . . the entire basis of American life is opportunity . . . no child can have an equal opportunity unless he has a basic minimum education." [15]

Taft and his cosponsors had negotiated well. Though the Chamber of Commerce and the National Catholic Welfare Conference opposed the bill, the CIO, the NEA, and the National Congress of Parents and Teachers supported it. In May the Education and Labor Committee reported it unanimously. But the bill aroused heated emotions among conservatives as well as Catholics; indeed, neither house had passed a general school aid bill in more than half a century. And House Republicans again promised to be unyielding. So Taft and his allies reluctantly gave up efforts to push the bill in the Senate and awaited more auspicious times.

Taft's support of federal aid to education seemed consistent enough to him. After all, equality of opportunity mattered above all else, which was why he had backed public housing and why he was also beginning to support modest federal aid to states for health — as an alternative to what he considered the excessive federal regulation involved in national health insurance.[16] As on the question of public housing, he did not worry that some called federal aid to education "socialistic." On the contrary, he said simply, "education is socialistic anyhow, and has been for 150 years." Though this statement directly contradicted his stand in 1943, Taft did not regard his change of heart as particularly exciting. Rather, he decided that he had been wrong, and he carried on without self-congratulation.

Yet his shift did seem remarkable to others — and properly so. While his conversion made him ultimately more attractive to many progressives, it earned him nothing but surprise from his conservative Republican colleagues in the Senate and amazement from the many Americans who were coming to regard him as the vanguard against government intervention. And his stress on aiding poor Southern states — throwing Northern money across the Mason-Dixon line, Northerners grumbled — made him few friends among politicians in the North. Indeed, his bill offered nothing at all to comparatively wealthy states like Ohio. It is possible that his near defeat in 1944 or his continuing presidential aspirations forced him to broaden his outlook, to realize the political futility of opposing attractive federal programs. But Taft acted primarily because he believed in equality of opportunity, because he took the time to apply his mind to the problem, and because he saw no alternative once he had done so.

His change of mind also seemed remarkable because he was able to move so easily from leading the opposition to directing the forces in support. Though he had not developed any strikingly original ideas on the subject — even the formula was similar to that which the Senate had rejected in 1943 — he worked so hard on the details that even veterans in the cause turned to him for help. Taft, said the NEA's legislative representative, had once been the enemy. But then he "crammed his mind with more facts and figures than any man I've ever seen. Before it was all over, he was giving *us* the answers." [17]

Taft's shift was also surprising to his critics because it seemed so rare. Though opponents had exaggerated in labeling him an unthinking reactionary — "the best eighteenth-century mind in America," they cracked — they were right in finding him often deaf to suggestion and so partisan that his political instincts sometimes clashed with his respect for facts. They were also right in stressing his argumentativeness — he had a problem for every solution, some people said — his reflexive revolts against new and costly government programs, his frequent reaction that no matter what the facts, they did not change what *ought* to be. Even his associates found him maddeningly sure of himself. "That's stupid, just stupid," he told them. "No, no, no, you're wrong, all wrong!" And his friends conceded that he was visually oriented, receiving information more readily through his eyes than through his ears. He could spend hours leafing through documents, his eyes spotting facts and figures that his mind absorbed and retained, but remain too preoccupied to listen to what his advisers — or even his family

— were trying to say. "He would *freeze* when disagreement comes," George Smith, his top aide on the steering committee remarked privately. "You can literally *see* it, for it is clear that his mind is elsewhere, going on to the next point. The next day, perhaps, he could have reconsidered, but not then, and there is no point in wasting time by arguing with him." [18]

Taft's views on social welfare surprised people for another reason: his apparent lack of warmth or humanitarianism. Smith, who admired him, remarked later that Taft was "too much occupied with facts, to the neglect of imagination and human values." Indeed, Taft's views on housing and aid to education did not stem primarily from emotional revulsion against poverty or from any sense of identification with the masses. Never having experienced such hardships himself, such identification was difficult for him, and he never pretended to be a tribune of the people. His unemotional approach to these issues suggested that his position was grounded in self-confident intellectual conviction, but it also made him sound almost detached in his support of causes that deeply moved other socially conscious Americans. It helped explain why he sounded more animated about price control and public spending than about social welfare, and it prevented him from carrying the cause to the people in a fervent manner that might have earned him wider admiration among contemporary observers.[19]

Yet Taft could support public housing and aid to education for the simple reason that he was not always so opinionated as he seemed. "His saving grace," wrote the liberal Arthur Schlesinger, Jr., "is a clear-cut logical intelligence and a basic respect for fact which undercuts his own impulses toward dogmatism." "Get him tied up in a subcommittee," a colleague added, "and rub his nose in the facts, then his automatic negative reaction starts melting away under the pressure of evidence." Taft in the company of old friends or the privacy of his books and statistics was cautiously open to new ideas, a man of the sort of integrity who can admit he knows nothing or that he could be wrong. Perhaps the glare of the spotlight still bothered him and turned a man who could be modest and reflective with friends into one who had to compete and who therefore seemed stiff, blunt, and abrasively assertive in public. Whatever the reasons for his public posture, it tended to obscure the core within and left people more surprised than they should have been when he changed his mind.[20]

In supporting aid to education and public housing, Taft showed that he could respond to the needs of American society, that in his mid-fifties he could change his mind, that on a few domestic issues he could move beyond his colleagues and ahead of his times. It was to be his misfortune as a presidential contender that he lacked the flair for publicizing his conversion and that the people more often heard his rhetorical and partisan outbursts than the lucid reasonableness of his views on social welfare. "I was wrong," was as much as he would say.

•

In October 1946 Kenyon College in Ohio sponsored a three-day convocation on the heritage and responsibility of the English-speaking peoples. The august gathering featured such participants as Crane Brinton, the renowned Harvard scholar of European history, and Harold Laski, a leading British socialist and intellectual. Taft also agreed to speak, even though he was heavily involved in the election campaign. Lacking time to prepare anything new, he strung together remarks he had made in February at Dallas.[21] Still, the speech came as close as any of his lifetime to setting out his fundamental convictions.

The key to the English-speaking heritage, Taft began, was the motto his father had had inscribed on the Supreme Court Building: "Equal Justice Under Law." In recent years, however, events were threatening this heritage. Powerful federal agencies such as the OPA and the NLRB had tried to interfere with individual liberty. In the wider world the United Nations was depending on force instead of on clearly stated principles of international law. Taft then went further. Another regrettable example of the use of arbitrary power to curb individual rights, he said, was the war crimes "trials" then being conducted at Nuremberg. The trials, Taft said, "violate that fundamental principle of American law that a man cannot be tried under an ex post facto statute . . . About this whole judgment there is the spirit of vengeance, and

vengeance is seldom justice. The hanging of the eleven men con-
victed will be a blot on the American record which we shall long
regret." [22]

Taft did not worry about repercussions from such phrases, for he
had used almost exactly the same words in his Dallas address without attracting attention. Indeed, while at Murray Bay in September, he had outlined his remarks to Martha and to his daughter-
in-law Barbara. Martha offered objections. His statements were
accurate, she conceded, but people might consider them pro-
Nazi — and that, in 1946, was devoutly to be avoided. Taft paid
no attention. "That's silly," he snorted characteristically. To Taft
such "trials" made a travesty of the law, and there was nothing
courageous about saying so.[23]

Americans, it seemed, disagreed. The New York *Times* featured
his speech on page one of its Sunday paper, and the wire services
spread it across the country. Critics jumped at the chance to denounce him, and Senate Majority Leader Alben Barkley announced that Taft "never experienced a crescendo of heart about
the soup kitchens of 1932, but his heart bled anguishedly for the
criminals at Nuremberg." The *CIO News* featured an angry-
looking photograph of Taft in its next issue. Adjacent to it were
pictures of Hjalmar Schacht and Hans Fritzsche, Germans ac-
quitted at the trials. "SENATOR ROBERT ALPHONSO
TAFT AND 'FRIENDS,' " read the caption.[24]

More disturbing was the reaction from lawyers and Republicans.
The *Times* reported that of fifty leading lawyers throughout the
world, none supported Taft's point of view. The trials, they contended, had ample justification from the League of Nations
Charter, the Versailles Treaty, and the Kellogg-Briand Pact of
1928. With the speech fast becoming a campaign issue, Republicans hurried to dissociate themselves from him. The Nazis, Governor Dewey said, had surely had a fair trial.[25]

Taft himself remained cool under fire. He had not tried to be
courageous, he insisted, but had merely stated his mind. Besides,
the press was reporting his remarks about the trials out of context
and was seizing on his unqualified sentence about the hangings as a
"blot on the American record which we shall long regret." His

own mail, he said, revealed 70 per cent approval of his stand.[26]

The Republican victories in November swept the controversy into the past and proved that the speech had done the party no serious harm. Yet in denouncing the trials, Taft had shown a disdain for popular reaction that permitted irresponsible critics to brand him as pro-Nazi. So long as he insisted on writing his own speeches and on speaking his own mind, he was destined to delight his opponents and to alarm many of his friends.

Most of his critics distorted his views of the Nazis. Far from sympathizing with the Nazi leaders, Taft made clear, both at Dallas in February and at Kenyon in October, that he found them repugnant. What he objected to was trying them ex post facto, for such a procedure sullied the courts. "I would almost rather see them executed by court-martial," he said at Dallas, "than go through the elaborate procedure of the Nuremberg trials." It would be all right, he added in a letter, for the Allies to "shut these men up for the rest of their lives as a matter of policy and on the ground that if free they might stir up another war. That was the basis for the imprisonment of Napoleon. My big objection is the use of the forms of justice to carry out a predetermined policy. This is the Russian idea of a trial . . ." Thus at Kenyon he also complained vehemently about quasi-judicial agencies like the OPA and the NLRB and about the absence of international law to guide the operations of the United Nations. All these institutions, he believed, typified the irresponsible pragmatism of the New Deal-Fair Deal years, and undermined the fundamental importance of the rule of law in the world.[27]

The proponents of the trials also failed to deal squarely with the issues Taft raised. Indeed, their reliance on the Versailles Treaty (which Taft at the time had criticized for laying war guilt on the Germans) and on the Kellogg-Briand Pact was disingenuous at best, for neither document provided for such trials of individuals, and neither sanctioned the concept, basic to the Nuremberg proceedings, that aggression was a crime. The trials so clearly rested on victor's "justice" that many experts later conceded the essential correctness of Taft's position. His outspoken view of the trials, like his defense of the civil liberties of strikers earlier in 1946, revealed the depth of his convictions on crucial issues. It was remembered long afterward — among others by John F. Kennedy in his *Profiles in Courage* — as among his finest hours.[28]

•

Like other senators in 1945 and 1946, Taft had to take stands on an almost bewildering variety of issues. It was, therefore, inevitable that he occasionally seemed philosophically inconsistent. Many observers, noting his antipathy to large-scale public spending, his outbursts against unions and price control, and his strict constructionism, concluded that he was "conservative" — or, enemies contended, "reactionary." Yet he also spoke for public housing and aid to education — programs that many of his fellow Republicans dubbed socialistic. What was his philosophy, and what core of faith, if any, held it together?

The answer was first that he was flexible. "We cannot blindly oppose every measure looking towards the improvement of conditions in the field of social welfare," he wrote a disapproving friend. He was also too intelligent to insist on the same governmental structure for all nations — Great Britain, he told friends privately, was small enough to function under socialism, the United States was not. And though he numbered among his admirers such extreme right-wingers as Robert McCormick, publisher of the Chicago *Tribune*, and George Sokolsky, the aggressively reactionary columnist, Taft carefully kept his distance from them. "What gives one pause in politics," he later said with wry amusement, "is the number of nuts who write you with approval." [29]

He also showed a singular lack of interest in abstract thought. On the contrary, he was in his way an activist, a politician concerned as much with the present and the future as with the past. Very occasionally he read treatises on government, such as his friend Thomas Hewes's vigorously Jeffersonian volume, *Decentralize for Liberty,* published in 1945. Even more rarely he inserted in his speeches quotations from John Stuart Mill's *On Liberty* — "Whatever crushes individuality is despotism, by whatever name it might be called," was a favorite. But even Mill served mainly as a convenient phrase maker, not as a guide for thought. A reporter later asked Taft whether he had read Russell Kirk's *The*

Conservative Mind. Taft shook his head and chuckled. "You remind me of Thurber's *Let Your Mind Alone*," he said. "There are some questions that I have not thought very much about, but I'm a politician, not a philosopher." [30]

Taft lacked many of the characteristics often assigned to the "conservatives" with whom he was conveniently lumped.[31] City-bred and widely traveled, he had as little in common with the hardened rural reactionaries in his own party as he had had with the Cornstalk Brigade in the 1920's, and he simply did not understand why some writers nostalgically glorified the agrarian style. Though as close to being an aristocrat as anyone in American public life, he showed little of the repugnance for mass society, for industrialism, for technological change, or even for rampant materialism which was characteristic of some conservative writers of the postwar scene. While he possessed a strong sense of family tradition — visitors to his office were always struck by the bust and photographs of his father — he exhibited no interest whatever in genealogy, and he ignored such organizations as the Daughters of the American Revolution. He was unsentimental about hoary traditions like the Yale Whiffenpoofs or even Skull and Bones, and he was largely indifferent to aesthetics, whether works of art, music, or even antiques. There was little of the collector about Taft, and still less of nostalgia. Secure in his world, he sought no traditions to place himself in, or mentors — save his father — to emulate.

Like most Republicans of his generation, Taft was often branded a spokesman for business enterprise. This vague label was often accurate, and businessmen — especially the smaller industrialists and entrepreneurs in the Middle West and South — applauded his stands on price control, labor policy, and corporate taxes. Yet those critics who wrote him off as a spokesman for privilege slighted his welfare policies, ignored his defense of the right to strike, and distorted his sincere belief that excessive taxation of business ultimately harmed all classes. They also neglected to stress his unconcealed animus against monopolists, idle speculators, the Eastern bankers. Like his grandfather Alphonso, he thought mere money making contemptible; like his father, he believed in the progressive dogma of battling the trusts and opening up opportunities for entrepreneurs. Taft was uncomfortable in the company of businessmen who could talk of nothing but their work, and he thought most of them unfit to handle broad governmental responsibilities. "I don't like the fact," he was to write about President-elect Dwight Eisenhower's cabinet selections in December 1952, "that we have so many big businessmen in the Cabinet." [32]

Many European conservatives have expressed two other beliefs that set them apart from Taft: a feeling that men are naturally depraved (or at least that the masses are) and a concomitant yearning for a hierarchical society and an elitist politics. The first belief Taft rejected. Like most Americans, he was prepared to accept the idea that men possess differing talents, but he believed neither in a Hobbesian view of human nature nor in the notion that racial considerations explained human differences. "Equality of opportunity is the important consideration," he insisted with characteristic American faith. "I see no reason to think that inequality of intellect or ability is based on racial origin." [33] The second belief he accepted only in the sense that he regarded some social gradations as inevitable. But he refused to be complacent about these gradations or to welcome the existence of distinct social classes. Taft believed passionately that the government must be run by the best men available, and he equated "best" with courage, intelligence, and political experience, not with social standing or even with financial success. And as an office seeker in democratic politics, he rarely doubted the desirability of representative government. Like most Americans, he wished to disperse political power, not to place it in the hands of some kind of elite.

European conservatives have also expressed disgust with the competitive ethic of Americans — and especially with the materialism and atomization that they think it engenders. They vastly prefer a traditional, evolving, organic society for which religious faith acts as a foundation. But Taft bluntly dissented. From boyhood he had been taught the joys of striving and of individual effort. Like most Americans, he also believed instinctively in the desirability, indeed the inevitability of progress; if a certain anomie developed as a result, it was unfortunate but unavoidable. And Taft simply remained unmoved by religious considerations. He did not trouble himself with the ultimate nature of man, the sublime meaning of life, or even the satisfactions of public wor-

ship. And though he was a nominal Episcopalian who occasionally
went to church, he was rare among national politicians in making
little pretense of being devout. Indeed, he chuckled to friends
about the religious foibles of other politicians — Thomas Dewey,
he laughed to his sister Helen, actually said grace before a private
luncheon for the two of them. What church did Bob attend on
Sundays, Martha was asked by reporters. "I guess," she said in reference to a Washington golf course, "you'll have to say the Burning Tree." [34]

Yet ultimately Taft was conservative in the practical sense ordinarily applied to mid twentieth-century American politicians. He
tended to equate the growth of the national government with the
curtailment of individual liberties, to view with suspicion expensive new programs aimed at the welfare of the masses, to rely on
evolutionary social development to alleviate most problems, and to
stress the importance of self-discipline. Above all, he insisted on
adherence to "principle" instead of to the opportunism adopted by
the Democrats since 1932. Among his principles were "peace,"
"no special privilege," "higher standards of living," and the prevention of "hardship and poverty." [35] Three general principles
supported all the rest. The first, "equal justice under law," had
been his theme at Kenyon. The second, equality of opportunity,
underlay his support of social welfare. This did not mean social
equality, but a system in which all men could rise from obscurity as
his grandfather Alphonso had done. Government, he concluded,
must provide the firm "floor," through which no man may be permitted to fall. This philosophy was closer to the enlightened no-
blesse oblige of conservatives like Disraeli and Burke than it was to
the probusiness materialism of many of his Republican admirers.

The third principle, "human liberty," was fundamental. Liberty meant "the freedom of the individual to choose his own work
and his life occupation." Pick a career in which you can be independent in your specialty, he told his sons repeatedly; don't drift
into a bureaucratic job in the government. Human liberty also
meant man should be free

to spend his earnings as he desires to spend them, to choose the
place where he desires to live, to take the job that fits him whether

some union official is willing that he gets it or not. It is the freedom of the local community to work out its own salvation when it
has the power to do so . . . It is the freedom of thought and experiments in academic institutions. It is the freedom of men engaged in industry to run their business as they think best so long
as they do not interfere with the rights of others to do the same.
Certainly, there are limitations which must be imposed by the state
to protect the liberty of others and more as our economy grows
more complex. But a party that believes in liberty will see that
such limitations are only imposed to the extent it is absolutely
necessary.[36]

In 1951 he stated it thus:

I do not like to talk much about "free enterprise." That has too
much the meaning that businessmen shall be able to do as they
please. The concept of liberty is a much broader one.[37]

Taft's libertarian philosophy, flexible on questions involving social welfare, was sometimes distorted by partisan and especially by
fiscal considerations. It often benefited narrow-minded businessmen battling federal regulation or reactionary state politicians
protesting federal guidelines. Indeed, Taft devoted more energy
to freeing people from quasi-judicial agencies than to using government to pull the masses from poverty, and his philosophy,
therefore, offered little to blacks, to poor people facing large medical expenses, or to others for whom equality of opportunity was
unavailable.

His critics argued that the right to social and economic security
was the greatest liberty of all, and to preserve that, government
must expand its scope.[38] Yet if Taft was sometimes wrong-headed
in the eyes of his critics, he was usually consistent and seldom unin-
formed. His opposition to the drafting of railroad workers and to
the war crimes trials proved that he not only thought for himself
but was also true to the fundamental faith in human liberty that
his entire education and experience had developed in him. More
than many of his contemporaries, he was even something of a
zealot about these ideals, and he was able to bring to them a force-

fulness, indeed a passion, which made him a formidable spokesman for his cause. By 1947, Taft's thinking on domestic affairs was set, his stature among his colleagues secure. It was time — at last — to put his ideas into practice.

CHAPTER 22

The Qualities of Leadership, 1947

THOUSANDS OF spectators thronged to Capitol Hill on January 3, 1947. Many arrived in time to pack the galleries and to stare at the scaffolding that workmen had erected to repair the ceilings of both chambers. People jammed the corridors so tightly that VIP's and their wives could not get through, and outside thousands more mingled in a cold drizzle. The Eightieth Congress, the first dominated by the Republicans since 1930, was getting under way.

The scaffolding may have served some as a reminder of the voters' demands in November: a restoration, a patching up, and a cleansing of things turned shabby and soiled in years past. For others, the drizzle may have promised the storms that lay ahead. Many Americans were edgy — about the activities of the Soviet Union abroad and of communists at home, about unions and prices, about such basic matters as decent housing and education. Few Congresses in American history have opened under circumstances that made the nation so restless.[1]

For Taft it was a time of vindication. Though Wallace White of Maine, an affable, courteous and self-effacing Republican veteran, was conceded the title of majority leader, observers knew he was a figurehead. "Taft is the man you want to see," White himself quietly told reporters.[2] Taft also assumed his first committee chairmanship, that of the newly christened Labor and Public Welfare Committee, and held the number two post on Finance. He served as the dominant member of the important group that determined Republican committee assignments. Capping his power was the chairmanship of the GOP policy committee, the new name given to the steering committee that he had headed since 1944.

Serving with him on this key group were other Republicans of Taft's persuasion — Wayland ("Curly") Brooks, a staunch conservative from Illinois, Homer Ferguson, a diligent partisan from Michigan, the volatile Kenneth S. Wherry of Nebraska, Wallace White, who served on the committee ex officio, Eugene Millikin from Colorado, a hard-working senator who was Taft's right-hand man, and two other acquiescent Republicans, Albert W. Hawkes of New Jersey and Guy Cordon of Oregon. Only Leverett Saltonstall of Massachusetts, who had arrived in the Senate in 1945, promised to offer any objections, and he was too isolated to worry about. With Millikin also in charge of Finance and with the economy-minded Styles Bridges of New Hampshire at the helm of Appropriations, Taft had men he could trust in most of the influential positions.

Indeed, Taft seemed radiant with confidence early in 1947. Well rested from a trip to Central America, he seemed hearty, healthy, prepared for the demanding attentions of the press. Though unsuccessful in trying to disguise his baldness, which by now had captured all but the rims, he looked little older than he had ten years earlier, and his unlined face and clear complexion showed no signs of fatigue. He still got up around 7 AM, devoured the New York and Washington papers over coffee and an egg, then drove his eleven-year-old Buick to work — somewhat absentmindedly and recklessly, his family complained. He arrived by 8:30 to read more papers, see constituents, and begin the awesome task of answering the five hundred to a thousand letters he received every day. Sometimes he had to break the routine to settle a problem, and once a surprised newsman discovered that Taft personally spent a morning tramping the corridors of the Pentagon to get revoked the orders of a sick soldier about to be sent to Europe. But usually he was in committee from ten until noon; then a quick but hearty lunch on the Hill; then to the Senate floor until late afternoon. Next he often went back to the office for more dictation and for appointments. Unless night sessions demanded his presence, he usually left for home by seven, but almost always with a battered briefcase stuffed with documents.[3] Few men at fifty-seven could take such a pace for long. But Taft was driven to serve and to excel, and he flourished with it.

In the early weeks of the session, Taft showed that his leadership could bring results. Even though the GOP numbered only fifty-one — or forty-nine without the belligerently independent William Langer of North Dakota or the unpredictable Wayne Morse of Oregon — he could still rely often on the Southern conservatives like Harry Byrd and Walter George, and he led his forces to a series of gratifying if minor triumphs in January. He also shrewdly persuaded the GOP policy committee to avoid unnecessary battles over presidential appointments. If some Republicans still resisted his appeals for aid to education and public housing, they were willing to follow his lead on almost everything else. Taft, one awed newsman reported in January, had more power over his party than any senator since Charles Sumner of Massachusetts eighty years earlier. "Congress," the *New Republic* grumbled a few months later, "now consists of the House, the Senate, and Bob Taft." [4]

•

Taft's dominance did not come easily. On the contrary, it rested on careful, often painstaking negotiations, required constant personal effort, and depended ultimately on qualities of character that made him one of the most respected senators of his time.

The first obstacle to party harmony stemmed from the Congressional Reorganization Act of 1946, which permitted a senator to serve on but two major committees and to be chairman of but one. "Every Senator wants a chairmanship," Taft complained privately to Mrs. Stanley Rowe, "and there is a lot of pulling and hauling." [5] Reluctantly, he left Banking and Currency, where he had worked in the past against such measures as Bretton Woods and price control. This left him the senior Republican on both Labor and Finance and forced him to choose which of the two to head. Because committee chairmen possess immense power in shaping legislation, the decision was important to him as well as to the nation.

Taft would have preferred to take the helm of Finance. He had always enjoyed dealing with numbers and statistics, and he was determined to cut taxes in the coming session. Besides, everyone knew that the Labor Committee would be, as one of his colleagues put it, a "HOT spot." Whoever assumed that chairmanship would have to do something to allay the alarm against unions. In the process he might bring down on himself the fury either of unions or management.[6] It was no place for anyone with presidential ambitions.

Taft knew this of course, but to take the helm of Finance would leave George Aiken of Vermont in charge of Labor, and Aiken, a ruggedly independent Yankee, seemed reluctant to curb the unions. So Taft tried to work out a compromise whereby Aiken would be passed over for the Labor chairmanship by the more conservative Joseph Ball of Minnesota. In return Aiken would receive the chairmanship of Agriculture. But Arthur Capper, a tired veteran from Kansas who was the senior man on Agriculture, refused to move out of Aiken's way. The impasse left Taft with little choice. The Labor job, he wrote Aiken lamely, "has more matters . . . on which I have taken an interest. Because of the labor bill, and my bills on federal aid to health and to education, I am somewhat inclined to take that rather than Finance." To John Hollister, who worried about the political consequences of heading Labor, he gave another answer. "They'll blame me for chickening out if I *don't* take it," he exclaimed. But Taft's real reason was his desire to keep the labor bill out of Aiken's hands. "If I had not taken it," he later explained privately, "it would have gone to Aiken and I doubt if he ever would have reported a labor bill. Since the success of the whole session depended on this job being done right, I thought I had to accept it." [7]

In the short run Taft had acted wisely. Not only was he free to run the Labor Committee, but in the process his friend Millikin moved up to the chairmanship of Finance. With Wallace White willing to do the unpleasant leg work as leader, Kenneth Wherry temporarily pacified as whip, and Arthur Vandenberg of Michigan holding the chairmanship of Foreign Relations as well as the post of president pro tem of the Senate, Taft could run the GOP policy committee while permitting others to have their share of the limelight. Given the constrictions of the Congressional Reorganization Act and the long wait for power by Senate Republicans, Taft's patient negotiations had proved eminently successful.[8]

But inevitably the outcome presented dangers, not the least of which was the battering he would undergo in the sensitive post of Labor chairman. The negotiations also left some of the more liberal Republicans unhappy. Among these, of course, was Aiken, who had to content himself with the lesser post as chairman of the Committee on Expenditures in the Executive Department, and others who resented the Taft wing's domination included Leverett Saltonstall, Wayne Morse, and Henry Cabot Lodge of Massachusetts, who returned to the Senate after a hiatus during the war. Taft's power also disturbed junior Republican senators. When the session opened, these newer Republicans, especially the sixteen-man "class of 1946," had no choice at first but to follow his leadership. They included such outspoken figures as Joseph McCarthy of Wisconsin, William Knowland of California, William Jenner of Indiana, Irving Ives, a liberal from New York, and Raymond Baldwin of Connecticut, and they quickly demanded more power. By March they were chafing so openly that Taft and Millikin had to promise them two posts on the GOP policy committee. For the next seven years, Taft was to have to contend with unhappiness, even incipient revolt, on the part of these newer men.[9]

Taft had to worry also about some of the more conservative members. John Bricker, who also arrived in the Senate in 1947, flatly rejected Taft's stand on aid to education and on public housing. So did Jenner of Indiana, who was later to vie with McCarthy of Wisconsin as red-hunter par excellence. Above all, so did Wherry, who was one of the most aggressive defenders of private enterprise in the Senate. "I like him [Taft], goddamit," Wherry told a reporter, "even if we have had a hell of a time to keep him from climbing up in Claude Pepper's lap . . . He doesn't want to make half the fight of it that I do."[10] Many of Taft's admirers, perceiving in their hero a man who gave no quarter to the New Dealers, failed to appreciate these tensions that often separated him from men like Wherry.

Taft's major concern was Arthur Vandenberg. A senator since 1928, Vandenberg was a power in his own right who had been mentioned for the presidency in the past and who was considered a prospect in 1948 as well. Before the attack on Pearl Harbor, he had opposed American involvement in war even more consistently than Taft, but he gradually changed his mind, and in 1945 he dramatically announced his conversion to a more interventionist position. Since then he had been the most influential spokesman for the internationalist branch of the party. In 1946, for instance, Taft had managed to secure eighteen Republican votes in the Senate against a proposed loan to Great Britain, but Vandenberg sided with the administration and helped find it seventeen Republican votes for passage. The vote symbolized the potential chasm between the two leaders and proved that Taft had to tread carefully on foreign policy matters lest he split the party.

Both men recognized these dangers and moved elaborately to avoid even the semblance of tension. When Vandenberg left to attend a conference in Paris in April 1946, he had been careful to send Taft a note. "I shall depend upon you," he said, "to 'save the country' in my absence." Taft, in return, was always careful to tell reporters to check with Vandenberg concerning Republican foreign policy. When newsmen reported trouble between them, Taft was quick to write his rival. "I suppose there may be some differences as there always are," he said reassuringly, "but I approve without qualification your whole position as far as I know it." He also congratulated Vandenberg on his recent work at a conference in Europe. "I am sure that you were the guiding hand in the whole procedure," he exaggerated. Vandenberg was gratified. "I deeply appreciate the spirit in which you have written," he replied. "It is typical of a relationship between us which — despite whatever differing opinions we may occasionally hold — will *never* amount to serious disagreements . . . I have followed you in the newspapers. You have been doing your usual splendid job." [11]

But this charade placed a strain on Taft, who remained adamantly opposed to bipartisanship in foreign policy — or in almost anything else. Strong parties, he had always believed, were the foundation of American politics. And the Truman administration was pursuing the active, expensive foreign policy that Taft had found so obnoxious in the Roosevelt years. Though Vandenberg almost always backed Taft on domestic issues, Taft simply could not bring himself to reciprocate regularly on foreign affairs.

Besides, neither man really felt comfortable with the other. The relationship, one reporter noted, was one of "courteous suspicion." Another reporter noted privately that Vandenberg found Taft's leadership so self-assured and domineering that he stood up during one Republican conference to criticize him.[12] And Taft, like many other senators, found Vandenberg loquacious, pompous, and end-lessly fond of flattery. If Taft was too circumspect to say so, Martha was not. "Your Father," she wrote her sons during the contest over the United Nations Charter in 1945, "thought Senator Vanden-berg was feeling that the Republicans did not sufficiently appreci-ate his work on the charter, so [he gave a] dinner in his [Vanden-berg's] honour, and your Father urged me to butter Van up. I tried manfully, but he buttered himself so thoroughly that I really couldn't find a single ungreased spot." [13]

·

As if these potential roadblocks to party harmony were not enough, Taft had also to contend with himself. This task was sometimes the most difficult of all.

Taft still struck many people as abrupt, cold, and inhumanly efficient. It did not occur to him to linger with colleagues, to swap stories, or to pause for a drink after work. Though he did his share of entertaining, he never grew very close personally to any of his colleagues. To an extent his failure to develop close friends stemmed from the difficulty most adults have in establishing truly warm friendships with new acquaintances, and to an extent it marked the kind of private man that he had always been. Besides, he had Martha to confide in, and he still relaxed most readily with his old college friends and with people like the Rowes from Cin-cinnati; not much desiring new intimacies, he simply did not trouble himself to look for any in the Senate. It was therefore not surprising that some of his peers in a body that treasured the conviviality of men like Alben Barkley of Kentucky and the courtly geniality of Richard Russell of Georgia found his often abrupt manners difficult to understand.

Taft also displayed this coolness to the members of his office staff. By 1947 his chief aide, Jack Martin, had made the office practically a model of efficiency, and Taft wisely relied heavily upon him. He also depended on Blanche O'Berg, the faithful personal secretary whom he had hired early in 1945 and who remained with him until his death. But Taft rarely relaxed even with them, and he hardly knew the names of his other coworkers, who labored hard six days a week under Martin's firm hand. Taft hurried in to work in the morning, disappeared quickly into his inner office, sat down at his desk (which faced away from the window), and plunged into the heaps of reports and documents that littered his desk and even the floor. A shy "Good Morning" was as far as he ordinarily progressed toward geniality with his staff.[14]

Even friends who stopped by found him abrupt. One such acquaintance on the Yale Corporation, James Lee Loomis, recalled a characteristic example. Loomis went to Taft's office to find out the status of a railroad bill in which he was interested, and Martin told him to wait outside the Senate floor. Loomis walked over there, and Taft appeared promptly. Would the bill reach the floor today, Loomis asked. "Over my dead body," Taft grimaced, then turned away. "And into the chamber he went," said Loomis. "No greeting, no friendly gesture, and above all no offense. His mind was charged with a public trust and there was no room for pleasantries." [15] Loomis was understanding; many others, including some of Taft's colleagues, were not.

Taft remained very much the preoccupied man who had distressed acquaintances in Cincinnati in the 1920's. Even his family found it hard to engage his attention. In late 1952 his son Bill conceived the ambition to become Ambassador to Ireland, and while visiting, he determined to communicate his plan to his father. But neither he nor his wife Barbara was able to shake Taft from his thoughts. So in the morning they arose early, went downstairs, and hid the morning paper. When Taft came down, he searched testily for the paper, gave up, and sat down at the table. Then, when he had nothing to read, Bill and Barbara were able to capture his attention. They had maneuvered well. MacAllister (Mack) Gray, who became the Tafts' houseman in 1948, knew how impenetrable his employer could be. "Never saw a man like the Senator," Gray said, recalling:

You take something like breakfast. He come down in the morning. He sit down at the table and he takes out his little book and writes in it — every morning he writes and writes in it. I say, "Good morning, Senator." No answer. I go out of the room and bring in the coffee. He still writing in that book. Finally he looks up and says, "Why, good morning, Mack," like he is surprised to see me. He hasn't heard me at all.[16]

Colleagues resented what they considered Taft's intellectual arrogance. Increasingly sure of himself after eight years in the Senate, he simply could not hide his annoyance with people who were slow to make themselves clear, and getting the *facts* wrong was a cardinal offense. "That is the most puerile thing I have ever read," he announced of an article written by a friendly reporter who had misconstrued a few facts. Repeatedly he glowered in his chair, muttered "goddam," twisted about impatiently, then stalked conspicuously from the chamber. Even in Republican conference he thought nothing of interrupting fellow senators, of lecturing them on their lack of information, of blurting, "why, that's nonsense . . . nonsense." One colleague, hoping to slow him down, stood up in conference to tell about a football player who centered the ball to himself, ran for a touchdown, and then led the cheering. Taft took the reproof in good humor, then continued as if nothing had happened.[17]

Acquaintances recoiled at his frightening candor. On one occasion, Harold Stephens, years earlier a classmate at Harvard Law School, approached Taft at a banquet, proferred his hand, and attempted to reintroduce himself. Taft looked at him and replied, "I have no recollection of you whatever." That ended the conversation. On another occasion Thomas Coleman, an important Wisconsin politician, was touched to receive from Taft a gracious wire of appreciation. When Coleman saw Taft shortly thereafter, he pulled out the telegram from his pocket, where he had kept it all the while, and started to express his thanks. "Oh that," Taft replied. "Never saw that wire myself, you know. Martin sends those things out by the dozen." [18]

This frankness was perhaps must unnerving at meetings of the Yale Corporation, which Taft usually attended, but which involved a world he lacked both the time and will fully to understand. When a high-level committee recommended the building of an art museum, an anthropological museum, and a plant physiology library, Taft was appalled. "Why should Yale have all these collections?" he demanded. "What *good* are they? Why do we need a *Titian?* And these dinosaurs. I don't know what you do with *dinosaurs,* but somebody has to *dust* them, don't they. *And that costs money!"* The corporation, stunned, managed to postpone the issue, and when Taft had the chance to hear more about the plans from a fellow member, he showed his capacity to listen to the facts and willingly supported the plan.[19] But the episode epitomized his tendency to blurt his opinions, to react to suggestions by asking about the cost, and to wonder about intellectuals outside the realms of science and medicine. In fact he ought to have been close to the academic world, for both his sister Helen and her husband Frederick Manning were college professors, as was his son Bill, who taught English at Yale before pursuing a career with the government. So, too, were such old college friends as Robert French, a Yale professor with whom Taft often stayed on his visits to New Haven, and Dr. Stanhope Bayne-Jones, who was for a time dean of the Yale Medical School. But though Taft appreciated the need for academic freedom, he was like many other men of affairs who wondered what academic people really did. It was a mark of his lack of feel for professorial opinion that when his son Horace later asked for suggestions on a graduate school where he might pursue a doctorate in physics, Taft sought out for advice and assistance General Leslie Groves, whose suspicious supervision of physicists on the atomic bomb program during the war had ruffled the sensibilities of practically every professor connected with the project.[20]

However harmless on the Yale Corporation, his habit of outspokenness and his uneasiness with intellectuals disturbed some of his younger Republican colleagues, who realized the contributions that academic people and idea men had made to the Democrats since 1933. And in February 1947 when he came out against the appointment of David Lilienthal, former chairman of the Tennessee Valley Authority, as chairman of the Atomic Energy Commission, he seemed particularly hasty and harsh. Lilienthal, said Taft, was a "typical power-hungry bureaucrat" who had run the TVA in a "secretive and arbitrary manner." Worse, Lilienthal was "soft on the subject of Communism." Taft's colleagues tried to change his mind, as did his old friend Lewis Strauss, then an AEC member.

So did his sister Helen, who made a rare attempt from Bryn Mawr to influence her brother. Though they failed, so, ultimately, did Taft, for Vandenberg and others declined to follow his example. After almost two months of acrimonious debate, the Senate refused, 52 to 38, to recommit the nomination to committee, and a week later Lilienthal was confirmed, 50 to 31. On the crucial vote to recommit Taft secured thirty Republican supporters, but Vandenberg led seventeen others to keep the nomination before the Senate. The controversy revealed Taft's occasional tendency, especially in matters involving foreign affairs, to plunge into controversies without consulting his peers — in this case even the GOP members of the congressional Atomic Energy Committee — and without controlling the severity of his rhetoric. And it did neither him nor the party any good politically. "There," grumbled a Republican senator anonymously, "goes the scientists' vote, the Jewish vote in New York [Lilienthal was a Jew], and a big chunk of the independent vote." [21]

•

This harshness was one side of Taft. But there was another, gentler side. If it surfaced too rarely to obliterate the overall image, it appeared often enough to confound the colleagues and newsmen who tried to set him in a mold.

Taft, first of all, had a shy and whimsical sense of humor. Contrary to the general impression, he enjoyed the banter of give and take, though only with old friends like Alice Longworth who refused to take him seriously. He also showed a modest talent for deflating pretense. One story about him concerned a colleague who had pompously declared, "honesty is the best policy." "He ought to know," Taft observed quietly, "he's tried both of them." The most widely told legend described an officious doorman who observed him leaving a fashionable Washington club. "Senator Taft's car," the doorman called haughtily. Unimpressed, Taft replied dryly, "It's a good car, but it won't come when it is called." [22]

Particularly in the privacy of his family, Taft seemed extravagantly pleased with his wit. "Children," he liked to needle his sons, "are relatively inexpensive until they become self-supporting." He enjoyed also joshing his daughters-in-law. At Murray

Bay one summer he was characteristically engrossed in a book while his family bustled about him. The book concerned the population explosion. Aware that two of his daughters-in-law were pregnant, he brightened. "Really, girls," he called out, "this indiscriminate multiplying must stop." Taft could never relax long enough on the stump to exhibit this brand of low-key humor — "I shall try to be funnier," he explained lamely to a friend. "One is under quite a strain in a debate . . . and unless something humorous comes up by itself, it is pretty hard to plan for it." [23] But those who knew him well recognized that he was not so stiff as he seemed.

Close friends realized also that Taft did find some things relaxing. They knew that he enjoyed his grandchildren, who appropriately named him "Gop" (after GOP), that he still found time to play poker occasionally with old friends like George Harrison or with Martha's brother, Tom, and that he took time personally to write letters of condolence and get-well cards. They knew, too, that he could get absorbed in the craftsmanlike mystery stories of Agatha Christie or John Buchan, that he could sing — off key — verses from Gilbert and Sullivan, that he regularly read the *New Yorker,* and that he occasionally recited from memory nonsense verse, such as the *Cautionary Tales for Children* by Hilaire Belloc:

> The nicest child I ever knew
> Was Charles Augustus Fortescue
> He never lost his cap, or tore
> His stockings or his pinafore.[24]

Journalists who persisted in portraying him as solemn, almost priggish, would have been surprised to discover that Taft could smile at himself. In 1950 he asked John Bullock, a senior lawyer for Taft, Stettinius, and Hollister, if the firm planned to make Bob, Jr., a partner. Bullock replied that "Bobby" had only one weakness — he was a "little too reserved." Bullock recalled that Taft said nothing for half a minute, then remarked, "I think you're right, John. As you know, we have four sons and Bobby is by far the most reserved of the four. I don't know where he got it from."

Some people sensed the warmth underneath the apparently frozen exterior. To the public, the newsman James Reston observed in 1950, Taft was cold and mathematical. "As a human being, however, the impression given is almost precisely the opposite," Reston related. "In private conversations or even in a press conference he is far less dogmatic than in the larger forum, more objective, more reasonable, more attentive, and far more amiable." Richard Rovere, a perceptive journalist who often found himself far removed from Taft's politics, tended to agree. Taft, he wrote, was "an odd, improbable combination of sweet reasonableness and ungovernable passion . . . The chilliness the public sensed in him was an illusion. He liked people very much and was shy and careful in all his relationships." And Edwin Lahey, a tough, profane newsman who covered the labor beat, was surprised after following Taft about in 1947 to discover "a gentle good soul . . . concealed . . . by his gruffness and his intolerance of stupidity." [25]

Newsmen also respected Taft's utter lack of pretense. He seldom embellished his speeches with appeals to the almighty, praise of the flag, or even with obeisance to the brilliance of his distinguished colleagues. He accepted, but quietly tried to avoid, the pomposities of official Washington. Though clean in dress, he was also careless, and he thought nothing of wearing what Martha wryly called his "all-purpose pants" — for the Senate, golf, and then a dinner party all in the same day. He was also simple — the sort of well-born but essentially plain man who not only drove his own car and filled its radiator but refused to let Mack Gray carry his bags up the steep stairs to his bedroom. Indeed, his simplicity sometimes seemed comic. Who else would put a napkin at his throat at a dinner party and then seem surprised when people laughed? How many other politicians would go to parties and provoke strong arguments over public policies? On one such occasion, a formal dinner, he grew animated and slammed the table with his fist. When Alice Longworth laughed and told him to stop, Taft looked up amazed. "Was I pounding the table?" he asked. Among family and friends he seemed relaxed, grateful for a drink, ultimately more comfortable to be with than was Martha, who for all her verve struck a few people as a little too sharp and too sarcastic to feel at home with.[26]

Though few of his colleagues on the Hill grew close enough to appreciate this side of Taft, they did perceive many other qualities that led them to offer him a respect given few members of the Senate. They recognized first that he possessed an astonishingly accurate and retentive memory. Fred E. Berquist, an economist who worked under him between 1947 and 1953 as a top staffman for the Joint Congressional Committee on the Economic Report, was startled to discover that Taft had not only read but was able to cite passages from such varied economists as Irving Fisher, William F. Foster and Waddill Catchings, and even Thorstein Veblen. Berquist also found out quickly that one did not try to give Taft off-the-cuff information instead of detailed statistics. Like others, he learned that Taft knew more about what Rovere aptly called the grubby economic issues such as taxes, controls, and labor law than other members of the Senate. As George H. E. Smith, chief staff man on the GOP policy committee, phrased it, Taft could "keep many things going at one time — and be able to switch readily from subject to subject." Unlike most senators, who were fortunate if they mastered one issue, Taft tried with marked success to be a generalist.[27]

Despite his intellectual arrogance on some matters, he showed himself willing to seek out and to use the advice of experts. As Berquist, Smith, and other aides discovered, he did not hasten to place his full confidence in them, and he never exerted himself to be intimate. Indeed, he did not call Berquist "Fred" for two years, and Berquist, like almost everyone else, never thought of calling the senator "Bob." Yet once Taft became persuaded of a man's intelligence, he made no secret of his willingness to rely on him. Sometimes this confidence in staff men irritated senators, for Taft, like a roving intelligence officer, often turned to an underling for information instead of to the senator himself. But his willingness to seek the advice of others on domestic issues helped him avoid blunders. It also gave his colleagues still greater confidence in his judgment. "Bob," senators explained to the journalist William S. White, "could give you a sense of security." [28]

Taft's faith in expertise produced especially fruitful results on the GOP policy committee, the chief source of his power and the fount of most official positions taken by Senate Republicans during his tenure. When Taft began with it in 1944, he had to rely almost entirely on George Smith and on part-time help. But year by year he fought for increased funds for it until by 1952 its staff included ten people and a total payroll of more than $50,000. Smith, an accomplished writer on economic matters, often turned to outside authorities, including scholars from Yale, where he had spent many years as a research associate. Taft himself worked closely with Smith, read most of the reports that formed the basis for position papers, and even corrected personally the minutes of the meetings.

The GOP policy committee met at least once a week, usually on Friday morning, in the conference room that lay directly across the hall from Taft's office in the Senate office building. It was an elegant room, perhaps the most distinguished in the building. Chandeliers hung from the ceiling, marble and gilt covered the walls, and large windows opened onto a balcony from which the senators could look down Constitution Avenue or across an expanse of lawn toward the city. Yet under Taft the senators had little time to enjoy the surroundings. He arrived promptly, adhered carefully to agenda that he had usually determined himself, described the reports that his staff had already prepared, allotted specified subjects to individual senators, and exacted the utmost from them whenever he could. Under Taft the Republicans developed a discipline and a preparedness that they had never enjoyed under Charles McNary, prior to 1944.[29]

Yet most of Taft's colleagues recognized that he was not trying simply to dominate. On the contrary, they often found him ultimately modest and unselfish. He was not only working for the party, but apparently willing to do so all day, every day. Repeatedly he opened meetings of the committee by asking how the party should stand on an issue. Just as repeatedly he was met with uncertainty. "We need more information," someone finally admitted. "Who'll study it?" Taft would respond. Excuses followed until someone said, "let Bob do it." Taft occasionally demurred, but he usually accepted the task. Thus while Bridges might be an expert on appropriations, Millikin on taxes, Aiken on farm legislation, and Vandenberg on foreign relations, only Taft had studied everything, only Taft could tie the package together. Furthermore, he did so in such an organized fashion that he kept the workload steady and manageable for all. His unselfishness, his willingness to work, and his capacity for retaining information forced his colleagues to rely on him, whether they liked him personally or not. His style of leadership could scarcely have differed more from the convivial approach of McNary and Barkley or from the shrewd and personable manner of Lyndon Johnson, but it was remarkably effective.[30]

His colleagues sensed another trait crucial to the success of his leadership: his trustworthiness. Taft, they realized, meant absolutely what he said, he never failed on his word, and if he seemed blunt, he was never personal. He played no favorites, adopted no cronies, shunned even the appearance of bowing to pressure groups. He was, they said, a man of integrity. By that they meant he was true to himself, that he was not only honest but forthright in an instinctive way they could only wonder at. Taft, said Walter Lippmann, "was the very opposite of the hollow men with their fabricated personalities. The inner man was the solidest part of Taft, and at the core he was so genuine and just, so rational and compassionate that he commanded the confidence of men when he could never convince them." [31]

Taft also seemed willing to bend, even to admit he was wrong. Indeed, though partisan, he refused to lead the party in a wholly negative direction. Republicans, he said, must be willing to compromise. Because the GOP had been in the minority for so long, his call for unity seemed irreproachable. And because he himself tended to stand somewhere near the middle of his congressional party, he was able to command a hearing from all but the few Republicans at either extreme. In this sense he was helped by circumstances. Both the uncertain nature of the times and the cautious expectations of his Republican colleagues did not call for the kind of leadership that would move the country in new, exciting directions but for the partisan yet usually reasonable course that he was prepared to steer.[32]

Some of his colleagues may also have sensed that Taft was, in a curious way, vulnerable. He projected an image of coldness, and he knew this well enough to regret it in an offhand way. But he could not be otherwise because he let no one penetrate his privacy. Even his sons felt their father's tight hold on his emotions. During the war Horace asked him to find out what had happened to an army friend who had been sent to Europe. Taft did so, but neglected to tell Horace. Then he visited his son at an army camp in Texas. Horace was about to be shipped to the Pacific theater, and his impending departure placed a strain on the meeting. Taft finally started talking about Horace's friend, ramblingly and hesitantly, then blurted it out: the friend had been killed. It was Taft's way of indicating his sorrow, and because he felt a little guilty about holding back the news, he did not handle the matter easily or gracefully. But Horace understood that his father was not cold or emotionless, but rather awkward and abrupt when forced to talk about personal things. "It stands out in my memory," Horace recalled, "as one of the instances of close communication between me and my father, and one of those instances where rather than being resentful at his preoccupation with other matters, I felt very sympathetic at the painful situation in which he found himself." [33]

In keeping his emotions to himself, in driving himself to compete and to serve, Taft paid the price of having to rely heavily on himself. He did not turn to the church, to friends, or to family. But if the strain bothered him, he was careful not to let others know, and it was a tribute to his self-control that he succeeded so well in depending on himself. This toughness was also a sign of the self-assurance that his repeated successes had maintained. If his makeup deprived him of joy and spontaneity, if it cost him that priceless serenity of spirit given to a few, if it thrust him into a spotlight that tightened him, it also gave him the satisfaction of accomplishment in the public career he had been trained to follow. Taft ate well, slept well, lived without pose, never grew melancholy, and seldom even second-guessed himself. He awoke each morning with a zest for the day's work, with the feeling that what he was doing was useful to the welfare of the republic, and with confidence which pulled colleagues into his orbit. Few men of his time seemed so well suited for or so content in their work. The Senate, as his handling of labor law was immediately to suggest, was for Taft an almost perfectly compatible way of life.

CHAPTER 23

Taft-Hartley

TAFT'S THIRD son, Lloyd Bowers, had finished his wartime service with the Navy and was starting work with Hulbert Taft's paper, the Cincinnati *Times-Star*. Now he was ready to marry Virginia Stone of St. Joseph, Michigan. They set the wedding for June 28, 1947.

They could not have anticipated what happened. Only five days before the wedding, the Senate overrode Truman's veto of the Labor-Management Relations Act of 1947 — the Taft-Hartley Act, everyone called it. Labor leaders rose in fury. A "slave labor act," they proclaimed. The "Tuff-Heartless Act." The morning of the ceremony in St. Joseph, pickets appeared about the church with signs that made known their feelings. "Taft," one read, "Divorced Himself from the American People." "TAFT IS A BAD BOY," said another. A third went further. "CONGRATULATIONS TO YOU," it hailed the groom. "——— TO YOUR OLD MAN."

The St. Joseph police, anticipating trouble, called in reinforcements from surrounding towns, and by the time of the ceremony only fifteen pickets remained. Taft himself was amused by the excitement and enjoyed the wedding.[1] But he was to encounter similar scenes repeatedly in the coming months and to contend with the epithet "slave labor law" for the rest of his life. The Taft-Hartley Act, his most enduring legislative monument, was as controversial as any law passed by Congress.

As Taft had recognized when taking the Labor chairmanship, some kind of revision of existing law seemed inevitable after the 1946 elections. Indeed, the number of man-days lost in strikes continued to hover between three and six million per month in late 1946. Though most of these strikes were called to obtain better wages — strikes that no statute in a democratic society could have prevented — congressmen were obviously determined to curb the unions. On the first day of the session in 1947, seventeen labor bills were dropped into the hopper. Truman himself two days later called for congressional action against jurisdictional disputes between unions that resulted in strikes, for the prohibition of secondary boycotts with "unjustifiable objectives," for machinery to help solve disputes under existing collective bargaining agreements, and for a temporary joint commission to study the labor situation and report by March 15, 1947. "Big Labor," like Big Business a generation earlier, seemed due for a comeuppance.[2]

The House ignored Truman's temperate requests. Instead, it relied on Majority Leader Charles A. Halleck of Indiana, who had spearheaded efforts to amend the National Labor Relations Act as early as 1939, and on Fred Hartley, a hitherto unnoticed Republican from New Jersey who became chairman of the House Education and Labor Committee in 1947. Drawing on years of attempts to change the NLRA — and on the 1946 Case bill in particular — they knew what they wanted, and few people were surprised when the House committee reported a stringent measure on April 11. Like the Case bill, it deprived foremen of the rights guaranteed employees under existing law, made unions liable for damage suits for violations of contract, created an independent Federal Mediation and Conciliation Service, and banned jurisdictional strikes, secondary boycotts, and mass picketing. It also outlawed the closed shop, prohibited industrywide bargaining (under which large nationwide unions were alleged to have too much power), enumerated and banned unfair union practices, denied recognition by the NLRB to unions whose officers refused to swear they were not communists, and authorized the President to proclaim "cooling-off" periods and strike votes by employees before walkouts. With but twenty-two Republicans opposed, this bill passed on April 17 by a vote of 308 to 107. Even Democrats favored it, 93 to 84. The House obviously was in no mood for moderation.[3]

These developments left Taft with mixed feelings. On the one hand, he recognized that the firmness of the House would strengthen the hand of senators anxious to curb labor. He was pleased that the House, in tying a number of individual proposals into a package — or omnibus bill — had left Truman with the unhappy choice of taking all or nothing. But Taft also worried about the harshness of Hartley's approach, which he feared would provoke a presidential veto. As he had already discovered in 1946 with the housing bill — and as he was to be reminded repeatedly in the future — the House Republicans took directions from no one.[4]

For the time being, however, Taft faced a more serious problem within his own Labor Committee in the Senate. Though Republicans controlled it 8 to 5, and though Allen Ellender, one of the Democrats, usually defected from his party on labor policy, Taft had to worry about Republican revolts from both directions. On his right stood Joseph Ball of Minnesota, number three Republican on the committee. Ball was a strong-willed senator who opposed not only the closed shop, but the union shop, under which workers could be hired providing they joined the union within a specified time, usually set at thirty days. He was to become the leader of a determined twenty-to-thirty-man faction in the Senate working for tougher measures than Taft was willing to sponsor.[5]

Taft had to worry still more about Republican committeemen on his left. Besides George Aiken of Vermont, he had to contend with Wayne Morse of Oregon, a maverick who was to turn Independent, then Democrat, in a long Senate career spanning 1945 to 1969. Morse had been something of a prodigy: dean of the Oregon University Law School at age thirty, labor mediator, then public member of the National War Labor Board. He understood the intricacies of labor legislation and shrank from major alterations in the Wagner Act. Fiercely independent, often waspish, he proved difficult to accommodate. "I have gotten on personally very well with Morse," Taft wrote privately in 1945, "but he certainly has a one-track mind." [6]

Another Republican committee member on Taft's left was Irving Ives of New York. Though a freshman senator in 1947, Ives arrived with unusual qualifications as former chairman of the New York Joint Legislative Committee on Industrial and Labor Conditions and as dean of the New York State School of Industrial and Labor Relations at Cornell University. More important, he was recognized as Governor Dewey's spokesman in the Senate. Because Dewey seemed a likely presidential candidate in 1948, Ives's pronouncements carried considerable weight.[7] If Morse, Aiken, and Ives lined up with four Democrats, Taft might find himself in a minority of 7 to 6 on his own committee. His job demanded tact and finesse of unusual dimensions.

Taft possessed several qualities that enabled him to rise to the challenge. The first was his willingness to seek out the facts, for he did not feel quite so much at home in the complicated field of labor law as he did on other matters. Early in January 1947 Taft had acquired the services of two experts, Thomas Shroyer, an NLRB regional attorney in Cleveland, and Gerard Reilly, a former NLRB member. Reilly was a skilled legislative draftsman, and both knew the field of labor legislation as well as anyone. Throughout the controversies that ensued, Taft constantly turned to them for the advice and draftsmanship essential in the preparation of congressional legislation.

Taft also impressed observers with his willingness to work. "I can recall innumerable conferences with Senator Taft beginning at six or seven P.M. and lasting until way after midnight," Shroyer later commented. The committee heard ninety-seven witnesses in almost daily sessions between January 23 and March 8, then turned to four weeks of executive sessions. Taft was always there to lead the struggle, and he seemed to thrive on the routine.[8]

Another of Taft's assets, an evenhanded fairness, surprised those who had previously noticed only his dogmatism. He not only gave each of his colleagues equal opportunity to express his opinion but tolerated blunt disagreement with what Reilly admiringly called "amiable composure." Taft's treatment of Ives particularly impressed newsmen, for he could easily have kept a freshman of such pronounced liberal views off the committee. He did not. "I felt," he told a newsman, "that the Dewey side had a right to a seat there." This decision was to cost Taft several narrow defeats in committee, but it brought Ives into the decision-making process and spared Taft the accusation of stacking the committee. In so doing he may have reassured doubting colleagues, and he avoided a damaging intraparty row in the process.[9]

Taft had another asset that proved the most elusive to define, yet ultimately the most important. It was his ability to persuade most of his colleagues that he was at once devoted to principle and yet willing to compromise. His principles were clear enough. First, he insisted on the right of labor to strike and to bargain collectively with management. This meant leaving the antagonists as free as possible from government intervention. He opposed the House provisions calling for government scrutiny of internal union operations — a task left to the framers of the Landrum-Griffin Act of 1959. "Unless there was a clear abuse to be remedied," he explained, "we had better not go too far into experimental fields." He also displayed relatively little interest in the House provision denying NLRB recognition to unions whose officers refused to swear anticommunist oaths. That problem, he argued, could be handled by unions and management themselves. And he seemed curiously uninterested in widely heralded efforts to provide the government with the authority to intervene in nationwide strikes. Walkouts, he said privately, "are not as serious as represented in newspaper headlines, and it is far better in my opinion to suffer the inconvenience of strikes than have a completely government regulated economy." [10] Though he consented to a clause authorizing injunctions that would permit delays of eighty days before allowing strikes imperiling the national welfare, he showed no enthusiasm for it. He also thought little of the Hartley bill's provision for government-supervised strike votes on employers' final offers. Workers, he predicted accurately, would always support their leaders in such situations. And he remained as adamant as ever against plans to provide the President with broad authority for seizure. When a strike created a national emergency, he said, Congress might vote special presidential powers for that particular situation — but only for that. In holding to these general principles, Taft was reiterating his lifelong opposition to extensive governmental intervention in the economy.

Yet Taft did not believe in absolute laissez faire in labor-management relations. Government, he thought, must act to preserve the equality of opportunity and the equal justice under law that he cherished. Because he felt the NLRB had been partial to industrial unions — an opinion widely, if not universally, shared — he regarded federal protection of individual workers against their leaders as the central task before the Congress. This did not mean a Draconian bill. "I am not anxious to make a bill so strong that it is regarded as punitive or destructive of unions," he wrote. But it did mean what he called restoring a balance between labor and management. The final bill, he insisted, must define unfair union practices to match the unfair management activities listed in the National Labor Relations Act. Such labor practices included jurisdictional strikes, the closed shop, and — as his father had contended a half century before — secondary boycotts.[11]

Given the temper of the times, it was possible that something like the Taft-Hartley law would eventually have cleared Congress. But Taft's judiciousness helped him to prevail during most of the major debates in the Senate committee. On April 17, the same day as passage of the House bill, his committee reported a moderate measure, 11 to 2. Aiken and Ives, though unhappy about several provisions, went along, as did Morse, who called Taft's bill a "constructive contribution." Even Senator Claude Pepper, one of the two Democratic dissidents, conceded that Taft had done "as good a job as has ever been done by the chairman of any Senate committee." This consensus was in itself a notable achievement.[12]

Yet Taft remained uneasy. The committee members had rejected four of his ideas, usually by 7-to-6 votes, and threatened even to force a floor fight against the omnibus approach. Determined to regain the ground he had lost in committee, he set about offering his own amendments on the floor. Two of these — to prohibit coercion of workers by their leaders and to require joint employer-union administration of union welfare funds — eventually passed, 60 to 28 and 48 to 40. But the others threatened to envelop the Senate in controversy so hot as to endanger the ultimate success of the bill. Taft's handling of these issues revealed his essential moderation as well as parliamentary skill of a high order.[13]

Taft strongly favored adopting an omnibus approach. Clearly the labor bill would have to be thrashed out in a House-Senate conference committee, and because the House had already tied all its proposals in one package, he felt the Senate must follow suit. So when Morse and others in committee balked at an omnibus bill, Taft adopted the rare and risky ploy of going over their heads. First he secured the backing of the GOP policy committee for an omnibus bill, then of the rest of the Republicans in the Senate. Fortified, he returned to the Labor Committee and presented the question as a matter of party loyalty. The omnibus approach carried, 7 to 6, with Ives voting loyally but unhappily with the majority. When the same issue was brought to the floor, Taft knew he was safe, and the omnibus plan carried again, 59 to 35. Only William Langer and Wayne Morse, ever the mavericks, bolted the party line, and they were more than outweighed by the eleven Democrats, all Southern, who joined the majority.[14]

The next controversy involved the proper means of controlling secondary boycotts and jurisdictional strikes — practices denounced by practically all senators. In the recent past employers seeking relief from such practices had had no recourse. Both employers and employees, Taft said, ought to have the right to seek injunctions from the courts. But Morse, Aiken, and Ives had argued that complainants should instead request injunctions through the NLRB and had succeeded in overriding him in committee. A struggle appeared imminent.

At this point Taft sensed the danger in his position. He might propose such an amendment on the floor, and he might win. But if Truman vetoed the bill, this clause alone — which many people believed would permit a return to the days of collusion between employers and antilabor judges — might induce the Senate to sustain the veto. Quietly Taft let it be known that he was open to suggestions for change, and after he had polled GOP senators, he decided to propose a more moderate amendment that merely permitted employers to sue unions for damages incurred by such practices. When Ball insisted on carrying the fight for the original amendment, Taft disavowed him and voted against it. Ball lost, 62 to 38, and Taft's more moderate substitute then won, 65 to 26. In agreeing to compromise, Taft had shown a moderation that gratified and surprised some of his enemies.[15]

A third disagreement provoked the sharpest fight. This involved the crucial question of industrywide collective bargaining. Morse, Ives, and the majority of administration Democrats contended that any interference with this practice would weaken nationwide unions. Unlike some of his Republican colleagues, Taft agreed — to a point. "A good many industries have had nationwide bargaining for years," he wrote, "and I would not like to disturb this relationship without further study." But in other industries he was not so sure, and he embodied his convictions in a compromise amendment that prohibited the NLRB from certifying national unions as bargaining agents unless locals called them in for the negotiations. His amendment also prevented national unions from imposing conditions preventing settlement on the locals. This approach, he conceded later, would "weaken somewhat the national collective bargaining practice" by making it possible for large corporations to outflank weaker locals. But, he maintained, it would not stop locals from getting together voluntarily, and it would enable some disputes to be settled where he thought they belonged: locally. Taft's approach typified his instinctive aversion to bigness, whether in business or in labor.[16]

Taft sensed the strength of his opposition on this issue, for Ives himself was openly leading it. But this time he decided to carry his amendment to the floor. On May 7, Ives corralled the votes of twenty-eight Democrats and fifteen other Republicans to sting Taft with defeat, 44 to 43. But Taft again showed his composure. He might have demanded another vote, and because five of his supporters had been absent on the previous roll call — to three of Ives's — he might have won. Instead, he sat momentarily at his desk, smiled, then walked over and warmly clasped Ives's hand in congratulation. Taft might have been well advised not to have contended at all. But he probably had to make the effort in order to satisfy his supporters, and by losing gracefully, he not only helped his colleagues avoid another parliamentary wrangle on a divisive day of debate, but cleared the bill of a clause that would have cut into the margin needed to override a presidential veto. Taft, said the New York *Times,* had been "urbane through a long and clamorous day." [17]

The bill had to surmount five more days of legislative hurdles, including a denunciation by Robert Wagner — his last speech as a senator. But the end was near, and on May 13 the Senate passed the bill, 68 to 24. The majority included all but three Republicans (Morse, Langer, and George Malone of Nevada), and twenty-one Democrats, seventeen of whom represented the South. Taft's strategy had paid off.[18]

But he still had to deal with Hartley. In some ways the House and Senate bills were easily reconciled. Both created a federal mediation service independent of the Labor Department, catalogued "unfair" union practices such as the secondary boycott, excluded foremen from the protection given workers on the NLRB, and outlawed the closed shop. Both also called for noncommunist oaths by union officials seeking NLRB certification, and both enabled the President to obtain temporary eighty-day injunctions against strikes threatening national health or safety. Both versions also contained different but easily resolved clauses separating the judicial and prosecuting functions of the NLRB — a goal of Taft's since the 1930's. But the House bill went further. It prohibited industrywide bargaining, permitted private parties to seek injunctions against secondary boycotts and jurisdictional strikes, outlawed strikes by government employees, sharply restricted the union shop, regulated internal union activities, and outlawed employer contributions to union welfare funds. It also made unions subject to antitrust laws, banned mass picketing, and prohibited union contributions in national primaries and elections. As the conferees met on May 15, the gulf between the House and Senate bills seemed formidable.[19]

Taft entered the negotiations with mixed feelings. The Senate bill, he told a confidant, "doesn't go as far as I think it should go. Except for Ives's position I believe we could have gotten a slightly more extensive bill." On the other hand, he added, "the whole thing is such a tremendous improvement over what we thought possible a year ago that I am doing everything possible to get it enacted into law." This, he realized, meant getting a bill that people as diverse as Joseph Ball and Irving Ives would vote to enact over a presidential veto. From start to finish Taft and his fellow Senate conferees refused to budge on the essentials.[20]

Taft's stubbornness irritated the House conferees, but Hartley knew that he had to give in — or risk a presidential veto that the Senate would fail to override. Taft and his colleagues receded on the questions of political contributions, strikes by federal government employees, and a few other lesser provisions. But the House conferees had to surrender their positions on permitting private parties to seek injunctions, on industrywide bargaining, welfare

funds, the union shop, and subjecting unions to the antitrust laws.
Though Morse remained critical of the result — a "far cry" from
the Senate bill, he charged — practically everyone else interpreted
the outcome of two weeks of hard negotiations as a triumph for the
Senate.[21]

The rest was anticlimax. Both houses quickly approved the conference report, by the overwhelming margins of 320 to 79 in the
House and 54 to 17 in the Senate. Two weeks later Truman ended
doubts about his position by issuing a veto. The labor bill, he
claimed, would not prevent nationwide strikes. It discriminated
against unions, complicated NLRB procedures, and introduced
excessive government interference to a field better left to the contestants themselves. But the House overrode him the same day,
331 to 83, and after Morse and Pepper led an exhausting twenty-
eight-hour filibuster, the Senate prepared to follow suit. On Monday June 23, 1947, with visitors packing the galleries, with hundreds milling about outside, and with scores of Representatives
watching from the rear of the chamber, Taft closed the debate with
a brief and dispassionate talk. Vandenberg, in the chair as president pro tem, sternly forbade demonstrations, then turned to the
clerk for a call of the roll. When George Aiken, first on the alpha-
betical list, called out "Aye," the outcome was clear. Morse,
Langer, and Malone held out against the bill, but Ives and Ball
joined a total of forty-eight Republicans who challenged the President. At 3:17 PM the tally was completed: 68 to 25 to override.
The bill immediately became law.[22]

·

Any assessment of Taft's role in the development of the only
major law to bear his name involves a complex series of questions.
Did the law reflect his thinking? Did it prove fair and workable?
And to what extent could he claim credit for its passage?

The first question poses no difficulties. Taft had spent years
in legislative politics, he was practical, and he knew he could not
have his way on every minor point. He also could not claim to
have developed any striking new approaches to labor law — most
of the clauses of Taft-Hartley stemmed from years of discussion.
But he was proud to have his name associated with the law. The

act, he said repeatedly, was fair. It preserved the right to strike, kept the government as remote as possible from labor-management relations, "restored the balance" disrupted by years of NLRB interpretations, and made labor law a "two way street." He doubted the workability and fairness of the anticommunist oath, claimed no credit for the provisions concerning strikes creating national emergencies or union contributions to political campaigns, and admitted that any act depended on its interpretation; if the law proved impractical, it could and should be amended. But in the meantime it must be applied. For the rest of his life Taft remained ready to embrace changes in the law, but not to accept repeal. Not even the furious attacks of organized labor forced him to repudiate what he regarded as one of his greatest accomplishments.[23]

Whether the law was fair became such a partisan question that no answer was to satisfy everyone. On the one hand, many businessmen and Republicans thought Taft had been too gentle on the unions. "Labor was never your friend, Bob," a Cincinnati Republican leader complained, "and playing with that crowd will never accomplish anything for you." Yet as Lloyd and Virginia discovered on their wedding day, the reaction of organized labor was immediate and explosive. CIO leader Philip Murray damned the law as "conceived in sin," and its promoters as "diabolical men who, seething with hatred, designed this ugly measure for the purpose of imposing their wrath upon the millions of organized and unorganized workers throughout the United States." AF of L chief William Green added that the bill was "conceived in a spirit of vindictiveness against unions." And more than 200,000 soft-coal workers immediately walked off their jobs in protest against the law.[24]

The passage of the years permitted somewhat more balanced appraisals. It became clear that the law contained a number of defects. The anticommunist oath discriminated against labor and proved of little use against strong unions, which did not need NLRB certification anyway. Though communist influence in American labor declined sharply in the next few years, it was not because of the Taft-Hartley law but because the cold war led the unions themselves to clean house.[25]

The law proved mistaken in other ways as well. The ban on the closed shop quickly proved unenforceable on the docks and in the building trades, where management had long permitted unions to determine hiring procedures; these industries simply evaded the law. The separation of the prosecuting and judicial functions of the NLRB at first resulted in almost as much confusion as efficiency. Strong unions, as John L. Lewis quickly proved, could also easily evade the law's strictures against strikes before the expiration of contracts by forcing management to grant such privileges in the contracts themselves. And the prohibition of union contributions to political campaigns merely encouraged organized labor to set up separate political arms supported by voluntary contributions. These, as Taft was ruefully to discover, could prompt unprecedented bitterness in political campaigns.[26]

The law showed that many of its supporters were wrong in assuming that workers distrusted their leaders. On the contrary, unions won 98 per cent of subsequent secret ballot elections on the adoption of union shops; the clause proved so time consuming and expensive for the government that Taft gladly sponsored its repeal in 1951. The act also had only limited success in encouraging individual employees to lodge complaints against their unions. Labor leaders themselves naturally discouraged such attempts, and management often proved more interested in avoiding conflict with union leaders than in defending individual workers. The act did not try to guarantee democratic union elections, to assure the honesty of union officials, or to prevent racial discrimination in union membership. Some of these problems had to await the findings of the McClellan Committee in the 1950's and the Landrum-Griffin Act of 1959; others, such as racial discrimination, festered long after that.[27]

The act failed even to achieve one of its stated objectives: balancing existing law so as to assure equality in collective bargaining. Unions in the Northern textile industry, for instance, were so strong that mill owners continued to relocate their plants in the South. In the South, however, the textile unions were so powerless that they were often unable even to organize the plants. The Taft-Hartley law, like the National Labor Relations Act, left many such economic realities untouched.

Unions also argued tenably against three clauses that they said could seriously damage the labor movement. One of these denied the right of strikers (over economic issues) who had been replaced by management to vote in bargaining elections during the course of the strike. It was this clause that Republican presidential nominee Dwight D. Eisenhower had in mind when he said in September 1952, "Americans want no law licensing union-busting. And neither do I." The second disputed clause involved secondary boycotts. Union leaders demanded amendments to permit boycotts against firms to whom struck employers sublet contracts. And the unions grew especially heated about Section 14-b. This provision, the so-called "right-to-work" clause, permitted states to outlaw all forms of union security, including the union shop, even though the Taft-Hartley law itself prohibited only the closed shop. By 1954, fourteen states had already taken advantage of this section, and the "right-to-work" issue was to become one of the most controversial of the 1950's.[28]

But Taft himself was careful not to insist on retaining all these provisions. Almost from the start he questioned the wisdom of the anticommunist oath, and he correctly predicted the wasted expense of government supervision of union-shop elections. With the passage of time he tacitly consented to what in fact were closed shops in the building trades and on the docks. In 1949, partly to counter strong congressional sentiment for repeal, he even supported government seizure of plants under extraordinary circumstances. In 1949 he also backed a move to abolish the office of general counsel, created under the Taft-Hartley Act to insure separation of the NRLB's prosecuting and judicial functions, and in 1953 he moved to let replaced economic strikers vote in bargaining elections held during the first year of the strike. His readiness to change the law suggested his cautious fair-mindedness. Edwin Lahey, the labor reporter, recognized this quickly. And Harry Lundeberg, boss of the Seafarers International Union, AFL, put it most succinctly. Taft, he said, "doesn't give you a lot of sweet con like the others." [29]

Scholars viewing the long-range effect of the law concluded that it was far from the "slave labor act" portrayed by the unions. On the contrary, it had little effect on the stronger unions so feared by the public in 1947, it did not stop unionization drives, and it did not culminate in "union busting." Although the law may have slowed the rate of growth in union membership, unions not only managed to live with the act but to increase their membership from 14 million to 17.5 million by 1957. Indeed, union membership as a percentage of the civilian labor force actually rose from 23 to 26 per cent during these years. One observer, contending that the act led union leaders to behave more responsibly, even argued that the law "greatly invigorated the trade union movement." [30]

In retrospect, it is clear that the unions grossly exaggerated the adverse effects of the law. But employers, similarly, had anticipated more than Taft could deliver. The lesson of the controversy proved above all what Truman had claimed in his veto: The economic power of unions and management would frustrate all but the most extreme legislative attempts at regulation. If Taft erred, it was not in trying to destroy unions — for he was neither anti-union nor pro-business and was more neutral on the subject than many of his Senate colleagues — but in mistakenly assuming along with many others at the time that a law could materially change these realities of power. That he of all people should have expected much from the central government was the ultimate irony of the struggle.

Whether the law harmed Republicans politically was another question. The unions thought so and kept up their attacks for years. Truman did also, and his veto seemed to infuse in him a fighting spirit that carried him through the amazing 1948 campaign for re-election. "Labor did it," he proclaimed when he won, and his vote in industrial states like Ohio, Illinois, and California, which he carried by 58,000 votes in a total turnout in these states of 10.6 million, gave some substance to his claim. So did the 1948 congressional races, which culminated in the defeat of nine senators who had voted for the bill. Among them was Joseph Ball, who fell to a young challenger named Hubert H. Humphrey.

But elections are uncertain phenomena. If "labor did it," so did the farmers. Indeed, Truman tended to fare worse than Roosevelt had in industrial regions, while outscoring him in the rural regions of the Middle West. Pollers were far from expert in 1948, yet their surveys consistently showed that voters were ill-informed and

confused about the law and that by itself Taft-Hartley was a relatively unimportant electoral issue. As Taft remarked in May 1948,
"I do not have much concern about the Taft-Hartley law, because
I find it is very generally accepted among the labor union members
and probably will cost us few votes. Those who are shouting so
loud always supported the Democratic candidate anyway." [31]

Perhaps so. But even if the law did not harm the Republican
cause, it gave Truman an excuse to brand Taft an enemy of labor.
Thus when the President credited labor with his victory in 1948,
many Americans hastily agreed that the law was a Republican liability and Taft the more so. What mattered therefore was not so
much the facts but what many people thought they were. For the
rest of his political career, Taft had to confront these suppositions.

Still, in 1947 Taft was content. His handling of the labor bill
had evoked widespread admiration. "Brilliant," one staff man
said. "Without his efforts," a scholar wrote later, "it is unlikely
that the law would have been enacted." As even his critics recognized, Taft's fairness, composure on the floor, and judicious blend-
ing of firmness and compromise not only steered the bill through
and enabled him to hold the party together but staved off more
extreme antilabor proposals that many observers had predicted
after the 1946 elections. It was the only major change in New Deal
legislation to pass Congress, and one of the few important bills ever
to be devised and passed wholly without the assistance of any
executive department. For all its weaknesses, it proved workable
enough to withstand repeated attempts at repeal and ultimately to
emerge as one of the lasting accomplishments of Taft's life.[32]

Taft was proud. For the first time since 1931, when he authored
the Ohio intangibles tax, he had devised an important piece of legislation and carried it through. It was pleasant once again to feel a
part of his times.

PART V

Mr. Republican

CHAPTER 24

The Perils of Prominence, 1947

BECAUSE THE STRUGGLE for Taft-Hartley consumed so much of Taft's time, he could easily have slighted other legislative matters without incurring too much criticism from his peers. Yet he was never a single-issue senator, and he possessed such energy that he injected himself into most of the other important controversies of 1947. He also found time to conduct another campaign for the Republican presidential nomination. Despite these pressures on his time, he spurred his Republican allies to a number of victories over the administration. Yet in leading his forces, he often took exposed positions that endangered his presidential candidacy. And in trying to field so many questions, he not infrequently revealed a partisanship that did little to enhance his reputation.

The first key issue in 1947 involved foreign affairs. Greece, President Truman warned congressional leaders in late February, would fall to communist guerrillas unless America provided military aid. On March 12, he pronounced what became known as the Truman Doctrine, the kernel of the containment policy that guided American leaders for many years thereafter. "I believe," said Truman, "that it must be the policy of the United States to support free peoples who are resisting attempted subjugation by armed minorities or by outside pressures." He then asked Congress for $400 million in military and economic aid for the non-communist governments of Greece and Turkey.

Taft had several reasons to support the request. Like his father, he bowed to no one in his instinctive anticommunism, and even during the war he had criticized what he considered the selfishness of Soviet foreign policy. Truman, he also felt, had committed the prestige of his office to aid of Greece and Turkey. Rejection of his public appeal could only strengthen communism in East Europe. When Truman — at Vandenberg's urgent request — belatedly included Taft in a White House conference concerning the question, Taft may have been confirmed in his inclination to cooperate. At any rate the invitation must have been gratifying. The conference, he commented four years later, was one of two at the Truman White House that he was invited to attend.[1]

But he recoiled instinctively from the idea of American involvement in such far-off places. Truman's request, he said the day of his visit to the White House, seemed to "accept the policy of dividing the world into zones of political influence, communist and anticommunist. Perhaps there is no other course." Then Taft ventured further. "If we assume a special position in Greece and Turkey," he said, "we can hardly longer reasonably object to the Russians' continuing their domination in Poland, Yugoslavia, Rumania, and Bulgaria." American aid might discourage the guerrillas, he conceded, but at what cost in American relations with the Soviet Union? The Soviets, he speculated, might feel compelled to go to war, "just as we might be prompted to go to war if Russia tried to force a Communist government on Cuba." [2]

As the days passed, the administration increased its pressure and in fact consciously sought to develop an air of crisis. Taft, however, refused to panic. When Vandenberg, who was cooperating closely with the administration, asked his colleagues for suggestions, Taft was quick to raise a host of embarrassing questions:

Did American military experts think the Soviet Union had the strength to wage war over the problem?

Could Greece, if given American aid, resist a Soviet invasion?

What was the evidence to suggest, as Truman seemed to claim, that a communist takeover of Greece would spread throughout the Middle East?

What evidence was there that American national security was threatened?

How would American policy be directed in Greece? Would Congress have much of a say?

Should America retain its influence in Greece if and when its aid achieved its immediate objectives?

Why not simply file a complaint with the United Nations, whether America provided aid or not?

Would America allow elections to be held in Greece, and would America accept the results of such elections if they proved unfavorable? [3]

Nothing suggests that Truman paid much attention to Taft's questions. In any event they were difficult for an administration bent on immediate action to answer at the time, and Taft gradually decided that defeat of Truman's request would signify American weakness. "I don't like the Greek-Turkish proposition," he wrote, "but I do recognize that perhaps we should maintain the *status quo* until we can reach some peace accommodation with Russia. I don't like to appear to be backing down." On April 10, 1947, he came out at last for the aid. But, he said carefully, "I do not regard this as a commitment to any similar policy in any other section of the world." America should "withdraw as soon as normal economic conditions are restored." [4]

Two weeks later the Senate approved the Truman Doctrine 67 to 23. Taft joined Vandenberg and thirty-three other Republicans in supporting it. The aid eventually helped to defeat the guerrillas, though not until 1949, when Yugoslavia's President Tito deprived them of sanctuary behind his borders. But Taft and others had raised some delicate questions that deserved more careful attention than they got in 1947. Were not the guerrillas more independent of the Soviet Union than the administration claimed? Was it not in America's national interest to disengage itself from autocratic governments such as existed in Greece? Would not such a policy promote the Cold War, which Americans were so quick to blame on the communists? In short, was not the Truman Doctrine a sign of the administration's exaggerated hostility toward the Soviet Union — and of the often irrational anticommunism, which was subsequently to distort the vision of makers of American foreign policy? The answer later given by many scholars to all these questions was "yes." [5]

Why then had Taft, who asked many of these questions himself, supported the administration? His stated reason, that Truman had already committed the country, was sincere. He was moved by his anticommunism. But he also went along because he was unsure of his grounds. "I am not an expert on foreign relations," he had properly conceded to Herbert Hoover privately in 1945. Busy with Taft-Hartley and other domestic questions, he knew little about the situation in Greece and Turkey, and he did not have time to inform himself. It was easier to submit to the judgment of Vandenberg than to lead his party along the path of obstructionism.[6]

Because Taft had given little thought to the question, he also lacked any cogent alternative. Some critics of the Truman Doctrine, like former Commerce Secretary Henry Wallace, were insisting that America first help Western, not Eastern Europe, and provide economic, not military aid. But these alternatives involved extensive spending overseas, which Taft had always opposed. Better, he concluded, to endorse short-run military aid and to announce, as he did, that he underwrote no commitment for the future. In taking this position, Taft was consistent, for he had demanded the end of lend-lease to the Soviets in 1945, opposed Bretton Woods, and tried to whittle down a loan to Great Britain in 1946. But it also suggested that he feared *any* long-term commitments, no matter how necessary or altruistic. His stand also satisfied neither the Wallaceites, who deplored the sending of military aid, the hard-core Republican opponents, nor the Eastern internationalists who controlled the GOP at presidential nominating conventions. The brief flurry of controversy over the Truman Doctrine did little to establish him as a thoughtful spokesman about the proper American course in the Cold War.

This question of foreign affairs temporarily taken care of, Taft found himself locked in a struggle with the administration over economic policy. Truman, he said, should curb inflation by carrying out a "plan of education" that would persuade labor to soften its demands, consumers to spend less, and businessmen to be careful about raising their prices. Above all, Truman should cut spending by at least $5 billion more than he seemed willing to do. The President, Taft charged, was "like a man tying down the safety valve while he speeds up the stoking under the boiler." [7]

Taft was wholly serious about cutting federal spending. Having agreed to head a new joint congressional committee on the economic report, he spent almost as much time collecting an able and professional staff, studying economic statistics, and issuing reports as he did on his other senatorial duties. He also seemed willing to offend all sorts of interest groups. Thus he opposed increasing the federal minimum wage beyond sixty-five cents even though spokesmen for organized labor insisted on a minimum of seventy-five cents.[8] Thus, too, he yearned to cut military spending by as much as $6 billion, even though Truman himself was already supporting a decrease from $12.9 to $9.5 billion. And he was willing to settle for expenditures of only $1 billion for his health, public housing, and aid to education bills — a figure that would have been insignificant in the overall Truman budget of $37.5 billion. The need for economy, Taft said, left the nation no choice.[9]

By the end of the 1947 session, Republicans had succeeded in cutting $2.8 billion from Truman's budget, but in the process they came to realize how economical the administration had tried to be. In the meantime, the real battle developed over tax policy. Though Congress had cut taxes in 1945, Republicans clamored for another reduction, and Taft gladly assumed the role as one of their spokesman. Federal, state, and local taxes, he charged repeatedly, constituted 30 per cent of the national income. "That means that on the average we are working three days out of ten for the government." Tax reduction, therefore, was "essential to the welfare of the country, because the present heavy burden of taxation is an evil in itself." In a statement typical of his lifelong concern for individual initiative, he claimed that such taxes discouraged "the use of brains, ability and hard work which lies at the very basis of developing our productivity, our prosperity, and our jobs . . . There is some point at which high taxes must lead directly to socialism, and I think thirty per cent of the national income is perilously close to that point." [10]

Assured of substantial Democratic support, Republicans in both houses moved for reduction, and Representatives passed House Resolution 1 in March 1947. It cut personal income taxes 30 per cent at lower income levels, 20 per cent in the middle, and 10.5 per cent at the top. In late May, Taft and his friends got a slightly more moderate and progressive reduction through the Senate, 54 to 32. The conference bill approved a few days later would have initiated the reductions on July 1, 1947, and was expected to save taxpayers $4 billion.[11]

At this point Truman struck back. Tax reduction, he maintained, would contribute to consumer spending, feed inflation, and deprive the government of $4 billion that ought to be used to reduce government debt. Finally, the President emphasized, the bill did little for lower income groups. Truman then vetoed it. When the House barely sustained him, Republicans hurried through a bill that was identical except for postponing the starting date of the reductions until January 1948. The compromise was enough to persuade the House to override Truman's second veto. But this time the Senate fell five votes short of the necessary two-thirds.[12]

The setback annoyed Taft. "The argument for tax reduction is overwhelming in view of the increased revenues," he wrote a friend, "and the President is simply playing politics by claiming that the bill is too favorable to the upper income groups." But he had grounds to be satisfied. Only Wayne Morse, William Langer, and George Aiken had rebelled at his leadership, and Senate Republicans had followed him on the two bills by the gratifying margins of 42 to 2 and 47 to 3. Besides, he anticipated that Americans would soon insist on reductions in taxes and that many Democrats might feel compelled by constituent pressures to approve a tax cut in the election year of 1948.[13]

The ironies of the battle of the budget were considerable. Truman, who was in the process of slashing the federal budget from $98 billion in fiscal 1945 to $33 billion in fiscal 1948, who opposed a tax cut because he wanted to reduce the government debt, and who succeeded in concluding the 1948 fiscal year with a cash surplus of $8.4 billion, was being accused of spending too much and of moving the nation toward socialism. Taft, who had so often called for higher taxes to balance the budget and for measures to reduce the debt, had opposed anti-inflationary price controls in 1946 and was now demanding lower taxes and maintaining that large-scale debt retirement could wait. Both sides believed what they said, yet Republicans in particular were talking politics as well as economics. The 1948 election, they recognized, might be won with the attractive issue of tax reduction.

Taft was actually more sophisticated and more consistent than he seemed. He did not blame postwar inflation solely on the administration, and he recognized that the government could not always balance its budget. What would you do, a reporter asked, if confronted with mass unemployment? "Deficit financing," he snapped unhesistatingly.[14] Taft also pointed out that he insisted on cuts in spending to accompany reductions in taxes, and he argued correctly that some debt retirement would be possible even with lower taxes. He may also have been right in suggesting that postwar consumer demand was already beginning to subside and that tax reduction would not unleash dangerously high consumer spending. At any rate the tax cut that Congress passed a year later, in 1948, proved noninflationary and probably stopped the economy from falling into a deeper recession than it did in 1949.

Yet Taft and most of his fellow Republicans had acted from questionable economic premises. Businessmen, who were prospering as seldom before, did not need tax cuts to stimulate their incentive to produce. Taft grossly exaggerated the likelihood of socialism in America, and in seizing on 30 per cent of the national income as the maximum tolerable tax load, he used an imprecise measurement that obscured the ability of many wealthy Americans to pay considerably more than that. Though the tax law of 1948 did apparently reduce the severity of the 1949 recession, the fact was that early in 1947, when Republicans were demanding reductions, practically all the experts were afraid that such cuts would promote inflation. Truman and his advisers at least acted on the basis of present indications. Taft and the Republicans, on the other hand, seemed willing to risk further inflation at a time when it was already serious. The ultimate irony of the struggle was that the tax cut, when adopted in 1948, appeared to most economists as foolish as it had seemed in 1947. Yet it worked to relieve the nation from an unexpected recession. Such was the level of economic expertise in postwar America.[15]

•

Taft had dinner guests at his Georgetown home on the evening of March 28, 1947. But it was not a purely social occasion, for the diners included prominent Republican politicians as well as personal friends. Some, like John Bricker, were powers in the party. Others — Ohio Congressmen George Bender, Clarence Brown, and Tom Jenkins — were seasoned professionals. Paul Walter,

Taft's loyal supporter in three earlier campaigns, was there, as were Fred Johnson, Ohio's Republican chairman, and Benjamin Tate, the conservative Cincinnatian who had served as Taft's finance chairman in 1944. Completing the gathering were three veterans of the 1940 campaign, John Marshall, John Hollister, and Martha's brother, Tom Bowers. It was as close to a summit conference of Taftites as was ever assembled.

The guests enjoyed their food and drink in the Tafts' spacious dining room, then settled back for the business at hand. What were his chances for the 1948 presidential nomination, Taft wanted to know? Bricker spoke optimistically; he would support his colleague. The others agreed. The Democrats had held the White House too long, Truman was stumbling, and the time was ripe. Taft did not commit himself — it was too early for that. But he set his men loose to estimate the odds. In the meantime he would assume the role of disinterested legislator until the session ended.[16]

Most of the guests needed no prodding, and they began to move in earnest. Walter reserved 140 hotel rooms and 16 suites in Philadelphia, site of the Republican convention scheduled for more than a year in the future. Brown, who gradually struggled to the top of the team, arranged for a newsman, John Gordon Bennett, to travel about the country and file detailed reports on political conditions. Other veteran Taft workers — Ohio national committeewoman Katharine Kennedy Brown (no relation to Clarence) and David Ingalls in particular — quickly set to work. And Clarence Brown even took it upon himself in August 1947 to promise Governor Dwight Green of Illinois a cabinet position. What Green — and Taft — thought about this was not clear, but it symbolized the drive of the Taft team well in advance of the convention.[17]

Taft himself had also needed no persuasion, for he had long kept open the possibility of running. "I do not really expect to be a candidate," he wrote a friend in November 1945, "but no one objects to being mentioned." "I have no real intention of running for the presidential nomination," he wrote two months later, "but I told Governor Bricker that I certainly would not take myself out of the running at the present time, or until after the election of 1946." Taft still hesitated — "I don't know what to do myself," he told Hollister in August 1946, "it seems to me I would have a lot of drawbacks as a candidate." Yet he could not bring himself to back out of the race.[18]

He also shrank from letting the other top contenders win the nomination. Bricker, who seemed a possibility to some in 1945 and 1946, struck him as unsuitable. "He hasn't got the ability to speak and say anything," Taft confided to Hollister in 1946, "and is almost certain to make a lot of mistakes." Fortunately for Taft, Bricker himself wisely refused to battle for the nomination, and said so openly as early as December 1946. By the time of the dinner meeting in March 1947 Taft already felt secure in Ohio.[19]

A much more irritating possibility was Harold Stassen. Tall, moon faced, only forty years old, Stassen had resigned the governorship of Minnesota to enter the Navy in the war and had returned to proclaim a vaguely liberal and internationalist philosophy. To many younger Republicans he seemed a dynamic alternative to men like Taft who had been in the headlines so long. Stassen was also tireless, well financed, free from the responsibilities of officeholding, and insatiably ambitious for the presidency. As early as December 1946 he announced what everyone had known already: He would run for the nomination in 1948.

Taft watched Stassen's movements with disgust. "It seems to me," he observed, "he ought to be spending his time and money to elect a Republican Congress instead of throwing it around the way he is doing on personal publicity and cocktail parties in Washington." Taft also found his rival's thinking "sophomoric." Stassen, he complained privately, "doesn't know what he is talking about. He wraps himself in a mantle of liberalism, but to the extent that his principles differ from those he attributes to the old guard, they are merely those of the Political Action Committee." Above all, Taft thought Stassen selfish and unreliable. "I may do him an injustice," he wrote Ingalls, "but I think he is a complete opportunist but basically a New Dealer and an internationalist." [20]

The chief contender, however, was once again Governor Thomas E. Dewey of New York. In the name of party harmony both men had tried to reconcile their differences after the 1944 campaign, and when Taft stopped in Albany in September 1946, the two Republican titans appeared even to enjoy each other's company. Taft graciously asked Dewey to criticize the text of a speech against socialized medicine, and the governor responded with elaborate praise. "You are making a great contribution," Dewey wrote, "toward clearer thinking on these proposals which would enslave our medical profession and set us back a century in medical care." Taft, too, was pleased with the meeting. "We did not get down to brass tacks," he admitted to a friend. But "it was a very friendly party and a good dinner."

Still, Taft recoiled from the idea of nominating Dewey. And the reasons in his mind were overwhelming. First, Dewey struck many regular Republicans like Taft as too accommodating to what was popular at the moment. "The Boy Orator of the Platitude," they called him. For this reason Taft doubted Dewey's willingness to wage a frontal attack on Truman. "I rather doubt if I am the candidate," he had explained to a friend in 1945. "On the other hand I do not want to see Mr. Dewey or Mr. Stassen [nominated] because they both seem to me New Dealers." Like many people, Taft also found the governor arrogant. ("I still think he is a son of a bitch," Roosevelt had said of Dewey in 1944).[21] And Dewey simply stood in the way. Taft had been raised to compete, to serve, and to excel, and he was not inclined to stand aside for such a rival. So it was that he called the meeting at his home in March, and so it was in early 1947 that he did nothing to discourage his friends.

•

When the congressional session finally closed in July, Taft hurried to Columbus to address the party faithful. Then he departed for Murray Bay. There he rested in the rambling house his mother had bequeathed him and Charlie, and relaxed with his sons, his three daughters-in-law, and his six grandchildren. He played golf, chatted with old friends, and watched the river flow by. Like his father forty years earlier, he also thought deeply about the presidential year ahead, and after taking his ease until mid-September, he decided to plunge ahead on a journey to the West to assess his chances.

Publicly, of course, the tour would have other goals. "I think it is important," he wrote Clarence Brown, "that the trip be played up as an attempt to publicize the action of Congress . . . It ought

not to be a presidential campaign trip." Yet this ostensible purpose fooled no one. When the train carrying him and Martha arrived in San Francisco September 12, it was met by some thirty-five
newsmen who clung to them through the remainder of their journey. Such coverage was not only unprecedented but proof, as if
proof were needed, of Taft's potential as a nominee.[22]

But the coverage was not the sort he wanted, for from start to
finish he seemed destined to make little gaffes and to encounter
situations that, when publicized, looked less than flattering. Far
from concealing these occasions, the reporters dwelt on them. The
results hurt.

Taft started off by inadvertently crossing a picket line to make a
speech the first day. The reporters duly recorded the occasion for
their readers. In Los Angeles a few days later, he remarked that
Republicans should await control of the White House (which
everyone expected would occur in 1949) before trying to enact
welfare programs. Again the press seized on the remark to make it
sound as if he opposed social reform. Hearing the reports, moderates like George Aiken protested, and a week later Taft felt
obliged to retract his statement.[23]

His chief gaffe, however, occurred during his first press conference, held at Santa Cruz on September 12, 1947. Earlier in the day
he had complained that excess demand was helping to promote
high food prices. Did he mean, reporters asked, that people should
consume less food? "Yes," Taft replied unhesitatingly. "Eat less
meat and eat less extravagantly." To Taft, who had helped Herbert Hoover promote "wheatless and meatless" days in 1917, such
an off-hand remark was simply common sense. But it was the first
day of the trip, and high food prices were a major issue. The New
York *Times* carried portions of the conference in a three-column
story on page one. Many others did likewise. And a few singled
out "eat less" for special attention.

The next day union picketers seized on the remark. "Tighten
your belt — eat less," they cried. One story then begat another.
Marie Antoinette had at least told the masses to eat cake, but Taft,
the cold-hearted defender of privilege, counseled people to starve.
More surprised than anything else, he held up Truman's economic report to prove that the President had said much the same

thing himself. Should profits be smaller, reporters persisted? Yes, Taft replied, if they were excessive. In any event, profits would decline when supply equaled demand.[24]

For most reporters that was the end of it. Indeed, many probably respected him for refusing to claim that he had been misquoted. But the unions continued to cry, and some papers kept the "news" near page one for days. One liberal paper, the New York *Post,* still found the episode newsworthy enough on October 6 to feature a full-page story under the headline, "SENATOR TAFT'S SEVEN DAY DIET. HOW HE FOLLOWS HIS OWN ADVICE TO EAT LESS MEAT." The story provided readers with a careful account of his meals for the preceding week. A two-column photograph capped the effort. It showed a grinning Taft eagerly slicing a thick piece of meat. The Democratic National Committee, which was already watching Taft warily, cut out the *Post's* account and sent it to its speakers later in the campaign.[25]

Taft had himself to blame for the infelicity of his remark. But he was powerless to prevent publicity attending the picketing by the unions. In San Francisco fifteen hundred pickets appeared. In Los Angeles three hundred sang while he made a speech. "TAFT'S CREED: MEIN KAMPF," read one sign widely reprinted in the media. "TAFT IS A SCHNOOK: HE BORROWED A LEAF FROM HITLER'S STORY BOOK," read another. In Seattle a few days later he encountered the roughest crowd of all. Arriving at the scene of a speaking engagement, he sat in his car while pickets splattered it with vegetables. When he tried to climb out, a fearful aide slammed the car door on his hand. White and bleeding, he struggled out of the car, only to confront a furious man who broke forward, thrust his chin at Taft, and shouted, "You goddamned son of a bitch." Taft's self-control amazed his aides. He turned away, demanded stitches for his hand, and carried out his schedule without interruption.[26] One can only wonder at the determination that carried him stoically through such demonstrations of the hatred and rhetoric of public life in the 1940's.

What distressed Taft most of all about these episodes was the coverage they received at the expense of his speeches, which he had laboriously drafted — as always by himself — during his sojourn at

Murray Bay. Yet the fault was partly his, for he still offered long and weighty expositions that bored reporters. "Taft," *Time* sniped, "is one of the best professors of government now in politics." [27] It was not surprising that many reporters despaired, that they turned to trivia or sensationalism in order to provide their editors with something. Whether the publicity on his trip West helped, hurt, or made no difference was impossible to say. But much of it was unflattering, and Taft could have prevented some of the distortions.

Still, he pressed on. After speaking in San Francisco, Los Angeles, Reno, and Seattle, he gave a carefully reported major speech in Tacoma denouncing administration foreign policy. Then to Gearhart, Oregon, Portland, Corvallis, Boise, and Casper, where he concluded his hectic three-week swing on October 2. Gradually he had worked out an effective, if tiring routine: up at seven, breakfast with local leaders, the morning dictating a speech, an extemporaneous talk at lunch, an afternoon press conference to accommodate the local reporters, more meetings and conferences, a set speech in the evening. Then back to the train or car for the trip to the next city. The reporters grew exhausted, dirty, and desperate for a shower and a change of clothes. But Taft, who had a private car, always appeared content, and he seemed never to tire.[28]

Martha proved as indefatigable as her husband. She appeared happy despite the interminable luncheons, the discomforts of Pullman cars, the awkward waits in hotel lobbies, the handshaking with hordes of minor politicians she had never seen before and might never see again. And she not only outshone Bob on the stump but left her audiences rocking with laughter. "We've got a 'highboy' government in Washington," she cracked — "one bureau on top of another, and the New Dealers are like termites in the drawers." Truman, she added, was "just one of the boys — and that's a fact . . . You've got to take him or leave him — and that's a suggestion." Well before the end of the journey, the reporters were giving her more attention than the featured performer.[29]

Taft did not seem to care. Some reporters, he noticed correctly, appreciated his bluntness, his candor, his awesome command of facts during press conferences. Some of the politicians had appeared impressed, and sizable crowds had heard his speeches. Though the public opinion polls showed him behind not only Dewey, but also Stassen and Vandenberg, he was so anxious to run that he saw only what he wanted to see. The trip, he wrote, was "not only encouraging but inspiring." "My general conclusion," he added, "is that Dewey is fairly easy to beat, but that I have to overcome the resistance to myself arising from the claim that I cannot be elected if nominated. All of our publicity efforts will have to be aimed in that direction."

On October 24, 1947, Taft announced his candidacy.[30]

CHAPTER 25

Pyrrhic Victories in the Senate,
1947–1948

TAFT HAD scarcely concluded his trip in October when Truman
called Congress into special session. Inflation, the President
claimed, demanded the imposition of new controls. And deteriorating economic conditions in Europe were opening the gates to
communism. Congress, Truman proclaimed, must provide $597
million in interim aid to France, Italy, and Austria, to last until
April 1, 1948. Later, he added, he would ask for more. The special session that followed — and the 1948 session after that — often
placed Taft on the defensive and confirmed an unwritten rule of
American politics: Any senator contending for the presidency
must tread carefully in the months before the convention.

Predictably, Taft opposed government controls. So did the
overwhelming majority of his Republican colleagues. But Taft
had not waited to assemble them, and he made no effort to sound
conciliatory. Export controls, he maintained, were necessary to increase domestic supply. But price control "is the police state con-
demned by the President himself a month ago. *This is the end of
economic freedom."* [1]

Most of Taft's fellow Republicans recognized correctly that
Truman's demand for controls was partly political, and they acquiesced in Taft's hyperbole. But Raymond Baldwin of Connecticut, Ralph Flanders of Vermont, and a few others chafed openly.
Since when could Taft speak for the party without going at least to
the GOP policy committee? Did he think he *was* the Republican
party? Trying to conciliate, Taft gradually backed off from his
negative stand and eventually supported a compromise bill that
continued Truman's authority to control exports and rail trans-

portation but offered him little else. Republicans backed the bill overwhelmingly, and Democrats, offered no choice, did likewise. It passed in December, 77 to 10. When inflation began to level off in 1948, the issue faded. But the controversy temporarily bruised the feelings of Taft's younger colleagues and left him exposed to the charge of negativism.[2]

His hostility toward aid to Europe — the European Recovery Program, or Marshall Plan, as it came to be called — was equally predictable. America, he wrote Herbert Hoover in July, ought to provide food and supplies "required to get the European economies operating." But Secretary of State George Marshall had invited the Europeans to state their needs, and this meant they would "gang up and make unreasonable demands." Taft also refused to accept the administration's bleak description of Europe. Citing Henry Hazlitt's *Will Dollars Save the World?* ("the best discussion on the subject and very convincing," he wrote his friends), he argued that Europe's needs were exaggerated, that the artificial injection of American money might do more harm than good, that Europe would recover only by restoring its own production. Like his father, Taft rejected the notion that the American government could materially improve domestic conditions in foreign countries.[3]

He also continued to resist the idea of bipartisanship. "Foreign policy," he wrote a friend, "should be one of the main issues in the next election, and the sooner we get free from the idea that we are bound to cooperate in everything, the better off we will be." Moreover, Marshall was "closely tied in with the Teheran, Yalta, Potsdam policy, which set Russia up as the power it is today . . . He made a complete failure of himself in China, and if his policy continues there it will hand China over to the Russians." Administration foreign policy, he added, "has brought the world to a state of complete bankruptcy." [4]

Here Taft's thinking took an interesting turn. Bungling diplomacy by the Democrats, he insisted, had strengthened the Soviet Union. Yet, he continued, the Soviets "do not want war within any reasonable period of years, because they know that in the end it would mean a serious defeat." Thus the real battle was not going to be military, but ideological. One way to stop the spread of communist ideology was to provide modest sums of money to nations that really needed help, and for this reason alone he grudgingly supported some American aid to Europe. But the only long-range way was to set an example at home: Keep America as free from state controls as possible. This was also the best way to develop healthy relations abroad. "If we throw our dollars around and try to run the show," he insisted, "we are going to give the Communists further arguments against us for trying to be imperialistic." [5]

Taft approached the whole question of aid to Europe from the perspective of the domestic economy. America had been suffering from inflationary pressures. Why? Because of a wage-price spiral stemming from the stresses of postwar reconversion and because of excessive demand. And whence came this demand? Partly, Taft concluded, from excessive American lending abroad. Such loans provided foreigners with the money to buy American goods, but this "artificial" foreign demand could not last forever — indeed, its breakdown in similar circumstances in 1929 had caused the Great Depression, and if continued would cause another. In the meantime the demand kept American prices up, introduced unwarranted government intervention in the economy, and unbalanced the budget. In opposing heavy public expenditures for foreign loans, Taft was thinking more about their effect at home than about what they might do for people abroad.[6]

These assumptions determined his course in the special session. When the GOP policy committee, again under the sway of Vandenberg on foreign policy matters, decided to back Truman's request for $597 million, Taft led a rump faction favoring an amendment reducing the figure to $400 million. Nineteen Republicans joined him, but twenty-seven followed Vandenberg, and the amendment failed, 56 to 30. Taft then unhappily supported the full appropriation, which passed easily, 83 to 6. When the special session finally adjourned before Christmas, Congress had compromised on $540 million (including $18 million for China). Round one had gone to Truman.[7]

Whether communism threatened France and Italy as much as the Truman administration maintained was debatable. It was also impossible to prove that the billions pumped into western Europe through subsequent congressional appropriations were the essential ingredient in the amazing economic recovery which Europe experienced after 1947. It was arguable, as some New Left historians later suggested, that Truman stirred Americans to new heights of irrational anticommunism, that the European Recovery Program accelerated the pace of the Cold War, and even that it drove a threatened Soviet Union to its coup in Czechoslovakia in February 1948. Indeed, in making some of these assertions Taft prompted Henry Wallace to state that he [Taft] was more likely than Truman "to keep peace during the next four years." Most subsequent observers, however, agreed that Western Europe desperately needed help in late 1947, that the Marshall Plan assisted her recovery, and that it therefore proved a humanitarian as well as realistic policy in the national interest. Because Europe's needs seemed so large at the time, Taft's position struck many people as shortsighted and selfish.[8]

As in his stance on the Truman Doctrine, Taft had seemed uncertain. During the summer he had acted cautiously. As the months passed, however, he grew steadily more critical; and as the election year approached, he seemed so hostile that he not only refused to abide by the recommendation of his own GOP policy committee but also called for a cut of $197 million in aid without giving a reasoned justification for picking such a figure. To many people the conclusion was inescapable: Taft had let partisanship and political ambition play important roles.

Worse, he seemed confused. Central to his thought was his belief that government lending abroad artificially stimulated demand and therefore inflation. Yet Taft then seriously compromised his argument. "Our loans," he said, "should be made to specific countries for specific purposes and only to pay for goods shipped from the United States." His insistence that borrowers purchase American goods would have stimulated foreign buying in the United States and in so doing have increased the very demand — and inflation — that he was earnestly trying to oppose.

Finally, Taft had contributed little to developing a policy for handling the most pressing issue of the age: dealing with the Soviet Union. On the one hand he seemed moderate — and correct, as it seemed to scholars in retrospect — in arguing that the Soviet Union did not want war. On the other hand, he had been delivering partisan speeches blaming the administration for being "soft" on the Soviet Union and international communism ever since the middle of World War II. It was difficult for Americans — and more difficult still for Europeans — to understand how he could claim to oppose communism and at the same time try to cut aid aimed at stopping it. The answer to this apparent contradiction was that he thought America militarily safe from the Soviet Union — and America came first — and that he worried above all about the domestic economy: If America stumbled toward statism, there would be no hope for the future. But the most influential groups in American life — labor unions, corporate leaders, the majority of Congress — were deeply frightened by what they perceived to be the threat of communism to western Europe. They thought the Marshall Plan would promote European prosperity, advance American economic interests, stop the spread of communism, and contribute to world peace. Taft's stand on interim aid to Europe left him more exposed than ever to the charge of isolationism at the very moment Americans were becoming alarmed about the prospect of another world war. His stand did little to reassure people about his understanding of world politics or to advance his claims for the presidency.[9]

The coming of the new year offered Taft little respite from his labors and ambitions. Indeed, he stepped up his presidential campaign, and by February 1948 he was paying several aides a total of $1600 per month in addition to employing the free services of the professionals at the top of his team. Ben Tate and others were having no trouble raising funds. And with the break for Lincoln's Birthday, Taft again took to the road. In one week he gave eight speeches in Indiana, Illinois, Minnesota, Nebraska, and Colorado. Returning to Washington for a week, he left again for a series of speeches in Michigan. In mid-March he went to Maine and barely escaped serious injury when his small plane made a forced landing on the snow-covered Kennebec River. As self-controlled as ever, he hiked to the road and carried out his schedule without interruption.[10]

The polls persisted in showing him behind his rivals, but he refused to despair. Stassen, he felt correctly, was too unpopular with GOP leaders to win the nomination, and Dewey was losing ground. Most encouraging of all, the Democrats seemed doomed. Henry Wallace had announced his candidacy on a Progressive platform, a move that was expected to lessen Truman's support from the Left; and angry Southern Democrats were threatening to desert the Democratic party unless Truman softened his stand for civil rights. In February, Taft chortled that "our friends, the Democrats, certainly appear to be completely demoralized here at the moment. I doubt very much if they ran regain any real unity in the campaign, and so I have become an optimist." By April a Gallup Poll reported that only 36 per cent of Americans approved of Truman's performance in the presidency, while 50 per cent disapproved. The Republicans, Taft needled Truman during a Gridiron dinner, "will do everything we can to see that you are nominated. We are like the little boy at the zoo enjoined to keep away from the lions. 'And always keep a hold of nurse, for fear of finding something worse.' " [11]

•

For all his travels, Taft still had to spend most of his time trying to run the second session of the Eightieth Congress. Because both parties approached legislation with the elections in mind, the battles that ensued proved unusually partisan, inconclusive, and exhausting. Taft emerged from the ordeal satisfied but bruised.

On some questions he still could not prevail. Chief among these once again was the European Recovery Program, for which Truman was requesting $17 billion over the next four years and three months. Vandenberg's Foreign Relations Committee then emerged with a bill authorizing $5.3 billion for the coming year. Though the Russian coup in Czechoslovakia attracted many Americans to all measures aimed at propping up western Europe, Taft opposed any commitment beyond one year and tried to cut the authorization to $4 billion. When the Senate defeated his amendment, 56 to 31, he then agreed to support the full amount on the grounds that some aid was necessary in the fight against communism. The bill passed in mid-March, 69 to 13. Once again

Vandenberg had led a bipartisan team of internationalists to victory.[12]

Otherwise, Taft's antiadministration forces continued to frustrate the President. Over Truman's veto they passed a bill relaxing antitrust restrictions on railroads. Over another veto they enacted a law that increased public assistance but excluded 750,000 workers whom the courts had recently made eligible for such help. They refused to heed Truman's requests for an increase in the federal minimum wage and for civil rights legislation, and they held the administration to a one-year extension of the reciprocal trade program. Most encouraging of all to Taft, Congress passed a tax cut only slightly less substantial than those vetoed by Truman in 1947. Truman vetoed it again, but the election was near, and this time both houses overruled him.[13]

Taft also thrust himself into two other key issues. On the first, Palestine, he continued to work closely with Rabbi Abba Hillel Silver and militantly insisted on partition and a United Nations force to back it up if necessary. When the British finally pulled out amid spreading violence on May 1, 1948, the Jews proclaimed the state of Israel, which the President recognized immediately. Taft's forthright support of Zionism tended to overlook the injustices that the Arabs, too, were suffering in the troubled Middle East, but he had long believed implacably in the justice of Zionist demands, and no one could accuse him, as they were to accuse Truman, of being a belated supporter in order to win Jewish votes. On the contrary, the creation of Israel marked the triumph of a campaign Taft had been assisting for years.[14]

On the second issue, farm policy, Taft at first spoke too frankly. Addressing farmers in Nebraska, he conceded that the government should encourage farm cooperatives, provide aid for soil conservation, and maintain "some minimum price comparable to the prices of other goods." Price supports, however, "ought to be at a much less percentage of parity than ninety percent," and "production controls . . . should be invoked only in the greatest emergency." His speech reflected his lifelong belief that high price supports cost the government money and occasioned the need for controls. But it took courage — or foolhardiness — to suggest lower sup-

Harry learns the hard way. *Reprinted, courtesy of the Chicago* Tribune

ports in Omaha, and the farm organizations, which had never warmed to his economy-minded outlook in the past, took sharp notice.[15]

Thereafter, Taft pursued a course more palatable to the farmers. Never much interested in farm policy, he let George Aiken engineer a compromise farm bill providing for 90 per cent supports until 1950, and sliding supports thereafter. The bill then passed both houses with large bipartisan majorities, and the Republican adjourned in 1948 feeling politically secure in the all-important farm belt.[16]

His most impressive achievements in the 1948 session concerned public housing and federal aid to education. On the housing issue he again had to battle Herbert Nelson, executive vice-president of the National Association of Real Estate Boards, who called him a "fellow traveller held captive by the bureaucracy which is running this government." We will "attack Senator Robert A. Taft on the public housing issue with all we have," Nelson concluded. "We will take Taft's presidential nomination away from him on this issue." Such excessive rhetoric, however, failed to impress the Senate; and as in 1946, it approved the Taft-Ellender-Wagner housing bill, again without even a roll call vote.[17]

Taft's $300 million bill for aid to education also encountered stiff opposition — from Catholics who sought federal aid for parochial schools in all states, from people who wished to exclude parochial schools entirely, and even from senators like Henry Cabot Lodge of Massachusetts, who demanded a formula offering more to wealthy states. Confronted with these cross pressures, Taft held firm on the religious issue by advocating federal aid to parochial schools in the nineteen states permitting such aid. And he shrewdly consented to an amendment that offered a flat federal grant of $5 per pupil to *all* states, rich or poor, providing they distributed it evenly throughout their school districts. Henry Cabot Lodge, Raymond Baldwin, and a few others with large Catholic constituencies continued to oppose the bill, as did John Bricker and other unyielding foes of the Fair Deal. But Taft's concessions proved more than sufficient, and on April 1, 1948, the Senate passed the first general school aid bill in more than fifty years by a vote of 58 to 22. The majority included not only thirty-one liberal Democrats but twenty-seven of the forty-four Republicans recorded on the issue. And included among the twenty-seven were many who were ordinarily conservative. Taft, *Newsweek* reported with only some exaggeration, "almost singlehandedly pushed [the bill] through the Senate." [18]

Unfortunately for Taft, House Republicans refused to support the housing and education bills. Many of them, indeed, agreed with Herbert Nelson that Taft had turned socialist. It was ironic that the bills failed to entice Deweyites to his side and at the same time earned him nothing but suspicion from conservatives. And the final irony was that the stubbornness of the House enabled

Truman to brand the Eightieth Congress as no good, do-nothing, and reactionary — and unfairly to blame Taft in the process.

One more struggle — again with the right-wing House Republicans — remained. The issue concerned the European Recovery Program. House Republicans had approved appropriations of $5 billion to last fifteen months, instead of the more generous sum of $5.3 billion to last a year, which had been passed by the Senate. Then the House stalled until the eve of the Republican national convention in mid-June. The Senate, it assumed, would have to back down rather than adjourn without reaching agreement.

At this point Taft intervened. After holding a meeting of the policy committee, he announced that the Senate would stay in session until its "moral commitment" had been met. Their bluff called, House Republicans had no choice but to back down. By taking such a forthright stand, Taft may have hoped to mollify Republican internationalists, Arthur Vandenberg in particular, on the eve of the convention. But he was moved also by broader political considerations: The party, after all, could not let Congress adjourn without providing the funds for a program it had agreed to authorize. Taft had tried to rescue his party from reckless partisanship, and this time he succeeded. It was fortunate for the later image of the Eightieth Congress that he did.[19]

•

The European Recovery Program bill was passed on Friday, June 19, 1948. But if Taft and his colleagues hoped to leave right away for the Philadelphia convention two days later, they were mistaken. Congress still had to approve the farm bill, and Taft battled until the very end trying to get the House to vote on public housing. Meanwhile Senator Glen Taylor, a Democrat from Idaho, staged a filibuster against the military draft bill. Desperate to adjourn, the Senate tried to break the filibuster by staying in continuous session. But William Langer of North Dakota came to Taylor's aid, and the debaters lasted through Friday night before surrendering to the inevitable. The Senate then prepared for a vote on a stopgap two-year draft.

The draft issue posed a serious dilemma for Taft. In 1940 and 1941 he had taken the lead against conscription, and since 1945 he had spoken heatedly against Truman's call for universal military training. Land armies, he pointed out, had not been required to invade Japan in 1945, and they might not be necessary in the future if America maintained "complete superiority in the air." Moreover, conscription cost money and cruelly interfered with the lives of the draftees. Yet 1948 was the year of the coup in Czechoslovakia, of the Berlin Airlift, and of rapidly escalating Cold War tensions; and practically all senators hesitated to oppose preparedness. As soon as the filibuster ended they voted, 78 to 10, for the draft, and Taft joined the majority. His stand dismayed many of his admirers, who blamed it on political ambition. But while he may have voted with the upcoming convention in mind, he also acted, as had many other senators, out of a sense of alarm at the course of world events. He was to acquiesce in a draft once again in 1950, a few days before the outbreak of war in Korea, and to vote for it a third time in March 1951.[20]

Though the draft issue concluded the most important business, the little skirmishes flared on. Spectators thronged the galleries and clogged Capitol corridors, and senators, sweaty and irritable, slept on makeshift cots and sofas in the cloakrooms. Still the session dragged on — through the sticky heat of Saturday morning and afternoon, then through violent electrical storms which crashed outside the chambers Saturday night. Finally, after forty-four consecutive hours in session — the second longest in American history (the longest, fifty-four hours, occurred in 1915 over Woodrow Wilson's ship purchase bill) — the regular session of the Eightieth Congress ground sullenly to a halt at 7:15 AM Sunday.[21]

Taft, who immediately drove Martha to Philadelphia, had little time to evaluate that historic Congress. On some issues he clearly had lost. During the 1947 and 1948 sessions Truman had succeeded on the crucial question of foreign aid. Congress had also given the President a makeshift farm program, extended rent control in modified fashion until April 1949, agreed to establish a Department of Defense aimed at unifying the armed forces, provided for civilian control of atomic energy, and granted another year of authority to alter tariffs. Finally, it had enacted a draft. As historians would later concede, the Eightieth Congress had approved some notable and lasting legislation.

But the Republicans had also dealt Truman some staggering defeats: universal military training, civil rights legislation, public housing, aid to education, broader Social Security benefits, and higher minimum wages. Above all, it had cut taxes and passed the Taft-Hartley law. Taft, even his enemies conceded, had been "Mr. Republican," a resourceful, flexible, and often successful captain in the heat of battle.[22]

But even as Republicans hailed Taft's legislative virtuosity Truman was riding the train throughout the West. The Congress, he was proclaiming, had been negative, unresponsive, reactionary. Taft, he said repeatedly, was the arch villain, the symbol of Republican reaction. Truman exaggerated grossly. But Taft had chosen to serve as Republican spokesman; he had lent his name to the labor bill; and he had let Truman, in calling for controls, pose as champion of the consumer.

And so Truman kept accusing. In leading the Eightieth Congress Taft had captured the affection of partisan Republicans as no party leader of his generation was able to do. But he had done so by taking unambiguous stands on many major issues of his era. Neither party had selected a congressional politician as its presidential candidate since Warren Harding — himself a discouraging example— in 1920. Whether the GOP dared to do so with someone as forthright as Taft remained to be seen.

CHAPTER 26

Can Taft Win?

DURING ALL these congressional wrangles in 1948, Taft remained optimistic about winning the nomination: The party would settle on him in June.

He had grounds for confidence. Thomas E. Dewey, though still favored in the polls, seemed vulnerable. Short, immaculately groomed, neatly mustached, he appeared prim, stiff, meticulous, and impersonal. "You really have to get to know Dewey to dislike him," it was said. He also seemed deliberately vague on many national issues. Besides, Taft's aides reminded people, Dewey had already proven a loser in 1944. "You can't make a soufflé rise twice," Alice Roosevelt Longworth reportedly said. Dewey's loss of the Wisconsin primary to Harold Stassen in early April seemed confirmation of his vulnerability at the polls.

Stassen was faring little better. By April he had traveled 160,000 miles, made 325 major addresses, and spent more than $1 million. But was he the "liberal" he claimed to be? Why did he favor the Taft-Hartley Act? Why did he seem to oppose public housing? Why did he want to outlaw the Communist party? Stassen, it seemed to many Republicans, lacked any consistent philosophy.[1]

Taft, by contrast, appeared to be earning the grudging respect even of journalists who did not share his views. *Life* and *Fortune* magazines, under the control of Henry Luce, printed more balanced stories about him than in the past. And Richard Rovere, while lamenting Taft's "parochial culture," lauded him in the April issue of *Harper's*. Personally "shy, quiet, and deferential," Taft was also the "ablest figure in American politics today, and in many ways the man of the firmest integrity and independence of mind." His "informed intelligence and massive sincerity of purpose," Rovere concluded, "make him seem, alongside the *papier mâché* statesmen of the period, almost a figure of granite." [2]

Taft thought he was succeeding in what was for him a remarkable effort to soften his image. As early as his western trip in September 1947, he had succumbed to entreaties that he replace (at least occasionally) his old-fashioned rimless glasses with horn rims. He also tried to unbend with reporters, even joining them on occasion for a drink or two. (The newsman Edwin Lahey, meeting Taft in a Columbus hotel room and seeing him in undershirt and socks, a glass of whiskey in hand, was amazed. "It was like seeing a priest without his vestments," he cracked later.) In Reno on his western trip, Taft also astounded newsmen by appearing with Nevada Senator George Malone in a gambling joint. "He looked like a preacher in a whorehouse," Lahey recalled. "He was amused and tolerant, and I supposed he was thinking, 'Well, there are these species of life.' He stayed for a few minutes and went on." [3]

Taft also showed a little more finesse on the stump. In the back of the pocket-sized appointment books that he carried with him on his travels he jotted down punch lines for use in his speeches. On a few occasions he even summoned the resolve to bring a personal touch to his talks. In Michigan in February, he compared that state favorably with Ohio, and added, "my son attended the University of Michigan last year. Two of my sons have married Michigan girls. I told Arthur Vandenberg that while he might be Michigan's favorite son, I propose to be Michigan's favorite father-in-law." [4]

He even looked to the field of public relations for help. As early as 1946 he had engaged the part-time services of William McAdams, a former newsman, to counteract the "left-wing attacks on me by the CIO, Communists, and New Dealers," and in 1947 he brought McAdams with him to assist in press relations on his western trip. Taft also relied for advice on Forrest Davis, who had helped in 1940, and on James Selvage, a publicity man who often worked for the GOP. And in late 1947 he even turned to John W. Hill, partner in the New York City public relations firm of Hill and Knowlton. With McAdams, Hill worked out an ambitious publicity program featuring everything from brochures to films.

The basic purpose of such an effort, Hill explained, would be to develop "emotional appeal." It would also stress Taft's "positive" programs such as public housing and aid to education, and it would feature "more drama and warmth." Backed by Martha, who took a personal interest, Hill also hired a writer to weave together Taft's speeches — changing a word here and there — with a view toward publishing a book.[5]

But Hill was a busy man with other clients, and McAdams proved unpopular with the press. At this point early in 1948, Selvage and Tom Bowers urged Taft to take on L. Richard ("Lou") Guylay, a young public relations man from New York. Taft summoned Guylay to Washington, talked to him, and finally placed him on the part-time payroll. Guylay still had to move carefully, for Taft lacked the heart to fire McAdams. Guylay also had to overcome the scruples of his new boss. "Jim," Taft remarked to Selvage, "I hope you have told Mr. Guylay that he was not brought in to HUMANIZE me." [6]

Guylay persevered. A disciple of Gustave Le Bon, the French author of *The Crowd*, he believed absolutely in the power of the media to influence mass behavior, and he set out to humanize his client. By April 1948 he had begun to win Taft's confidence, and he was to serve in both 1950 and 1952 as chief adviser in the realm of publicity.

The results in 1948 were mixed at best. Some of Guylay's efforts, such as "My Political Credo," a pamphlet setting out Taft's stands on the major issues, were straightforward enough. Others, such as a series of radio spots used in the Ohio primary in May, more directly revealed Guylay's belief in the group behavior of voters. One of these featured a veteran giving his opinions. "I went through Saipan and Guadalcanal," the radio voice said, "and was wounded doing it. Then I came home and found my family in the street . . . Bob Taft is the first man who has really done something about it . . . Put a housing bill through the Senate . . . All the vets at my post are voting for Taft at the primary next Tuesday." Another spot appealed to young voters. "I'm a young man," said the voice. "Just voting for the first time. I'm giving my vote to Bob Taft next Tuesday. My folks went through the New Deal and are still paying. I figure this way . . . We need a good

program of housing, education and health, like Bob Taft is working for . . . A strong foreign policy to fight communism abroad
and prevent a third world war." A third spot even ventured to
woo the union vote. "I'm a working man — belong to the union,"
the voice proclaimed. "President Truman wanted to draft strikers
in the army . . . that would have been slave labor — just like
Hitler did. Bob Taft was the fellow that stopped it . . . What's
more, us workers and union men have found out the Taft-Hartley
bill is a good thing for us . . . Taft's the man for me." [7]

A more light-hearted effort by Guylay produced a campaign
song to the popular tune of the day, "I'm Looking over a Four-Leaf
Clover." One verse went like this:

> We're looking over a four-leaf clover
> That we overlooked before;
> One leaf is courage, the second is fight,
> Third is our party, that always is right;
> No need explainin' the one remainin'
> It's Bob Taft whom we adore.
> Let's put Taft over — the four-leaf clover
> That we'll overlook no more.[8]

Guylay also produced a film to be shown, it was hoped, with
newsreels in the theaters. It showed Taft working at the Capitol,
being served by Martha (smiling lovingly) at home in Georgetown, and walking into his office and having his secretaries chorus
"Hello" as he passed by. Then it featured a happy family gathering at Indian Hill. Taft showed Lloyd his golf swing, played with
his grandchildren, showed one of them the chickencoop in the
yard, and even picked a flower for Martha. The reel ended with
Taft and Martha quietly sipping tea before a fire in the living
room.[9]

The ultimate in the humanization of Robert Taft was a widely
distributed pamphlet, "The Story of Bob Taft." Attractively done
on glossy paper, it featured domestic photographs lifted from the
movie. It also showed his love of the soil: The closest thing to an
argument that Bob ever had with Martha, it added, was when she
insisted on planting flowers in clumps, and he wanted to plant
them in rows. The pamphlet also stressed the valor of their four

sons during the war and even featured a passage on his civic mindedness at Murray Bay. Taft's "fluent French," the pamphlet
added, "makes possible spirited talk, either on the 'big ones that
got away,' or camp-fire reminiscences of former days." The passage concluded that he liked to sing hymns in church. "He is an
Episcopalian."

But everyone has his faults, and the pamphlet pointed these out.
Taft, it said, was a "devotee of symphonic music . . . but not
much of a performer . . . As a boy he took a few piano lessons.
Now he remembers one piece. It is a noisy thing called 'The
Storm,' which he trots out once in a while at family insistence —
and strictly for family consumption." Worse, he lacked self-
control. "Taft," it concluded, "doesn't smoke, but he does admit a
secret 'vice.' It is eating candy. He keeps a supply in a desk drawer
at the office, and munches frequently while he works." [10]

Much of this was inaccurate or misleading. Taft could not speak
"fluent" French. He was hardly a "devotee" of symphonic music;
he could not play the piano; and he was a Sunday morning golfer,
not a church-going Episcopalian. Why he tolerated such exaggera-
tions was unclear — perhaps because they were so frivolous in nature.[11] But he not only accepted the pamphlet but permitted it to
be distributed widely. The man who in 1940 had held up a putrescent fish before the camera was trying slowly to learn, the second
time around.

.

It is impossible, the wise men said, to make a silk purse out of a
sow's ear. Unfortunately for Taft, they seem to have been right.

One obstacle in the way of humanization was his supporters.
Some of them, such as his brother Charlie, Jack Martin, and Paul
Walter, appreciated his stands in favor of social welfare. Others,
like Ben Tate and David Ingalls, were devoted admirers without
major political ambitions of their own. But many were men like
John Bricker who championed Taft not as a reasoned spokesman
for social welfare but as a dedicated foe of all New and Fair Deal
measures. Any political candidate is identified partly by his friends
and his supporters, and Taft, deified by the Republican party's
largely noninterventionist Midwestern wing, was too loyal to his

backers to break away from this unimaginative and often reactionary congregation.

A larger obstacle was Clarence Brown, his campaign manager. A
huge, corpulent, jovial man, Brown was a former semiprofessional
football player who was the archetype of stand-pat Ohio Republicanism. He had been Ohio's lieutenant governor as early as 1919,
its secretary of state from 1927 to 1933, an unsuccessful gubernatorial candidate in 1934, and congressman from his rural district in
southwest-central Ohio since 1939. Though he was a Republican
power in the House by 1947, Brown's brusque, domineering
manner offended some people, and he had often crossed swords
with moderates like Paul Walter. Even Taft, who studiously
avoided criticizing fellow Ohio Republicans, had found Brown
difficult on occasion. In 1936, when Frank Knox seemed about to
enter the Ohio presidential primary, Taft complained that Brown,
"who wants to run everything," was behind the effort.[12]

Brown was also as reactionary as anyone in the House, and he
surrounded himself with congressmen and party workers who
thought as he did. He spurned Stassen emissaries who talked of a
coalition against Dewey, refused to let Charles Taft — or other
Ohio moderates like him — play important roles in the campaign,
and remained too busy with congressional duties to devote the full
time which direction of a presidential campaign demanded. Cautious about spending money, he vetoed Hill's idea of a book.
"What we should do," he argued, "is a short, straight selling job of
Bob Taft's good qualities, and I don't think we should try to sell
him as a 'liberal.' " When Taft tried to get Brown, the ranking
Republican member of the key House Rules Committee, to report
the public housing bill in the last frantic days before the convention, Brown abruptly refused.[13] What Taft might have accomplished with a different team was conjectural; with Brown and
his ilk he seemed the prisoner of the party's extreme right wing.

Ultimately the blame for accepting such a situation lay with
Taft himself. Indeed, he had long recognized the dangers of relying on organization Republicans in Ohio. They had opposed him
in the 1938 primary and offered him little assistance in 1944, and
yet he depended on the regulars for a variety of reasons. In the
first place, Brown was too demanding to be put off easily. "The

time has come," Brown insisted as early as August 1947, "when it has to be made clear that I am either running this campaign or I am not." Taft thought nothing of combating New Dealers in committee rooms, but like many reticent people, he disliked unpleasant personal confrontations with friends, and he shrank from discharging someone as strong-willed as Brown. Many of Taft's friends admired this undeviating loyalty to old political associates — unlike Dewey and many other presidential aspirants, Taft did not cast supporters adrift. His admirers also understood that his gentleness with friends belied the image of coldness which the media purveyed. But people like Paul Walter also despaired at the contrast between Taft's fearlessness in partisan encounter and his timid toleration of old-guard professionals like Brown.[14]

Taft was used to making the key decisions for himself anyway. He had been raised to be self-reliant, to prove himself on his own. And he persisted in thinking that the issues mattered at least as much as organization and tactics. Thus he reserved to himself all decisions about the issues and refrained from bothering Brown about the details of professional politics. Indeed Taft's habit of handling the ideas himself explained why more imaginative and less political men than Brown did not join him. And it led a few friends to wonder whether he had the capacity to delegate responsibility that is necessary in the White House.

Above all, Taft stayed with the Ohio team because he was temperamentally incapable of doing otherwise. Instinctively, he preferred the routine path, the accepted way, the "sound" procedures of organization politics. He did not reach out for new ideas or for new advisers, and he was far from being a rebel. Brown might be stubborn, but he was a tested veteran of the hustings, an important Ohio politician whom it made no sense to antagonize, and a vigorous foe of Truman. So Taft placed Brown in charge. After the convention, Walter exploded in protest. Taft nodded and seemed to acquiesce. But in 1952 the old guard was again high in his councils. Taft, like his father before him, was ever a regular.

Taft was his own worst enemy in other ways as well. He still insisted on dictating his own speeches and on boring his listeners with statistics. And he refused to soften his public statements. "No one is a greater admirer of Bob Taft than I," an old friend from Cincinnati complained, "but I just get frightened when I think of what can be done by the Democratic Party with the many statements, unwise statements, that he has made. He is intelligent, courageous, and honest, but how he could make so many statements that are so bad like the one about the Nuremberg Trial . . . is beyond me." [15]

The politicos also worried about his personality, which Guylay's efforts failed to brighten. In late 1947 Congresswoman Frances Bolton of Ohio wrote her colleagues for their opinions of him as a presidential nominee. Most of the answers were either favorable or noncommital, but one, from Representative Angier Goodwin of Massachusetts, offered a common complaint from Taft's peers on Capitol Hill. "I have for the past year served on a special joint committee with the Senator," Goodwin wrote, "and as a result of sitting in on these meetings, I doubt very much whether any House member feels that the Senator even knows those who serve on the committee with him. This is something which the Senator probably cannot help, but apparently the people feel he lacks something by way of friendliness of personality." [16]

Such critics overlooked Taft's warmer side. Still, the failure was Taft's, for he did not let them get close enough to see it. On one occasion he infuriated Martha by appearing at a lavish engagement party in his "all-purpose trousers," then proceeded to sit by himself. The guests, anxious to meet him but afraid to interrupt, left him alone. On another occasion, aboard the train on his western trip in 1947, it was rumored that the chef prepared a large beautifully decorated cake in honor of Taft's fifty-eighth birthday, carried it, singing "Happy Birthday," down the aisle, then set it down on Taft's table. Taft looked at the cake, glanced at the chef, and remarked with wonted precision, "Thanks. My birthday was yesterday." [17]

Perhaps his greatest liability continued to be his relationship with the press, particularly the national correspondents, columnists, and radio broadcasters, whom he regarded as New Dealers. "Reporters," he complained, "think they are impartial, but the fact is they are not, either towards the Republican party or towards Congress as an institution." Taft thought nothing of feuding openly with such powers of the pen as Walter Lippmann, Norman

Cousins of *Saturday Review*, Joseph and Stewart Alsop, Doris Fleeson, Raymond Brandt, and — again and again — Drew Pearson.
And he found the New York *Times* (which he persisted in reading) insufferable. "It is extraordinary," he wrote, "that a newspaper of the standing of the *Times* should have an editorial policy
as stupid and as unintelligent as theirs. It is dominated by prejudice, but without the knowledge or mental capacity to express its
prejudices intelligently." [18]

Taft may have been justified in grumbling about some of the
columnists. Many of them did have a more progressive philosophy
than he did. Some in fact used anti-Taft propaganda fed to them
by the Democratic National Committee, which for a time regarded
him as the most dangerous foe in 1948. "Don't make the mistake
of underestimating Taft," Robert Hannegan, a former Democratic
national chairman said. "Many people think he'd be easy to beat.
But that's because they see in his nomination the simple matter of
a clear division between the parties. The fact is that Taft is a
fighter and will make a terrific fight for what he represents." [19]

Taft was probably accurate in suspecting that some top magazines and newspapers were subtly undermining him while pretending reportorial objectivity. Surely, he thought, the flaps over the
Nuremberg trials and "Eat Less" had not deserved such exposure.
What about the ugly cartoons showing him with big sharp teeth,
scowling visage, heartless intent? Why was it that *Life,* which
placed him on its cover for the first time in February 1948, used a
photograph which emphasized his baldness and which portrayed
him in the old rimless glasses he had largely discarded some months
before? [20]

Such feuds with a handful of columnists were commonplace
enough for people in the public eye. "*Life, Time,* and *Fortune*
magazines," Truman complained to Henry Wallace in 1946, "take
particular delight in garbling anything that you or I have to say,"
and Roosevelt himself, the master of relations with the press,
once complained, "Those newspapermen are a bunch of Goddamned ghouls." [21] But Taft made little effort to ingratiate himself with the working reporters who had to follow him around, and
he did not hesitate on occasion to speak out. "No, your question
completely confuses the issue," he would say. "No, I think you are

entirely wrong." More often he simply paid newsmen little attention. When Glenn Thompson, a reporter from the important Cincinnati *Enquirer*, became Washington correspondent for his
paper, he decided to start by presenting himself. Taft answered
questions easily and frankly, but he kept shuffling papers, and he
hardly looked up. After a while, Thompson left; the "interview"
was over. Taft, Lahey commented unhappily, was a "complete
washout in the field of public relations. He won't truckle. He
won't explain, he won't polish apples with any group." [22]

In one sense his problems with the press may have made little
difference. After all, he was true to himself — a trait admired by
some of the newsmen — and no amount of image-building would
have been likely to turn him into a colorful man of the people.
But doubts remain. Suppose he had recognized the press as a potential asset? Suppose he had let reporters see more of the mellow
side that discriminating newsmen like Lahey and Rovere managed
to penetrate? If he had been willing to do so — as other American
politicians somehow managed to do — he might have softened his
image. And he might then have lightened the heavy burden which
dragged him down wherever he went. Taft, the politicians were
saying, was too outspoken, too colorless. "Much as I admire Taft,"
Bruce Barton of New York explained privately, "I do not believe
he can be nominated. His place is in the Senate." [23] Taft was able,
but — "he can't win!"

•

Taft had hoped to save himself the trouble of battling for delegates in the primaries. He had two excellent reasons for wanting to
do so: the press of business in the Senate, and the poor showing he
continued to make in the public opinion polls. But in April 1948
he found himself involved in the primary in Nebraska, and in May
in Ohio. Neither one helped his cause.

He could hardly avoid the Nebraska battle, for a committee had
placed the names of all the leading contenders on the ballot. Besides, Hugh Butler, his Republican senatorial colleague from Nebraska, offered him the support of his organization. Butler not
only kept his word, but planned a three-day schedule in early April
that called for Taft to give twenty-five speeches in as many differ-

ent towns. Somewhat reluctantly ("the Nebraska primary is a tricky kind of popularity contest," he wrote in March), Taft consented, and he and Martha carried out their end of the bargain with their usual indefatigability.[24]

He should have conceded the race without a contest. As John Hollister warned him in January, there was no guarantee that Butler could transfer the allegiance of his constituents to someone else. Furthermore, Dewey seemed strong there, and Stassen, the winner of the 1944 Nebraska primary, was well known in the state and was barnstorming it throughout early 1948. Indeed, late in 1947 Taft had authorized a secret poll — he simply refused to believe the public ones — that showed Dewey with 26 per cent of the voters, Dwight D. Eisenhower with 15 per cent, Taft with 14 per cent, and Stassen a point behind at 13 per cent. He had then compounded his problems with his speech in February 1948 at Omaha critical of farm supports.[25] The result in mid-April proved the folly of his course. Stassen won a dramatic victory by polling 79,000 votes. Dewey finished second with 63,000. Taft trailed with 21,000, and Vandenberg, who was not even an avowed candidate, got 9000. The result, Taft admitted wistfully, was a "great disappointment, because I saw no reason to expect it. For some reason no one seemed to care anything about issues and voted on the whole business merely as if it were a popularity contest." The vote seemed to confirm what the press and the polls had said all along: *Taft Can't Win*.[26]

Having to face a primary fight in his home state had at first seemed the remotest kind of possibility. Ohio, after all, was solid for him, and political etiquette dictated leaving a candidate alone in his native state. But Stassen had other plans. Unable to win much support among the party professionals, he came to believe that he had to win the primaries. Taft, divining Stassen's intentions, took the unusual step of asking him to desist. First in snowy Cincinnati, then at the Statler Hotel in Washington, the two men conferred, and Taft tried to explain the situation. You cannot win, he told his rival, and you will infuriate all my friends if you try. Stassen listened and promised to think it over. But on January 25, the morning after the conference in Washington, Stassen announced he would file in Ohio.[27]

Stassen's unorthodox move angered Taft. "He is a stubborn gentleman," he confided to a friend, "and has been led astray." Stassen's decision, he explained to another friend, "will cost us a lot of time, money, and effort which ought to be spent elsewhere . . . It seems to me that it is unfortunate to try to stir up party dissension when we are doing our best down here in Washington to keep the Party together." [28]

Taft also knew he had to fight. "We can't take a chance," he wrote. "Victory . . . will be the best method of meeting the argument that I can't be elected, which is supported by the Gallup polls. We have checked those polls and find them quite unreliable, but they do affect the politicians." Stassen, he noted, was shrewdly focusing his strength by entering but twenty-three delegates in the contests for Ohio's fifty-three convention seats. One of these twenty-three, a respected former chief justice of the Ohio Supreme Court, was to seek one of the nine at-large seats; the other twenty-two were to run in eleven carefully selected districts in places like Youngstown, Akron, Dayton, and Cleveland. Workers in these strongholds of industrial labor, Stassen reasoned, would surely vote against the coauthor of the Taft-Hartley Act. And because nothing prevented Democrats in these ordinarily Democratic regions from voting in the Republican primary, he might also corral the vote of many partisan opponents of Taft.[29]

After the Nebraska primary early in April, Taft cut short other engagements and hurried back to Ohio, where he discovered that Stassen had made serious inroads. Grimly Taft set out to turn the tide, and from April 17 until primary day on May 4 he spoke eight to ten times a day. He ridiculed Stassen's vagueness on the issues, denounced universal military training, reminded voters of his public housing and aid to education bills, and made no effort to hide his pride in the Taft-Hartley Act. He was meeting the issues head on.

It was springtime in Ohio, and campaigning could have been pleasant amid the blossoming crabapples, the rows of daffodils, the flowering redbuds, and the radiant star magnolias. It should have been flattering, too, to step out of his car in the courthouse squares, to climb steps to the bunting-bedecked platforms, to hear out the high school bandsmen, sweating in their heavy uniforms as they pumped out "I'm Forever Blowing Bubbles," "Put On Your Old Gray Bonnet," and even the tiresome strains of the campaign song, "I'm Looking Over a Four-Leaf Clover." But Taft was running too hard to enjoy himself. He grimaced visibly at the line, "It's Bob Taft Whom We Adore," and he noticed the sullen workers who often paced and picketed across the squares. He waited until the bands had finished, stood up, stated his piece, and hurried on to Cleveland, Youngstown, and Akron, where the crucial votes had to be won. Then up at dawn the next morning for another eighteen hour ordeal.

As primary day approached, it was not clear whether his efforts had succeeded. "The Stassen thing has me petrified," Brown conceded privately. Even Taft expected some defections. And Stassen was anticipating another victory to add to those in Wisconsin and Nebraska. If Taft lost even eleven or twelve of the contested twenty-three delegates, the Stassen forces said, it would finish him as a candidate.[30]

The results proved more satisfying than that to Taft. Stassen's delegates won only nine of the twenty-two district races, and his candidate for delegate at large finished last. Taft, said *Newsweek*, had received a "new lease on life." Stassen, observers agreed, had not only been derailed but had thoroughly antagonized the Taft wing of the party by daring to enter at all. Taft was gratified by the support he had received in the industrial regions, and he rejoiced at his rival's comeuppance. Stassen, he wrote, "is definitely discredited with many Republicans, and my chances seem to be much better." [31]

Taft, however, was a great deal less happy in private than in public, for he knew he had won less than a sweeping triumph. As the columnist James Reston put it accurately, "one more 'victory' like this one would be the undoing of both candidates." Indeed, the only winner in the Ohio primary was Dewey, who had had the good sense to let his rivals cut each other up. Two weeks later Dewey added to his luster by whipping Stassen in a hotly contested primary in Oregon. Stassen, Taft agreed with the experts, was now "entirely out of it." With the primary season then over and with the convention scheduled to open June 21, the long battle had narrowed to a confrontation between Dewey and Taft, with Stassen and a few dark horses such as Vandenberg and Governor Earl Warren of California holding the balance of power.[32]

By then Taft was busy trying to close the congressional session, and he cut short his schedule outside of Washington to ponder his chances. Generally he exuded optimism. "I think I will have more votes on the first ballot than either of the other candidates," he wrote his friends, "and I believe we have a majority of the delegates who will vote for favorite sons for one or two ballots." But he knew Dewey would be extremely difficult to beat. "I do need a lot of second choice votes," he admitted to delegates.[33] The polls also persisted in showing Dewey ahead with the voters — and politicians had an irritating habit of listening to the polls. ("It would be a tragedy if Mr. Gallup came to run the political parties," Taft confided.) [34] Above all, he knew how hard it would be to convince the delegates that he could win if nominated. As time for the convention approached, the same handicap pulled him back. Could he win?

CHAPTER 27

A Second Defeat at Philadelphia

EVERYONE KNEW that 1948 was a Republican year, and Philadelphia threw open its gates to the winners. Bunting decorated the downtown buildings, bands marched in the streets, crowds packed the hotel lobbies and intersections. In Convention Hall, where Willkie had staggered the regulars eight years earlier, workmen were installing the cameras that would make the convention the first in history to be televised. Even the weather — warm but far less humid than it had been in Willkie's hour of triumph — seemed to be cooperating for the Grand Old Party.[1]

All was prepared too, for the grand entrance of Taft. His forces had reserved three floors of the Benjamin Franklin Hotel, plastered the lobby and ballroom with decorations, and strung banners — "WIN WITH TAFT," they proclaimed — to the hotel from across the street. They had prepared lists of delegates and had placed key men in charge of blocs of delegations. These included John Hollister, David Ingalls, Paul Walter, Ohio State Chairman Fred Johnson, and many other stalwarts from Ohio. They also included Richard Scandrett of New York, who had worked for Taft in 1940, Harrison Spangler, former GOP national chairman, Monte Appel, a Minnesota lawyer who had been a friend since his days with Taft at law school, Perry Howard, boss of the Mississippi delegation, Hugh Butler of Nebraska, and Eugene Millikin, his Senate colleague from Colorado. At the last moment Taft also secured the services of John Hamilton, a former GOP national chairman who had taken a job with a prestigious Philadelphia law firm. And available to run important errands were Bill, Bob, Jr., Lloyd, and Horace. Even neutral observers conceded him a chance in what they expected to be a lengthy convention.[2]

Because the Eightieth Congress had remained in session until 7:15 AM Sunday, the day before the convention was scheduled to open, Taft was unable to supervise the advance planning as he had hoped. The struggles in Washington had permitted him a total of but three hours sleep Friday and Saturday nights. Still, he ate breakfast Sunday with Martha, drove his car to Philadelphia, attended a luncheon in the suburb of Rosemont on the way, and looked remarkably fresh as he climbed out in front of his hotel early in the afternoon. With that a brass band started to blare, horns and sirens screamed, and a crowd broke out in "I'm Looking Over a Four-Leaf Clover . . ." His triumphal moment had come.[3]

Or so it seemed. In fact, his aides had already proved fallible by buying 10,000 copies of "This Week in Philadelphia" and then— and only then — realizing that the magazine showed Dewey's picture on the front. They also cheapened their candidate by securing a 500-pound baby elephant, whom they named "Eva Tfat" ("Taft" spelled backward) and pulled through hotel lobbies. Eva wore an anagram placard that read "Renounce Obstinate Bureaucracy, End Roguish Tactics, and Tally Americanism, Freedom, Truth" (R-O-B-E-R-T A. T-A-F-T). When Taft entered the hotel, Eva was there to greet him, and aides urged him to shake the creature's trunk for the benefit of photographers. Gamely, he did so. "Shake it again," a cameraman pleaded. "It's your baby." Again, grimly, he complied. Then he endured the tiresome refrains of his campaign song. As his biographer William S. White later remarked, it was ironic that Taft of all people was saddled with hucksterism while Governor Dewey remained remote in his dignity.[4]

The contrast between the Dewey and Taft forces was obvious in other ways. Clarence Brown seemed no match for Herbert Brownell, an affable, shrewd, and highly efficient lawyer who ran the governor's operation. While the Dewey forces were busy flattering delegates and hinting at promises of patronage, Brown was still worrying about such mundane matters as hotel rooms and seats in the gallery for his friends. "There is more cussing of Clarence Brown," wrote one newsman, "than there has been heard in any political ruckus in recent times . . . the vast bulk of Clarence Brown has blocked every road to effective action." [5]

Proof of the Taft organization's clumsiness surfaced over a confrontation Monday afternoon, opening day of the convention, between two rival delegations from Georgia. Prior to the convention the Republican National Committee had ruled, 48 to 44, for a predominantly Dewey delegation from Georgia, but by convention eve the Stassen forces had tentatively agreed to support the Taft slate in the contest before the convention's credentials committee. Because this committee consisted of one delegate from each state, and because Taft and Stassen between them controlled a narrow majority of the state delegations, Taft naturally assumed he would win, and he even refused to entertain Dewey's offer of compromise to divide the Georgia delegation, 8 to 8.

When the committee met, Stassen's delegates voted as expected. But the delegates from Taft's states of Illinois, Tennessee, and Mississippi jumped the track for Dewey. The final vote was 26 to 24 for the Dewey slate. Exactly what happened never became clear. Some people blamed the Taft forces for backing a "lily white" delegation, and others pointed to well-placed promises by Brownell. Whatever the case, the fiasco marked, as Scandrett complained, "the most inexcusable kind of mismanagement" which the Taft organization could have prevented by making sure that every committeeman was absolutely reliable. The struggle revealed Dewey's superior generalship and presented him with a psychological lift at the very start of the convention.[6]

The next day, Tuesday, June 22, the Dewey team's hard work — opponents said promises — began to bear fruit. Senator Edward Martin of Pennsylvania, nominally a favorite son, conferred with Dewey, then announced he would make the nominating speech for the New York governor. Martin, whose faction had favored Dewey all along, probably needed little coaxing. He also was unable to bring his entire delegation with him; approximately thirty were expected to remain with Governor James H. Duff in support of Arthur Vandenberg or someone else. But Martin's early defection brought Dewey some forty votes. Taft would have to move quickly to avert a stampede.

There was but one way he could do so: Combine with Stassen, Warren, Vandenberg, and other favorite sons in a "Stop Dewey" alliance. Indeed, many observers had suspected Taft of just such a strategy well before the convention, and Colonel Robert McCormick, the crusty publisher of the Chicago *Tribune,* had dined with Stassen ten days earlier and emerged to suggest a Taft-Stassen alliance against Dewey. Though Stassen had openly spurned such talk, he had cooperated on the Georgia question; so Taft picked up the phone to call him. Leaving nothing to chance, Taft also called Duff, Martin's rival in Pennsylvania politics. Both men agreed to confer with Taft that evening, and John Hamilton offered the use of his Philadelphia apartment as a meeting place. The stage was set for a deal in a smoke-filled room.[7]

The deal never materialized. With characteristic candor, Taft proposed that everyone unite behind him. Duff was happy to form an alliance of convenience to stop Dewey, and his forces later gave Taft twenty-eight votes on the first ballot. Stassen, however, refused to go along. He had gone out of his way to contest the Ohio primary, he explained: How could he cynically turn about a month later? Stassen then urged an alliance behind Vandenberg. To this Taft demurred. Ohio delegates, he explained, would back Bricker before Vandenberg, and most of his other delegates preferred Dewey as their second choice. The three men talked into the morning, but could reach no agreement other than to hold their forces in line and to meet again at ten the following morning. The essence of their impasse was simple: neither Stassen nor Taft hated Dewey enough to withdraw, and neither man thought he could get his delegates to follow if he did.[8]

The next day the Dewey steamroller pressed on. Governor Alfred E. Driscoll of New Jersey, another favorite son, announced he would support Dewey after the first ballot; that would mean at least twenty of New Jersey's thirty-five votes. So did James P. Kem of Missouri, who regularly sided with the right-wing Republicans in the Senate, and Governor Robert F. Bradford of Massachusetts. Dewey was to get thirty-four of the sixty-eight votes in these two states on the first ballot. Most alarming of all was the surprise from Indiana. Representative Charles A. Halleck, also a nominal favorite son, announced he was withdrawing, that he would second Dewey's nomination, and that Indiana's twenty-nine votes would go for Dewey at once. Halleck, who was frankly ambitious, believed that Dewey's lieutenants had offered him the vice-presidency if he delivered the Indiana delegation. Later, when the vice-presidential nomination was denied to him, it was clear that he had been deceived. But Halleck's action cost Taft at least ten votes in the delegation and revealed again the aggressiveness of the Dewey lieutenants. It looked now as if the New Yorker would run away with the convention.[9]

With this thought in mind Taft, Duff, and Stassen decided to broaden their alliance. After meeting briefly in the morning, they scheduled an afternoon conference in Hamilton's apartment with Governor Kim Sigler of Michigan, Vandenberg's manager, and Harold E. Mitchell, the Connecticut national committeeman who was holding nineteen votes for favorite son Raymond Baldwin. When the meeting was over, Taft emerged to give an optimistic statement. The "Dewey blitz," he told reporters, "is already stopped. I feel very much encouraged. I feel that if the delegates have a perfectly free hand I will be nominated in due time." But it was abundantly clear that none of the conferees had been willing to quit. As Taft explained unconvincingly, "we decided it was not our job to agree on a candidate. The real purpose was to keep everything open so the nomination will develop in a free and un-controlled way." Dewey, he might have added, was still free to pick off his adversaries one by one.[10]

There remained little to do but to endure the tedium of nomi-nating speeches, which began at 9:20 that evening. Martin, as promised, nominated Dewey, and Halleck offered a second. Bricker and four others followed for Taft. Then came intermi-nable oratory for Warren, Stassen, Baldwin, Vandenberg, and finally for General Douglas MacArthur, who was in Japan. At 4:30 AM the delegates staggered home to bed.

The balloting began the next afternoon, Thursday June 24, three days short of eight years since Taft's failure in 1940. The weather, cooperative until then, suddenly turned frightfully hu-mid, and the thermometer climbed above one hundred degrees in the packed convention hall. Delegates loosened their ties and shirts, mopped their heads with towels, and cursed audibly. As everyone expected, Dewey jumped into the lead on the first ballot with 434 votes. Taft received 224, Stassen 157, the favorite sons 276. With only 548 votes necessary for a majority, Dewey was close to victory. On the second ballot the forces for Vandenberg, Warren, and Baldwin held firm, but Dewey still gathered 81 new votes to close at 515. Taft, picking up 50 votes in Illinois previously promised to him by Governor Dwight Green and Colonel McCormick, moved to 274, and Stassen, slipping already, fell eight votes to 149. Dewey needed but 33 more votes to win, and everyone knew the California and Connecticut delegations were chafing to be released.[11]

At this point Dewey's foes frantically called for a recess. Dewey supporters, wilting under the heat, just as loudly shouted for an immediate, presumably decisive, third ballot. Convention chairman Joseph Martin of Massachusetts banged his gavel, called for the ayes and nays, could not decide who had won, and was rescued only when the confident New York delegation suddenly declared it would consent to a recess. Grateful for a reprieve, the delegates went off at five o'clock for supper.

Taft, comfortably ensconced in an air-conditioned room at the Franklin, had been spared the frightful heat of convention hall. With Martha, Jack Martin, and his sons, he had enjoyed the luxury of television to keep him abreast of events. When the recess began, he emerged from his privacy to confront the ever-present reporters in the hall. "I think it is wide open," he said with no sign of strain. "He [Dewey] is close so I might be right and I might be wrong." Soon his perspiring lieutenants streamed back from convention hall. What was the outlook, Brown was asked. "I don't know," he panted, "I'm just so damned tired I don't know." [12]

But Taft understood that his chances were desperately slim. Indeed, everyone knew Connecticut's nineteen votes would go to Dewey on the next ballot. California, with fifty-three votes, was also expected to be released and to turn heavily for Dewey. Apprised of these developments, Taft did not hesitate. He called Stassen and asked him to withdraw in his favor. No, Stassen replied, it was not over yet, wait one more ballot. That was enough for Taft. Consulting no one, he sat down to draft a statement on long yellow legal paper.[13]

As the delegates swarmed back into the hall, a furious thunderstorm struck the city. It ripped the bunting from buildings, smashed windows, flung broken glass into courtyards, and sent crackles of static across the thousands of radios around which Americans were huddled for news of the convention. It was in this atmosphere that John Bricker, chief of the Ohio delegation, arose to read a statement. It was Taft's. "A careful analysis of the situation," it said, "shows that a majority of the delegates will support Governor Dewey on the third ballot. I therefore release my delegates and ask them to vote for Governor Dewey . . . He is a great Republican and he will be a great Republican President." [14]

The statement at first surprised the delegates. But they knew it meant harmony at last, and they broke out in applause. In rapid succession the other candidates withdrew as well, and the convention chose Dewey unanimously. The governor had won the nomination for the second time, and this time everyone knew he would win the election.

After calling Dewey to congratulate him, Taft stepped out into the corridor once again. To reporters, he seemed almost relieved in his hour of defeat. "Hello, boys," he greeted them. He then explained diffidently why he had surrendered. "The evidence was in," he said. "Simple arithmetic," he added. But when he remarked that it would be his last try for the presidency (like everyone else, he expected Dewey to hold it for eight years), the size of the blow which had befallen him struck the crowd, and his partisans began to sob. Even veteran reporters brushed away their tears.[15]

.

The presidential nomination disposed of, the convention settled back to hail its nominee, then to acquiesce in Dewey's selection of Earl Warren as his running mate. As the delegates returned home, the experts asked why Taft had lost.[16]

Many attributed the outcome to the selfishness of Dewey's opponents. Had Vandenberg or Warren agreed to deal, had Taft been willing to offer promises in return, above all if Stassen had not insisted on holding out in a hopeless cause, they argued, Taft might have deadlocked the convention.[17] Other observers blamed the inflexibility and inefficiency of the Taft organization.[18] And Taft's friends complained bitterly that Dewey had won to his side such powerful right-wingers as Martin of Pennsylvania, Kem of

Missouri, and Halleck by concluding flagrant deals. "To the best of my knowledge," James Selvage recalled, "there was never a single person working intimately with him [Taft] who ever knew whether he would be offered any post if Taft were elected." [19]

Other observers discounted these assessments. Warren, Stassen, and Vandenberg, they pointed out accurately, opposed Taft's position on foreign policy and doubted his ability as a vote getter. Even if Taft had tried to entice them with promises, it was hardly likely that he could have drawn in their delegates. And while deals may have helped to bring Dewey the victory, it was doubtful that he could have succeeded in making them, had not people like Halleck already regarded him as the likely winner. Taft's weakness, these observers concluded, was not so much organizational as political.

In retrospect it appears that they were right, for two reasons. First, Taft's delegate strength was heavily sectional. At the peak of his strength on the second ballot he had 44 votes in Ohio, 50 in Illinois, and 29 (thanks to the continued friendship of Boss R. B. Creager) in Texas. He also had 63 of the remaining 156 votes from the South and 40 of the 181 votes in the mountain and border states. But he captured only 3 of the 84 votes from the West Coast, 5 of 92 in New England, and aside from the 29 votes that Duff brought him temporarily, only 3 of the 205 votes in New York, Pennsylvania, and New Jersey. Dewey, by contrast, stayed close to Taft in the South and Midwest, and overwhelmed him in the East with 252 votes before Baldwin even delivered his delegation. As in 1940, Taft's attacks on the administration brought him the support of parts of the South and Midwest. But they cost him the votes of the crucially important delegates from the East. These people had preferred Willkie to Taft in 1940, Dewey to Bricker in 1944, and now Dewey in 1948.

Taft's second political handicap was the feeling that he could not match Dewey as a vote getter. He had failed to develop a winning image, had taken potentially harmful stands on the issues, and trailed steadily in the polls. The delegates desperately wanted a winner in 1948. "I have the highest regard for Senator Taft," wrote Kentucky's Republican national committeeman in late May, "but he is the only candidate spoken of for President that would cause us to lose Kentucky this fall." Taft lost, explained Brown, because of the "polls and the widespread propaganda and belief that he was a poor vote-getter." [20]

For all his poise before the reporters, Taft at first was critical of others. While watching the balloting over television, he sat quietly, scratching out the reasons for his weakness on his long yellow pad. The defection of conservatives like Martin and Kem he blamed partly on his "progressive ideas" in domestic policy. But he was also critical of others:

> Georgia contest . . . bad organization; Martin — Pennsylvania — progressive ideas, fear of polls, etc; Indiana — Dewey's unscrupulous tactics; Missouri — Kem — progressive ideas, Dewey's promises; West Virginia — Walter Hallanan double-cross, progressive ideas, polls; California — Warren's stupidity; Stassen — internationalist and stupidity.[21]

With the convention over, he continued to mull over his defeat. To one friend he blamed the "continuous knocking of the New Deal columnists and the New Deal press." To another he admitted that "various matters . . . might have been better handled." To a third he complained, "I rather resent the defection of the conservatives like the Pennsylvania Manufacturers Association, the Du Ponts, and Senator Kem." And to a fourth he responded cryptically, "You asked who 'double-crossed me' at Philadelphia. I could give you a list of a few." [22]

But Taft never exposed his feelings publicly, and usually he refused to blame individuals even privately. His reticence stemmed from a combination of self-containment, good sportsmanship, and political wisdom. But it flowed also from his recognition that the delegates had wanted a winner in November. "I had to struggle constantly against the idea that I could not be elected," he wrote. "We could usually persuade people over after we could sit down with them, but they were always easily unpersuaded." Many people, he added, "felt I would not be a strong candidate. Politicians are not very courageous, and they saw no reason to take a chance." [23]

Above all, Taft was too realistic a politician to have overlooked Dewey's strength, and after the convention he confessed he had doubted his chances ever since the Nebraska primary in April.[24] Having anticipated the possibility of defeat, he was prepared for it when it came, and he was therefore able to withdraw smoothly at the critical moment. In doing so, he probably made more friends than he would have by protracting the struggle. "Senator Taft," remarked newsmen Joseph and Stewart Alsop, "comes out of the convention . . . with increased stature. From start to finish he showed unfailing strength of character, good sportsmanship and an odd attractive kind of impersonal common sense." [25]

CHAPTER 28

Surmounting Disappointments,
1948–1949

THE CONVENTION over, Taft drove back to Washington to clean up some unfinished work. Whatever his inner feelings, he remained cool and confident with his friends. "Dewey and Warren will win this year," he wrote flatly. "The general prosperous condition of the country is in favor of Truman, but he does not have the personal hold which Roosevelt was able to maintain." With but a few details to worry about, he looked forward to getting away quickly to Murray Bay for his first vacation in a year.[1]

Truman quickly dashed these expectations. Less than three weeks later, he electrified the Democratic convention by announcing he was calling Congress back into special session — "to get the laws the people need," he said shrewdly. Truman's move widened divisions within the Republican party and turned relations between Taft and Dewey from suspicious collaboration to barely concealed disgruntlement. Then when Truman won in November, Taft blamed Dewey; the Dewey partisans blamed Taft. The events of summer and fall 1948 cast a pall over what might have been a satisfying period in Taft's life. They led directly to a sharp intraparty skirmish in the Senate in 1949. And they left a gulf between the Taft and Dewey wings of the party that Taft was never able to bridge.

•

Truman's call for a special session was politically astute. In demanding that the Republicans curb high prices, increase the minimum wage, liberalize immigration of displaced persons, and enact public housing and aid to education, he immediately placed them on the defensive. Either the GOP did as he commanded — in which case he would claim the credit — or it must accept the blame for depriving the people of presumably vote-catching measures in an election year.

Confronted with this dilemma, Republicans argued over the proper response. One alternative was to adjourn the session as soon as it met. But Taft and his fellow Republicans shrank from this bold course: The party must not seem wholly negative, especially on the sensitive issue of inflation. Another alternative was to meet Truman halfway. After all, Senate Republicans had already passed aid to education and public housing; perhaps House Republicans would follow suit. But this option, too, seemed dangerous. It would give the President credit for the legislation and re-open divisions that had hurt the party in the regular session. Only one response remained: listen to Truman's demands, denounce them as politically inspired, enact a few minor measures to combat prices, and go home as soon as possible.

Having pressed for such a strategy, Taft steadfastly carried it out. When the two-week session closed on August 7, Truman had received additional power to control consumer credit and to increase bank reserves. He also signed a bill liberalizing credit for private builders. But Congress gave him nothing on minimum wages, aid to education, displaced persons, or public housing. The Republicans had accomplished their mission, and Taft set out for Murray Bay at last.[2]

He might have done better to have gone in June, for most observers agreed that Truman had triumphed politically. Indeed, Taft himself emerged bruised from the session. Anxious not to open old party wounds, he told House Republican leaders that he would oppose bringing his public housing bill to the floor at that time. But liberal Republican colleagues refused to be bound by such a strategy, and they reported the measure. Taft then felt obliged to fight his own bill, and Democrats gleefully pounced on him. "The Senator from Ohio apparently has surrendered his position," mocked minority leader and vice-presidential candidate Alben Barkley. Taft, grimly pressing on, got enough Republicans to defeat public housing, then to pass the innocuous measure for private builders that Truman signed. But the President did not let him forget. "After his defeat at the Republican convention in Philadelphia," Truman proclaimed in Cincinnati, "Taft didn't have to carry on his pretense of caring about the needs of the people. He could act in his real character — as a cold-hearted, cruel aristocrat." Although these charges were much too exaggerated to be convincing, Truman probably scored effectively by branding the special session as "do-nothing" and by labeling Taft as chief conspirator in a plot against the people.[3]

For the time being, however, Taft had to worry almost as much about Dewey as about Truman. After the convention, Taft at first seemed cautiously friendly to his successful rival. "Tom Dewey's own ideas on government," he wrote a friend, "are about the same as mine." But he complained privately that Dewey had refused to consider Governor Dwight Green of Illinois as the vice-presidential nominee. "I urged your name on Tom Dewey," Taft explained to Green, "but I got little response except that you were too closely connected with the Chicago *Tribune*. Tom's whole concern seemed to be about carrying the Atlantic seaboard, and he seemed to be afraid of all midwestern candidates because they were too 'isolationist.'" And Taft worried generally about Dewey's low-key campaign. "I am chiefly afraid," he wrote, "that he will pay too much attention to the Eastern newspapers, which seem to have created a lot of wholly false issues." [4]

Hoping to narrow the gap, Taft met with Dewey in New York on July 13. Taft offered his services, then discussed the legislative program for 1949 — so sure were the two chiefs of victory! They then parted amicably enough. But Taft was distressed about Dewey's campaign plans, and he jotted down his feelings in note form:

Tone of campaign. Sweetness and light — always successful — better than attacks on other fellow — evidently intends to avoid issues unless campaign gets doubtful.[5]

When Truman issued his call for a special session, it was Dewey's turn to be distressed. Like Taft, Dewey did not want Truman to profit much from calling Congress together, and he made no effort publicly to support such legislation as public housing or aid to education.[6] But he encouraged Herbert Brownell, his chief aide, and Hugh Scott, the Pennsylvania congressman whom he had picked as GOP national chairman after the convention, to talk with Taft. Both recommended that the Eightieth Congress at least placate the important ethnic vote by liberalizing the Displaced Persons Act. But Taft, according to later accounts by Brownell and Scott, was deaf to their suggestions. "No," he snapped to Scott, "we're not going to give that fellow [Truman] anything." From then on, Dewey was even more disposed than before to dissociate himself from Taft and the congressional wing of the party.[7]

Then the gulf widened. Dewey's campaign team, convinced that Taft was a liability, forced the senator to content himself with speaking appearances in Ohio and in such Democratic strongholds as Little Rock, St. Petersburg, Nashville, and Dallas. Dewey also made no effort to defend the record of the Eightieth Congress, and he even called on Stassen to answer charges against the Taft-Hartley law. Taft, meanwhile, grumbled privately about Dewey's bland campaign. "I doubt if Dewey's campaigning really does the 80th Congress any good," he confided in October.[8]

Perhaps the most glaring example of the growing hostility between the rivals occurred at the end of October, when Dewey paid his only visit to Ohio. Taft boarded the campaign train in Toledo, rode it stoically to Cleveland, then appeared with Dewey in the Cleveland auditorium. There he praised Dewey and the GOP ticket in Ohio, then sat on stage to listen to the nominee's speech, which was being broadcast around the state. But Dewey ignored Taft's laudatory introduction, launched into a plea for extensive aid to Europe, and said nothing about Taft or the Ohio ticket. Taft, an observant reporter noticed, looked straight ahead, clasped his hands tightly, applauded only once or twice. To the reporter Edwin Lahey, Taft let himself go. "I don't understand why he hates me so," he said plaintively.[9]

Even in hindsight his question could not receive a simple reply. At the root of the rivalry was the sectional-ideological split in the party that had pitted the Taft-Bricker-Midwestern wing against the Willkie-Dewey-Eastern wing as early as 1940. Dewey, like his

"Yes suh, he's a real sho nuff ol' houn' dawg."
From The Herblock Book (*Beacon Press, 1952*)

internationalist supporters, found Taft irritatingly self-assured, surrounded by reactionaries from beyond the Hudson, and abrasively partisan. They saw him also as an isolationist whose views threatened the Republican ticket in the coastal states. Regarding themselves as the modernist wing of the party, the Deweyites were quick to dismiss the Taftites as reactionaries, isolationists, and political liabilities.

But the ideological differences between the two wings were not unbridgeable. Both men, indeed, were flexible enough politicians to have accommodated each other, and in September Taft even observed quietly to a friend that Dewey might turn out to be "more conservative than we true liberals." The feud was also personal, born of unavoidable competition between two men with conflicting ambitions, clashing personalities, and zealous supporters who did little to improve relations. Above all, Taft saw in Dewey the traits he especially distrusted in a Republican politician: a willingness to accommodate the New Deal, and a lack of political courage (the kind he, like his father and Herbert Hoover, had often displayed). And though he was too circumspect to say so, Martha was not. Dewey, she wrote a friend after the campaign, "actually told Bob that he had found that when he got into controversies he lost votes. About the housing bill, he said, 'You'll never win any votes on that . . . Why, I supported a big housing project out on Long Island and when I ran for governor all the tenants voted against me.'

"You can imagine," Martha concluded, "how pleased and impressed Bob was by that high-minded argument." [10]

Truman's surprise victory in November destroyed what amity might have developed between Taft and Dewey and between their respective wings of the party. The journalist William S. White recalled that Taft — after the election — told him he had expected the ticket to lose. "I knew it for certain," White quoted him, "when Martha told me she could no longer listen to Dewey's speeches or listen to him on the television." Yet on election eve, Taft was optimistic enough to send Dewey and Warren notes of congratulation, then to sail with Martha for a European vacation.[11] When he heard the election results, he loyally said nothing for publication. But he had spent ten years in Washington anticipating a Republican victory, and Dewey's defeat, carrying GOP congressmen and senators with him, hurt so much that for weeks and months thereafter he let his friends know how he felt. "The only way to handle Truman," he wrote, "was to hit him every time he opened his mouth." But Dewey had stupidly refrained from doing so. "The result of the election was a tragedy," he wrote, "largely because it was entirely unnecessary. Dewey could have won, and we could have elected a Republican Congress if the right kind of campaign had been put on." The corollary to this reasoning was that he himself could have triumphed. "I could have won the election if nominated," he told his friends. "I am absolutely certain that Dewey could have won if he had put up any kind of fight at all and dealt with the issues before the people." [12]

Because Dewey had come close (a switch of less than 30,000 votes in Ohio, Illinois, and California would have given him the electoral college), and because he had seemed such a certain winner earlier in the year, many experts agreed that his platitudinous campaign had cost him the election. "No presidential candidate in the future," chortled the Louisville *Courier Journal* about Dewey, "will be so inept that four of his major speeches can be boiled down to these historic four sentences: Agriculture is important. Our rivers are full of fish. You cannot have freedom without liberty. The future lies ahead. (We might add a fifth . . . the TVA is a fine thing, and we must make certain that nothing like it ever happens again.)" Harold Ickes, Roosevelt's cantankerous Interior Secretary, went further. Taft, he said, was the "Babe Ruth" of the Republican Party. With Dewey, the GOP "sent in a batboy with the bases full and only one run needed." [13]

Later analysts agreed that Dewey had waged an uninspiring campaign. Indeed, the low Republican turnout (21.9 million, as opposed to 22 million in 1944 and to the 33.9 million who voted for Eisenhower four years later) suggested that he had failed to draw even GOP regulars to the polls. His poor showing in the potentially Republican rural farm regions also suggested his weakness among the party faithful. By contrast, he fared better than he had in 1944 in industrial areas, prompting Taft to contend that the Taft-Hartley Act was far from a liability to the GOP.[14]

Yet these analyses told but part of the story. A decline in political interest and voter turnout often follows a war. Taft, therefore, might have done no better than Dewey in attracting voters to the polls. Moreover, in the agricultural regions Dewey was the unfortunate victim of falling farm prices, which Truman shrewdly if unfairly blamed on the Eightieth Congress. Anti-Dewey analysts also refused to assess the role, however hard to determine, of the President's remarkably energetic campaigning. In Ohio, which he won by only 7000 votes, he gave eleven speeches in one day and scored better in these places than Roosevelt had done four years earlier.[15]

Above all, Taft's view of the election overlooked some hard facts of political demography. Chief among these was the large advantage in voter registration which Roosevelt had bequeathed to the Democratic party. Any Republican who hoped to win a nationwide election not only had to retain the core of regular party voters but to appeal to independents and to the millions of ethnic voters, urbanites, blacks, and unionists who formed the powerful coalition that had four times elected Roosevelt. Subsequent presidential elections suggested that for a long time only a popular hero like General Dwight D. Eisenhower or unusual circumstances (the crisis within the Democratic party in 1968) would enable Republicans to win.[16]

Given these facts of political life, Dewey was probably wise in trying to evade Truman's charges about the congressional Republicans. It was similarly most improbable that Taft, "Mr. Republican," the most partisan of all Republican possibilities, the candidate who had trailed in the polls, could have run better than Dewey, let alone have beaten Truman. Far from convincing people that Taft could have done better, the election forced them to look for fresh new possibilities like Eisenhower — someone who was sure to attract the uncommitted. Mr. Republican had still to confront the dire prediction: "Taft Can't Win."

•

A week before Christmas, Bob and Martha returned from their trip to Europe. They had visited Naples, Rome, Florence, Switzerland, Germany, the Netherlands, Paris. Taft had had an audience with the Pope, conferred with American generals, and visited the Ruhr to assess the rate of European recovery. Disembarking in New York, he complained of the excessive regulation and "red tape" in European governments, called for cuts in the European

Recovery Program, and hurried to Washington. It was time to set to work again.[17]

The coming congressional session promised to be controversial. The elections had enabled the Democrats to gain nine seats in the Senate and seventy-five in the House; they would control both houses, 54 to 42 and 263 to 171. Truman, buoyed by his victory, was already demanding enactment of public housing, aid to education, inflation controls, a tax increase, and repeal of Taft-Hartley. And to help him, he had able new men like Hubert Humphrey of Minnesota, Paul Douglas of Illinois, and Lyndon B. Johnson of Texas. Taft, who returned as the third senior Republican (behind Arthur Vandenberg and Styles Bridges), was once again in the minority.[18]

The Democrats were but a part of Taft's worries. While he had been in Europe, his junior Republican colleagues began to stir restlessly. Led by Henry Cabot Lodge, Irving Ives, and William Knowland, they let it be known that the negative record of the Eightieth Congress had driven Dewey to defeat, that the party needed fresh leadership in the Senate. Because Senator Wallace White of Maine, the nominal Republican leader early in 1948, had retired, Lodge and his allies quietly tried to line up votes in the weeks before the opening of the session to oust Taft from his chairmanship of the GOP policy committee and to prevent the election of Kenneth Wherry as the party's floor leader.

Most newsmen reported accurately that the revolt was hardly the battle of progressives against reactionaries which the rebels liked to call it. Some of the dissidents — Wayne Morse, George Aiken, William Langer of North Dakota, Ralph Flanders of Vermont — had indeed voted for Fair Deal programs more regularly than had Taft. But Lodge had opposed the aid to education bill, and many of his colleagues — like Ives and Knowland — had regularly followed Taft on the key issues of the previous congressional session. All but Morse and Langer had voted to override Truman's veto of Taft-Hartley. What the dissidents wanted was not so much a new approach to the issues, but increased power in decision making. If they embarrassed the Taft wing of the party, so much the better.[19]

When the session opened, the rebels offered their own slate: Lodge for policy committee chairman, Knowland for floor leader,

Boys will be boys. *L. D. Warren, Cincinnati* Enquirer

Leverett Saltonstall of Massachusetts for whip. But Taft had had time to organize his followers. First they amended the rules to enable him to repeat as chairman of the GOP policy committee, then they returned him to the job by a vote of 28 to 14. After voting Wherry in as floor leader by the same margin and unanimously naming Eugene Millikin as chairman of the Republican conference, the party softened the blow by selecting Saltonstall as whip and adding him and Ives to the policy committee. Taft thus retained control of his party in the Senate; the dissidents were never again to offer such a challenge. But the insurrection had annoyed him — so much so that he even shyly thanked newsmen who downplayed the story.[20] The whole episode seemed to him but one more example of the phony "liberalism" of the Dewey wing of the party.

.

Deprived of the Republican majorities he had confidently anticipated, Taft might well have turned sour. Privately, indeed, he seemed subject to unaccustomed moods of bitterness, to what one close observer later described as a "blood in the nostrils" approach to the Truman administration.[21]

On most matters of policy, however, he did not turn angrily to the right; on the contrary, during the long session that followed, he talked and acted much as he had in the past. He continued to oppose a compulsory FEPC, while at the same time futilely supporting cloture to break a filibuster against it. He voted for unsuccessful amendments against rent controls, then surrendered to the inevitable by approving controls for another year. He supported a successful increase in the minimum wage from forty to sixty-five cents while at the same time joining a majority to exempt some hotel and restaurant workers from coverage. Although he approved the quota system of limiting immigration, he quietly supported efforts that culminated in 1950 in the liberalization of the Displaced Persons Act.[22]

Taft also hewed to his tough stance on federal spending. Public works, he conceded, would be necessary if the developing recession of 1949 continued, but until then the government should cut back. With this in mind he tried — and failed — to cut each appropriation bill by 5 per cent, and exulted when the Senate reduced the army appropriation bill from $15 to $14 billion. "There's more waste in any army," he said, "than in any civilian organization I

From The Herblock Book (*Beacon Press, 1952*)

know." When Secretary of Agriculture Charles Brannan proposed a plan calling for high income supports for farmers, Taft and almost all his Republican colleagues denounced it in favor of sliding price supports. The plan, which became a divisive issue, never passed the Senate.[23]

He proved especially resourceful on one of the most controversial issues of the session: Taft-Hartley. Sensing their opportunity, union leaders demanded repeal of the law, and the administration felt bound to go along with them. Taft, who had long admitted some deficiencies in his handiwork, coolly offered a substitute bill which called for twenty-nine changes in the law. Many of these amendments were minor, but some represented substantial responses to criticisms. Taft agreed to increase the size of the National Labor Relations Board from five to seven members, to eliminate the requirement that workers vote to authorize union shops, to moderate the ban on secondary boycotts, to permit strikers to vote on contract offers even if they were not entitled to reinstatement, and to apply the noncommunist oath to employers as well as to unions. And he shrewdly included two crucial amendments to swing uncommitted senators to his side. One abolished the office of general counsel of the NLRB, thus restoring to the board the prosecuting and judicial functions it had enjoyed under the Wagner Act. The other authorized the President not only to seek injunctions in strikes affecting the national welfare but also to seize plants. For Taft, who had stood up to prevent such authority at the time of the railroad strike in 1946, this was a large and painful concession.[24]

But it worked. The unions, refusing to compromise, decided to fight his injunction-or-seizure amendment by substituting an amendment authorizing seizure alone. At the same time, John L. Lewis brazenly called a walkout of his mine workers, a tactic that did nothing to assuage the moderates in the Senate. (Taft, hearing news of the walkout, was described as "grinning broadly," the administration as "sputtering in rage.") Intricate parliamentary maneuvering then dragged on into late June, when the Senate defeated the unions' substitute, 46 to 44, approved the Taft amendment in its place, 50 to 40, and passed his other amendments, 51 to 42. Still unbowed, the union leaders persuaded House Democrats to recommit a comparable bill, leaving Taft-Hartley unscathed for the session. They were never again to have such an auspicious opportunity for repeal.[25]

The survival of Taft-Hartley under the onslaught of a Democratic Congress stemmed primarily from the uncertainty of the administration and from what one impartial authority described as the "arrogant and unreasonable" behavior of the unions. Taft had also failed to impress some of the eastern Republicans, and Ives complained to Dewey that Taft's alliances with southern Democrats were "not likely to prove helpful to the Party in the 1950 elections." Yet Taft had once again proved himself a skillful and pragmatic legislative leader — so temperate that even Morse hailed his "fair-minded objectivity" and so knowledgeable that the columnist Joseph Alsop, no admirer, described him as the most technically efficient Senate leader since the days of James F. Byrnes of South Carolina in the late 1930's.[26]

Taft also carried on his efforts for a social welfare program which would provide proper "food, clothing, and medical care for those who cannot help themselves." This meant, first of all, resubmitting his bill setting up a national health agency to administer $280 million in grants for medical and hospital services to states that matched the federal grants. Because the administration favored national health insurance, it naturally refused to support this conservative alternative. But Taft's proposal revealed his recognition that there were limited areas in which the federal authorities might help.[27]

Social welfare also meant improving the schools, and Taft wasted no time in joining again with Elbert Thomas of Utah and Lister Hill of Alabama to introduce their federal aid to education bill. Almost identical with the measure that had passed the Senate in 1948, it called for $270 million (or 10 per cent less than the $300 million the year before) in federal grants. If passed, Taft estimated, it would increase the average payment per pupil in Mississippi, the poorest state, from $54 to $84.50, in Alabama from $70 to $93, in North Carolina from $89 to $110.[28]

As in the past, the bill encountered criticism from all sides. Fiscal conservatives like Harry Byrd of Virginia hit him with the charge of inconsistency on the issue of economy. Lodge and other senators tried to change the formula to give all states, rich or poor, a minimum federal grant of $10 per pupil. Because Taft and Thomas had already undercut such criticism by again authorizing minimum grants of $5 per pupil to each state, Lodge failed in his attempt. Unbowed, Lodge then tried to kill the bill by denying aid to states that practiced racial segregation in their schools. But even senators favoring federal guarantees of civil rights refused to be sidetracked, and Lodge lost again. With Taft in full command of the debate, the bill passed early in May 1949 by a vote of 58 to 15. Though the religious issue then stymied the measure in House committee — even John F. Kennedy, a young Democratic congressman from Massachusetts, opposed the measure on such grounds — passage in the Senate was a milestone that resulted in part from Taft's support.[29]

The housing issue offered the clearest indication of Taft's basic constancy on matters of policy in 1949. Democrats, cavalierly assuming they could enact a public housing bill by themselves, drew up a draft at the start of the session, then gave Taft but one hour to study it before they introduced it. Taken aback, he refused to lend his name to it, and joined Ives and Flanders in submitting a plan of his own. For a time it seemed as if partisanship might endanger passage of any bill at all.[30]

Both sides, however, had waited too long to haggle over minor differences, and by March they compromised on a proposal that called for construction of 810,000 public housing units over a six-year period. "The current bill is somewhat more extensive than I would undertake at this time," Taft apologized to one of many conservative friends, "but I am definitely committed to support it." He then faced the perennial task of trying to persuade colleagues like Bricker to join him. "I had a pretty strenuous argument with John Bricker in the Republican conference yesterday on the subject of the Republican attitude toward public welfare measures like housing, health, and education," Taft wrote a friend, "and he seems to harbor some resentment still, though I tried to talk with him afterwards." [31]

Bricker and a handful of supporters continued to resist. But the Senate had already passed the measure twice before, and soon it did so again, by a vote of 57 to 13. Republicans, following Taft's lead, voted for it, 23 to 11. The House, long the stumbling block, finally forced the bill to the floor for the first time, approved the public housing section, 209 to 204, and passed the measure late in June,

227 to 186. After years of controversy Congress had finally enacted a public housing law. It was the high-water mark of Truman's Fair Deal.

Like many welfare measures passed in midtwentieth-century America, the housing bill fell woefully short of the sponsors' expectations. Real estate lobbyists continued to harass and to influence the administrators charged with carrying it out. Limits on costs sometimes forced the construction of barrackslike dwellings or of sterile high-rise apartments. Income limits on people eligible for public housing, while providing vacancies for those in need, occasionally proved demoralizing and self-defeating. And bureaucratic regulations — to say nothing of the difficulty of getting subsequent Congresses to provide adequate appropriations — seriously impeded construction. Twenty years after passage of the law only 530,000 public housing units had been built.

Still, Taft and his cosponsors had studied the problem as best they could, had come up with what almost all the experts thought to be the most promising solution at the time, and had shown themselves adept at pursuing the art of the possible. If their approach ultimately proved deficient in some ways, it also seemed realistic enough a generation later to strike urban experts as one of many necessary remedies for the sickness of American cities. Truman himself recognized Taft's important contribution to the cause. "No one," he wrote Taft warmly on signing the bill, "has taken more interest in this subject than you have . . . I believe it will contribute to the public welfare." [32]

•

Taft's reasoned approach to questions of social welfare did not surprise people who had followed his development over the years. On the contrary, it forced even progressives to offer him grudging praise. But foreign problems persisted in intruding. Before the end of the session of 1949, they had widened the break between him and the internationalists in his party.

His stance on the first major foreign policy issue of the session, aid to Europe, surprised no one. From the moment of his return from Europe in December 1948, he had questioned the level of spending, and when the European aid bill reached the floor in late

March he joined with Richard Russell of Georgia in calling for a
10 per cent cut in the $5.58 billion requested by the administra-
tion. From the point of view of fiscal policy, Taft was consistent.
Indeed, he had even cut funds for his own aid to education bill by
10 per cent. But the difference on the foreign aid bill was that he
again had made little effort to approach the question from the
standpoint of needs abroad. Why, his adversaries asked, do you
settle on an arbitrary cut of 10 per cent? "Why not?" Taft shot
back. "I want to save us a tax increase." [33]

It was a characteristically blunt and honest answer. But it
gained him no converts, and the Taft-Russell amendment was defeated by bipartisan majorities, 54 to 23. His attitude also exposed
again his nationalistic approach to foreign affairs. The aid, he conceded, was helping to stop the spread of communism. Yet that objective, he seemed to say, was less important than cutting spending.
Perhaps because he had taken a similar stand in 1947 and 1948,
perhaps because he was far from getting the votes to support his
position, he did not attract much attention. But he did accentuate
his distance from the internationalists. "I get so damned sick of
that little band of GOP isolationists who are always in the way,"
grumbled Vandenberg to his diary a few months later, "that I
could scream." [34]

Where Taft really exposed himself was over ratification of the
North Atlantic Treaty Organization (NATO), which the administration had negotiated in April with nine Western European
countries, Iceland, and Canada. Designed to emphasize America's
commitment against Soviet expansion, it contained a key clause
stating that an attack against any of the signatories would be regarded by the others as an attack against all. It thus committed the
United States — for the first time since its pragmatic alliance with
France in 1778 — to war in defense of other nations outside the
Western Hemisphere.

From the start he had been careful not to adopt a wholly negative
response. America, he said, ought to state its commitment to combating Soviet aggression. Indeed, he said, the principle of NATO
resembled that of the Rio de Janeiro Pact of 1947, which he had
supported and which obligated the United States to protect Western Hemispheric signatories from aggression. In supporting this

principle — what he called a Monroe Doctrine for Western Europe — Taft was proving himself willing to depart from the historic American refusal to entangle itself abroad.

Or was he? Instinctively he worried about delegating to the executive branch the freedom for twenty years to drag the nation into war without specific congressional action. He wondered also about committing America to such small nations as Portugal and Luxembourg. And what if one of the signatories went communist or fascist; was it then still America's duty to defend her if attacked?

Taft hesitated most over the question of providing arms and equipment to Europe. Though the treaty did not require the United States to grant such aid, it did say that the "parties separately and jointly by means of continuous and effective self-help and mutual aid will maintain and develop their individual and collective capacity to resist armed attack." It was also an article of faith for many Americans that Europe needed such military aid to make the deterrent meaningful. As the State Department conceded reluctantly in May, military aid was a "very vital corollary" to the pact.

This is precisely what Taft refused to concede. "A completely effective military defense," he argued, would cost $30 billion. Moreover, the Soviet Union, which he said did not want war, was already checked by America's possession of the atomic bomb. "A few more obsolete arms in Europe," he charged, "will not concern them in the least." Taft concluded that the pact would "give the Russians the impression, justified at least to themselves, that we are ringing them about with armies for the purpose of taking aggressive action when the time comes." Thus the alliance, "instead of being a deterrent to war, might become an incitement to war, and make it more probable instead of less." It would "make permanent the division of the world into two armed camps." [35]

In early July, with a vote on the treaty imminent, Taft remained undecided. If he could be assured the pact carried no legal or moral obligation to provide arms, he explained, he would vote for it. Such an alliance, he said, would be enough to warn potential aggressors of America's determination to fight in a crisis. But the administration, though deliberately vague on the treaty's ultimate implications, offered no such assurance, and Taft arose to announce his opposition. Fellow Republicans, impressed by the candor and thought which went into his speech, arose to applaud him when he was through. But Vandenberg's response was more typical of internationalists: "My friend from Ohio," he confided, "has given me a first class headache tonight." A week later a majority of both parties voted down an amendment barring arms aid, 74 to 21, then passed the treaty, 82 to 13.[36] Taft voted against the treaty, then two months later, consistent to the end, led a futile attempt to cut the military assistance program.[37]

Given Taft's previous thinking on foreign affairs, his position was not surprising. He had always shrunk from expensive and long-range American commitments in Europe — and surely NATO was the most far-reaching of all. He had also been quick to point out the imperialistic overtones of such commitments. "Today," he had said in January, "we have quietly adopted a tendency to interfere in the affairs of other nations, to assume that we are a kind of demigod and Santa Claus to solve the problems of the world . . . It is easy to slip into an attitude of imperialism where war becomes an instrument of public policy rather than its last resort." [38]

In adopting this perspective he showed courage, for 1948 and 1949 were among the most frightening years of the Cold War. First the communist coup in Czechoslovakia, then the Berlin blockade, then testimony about Soviet espionage in the United States. With the administration repeatedly sounding the alarm, NATO seemed to many people the only way to prevent a return to the appeasement of the 1930's. Taft could have bent to the popular mood by voting for the pact, then saved his fire to fight the military assistance bill that followed two months later. That he did not, that he insisted instead on drawing attention to the long-range possibilities of such a pact, that he even raised the heretical notion that the United States was imperialistic, attested to his integrity, his sense of responsibility, and even his gift for prophecy.

Many of his arguments seemed sound to subsequent historians. As he predicted, NATO, even with the arms (and later the troops) that the United States sent to Europe, was hardly a credible military deterrent. Because Europe was still recovering economically from the war, NATO also failed to push the Europeans into appreciably greater military expenditures of their own. It was also doubtful that Europe required a commitment like NATO to persuade them of America's willingness to resist Soviet aggression. Above all, Taft was probably correct in arguing, as did such contemporaries as the diplomat George Kennan, that the Soviets posed no military threat to western Europe. On the contrary, the Soviet Union had lost some twenty million men in World War II, and it had no wish to repeat the performance. NATO, some of these critics pointed out, may indeed have had the effect — as Taft said it would — of forcing the Soviet Union to mobilize at the very time it hoped to channel its resources into more productive directions, and of freezing the postures of both sides in the Cold War for years to come. The lid of secrecy on Soviet behavior has made such speculations hard to prove. But the benefit of hindsight makes it arguable that the formation of NATO was a provocative step that escalated the Cold War.[39]

Yet at the time, Taft's position struck many people as unwise. An American Monroe Doctrine for Europe, as Taft himself was frank to admit occasionally, hardly seemed a credible deterrent unless backed up by the commitment to provide arms. Indeed, failure to supply the European nations with the means to fight would leave America's atomic bombs as the ultimate defense. The threat of using such weapons in Europe, critics noted, offered the coldest kind of comfort to the Europeans themselves. For this reason Taft's position, which assumed that American bombers were the ultimate deterrent, was probably at least as provocative (and as doubtful as a believable deterrent) as NATO itself.

Taft also seemed inconsistent on the question of American responses to aggression. For years the Nationalist Chinese under Chiang Kai-shek had been waging a losing battle against communist forces, and by 1948 many critics were demanding that the Truman administration "save" China. Taft, who had never paid much attention to Asian affairs, was far from prominent among such critics. But by 1948 he, too, edged into their corner. "I believe very strongly," he said, "that the Far East is ultimately even more important to our future peace than is Europe." He also approved of military aid to China, and implied that Truman ought to have done more. Taft's message seemed clear; he was willing to oppose communism in faraway East Asia, but reluctant to do so in Europe. Given the historic ties of America to Europe, to say nothing of the enormous economic and strategic importance of the Atlantic world, his position, like that of the so-called "China Lobby" with which he was allying himself, struck many as both inconsistent and partisan.

Taft's statements raised other questions. For one thing, how could he claim to know Soviet intentions? Four years of scare headlines about the Cold War had thoroughly frightened many Americans. Indeed, Taft himself had long ago joined the anti-Soviet chorus by accusing the Democrats of being "soft" at Teheran and Yalta. How could he reconcile his denunciations of communist behavior with his opposition to NATO, an instrument intended to stop Soviet expansion? The answer was that he could not.[40]

In his reflective moments Taft conceded he might be wrong, and he was too intelligent to be unaware of the pitfalls in the path he was taking. Yet his stress on maintaining a free hand for America was cutting him off from the influential internationalists who were already girding themselves for 1952. "A new appeasement," editorialized the New York *Times*. "His stand on the treaty is quite in keeping with his whole record on foreign policy, which is the record of a man who would apparently like to be an internationalist but often plays the role of a Hamlet who cannot make up his mind." [41]

The ultimate complaints came from Vandenberg and from Taft's brother Charlie, who had long aligned himself with the internationalist wing of his party. In November Vandenburg wrote Charlie about Taft:

> I would feel much more comfortable for the country if he and I did not seem to be drawing farther apart in respect to "foreign affairs." I hope we can find common ground upon which to reverse this trend. This is a very *personal* comment in your very *private* ear.

Charlie replied:

> You and I are in complete agreement, and I am just as much disturbed as you are.[42]

At the beginning of 1950, a year and a half had passed since the Dewey forces captured the presidential nomination. More than a year had gone by since these same forces fell to President Truman at the polls, leaving congressional Republicans again in a minority. Privately Taft suffered under this string of disappointments. Yet all the frustrations of 1948 and 1949 really had not changed him much. "There was not the slightest difference in his manner, or his apparent self-confidence, from the days of the Eightieth Congress," the *New Republic* reported with some surprise. Truman, whose combativeness helped him understand that of his foe, agreed. Taft, he told a friend, "is a high class man. He is honest, intelligent, and extremely capable . . . There is nothing devious about Bob Taft." And 211 Washington newsmen in September 1949 voted him "best Senator." (He got 110 votes, to 70 for Vandenberg, to 60 for Paul Douglas; Bricker outpolled William Jenner of Indiana for "worst.") [43] Despite the complaints from internationalists, Taft at the start of 1950 enjoyed a higher reputation for integrity, conscientiousness, and intellectual power than ever before, and he had proved that he could rise above disappointments. He had reason to feel proud and to look forward to the future.

CHAPTER 29

A Troubled, Partisan Taft, 1950

THE EVENTS of midcentury sharpened the tensions that had been gathering since the war. In New York, Alger Hiss, a former State Department official whom ex-communist Whittaker Chambers had accused of espionage for the Soviets, underwent two protracted and sensational perjury trials. In China, Mao Tse-tung ripped up the last shreds of Nationalist opposition and threatened to dislodge Chiang Kai-shek from his refuge on the island of Formosa. And in the sky, American planes collected an unusually radioactive air sample. Three weeks later, on the morning of September 23, 1949, President Truman called in the press and told them the news. "We have evidence," the President announced solemnly, "that within recent weeks an atomic explosion occurred in the U.S.S.R."

Taft's sixtieth birthday occurred in the midst of these disturbing events. The passage of years seemed to leave him unmarked. He acted as alert and as competitive as ever, and he had lost none of his remarkable vigor and good health. With his sons establishing themselves — Bill as a foreign aid administrator in Ireland; Bob, Jr., as a lawyer with Taft, Stettinius, and Hollister; Lloyd with the Cincinnati *Times-Star;* Horace finishing his senior year at Yale — he had few worries at home. He had time to play golf on Sundays, to relax in the evenings with Martha and friends, and occasionally to read detective novels late into the night. Not all sexagenarians could count so many personal comforts.

Yet Taft was a public man, and he could not rest long. Above all, he had to worry about his future. In November 1950 he had to face the voters again in a contest that the labor unions had long

threatened to invade. As early as December 1948 he had set up an
organization for the campaign. In April 1949 he had hired Lou
Guylay as his public relations man at a monthly retainer of $1500.
In May he had started a series of weekly radio broadcasts on some
90 Ohio stations, in June he began writing a weekly column carried by more than 150 Ohio papers, and in September he embarked on the first of what were billed as fact-finding tours of
Ohio. In December 1949, when he finished his "100 Days" of
travel, he had visited seventy-five of Ohio's eighty-eight counties
and spoken to more than 300,000 people, all the while driving
from town to town himself and without missing a weekly column
or news broadcast. Taft was tireless. He was aroused. And, remembering his narrow victory in 1944, he was scared. For Taft,
1950 promised to be the crucible of will, the ultimate test of fire
against the enemy. Before it was over, he seemed a changed man.[1]

•

When the new congressional session started in January 1950,
Taft seemed happy about the results of his travels through Ohio
and well rested from a Christmas break. But when Truman used
his State of the Union message to pursue his long-elusive goals —
the Brannan Plan for agriculture, repeal of Taft-Hartley, tax increases, national health insurance — Republicans guffawed and
hooted, causing the President to flush angrily. Taft, who sat stonily in the front row, wasted no time in asserting that the duty of the
opposition was to oppose. Truman, he said, had sounded reasonable. But, "most of the Socialist handout program is still to be
found in very innocent sounding language." It reminded him of
the quote from Byron:

> The mildest manner'd man
> That ever scuttled ship or cut a throat.[2]

Taft then joined a growing chorus of Republicans who were denouncing administration policies in East Asia. The United States,
he insisted, ought to commit its navy to the defense of Chiang Kai-
shek on Formosa. Such a policy would not cost much and would
be consistent with America's stated willingness to stop the advance
of communism. Using the navy would also involve minimal risk.

There was "not the slightest evidence," he declared, "that Russia will go to war with us because we interfere with a crossing to Formosa." [3]

Taft was probably correct in these contentions, but when the administration refused to commit itself, he and other Republicans went further. The State Department, he charged, "with its pro-communist allies" was "liquidating" the Chinese Nationalists, and was "guided by a left-wing group who have obviously wanted to get rid of Chiang and were willing at least to turn China over to the Communists for that purpose." In repeating such an accusation during the coming months, Taft fanned the passions that inflamed Americans following the Chinese Communist triumphs on the mainland. But his innuendo about communist infiltration of the State Department not only lacked solid proof but also cast the debate over China policy into an unproductive search for scapegoats and prevented any reasoned discussion of alternative approaches. Arthur Vandenberg cautioned him, "Let's not slam the door against the right kind of bi-partisan cooperation in foreign policy." [4] But Taft, who had long attacked the administration's "softness" toward communism, thought the administration's Asia policy craven. It appeared vulnerable. And 1950 was an election year.

He also sounded hostile to Truman over domestic policy. He helped block national health insurance, lambasted the Brannan Plan for agriculture, continued to oppose a compulsory Fair Employment Practices Commission (though twice voting unsuccessfully to stop southern filibusters against it), and voted against extending rent control another six months to January 1951.[5] Above all, he stepped up his campaign against heavy federal spending. A recession that had descended late in the spring of 1949 was threatening to turn the $8.4 billion surplus of 1948 into a more than $3 billion deficit for fiscal 1950. Alarmed, Taft tried again to cut all federal appropriations by 10 per cent or more. Reduced spending was so vital, he told the Ohio College Association in April, that even aid to education ought to be deferred.[6] Congress should also cut spending for foreign aid. Undaunted by his failures in previous sessions, he led a fight to slash such funds by $500 million, or 17 per cent of the $3.1 billion requested by the administration. He also tried to trim funds for Point Four, Tru-

man's new program calling for technical assistance abroad. Because many senators shared Taft's worries about the budget and
because Europe seemed on the road to recovery, his amendments
almost passed. But administration Democrats held firm enough to
beat them by narrow margins. On European policy the bipartisan
coalition behind the President was trembling but still in command.[7]

The ultimate manifestation of Taft's aggressiveness in 1950 concerned Senator Joseph McCarthy of Wisconsin. Crude, tough, ambitious for the spotlight, McCarthy had chafed under his obscurity
since reaching the Senate in 1947. Then on February 9, 1950, he
flew to Wheeling, West Virginia, for a speech. It was less than a
month after Alger Hiss's conviction for perjury and but six days
after the British announced the confession of spying by Dr. Klaus
Fuchs, an atomic physicist who had worked on the bomb between
1943 and 1947. America's dilemma, McCarthy told the ladies of
the Wheeling Women's Republican Club, did not come from foreign enemies but from "the traitorous actions of those who have
been treated so well by this nation." The worst offenders were the
"bright young men with silver spoons in their mouths . . . In my
opinion the State Department, which is one of the most important
government departments, is thoroughly infested with Communists." McCarthy closed by brandishing a piece of paper that he
said listed 205 names — some reporters later said 57 or 81 names
— of American policy makers who were members of the Communist party.[8]

McCarthy's charges drew little attention at first, but he then repeated them in Salt Lake City and Reno. Recognizing sensational
news, the press quickly spread his charges across page one. And
worried Americans seemed to grasp at the answer McCarthy held
out to them. It did not matter that he was reckless, that he
smeared those who dared to dispute him, that he blackened the
name of the American State Department, that he seemed unable to
furnish evidence to uncover one, let alone 57 or 205 communists in
government. What mattered was that he claimed to have hard evidence and that he was offering a simple explanation for America's
complex international difficulties. In a few weeks McCarthy had
attracted enough attention, adulation, and disgust to satiate the

most ambitious of men. McCarthyism was suddenly a term in itself, a fact of political life that was to tear America apart for the next five years.

Though McCarthy had been a Republican senator for three years, Taft had not paid much attention to him. Indeed, in April 1946, when McCarthy was engaged in a bitter primary against Robert La Follette, Jr., for the Republican senatorial nomination, Taft had sent a letter — made public by its recipient — expressing his preference for La Follette, who was his personal friend and fellow anti-interventionist. McCarthy, in turn, had served as Stassen's floor manager in the 1948 presidential convention. And when Taft and his friends announced Republican committee assignments in January 1949, McCarthy complained bitterly. His second-rate assignments, he protested, "will be extremely embarrassing to me in my State." The whole operation, he insisted, was an "awfully foul deal." [9]

When McCarthy launched his crusade a year later, Taft was therefore as surprised as anyone else. McCarthy did not consult Taft — or any of the top Republican leaders — and he refused to moderate his accusations or verify his facts. As Taft explained privately, McCarthy "doesn't check his statements very carefully and is not disposed to take any advice so that it makes him a hard man for anybody to work with, or restrain." [10] Like many of his colleagues, Taft found himself trying to deal with an individualist who ignored the folkways and civilities of the Senate.

As if these were not reasons enough to disavow McCarthy, Taft had himself compiled a creditable record in the field of civil liberties. He had opposed the Ku Klux Klan, objected to compulsory Bible reading in the public schools, courageously defended alleged seditionists against government prosecution in World War II, and objected to Truman's attempt to draft strikers in 1946. As a member of the Yale Corporation, he had occasionally tried to block appointments of left-wingers to the faculty, but had stoutly resisted efforts by friends and alumni to remove professors for political reasons. He had also agreed with Zechariah Chafee, his law school classmate turned Harvard law professor, that "we cannot make it a crime to be a Communist or to teach communism." [11] When McCarthy began accusing individuals of communist sympathies, Taft might well have denounced him — or at least have been careful to dissociate himself.

At first he seemed to do so. McCarthy, he said privately, was putting on "a perfectly reckless performance." But when McCarthy continued his crusade, the GOP policy committee felt obliged to take a stand. Emerging from the committee on March 22, 1950, Taft explained to reporters that his colleague's charges were "not a matter of party policy." But instead of stopping there, he ventured his own opinion. Though McCarthy had not yet found any communists, Taft said, he should not despair. He should "keep talking and if one case doesn't work out, he should proceed with another one." Individual Republican senators, Taft added, were free to help McCarthy do so.[12]

Privately, Taft still had his doubts. McCarthy, he complained to a friend, "overstated a good case . . . he made allegations which are impossible to prove which may be embarrassing before we get through." But publicly, Taft refused to change his stance, and he even endorsed his embattled Republican colleague as:

a fighting Marine who risked his life to preserve the liberties of the United States. The greatest Kremlin asset in our history has been the pro-Communist group in the State Department who surrendered to every demand of Russia at Yalta and Potsdam, and promoted at every opportunity the Communist cause in China until today Communism threatens to take over all of Asia.

Twelve days later Taft reiterated his faith. "Whether Senator McCarthy has legal evidence, whether he has overstated or understated his case, is of lesser importance. The question is whether the Communist influence in the State Department still exists." [13]

Reporters were not wholly surprised by Taft's position. Although he never went so far as to talk of "treason" in the State Department or to name individuals, he had joined other Republicans in damning communism in American life even before McCarthy carried this tactic to its extreme. "It is astonishing," he had written in February 1945, "how many professors and other so-called intellectuals have been converted to a sympathy with the Russian system." The Political Action Committee of the CIO, he charged during the 1946 campaign, "is so dominated by Communistic thinking that it is compelled to be more Russian than American." [14] By 1947 he had turned his attention to the government. "We have an administration so soft toward communism," he said in October, "that apparently the government is riddled with them. Otherwise the President wouldn't have had to ask for a great sum of money to get rid of them." In preparing for the 1948 campaign Taft had urged an aide to "make every possible issue" of communism in government and "show that the Democrats have fostered Communism and Communists right through the war." [15]

Taft refused to concede that citizens possessed the right to conceal communist affiliations. He warmly defended the work of the House Un-American Activities Committee, a body widely criticized by civil libertarians, and defended the anticommunist affidavit required under the Taft-Hartley Act. He favored defining communism, requiring party organizations and fronts to register with the government, and banning party members from the ballot and from jobs with the federal government. To outlaw communism, he proclaimed, would be to "abandon the principles of liberty found in the Bill of Rights," but forcing party members into the open was essential. "I don't know what civil rights there are," he argued, "that entitle a man to pretend he is not a communist, and then spread Communism through labor unions . . . and through the movies and publications." Thus before McCarthy launched his movement, Taft himself was moving in the same direction. "The revelation of the Fuchs treason," he wrote five days before McCarthy's speech at Wheeling, "shows that we were right about Lilienthal and his softness towards Communists. The situation has been so bad that it may become the major issue in the next election." [16]

Early in May, Taft again developed second thoughts, and even tried to deny his earlier statement advising McCarthy to "keep talking." The columnist Stewart Alsop, interviewing Taft later in the month, noted how the whole subject seemed to trouble him. Taft never felt comfortable with his crude and undisciplined colleague.[17]

But as Richard Rovere was to point out later, Taft confronted McCarthyism as alcoholics battle the bottle: It was bad but irresistible. The reasons for his weakness were complex. First, McCarthy's accusations seemed perilous for politicians to assault, and even Democrats refrained from doing so. "McCarthy may have something," said Congressman John F. Kennedy. Many others, especially those from heavily Catholic areas such as Kennedy's, felt bound to agree, for it seemed foolhardy to breast the tide. In June, when seven liberal Republican senators criticized McCarthyism in a "Declaration of Conscience," they were lost like voices in a wilderness.[18]

Second, Taft sincerely detested the drift of administration foreign policy since 1940. The Democrats, he had said repeatedly, had proved "soft" on communism at Teheran and Yalta, and they had done little to "save" China from the communists. It was plausible for him to assume that communist sympathizers existed in the State Department, and not impossible for him to entertain McCarthy's charges that some of these sympathizers were traitors. These charges were slanderous, and they hardened America's posture in the Cold War. But Taft's passionate feelings about administration foreign policy conquered lingering doubts.

Third, 1950 was a time when his opponents in Ohio were threatening to eliminate him from public life. "We have not warmed up yet," one angry union official snapped at him during a congressional hearing in 1949. "The boys in Ohio tell me that they will take care of things — including you — pretty well in the next election." By July 1949 the AF of L's Labor League for Political Action had already singled Taft out as its number one enemy and had called for $2 contributions from each of its eight million members for the purpose of defeating him.[19] Though Taft feigned unconcern (the unions, he wrote a friend, seem "to have really opened the pocketbooks of the conservatives"), he felt himself on the defensive against not only the unions but also such pressure groups as the NAACP, which opposed him for his stand on FEPC, and Catholic bishops, who resented his stand on aid to parochial schools.[20] And he possessed a more sensitive hide than many people suspected. At a dinner party a guest complained of the unfair methods used by the House Commitee on Un-American Activities. "What difference does that make?" he flared. "*I* am always being unfairly attacked and confused, for that matter." [21]

Above all, Taft shared his father's instinctive hatred of bolshevism. The great struggle of the age, he had always believed, was ideological, not military. It pitted democracy and capitalism against communism. Unless America rooted out communism from the government, it could never hope to serve as an example of capitalist virtue to the rest of the uncommitted world. Taft, a close friend ruefully recalled, "was rabid on the subject of communism. Just the word would make him furious about it. And that was a part of a great conservatism that was not too attractive." [22]

Taft always maintained that he could not have stopped McCarthy in 1950. "You are mistaken when you suggest that I have an influence on McCarthy," he wrote a friend in mid-1951. "From the beginning of his attack on the State Department we tried to stir him somewhat, but found it was impossible." [23] He was surely correct, for McCarthy listened to no one. Yet Taft, who had defied the popular will in the past, who often showed a dogged and painstaking respect for facts, who revered the law, and who had occasionally restrained his right-wing admirers, had done nothing to intervene this time, and had even publicly defended McCarthy. That he did so was a mark not only of his own fervent anticommunism but of his party loyalty and aggressive partisanship in an election year. The temptations of politics, more than anything else, had turned Taft toward irresponsibility.

•

In these troubled times, Taft also suffered the deepest personal blow of his life. While making a speech late in 1949, Martha had suddenly felt so tired that she sat down. She had a long history of high blood pressure and perhaps had suffered a mild stroke. Her doctor told her to rest, and early in 1950, while her husband took to the campaign trail in Ohio, she relaxed weekends at Indian Hill. Concerned, Bob got friends to stay with her while he was away — most often Darrah Wunder, Martha's old friend in the League of Women Voters in Cincinnati. Mrs. Wunder, then the executive secretary of the League, was long divorced from her husband and free to take care of Martha on weekends. Warm, lively, deeply interested in politics, Mrs. Wunder was perhaps an ideal companion for Martha in the early months of 1950.

But in March, Tom Bowers, Martha's brother, succumbed unexpectedly to phlebitis. Early in May, Clarence Dykstra, the husband of her close friend Lillian, also died suddenly. Though deeply upset, Martha went with Alice Roosevelt Longworth to the Senate gallery on May 16. On Martha's return home to Georgetown, it began to rain, and she ran up the steep stairs to see if the windows were closed. On the way up she fell, and she felt a headache. When Taft got home that night — after excoriating Truman over four radio networks — he found her all right. But that night she twice fell out of bed, and in the morning she awoke paralyzed. He hurried her to the hospital, where he learned that Martha, like his mother forty years earlier, had suffered a severe stroke. It was to be July before she was permitted to leave the hospital — and then only with nurses watching her around the clock.[24]

At that point Taft took her home to Indian Hill. He also secured Mrs. Wunder as her companion for the rest of the campaign. But the stroke had afflicted Martha cruelly. Though she no longer had the blackouts and convulsions that had accompanied the early days of her illness, she was unable to walk, and he had to fix up the house to enable her to get about in a wheelchair. The stroke also seemed to affect important centers of the brain and to change her personality. Martha, once so vibrant, bright, and uncomplaining, was no longer able to concentrate, sometimes unable even to comprehend or to remember what was read or said to her. She resented her husband's absences, yet hardly seemed aware of his presence when he hurried home. And she lapsed into spells of profound depression, bitterly bewailed her fate, refused to be consoled, and demanded the unsparing solicitude of nurses, of Mrs. Wunder, of Taft himself. It was her fate to be cut down in the midst of the campaigning she loved, and Taft had to suffer her querulousness. He was ever after to campaign alone.[25]

With characteristic self-control, he refused to break down, to lean on the shoulders of family or friends, or even to inform his son Horace, studying for his doctorate in physics at Zurich, of the seriousness of her illness. Perhaps because it was clear after a few days that she was in no danger of dying (indeed, she lived on, in much the same condition, until 1958), he also carried on in the Senate with hardly a break. And he gave no serious thought to withdrawing from his Senate campaign. Healthy, vigorous, ambitious to serve and to excel, he saw no reason to remove himself from public life.[26]

Whether her illness affected his actions in the remaining months of his campaign was doubtful. Some people guessed that her stroke embittered him, made him more remote, and led him to new heights of partisanship. Others, however, speculated that the tragedy, the first of any consequence ever to affect him, gradually broadened his sympathies and softened his personality. Yet Taft did not seem embittered, and he was no more partisan after her illness than he had been before it. He gave no appreciable signs of relaxing on the stump or of sharing his emotions with others. Like his father in 1909, he held stoically to the carefully controlled course on which he had embarked.

Yet there was no denying that Taft suffered. He called Martha every night he was away — often to discover that she hardly knew he was gone. He cut short conferences and weekend engagements, returned home early when his travels took him near Indian Hill, and read to her, even though she often seemed unaware of what he was reading. He pushed her about in her wheelchair, personally lifted her heavy frame in and out of cars, endured her complaints, tenderly did his best to make her feel comfortable and happy. She had been the one person with whom he shared everything, and no one could begin to take her place. As his sister Helen Manning was to phrase it later, it was probably the first time in Taft's life that he had been actively unhappy, and he was helpless to do anything about it.[27]

•

In the early dawn of June 25, 1950, soldiers patrolling the Thirty-Eighth Parallel dividing communist North Korea from South Korea observed unusual movements. Quickly they understood why. North Korean soldiers stormed across the border through the outnumbered South Koreans. The fury of the attack clearly suggested aggression. Either the United States had to respond in kind, or it would seem to pursue appeasement in response to the use of force.

Truman wasted no time. Without seeking congressional assent, he secured a United Nations resolution accusing North Korea of armed invasion, demanding a cease fire, and calling on UN members to assist in the execution of the resolution. He then authorized the dispatch of American air and naval forces to Korea. When these forces proved inadequate, he invoked his authority as commander in chief to send American ground troops under the direction of General Douglas MacArthur. Truman's quick response evoked praise and relief from American leaders throughout the country. At last, it seemed, America was taking a stand against aggression.

Taft, like everyone else, had not anticipated the Korean war. Indeed, he had paid the peninsula rather little attention, perfunctorily going along with the rest of Congress in agreeing to the gradual withdrawal of American forces from South Korea after World War II and in assenting to limited economic aid after the creation of the Republic of [South] Korea in 1948. Though he had insisted early in 1950 that America protect South Korea in case of attack, he had not been enthusiastic about such an adventure. Compared with the limited effort necessary to hold Formosa, which he insisted America could and should defend, protection of the South Korean mainland struck him — as it struck many others in 1950 — as a much more costly and formidable task.[28]

When Truman reacted decisively, Taft was caught with divided emotions. During the early debate he sat, pensive and inscrutable, in his seat on the floor of the Senate. But on June 28, three days after the invasion, he stood up to offer the speech his colleagues had anxiously awaited. The North Korean invasion, he said, was "an outrageous act of aggression" which "in all probability was instigated by Soviet Russia." The "time had to come, sooner or later, when we would give definite notice to the communists that a move beyond a declared line would result in war." This, unquestionably, was the time. Were Truman to request a congressional joint resolution approving his dispatch of the air and naval forces, Taft concluded, "I would vote for it."[29]

Taft repeatedly reiterated his support of the administration during the next week. "The general principle of the policy is right," he told Ohioans the next day, "and I see no choice except to back up wholeheartedly and with every available resource the American

men in our armed forces who have been moved into Korea."
There was "no alternative to what the President has done," he
proclaimed over the radio three days later. "I thoroughly approve
of it. I am in favor of backing up the policy which he has now
adopted." Administration officials, gratified at such support from
their most feared enemy, relaxed. "My God," said presidential
press secretary Charles Ross, "Bob Taft has joined the U.N. and
the U.S." [30]

Or had he? When Senate Republicans caucused immediately
following the invasion, *Newsweek* reported, Taft privately cautioned that the GOP "shouldn't be stampeded into war" over
Korea. Persuaded in the next two days that the United States had
no choice but to fight, he then denounced Truman at the same
time that he was supporting him. The President's firmness, he said
in his speech on June 28, represented a "complete change in the
programs and policies heretofore proclaimed by the administration," for in previous months both Secretary of State Dean Acheson and Tom Connally, the Democratic chairman of the Senate
Foreign Relations Committee, had implied that America would
not aid South Korea in case of attack. Taft, who had served on the
Yale Corporation with Acheson since 1937, had never suffered his
cool air of superiority gladly, and he demanded that Acheson resign as secretary of state. The United States, Taft added, should
have left fighting troops in South Korea and "should have given, a
year ago, the notice which the President has given today." He continued:

> With such a policy, there never would have been such an attack
> by the North Koreans. In short, this entirely unfortunate crisis
> has been produced, first, by the outrageous, aggressive attitude of
> Soviet Russia, and second, by the bungling and inconsistent for-
> eign policy of the administration.[31]

Taft then hit the administration on other grounds. Dividing
Korea at the Thirty-eighth Parallel, he said, was typical of the Roo-
sevelt-Truman softness toward the Soviet Union. The failure to
stand behind Chiang Kai-shek and to guarantee the safety of Formosa had given "basic encouragement to the North Korean aggression." And now the administration was committed to fight a war,

not in defense of Formosa, but of Korea — "a very difficult military operation indeed." Finally, why had Truman not requested congressional approval before authorizing American defense of South Korea? As in 1941, Taft upheld the right of Congress to declare war and accused the President of abusing his constitutional powers.[32]

With the war proceeding badly for American troops in July, Taft continued to speak with divided mind. He called for a substantial tax increase and ultimately voted in early September for a successful bill that provided an estimated $4.7 billion in new revenue. Pay as you go, he argued, must be the economic policy of the war. He also called for decreased domestic expenditures in order to ensure a balanced budget. Yet he balked at letting the war lead to new economic policies, opposed an excess profits tax, and attacked efforts to give Truman tough controls over prices and wages — what Taft called "arbitrary and dictatorial control over the entire economy." The Korean war, he argued, was "not any particular strain on the economy of this country." Faced with evidence to the contrary, Taft eventually refrained from trying to defeat the Defense Production Act, which passed both houses in September and which gave Truman standby controls over wages and prices. But he did sponsor a successful amendment requiring the President to control wages as well as prices. To Taft, the Korean war was not to be a long-term commitment requiring stringent economic controls.[33]

Taft's speeches scored some points. By publicly excluding South Korea from America's so-called "defense perimeter" in East Asia, the Truman administration may in fact have encouraged the North Koreans to think they could safely attack. In then responding with American troops, the President involved the United States in a war for an area of little economic or strategic value. And in neglecting to get congressional assent for such a major military adventure, Truman had stretched his powers as commander in chief. When the bloody "police action" dragged on into 1951 and 1952, Truman's failure to consult Congress cost him severely.

Yet Taft also seemed inconsistent — caught amid his anticommunist militancy about Asia, his lifelong hostility toward extensive overseas involvement, and his partisan opposition to Truman. On

July 6 he agreed that UN forces would have to "march right on over the thirty-eighth parallel and at least occupy the southern part of North Korea." Yet three weeks later he complained privately that America was "in real danger of becoming an imperialistic nation. The line between imperialism and idealism becomes very confused in the minds of those who operate the system." [34] Early in September he alarmed even his admirers by voting against confirmation of General George Marshall as secretary of defense. The appointment, he said, was a "reaffirmation of the tragic policy of this administration in encouraging Chinese communism which brought on the Korean war." And privately he revealed his partisan emotions. "The only way we can beat the Democrats," he wrote:

> is to go after them for their mistakes. We were making some progress in this when the war came and forced a change in policy. There is no alternative except to support the war, but certainly we can point out that it has resulted from a bungling of the Democratic administration.[35]

Whether Taft's "yes, but" approach to Korea helped or hurt him in his campaign was unclear. In any event, when MacArthur's forces staged a dramatic counteroffensive in September, the war faded temporarily as an attractive electoral issue for the GOP. But to some people, Taft had once again seemed excessively partisan, ever too ready to bark, "I told you so," and only grudgingly prepared to accept strong measures against what most Americans regarded as unprovoked communist aggression. With so many other problems to distract him in 1950 — the unpredictability of McCarthy, the militance of the unions, above all Martha's illness — the Korean war was a conflagration for which he was unprepared and which he could well have done without. It was also the most baffling in a series of issues — China, McCarthy, aid to Europe, spending and controls — which impelled him to the politics of attack. The tensions of midcentury — and the pressures of campaigning — were worrying him. And they were bringing out the more combative, rougher sides of his personality.

CHAPTER 30

A Magnificent Triumph

AMID so many tribulations Taft might have been tempted to despair. But chance both frowned and smiled on him in 1950. Like most successful politicians, he had more than his share of plain good luck in the campaign.

Fortune first shone on him when it left Joseph T. Ferguson as his Democratic opponent. Ferguson, short, slight, sandy-haired, was fifty-eight years old in 1950. The oldest of four children, he had grown up in the small southern Ohio town of Shawnee, the son of a precariously employed coal miner. He had helped support his family by selling papers, worked in business and as an auditor for the state, married, had eight children, and become state auditor in 1937. Hard working, affable, careful with state money, devoutly Catholic (he had not missed a Sunday or holy day mass in fifty-two years, he told voters in 1950), he also let few opportunities pass to publicize himself. His winning softball team, the "Ferguson State Auditors," brought him wide recognition, and his habit of sending out Christmas cards — 100,000 annually by 1949 — depicting his family added to his renown over the years. By 1950 Ohioans had re-elected him auditor three more times, in 1948 by a margin of nearly 292,000 votes over his Republican foe, the largest victory ever given a Democratic office seeker in Ohio history. He seemed a formidable contender in 1950.[1]

But only on the surface. Almost all observers agreed that either Governor Frank Lausche, one of Ohio's most successful vote getters, or Murray Lincoln, a liberal farm leader and the choice of organized labor, would have made a much stronger candidate. But Lausche, an independent and conservative Democrat, decided to run again for governor instead, and Lincoln declined to combat so solidly entrenched a party man as Ferguson. Their decisions left Ferguson the standard-bearer, but many Democrats wondered about his chances of carrying it through the elections in November.[2]

They worried with good reason. Ferguson wore glasses, had a prominent gap in his front teeth, and grinned in the wide goofy manner of the comedian Joe E. Brown. Though small in size, he possessed a loud platform voice, an ebullient manner, and a fondness for glad-handing that had already won him the derisive nickname of "Jumping Joe." He also sounded crude, ungrammatical, unsophisticated. "I'll beat the pants off Bob Taft," he liked to say. "I got the people in mind, and when you got the people in mind, you got the cat by the tail." Ferguson, said the journalist Stewart Alsop in calculated understatement, had "an imperfect acquaintance with his mother tongue." [3]

Even these handicaps might not have proved fatal. Ferguson was likable, upright, wholly loyal to Truman's Fair Deal. (Indeed, he seemed so well qualified for state auditor that he emerged from obscurity in 1970 to capture that office again.) But when he thrust himself into the glare of the senatorial contest, it became clear how little he knew about national issues. "As a representative of the long American liberal-radical tradition," Alsop added, "he is a joke." The Wooster, Ohio, *Daily-Herald* was even harsher. Ferguson's grasp of state and national issues, it editorialized, was "primitive . . . As for his comprehension of international affairs . . . we would rather put our trust in a high school sophomore . . . We are in favor of everybody taking twenty-four hours to do their laughing and then getting behind a campaign to keep Joe Ferguson in Ohio henceforth and forever more."

Soon the reporters grew nastier. What was Ferguson's foreign policy, they queried. "Beat Michigan," was their response. "How would you handle Formosa?" they asked him. "I'll carry that county, too," Ferguson was supposed to have replied. "The smartest thing the Democratic national committee could do," said a reporter for the important Cleveland *Plain Dealer,* "is smuggle their nominee, Jumping Joe Ferguson, out of Ohio and keep him hidden until after the November election. Just buy him a ticket for a long trip — South America, Hawaii or anywhere — so the voters can't come in contact with him." [4]

Ferguson was not quite so inept as that. But he was easily carica-tured by the predominantly Republican press of Ohio, and he seemed an especially crude contrast to a man of Taft's experience. Although the size of Taft's eventual margin suggested that no Democrat could have beaten him in 1950, it was also true that Fer-guson, even more than Bulkley and Pickrel before him, symbolized the mediocrity of the Ohio Democratic party. It was Taft's good fortune that he never had to face a truly formidable foe in Ohio.

.

If Ferguson proved a less than scintillating candidate, the labor unions behind him often seemed unfair. John L. Lewis of the United Mine Workers typified their approach. Taft, he said in August 1950, was "a relentless, albeit witless tool of the oppressors of labor." If Taft tried to enter the mines, the workers should keep him out. The air underground, Lewis said with characteristic flourish, was close, and "the effluvia of the oppressor is ever dis-agreeable and could enrage the men to the point of evacuation of the mines." [5]

Lewis was moderate compared with the United Labor League of Ohio, a political arm of most of Ohio's unions. Early in the cam-paign it performed the prodigious feat of producing *The Speaker's Handbook,* a 218-page study of Taft's life, which it distributed to some four hundred key Democrats in its first edition, then to five thousand in a slightly amended second version later in the cam-paign. Seemingly a job of careful research, it listed more than nine hundred of Taft's votes as state and national legislator and was re-plete with his outspoken comments over the years.

Chapter One of the first edition left no doubt of the tone of the book. "As a baby," it reported, "Robert Alphonso was greedy for oatmeal." It continued:

> His nurse tried to curb his appetite by giving him plain milk in-stead of rich cream served at the Taft breakfast table. When that didn't work, the nurse held out on the sugar. These tactics must have made a deep impression on the young heir . . . Fifty years

later he was using them himself. When Taft found he couldn't block certain welfare measures in the Senate, he tried to take the good parts out of them.

Taft, the book continued, then went to the Philippines, only to be stung by a jellyfish. "This, too," the handbook concluded, "must have made a deep impression on Taft. It may have been the start of his fear, distrust, and dislike of foreigners, of immigrants, of all things that are not demonstrably third generation America." The handbook proceeded to show how he had voted against public housing in the August 1948 special session — without explaining that he had felt obliged to give his word to the House Republicans. It went on to describe him as opposing a sixty-five-cent minimum wage without bothering to report that in 1949 he had supported a seventy-five-cent minimum wage instead.[6]

The handbook probably influenced few voters. Indeed, most of the extreme sections, including the parts about the oatmeal and the minimum wage, disappeared under fire from Taft and his supporters in the second edition. But labor's other magnum opus, a comic book entitled "The Robert Alphonso Taft Story: 'It's On the Record,'" went to 1,500,000 Ohioans. It was short enough — sixteen pages — and simple enough to be read by even the most apathetic voter.

The comic book was beautifully clear. On the cover stared Taft, a bug-eyed, pink-skinned, simpering child of the rich. Inside was J. Phineas Moneybags, a fat, mustachioed, cigar-chomping spokesman of privilege who was charged with the task of running a local Taft campaign committee. Phineas, bluff and decisive, had hit on the idea of making a film of Taft's career, and his smirking co-conspirators rubbed their hands in glee at the prospect. "We'll make 'em show it in schools, factories, union league clubs," chortled Phineas. "OOPS — excuse that dirty word, 'UNION,' boys!"

But Phineas and his friends soon ran into difficulties. Voters, they felt, might not like the story of Taft's early life — "pretty dull . . . exclusive private schools . . . avoided sports . . . didn't have to work of course," mumbled Phineas. His term in the state senate was also a little embarrassing. "Remember those days, J.P.?" asked a wing-collared associate. "Remember?" Phineas chuckled, "How could I forget? One of the first things Taft did was pass that bill taking a cool million and a half off our corporations' taxes." Out came Phineas's scissors to cut the offending portions of the film.

The rest of the comic book followed this simple format. Phineas and his friends had to cut out Taft's stand on foreign affairs in 1941, his remarks on the soldier ballot in 1944, all of his comments about taxes and controls. ("Oh, the LOVELY PROFITS we made after Taft helped kill those controls! And the housewives didn't know what hit them until it was too late.") "Cut!" "CUT!!" "CUT!!!" By the end of the comic book the conspirators had to destroy everything and turn instead to "see what dirt we can dig up on FERGUSON." But this, too, proved disastrous. Ferguson, it seemed, was a wonderful family man, the people's choice. The comic concluded with pictures of Ferguson's well-groomed, attractive children, then with a perspiring Phineas putting on the last piece of film. It showed a smiling, youthful-looking Ferguson. "The people," said the Democratic nominee, "will beat the pants off Senator Taft . . . and they'll do it by a quarter of a million votes."

"Cut!"

"Cut!"

"Cut — (shudder)."

"Gulp!" [7]

Some expert observers, including columnist Ernest Lindley of *Newsweek* and Samuel Lubell, a perceptive analyst of electoral trends, thought labor's extraordinary effort in Ohio energetic and imaginative. But as Lubell also pointed out, the unions acted so militantly that they became key issues in themselves.[8] Taft, aware of labor's excesses, was careful not to explode in anger. *The Speaker's Handbook,* he wrote a friend, "is not very effective, largely because the opening chapter is so silly." But he had his aides go through the handbook vote by vote, and they uncovered forty-five "lies" and eleven "things to explain." He then passed on the appropriate factual responses to his supporters, who responded with honest outrage. Charlie Taft, who worked hard to pull reluctant Charterites into his brother's campaign, typified this sort of reaction. The handbook, he fumed to a labor leader, was "a tissue of lies . . . reminiscent of Goebbels at his worst, and clearly resembles the propaganda of hate pouring out over Moscow radio, *Izvestia,* and *Pravda* from the Kremlin." [9]

The comic was more absurd than anything else, and it was doubtful that many people took it seriously. But this was of course the point. In openly trying to remove Taft from public life, the unions probably struck many Ohioans, including some workers themselves, as vindictive. They lowered the tone of what was already an unedifying Democratic campaign, left Ferguson open to the charge of being "run" by others, and enabled Taft to ignore his opponent while accusing organized labor of trying to dictate to the people of the sovereign state of Ohio. The union attack probably drew formerly apathetic suburbanites to the polls and helped Taft more than it hurt.

·

Taft welcomed the blunders of his opponents. But he was too experienced in politics to depend on them alone. From the start in 1949, he seized every opportunity.

His first important move was to change the Ohio ballot. As Paul Walter never tired of telling him, thousands of Democrats in 1944 had selected Frank Lausche at the top of the ballot, then voted a straight ticket. With Lausche again slated to run for governor, it seemed foolish not to press for adoption of the Massachusetts ballot, by which voters had to make individual choices for all offices. Mobilizing during the spring and summer of 1949, Walter and his friends labored hard to place the issue on the ballot, and they received ample support from the League of Women Voters and other nonpartisan groups. When the voters approved the constitutional change in November 1949, all observers reckoned the Massachusetts ballot would save Taft more than 100,000 votes in 1950.[10]

Taft worked more closely with the state organization than ever before, partly because it was then led by Ray Bliss, a quiet, effective political organizer from Akron. A believer in careful precinct work, Bliss was to build a national reputation culminating in his selection as GOP national chairman for Richard Nixon's presidential victory in 1968. But Taft also recalled vividly his past troubles with other people's organizations, and he determined to rely primarily on his friends. These included Paul Walter, who was in charge in the north, Willis Gradison, an old Cincinnati friend who became his campaign manager, and many others. He also set up a whole series of fronts such as Farmers for Taft, Teachers for Taft, and Labor for Taft. Well before 1950 the structure was so self-sufficient that some of his running mates grumbled about his lack of teamwork.[11]

Partly because organized labor insisted on attacking him, Taft also found it easy to raise funds. Indeed, so many thousands of people from other states wrote to enclose checks that he felt obliged to intervene. Save your money for Republicans in your own state, he told them; there was more than enough in Ohio. As indeed there was. Using a mailing list provided by *Reader's Digest*, Taft's fund raisers secured seventy thousand $1 contributions. Meanwhile, Ben Tate, his finance chairman, was working wonders with wealthy businessmen, especially in the Midwest. Before the campaign ended, Taft's own organization had raised at least $500,-000, more than three times the $150,000 he had been blamed for spending to win both a primary and an election in 1938. The Ohio GOP raised $1.3 million more — at least $100,000 of which went directly to Taft, and much more of which aided him indirectly. And Taft had no hesitation about spending it. Even if it cost $10,000 a month for office expenses alone in 1949, he wrote Gradison that February, "I think it will be well worthwhile. This is not going to be a pink tea." [12]

Taft also worked hard to win the press. His first move on entering a town was to see the local publisher, explain his views, and ask for support. Well before the summer of 1950 it was clear that the publishers needed little persuasion, and by November only three of Ohio's major papers — the Dayton *News*, the Springfield *Sun*, and the Lancaster *Eagle Gazette* — endorsed Ferguson. Some of the others actually doctored syndicated columns in their effort to wreck the union drive in Ohio. And Taft got help from the national press as well. *Collier's* let him write an article, *Newsweek* twice placed him on its cover, and even *Time*, so critical in the past, gave him a favorable cover story in the issue before election day. The thought of Ferguson as a senator probably accounted for much of the favorable attention Taft received. But it was nonetheless gratifying to get it. The 1950 campaign was one in which he could not complain of bias from the press.[13]

In the course of his efforts to gain favorable publicity, Taft moved closer than before toward the world of public relations. In late 1950, Guylay and seven or eight other paid staff members moved to Cincinnati for the campaign. Making free use of polls, Guylay concluded that Taft himself was the issue of the campaign, and he set out to humanize him. "T-A-F-T" — "Tried And Found True" — became a central theme. At first, Guylay recalled, Taft resisted his efforts. Though agreeing to do the weekly news column, he balked at cutting his newspaper articles to the maximum of 650 words which Guylay had arranged with the local papers. "I can't cut it," Taft complained. But Guylay insisted, and gradually, grudgingly, his candidate learned the merits of brevity. Taft also learned to dictate columns quickly and efficiently, and he never missed a deadline, even while on the road. At the peak of the campaign "Washington Report," attractively set out in two columns under his picture, brought the readers of nearly two hundred Ohio papers his views on the issues.

Taft was slower to learn the art of mastering the question-and-answer format of his weekly radio broadcasts. Though his own staff prepared the questions in advance, he seemed at first tense and uncertain. His voice sounded twangy, nasal, occasionally loud and harsh. And he insisted on being himself. There was little humor, much abstract talk about "liberty" versus "socialism," heavy doses of statistics, no attempt at folksiness. Franklin D. Roosevelt, a genius over the air, had told the people what he was trying to do for their lives; Taft persisted in talking about principles.[14]

Beginning in August 1950, Taft dropped all pose of using the radio merely to inform the voters. As he did so, he spoke more extemporaneously, more aggressively, perhaps more effectively. Guylay, still anxious to humanize his man, also insisted on including occasional personal questions. "I suppose you're looking forward to your annual visit to Murray Bay," the announcer asked kindly. "Yes," Taft replied evenly, "because it's a chance to see all my grandchildren." "Senator," the announcer said, "you are the best informed man in Washington. What do you think about . . . ?" "Well," Taft drawled modestly, "I'm not the best informed man in Washington, but I see those who are every day, and I . . ." The broadcasts may have done little more than confirm what many people already thought about him. Yet they probably did him no harm, and revealed his determination to try almost anything the publicists thought necessary to win.[15]

All these efforts, impressive as they were, paled in significance to his traveling. Until September, Senate business kept him in Washington more often than he wished, but he still flew to Ohio as frequently as possible. "I don't think Ferguson is the most formidable candidate in the world," he explained, "but he is not to be laughed off as a candidate, whatever kind of a Senator he might make." By springtime he had visited the few counties he missed in 1949, and by late summer he was preparing to visit all eighty-eight counties a second time.[16]

During the ensuing campaign tour, Taft occasionally seemed more relaxed and folksy than in the past. One newsman watched him talk warmly with people at a county fair and concluded that he was a "new Taft." Reporters also found him a little readier than in previous campaigns to stop, talk, and even to joke a little with them. After touring a grimy Hamilton foundry, he went into the men's room to wash the dust from his hands. "What do you think now of campaign dirt?" he quipped to newsmen. On another occasion a reporter eating with him in an expensive restaurant watched his awkward pleasure when half a dozen people stopped by the table to wish him luck. "You know," Taft laughed, "sometimes I think it a pity that voting is not restricted only to the fat cats. If that were only so, I could be elected to anything." [17]

Most of the time, the pace of campaigning gave him little rest, and his energy astounded even his old friends. Up at dawn, he pushed himself until late at night for five, sometimes six days a week before returning to Indian Hill to be with Martha. Often driving his car himself, he thought nothing of making three or four major speeches a day, of marching through factories to shake hands with the union men who were being taught to hate him, of standing uncovered in the rain, of nourishing himself on cold and unpalatable food. What are your main assets as a candidate, he was asked. "A cast iron stomach and good digestion," he answered drily. By election day, he reckoned later, he had given 873 speeches, spoken 147 times over the radio, and toured 334 industrial plants since starting his first tour in 1949. And late at night he pored over election statistics and personally informed county chairmen how many votes he expected them to produce in November. "His endurance impresses everyone who tries to keep up with him," *Newsweek* reported. "Probably no other candidate in the history of Ohio politics," an Ohio newsman added in November, "has made so many speeches, travelled so many miles, or was face to face with so many voters as has Taft in the now ending campaign." [18]

.

With both sides fighting hard to win, it was not surprising that the Senate race in Ohio, like many others in the country that unhappy autumn, degenerated into a brawl well before November. And both Taft and Ferguson seemed willing to engage in it.

Taft had at first hoped to keep to a high plane, to approach people directly, to explain the Taft-Hartley Act, to win through sheer hard work. But he noticed the rapport he engendered when talking about communism, and soon he was sounding almost like McCarthy himself. "Because of the administration's strong Communist sympathies, which apparently existed before and about the time of the Yalta conference," he charged in Dayton, "we have placed Russia in a commanding presence in Europe . . . and in China." The demands of the Korean war, he emphasized over the radio, "may well require the drafting of every American boy of nineteen for two years' service in the Army. They will certainly involve taxes higher than we have levied on our people before. These sacrifices result directly from the fact that this administration has lost the peace after the American people won the war." [19]

He also spoke bitterly of the CIO-PAC. "The technique used by the Political Action Committee," he proclaimed in Euclid, "is strictly the Communist technique . . . The PAC campaign has been identical with that of the Communist Party." The PAC, he insisted, "was conceived in Communism, had Communist midwives assisting at its birth and was carefully nurtured in its formative period by Communist teachers." Taft was careful never to say that the PAC was then communist, but he encouraged voters to think that communists had dominated it at the beginning. Some Republicans really believed this, but there was abundant evidence to the contrary, and in repeating such a charge Taft was letting partisanship override his respect for facts.[20]

Why Taft waged such a rough campaign puzzled some people who had always admired his decency and focus on the issues. But the reasons seemed compelling to him and his friends, and no one in the Taft camp seemed to doubt them. The unions had invaded, the party must win, Trumanism must be discredited. Taft, like Republicans throughout the nation in that acrimonious and frustrating year, yearned for victory against a foe which he passionately believed was destroying the country. The end, it seemed without much reflection, justified the means.

Besides, he could not match the excesses of his opponents, who reached remarkable heights of superpatriotism. Taft, said a United Auto Workers flier, "votes the Communist line on foreign policy matters. Yes sir, every time Congress was asked to shell out money to fight Communism, Taft was against it . . . You can take his vote against the Marshall Plan, the arms assistance program — and it [sic] fits exactly with what the Daily Worker approves." [21] Not to be outdone, the Ohio State Council of Carpenters produced a pamphlet including such headlines as "How He Helped Hitler" and "Why Commies Love Him," and the Citizens Committee for Ferguson of Cincinnati published a tabloid likening Taft's voting record to that of Vito Marcantonio, a New York congressman who usually voted the communist line. When even these tactics seemed insufficient, Taft's opponents freely circulated a photograph showing him with Earl Browder, once America's top Communist party leader. In so doing, they conveniently neglected to explain that the photo was taken in 1936, when Taft appeared on stage to debate Browder before the American Youth Congress.[22]

Ferguson himself, a veteran of Ohio politics, did not shrink from the fray. Taft's remarks about Korea, he said as early as August 10, are "the stuff that treason is made of. I believe the time has come when a spade should be called a spade." Two weeks later he elaborated on this theme. "While American blood is flowing in Korea," he said, "Taft is playing politics as usual . . . It is my personal

belief that Taft right now is secretly hoping for an American defeat in Korea as his last desperate chance for reelection." On October 21 Ferguson abandoned all scruples. If Taft wanted to be "fair
and frank," Ferguson proclaimed, "he would explain to the people
of Ohio his own association with communist leaders." Commenting on the photograph of Taft and Browder, he continued, "What
other Communist has he been associating with? Was he in sympathy with the Russian efforts in our behalf in the war? Why is the
record of Senator Taft during the years he has been in the United
States Senate similar to that of Congressman Vito Marcantonio of
New York, widely known exponent of the views of the Kremlin?" [23]

Sporadic acts of violence and intimidation accompanied these
rhetorical excesses. In Waynesburg someone splattered Taft in the
chest with a tomato. In Dayton thugs beat a Taft worker uncon-
scious. In Cincinnati they threw rocks through a car window. On
other occasions they let the air out of the tires of cars at GOP rallies, defaced Republican billboards, and intimidated workers who
did not contribute money to fight Taft's campaign.[24] And at the
strife-ridden Youngstown Sheet and Tube Company, union leaders
called a strike that shut down the boiler room and threw some thirteen hundred of the men out of work a few hours before Taft's
announced visit. When he arrived at the grimy gates later that
morning, worried officials informed him of the potentially violent
picket line outside the plant. Cheerfully, Taft ordered his car into
the dusty heat of the valley. When he reached the pickets, he
found them milling about in his way, jeering, catcalling. The
mood was tense and ugly. But he told his driver to stop, leaned far
out of the car window, and waved. "Hello there, fellows," he
called out. Taken aback, the workers fell silent. He then moved
on, entered the plant, and held out his hand to those men still at
work amidst the roaring flames and giant rollers of the mill. Some
ignored him, but many more, perhaps angered by the union's precipitate action, responded. "Sure, I'm going to vote for Taft," one
told a reporter. "I did before, and he's a better man now than
before. I can't understand these other guys. They say he hates
labor but they clam up when you ask them for evidence." [25]

As if in triumph, Taft strode an estimated four miles through the mills that day, and the next day he marched through plants in Warren and Ashtabula. Apparently oblivious to danger, he persisted in visiting factories throughout the campaign. After Youngstown no one doubted his personal courage.

•

By election day, November 7, 1950, MacArthur's forces were already discovering Chinese Communist soldiers in North Korea. But the general remained confident; they were "volunteers." With Americans racing toward the Yalu River, the war would soon be over. American boys might be home by Christmas.

Perhaps because of America's apparent success in the war, perhaps because of the uncertainty of the times, most analysts refused to discount Ferguson's chances. "An even-money bet," *Newsweek* declared a week before the election. "A close race . . . Few bets were being placed on the outcome," added the New York *Times* on November 6.[26] Taft himself had reasons to be more confident, for Guylay's polls had consistently shown him with 60 per cent of the vote.[27] But Taft shrewdly preferred to keep the polls confidential in order to sustain the drive of his supporters. Like most politicians, he also wondered and worried. At the last minute he even wired Arthur Vandenberg for help. In view of rumors to the contrary, Taft said, would you send a statement "of your belief that my presence in Congress would contribute to wise decisions on foreign policy as well as on domestic matters?" Vandenberg, weak with the cancer that was to kill him five months later, gamely complied. Taft, he wired Ohioans, "is unquestionably needed in the United States Senate, and I hope he wins." [28]

Election day was mild and pleasant throughout most of Ohio, and the voters thronged to the polls. Taft stayed at Sky Farm, then set off after supper for his headquarters at the *Times-Star*. With him were Bob, Jr., Lloyd, their wives, his brother Charlie, cousin Hulbert, and even Martha, who seemed well enough to leave her wheelchair and get about with cane in hand. Early in the evening Taft knew he would win, at midnight he predicted a 250,000 vote margin of victory, and at 2:15 AM Ferguson conceded. "You not only handed me a licking," Ferguson said, "but also gave me the greatest surprise of my life." Overjoyed, Republicans celebrated far into the morning.[29]

The completed returns revealed a victory even more astounding than Taft had predicted election night. Lausche retained the governorship by a margin of 152,000 votes. ("The extraordinary popularity of Mr. Lausche," Taft grumbled privately a few days later, "is wholly undeserved . . . businessmen . . . can't seem to understand that the victory of a conservative Democrat can often do more harm in the long run than that of a left-winger.") But Republicans won practically everything else, including fifteen of Ohio's twenty-three seats in the House of Representatives. Taft himself, running well ahead of his ticket, rolled up 1,645,643 votes to Ferguson's 1,214,459. His plurality of 431,184 was the second largest in the history of Ohio senatorial elections (next to Theodore Burton's 572,000 in the Hoover landslide of 1928), and his total vote was the biggest ever accorded a Republican office seeker in the history of Ohio. Most remarkable, he carried eighty-four of the eighty-eight counties, including all the major ones with heavy industrial concentrations. In the eighteen largest counties with populations of 75,000 or more, he won by an average margin of 53 per cent. By any standard — his own narrow margin of 17,000 in 1944, Dewey's loss of the state by 7000 in 1948, Ferguson's triumph as auditor in 1948 by 291,000 — Taft had scored the most resounding victory of his career and the most impressive triumph, given the militance of his opponents, scored by any Republican senator in 1950.[30]

In retrospect the analysts agreed on a number of elements behind the victory. One of these was Ferguson himself. Even before the election labor leaders had observed the reluctance of the rank and file to contribute to his campaign and had watched many ordinarily regular Democrats desert to his opponent. Lausche himself, silent to the end, was widely presumed to have voted for Taft at the polls.[31]

The new ballot also helped — probably in two different ways. First, it forced voters to look at the names of the major candidates, and in so doing worked to the advantage of well-known incumbents. Second, it facilitated split ticket voting. Lausche carried

Cuyahoga County by some 161,000 votes — or more than the plurality by which he won the state as a whole. Yet Taft also won it (for the only time in his life) by nearly 23,000. After the election he estimated that the ballot gave him between 100,000 and 200,-000 of his 430,000 vote majority. Although it is impossible to verify this estimate, observers later accepted 100,000 as accurate.[32]

The experts also agreed that he had waged an extraordinarily aggressive, well-organized campaign — in short, that he was an effective vote getter in his own right, irrespective of opponent or form of the ballot. As they correctly observed, he was a senator, right or wrong, of stature. He had also campaigned tirelessly, cooperated with the regular organization, shrewdly pushed voter registration drives into the suburban and middle class wards while leaving labor precincts alone, and relied on reaction against union excesses to draw out thousands of ordinarily apathetic voters. The result was that the turnout in his race was 2,860,000 — 500,000 more than had ever voted in nonpresidential years before in Ohio, and almost 640,000 more than had cast their ballots in the off-year senatorial race of 1946. "Of the 500,000 votes over and above all previous off-year elections," Taft concluded, "400,000 came from the program of organization which we set up." Again, Taft's claim was impossible to prove, especially since Lausche and his opponent Don H. Ebright had attracted 30,000 more voters than had Taft and Ferguson. Yet the gubernatorial vote usually exceeded all others in off-years, and there was no denying that voters had turned out in record numbers or that Taft received more votes than anyone else from either party. Perhaps he was a vote getter after all.[33]

Two other elements probably added to his margin. First, 1950 was a Republican year, as had been 1938, when he entered the Senate. Americans worried about communist influence at home, its apparent extension abroad, and perhaps about the reports of Chinese soldiers crossing the Yalu. They chafed at inflation, at the pressures of postwar life. Taft, like Richard Nixon, who captured a Senate seat in California, like Everett Dirksen, who overwhelmed Scott Lucas, the Democratic Senate leader from Illinois, and like many other Republicans in 1950, benefited from a tide that was sweeping many Democrats out of office and that was to leave the

Truman administration defending itself against partisan on-slaughts for the next two years.

Second, Taft seemed to benefit from the excesses of labor. Some analysts exaggerated the effect of these excesses. Indeed, Taft him-self estimated that Ferguson had not only swept the lower class black wards but had captured 60 per cent of the labor vote. Yet considering the union campaign against him, Taft had done well indeed to capture 40 per cent, and in some areas — as in the four heavily unionized precincts in Youngstown — he won 63 per cent of the vote compared with Dewey's 44 per cent in 1948. "We didn't want labor to go too far," one worker explained. "Ferguson would have been a yes man for the labor party," said another. The election, Taft concluded with some justification, "seems to show that the American workingman will reject a strictly class appeal." [34]

Above all, the figures suggested that he had succeeded in mobi-lizing suburbanites, farmers, and residents of small towns. Many of these people bitterly resented the politicking of the unions, and their record-shattering turnout accounted for the remarkable in-crease in the overall vote. Victory, Taft explained in a thank-you note to Vandenberg, stemmed from the frontal attack against Tru-man and from "resentment against the labor union crowd." [35]

•

Six days after the election Taft strode into a press conference in Washington. Reporters, cameramen, and photographers pressed against him. Klieg lights shone into his face. Excited onlookers jammed the corners of the room. It was Taft's triumphal return to Washington, the high point of a long and successful career in poli-tics, the homecoming of the senator whom Republican state chair-men had already picked as their favorite for the GOP presidential nomination in 1952.[36]

Taft did not disappoint the crowd. Remarkably fresh after the ordeal of campaigning, he seemed relaxed, casual, unusually at ease in the spotlight. He beamed, smiled, joked with the press, and charmed the assembled multitude.

Yet victory did not soften him. On the contrary, it confirmed his faith that the hard line of 1950 offered the best way of ousting the

Going to be rough sledding. *L. D. Warren, Cincinnati* Enquirer

Democratic administration. And privately he was already looking ahead. "I don't think there is any solution to the present problem," he wrote, "except to throw out the present administration at the first opportunity. Their policies have led America into a dangerous situation, and they are utterly incapable of getting us out." [37] For the son of William Howard Taft, for the apostle of Republicanism, there was no euphoria, only the competition ahead.

Yet in this partisanship, this competitiveness, lay the seeds of trouble. Had he stopped to reflect, he might have wondered about the real meaning of his mandate. What, indeed, had the voters approved? Were they really furious at what he repeatedly described as the administration's "socialistic" principles? Almost reflexively, he thought so, and instead of mellowing or trying to appeal to moderates, he stepped up his partisan attacks. For Taft, 1950 ended on a partisan note as it had begun.

In eschewing the politics of accommodation, Taft gladdened the hearts of the Republican stalwarts who had come to revere him since 1938. But what of the millions who had elected Democrats since 1932 and who had nominated Republican moderates for the presidency since 1936? While Taft exulted in Washington, Henry Cabot Lodge, Jr., handsome, articulate, shrewd, watched disapprovingly in the Senate. Sherman Adams, cool and cautious, waited restlessly at the State House in New Hampshire. Tom Dewey, winning a third term as governor of New York, stonily awaited the future. And Dwight David Eisenhower, president of Columbia University, already Dewey's choice for 1952, observed quietly but uneasily from Morningside Heights.

CHAPTER 31

Foreign Policy Moves In, 1951

"I AM going to have to learn more about foreign policy matters than I have known in the past."

"People have accused me of moving into foreign policy. The fact is that foreign policy moved in on me [laughter]." [1]

Both statements were Taft's, the first in a letter to an old friend after the 1950 elections, the second to the annual convention of the United States Chamber of Commerce five months later in Washington. Together they revealed his awareness that foreign policy questions were becoming so pressing, so controversial, and so politically beneficial to the Republican party that they could not be ignored. With Arthur Vandenberg's life ebbing away in Michigan, Taft felt he had to involve himself. Foreign affairs were again to drag him from his lifelong preoccupation with domestic problems.

He was less than happy about this turn of events. "I wish I could just stay out of that," he complained to a reporter, "but of course I can't." He meant it when he said that "foreign policy moved in on me," and he even refused to take a place on the Foreign Relations Committee. "I do not feel that a position on that committee is of the importance attributed to it by the public. The truth is that the President has very wide power in foreign relations . . . I think I can maintain more freedom on basic questions if I am not a member of that Committee." [2]

His uneasiness in his new role stemmed partly from lack of preparation. As he had been modest enough to recognize, he knew relatively little about foreign affairs, and he had scorned the Pentagon and State Department over the years. There were few experts he would turn to for help, and in January he admitted it. Who are your advisers, a reporter asked? "The same as yours," Taft retorted. "You read the advice from military critics in the newspapers every day. That is my best source of information." Taft, who had spent so much time on domestic matters, leaped into the fray of foreign policy in 1951 without finding the time to brief himself.[3]

Perhaps for this reason his statements sometimes sounded inconsistent. He denounced the communists as vigorously as ever and continued to blame the administration for softness and stupidity dating back to the Teheran conference in 1943. Soviet behavior, he told a friend, was "truculent beyond any American's imagination," and the United States must build up its air force to "where it is clear that we could drop atomic bombs if they began a war." Similarly, he derided the United Nations. It was finished, he wrote, "as far as an agency for the prevention of aggression. The veto power has killed it." America, he said, "might consider the dissolution of the U.N. and the formation of another U.N. without Russia." [4]

Yet Taft sometimes sounded conciliatory toward the Soviet Union. "I am far more optimistic than you," he responded to pacifist leader A. J. Muste, who had written him for his views. "I have never given the same importance to the Russian military position as have many other Americans." The Soviets, he continued, had grievous internal problems, and if the United States held firm, they would shrink from aggressive behavior.[5] And to the Socialist leader Norman Thomas, whose pacifism both Taft and Martha had long admired, he complained about administration rhetoric. "I see no reason for the President and the Secretary of State and everybody else calling the Russians names on every occasion. I realize that they are impossible to deal with, but I really do not believe they intend to start a third world war." For all his hatred of communism Taft sounded ready to proclaim a policy of what was later called peaceful coexistence.[6]

Still, two basic beliefs continued to form a fairly consistent core to Taft's thinking on foreign policy. First, he insisted on limiting America's overseas commitments. "Nobody today can be an isolationist," he wrote in January. "The only question is the degree to which we shall take action throughout the entire world." America had obligations that it had to honor — such as NATO — and it could not turn a blind eye to such countries as Formosa or Israel. But the United States had limited funds and problems at home and must therefore curb its commitments. "If the Republicans take over," he wrote late in 1950, "their policy will be sound and constructive — probably not so liberal in giving away American money, but certainly not one of isolationism." [7]

This fear of overcommitment was rooted in Taft's even deeper faith in liberty, which made him shrink from a foreign policy that would cost large sums of money, increase the power of the military, and transform American society into what he called a garrison state. The way to counter communism abroad was therefore not to thrust American men and money overseas (though he voted reluctantly to extend the draft in March), but to adhere to libertarian practice at home and to demonstrate to the world the source of America's greatness. This trust in the power of example had long exposed him to criticism from the internationalists, who said he was placing his bets on words, not on believable commitments abroad. But Taft ignored such criticism. "I am convinced," he wrote Muste, "that if we are smart enough we can so present the advantages of freedom to the world that gradually communism itself will be driven back into the borders of Russia and liberty will again become the ideal which it was in the nineteenth century." [8]

·

It was one thing to adhere to certain suppositions about the world, another to arrive at prudent and politically possible practices. With the Cold War more frigid than ever and Chinese Communists driving into South Korea, finding workable policies seemed more difficult to do in the early 1950's than at any time in the past. Americans recalled the sacrifices of World War II, trembled at the apparent growth of communist power, and oscillated between withdrawing to the security of the Western Hemisphere and striking out against the "enemy" wherever he was imagined to be. As Taft let foreign policy "move in" on him, he stepped into a quicksand.

Taft himself helped precipitate the first major foreign policy controversy of 1951, over the military implementation of NATO. Having voted against the pact in 1949 because he opposed sending arms to western Europe, he grew alarmed late in 1950 to learn that the administration was thinking of dispatching American troops as well. "The most important question before Congress," he wrote Vandenberg in November 1950, "is the size of the armed forces required for safety . . . It seems to me that the whole policy of building up very large land forces with the idea of throwing several million men into Europe in case of a Russian attack ought to be carefully studied." [9]

For the next month Taft continued to worry. "The thing about Europe," he wrote, "is can you defend it? If Russia has the atomic bomb, can't they knock the devil out of Europe?" Taft stated that he did not know the answer to his question, but that foreign policy "ought to be re-examined." (A "re-examinist," Acheson retorted contemptuously, "might be a farmer that goes out every morning and pulls up all his crops to see how they have done during the night.") Taft still resisted the idea of American troops committed to Europe under the nose of Soviet atomic weapons. "It seems to me," he explained to his old acquaintance John Foster Dulles, "that a large land force is of dubious value and that the defense of this country as well as the deterring of Russia rests far more on an all-powerful air force." [10]

On January 5, 1951, Taft publicly revealed his doubts by taking the Senate floor to deliver a ten-thousand-word speech. It was by far his most comprehensive address on foreign policy, and the most widely noted in the press. It also intensified what reporters dubbed the Senate's "Great Debate" over foreign policy.

His arguments were simple enough. The Soviets, he argued, did not want war. Yet Truman had already called General Dwight D. Eisenhower back into uniform and was preparing to send him to Europe, presumably as commander of NATO forces. Truman was also covertly planning to send 300,000 American combat soldiers to Europe and perhaps twice that many support troops. America, Taft was careful to say, must honor its NATO commitment, and it might well station a token force in Europe, but only after careful study, for such troops would strain the American economy and encourage the Europeans to depend on America instead of on themselves. The Soviets, he pointed out, had refrained from invading western Europe when it lay helpless; why provoke them unnecessarily? Besides, no conceivable number of American troops could hope to contend with the millions of Russian soldiers massed in Germany. Instead of trying to match the Soviet Union where it was strongest, America should build up its air and naval forces. Truman's ill-concealed plans, Taft concluded, were provocative, and they were unconstitutional. The President had no right to commit American troops abroad in peacetime without the prior approval of Congress.[11]

Those who had followed Taft's approach to foreign policy over the years admired his consistency. He had always criticized extensive American commitments abroad, supported what he called the policy of the "free hand," insisted on partisan debate over foreign policy, and demanded a meaningful congressional role in foreign policy making. But while he was speaking, Eisenhower was getting ready to fly to Europe to tell his old companions in arms of America's friendship. Paris, said the New York *Times,* was "amazed," the communists overjoyed, at the speech. And across the globe Chinese troops churned through the snow into Seoul, capital of South Korea. In such a frightening world a direct challenge from as important a senator as Taft could not be ignored.

Truman's supporters reacted sharply to Taft's speech. Democratic Senators Herbert Lehman of New York, Paul Douglas of Illinois, and J. William Fulbright of Arkansas repeatedly challenged him. They argued that he was offering Europe the prospect of getting bombed again by American planes. Taft, they added, said that American boys would not help and that despite the lesson of Korea air-sea forces could contain aggression. The State Department then unearthed a long-forgotten book to show that William Howard Taft, in his *Our Chief Magistrate and His Powers* (1916) had defended the authority of the President "to order the army and navy where he will." [12] Senator Lyndon B. Johnson of Texas, already the assistant Democratic leader after but two years in the Senate, compared Taft's analysis of Soviet intentions to that of Senator William Borah of Idaho concerning the Nazis in the summer of 1939. Borah, Johnson reminded the Senate, had coolly insisted the Germans did not want war. And Thomas Connally, the

Our new joint chiefs of staff. *Courtesy, The Washington (D.C.)* Star

loquacious, flamboyant Texan who was chairman of the Senate Foreign Relations Committee, said that Taft failed to sense the urgency of a strong stand against the Soviets, whose "puppets" were killing Americans that very day in Korea. "In Texas," he closed with characteristic flourish, "we are strongly of the opinion that when a person shoots at you, he is being unfriendly." [13]

Some Republicans also rejected Taft's arguments. Chief among these were Henry Cabot Lodge and William Knowland. Taft, they said, did not understand that Europeans could not handle their burden alone, that the prospect of American "defense" of their soil by bombers appalled them. Lodge also pointed out that Taft argued both that American troops might provoke the Soviet Union and that the Soviets could overwhelm such troops. But if this latter assumption was correct, why should the Soviets regard

American soldiers as a threat? American forces, Lodge argued, would contribute to the security of western Europe, stimulate America's allies to greater defense efforts, and deter instead of provoke the Soviet Union.[14]

From the start Taft avoided a wholly negative stand regarding the troops. Appearing before "Meet the Press" on January 7, 1951, he said that he would not object to two or three American divisions in Europe, and privately he told friends he would agree to as many as five.[15] In a speech to the National Press Club on January 9 he startled some of his listeners by proclaiming himself "quite prepared to sit down with the President of the United States" or anyone else of authority in the administration who wished to discuss foreign policy. To no one's surprise neither Truman nor Acheson responded enthusiastically to this uncharacteristic offer. But reporters noted that Taft had spoken seriously. Had the administration seized his feeler, it was conceivable, though unlikely, that he could have edged gingerly into the role that Vandenberg had played before him.[16]

Instead, Taft was left free to pursue his own instincts, and these proved hostile to the administration. Defense policy, he complained privately, "has been dominated by those who believe in land warfare. It is they who are responsible for this European adventure, which seems to me so dangerous." The "welfare state," he wrote another friend, "means equal misery for all . . . At the present moment, however, we seem to be stepping from the welfare state into the garrison state." And he proved as hostile as ever to Acheson. "He probably has as bad judgment as anyone I have ever seen in that position," he told a friend.[17]

Taft also refused to let his father be used against him. His book had noted the *power* of the President to dispatch troops, not his *right*. Truman lacked constitutional authority to order troops to Europe without congressional consent, just as he had lacked it in sending them to Korea in 1950. In this frame of mind Taft backed a resolution introduced by Kenneth S. Wherry on January 8. It proclaimed that it was the sense of the Senate that no United States ground forces be assigned to Europe for NATO purposes until Congress so authorized. While presumably not binding on Truman, the resolution could have forced him to defy the Senate. From the start it became the key issue in the debate.[18]

After the initial charges and countercharges the antagonists settled down to weeks of talk on the Wherry resolution. But when Eisenhower seemed ready to settle for four American divisions, or approximately 100,000 men, it was clear that the two sides might compromise their differences. When the debate ended in early April, it left Eisenhower in command of a defense force that was to include four new American divisions in 1951. If Truman wanted more, he was to come to Congress for prior approval. Taft was pleased to join thirty-seven other Republicans in passing the amendment, 49 to 43, which called on Truman to come hat in hand in the future. But he then felt obliged to approve the four divisions, and he joined a majority of 69 who voted — against 21 holdouts — to table a revised version of Wherry's amendment. The great debate had ended with the administration in tenuous command of its policy.[19]

Taft and his friends had scored some impressive points during the debate. He had raised the question, though not pointedly enough to satisfy the Left, of the effects of military spending on "progress of every kind of education, social welfare, and many other matters in which the Americans are vitally interested." He was correct and surely relevant in arguing that the Founding Fathers had not intended to give the President the powers he was invoking; indeed, Truman might have avoided the debate entirely had he sought congressional authorization from the start. Taft was right in insisting that the administration had deceived the Senate when it claimed in 1949 that no American troops would be sent. He predicted that NATO could never match Soviet ground forces in Europe — and that the effort to try would fire the arms race. And in maintaining that the Russians did not want war, he stated a point of view which, given Soviet secrecy, was impossible to disprove.[20]

Yet the issue was not so simple. The uneasy peace that hung over western Europe in the decades after the great debate may have stemmed as much from American firmness, Truman's included, as from Soviet moderation. Subsequent events also proved Taft an alarmist in suggesting the troops might provoke the Soviets to attack; Russia watched, angrily but peacefully, as NATO forces expanded slowly and even as German troops were integrated into them.

In the course of the debate Taft also assumed militant positions that distressed pacifists and isolationists as well as internationalists. He proclaimed himself ready to defend such places as Britain, Japan, Formosa, the Philippines, Indonesia, Australia, and New Zealand, and perhaps even Spain, Singapore, and the Malay Peninsula. Taft's rationale was that American air-sea forces could easily protect these insular and peninsular regions. But many friends of western Europe argued that he was placing defensibility ahead of the national interest, and pacifists and old-line isolationists were appalled that Taft, the apostle of restraint, had moved so far toward globalism. "For isolationists," Muste commented, "these Americans do certainly get around." [21]

Allies such as Wherry also emerged pained at Taft's support of four divisions. Some of them had never reconciled themselves to the NATO pact, and all of them refused to endorse the sending of troops. If Taft really believed American soldiers were provocative, they argued cogently, why send any at all? Because Wherry and the twenty others who voted against sending the divisions saw Taft as an ally against the Eastern internationalists, they did not break openly with him. But these wholly disenchanted foes of NATO recognized that Taft was closer to the bipartisan consensus on foreign policy than many people realized.

The internationalists, however, also remained dissatisfied with Taft's performance. In the midst of the Cold War how could he claim to be against communism, yet refuse to support concrete measures to stop it? Were not a strong navy and a powerful air force more provocative to the Soviets than a few divisions in Europe? As the newsman James Reston pointed out, Taft had taken a precarious position that exposed him to criticism from Democrats, liberal journalists, expansionists, and internationalist Republicans.[22] "Taft," one angry citizen wrote Truman, "is current Colonel McGoofus . . . Why not publicize his errors in judgment the past ten years? No one in public life has made more mistakes." Another went further. "Call in some exterminators," he wrote, to try to rid the Senate of the odor left by the following Senators especially the one from Ohio, R.A.T., his initials spell his true self . . . If they want to live in isolation, can't you do something to help them get into Siberia? [23]

Truman's friends — to say nothing of the internationalist Republicans — no doubt anticipated Taft's stand. They were suspicious of the Soviet Union, afraid of any communist gains in Europe, and convinced from recollections of appeasement in the 1930's that firmness was the way to deal with potential enemies, and they perceived in his arguments merely confirmation of what they had always thought him to be — a harsh, quibbling, partisan isolationist. Whatever Taft did, it was hardly likely that men like Dean Acheson, Henry Luce, and Thomas E. Dewey would have applauded him.

Yet if these people did not matter too much, Eisenhower did. Widely respected for his generalship in World War II, "Ike" possessed so much personal warmth and genius for conciliating people that politicians of both parties were turning to him as their candidate for 1952. Dewey had already announced his support in 1950, and many others were known to be ready to follow suit if the general would offer them any encouragement. Obviously, it behooved Taft to keep such a rival out of the race.

Eisenhower would perhaps have been glad to steer clear of electoral politics. He believed firmly in Truman's plans to commit American troops and seemed prepared to spend the next few years in Paris working on the defense of western Europe. But before taking himself out of the presidential race, Eisenhower determined to check congressional sentiment; as he told the story later, he asked to see Taft during the debate. When Taft volunteered to come unannounced to the Pentagon, the general was so encouraged that he called in two aides to draft a statement to be issued that evening. "Having been called back to military duty," Eisenhower remembered saying, "I want to announce that my name may not be used by anyone as a candidate for President — and if they [sic] do I will repudiate such efforts." Pleased, Eisenhower folded up the statement and stuck it in his pocket.

When Taft arrived at the Pentagon, he was quietly whisked to

Eisenhower's office. There the two men had what the general later called a "long talk" — the first extended tête-à-tête they had ever had. Eisenhower recalled that he wanted to know but one thing: Would Taft and his congressional associates "agree that collective security is necessary for us in Western Europe — and will you support this idea as a bipartisan policy?" If the answer were "yes," Eisenhower continued, he would spend his "next years" in Europe carrying out the policy. But if it were "no," "then NATO would be set back, and I would probably be back in the United States."

Eisenhower thought his message was clear. But Taft refused to commit himself. "This," the general remembered, "aroused my fears that isolationism was stronger in the Congress than I had previously suspected." When Taft left, Eisenhower called in his assistants, took the statement from his pocket, and tore it up. It seemed that Taft had thrown away a perfect opportunity to keep his major rival out of the race.[24]

Eisenhower's story may have claimed too much. It was not entirely clear from his retrospective account (Taft left none) exactly when the meeting occurred, or who the aides were who allegedly witnessed the destruction of the statement. Could he really have expected Taft, who was leading the debate, to make a commitment to collective security in Europe, let alone involve his colleagues in it? If he had hoped for such a promise, why did he not actually tell Taft he would issue his statement that very night? Finally, how unequivocal would the statement have been? Given Eisenhower's enormous popularity, it was doubtful that his avid supporters, who later refused to be discouraged, would have paid much attention to it. It was also not surprising, given the magnitude of the request, that Taft was (as Eisenhower phrased it) "a bit suspicious of my motives," or that he refused to bind himself to a policy Republicans had been questioning in the Senate. Thus Taft's response was neither a blunder nor — the reverse — an act of political integrity. It was an episode that symbolized the political vulnerability to which Taft's views on foreign policy had exposed him.

·

Whatever the wisdom of Taft's stand on western Europe, it was largely consistent with his past statements. He had opposed American military commitments to Europe in 1940 and 1941, tried to cut funding for the Marshall Plan, and voted against NATO. By 1950 and 1951 he still favored preserving a relatively free hand and keeping American soldiers at home.

Unfortunately for his reputation as a thinker on foreign policy, his position on Asia in 1951 showed no such consistency. Before the year had ended, he had contradicted himself more than once. He was not alone in doing so; many Americans were frustrated after the Chinese streamed across the Yalu River in the fall. But he was at center stage in the Senate, and his uncertain path on Korea left critics doubtful of his motives and of his ability to understand.

Like most Americans, Taft had supported the fateful American decision in 1950 to pursue the enemy toward the Yalu. "We had to cross the 38th parallel," he wrote in January 1951. "I don't see how we could permit an aggressor to retire behind his boundary and remain unpunished." Like most Americans, he assumed the Chinese would stay out.[25]

When the Chinese moved in, he quickly grew alarmed. "Everyone here in Washington is tremendously upset by the developments in Korea," he wrote Horace in early December. "There seems to be no alternative today from a complete withdrawal from Korea." Worried because Horace was still in Zurich doing graduate work, Taft concluded: "If we are forced out of Korea, it will be very difficult to defend Japan. If Japan goes, I would not be surprised to see a pretty aggressive move by Russia in Europe, so figure out how you can best get home if necessary." [26]

Less than a month later Taft began professing his fears in public. "What would you have done about Korea if you had been President in June 1950?" reporters asked him in early January. "I would have stayed out," Taft replied. "You have my speech on the Korean war." "What would you do now?" they persisted. "I think I would get out and fall back to a defensible position in Japan and Formosa," he answered. "I certainly would if I thought that there was danger by staying of losing any considerable number of men." The United States, he added, should take the "shackles" off Chiang Kai-shek and help him make a "full scale diversion action" in Korea or South China. In yearning to pull American

"You can still catch the boat if you hurry."
From The Herblock Book (*Beacon Press, 1952*)

troops from the Asian mainland, Taft was following his basic position against committing soldiers abroad.[27]

In April, however, President Truman dismissed General MacArthur from his command. MacArthur had publicly demanded stronger action to end the stalemate that was descending on the battlefield. America, he argued, must unleash Chiang Kai-shek's forces, bomb Manchurian installations, blockade China, and fight on to victory, even if such an effort meant protracted warfare. Truman, who feared for the security of western Europe, shrank from such a war in Asia, and with MacArthur openly insubordinate, had no choice but to fire him. For many Americans, however, MacArthur was a symbol of firmness in Asia, a heroic figure snatched from his command by a vacillating administration. When MacArthur flew to the United States a few days later, he received near hysterical greetings, and when he addressed Congress, millions of Americans felt him pull at their heartstrings: "Why, my soldiers asked of me, surrender military advantages to an enemy in the field? [Pause.] I could not answer . . . Old soldiers," MacArthur concluded, "never die; they just fade away."

MacArthur's dismissal seemed almost criminal to a band of congressmen and senators who had been demanding American militance in Asia. Labeled "Asia-firsters" by their critics, they actually differed considerably among themselves. Some complained that America — "winner" of all its wars — was not victorious in this one. Others thought the administration soft on communism at home and abroad. With MacArthur, many held that the crusade against communism must be waged in Asia or it could not be won anywhere else. Most of these "Asia-firsters" were Republicans — men like Kenneth Wherry, Styles Bridges, and William Jenner who had long denounced Truman's foreign policies. When Jenner and Joseph McCarthy heard of MacArthur's dismissal, they demanded Truman's impeachment.

Taft contented himself at first by saying that American soldiers had lost a "great general." But he also had reasons to join the Asia-firsters. Despite the coolness between his father and MacArthur's father in the Philippines, he had always esteemed the general highly. "The ablest general that we have," he had written a friend in March 1945, "and a general most likely to avoid unnecessary sacrifice of life." Six months later, when MacArthur began his administration of Japan, Taft added that the general "seems to understand the psychology of other people and I doubt if anyone could handle the Japanese better than he. Also, he has a fine sense of the dramatic." MacArthur had later responded in kind. "I cannot tell you how greatly I admire your handling of affairs on the home front," he wrote Taft during the battle over price control in 1946. "Like your great father, you see clearly and act with courage and effectiveness." Though the two men corresponded only sporadically in the next few years, they shared a common antipathy to the Truman administration.[28]

Taft was moved still more by his disgust with the administration's general policy in Asia. Truman, he conceded, "had every right" to dismiss MacArthur. But the President had "invited the war" prior to June 1950. He had then reversed himself to fight the North Koreans, only to refuse to punish the Chinese. Three courses, Taft continued, now remained open. One, ending the war by "appeasement," he rejected. A second was Truman's "Maginot Line policy," which called for a "stalemate war." It was "like a football game in which our team when it reaches the 50-yard line is always instructed to kick. Our team can never score." Clearly, Taft said, America must pursue a third course. This called for using Chiang Kai-shek's troops in Korea or South China and for the bombing of Chinese communications.[29]

Taft's quick support of bombing marked a significant new trend in his thinking, and MacArthur's triumphant homecoming then sustained it. "We listened to MacArthur today," he wrote after the general spoke to the Congress, "and he made a most effective speech. I cannot help but feel that the whole episode was completely to the advantage of the Republicans, and that Truman's efforts to pose as a man of peace will be easily exposed." By the end of April Taft was vigorously championing MacArthur's cause. The stalemate in Korea, he said, "could not go on forever." On the contrary, America "ought to try to win that war by every means at our command." This meant using Chiang Kai-shek's forces, bombing rail lines in Manchuria, going "the limit" in assisting Chiang against his communist foes, and perhaps imposing a blockade on the Chinese mainland. It also meant dismissing "any hesitation about the possibility that the Russians may come into the war." [30]

In the next six months Taft was usually careful to set some limits on American policy in Asia. He opposed putting American troops in China, recoiled from the idea of using atomic weapons, and continued to have doubts about imposing a blockade. Upset, a more militant Wherry exploded to a reporter, "Taft! Taft! That's all I hear — *Taft!* What will Taft do? How does Taft feel? What does Taft think? I don't care what Taft will do! I'm telling you what Ken Wherry will do!" As the fighting stabilized in July, Taft also conceded grudgingly the possible virtues of a settlement of boundaries at the Thirty-eighth Parallel.[31]

Yet most of Taft's statements about Asian policy in 1951 echoed the militant tone he had established in April. "I see nothing to do," he wrote in June, "except to clean up that war while using every means within our power." America should not make peace "until we are safely guaranteed a complete Korean republic covering all of Korea." Truman, he charged, got America into Korea "in one of those convulsive movements so typical of our foreign policy . . . This Korean War is a Truman war." It was "useless and expensive." The "net result of the whole proceeding," Taft exclaimed in August, "is the loss of 80,000 American casualties and billions of dollars and the destruction of the very country which we undertook to defend." Recklessly, Taft then insisted that "we abandoned Chiang Kai-shek . . . the State Department absolutely wanted the Communists to win in China." "Do you really mean that?" a reporter pressed him. Yes, Taft replied, "I think Secretary Acheson and the Far Eastern Division of the State Department did." "Why?" the newsman persisted. "Because in the State Department for a long time there's been a strong Communist sympathy, as far as the Chinese Communists are concerned." [32]

·

American policies — in particular Dean Acheson's failure early in 1950 to include Korea in a public description of America's probable defense perimeter — had perhaps encouraged the North Koreans to think of South Korea as a "soft spot" which the United Nations would not defend; in this limited sense the Korean war might have been the "unnecessary" conflict that Taft repeatedly called it. It was also "useless" in that UN forces failed to push the Chinese back to their borders.

But Taft otherwise presented a weak case. In addition to making McCarthy-like remarks about the State Department, he neglected to admit that he himself had proved relatively quiet concerning the fate of Chiang Kai-shek prior to 1949, that he had supported American intervention in June 1950, that he had offered no complaint against the decision to press on toward the Yalu, and that he had even talked of a withdrawal of American forces when they were being driven back early in 1951. Yet when Truman removed MacArthur, Taft turned about and called for military escalation (which he was simultaneously deploring in Europe), and demanded the use of Chiang Kai-shek's forces when most thoughtful critics knew they would be of little use against Mao Tse-tung. Taft's arguments, full of hindsight, represented a departure from his counsel of restraint in the rest of the world.

He also failed to offer a coherent rationale for the militant policy he demanded after April 1951. Occasionally he seemed to base it on his view of Mao Tse-tung, whom he termed a "sincere Communist, perhaps even more aggressive in his military intentions than is Stalin . . . We must treat him as a determined Communist fully sympathetic with the idea of a Communist domination of the world." And occasionally he seemed to agree with MacArthur that a noncommunist Asia was essential to American security. "The Far East," he had said in 1948, "is ultimately even more important to our future peace than is Europe." But if he truly held such views, he did not belabor them at all before April 1951, and unlike some of the "Asia-firsters" he was not sentimental about China. Why, critics asked, had he not sounded concerned about Korea before MacArthur's dismissal? And why did he not fashion a consistent view of American interests in the Orient? On this central question, indeed, he was inarticulate.[33]

Taft proved confusing on another major question underlying the debate over Korea: What would be the consequences of expanding the action? Truman argued that bombing Manchuria or blockading China might trigger Russian intervention in Korea or even in Europe. But Taft, who was then insisting that the presence of a few American divisions in Europe would antagonize the Soviet Union, refused to believe the Russians would be provoked to war by actual fighting and bombing near its borders in Asia. Even if they were, he added, "we have repeatedly assumed the risk of war in Europe, and there is no reason why the same policy should not be followed in Asia." [34] He may have been right in assuming the Soviets worried primarily about western arms in Europe, which was nearer to their heartland than was the Yalu, but his critics were quick to point out that he had himself blamed the Soviets in 1950 for the North Korean invasion. If that was so, why should they back down in 1951? His critics maintained also that his argument meant one of two things: either that firm American commitments were foolish in Europe but wise in Asia, or that what was wrong in Europe ought to be applied anyway in Asia, presumably for consistency's sake alone. "Taft is very badly discredited by the MacArthur show," a friend of Tom Dewey was happy to report, "and has forfeited his reputation for intellectual honesty." [35]

Two irreconcilable impulses upset Taft's sense of balance over Korea. One was his aversion to American troops on foreign soil. Before MacArthur's dismissal this instinct had led him to criticize retrospectively American intervention, then to consider withdrawal to island bastions in the Pacific. He wanted to keep Americans out of land wars in Asia as well as in Europe, to force Chiang's troops to bear the burden, and to bomb Manchuria to conclude the war, not to expand it. So he found himself in the awkward position of supporting some of MacArthur's military recommendations while simultaneously hoping for early removal of American troops.

The second impulse explained why he persisted in his course: politics. MacArthur, he conceded privately, might not be entirely right, but "I think the people fully agree with him." And Republicans could not rely on domestic issues. "We cannot possibly win the next election," he wrote in July 1951,

unless we point out the utter failure and incapacity of the present Administration to conduct foreign policy and cite the loss of China and the Korean war as typical examples of their very dangerous control. We certainly can't win on domestic policy, because every domestic policy depends entirely on foreign policy.[36]

Such remarks were not entirely crass and opportunistic, for Taft, like other Americans, deeply lamented the inability of the Truman administration to stop the Chinese communists. Without saying so explicitly, he also reflected the view of many Americans that western technology — above all, air power — could force the Asian enemy to collapse. But he was also thinking, however shortsightedly, of the future of his party. With another presidential election ahead that might also mean the political welfare of Robert A. Taft.

•

By mid-summer 1951 Taft could no longer say that foreign policy had "moved in" on him. On the contrary, he had leaped into foreign affairs with the same forcefulness that had marked his lifelong ventures into domestic issues. It remained only for him to cap his efforts by drawing his thoughts together, and when Lee Barker, an editor for Doubleday & Co., urged him to write a book, Taft consented to do so. The result, after painful labors of dictating and rewriting during the summer, was *A Foreign Policy for Americans,* which appeared in November. It was ironic that Taft, sometimes labeled an intellectual in politics, wrote only one book in his lifetime and that it concerned foreign policy alone.[37]

The book, only 121 pages long (plus a brief appendix), was hardly a detailed account of past policy or even a thorough analysis of alternatives that lay ahead. Indeed, Taft made no such claim; on the contrary, he called it an exposition of his views at that time and a critique of the policies of his opponents.

In two respects it differed slightly from most of his earlier statements. First, he called more explicitly than before for an aggressive "propaganda campaign on behalf of liberty" — a drive that would even include infiltration by secret agents into communist countries. Such a policy, he conceded, was "not in accordance with American tradition and is no part of a permanent foreign policy," but ought to be tried under present circumstances. This support of fifth-column activities foreshadowed what was shortly to become known as the policy of "liberation" and contrasted rather sharply with his previous distrust of interference in the domestic affairs of other nations. It was another sign of his greater militance in 1951.[38]

The second new emphasis concerned European policy. Though Taft reiterated his opposition to sending arms or large numbers of troops to NATO nations, he sounded more willing to accommodate the Europeanists than before. He supported an alliance with England, glided over his attempts to cut funds for the Marshall Plan, and stressed, as he had since the close of the great debate, his willingness to support reasonable numbers of American troops on European soil. "We have no choice," he wrote, "except to complete as rapidly as possible the arming of Western Europe if it desires to be armed." His past worries about provoking the Soviets, he admitted, "do not seem to have been borne out up to this time." Taft hedged his argument by concluding that "our aim should be to make Europe sufficiently strong so that American troops can be withdrawn from the continent of Europe." [39] Nevertheless, the tone of his remarks sounded so willing to accept American presence in Europe — as well as in islands and peninsulas around the world — that the thorough-going isolationists and pacifists continued to be alarmed. As in the great debate, he showed that he was far from being an isolationist — and that he was defending positions which he could hardly have imagined in 1940.

Otherwise, his book merely wove together past speeches. He used his father's writings to rebut Truman's interpretation of the powers of the commander in chief, pronounced the United Nations incapable of halting aggression by large nations, extolled air power as the basis for American defense, reminded readers that Alger Hiss had been at the Yalta conference, and spoke of the "pro-Communist policy of the State Department" in Asia. America, Taft insisted, must consider the advantages of the "free hand," and recognize limits to what the nation could do. ("WE SHOULD STRIVE TO LIMIT FEDERAL EXPENDITURES DURING THE EMERGENCY TO ABOUT 75 BILLION DOLLARS," he wrote.)[40] Above all, policy makers must think of America first, especially American *liberty* and *peace*. They ought not to try to save the world, but to preserve the American system and let its blessings shine across the seas. "We do not need to seek further than the Sermon on the Mount," Taft proclaimed in a rare resort to Biblical authority, "to know the first step we must take if freedom under God is to survive in our country and in the rest of the world:

"A good tree cannot bring forth evil fruit,
   neither can a corrupt tree bring forth good fruit.

"Every tree that bringeth not forth good fruit
is hewn down and cast into the fire.

"Wherefore by their fruits ye shall know them." [41]

Taft had reason to be pleased with his book. *Look* paid him to
summarize it in an article, and nearly a hundred newspapers with a
total circulation of eight million serialized it. Sales (at $2 per
copy) started so quickly that for a time in December it joined Herbert Hoover's memoirs and James Forrestal's diaries on the best-
seller list. "My book seems to be going very well," Taft wrote his
sister Helen in late December, "and probably I shall make something like $25,000 on it, although the government is going to take
the greater part of it." By March 1952 sales were falling off
sharply, but the book eventually sold 39,234 copies, earning him
$10,947.21. Because he also received more than $6500 from syndicated sales, he grossed $17,733.61.[42]

A Foreign Policy for Americans received some favorable reviews.
Taft's friend Walter Trohan of the Chicago *Tribune* wrote that
the book was "far and away the best thing he has ever done in the
way of speaking, writing, or statecraft." And MacArthur wrote to
term the book "masterful." Your stand, he said, will "greatly
strengthen your position with the American people." If Taft's
ventures into foreign policy had done nothing else, they had tightened his grip on the partisans of Douglas MacArthur.[43]

Still, *A Foreign Policy for Americans* failed to impress most of
the reviewers in the mass circulation magazines and Eastern press.
Some noted accurately that he contradicted himself on whether
the Soviets were capable of delivering atomic weapons. Others dismissed his writing as a campaign document. More revealing reviews came from Henry Luce's *Time* and from McGeorge Bundy,
associate professor of government at Harvard. *Time* recognized
that Taft could no longer be called an isolationist, but complained that he still failed to appreciate the role America must
play in the world. He "lacks any dynamic sense that United States
efforts can help make the world situation less unsatisfactory."
Bundy, who was later to serve as one of President John F. Kennedy's key aides, stressed that Taft's emphasis on peace and justice
overlooked the tough question of *power*. These were times, Bundy

added, of great global struggle, and Taft's views simply did not fit. To these advocates of containment Taft seemed as reluctant as ever to impose the benefits of American power on the world.[44]

Perhaps the most perceptive comments in this vein came from Francis P. Locke, reviewer for the Dayton *News*. Locke carefully observed Taft's habit of devoting a paragraph or two in favor of some internationalist position, then following with much longer passages of a critical nature. The book, Locke said, showed the old Taft penchant for "yes, but" and proved that he had reached only an "intellectual acceptance of limited internationalism. On the surface is a layer of reasoned thought which is genuine, but which is extremely thin. Scratch it ever so lightly, and Taft's emotions are laid bare." [45]

Locke and others like him perhaps criticized Taft too harshly. Indeed, as many such reviewers conceded, Taft had tried harder than most prospective presidential candidates to summarize his position. The book also reflected the man: earnest, hard hitting, and partisan. His more moderate posture toward Europe aside, it accurately portrayed his mature views on foreign policy. And because he was to change little in the next two years, the book was to remain the most reliable single guide to his thinking.

The critics might also have listened more carefully to one of Taft's central tenets that set him apart from many of the more enthusiastic internationalists: that America could do only so much to better the world. Thus he doggedly insisted on holding down military spending, on giving greater attention to domestic needs, on controlling presidential discretion in dispatching troops, and on questioning the wisdom of long-term defense pacts. Like Senator Fulbright, who was much later to warn of the "arrogance of power" and of the "Pentagon Propaganda Machine," Taft was reminding Americans of their limitations, of the dangers of moralistic globalism. Had he sounded this warning unambiguously he might have shaken policy makers from their ethnocentric assumptions about the beneficence of American influence abroad.

The trouble was that he did not stop there. Instead, he called for a militant pose in Asia and demanded worldwide propaganda, including infiltration of communist lands. He persisted in adopting a moralistic stance about communism, especially in Asia.[46] And he seemed unable to resist irresponsible assault on the Democrats. Had he avoided these inconsistencies — which had coexisted in his thought for many years — he might have stimulated the real debate over foreign policy that the nation needed in 1951. Instead, he often offered the sort of moralistic militance that was to sustain the "liberation" policy of John Foster Dulles in the 1950's and the anticommunist ventures of American political leaders in the 1960's. Foreign policy had moved in on Taft, and he had let the Cold War carry him some distance from his noninterventionism of 1940. But he had not broken the bipartisan containment policy or persuaded the internationalists of his wisdom.

Robert A. Taft

Robert Taft's birthplace, East McMillan Street, Cincinnati

Bobby, approximately
one year old

Helen Herron Taft,
Bob's mother, c. 1905

Charles P. Taft, Bob's uncle, and William Howard Taft, c. 1907

The Taft family, c. 1909. Children, from left, are Helen, Charlie, Bob

Martha Bowers Taft, 1914

Taft as Ohio legislator, 1923

Three generations. Adults, from left, are Martha Taft, Robert, Mrs. William Howard Taft, the Chief Justice, Mrs. Charles P. Taft, 2nd (front), Mrs. Helen Taft Manning, Charlie, and Fred Manning

Taft in Washington for his father's funeral, 1930

The Taft home, Sky Farm, Indian Hill, Ohio

The Taft family, late 1940's. In middle row, left to right, are Bob Jr.'s wife Blanca, Horace, Bill's wife Barbara, Lloyd, Lloyd's wife Virginia, and Bill

Candidate Taft in Texas,
December 1939. He changed
back into business clothes
before this picture was shot

Taft with other GOP powers, 1940. Left to right are Taft, Wendell Willkie, Senator Warren Barbour (New Jersey), Senator Charles McNary (Oregon), Willkie's running mate, Representative Joseph Martin, Jr. (Massachusetts), and Senator Arthur Vandenberg (Michigan)

With his mother, 1940 convention

With Senator Burton K. Wheeler of Montana, a fellow foe of war, in 1941. *Below:* with Senator Arthur Vandenberg, 1947

Unhappy unionists surround Taft, Los Angeles, September 1947

At the GOP convention, 1948. Left to right are Harold Stassen, Representative Joseph Martin, Jr. (Massachusetts), Governor Thomas Dewey of New York, Taft, Governor Earl Warren of California, and Senator Edward Martin (Pennsylvania)

Yale Alumni Dinner at Mayflower Hotel in Washington. Left to right are former Senator John Sherman Cooper, Senator Taft, President Charles Seymour, Marvin J. Cole, and Dean Acheson

Nixon and Taft, c. 1951

With Senator
Everett Dirksen, 1952

Clashing with United
Mine Workers leader
John L. Lewis, 1952

Eisenhower and Taft
at Morningside Heights,
September 1952

Golfing with Eisenhower,
April 1953

Taft turns over Majority Leadership to Senator William Knowland, June 1953

Taft in the Capitol, 1953

PART VI

Reaching for
the White House

CHAPTER 32

The Last, Best Chance

EARLY ON OCTOBER 16, 1951, Taft hurried to the Republican conference room across from his office, where he had called a press conference. Anticipating important news, two hundred reporters, photographers, and television and newsreel people jammed the ornate chamber. They were not disappointed, for as one newsman put it, Taft "sparkled" with confidence. A majority of Republicans throughout the nation, he said, "really desire me to be the candidate of their party." Bowing to this demand, he would try again for the presidential nomination and conduct an aggressive campaign for "liberty rather than the principles of socialism," for "restoration of a Government of honesty and integrity in Washington," and for a foreign policy that would avoid the "fatal mistakes . . . in the buildup of Russia and the Korean war and other disastrous occurrences." [1]

Though it was early for an announced presidential candidacy, his declaration surprised no one. Since 1948 he had struck many Republicans as the obvious choice, and by 1950 staunch partisans such as the Chicago *Tribune*'s Colonel Robert McCormick were already pressing him hard. Taft had parried McCormick's appeals. "I myself would be entirely satisfied with six years in the Senate," he replied, "at which time I will be 67 years old and have always expected to retire from politics . . . I have been campaigning, it seems to me, for the last ten years. In any event, I do not wish to make any decision until after the 1950 election." [2]

His triumph over Joseph T. Ferguson merely increased the pressure on him. McCormick wrote again that the election "makes you the logical candidate for the Republican nomination," and veterans of Taft's 1940 campaign like John Marshall and Richard Scandrett began writing letters to gather support. In March 1951, Marshall reported that he had convened forty wealthy men, including steel magnate Tom Girdler and Alfred Sloan, chairman of the board of General Motors, and that they had pledged $1 million to help Taft get organized.[3]

Yet Taft declined to commit himself, and one reason for hesitating was Martha. When she returned to Washington after staying at Sky Farm during the 1950 campaign, she seemed reminded of past triumphs and pleasures in the nation's capital, and her doctor observed that she "went promptly into a rather serious emotional decline . . . characterized by periods of uncontrollable crying, weeping, profound depression, increased demands upon the people around her and a retrogression in her physical activities." As Taft phrased it to Barbara, his daughter-in-law, Martha was having frequent "fits of depression . . . It makes it pretty hard, because almost anything produces tears, and she is particularly concerned as to where I may be and as to whether I am likely to come home within a reasonable time, safe from the perils of travel." [4]

Taft did what he could. He had a bathroom installed on the ground floor of their house, then added special railings on the stairs to enable her to move by herself to the second floor. To accommodate the nurses whom she had to have twenty-four hours a day, he moved upstairs to the third floor. He also acquired a dictating machine so that he could come home earlier and so that he could undertake the correspondence with their sons which Martha had ordinarily handled in the past. Listening to dictation "enables your mother to keep up somewhat with current events," he wrote his son Horace, "and also enables me to keep up my correspondence much better than I have ever done." Martha's illness, he added a little lamely, made life "a good deal simpler than in the past, and I don't think I will mind missing the continuous dinners which we usually attended." [5]

A few close friends and relatives recognized that he continued to suffer more deeply than he let on under the blow which had wrecked his domestic life. Indeed, his quarters at the top of the steep staircase to the third floor were barren and drafty. When he worked nights — which was often — he sat in a straight-backed chair at a table heaped with books and documents, and he hung up his clothes on a rack behind a curtain. "Little America," he jokingly called his new abode. "A monk's cell," his friend Stanley Rowe described it. And Martha's lack of emotional balance left her unpredictable. On some days she was gay, lucid, even able to move about with the aid of leg braces and a cane. More often, however, she remained in her wheelchair, succumbed to tears, and even exploded angrily at friends and visitors.[6]

Her remoteness threw Taft even more than before back upon himself. But he still showed no signs of flinching under such a burden. He refused to break down, to seek solace from others, or even to alter substantially his pace of work. And because he was powerless to do much for her, he found no reason to rule out another presidential campaign. He would simply have to run again without her.

.

Accordingly, he kept his options open, and except for his militant statements about foreign policy, he tended to avoid positions that would expose him or his party to unnecessary criticism. Indeed, in 1951 Taft, whom Democratic Senator Paul Douglas called "the uncrowned leader of the Senate" in July, managed to sound more accommodating on domestic issues than earlier.[7]

One such issue was the Taft-Hartley law. When the Supreme Court early in the year invalidated more than three thousand union shop elections because they had been held before the signing of noncommunist affidavits, Taft joined with Hubert Humphrey, a fellow Labor Committee member, to introduce an amendment validating these elections and rendering them unnecessary in the future. Because he had long considered such elections foreordained for the unions, his willingness to work with Humphrey was neither surprising nor controversial, and when their amendment passed later in the year, Truman quickly signed it. It was the only change made in the law during Truman's presidency.[8]

Taft bent further under the pressure from farm interests. This did not mean supporting proposals calling for high and inflexible price supports or even pretending any expertise. When a constituent wrote to ask whether his father had kept a cow on the White House lawn, Taft replied that he did not know. "I never had con-

"You must be new around here, son." *L. D. Warren, Cincinnati* Enquirer

tact with the cow," he volunteered, "and I am afraid I could not have milked it if I had to." But he did insist on pacifying the politically potent farm cooperatives by supporting a bill that taxed them as partnerships, not more heavily as corporations. Some of his businessmen supporters complained vigorously at what they considered favoritism. But Taft held his ground. My position on the issue, he wrote a Texas politico in November, can be defended on its merits. But:

> undoubtedly the strongest argument is the political situation. It is not my own future; it is that of the Republican party. The Republicans have antagonized the labor unions and must continue to do so because they are supporting a socialist program. It cannot afford also to alienate the farmers . . . In 1948 Dewey lost in the rural districts. He lost because the farmers felt that Truman had done a fairly good job for them, and that Dewey had no sympathy whatever for the farm position.[9]

Taft was careful not to sound so politically calculating in public. But for him to be so frank even in private was rare. The 1952 presidential sweepstakes were already under way, and they were impressing him with the need for political finesse.

Another change of pace in 1951 involved Joseph McCarthy. Like most senators, Taft still refused to denounce him, but Taft did edge away. McCarthy's statements, he told a newsman, were "bunk . . . I thought if he was going into this fight he ought to be carefully prepared and get some experts to help him. He agreed in principle but never did much about it." [10] When McCarthy expanded his charges to accuse General George Marshall of taking part in a "conspiracy so immense, so black, as to dwarf any in the previous history of man," Taft demurred openly. Marshall, Taft said in June, had followed "the most stupid possible policy [as secretary of state in 1947 and 1948] . . . and subsequent events in Formosa and Korea stemmed directly from it." But "I do not agree with Senator McCarthy's accusations of conspiracy or treason." Five months later he added, "I don't think one who overstates his case helps his own case. There are certain points on which I wouldn't agree with the Senator. His extreme attack against General Marshall is one of the things on which I cannot agree with McCarthy." Informed of this statement, even McCarthy was surprised. "I will not believe it," he told reporters, "until I get his word that he said it." [11]

Taft even seemed to soften his assaults on administration economic policy. Again, this did not signify any turnabout in his thinking. He denounced excessive military spending and temporarily dropped his support of federal aid to medical schools — it was too expensive during the Korean war. Yet he was careful not to seem reactionary. "I believe that we can increase further the taxes on big business, and will have to," he wrote a friend in March. A few months later he urged businessmen to drop their demands for a federal sales tax. A temporary sales tax might balance the budget, he admitted privately, but even if Congress approved one — which was unlikely — Truman would veto it. Besides, Taft added, sales taxes would be "practically as inflationary as a limited amount of borrowing." There was but one course — which he was distastefully prepared to swallow: "deficit financing for several years while the defense production program is at its height." [12]

He reached equally unpalatable conclusions about controls, which he argued must be maintained to prevent inflation. To Republican friends he added another reason: "Some fairly strenuous control will be justified by next November. If we refuse to give it now and prices go up as I feel confident they will, the Republican party would have assumed complete responsibility for that rise, and they would never hear the end of it." [13]

Union shop elections, farm cooperatives, taxes, controls. These issues failed to excite the media — or, apparently, the people. Yet in reacting quietly to them, Taft proved willing to muffle partisan debate, and even to admit partly political motivations for doing so. The Grand Old Party — and Taft himself — need not founder in 1952 as it had in 1948.

During the early months of 1951 he was also careful not to discourage his supporters. "I don't say I wouldn't take the nomination if it were offered to me," he wrote, "but I shall make no campaign to get it." He also denigrated other likely contenders. Of California Governor Earl Warren, who was ultimately to become a rival, Taft was caustic. "It is hard for me to see how any real Republicans could be for Warren today," he commented. "He certainly represents all the New Deal principles, and does not even recognize that there is any difference in principle." [14]

Taft turned again to his cousin David Ingalls for help, and Ingalls, an accomplished pilot, gladly agreed to tour the country and assess the political climate. By August, Ingalls, who was often joined by Ben Tate, Taft's Cincinnati neighbor and perennial fund raiser, had traveled some thirty thousand miles and had visited politicos in twenty-eight states. He was to visit many more before the end of the year.[15]

Ingalls was loyal, genial, and almost boyishly enthusiastic about his cousin's prospects. And in New York, Lou Guylay, Taft's public relations man, agreed. Let's undertake "an accelerated program of activity from the 'pros,'" Guylay counseled in July. "It should be positively stated — not once but a million times that Taft is the greatest vote-getter the Republican party has by actual performance." [16] Still, the senator hung back. One reason for hesitating was the political wisdom of keeping people guessing. But he also wished to be sure. "He really wants to know if people are going to help him or not," Ingalls complained, "and it is always hard to get a pledge so far in advance." Taft told his friends he would consider running only if he could count on the support of a "majority of Republicans." He added, "I do not look forward to this campaign or to the job itself with anything like the enthusiasm I once did." [17]

By September, however, Taft felt he had to make up his mind. Eisenhower, Taft's only formidable opponent, seemed the voters' choice in most of the polls, but the general was carrying out his assignment for NATO in Paris and giving his anguished admirers no encouragement whatever that he would run. Besides, Ingalls and Tate claimed to have secured more than 400 of the 604 delegates necessary to nominate. If Taft hoped to get additional delegates before Eisenhower changed his mind, he ought to do so soon. And the anti-Dewey regulars in the party gave Taft little rest; surely, they said, he would not desert his supporters in 1952. Perplexed, he pulled out a sheet of lined paper in September and scrawled out the pros and cons:

1. Against — Too old; serious effect on health, and not as good as should be.
   Job too hard to accomplish anything substantial, and problems insoluble.

No relaxation for pleasure.
Smearing and unpleasantness in the campaign.

2. For — Opportunity to accomplish many things I am deeply in-
terested in.
Opportunity to save liberty in U.S.
Demand of enthusiastic supporters.
The *duty* to do those things which are imposed on you.[18]

As late as October 11, 1951, only five days before Taft announced his candidacy, he still refused to tell even Ingalls what he
planned to do. But on September 20, Taft had begun a strenuous
speaking schedule, and the pressure continued to mount. Clearly,
the "fors" were carrying the day, and on October 16 they did.
Given his aspirations, his ambitions, and the sense of service instilled him long before, it would have been surprising had he decided otherwise.[19]

•

From the very start of his campaign Taft had to confront a series
of minor irritations. The first followed publication in *Life* on October 15 of excerpts from the diaries of James Forrestal, Truman's
former secretary of defense. At the top of one page *Life* carried a
photograph of Taft, Dewey, and Vandenberg over the caption,
"HOW SINCERE THE SMILES of Tom Dewey and Robert
Taft, meeting at G.O.P. dinner with late Senator Vandenberg, is
exposed in diaries." *Life* then prefaced an excerpt from the diaries
with the explanation that it would prove "embarrassing to Taft
Republicans." The passage described a visit of Forrestal to Truman following the 1948 election. At this meeting, Forrestal recorded, the President said that Taft had written him a letter of
congratulation, which suggested that "neither he [Taft] nor his
wife were particularly disappointed in the result of the election." [20]
Life correctly stressed that this disclosure would prove "embarrassing," for it seemed to demolish the image of "Mr. Republican."
But if *Life* hoped to ruin Taft, it reckoned without the integrity
of President Truman, who immediately sent Taft a copy of the
letter and added, "I see you have thrown your hat in the ring and I
suppose you will have all the fun that goes with that sort of a deci-

sion." Armed with the original, which was nothing more than a routine letter of congratulation (Forrestal obviously had misconstrued Truman's remarks), Taft sent Dewey a copy and responded jocularly to Truman. "Whether my recent decision will involve any fun for me is somewhat doubtful but perhaps if you feel that way about it you may consider joining the merry throng before many months." [21] The brief exchange of correspondence revealed that the two men, alike in their partisanship, had managed to retain a measure of respect for each other. But the brief flurry of excitement also suggested that *Life,* never in Taft's camp, had at the least not bothered to do its homework, at the most had taken an insignificant portion of the diaries and given it undue prominence. Taft was again to have his problems with Eastern internationalist magazines.

A more irritating interruption involved hearings conducted in late November by a Senate subcommittee investigating the 1950 campaign in Ohio. The hearings originated in complaints from Ferguson, who testified that he had spent but $171,000 during the campaign, to Taft's "more than $5 million." Ferguson also repeated his charge that Taft associated with communist leader Earl Browder. In response, Taft had to prepare a detailed statement and to spend part of a day refuting Ferguson. When the subcommittee finally finished its work in March 1952, it succeeded in showing that Ben Tate's sloppy bookkeeping methods had concealed substantial sources of funds — hardly an unusual practice in American elections. The episode brought Taft publicity he would have been happy to do without.[22]

Much the most delicate problem of late 1951 involved his brother. By 1951 Charlie had established a distinguished name for himself. Besides having served seven years on Cincinnati's city council, he had worked for the Federal Security Agency and the State Department during World War II, and presided over the Federal Council of Churches of Christ in America from 1947 to 1948. He had also found time to write four books and to engage in a wide variety of civic causes in Cincinnati. Convivial, public spirited, idealistic, he struck many people as the more appealing, if indeed not the more able, of the two Taft brothers. Now he hoped to cap his political career by running for the governorship of Ohio.

The partisans of Robert Taft vehemently opposed Charlie's ambition. Far from abandoning the Charterites, Charlie had run for
city council on their tickets, fought the regulars in campaign after
campaign, and published a book in 1936 entitled *You and I — and
Roosevelt.* "I shall probably vote against Mr. Roosevelt," he proclaimed therein, but "I can't and I won't damn F.D.R. and all his
works . . . Some of the Republican orators who do give me a pain
in the neck." Charlie even defended the CIO in a series of legal
battles in Ohio, and he had infuriated some of the lawyers at Taft,
Stettinius, and Hollister by making the firm's hallways a refuge for
the unemployed. Though he had left the firm in 1938 ostensibly
to avoid conflicts of interest while a city councilman, the bonds
between him and John Hollister had long been frayed. To the
regulars in Cincinnati — and to other conservatives such as Clarence Brown — the thought of Charles Taft heading the state ticket
in 1952 was distasteful in itself. They also reckoned that Charlie
would lose to the popular Lausche. When Charlie persisted in his
course, they turned to Bob for the ultimate in persuasion.[23]

For Bob the confrontation was unpleasant. Charlie had loyally
supported him during his quests for the presidency and the Senate.
But Bob had always disapproved of Charlie's association with the
reformers, and he frowned at his more liberal stand on such issues
as the tariff and foreign aid. "I don't see why he [Charlie] is always on the wrong (or at least the opposite) side," he had complained to Martha in 1941. Where Bob tended to look suspiciously
on new programs, Charlie often responded with what seemed to
Bob careless and evangelical enthusiasm; in their approach to
problems the two brothers could hardly have offered a more vivid
contrast.[24]

Like most cautious politicians, Bob had also tried to save his endorsements for candidates duly nominated by the party. For the
sake of consistency, he preferred to remain silent until the outcome
of the gubernatorial primary in May 1952. He worried also about
the reaction of Ohioans faced with two Tafts on the ticket in November. To Bob, as to his supporters, the answer was clear: Charlie's candidacy would be an embarrassment. And Bob told him
so.

Charlie, hoping for a change of heart, pressed harder for his

brother's support. But Bob bluntly asked him not to run and pre-
cipitated the most heated political argument the two men had had
since the 1920's. Convinced of the futility of further discussion,
Charlie then drafted a statement of neutrality for his brother to
issue, and Bob, after altering it in minor particulars, added a final
plea. "To be frank," he wrote at the end of October, "I would
rather not have you run . . . However, I certainly do not feel I
have the right to interfere with any action you determine to
take." [25]

This letter ended the matter. Bob stayed neutral while his
friends among the regulars did their best to defeat his upstart
brother. Undaunted, Charlie stayed in the race and whipped the
organization in the May primary, only to lose badly to Lausche the
following November. But the episode left Bob somewhat bruised,
for his neutrality prior to the primary, however pleasing to his
friends, struck some others as ungracious and selfish. It was another controversy he could well have done without.

•

These interruptions did not prevent Taft from seeming cool
under a formidable schedule of travel in the last months of 1951.
Indeed, by the time of his formal announcement October 16, he
had already spoken in the Dakotas, Iowa, and Nebraska. On October 23 he set off again — to South Dakota, Pittsburgh, Cincinnati,
Knoxville, Providence, and Chicago. After a three-day break he
flew on November 6 to Birmingham, Alabama, then to Biloxi,
New Orleans, Kansas City, and Tulsa — all in five days during
which he delivered twelve major speeches, appeared twice on television, and staged seven press conferences. Despite sixteen-hour
working days, he struck newsmen as well rested, affable, even genial; Martha's absence, one reporter noted, did not seem to bother
him.[26]

Getting the South behind him became a major effort in these
months. He encouraged oil executives in the gulf states who were
battling against federal ownership of offshore mineral rights, told
audiences that he would campaign throughout the South if nominated, repeatedly denounced a strong Fair Employment Practices
Commission, and opposed federal action against racial segregation

"Maa-aa-my." *L. D. Warren, Cincinnati* Enquirer

in primary schools. "As long as states provide equal educational facilities for whites and colored children in the primary schools," he explained in adhering to the Supreme Court's decisions on the question, "I do not think the Federal Government has the constitutional power to require a state to change the established system of education." [27]

Taft also used these early months of the campaign to create an organization. Many on whom he came to depend were powers in their states who had supported him in the past. These included national committeemen Perry Howard of Mississippi, Wallace Townsend of Arkansas, Walter Hallanan of West Virginia, John Jackson of Louisiana, and other veteran operators who ran tightly knit organizations in the smaller states. He also used old friends such as John Hollister and Paul Walter in Ohio, Walter Tooze in Oregon, and Vincent Starzinger, a law school classmate, in Iowa. He continued to rely on Lou Guylay for publicity and more heavily than ever on Jack Martin, his administrative assistant in Washington. David Ingalls, his campaign manager, and Ben Tate, who again handled the purse strings, stayed on as keys to the operation.

He also turned to newcomers. One addition was Congressman B. Carroll Reece of Tennessee, a veteran political operator who had served as GOP national chairman from 1946 to 1948. Reece was a quiet, methodical conservative with wide contacts and experience. Taft knew him well from the Hill, felt comfortable with him, and entrusted to him the responsibility for the Southern states. A second newcomer, Victor A. ("Vic") Johnston, took charge of organizational work in offices that Taft rented at the foot of Capitol Hill. Johnson, a publicity man turned political professional, had first achieved prominence as Harold Stassen's publicity director from 1938 to 1944. He had then helped Joseph McCarthy in his race for the Senate in 1946 and served briefly as McCarthy's administrative aide in 1947. Returning to assist Stassen in 1948, he had worked since then as executive director of the GOP Senate campaign committee, where he necessarily crossed paths with Taft.

Still, Taft felt the need for more new faces, and by the end of 1951 he was relying heavily on two other political pros. The first, John D. M. Hamilton, was a veteran organizer who had served as GOP national chairman from 1936 to 1940 and later as paid executive director of the national committee. He had moved to Philadelphia, where he had impressed Taft with his energetic assistance during the 1948 convention. When Hamilton proved eager to help, Taft gave him responsibility for the Eastern states. With Ingalls and Tate he was to serve on the highest boards of strategy.

The other newcomer to the Taft team was Thomas E. Coleman, a quiet, white-haired, distinguished-looking manufacturing executive from Madison, Wisconsin. Fifty-eight years old in 1951, Coleman was the Mr. Republican of Wisconsin politics who had led McCarthy's battle against Robert La Follette, Jr., in the 1946 senatorial primary. In 1948 Coleman had backed Stassen, but by 1951 he was letting Ingalls and Jack Martin know of his availability. Taft gladly adopted him, and Coleman joined Ingalls, Hamilton, and Tate as the key men of the campaign. At the national convention in 1952 he was to be floor manager.[28]

As in the past, Taft had not searched far and wide for bright young men to hold key positions on his staff. He also made no effort to bring into his top echelons any of the more progressive Eastern Republicans who were lining up behind Eisenhower. On the contrary, men like Reece and Tate reflected the GOP's right wing. Ignoring the protests of Walter and Martin, he refused to ignore the Ohio organization, and he even kept on such veterans of his 1948 campaign as Clarence Brown. Taft had added some new people, but he had not appreciably broadened the spectrum of thinking within his organization. Later, when his advisers employed heavy-handed tactics in a few key states, their limitations became apparent.

He failed also to change his method of dealing with his advisers. As before, he tried to meet with them when he could, and he listened to criticism when it came from old associates like Ingalls or Tate. Aware of the political contacts of veterans like Coleman and Reece, he also delegated to them considerable authority — too much as it turned out. But Taft still made most of the key decisions alone, insisted on writing his own speeches, and thought nothing of driving his car to Maryland or Pennsylvania to confer with individual delegates. As ever, he tended to keep his own counsel, to discourage the burdensome benefits of intimacy.[29]

Still, his willingness to include new men suggested he had learned something from the mistakes of 1948. He was also careful to assign his advisers clearly defined responsibilities — Tate finances, Hamilton the East, Reece the South, and Coleman most

The little artist. *Reprinted, courtesy of the Chicago* Tribune

of the Midwest. Ingalls, genial and inoffensive, became the front man who nominally headed the team. Except for the usual squabbles that flare up in any organization, the group functioned harmoniously, and it was united ideologically behind Taft's principles. He had every reason to think that he had drawn together as technically proficient a team as any during his lifetime.

With all these advantages the candidate had but one worry as 1951 drew to a close: Eisenhower. As early as June a group of powerful professionals, many of whom had served Dewey in the past, had met to coordinate a campaign for the general. Among them were James Duff, then senator from Pennsylvania, Hugh

Scott, the former national chairman whom Dewey had installed in 1948, and James Hagerty and Herbert Brownell, two of Dewey's ablest advisers. Still more influential were Henry Cabot Lodge and, above all, Dewey himself, who was certain to control the large New York delegation at the convention. In September when Governor Sherman Adams of New Hampshire announced that Eisenhower's name would be entered in the New Hampshire primary in March 1952, many influential senators and governors openly endorsed the general's candidacy.[30]

Many Eisenhower supporters acted in part from uneasiness about Taft. One of them, Senator Alexander Smith of New Jersey, explained later that Taft seemed to support policies "rather negatively than aggressively. And I was a little doubtful . . . whether Taft could be elected . . . I felt that in light of the international issues . . . we really needed a man of Eisenhower's calibre." Governor Howard Pyle of Arizona reluctantly agreed. Taft was "the best qualified man in America today . . . he not only has the know how but he has the stability." Yet "he hasn't the personal appeal and that is not the only thing . . . He has been completely on the 'agin' side, and I question like hell whether he can revise his thinking and be positively for something." [31]

The public opinion polls helped sustain these opinions. A Gallup survey in August had shown that five of six Republicans held favorable opinions of Taft, but that slightly more than half of the people calling themselves Independents disapproved of him, and that only 20 per cent of all those questioned said he would make a good President, compared to 27 per cent who thought he would not. Other polls reflected the same sort of divisions: Taft was the heavy favorite of party regulars and Republican senators, but Eisenhower was strong with rank and file Republicans and was the overwhelming choice of Democrats and Independents who were asked about Republicans. In January 1952 a Roper poll revealed that even Cincinnatians who said they had voted for Taft by 60 to 40 per cent in 1950 now favored Eisenhower over him by 43 to 39 per cent. The polls left little doubt that Taft, for all his strength in 1950, lacked Eisenhower's broad appeal.[32]

At first Taft had tried to dismiss the Eisenhower phenomenon. "I don't think he has any basic knowledge of the principles of government," he wrote a friend late in 1950. "Consequently he is likely to accept the advice of those who happen to be intimate with him at the moment." To Guylay he added that Eisenhower "always makes a good impression," but that "I have no confidence in his judgment on matters which he does not really understand and does not seem to want to understand." And to Katharine Kennedy Brown, Ohio's perennial national committeewoman, Taft confided that "if we get Eisenhower we will practically have a Republican New Deal Administration with just as much spending and socialism as under Mr. Truman." [33]

By October 1951, however, he was changing his pose. Instead of describing Eisenhower as a would-be New Dealer, he tried to minimize the differences which separated them, presumably in the hope that the general would not feel compelled to run. Thus he wrote that he favored the presence of six American divisions in Europe, and "even some reasonable addition." He also had General Bonner Fellers, a zealot for air power who had connections at the Pentagon, inform him of Eisenhower's plans and movements. Taft's friends plied Eisenhower's aides in Europe with clippings indicating what an uphill struggle the general would have. And Taft's advisers ridiculed the public opinion polls. "Eisenhower would not make as good a run as Taft," Ingalls said. "You hardly pick a man from the bush leagues to pitch in a World Series, and Eisenhower has never been tested in a campaign as yet, and Taft has never been licked." [34]

Thus even the shadow of Eisenhower failed seriously to disturb Taft's equanimity at year's end. After all, the Truman administration, already enmeshed in a drawn-out war, grew increasingly compromised by revelations of corruption among some of its officials. And Eisenhower was adamantly refusing to commit himself.[35] When Stassen entered the race in December, Taft could barely conceal his amusement. "The reporters," he wrote Butler of Nebraska, "seem to think he is slightly off the beam. Nevertheless, I suppose his very stupidity will lead him to file in various states." Relaxed, he took Martha home to Cincinnati in early December to celebrate Christmas with his sons, daughters-in-law, and grandchildren. At the same time Darrah Wunder, who had remained in Cincinnati during 1951, agreed to be Martha's companion during the months of campaigning ahead. She was to remain with the Tafts — and then with Martha alone — until Martha's death in 1958.[36]

Taft also had his tonsils taken out, an operation which Dr. Johnson McGuire, his personal physician from Cincinnati, had been recommending for several months as a precaution against the more frequent colds and sore throats that he seemed to incur on his travels. The operation necessitated a break in campaigning, and Taft did not resume his heavy schedule until mid-January. But he had planned it that way, and after the operation proved successful he enjoyed gesturing to friends that he should not talk. "All of the doctors apparently were Republicans," he quipped, "and everything went all right at the hospital." "The way things line up today," he added, "I can't quite see how Eisenhower is going to cut in to any substantial extent on the 600 or so delegates who are clearly favorable to me at the moment." [37]

Taft wrote this letter on January 1, 1952. At that time the new year promised to be the most rewarding yet of an active and productive political life.

CHAPTER 33

The Tensions of Campaigning

"A NATIONAL campaign for the presidency," William Howard Taft
had complained, "is to me a nightmare." [1]

If his son thought so, he gave few signs of it during the first
weeks of 1952. As soon as his throat permitted, Taft took to the
road again, and between January 21 and February 22 he spoke in
eleven states from Oregon to Florida to Vermont — all while succeeding in maintaining an attendance record in the Senate which
though the poorest of his career was considerably better than that
of such Democratic contenders as Estes Kefauver of Tennessee,
Richard Russell of Georgia, or Robert Kerr of Oklahoma. Before
he concluded his travels in late June he visited thirty-five of the
forty-eight states. A New York *Times* reporter observed on May
11 that since October Taft had paused for only two rounds of golf,
made some 550 speeches, traveled fifty thousand miles, and been
seen by approximately two million people. His campaign was one
of the most vigorous in American history.[2]

It was also one of the most efficient. Some two thousand letters a
day deluged his office, and he instructed his staff to answer all of
them. One of his office workers explained that "we thank all who
met him — from the big operator to the lowly operator . . . He
writes the Governors, head arrangers, national committeemen, etc.
down to the taxi cab driver who took him to his train or the man
who happened to see him on the street . . . That's one way we
can get the Senator over to the 'little people.' " [3]

As in past campaigns Taft readily offered his views on the issues.
He favored Hawaiian statehood, aid to education, modest agricultural price supports, the Taft-Hartley law. He opposed statehood

for Alaska, suspecting that it would go Democratic once admitted to the union. He cosponsored a joint resolution in May for a constitutional amendment to limit nonmilitary expenditures to 5 per cent of the national income.[4] And he continued to woo the South. If elected, he proclaimed, he would name at least one Southern Democrat to the Cabinet. His father, he reminded southerners, had served as a United States Court of Appeals judge in Tennessee, spent winters in Georgia, and appointed three southerners to the Supreme Court. "He ate, and claimed to have enjoyed, possum meat. He used to say that the southerners would do anything in the world for him except vote for him." [5]

Elsewhere, Taft moved cautiously. He discouraged California supporters from contesting Governor Earl Warren, a favorite son who was clearly unbeatable in his home state. He assigned Tom Shroyer, one of the experts who had helped draft the Taft-Hartley law, to try to secure the support of Nixon. He let aides handle — and mismanage — delicate bargaining for delegates in such divided states as Iowa and Oklahoma. He even tried to build bridges to Harold Stassen, only to be rebuffed. Stassen, he complained, "seems to be imbued with a sense of hostility to me. His course in general has apparently been directed in such a way as to assist General Eisenhower." [6]

Caution also dictated his approach to the Eisenhower boom, which had swelled after Henry Cabot Lodge announced on January 6 that the general would remain in the New Hampshire primary. Taft, far from attacking his potential opponent, tried to avoid statements that would drive him more openly into the fray. "I am opposing him for the nomination," he explained to reporters in late February. "But I want a Republican to win in November and would support him if nominated . . . I hope he would support me, too." [7]

In this spirit he let intermediaries try to persuade Eisenhower people of his reasonableness. In late January he conferred with Charles White, the head of Republic Steel, and acquiesced unenthusiastically in White's plan of urging the general to accept a Taft-Eisenhower ticket. He also encouraged a supporter who was trying to use John Foster Dulles as an avenue toward conciliating Dewey. "It is just possible," Taft wrote, "that if he [Dewey] thinks the

Eisenhower boom is going to blow up he may be willing to cooperate." And Taft took special pains to sound cooperative on the crucial question of NATO. "I have written a letter which has been shown to the General assuring him that I am anxious that the European Project be carried through to completion," Taft wrote in January. "That seems to be his great interest, and I can see no difference between us on that subject. I can renew that assurance from time to time." [8]

Trying to conciliate the Eisenhower partisans infuriated Taft's advisers, who resented the adulation showered on a general who comfortably played the role of reluctant candidate in Paris and who seemed ignorant of the issues. One of Taft's aides, anxious to combat the ubiquitous slogan, "I Like Ike," urged distribution of five thousand buttons labeled "But What Does Ike Like?" Others encouraged Taft to spread the rumor that Eisenhower had carried on an extramarital affair during the war, and David Ingalls publicly demanded to know whether the general's advisers planned to run their campaign on "sex appeal." If so, they should "select a good-looking mortician to preside over the funeral rites." Thomas Coleman and John Hamilton, more devious than Ingalls, had aides put together a file labeled "Anti-Eisenhower Material." This file contained such harmless information as that Eisenhower had never spoken as a Republican, and that generals-turned-President offered scarcely encouraging precedents. It stated that Hamilton's agents in New York had secured photostats of Eisenhower's voting registration in 1949 and 1950. These allegedly showed that he had returned his slips blank: the general, it seemed, was either an Independent or a nothing.[9]

Taft, however, was careful not to engage in personal attacks on his rival. Spreading a rumor about Eisenhower's love life, he told Darrah Wunder, would backfire, and calling attention to his nonpartisanship — which was well-known anyway — would serve no purpose. Ingalls, he wrote a friend, had gone "somewhat too far . . . he could have presented the arguments in a somewhat different tone"; henceforth, he told Guylay, all statements about other candidates must be cleared before publication. Taft well knew that it made political sense to sound as accommodating and as inoffensive as possible. At least until Eisenhower definitely committed himself as a candidate it was better to walk the high road to the nomination.[10]

Besides, Taft remained in the benign, relaxed mood in which he had started the New Year. "Bob arrived home from a whirlwind ten-day trip — Chicago, Wisconsin, Washington, Oregon, Idaho, Minnesota, Wyoming, and Denver —" Mrs. Wunder recorded in her diary February 17. "He is gay and confident and enjoys it." "I don't get as tired as I used to," he told a reporter. "In the 1950 campaign my knees used to get tired. But I had my tonsils out, and I'm feeling much better." He continued to sleep well, to eat whatever was placed before him, to laugh off disparaging remarks about the somewhat battered hat that he had worn since his 1950 campaign. "Bob," Mrs. Wunder added, "isn't accustomed to flattery at home . . . The Tafts care so little for clothes. Bob is never upset over trifles which would annoy other men." [11]

Reporters, marveling at his composure, even started talking about a "new Taft." "It's a different candidate this time," a newsman who had followed him in 1948 observed. "He is assured and relaxed and happy to talk at the drop of two potential voters from any given alley. He seems to approach this thing as a crusade." The columnist Marquis Childs noticed that Taft tramped contentedly through factories and work rooms. "If there are any signs of friendliness, he stops to shake hands and say a friendly word or two. If his presence produces obvious hostility or embarrassment, he walks on undaunted. The suggestion that this might be undignified in a candidate for President has apparently never crossed Taft's mind. That is one of the disarming things about the man; he is so completely without pretensions." [12]

In this happy mood Taft even took time to laugh at himself. In January the Circus Saints and Sinners, a group which liked to rib prominent personalities, put on a skit in New York featuring him as its "fall guy." Warned not to go by anxious friends, Taft nevertheless joined a thousand other guests who sat through the three-and-a-half-hour show. One scene dubbed the "Aft-Tartly Act" featured two showgirls bumping and grinding. Another showed Major General Harry Vaughan, an aide of Truman who had been accused of peddling his influence for favors, entering Taft's home.

Vaughan asked a maid if Mrs. Taft wanted a "deep freeze." "Does she need a deep freeze?" the maid replied incredulously. "She married one." Taft told Darrah Wunder that the "deep freeze joke was hard to take." But he took it well and laughed heartily throughout the show.[13]

Reporters speculating on the reasons for Taft's affability properly stressed two: He yearned for the nomination, and he thought he would win. But they might have added a third: the reassurance he had in knowing that Darrah Wunder was helping with Martha. Indeed, Martha, far from regaining her emotional balance, continued to be confined to her wheelchair, to be impatient and sharp-tongued, and to show little interest in his campaign. She also began suffering convulsions, and on one frightening occasion in February he had to hold her tongue until the doctor arrived to put her to bed. Taft interrupted whatever he was doing to call Martha at six every night he was away, but knowing Darrah Wunder was at home to help removed some of the burden of worry.[14]

Mrs. Wunder, vivacious and warm-hearted, also took some of the gloominess out of the home life he had led since Martha's stroke almost two years earlier. When he returned home after his travels, she was there to give him the human companionship he had been lacking. When he had time, he sat with her and talked of his work, and because she liked politics she was happy to listen. "How few people really know him," she confided to her diary after one such conversation. "He is a shy, reserved man, but so kind, so thoughtful, so concerned that I am happy and having a good time." [15]

Mrs. Wunder also took pains to help Taft relax. On one occasion she amused him by reading snatches from the "nut" mail that poured into the house. One such letter asked Taft what he would do as President about the 200,000 "Truman bastards" sired by American soldiers in Japan. Taft laughed. Another letter came from a dentist's wife who complained that Taft's smile was "too tight." Her husband, she added, once helped a patient who had been kicked by a horse by placing a pad in his mouth. You should do the same, she told Taft. On another evening Mrs. Wunder told of taking Willy Taft, Bill and Barbara's son, on a tour of the Lee Mansion and the Tomb of the Unknown Soldier. At this point

Willy intervened to say, yes, he had seen the Tomb of the Unknown Soldier — Robert E. Lee. Taft smiled. "There," he concluded, "goes the Southern vote." [16]

As the campaign quickened in March and April he had fewer light-hearted moments. But Mrs. Wunder stayed on, and the domestic scene remained stabilized. Despite his fearsome schedule he was probably as relaxed and content in early 1952 as at any time during the trials of the previous two years.

•

In March an unaccustomed excitement jolted New Hampshire natives from the stillness and serenity of wintertime, for the partisans of Eisenhower, Taft, Stassen, and even MacArthur were loudly stumping the state in advance of the nation's first important presidential primary on the eleventh. The Taftites, in a caravan of buses and sound trucks which wound over the snow-covered hills, were the noisiest of all. "Bob Taft's victory tour," bellowed the lead vehicle. "The next President of the United States, Bob Taft, is in the gray sedan just behind us."

The caravan started early in the morning of March 6 on the streets of Manchester, the state's largest city, then hurried twenty miles north to the state capital of Concord. There Taft talked with union officials and endured a staple of the tour — being photographed with an elderly native who had voted for his father. The procession continued north to Laconia, where he received a three-foot key to the city and a plaque from two Indians. Impatient with such tomfoolery, he refused to don an Indian headdress for photographers, returned to his car, and pressed on forty miles northeast to Conway, capital of the ski country, and to Berlin, the state's northernmost city. There he addressed a thousand people, visited a mill, shook hands with the workers, and went to bed a few minutes before midnight. Hoarse but vigorous, he arose at six the next two mornings for repeat performances. Before leaving the state early on the ninth he had traveled five hundred miles, given more than thirty speeches, and left his supporters amazed at his stamina.[17]

Many people thought this strenuous odyssey had moved the people. F. E. Johnston, his local campaign manager, proclaimed that Taft would take the presidential preference primary by five thousand votes and win six of the fourteen contests for delegates. And MacArthur, apparently repudiating his supporters, recommended they vote for Taft instead. "Bob," Mrs. Wunder remarked in her diary March 9, is "gay as a bird, and much encouraged by the crowds in New Hampshire. He says if he gets four delegates out of fourteen he will be satisfied." [18]

The returns shattered this euphoric mood. Taft carried the city of Manchester, probably because of repeated endorsements by the important Manchester *Union-Leader*. But he lost the state's other eleven cities by substantial margins and trailed in 148 of the 223 towns. Eisenhower captured all fourteen delegate contests and won the preferential primary with 46,661 votes to Taft's 35,838 and Stassen's 6574, while MacArthur got 3227 write-ins. Eisenhower had done better than his three opponents combined. "We are pretty low today," Mrs. Wunder noted.[19]

Taft, then seeking votes in Texas, grimly explained to reporters that "our campaign started too late to reach back into the many small towns which, with Concord, gave most of the Eisenhower majority." "I was a little disappointed," he added. "I was expecting a horse race." As he recognized, the New Hampshire primary had shot renewed enthusiasm into the ranks of the Eisenhower supporters, and suggested what Taft had steadfastly refused to concede: Eisenhower, the war hero extraordinaire, could win. Few things that happened in the preconvention campaign were to prove more damaging to Taft's cause.[20]

In conducting post-mortems many reporters faulted Taft for implying during the primary campaign that the general was the captive of Harry Truman's policies; such "attacks," the reporters concluded, were unfair to a man in uniform, and they offended the New Hampshire sense of fairness. Other observers, forgetting the praise that his campaigning had engendered, argued that Taft had seemed as chilly as the weather. On one occasion, a reporter recalled, Taft came out of the cold into a small coffee shop. Patrons and waitresses immediately crowded around to shake his hand. But Taft, thinking ahead as always, had already sat down to study notes for his next speech. Hardly looking up, he ignored the people around him and called out, "Coffee please, and make it hot." All the waitresses, the reporter claimed, later voted for Eisenhower.[21]

Taft himself privately criticized his New Hampshire leaders. "Our publicity," he wrote a friend, "was very poorly managed by the local people who insisted that everyone else keep out of the state." Yet he was really too busy to do a careful post-mortem, and he admitted his befuddlement. Private polls, he explained to F. E. Johnston, had never showed Eisenhower more than 5 per cent ahead, "and I still don't know exactly what happened to them." Careful not to offend, he congratulated Johnston on having mobilized a "first-class organization." [22]

Both Taft and the reporters tended to pay less attention than they should have to his greatest error: deciding to enter the primary at all. Indeed, he had originally intended to avoid contested primaries save in Wisconsin, where Coleman promised the support of the state organization. Forcing the issue in New Hampshire, where Governor Sherman Adams was certain to oppose him, and where he could win a maximum of fourteen delegates, would absorb much-needed time, to say nothing of money.

Until sometime in January Taft adhered to his sensible strategy. But John Hamilton, in charge of the East, demurred. His polls by post card, he explained, showed Taft with approximately 50 per cent of the vote. Hollister, who was also testing opinion in New Hampshire, cautiously added his voice to Hamilton's. "To avoid New Hampshire," he wrote, "is to belie in you the characteristic of courage which is the attribute bringing these people to your cause." Taft still resisted, but he discovered that he could rely on an active anti-Adams faction led by Wesley Powell, later to become New Hampshire's governor. In late January Taft announced that he would compete.[23]

Having agreed to stay in, Taft could still have feigned indifference to the result. Conversely, he could have thrown all his efforts into the struggle. Many reporters argued that he should do the former. Others recommended the second option on the grounds that he should make the most of this opportunity to overcome Eisenhower once and for all. Instead, Taft took the uneasy middle course of relying on Powell's men until the last week, then conducting his whirlwind three-day tour, then incautiously permitting his aides to predict a great victory. These decisions compounded the original one of staying in, for he ended not only by losing but also by being unable to offer any credible excuse for doing so.

Ultimately, of course, it was the magic of Eisenhower's name that decided the outcome in New Hampshire — and that overwhelmed the Democrats for the next eight years. Taft, like almost everyone else, could not have predicted the size of this appeal in January 1952. Yet there were two ironies to the contest. The first was that a man who professed contempt for polls proved willing to be persuaded by Hamilton's crude post cards. The second was that he himself seemed to expect so little from staying in. "I probably will lose the presidential preference primary," he conceded privately only a week after agreeing to remain in it. To risk so much on such polls exposed the limitations of his supposedly professional staff, to say nothing of his own lack of sophistication in such matters. To wage a battle when even he doubted he could win was still more astonishing.[24]

Why did he do so? Although Taft never offered a complete explanation, two of his letters in February suggested partial answers. The first observed that he could at least make the result "inconclusive." The Eisenhower "propaganda machine," he remarked, "was going to make about as much publicity on a default victory as an actual one. Furthermore, there is a good gamble on some success." The second simply elaborated on this argument. "I don't know what may happen in New Hampshire," he said, "but I thought we had everything to gain and nothing to lose." Henceforth he was to think twice before entering a primary; the question was whether he began to think too late.[25]

·

During the next two months the campaign for delegates intensified. Stassen and Warren, praying for a deadlock at the convention, occasionally joined the skirmishing, but practically everyone anticipated a fight to the end between Taft and Eisenhower. These months kept the Taftites apprehensive, occasionally even desperate.

The first test took place in Minnesota only a week after New

Hampshire. Earlier, most people had conceded the twenty-eight delegates to Stassen, the state's former governor and the only major candidate on the ballot. But the Eisenhower enthusiasts, buoyed by New Hampshire, mounted a vigorous write-in campaign, and when the results came in, even they were astonished. Stassen won the contest with 120,000 votes and gained an estimated twenty-four delegates, the only substantial bloc he was to get during the entire campaign. But so many voters turned out to write in Eisenhower's name that election officials had to accept slips of paper in place of ballots. In all, the war hero got 108,000 write-ins and four delegates. Taft, by contrast, amassed but 24,000 write-in votes. The results in Minnesota again suggested the general's great popularity at the polls.[26]

The result of the Minnesota primary may have had an even more significant consequence: It moved Eisenhower, who had still refused to commit himself, to take the first step toward coming home. The primary, he told reporters, was "forcing me to re-examine my personal position and past decisions." Whether Minnesota by itself did this was impossible to prove; indeed, he had been moved by New Hampshire, and — perhaps — he was bitten by the presidential bug. His unsatisfactory meeting with Taft over NATO a year earlier also had alarmed him. Taft, C. L. Sulzberger of the *Times* recorded the general as saying, was a "very stupid man. He might have a memory . . . but he had no intellectual ability, nor any comprehension of the issues of the world." Whatever Eisenhower's motives, Minnesota seemed to force his hand. Two weeks later he asked President Truman for permission to resign as NATO commander, and on April 12 the White House relieved him as of June 1.[27]

Another blow hit Taft in mid-March, this time in New Jersey, where Hamilton had been constructing a slate of delegates for an April primary. But on the eve of the balloting in Minnesota, New Jersey's Republican governor Alfred E. Driscoll endorsed Eisenhower. Busy campaigning in Wisconsin, Taft seemed unimpressed at first by Driscoll's statement. "We've known Governor Driscoll has been for Ike for months," he declared, "but I still think we'll elect a considerable number of delegates in New Jersey." With the news from Minnesota, however, Taft changed his mind. Driscoll, he charged angrily, had pretended to be neutral until the deadline for pulling out of the primary, then had "broken his word and . . . obviously taken steps to corrupt the intent of the preferential primary." Therefore, Taft added, he was withdrawing from the race in New Jersey.[28]

Having made his decision, Taft adhered to it in the three weeks remaining before the New Jersey primary April 15. The courts, however, ruled that the deadline for withdrawing had passed; his name must stay on the ballot. Determined to do the best they could, some of his local supporters continued to press his cause. But Taft refused to campaign, and long before the primary he knew he was destined to lose. His decision showed that he had learned the folly of combating a state organization and of claiming too much. But suspecting Driscoll's position from the beginning, he should never have entered a slate at all. In then pulling out, he had had to sound petulant against Driscoll. Once again he had miscalculated.[29]

These repeated setbacks started talk of what *Newsweek* called a "potentially runaway Eisenhower boom." They also shot so much gloom into the Taft organization that Ingalls carelessly admitted, "if we were to be beaten badly in Wisconsin, the Senator might as well get out." Many agreed that Ingalls, for all his artless candor, spoke the truth. Unless Taft won a primary — and impressively — he could never claim to be a vote getter.[30]

Like everyone else, Taft had long known where this crucial test must occur: Wisconsin on April 2. From the start he had proclaimed his intention to enter the primary, and Tom Coleman had made no secret of his elaborate plans. Taft visited the state four times for a total of twenty-two days, gave an estimated 250 speeches, traveled approximately three thousand miles throughout the state, and endured cold and snowy weather; once his car spun around two times and barely stopped before an oncoming gasoline truck. When he concluded his campaign, his organization had spent some $100,000.[31]

The results justified his efforts. In a large turnout he amassed 315,000 votes and captured twenty-four of the thirty delegates. Warren, who had briefly toured the state, carried some of the urban wards in Milwaukee and Madison to receive 262,000 votes and the other six delegates, and Stassen trailed with 169,000. Doubters noted that Warren and Stassen combined had gotten a plurality of 115,000 votes, that neither had exerted as much effort or spent as much money as Taft, that Eisenhower had not even entered. But Taft argued, probably justifiedly, that Warren had come as close as he did partly because Democrats had crossed over to vote in the Republican primary. To some observers this voting pattern reaffirmed Taft's dangerous weakness among independents and Democrats. But the statistics told the important story. Taft, faltering after New Jersey and Minnesota, had proved he could win.[32]

On the same day he also triumphed in Nebraska. Like the race in Minnesota, it had at first attracted little attention. But after Eisenhower won in Minnesota, his partisans staged another write-in campaign. Taftites, not to be outdone again, did the same, depending (as in 1948) on the machine of Senator Hugh Butler. When the ballots were counted, Taft emerged the winner with 79,000 votes to Eisenhower's 66,000. Stassen, the only major candidate on the ballot, finished third with 55,000. Some interpreters concluded that Butler's organization had made the difference, or that Nebraska, deemed conservative and isolationist, was Taft territory. Perhaps so, but what mattered to Taft was that he had won, getting thirteen or fourteen of Nebraska's eighteen delegates in the process. If Eisenhower ruled the cities and the coastlands, Taft remained a threat in the interior.[33]

For the next month voters confirmed this sectional pattern. Taft won the Illinois primary April 9 against token opposition, but Eisenhower took New Jersey a week later. With Taft declining to enter, the general also carried the nonbinding Pennsylvania primary April 22. When Eisenhower partisans scored another impressive write-in victory in Massachusetts April 29, Taft loyalists again accused Democrats and independents of crossing over. But such complaints changed nothing, and the next day Eisenhower also gained eight delegates from Missouri to take a 278 to 274 lead in committed delegates. Taft struck back to conquer Stassen for the fifty-six votes of his native Ohio and to subdue the Eisenhower forces at state conventions in West Virginia, North Dakota, and Wyoming. Eisenhower then won in Oregon, Rhode Island, and

Vermont. By May 18 the Associated Press gave Taft a lead of 374 to 337 in committed delegates; United Press International figured it at 378 to 359. By making the most of his strength in the Midwest, the South, and in scattered states throughout the Plains and Rocky Mountains, Taft had clung to the lead. But Eisenhower, without devoting a minute to active campaigning, controlled all of the populous northeastern states which had proved essential in previous Republican conventions. For Taft, the trail that had begun treacherously on the icy hills of New Hampshire had remained slippery thereafter.[34]

.

During the happy days of January and February Taft had seemed relaxed, available, and undisturbed, as Mrs. Wunder had noted, by "trifles." How had the adversities of March and April affected him?

From the standpoint of domestic issues, not much. Though he went so far as to call for the President's impeachment when Truman tried to seize the steel mills in April, Taft seemed content to leave the matter to the courts, which quickly ruled against the President's precipitate action.[35]

Instead, he continued to concentrate on foreign policy. Often quoting his book, he was careful to dissociate himself from Herbert Hoover, who was calling for a "Gibraltar" concept that would recall American defenses to the Western Hemisphere. "I don't believe that anyone who is actually responsible for foreign policy in early 1953 could at that time take as drastic action as you propose," he told his former mentor. Taft also continued to sound accommodating regarding American troops in western Europe. And he was careful to caution against the use of American soldiers in Indochina, which was then in the throes of revolt against the French. "No United States troops," he said unequivocally in January, "should be sent to that strife-torn region." [36]

Most of the time, however, Taft harped on administration "failures." He criticized Truman's Point Four program, tried to cut funds for economic aid to Europe, and appealed again for a "crusade of propaganda for liberty throughout the world." He read the record of administration mistakes in foreign policy since 1943 and missed few opportunities to support MacArthur. Truman, he charged, seemed to believe in "war without victory. That is a doctrine I abhor." [37]

In this spirit Taft moved gradually toward the politics of confrontation with Eisenhower. Though he still refrained from a direct attack on his silent foe, he began complaining freely to friends that "the main Eisenhower men seem to be the international bankers, the Dewey organization allied with them, Republican New Dealers, and even President Truman. Apparently they want to be sure that no matter which party wins, they win." By the end of May he was beginning to consider linking Eisenhower with the failure of American armies in 1945 to secure an ironclad corridor to Berlin.[38]

During the Wisconsin primary he also sounded friendlier to Joseph McCarthy than he had at times during 1951. First he worked with Coleman in a quiet effort to get McCarthy's endorsement. "I have talked over the matter at length with Tom Coleman," he wrote Hoover, "and he feels that he can bring McCarthy around." To an influential Wisconsin leader Taft added that he approved of McCarthy's "campaign to eliminate Communists from the government." And during his travels in Wisconsin he repeatedly backed his embattled colleague. "Senator McCarthy," he said, "has dramatized the fight to exclude Communists from the State Department. I think he did a great job in undertaking that goal." [39]

McCarthy, however, refused to cooperate. He has developed a "Christ-like complex," Ben Tate complained. "Before he would come out for you you would have to support him in everything he stood for." Unwilling to go quite that far, Taft never received McCarthy's endorsement. But McCarthy did not oppose him either. Like many other office seekers in 1952 — including Eisenhower himself during the campaign in the fall — Taft had pursued the course of political expediency, and he brought himself no garlands for courage. The "man of integrity" continued to prove himself opportunistic concerning McCarthy.[40]

The most revealing development regarding Taft's campaigning in the spring of 1952, however, was not his position on the issues — or even on McCarthy, whom he had excused in the past. Rather, it was his sharp reaction to barbs flung at him by the media. By mid-May whatever good relations he had curried with the press had evaporated, to be replaced by distrust and recrimination.

In part the trouble stemmed from increasingly harsh criticisms of his views on foreign policy. The *New Republic* ran a series entitled "Concentrated Tory — Robert A. Taft," and concluded that he "set out grimly to give the appearance of warmth. But he has abandoned a deeper virtue, his integrity." *Christian Century* termed him irresponsible and alarming. And Arthur Schlesinger, Jr., and Richard Rovere, both of whom had conceded his sincerity in 1948, joined the chorus of criticism. Schlesinger, placing Taft among a breed he called the new isolationists, described him in the April *Atlantic* as a "man of transition trying hard to come to terms with the modern world." Taft's foreign policy, Schlesinger said, represented the "last convulsive outbreak of an old nostalgia." Rovere remarked in *Harper's* that Taft's comments on foreign policy and on McCarthy showed that he was "capable of taking to demagogy and of doing it with breathtaking abandon." Ambition had not caused the change, Rovere argued, but "deep, unexpected, and sometimes ungovernable passion" against the Truman administration. Taft wanted so desperately to run the Democrats out of office that he had let ends justify his means.[41]

Perhaps expecting as much from such sources, Taft did not worry too much about them. "I really do not enjoy reading any of them, no matter how good or bad they may be," he had written his sister Helen earlier. In the same spirit he never bothered even to look at drafts of an admiring brief "biography" then being prepared by an Illinois woman, Caroline Harnsberger. "He says he doesn't want to read about himself," Mrs. Wunder noted.[42] But he continued to resent the editors of *Time,* who always wanted to "show the people how smart they are," and of the New York *Times* and the New York *Herald Tribune,* which had already endorsed Eisenhower. "My greatest handicap in this whole campaign," he complained on April 30, "has been the solid backing of General Eisenhower by many of the eastern papers and others throughout the country as well as a majority of the national magazines and syndicated columnists and commentators." [43]

What irritated him most was the way the media handled the sensitive question of his vote-getting ability. The press, he complained, uncritically accepted what he termed the "deliberate propaganda campaign" of pollers like George Gallup, and it distorted the straight news, crediting him, for example, with but twelve delegates in Florida when the delegates themselves set the total at fifteen. When he won fifteen of West Virginia's sixteen delegates in early May, he expected recognition of his popularity. Instead, he noted, the New York *Times* carried the story on page 18 under the heading, "TAFT SWEEP FAILS IN WEST VIRGINIA." He complained: "It would take a diligent search in most of the eastern seaboard newspapers to uncover the fact that we have a great lead, both in the number of delegates and in the number of primary votes cast for the various candidates." [44]

His irritation was understandable, because it was hardly flattering to trail an absentee rival who had never involved himself in electoral politics. "I would be a stronger candidate than Eisenhower would be," he grumbled, "but businessmen seem to fall for the glamour stuff even more than women do." [45] But his petulance stemmed from dubious premises. The polls, whatever their shortcomings, bore no special animus toward him. Moreover, he was ready to use them when they suited his purposes; and he was even then distributing surveys by the Chicago *Tribune,* which had queried only House Republicans, an extremely small sample of known party regulars.[46] The facts were that both polls and primaries revealed an unmistakable groundswell of popular enthusiasm for Eisenhower, that many editors and columnists, whatever their personal opinions, felt duty-bound to report what the pollers had uncovered, that large circulation papers such as the Chicago *Tribune* and the New York Daily *News* carried editorials for him, and that the media's power to change people's opinions, while debatable, was probably less important than Taft believed. In complaining about the press in the spring of 1952 he revealed more about his own inner tension and growing sensitivity to criticism than about reality.[47]

Because of these tensions he also seemed less relaxed on the stump than he had been earlier in the year. Hostile columnists noted that he often refused to smile for photographers or to kiss babies. When people crowded around for autographs, he sometimes blurted, "no, no." Autographs took three times as long as a handshake, he told them; if you want my signature, send a letter and ask for it. As Edwin Lahey recalled sympathetically, Taft simply lacked the common touch. After a press conference in North Dakota, Lahey remembered, a high school newspaper editor mustered the courage to introduce herself. "So they shook hands," Lahey continued, "and then there was this Mendenhall Glacier over there — everybody uncomfortable. Finally he said, 'Well, what can I do for you?' Very pleasant but very stiff . . . 'Senator,' the girl asked timidly, 'could you tell us some of your humorous experiences?' Well," Lahey concluded, "I had to leave. I couldn't stand it. This was terrible. It was like a man's pants falling off or something. You get embarrassed for them." [48]

Mrs. Wunder, faithfully recording her experiences, reinforced Lahey's impressions. When Taft returned from a meeting in mid-April, she asked him how things had gone. " 'Oh, fine,' " she quoted him, " 'except there were a lot of those crazy women there.' 'You mean Eisenhower women?' " she asked. " 'No, Taft women.' " "Bob," she concluded, "does get embarrassed by mass admiration." Both she and Lahey recognized that Taft had changed little over the years. He still found it hard to chatter, tell stories, unbend with reporters, even to accept the plaudits of a crowd. He remained the enigmatic politician who at once could display becoming modesty and breathtaking curtness and self-assurance. [49]

Well-wishers frankly offered advice. Talk slower, wrote the veteran actor Adolphe Menjou, and pause at the end of phrases to let your points sink in. Don't race through your speeches, John Hamilton cautioned in a lengthy memorandum. "Your principal difficulty lies in a state of mind in which you are more engrossed in the context of the sermon than in the method of delivering it." Strive for personal warmth, another supporter advised.

> The voter . . . sees that same dryness — or shall I say arrogance — which has been typical of the Taft campaigns in the last twelve years. Bob Taft has a good smile but he does not know how to use it. Eisenhower does, and the people fall for it. Taft can be simple, he can be kind; why isn't he his own self when he speaks to the voter? [50]

Why indeed? The answer was that he had always been that way: decent and reflective in private, yet stiff, partisan, and fiercely loyal and competitive in public. With the enemy now threatening to deprive him of his goal, he had to strain himself, and he became ever more engrossed in the public man. In April he got the sad news that the family homestead in Murray Bay had burned to the ground. And sometimes he even grew testy at home. "Poor man," Mrs. Wunder noted on May 6. "He hurt his back lifting Martha last night, had a busy disappointing day, came home tired and found the living room set up by photographers. He was very cross, and I felt very sad." [51]

The tensions of early spring were starting to take their toll.

CHAPTER 34

"Stealing" Delegates

WITH TAFT AND EISENHOWER neck and neck as the race turned into June, both sides fought harder than before. By early July neither had succeeded in pulling out in front. But in their desire to win, Taft's aides played rough, and Eisenhower's team counterattacked. By convention time, July 7, the struggle had become one of the roughest in years.

At the beginning of the stretch Taft anticipated a somewhat more gentlemanly finish. "The chances still are in favor of my nomination in spite of the defeats in the East," he cautiously informed an old friend from Murray Bay. "Our campaign appears to be in good shape," he added on June 9. "Our efforts are now being directed toward holding our delegates in the face of the 'blitz.'" With so much money pouring in that he was later able to return many contributions, and with his organization functioning well, he had grounds for optimism.[1]

The last of the primaries, in South Dakota June 3, added to his sense of well-bring. Taft had expected to profit from an agreement to divide the fourteen-man delegation ten for himself and four for Eisenhower. But the general's enthusiastic supporters waged a spirited campaign that cost an estimated $44,000 and brought in a host of prominent politicians to speak on his behalf. Quickly accepting the challenge, Taft invaded the state at the end of May for a five-day tour. To farmers he talked of his stand on farm cooperatives, and to Mennonites he denounced universal military training. ("Draft Ike And He Will Draft You," read stickers distributed by his local supporters.) Responding on primary day, the agricultural areas gave him majorities, while one heavily Mennonite county voted for him by a margin of four to one. The final tally gave him 64,695 votes to 63,879 for Eisenhower. It was hardly a ringing victory in an area long believed to be Taft country. But at least he had won. When he secured thirty delegates from the Indiana state convention a few days later, AP credited him with 462 committed delegates, to Eisenhower's 389. With but 604 needed to nominate, Taft was coming close.[2]

Unfortunately for Taft, the Eisenhower forces stepped up their pace. On June 1 the general flew home, and on June 4 he launched his campaign with an elaborately staged "homecoming" in Abilene. Taft, at last, had to worry about the active candidacy and presence of his rival.

Actually, Eisenhower proved far from impressive in his early appearances. He had suffered from a strep throat and pinkeye in May, and he arrived home tired. Unprepared to deal with the issues, he shocked a group of conservation experts by asking what parity payments were. And at Abilene people had to stand ankle deep in rain and mud to listen to him mutter bland generalities over nationwide radio and television. "It looks like he's pretty much for mother, home, and heaven," chortled Carroll Reece. Eisenhower, the New York *Times* agreed June 15, had scarcely "started a real prairie fire" of enthusiasm.[3]

But the excitement surrounding Eisenhower's return tended to obscure his inadequacies, and Taft again complained of the extraordinary attention his rival received in the media. The New York *Times* devoted pages to tell its readers everything Eisenhower did during his first weeks in the United States. *Newsweek* placed him on its cover June 9, as did both *Life* and *Time* a week later. The radio and television networks followed him so assiduously that Taft made an issue of demanding equal time (for the Abilene speech) from the Federal Communications Commission. And from July 1 through July 3 the *Times* ran editorials entitled "MR. TAFT CAN'T WIN."

Editorially at least, the New York *Times* pretended no objectivity. Neither did such publications as *The Nation*, which pronounced Taft the "leader of an aggressive neo-fascist coalition," nor *Progressive*, which branded him "the last of the old breed . . . Already he begins to take on the slightly glazed look of the high-

"I may decide to run." *L. D. Warren, Cincinnati* Enquirer

button shoes and nickel beer era."[4] But *Life* attacked him more
deviously on June 23. Its story, entitled "The 1912 Overture to
1952," described Eisenhower leaders holding "strategy meetings,"
while Taft backers "huddled to plot strategy." It printed a cartoon

of Taft running a steamroller over delegates. It showed him holding a hot dog, then added, "he posed with it but didn't eat it."
Taft, *Life* added, pursued the "emotionless and systematized style
of a good club fighter," while Eisenhower, a genial man, rested in
his "modest red-barned farm near Gettysburg." By its use of words
and juxtaposition of photographs *Life,* which typified the attitude
of many Eastern internationalists hostile to Taft's foreign policy,
showed "objective" picture journalism at its most insidious.[5]

It was again difficult to say, however, whether Taft fared much
worse in the media than his rival. How often, after all, did a war
hero contend for the presidency a month before the convention?
And Taft did receive considerable attention. *Newsweek* had
placed him on its cover in April, and *Time* followed on June 2,
two weeks before it did the same for Eisenhower. The New York
Daily News, which claimed the largest circulation of any newspaper in the country, endorsed Taft on June 21. Even *Life* devoted a picture story to him in late May.[6] His problems in June
1952 stemmed less from machinations in Times Square or Rocke-
feller Center than from the bumbling of his own men two thousand miles to the southwest. Nothing that happened during the
campaign — not even New Hampshire — was to hurt him so
much.

•

Texas Republican politics, like those in other southern states,
mocked the American two-party system. Candidates had long
understood that the state was almost certain to vote Democratic in
a national election. Yet Republican national conventions regularly allocated Texas and the other southern states many delegates,
and nominees had contested bitterly for the support of the
tiny organizations that lived primarily for patronage from Republican Presidents. "All rank and damned little file," aptly characterized these organizations. Factional struggles within these
groups had often culminated in rival delegations, and in 1912 the
Republican convention's credentials committee had settled such a
contest in Texas by seating regulars partial to William Howard
Taft. The decision, hotly denounced as a "steamroller," offered
Theodore Roosevelt a pretext to walk out, then to form the Pro-

gressive party that divided the Republican vote and led to the victory of Woodrow Wilson in the election. Despite such unhappy precedents, the Republicans in 1952 allocated Texas thirty-eight delegates, which tied it with Massachusetts and New Jersey as the sixth largest delegation at the convention.

Well before 1952, it was obvious that trouble loomed ahead for the Republicans in the Lone Star State. Colonel R. B. Creager, long the local party's dominant figure, had died in 1950. In the ensuing factional struggle Henry Zweifel of Fort Worth, who had led the Dewey forces in 1948, bested H. J. ("Jack") Porter of Houston for national committeeman. By late 1951 the Zweifel faction, predominantly pro-Taft by then, controlled the party's executive committee — and therefore its central machinery. But Porter, assisted by Dallas leader Alvin H. Lane, refused to quit, and factionalism rent the party.[7]

The Taft managers had coveted Texas from the beginning, and Ingalls had visited the state as early as January 1951. There he discovered widespread sentiment for Eisenhower. "If Ike was an active candidate," he wrote frankly, "at least as of today not many of the delegates could be held for Taft." Operating on this assumption, Ingalls struggled to negotiate a compromise. But Porter proved intransigent, and Marrs McLean, an influential San Antonio politician, Taft supporter, and member of the National Finance Committee, called for a fight to the end. "When the show down comes," McLean told Taft, "I believe you will have 85% if not more." Faced with such implacable divisions, Ingalls lamented to Porter that "the thing that astonishes me is the fact that with so few Republicans as you have in Texas . . . you can't get together." In September, 1951, Ingalls finally conceded the impossibility of compromise. There will be, he prophesied, "a bitter fight for the delegation."[8]

By early 1952 the two factions were fighting openly, and Zweifel was turning repeatedly to Ben Tate for financial help. But after touring the state in mid-March, Taft grew more optimistic. "Zweifel," he wrote, "is 100 per cent for me and . . . he will have a very large majority of the delegation with him." When he discussed the Texas situation with Ingalls, Jack Martin, and Tom Coleman a few days later, all agreed that prospects looked bright.

"Our chances for thirty out of thirty-eight delegates," Coleman concluded on March 17, "are very good." [9]

The Porter faction then committed the ultimate heresy of turning to Democrats and independents for support in the precinct conventions that were to start the complex process of delegate-making in May. Hoping to stop such activity, Zweifel unearthed a little-noted section of the state elections code that appeared to restrict participation in such conventions to party members. He also designed a pledge for participants in the conventions. "I am a Republican," it said, "and desire to participate in Republican party activities in 1952." Porter struck back by noting that the Texas Supreme Court had held that present intent, not past voting behavior, determined one's eligibility to participate in the nominating process. Democrats, he argued, could attend Republican conventions. "If asked to sign a declaration that you will support the Republican nominee," Porter's faction advertised widely, "SIGN IT! . . . You CAN vote in BOTH Democratic and Republican elections — DO NOT BE INTIMIDATED!"

Because of the ambiguities of the election code, it was difficult to know which side was right. But by instructing its followers to sign the pledge, the Porter faction had gained an immeasurably important tactical advantage, and when the precinct conventions convened May 3, it made full use of it. Republican regulars in San Antonio and in some rural areas controlled matters as they had in the past. But in most urban precincts they were overwhelmed by droves of newcomers pledging themselves Republican and trumpeting their affection for Eisenhower. Some of Zweifel's men even tried to hold the conventions in their homes, only to find hordes of people overflowing into the warm Texas darkness. At some such meetings, where rival partisans shoved and punched each other, the atmosphere grew ugly. At others it turned ludicrous, as the factions adjourned to lawns or parking lots, peered suspiciously at each other through the night air, and tried to count noses.

To the Taft forces the conventions posed a terrifying threat. Zweifel himself had been one of those who had called a meeting at his home, only to be forced to his front yard when a hundred Eisenhower supporters thronged to his door. Like most other regulars outnumbered by the enemy, he responded by naming a rival

Taft delegation. When the turbulent meetings were over, the Associated Press estimated that 426 precincts favored Eisenhower, 155 Taft, and that 168 were uninstructed. But the Taft forces were ready with rival delegations of their own.[10]

The county conventions a few days later witnessed the same performance. Taft partisans, confronted with Eisenhower majorities in most of the counties, angrily stormed out to hold rump meetings. "Farewell, New Dealers," they shouted. "We Like Ike," their foes jeered back. Both sides then instructed delegates for the ultimate confrontation — the state convention at Mineral Wells May 27. As the protagonists gathered for the final round it was clear that a contest was inevitable.[11]

The scene at Mineral Wells, a spa west of Fort Worth, resembled no other Republican gathering in Texas history. More than four thousand people poured into the town which had beds for no more than a thousand; the unlucky ones had to sleep forty to fifty miles away. Washington reporters, covering the Texas drama for the first time, watched closely over the proceedings. Herbert Brownell hurried down for the Eisenhower forces, and both David Ingalls and Carroll Reece were on hand for Taft.

Those few Texans still neutral enough to work for compromise were quickly disillusioned. Zweifel's executive committee plunged into its task of hearing repeated complaints from the Eisenhower leaders. In precinct 176 of Harris County, these leaders testified, Eisenhower people outnumbered Taftites 472 to 4; in precinct 38, they led 334 to 6; in precinct 70 it was 256 to 4. The Taft forces countered that their rivals were Democrats who had signed pledges they intended to repudiate. Accepting this argument, the executive committee systematically unseated the Eisenhower delegates, and after almost twenty consecutive hours in session gave the Zweifel faction 596 of 606 disputed seats.

The next day the regulars completed their work. With the 596 disputed Taftites voting on their own fates, they were seated, 762 to 222. The Eisenhower forces waved signs — "Rob With Bob," "Graft with Taft." They chanted, "We Like Ike." And once again they stomped out. The regulars then named a delegation to the national convention which, while technically uninstructed, was expected to hold between thirty and thirty-four of the state's thirty-eight votes for Taft. The dissidents held a rump session to instruct thirty-three for Eisenhower, five for Taft. Brownell fired the parting shot. "The Taft forces," he exclaimed, "are now convinced that he cannot win the nomination — so now they are out to steal it." [12]

．

Neither faction crowned itself with glory in Texas. The Porter forces had been brazen in advising non-Republicans they should feel free to pack the precinct conventions in May, then to vote as they wished in November. To Taft, committed in principle to party government, the Eisenhower people were bringing "an end to the two party system, the basis of stability in modern government." Using an analogy suggested to him by John Hamilton, he later likened Porter's strategy to that of a minister who tells his flock to attend another church the following Sunday and name his friends as deacons.[13]

Yet Zweifel's overzealousness made Porter look clean. Having noticed the surge for Eisenhower, he tried to stay it by requiring people to sign pledges. When Porter's followers shrewdly agreed, Zweifel was trapped, but instead of admitting that many of the pledge-signers were sincerely pro-Eisenhower (the GOP carried Texas in November), he ran roughshod over his opponents. Zweifel's excuse — that only tested Republicans should vote in GOP meetings — also conveniently overlooked the fact that many Republican regulars had publicly supported Democrats in the past. In trying to keep the party a preserve for the rare birds who had always occupied it, he stood in the way of the Texas party's first chance in years for victory. Obviously, Taft's attention to the South did not signify a desire to broaden the base of the national party, but to capture delegates.

Taft himself, campaigning elsewhere in April, at first did not give the festering controversy the attention it deserved. Jolted into thinking about it after the precinct conventions early in May, he inclined toward compromise. "I am sorry about the mess in Texas," he wrote McLean May 6, "but I understand that something may still be worked out." "I would rather like to make a compromise if we can," he added two weeks later, "because I don't like the idea of contests and the bitterness which is always brought about by them." Intent on other matters, Taft regarded the imbroglio in Texas as a "mess," as a matter for politicians to settle in good time.[14]

He had every cause to know better. As time for Mineral Wells approached, his office received a deluge of letters and telegrams protesting the Zweifel steamroller. Yet he listened instead to McLean, who was breathing fire. "This setup," McLean wrote of the forthcoming executive committee meeting over the contested delegates, "gives us a chance to rough it up with them so that they will likely bolt the convention, as we do not propose to seat any of the delegates." Taft replied that he would still prefer a compromise, but instead of restraining McLean he encouraged him by describing plans to capture a majority on the credentials committee of the national convention. Neither then nor later did he try to stop McLean and his fellow operators.[15]

The intransigence of both factions made it highly unlikely that he could have avoided some kind of a confrontation at Mineral Wells. He was also served poorly by his advisers — not only men like Zweifel and McLean but professionals like Reece and Ingalls. And he understandably found it difficult to admit that the Eisenhower tidal wave had swept loose the old politics of the South. But after the precinct conventions he should have alerted himself and disavowed Zweifel's tactics. In failing to do so he lent himself to one of the more clumsy grabs for delegates in recent American history.

Thus at the very time he was capturing the South Dakota primary he found himself slammed to the defensive. Columnist Joseph Alsop, taking up where Brownell left off, attacked the Taft managers for "a system of rigging as grossly dishonest, as namedly anti-democratic, as arrogantly careless of majority rule, as can be found in the long and often sordid annals of American politics." Raymond Moley, the veteran *Newsweek* columnist who had written favorably of Taft during the campaign, criticized the "stupid" Taft organizers who "have been unworthy of him and have perhaps fatally injured his cause." And Herbert Block, the widely syndicated cartoonist, drew a much reprinted cartoon that captured the mood of many observers. It showed Taft and MacArthur in a tank labeled "Taft Machine." Taft looked puzzled. "Who's using a steamroller?" he asked.[16]

Strangely enough, the Eisenhower people were a little slow to pursue Brownell's lead. But when the general moved to the offensive, he took off the gloves. "The rustlers," he said, "stole the Texas birthright instead of Texas steers." Soon the Eisenhower managers were talking of nothing else. It was 1912 all over again; Taft, they said, had perpetrated the great "Texas steal" of 1952. Alsop later estimated that the Eisenhower partisans spent more than $3 million publicizing the Texas "steal." [17]

Taft's strategists, shaken gradually from their complacency, offered all kinds of advice to counter these accusations. Hamilton recommended making an offer of arbitration. "Thus we could avoid the washing of dirty linen before the eyes of the public." John Hollister insisted on getting control of the credentials committee in Chicago. "ANYTHING," he urged, "should be traded for votes in that committee." And Paul Walter stressed the futility of trying to compromise the issue at this late date. Such an effort, he insisted, would imply wrongdoing and establish the moral position of the opposition.[18]

At first Taft indignantly rejected the accusations. "The Eisenhower people are shouting about Texas," he wrote, "but all over the country they have used the most ruthless methods of eliminating Taft delegates." He told reporters that participants in the nominating process ought to swear that they had voted Republican in the last election — or that states should allow people to change their voting registrations only "up to a certain date." The Texas fight, he told a friend late in June, had come from "internal rows in the organization there." Eisenhower, he added, "is pretty sore, which arises out of the fact that he does not really understand what politics is about." [19]

Yet when the Eisenhower forces intensified their assault, Taft began to bend. He had always prided himself on his uprightness, and the accusations of thievery gradually shook him. When Walter persisted in calling for a strategy of no compromise, Taft flared angrily at his long-time aide for one of the few times in their association. Taft then acted in character. The Texas affair, he believed, was not a moral but a mathematical issue. Careful study would discover the proper ratio of delegates. There were three categories of delegates, he concluded. The first, numbering nineteen, was composed of bona fide Taft men. The second, thirteen in all, was contested; these he would give to Eisenhower. The other six delegates were chosen at large, and these, for the sake of "unity," ought to be divided three to three. The final tally: Taft twenty-two, Eisenhower sixteen.[20]

Taft's numerical division was not wholly unfair, for scholars later decided he was entitled to sixteen delegates, eleven more than the Porter faction was prepared to grant.[21] But his mathematical approach failed utterly to prevent the Eisenhower people from making Texas a moral issue or from linking Texas with a series of decisions by the Taft-controlled national committee. Two such actions named Walter Hallanan, Taft's leader in West Virginia, as temporary chairman of the convention, and General MacArthur as keynoter. Then on July 1 the committee outlawed radio and television facilities from its deliberations — a decision which went counter to Taft's own advice, infuriated the media, and enabled the Eisenhower managers to rage againt clandestine operations. The committee then seated disputed Taft delegates in Georgia, Mississippi, and Louisiana. When it concluded its work on Independence Day by accepting Taft's twenty-two to sixteen division of the Texas delegates, it goaded the Eisenhower supporters to new rhapsodies of rhetoric and set the scene for one of the bitterest conventions of recent times.[22]

Governor Dan Thornton of Colorado, shrewdly capitalizing on the Texas issue, was meanwhile applying the coup de grâce. Gathering the twenty-three Republicans at the annual governors' conference, he and Dewey got them to sign a manifesto. Republicans, it said, should not permit contested delegates to vote on the seating of other delegates. If accepted, the manifesto would overturn the existing rule established to aid William Howard Taft in 1912. But no matter, for Texas had been a "steal." Every governor at the conference, Taft supporters included, felt obliged to sign.[23]

•

The governors issued their manifesto on July 2, five days before the convention. Taft still seemed so strong that AP gave him a lead in committed and undisputed delegates of 458 to 402. (Figures including disputed delegates in the South made the totals 530 to 427.) Half of the nation's fifty top political writers also thought he would win.[24] Relieved that the primaries were over, Taft spent a little more time at home with Martha, Darrah Wunder, and Lillian Dykstra, who was to accompany Martha to the convention. Bob, Mrs. Dykstra wrote, seemed "relaxed and doesn't look too tired." On July 4 he even played eighteen holes of golf before returning to his Georgetown home for supper on trays with the women. That evening several people telephoned, including Harold Stassen. "Bob," Mrs. Dykstra was pleased to say, "was amused. He won't promise him [Stassen] anything." [25]

But Eisenhower led the Gallup polls of independent voters by seven to one and of Republicans by a margin of 44 to 35 per cent. As the New York *Times* was proclaiming in its "Mr. Taft Can't Win" series, much of Eisenhower's delegate strength lay in the pivotal northern states, Taft's in southern and border states that had gone Democratic since 1932.[26] And Eisenhower had the "moral" issue of Texas. "For years," one of many outraged citizens cabled Taft on Independence Day, "I have been a great admirer of you . . .

> I come from three generations of Yale men and voted for you in the primary. Your recent actions . . . turned my stomach and make me feel there is little hope for our beloved country. What is the use of changing one corruption for another. God help us.

Another added:

> We progress from the smoke-filled room to the stench-filled convention. I had planned to vote for almost any Republican nominee including you to sweep the Democrats out, but if the hard-shelled pro-Taft interests get away with this stuff I will vote for the Democrats even if it's Harry.[27]

After so many months of struggle, had it all come to that?

CHAPTER 35

Defeat at Chicago

WHEN THEODORE ROOSEVELT arrived in Chicago before the Republican convention of 1912, he angrily assailed the tactics of the organization behind William Howard Taft, his former political comrade. The regulars, he charged, were stealing delegates and steamrolling the convention. Despair not, he exhorted his excited supporters. "We stand at Armageddon and we battle for the Lord." [1]

Forty years later, July 5, 1952, Bob Taft slowly descended the ramp from his plane into an atmosphere that was uncannily similar in its moralistic bitterness. Outside the Conrad Hilton Hotel, which was to be his headquarters while in Chicago, a sound truck was already moving back and forth, blaring "Thou Shalt Not Steal." And infighting was ravaging many of the delegations as soon as they landed in the hot and humid city. When a revolt by a minority of Taftites threatened Dewey's control of New York, Dewey reminded them openly that he would be "governor for the next two and one half years, and I mean that." The restless New Yorkers sullenly held firm, but Dewey's very presence infuriated the Taft people. "He is just about the nastiest little man I've ever known," Mrs. Dykstra wrote. "He struts sitting down." [2]

Taft, upset by the attacks on his integrity, was sounding a little plaintive in private. "Why do they hate me so?" he asked a newsman. "There seems to be such violence to it, yet our political differences are merely matters of degree." He also resented the ascending refrain, "Taft Can't Win," which the New York *Times* editorials helped to amplify. And he worried about Martha, whom he had decided to bring along but who required constant attention from her nurse, from their houseman-chauffeur "Mack" Gray, from Lillian Dykstra, from Darrah Wunder — herself in an ankle cast as a result of a recent fall — and occasionally from his four sons. As he followed Martha's wheelchair down the ramp to the hot and dirty pavement at Midway Airport he might well have looked nostalgically to the happier campaigns of the past — or even to have questioned the drives which had taken him this far.[3]

If he harbored such doubts, he told no one at the time. Besides, the scene at Midway left him no time for reflection. As soon as he stepped off the ramp, he was surrounded by his brother Charlie, his son Lloyd, Senator Everett M. Dirksen of Illinois, and a throng of four thousand enthusiasts who cheered and chanted "Taft for me, Taft for you, Taft Will Win in 'Fifty-two." Cameramen shouted for pictures, and well-wishers pushed him in front of a microphone, where the crowd pressed so tightly that police had to lock hands around him. Taft smiled broadly, spoke confidently to the crowd, and climbed into a waiting car for a triumphant motorcade into downtown Chicago.[4]

He had some grounds for confidence, because his organization had outdone itself in making arrangements. During the convention he was to stay with Martha and her entourage in the five-room presidential suite of the Congress Hotel. (*Life,* in a basically mindless story, devoted pages to the lavishness of the suite and carried one large photograph of the $2500 bed on which Taft would sleep.) But these were solely living quarters, acquired to give Martha some privacy and him a chance to dine with his family in the evenings. His organizers had also reserved the ninth floor of the nearby Hilton as his convention headquarters and had established a "Taft Town" in the Hilton's Grand Ballroom. The "Taft Town" featured a complete press headquarters, music by Sammy Kaye's orchestra, and appearances by such movie personalities as Glenn Ford, Gary Cooper, and John Wayne. The Taft leaders were determined not to let the Eisenhower forces monopolize the glamour.[5]

They had prepared meticulously for the more important task of keeping in touch with delegates. As delegates arrived they were welcomed by Taft supporters, accompanied to their rooms, and apprised of coming events. The Taft leaders also compiled notebooks listing every conceivable sort of political information and personal gossip. "Cannot be trusted, has reputation for being swayed," one delegate was described. "Wonderful chap, fine and strong for Taft, but does not know practical politics and cannot be much help," was the line on another. "Widow, likes flattery, good time. Right type flattery might win her over," a notation portrayed a third. If the convention were to develop into a struggle for handfuls of delegates, the Taft people were as ready as anyone.[6]

Still another development encouraged Taft as he arrived in Chicago: the likelihood that General MacArthur would agree to become his running mate. Neither man committed himself to such an eventuality, and many of Taft's friends later insisted that he would have ended by selecting someone else — most likely Dirksen or William Knowland. Yet on the eve of the convention MacArthur was reported ready to take the job, providing it involved larger responsibilities than merely presiding over the Senate. And Taft had seriously discussed the vice-presidency with the general's aides as early as March. Would you like to have MacArthur run with you? reporters asked on June 29. It would be "quite a ticket," Taft replied enthusiastically. "It would be entirely up to General MacArthur, and I don't know whether he would accept." Though Taft stopped short of a commitment, he had every right to expect the backing of the five delegates openly endorsing MacArthur, plus the good will of scores of others who admired him.[7]

Above all, Taft knew he could count irrevocably on the support of 500 of the 604 delegates needed to nominate. Many of these 500 represented southern states that rarely voted Republican in an election. But they were delegates nonetheless, staunch party regulars who revered him. Most of the 500 also hated and feared the eastern "Dewey wing," which had outgeneraled them in three consecutive conventions. They considered Taft the epitome of integrity, dependability, and undying hostility to the Fair Deal; and they freely and bitterly admitted that this was his last, best chance. As Taft carried through a busy round of appearances, fittingly sporting a colorful tie with elephants on it, reporters could not help but observe the depths of emotional attachment that he aroused among these delegates. When he strode into a basement exhibition hall of the Hilton on Sunday evening July 6, he awed even veteran observers by clutching aloft some five hundred telegrams from delegates who had bound themselves to remain with him until the end and who then offered him a tumultuous ovation. "It was perhaps the most impressive display of personal strength," wrote Richard Rovere, "made by any political leader in American history." [8]

.

Only one thing was lacking: another 100-odd delegates to give Taft the majority he needed. Because Eisenhower was thought to have nearly 450 delegates himself — and because strong men like Dewey were holding backsliders in line — there were but few places Taft might find the elusive majority of 604.

The first lay in the favorite son delegations of Minnesota, which was expected to give most of its twenty-eight votes to Stassen, and of California, whose seventy votes Knowland was holding for Governor Warren. But Minnesota, scene of the extraordinary write-in vote in March, was expected eventually to go to Eisenhower. California, the second largest bloc of votes at the convention, seemed more promising, and Taft had carefully avoided offending Warren or Knowland. But he never offered California anything, whereas the Eisenhower people had made it clear that Senator Richard Nixon would be an excellent running mate. Indeed, on the train that carried most of the California delegates to the convention this talk had already begun to alarm the Warren loyalists, who distrusted Nixon. In any event both Knowland and Warren insisted that they were staying in to the finish. For the time being at least Taft had to reckon without California. [9]

Another potential source of support lay in the important delegations from Michigan and Pennsylvania. The forty-six-man Michigan delegation arrived in Chicago with six partial to Taft, seven to Eisenhower, and with national committeeman Arthur Summerfield holding the balance uncommitted. Tom Coleman, a personal friend of Summerfield and his family, kept Taft apprised of every development. At first Coleman had despaired — the industrialists of General Motors and Ford, he complained, were forcing Eisenhower down the throats of their employees. But months of careful work with Summerfield had changed his mind, and in April he had written Jack Martin that "I firmly believe right now 28 or 30 Michigan delegates are for Taft and will vote that way now." By July Coleman still seemed confident, and Taft, reluctant to interfere with the activities of his advisers, looked for a happy outcome in Michigan.[10]

Pennsylvania Republican politics were more confusing. The primary, which Eisenhower had won over token opposition, bound no one, and the seventy-man delegation arrived in Chicago badly split. Approximately twenty-five were expected to follow Senator James Duff and vote for Eisenhower. Another thirteen to eighteen, taking their cue from Senator Edward Martin, would back Taft. But the remaining thirty-odd delegates were awaiting word from Governor John Fine, who was known to admire MacArthur, but who was vacillating at convention time.

Recognizing Fine's importance, Taft had sent him photographs and campaign literature and had written to refute the public opinion polls that Fine followed closely. Taft had even driven to Harrisburg himself to confer with the governor. On the eve of the convention, however, Fine still had not committed himself, and when he arranged to dine with Summerfield in Chicago, reporters predicted that both men would come out for Eisenhower. The "Taft Can't Win" argument, *Time* explained, had cut deeply. "We've got a lot of people who, after twenty long years, don't want to take any risk at all," it quoted Fine. But Taft had to hope for the best; perhaps Pennsylvania and Michigan could lift him over the top.[11]

The last potential source of votes involved contested seats, thirty-eight in Texas, seventeen in Georgia, and thirteen of the fifteen in Louisiana. Taft enjoyed the blessing of the National Committee, which had not only accepted his compromise of 22 to 16 in Texas but awarded him all seventeen in Georgia and eleven in Louisiana — or fifty of the sixty-eight disputed seats. He knew also that the convention's credentials committee would sustain him at the next stage of the controversy. But the convention as a whole could overrule the credentials committee, and the sound truck was continuing to blare, "Thou Shalt Not Steal." As both sides recognized, roll calls on the contested southern delegations would reveal which side really controlled the convention. And such a test could unleash a bandwagon psychology culminating in the nomination. On such mundane issues, the fate of the party was to rest.[12]

•

Convention hall, the International Amphitheater, was air-conditioned, and it spared delegates a repeat of the inferno at Philadelphia in 1948. But it was located in the stockyards section of the city, several miles from the hotel headquarters of the candidates, and it was set up so tightly that delegates could hardly squeeze by the throngs of photographers and newsmen who jammed the passageways to the stage. When National Chairman Guy Gabrielson opened the proceedings in the early afternoon of Monday July 7, the delegates were packed elbow to elbow in their seats, and the noise was so loud that speakers on stage had to shout. Taft, comfortably ensconced before a television set at his headquarters in the Hilton, was spared these physical discomforts. But he was also far from the scene and able to communicate with his aides by telephone only. They in turn had to thread their way to contact each other. He was shortly to discover that easy communications were almost nonexistent.

Gabrielson opened the convention by calling upon John Bricker, who headed the Ohio delegation, to move temporary adoption of the convention rules as practiced in 1948. In past conventions such a routine motion had occasioned little comment. But this time Governor Arthur B. Langlie of Washington arose to propose a substitute. It resolved that no disputed delegates (except those authorized by at least two-thirds vote of the National Committee) be permitted to vote on any contests until the delegates from the nondisputed states had agreed to seat them permanently. This substitute resolution, which the Eisenhower people shrewdly designated the "Fair Play" amendment, stemmed from the manifesto issued by the Republican governors a few days earlier. If passed, it would change the previous rules that had allowed contested delegates temporarily validated by the National Committee and credentials committee to vote on disputes other than their own. It would deprive Taft, at least temporarily, of a net advantage of thirty-two votes (his fifty minus Eisenhower's eighteen) on ballots to determine the permanent seating of the sixty-eight disputed delegates from Texas, Louisiana, and Georgia. This loss, in turn, might give Eisenhower the margin he needed for the nomination.[13]

The Taft leaders had anticipated some such move by the opposition. Ingalls, Coleman, who was serving as floor manager, and Clarence Brown, who as Ohio's national committeeman was again in the forefront, had spent much of the night and following morning talking with Gabrielson and haggling with Lodge, who was Eisenhower's manager. Lodge, however, refused to surrender Eisenhower's moral issue in Texas; the general, he proclaimed, was a "no deal man."

Finally accepting the inevitable, Coleman and Brown conferred hurriedly outside Gabrielson's office just before the convention opened. Here they hatched an elaborate plan. Instead of risking a roll call on the anticipated amendment to the rules, Brown would take the stage to demand a point of order on Louisiana's seven district delegates. Because party rules specified that state committees should decide contests involving delegates chosen by districts, and because the Louisiana state committee had done so, Brown and Coleman contended that the national convention lacked authority to settle them. Gabrielson, a Taft supporter, would presumably recognize their point of order, and the convention would then have to vote against the chair to overturn it. Because Brown and Coleman thought the delegates would be reluctant to challenge the chair, they expected the point of order to save seven votes for their candidate. To avoid a potentially damaging vote on the Langlie substitute itself, Brown could then magnanimously move its adoption.[14]

Neither Coleman nor Brown seemed to realize that such a strategy promised little: Why haggle over technicalities when the most to be gained was seven votes? But before they had a chance to attempt their plan the fast pace of events overwhelmed them. Lodge showed them the Langlie resolution only a few minutes before the convention opened, then refused even a fifteen-minute recess. Bricker, unaware of the strategy that Coleman had devised, then routinely offered his motion on the rules, and Langlie followed immediately with his substitute. Before the Taft men had fully coordinated their thinking, a key issue of the convention demanded to be resolved.

The Langlie resolution also threw the convention into a turmoil. The Taft partisans booed loudly, Eisenhower delegates shouted back, and delegates overflowed excitedly into the already crowded aisles. Gabrielson, trying to restore order, furiously called on the sergeants at arms to clear the passageways. But the delegates paid little attention, and during the heated debate that followed few people could make themselves heard over the din of the crowd.

Brown then took charge. He rose from his seat, was recognized, and struggled through the throngs toward the stage. But by the time he reached the podium he had developed second thoughts about offering a point of order, for Gabrielson, who was under severe pressure from the Eisenhower forces, seemed an uncertain quantity. Thinking fast, Brown grasped the microphone and told the convention, "there is a question in my mind as to whether or not the amendment is subject to a point of order." A chorus of "nos" from the carefully instructed Eisenhower delegates then overwhelmed him, whereupon he abandoned the plan for a point of order, and offered instead an amendment to exc...de from the Langlie resolution the seven district delegates from Louisiana. Quickly seconded, it became the focus of the rancorous debate that ensued.[15]

The Brown amendment, as everyone called it, rested on the valid technicality that the Louisiana state committee had followed existing procedure. Taft partisans also stood on tenable ground in complaining about attempts to change suddenly rules that Dewey himself had found satisfactory in 1944 and 1948. But the Louisiana controversy, like the one in Texas, had long ago become an emotional issue. Indeed, most people recognized that the Taft-controlled state committee had ignored evidence of Eisenhower majorities resembling those in Texas. Yet here was Brown standing before a nationwide television audience and calling for the delegates to besmirch the image of the party by opposing "Fair Play."

Taft gasped when he saw Brown heading toward the stage. Then he got on the phone to Paul Walter, who recalled that Taft "virtually went out of his mind. I have never seen him in such a state of frustration." But Brown was already out of reach, and the Taft team had not yet established a network to overcome the obstacles of noise and crowded aisles. Thus Brown, his speech punctuated by boos and catcalls, meandered on, and when he finished Coleman had no choice but to dispatch Ingalls, Bricker, and others to reinforce his argument. But pandemonium ruled, and the delegates impatiently awaited the roll call.[16]

When it finally occurred late in the afternoon, it was decisive. With all 1206 delegates voting (including the disputed 68 temporarily seated by the National Committee) Brown's amendment lost 658 to 548. Aware of the futility of fighting on, the Taft leaders then moved unanimous adoption of the Langlie resolution, which quickly passed. Technically, the battle had settled only the procedure for later votes on the contests. But it had also tipped the hand of the uncommitted states. Michigan voted against the Brown amendment, 45 to 1, California 70 to 0, Pennsylvania, 57 to 13, Minnesota 28 to 0.[17] This did not necessarily mean they would support Eisenhower, but it did suggest they would later vote against the disputed Taft delegates. Brown's amendment revealed that his candidate, even with the contested 50 votes from the South, had a maximum of 548 votes. It unleashed a demoralizing round of recriminations within the Taft organization. And it infused the Eisenhower partisans with joy and confidence. At the very first session of the convention the unpleasant truth was revealed: Eisenhower had the votes, Taft did not.

For Taft things could scarcely have been managed more ineptly. Despite the usual braggadocio about delegates, his managers knew that he lacked a solid majority on the floor. Having failed to get Lodge to compromise, they should not have risked a roll call so early on such an emotion-laden issue, let alone for but seven delegates. Instead, they should have pretended magnanimity, accepted the Langlie resolution, and postponed a revealing roll call until later. That they did not was the fault of Brown, who again proved his limitations, and ultimately, of Taft himself, who had not learned the lesson of 1948: When the stakes are high, do not rely on subordinates to handle such matters by themselves.[18]

·

Taft knew enough about politics to hide his feelings, and except for his outburst over the phone to Walter he refused to criticize his aides. Reporters still found him easy and accessible, and he carried on his busy schedule as if assured of the nomination. With Douglas MacArthur and Herbert Hoover slated to speak the next two evenings, with the credentials committee preparing to back his Southern delegates, and with his supporters as devoted as ever, he refused to surrender hope. "Everything is relaxed and hilarious," Mrs. Dykstra noted in her diary. "How I wish everyone could see Bob this way — so amusing and warm." [19]

But the next two days brought repeated disappointments. Recognizing the inevitable, Taft felt obliged to give up all thirteen disputed seats in Louisiana, and he watched unhappily as MacArthur gave a pedestrian keynote speech. Most ominous of all, John Fine and Arthur Summerfield were rumored to be working for Eisenhower. Taft's strength seemed to be ebbing fast.[20]

On Wednesday night came another blow, this time over the disputed Georgia delegation. This case pitted two factions that had already hauled their dirty linen to the national convention in 1948. The group behind Eisenhower enjoyed the status of having been officially recognized in 1948 by the GOP national committee. But it had not tried to start a pro-Eisenhower groundswell like those which had rolled through Texas and Louisiana. Thus when Taft supporters drew up a slate in 1952, they believed they had a tenable case, and by July 9 they still felt that way. If the senator could triumph in Georgia, he might win in Texas as well.[21]

Debate on the issue quickly grew heated. Dirksen, who was emerging as one of Taft's most stalwart supporters, stunned the convention by pausing in the course of an emotional address to say a "special word to my good friends from the Eastern seaboard." Calling on the New York and Pennsylvania delegates to hold up their hands, he looked hard at Dewey and reminded everyone of 1944 and 1948. "Reexamine your hearts," he told the easterners, "before you take this action . . . we followed you before and you took us down the path to defeat." The Deweyites shouted in protest, fights broke out on the floor, and even Dirksen, who seemed taken aback by the response, pleaded for understanding.[22]

Dirksen's speech, however inflammatory, probably did Taft no harm, for most of the delegates cared little for the merits of the shabby battle. When they finally voted late that night, they seated the Eisenhower faction, 607 to 531. The margin of 76 was 34 closer than it had been on the Brown amendment, because a few of the uncommitted delegates thought Taft had a valid case. But again the doubtful states overwhelmingly supported Eisenhower's cause, even though they knew they were diminishing chances for the deadlock which their favorite sons needed. Even if Taft had had the support of his contested delegates from Louisiana and Texas (votes excluded by the Langlie resolution), he would have fallen short of victory.[23]

As most observers recognized immediately, the vote on the Georgia delegation sealed Taft's fate. Fine quickly ended doubts about his position by endorsing Eisenhower, and Taft's managers resignedly gave up the fight for Texas. At 1:30 on Thursday morning the convention unanimously seated the Porter delegation of thirty-three for Eisenhower, five for Taft. The long night of acrimony had cost Taft thirteen in Louisiana, seventeen in Georgia, and seventeen (he got five instead of twenty-two) in Texas — forty-seven in all. It had shattered the southern strategy. And it left him with little but time before the end of the trail.[24]

Privately Taft seemed to know he had lost. After watching the roll call on the Georgia vote, he had turned to get Martha ready for bed. "He kissed her," Mrs. Dykstra recorded, "and hoped she would have a good night." Then he added calmly, " 'if I'm not nominated, you'll have more quiet nights, dear.' " But the end was approaching, and as the nominating speeches droned on into Thursday night even Ingalls, normally genial and even-tempered, signed his name to a broadside circulated to the delegates. "SINK DEWEY," it said. "TOM DEWEY IS THE MOST COLD-BLOODED, RUTHLESS, SELFISH POLITICAL BOSS IN THE UNITED STATES TODAY. He stops at nothing to enforce his will. His promises are worthless. He is the greatest menace that the Republican party has." As Richard Rovere perceptively observed, it was a mark of the hate rending the party that this extraordinary diatribe barely attracted notice.[25]

The next morning the balloting was to begin at last. Still outwardly confident, Taft assembled his supporters and told them not to despair. "I've been sitting up most of the night making figures and calculations," he said characteristically. "I feel that we have an excellent chance of winning today." Aroused, his delegates sang "Onward Christian Soldiers" as they marched into convention hall. Taft then returned to his headquarters to watch the proceedings on television. When the balloting started, he phoned Vic Johnston at the convention. "Go to Senator Knowland," he said, "and tell him I'd like to talk to him after the first ballot is over. Maybe we can work something out." [26]

What Taft had in mind — perhaps the vice-presidency — was left unsaid. But it did not matter, for Johnston quickly returned to the phone. "Knowland," he reported, "says there isn't going to be any second ballot." Knowland was right, for the first ballot moved quickly. Eisenhower, like Willkie and Dewey before him, swept the delegate-rich northeastern states and held enough elsewhere to get 595 votes, to Taft's 500, Warren's 81, Stassen's 20, and MacArthur's 10. Minnesota then switched 19 Stassen votes to Eisenhower. Other states followed, and the final tally gave Eisenhower 845, Taft 280, Warren 77, and MacArthur 4. Bricker then moved the nomination be made unanimous. It was the third time in twelve years that he had carried out this task for his Ohio rival and colleague.[27]

·

What had gone wrong?

As usual in such cases, there was no shortage of theories. The first, devoutly held by many of Taft's friends, pointed to mistakes by his staff. "Somehow or other Bob never seems to be able to organize for a convention," one well-wisher wrote. "Every bloody time he gets into the convention his organization falls down and the other fellow takes it away from him." *Newsweek,* concurring, spoke of his advisers' "egregious errors," while Governor Warren, no stranger to politics, still felt many years later that blunders cost Taft the nomination. And Coleman, probably Taft's ablest adviser, agreed that "in our group there were some whose job left much to be desired." As he warned Taft's son Bob in 1963 — when "Young Bob" was himself preparing to run for the Senate — "I was in a good position to judge the harm that some of your

Father's old supporters could do to him and did do to him. Your Father had a tremendously loyal attitude toward people who had been loyal to him, and I am afraid that it did him some damage." [28]

This line of thinking rested on undeniable facts, for Taft had again shown himself so careless a judge of men that people questioned what kind of a President he would have made. Hamilton had badly overestimated chances in New Hampshire. Coleman himself had proved overconfident about Summerfield. Mismanagement by many top leaders, Ingalls and Reece included, had led directly to the "Texas steal." And Clarence Brown, who had fumbled in 1948, had found a way to do it again by overriding Coleman and Taft himself in barring television from the deliberations of the National Committee and by following with his inopportune amendment to the Langlie resolution. Capping an unenviable performance, he proved the only member of the Taft team to complain publicly about his allies. "If anyone is at fault," he remarked defensively after the convention, "it's Tom Coleman. He was Taft's floor manager. He was in on all the meetings, and I didn't hear him object." [29]

But pointing to mistakes in strategy overlooked two things. First, by most standards of comparison — including Taft's effort in 1948 — his organization had functioned efficiently. Ingalls and Tate had canvassed carefully for months before Taft committed himself. Guylay had proved competent at publicizing Taft's appearances. Tate had amassed more than enough money — at least $7 million. Coleman's direction of the Wisconsin campaign struck observers as masterful. And Walter, Johnston, and others proved thorough in handling organizational and delegate work. Because Taft crashed in the end, it was easy to sift through the wreckage and pick up small parts which had malfunctioned. But the body of his campaign was better constructed than that of many presidential aspirants in the past, and it came remarkably close to collecting the nomination.[30]

The second fallacy was to assume that the grossest blunder, Texas, by itself cost him the nomination. Surely, it hurt badly. If he had repudiated Zweifel, he would have deprived Eisenhower of the moral issue, and Lodge and Langlie might not have dared to try to change the rules over the lesser controversies in Georgia and

Louisiana. But these were might have beens, for every vote taken at the convention revealed the overriding fact that Taft simply lacked enough delegates. Even with his contested 50 seats on the Brown amendment he amassed but 548 votes. To have written off Texas might have preserved Georgia and Louisiana, but nothing suggested that such a move would have given him Michigan, Minnesota, Pennsylvania, or California. Without these crucial delegates Taft could not have won, and that was that.

The truth was that Taft suffered from the same burden that had held him down in 1940 and 1948: weakness in the populous northeast and Pacific Coast. On the Brown amendment — his best showing — he led in the South, the Plains, and the mountain West, and he swept Ohio, Indiana, and Illinois, 145 to 3. But he lost the West Coast states, 108 to 4, New England, 96 to 14, and the five Middle Atlantic states from New York through Maryland, 211 to 29. As in 1940 and 1948, he had collided with a keystone of political demography: At convention time it was often the important eastern states that ruled the Republican party.[31]

This repeated Eastern domination accounted for the fury of his friends. Frustrated by defeat, they persisted in blaming Dewey's ruthlessness, the power of Wall Street money men over industrialists, or some combination of the two. Yet the real problem was that coastal Republicans had long distrusted Taft's views, especially on foreign policy, and his voting record since 1948 had done nothing to set their minds at rest. Indeed, William White's biography of Taft labeled the years 1949 to 1952 "the sad, worst period" of his life. While White distorted matters a little — Taft had proved accommodating on many domestic issues in this period — he described a widespread belief among Eastern Republicans that Taft lacked the necessary understanding to conduct America's foreign relations in the dangerous postwar world. One Deweyman wrote: "I believe he [Taft] would make a splendid President for a stable, prosperous country in an orderly world — say in 1925. I suspect, however, that, as has happened to many other able and patriotic men, his political serviceability has been repealed by World War II and the rise of the Third International." [32]

The Easterners also turned from Taft because they did not want to risk losing in November. Eisenhower, the military hero, the

"Don't be ridiculous. Nobody is a dinosaur any more."
From The Herblock Book (*Beacon Press, 1952*)

captain of NATO, excited the voters. Only he could overcome the
Democratic lead in voter registration that had overwhelmed Republicans in the populous urban regions of the Northeast since
1932. So many of the delegates admired Taft that Rovere, among
others, was certain a majority yearned to nominate him. But they

were practical men and professional politicians who had watched
their party go down to defeat in presidential elections for twenty
years and who thought he would run poorly in their states. Eisenhower's amazing appeal, with the refrain "Taft Can't Win," hurt
Taft badly in 1952.[33]

In this ultimate sense Taft had fallen out of step with his times.
Too much himself to soften his profile, he happened on the national scene at the same time that Franklin D. Roosevelt was dem-
onstrating the magic to be wrung from the mass media. Myopic
and somewhat disdainful about the importance of "image," he
struggled to prominence just as public opinion polling developed
into a powerful tool for his opponents. Instinctively partisan, he
tried for the presidency after the depression had helped the Democrats build an electoral coalition that forced Republicans to turn
to Dewey and even to such unpartisan figures as Willkie and Eisenhower. Fearful of commitments abroad, he reflected broad cur-
rents of thought about foreign policy more suited to the 1920's —
or even the late 1960's — than to the frightening years spanned by
Hitler and Stalin. Like the two men who had affected him most,
his father and Herbert Hoover, Taft had clung steadfastly to a set
of assumptions about the world. Like them again, he had been
swept aside while new men of destiny — Wilson, FDR, Eisenhower — came in to fill the void. When the delegates whispered,
"Taft Can't Win," they were talking not only about a man who
lacked charisma but about a figure who seemed uncomfortable
with the world of 1952.

•

Two tasks remained before the convention adjourned — recon-
ciling the two factions, and naming a vice-presidential candidate.

Eisenhower gamely undertook the first. After the balloting he
phoned to ask Taft if he could pay a visit. Then he left his room at
the Blackstone Hotel and fought his way across the crowded street
to the Hilton, where workmen were already dismantling "Taft
Town." Finding an elevator, he rode to Taft's headquarters on
the ninth floor, only to be staggered by the scene before him.
Women were wailing, men snarling. "They ought to pick Dewey
for Vice-President," one said, "and let him run the whole show."

"I'll never vote for anyone who calls himself a Republican again," cried another. "We Want Taft," the crowd chanted. The mob — for that is what it was becoming — was packed so tightly that security men had to force a passage so that Eisenhower could reach the door of Taft's room.[34]

Once inside, Eisenhower found his rival remarkably composed. Indeed, even before losing Taft had drafted a statement of defeat (as well as one of victory), and during the balloting he had sat quietly. When his fate was sealed, he simply remarked, "Well, our figures haven't stood up." Then he had called Martha, who was at their suite in the Congress, to find her undisturbed — she was really too self-concerned to care — by the course of events. When Eisenhower finally arrived, Taft asked only if his three sons could be present (Horace was with Martha), then welcomed him to his rooms. After calming his rival down — Eisenhower was in a highly agitated state following the excitement of victory and the shock at the scene in the hallway — he ushered his foe outside to face newsmen.[35]

Once in the hallway, both men were almost mauled by the throngs outside the door. Visibly ill at ease, Eisenhower turned in alarm to his rival. "You'll get used to it," Taft replied laconically. "I was telling my wife," Eisenhower responded, "that when I really have a nightmare it's when I imagine I have been nominated — and elected." Again Taft sounded composed: "You'll win the election all right." Newsmen noted that it was Eisenhower, the winner, who looked drawn, his eyes moist with emotion, while Taft, the loser, seemed poised and dry-eyed.

Perhaps because Taft was among his friends, he also took charge. He waved his hands and shouted for attention. "Everybody, please be quiet!" With flash bulbs popping and microphones thrust roughly over his shoulder, he calmly made a statement. "I want to congratulate General Eisenhower," he said. "I shall do everything possible in the campaign to secure his election and to help in his administration." Eisenhower followed with a tribute to a "great American," then struggled to the elevator and was gone.[36]

The moments of drama over, Taft too squirmed back to his headquarters. Outside his door the crowd began to disperse, but only slowly. Newsmen found Coleman and asked for his views.

No comment, he replied tersely. Tate, spying Dewey in a hotel lobby, had to be physically restrained from hitting him. Men and women continued to weep in the hallway, the elevators, the lobby downstairs. For the stalwart five hundred and their allies, the loss to Eisenhower was almost too much to bear.[37]

Yet Taft seemed calmer than ever. "I can take it," he joked to the well-wishers who filtered in and out of his headquarters that afternoon. "After all, I've had plenty of practice." "He won, we lost," he told a reporter. "Quit politics?" Then he laughed heartily. When he got back to see Martha in their private suite, he kissed her and Mrs. Dykstra, then said calmly, "Well, this was always one of the alternatives." As in 1940 and 1948 he impressed all who saw him with his strength and graciousness in defeat. "He had no petty jealousy and hatred," the newsman Edwin Lahey remembered. "He was freer of them than almost any man I've ever seen in public life." [38]

How he managed such poise in the aftermath of his cruelest disappointment defied precise explanation. Perhaps he had not had time to absorb the full meaning of the shock. Probably he had confronted the possibility of defeat more seriously than he had let anyone know. Perhaps, as his subsequent public life was to suggest, he felt a burden removed from his back: Freed from towering ambitions and aspirations, he could continue as senator in a life he knew as well as anyone in America. And certainly he was displaying the same tight hold on his emotions that he had maintained in public ever since being thrust into the spotlight as a child. At any rate, the columnist Arthur Krock wrote for many when he concluded that Taft seemed at peace with himself. "This was his finest hour . . . even had he become President, he could have left no finer memory to the people." [39]

•

In the midst of consoling his admirers Taft also had to think about the vice-presidency. Indeed, Alexander Smith, his Senate colleague from New Jersey, had already been pressing him to take the job if Eisenhower won the presidential nomination, and Taft, according to a diary Smith was keeping at the time, had been "willing to consider the matter if it would help to heal the wounds and enable the party to move forward." When the Eisenhower leaders — Brownell, Adams, Lodge, Senator Frank Carlson of Kansas, and others — met to pick a running mate, Smith joined the group and immediately suggested Taft. Brownell and Lodge, Adams wrote later, "made no move to oppose it," and Summerfield, who was to replace Gabrielson as national chairman the next day, "thought it was a fine idea." For a few fleeting moments it seemed that the impossible might be considered: an Eisenhower-Taft ticket.[40]

Unfortunately for such dreamers, Eisenhower himself had already told his associates that he favored younger men like Knowland, Driscoll of New Jersey, or especially Nixon. At the meeting Sinclair Weeks then argued that Taft would be more useful in the Senate. And Russell Sprague, one of Dewey's veteran aides, observed that with Taft on the ticket the party could not carry New York. With this remark the group turned to other names and quickly settled on Nixon. That evening the Californian was nominated by acclamation, and at 8:20 PM the convention adjourned, sine die.[41]

Smith, disappointed, noted in his diary the next day that he had seen Taft and found him "sorry that he had not been asked to be Vice-President. He probably would have accepted." It was possible that Smith was right, that Taft, like Lyndon Johnson eight years later, would have surrendered a position of power in the Senate to take second place under a victorious rival.

Possible, but unlikely. The preconvention campaign had left angry scars on Taft's supporters, many of whom would have blanched at such a marriage of convenience. Indeed, Smith seems to have been the only one who really thought Taft would take the job. Taft had even called up Carlson during the afternoon deliberations and suggested — of all people — Everett Dirksen, who had done more than anyone else during the acrimony at Chicago to infuriate the Deweyites. Had he tried, Taft could hardly have spoken more eloquently of the chasm that divided the two wings of the Republican party and that made an Eisenhower-Taft ticket the sort of combination on which idle dreams are made.[42]

Taft did not go to convention hall for the acceptance speeches that concluded the festivities. Instead, he returned to his suite at the Congress and dined with Martha, his sons and daughters-in-law, Mrs. Wunder, Mrs. Dykstra, and his friends the Stanley Rowes. It was perhaps a characteristic of politics that almost no one save Senator Millikin and John Foster Dulles (who had known him and Martha for more than forty years) stopped by to talk in his hours of defeat. Yet Taft's grace placed everyone at ease. "He was the gayest and most amusing of all," Mrs. Dykstra noted. At one moment, she marveled, Dulles lightly placed his arm around Taft and quipped, "How many of you can tell me who was President when Webster, Clay, and Calhoun were functioning?" No one, Mrs. Dykstra noted, had the answer. But Bob laughed and said, " 'Some of my friends have been trying to retire me to the Vice-Presidency, but Foster, you're trying to retire me to history.' " [43]

The next morning he crossed to the Hilton for a farewell visit to his staff. Arriving at headquarters, he found workmen replacing his posters with those of Richard Russell, the senator from Georgia whose headquarters for the imminent Democratic convention were to be established there. Taft also found his secretaries and office workers as teary as the day before, and the scene seemed to affect him. "This is the last time I'll ever run for President," he told them. "I'll be too old." Waving to his staff, he turned to the elevator. "Well, good bye," he saluted them. Reporters noted that he seemed to have a lump in his throat.[44]

That Saturday afternoon, instead of resting, he joined his nephew Lloyd Bowers for eighteen holes of golf in sweltering heat and humidity. And on Sunday, a gloomy, humid day with temperatures in the nineties, he collected Martha for the drive to the airport, where they were to board a plane for Murray Bay. Enroute to Midway the clouds thickened, it threatened to rain, and the streets which had echoed with cheers on his entrance ten days earlier were silent and deserted. Martha, who was not feeling well, began to weep. Taft placed his arm about her, consoled her softly, and awaited the end of the ride. When they arrived at the airport, no one was on hand to send him off. He lifted Martha out of the car and followed her wheelchair onto the plane.[45]

PART VII

Responsibility

CHAPTER 36

Fencing with Eisenhower

TAFT HAD hardly settled his wife in Murray Bay when he flew off again for Washington. There he cleaned up his desk, conferred with aides, and dined with Alice Longworth and other friends. Then he drove slowly north, stopping to visit the Stanley Rowes at their summer place in Rhode Island and to see the Robert Blacks, old acquaintances from Indian Hill, at their home in Maine. His friends noticed that he brightened when people recognized him — in Boston, where he drove with Rowe to do some shopping, he was touched when a store owner insisted on selling him a record player for Martha at half price. But both the Rowes and the Blacks also observed that he sometimes seemed upset and that he refused to say whether he would support Eisenhower in November.[1]

Back in Murray Bay by July 23, he stayed for the summer at the home of relatives, the Semples. Their house, roomy, ivy covered, and flanked by a wide porch overlooking the St. Lawrence, was next to the Taft family place which had burned down that spring, and he felt comfortably at home in it. The weather was cool and refreshing after the sticky heat of Chicago and Washington, and he reveled in the fresh air. He played golf every morning, took Martha and Darrah Wunder driving in the afternoons, joined old friends who stopped by for tea, and happily endured the bedlam created by nine grandchildren. With Congress adjourned, with no campaign to plan, he for once had little to do.[2]

Camping offered special pleasures. Almost childlike with enthusiasm, he went off in August to the Laurentian wilderness with Bob, Jr., his wife, Blanca, and Bill's wife, Barbara. There he fished for four days, and in the evenings, instead of immersing himself in a book, he told nonsense stories, joked with his daughters-in-law, and gaily mixed drinks before climbing into his sleeping bag for the night. Returning to Murray Bay, he surprised Barbara by suggesting they all go out again, and when she declined — she and Blanca had to tend to their children — he complained unhappily. It had been years since he had taken such time to enjoy the pleasures of his childhood.[3]

Yet friends occasionally noted a certain melancholy. As if too bruised to bare his feelings, he evaded serious talk about politics. He also admitted to a friend that he was "greatly disappointed . . . I think a President today has a hundred times the power of a Senator, and I believe that only through the Presidency can one secure the carrying out of the policies in which you and I believe." [4]

It was impossible, too, to ignore the letters that poured in from the faithful. "If there is anything I do not like, Bob," an admirer wrote, "it is an ingrate, and you have suffered at the hands of an ingrate in your own party, and they surely nominated an ingrate. I will do everything I can to defeat General Eisenhower and I know there are many other men like me." "On July 11," his cousin Hulbert Taft wrote, "something went out of the lives of a lot of millions of Americans. Now we have moderates and conservatives in the background, with Mr. Roosevelt's New Dealers, Mr. Truman's Fair Dealers, and General Eisenhower's socialist Republicans in the foreground. Maybe a third party wouldn't be so bad after all." When Senator Smith of New Jersey, who was also vacationing in Murray Bay, stopped by to pay his respects, Taft took him into the house and showed him three huge stacks of mail — one calling on him to support Eisenhower, another telling him to sit quietly, the third urging that he pull out of the party. There was no way he could have put the convention out of his mind.[5]

Indeed, while in Washington after the convention he had already set down his interpretation of the campaign, and in Murray Bay he used spare moments to enclose it with letters to his friends. This interpretation, a 2200-word essay which he entitled "Analysis of the Results of the Chicago Convention," offered some insights into his thinking. The accompanying letters, written over the course of the next two months, told even more.

The analysis began by deploring newspaper accounts that blamed his advisers. As he properly (and loyally) insisted, no "striking move would have solved the whole problem." On the contrary, he continued, two insidious influences had brought defeat. The first was "the power of the New York financial interests and a large number of businessmen subject to New York influence who had selected General Eisenhower as their candidate at least a year ago." The second was the press. "Four-fifths of the influential newspapers in the country," Taft wrote, "were opposed to me continuously and vociferously and many turned themselves into propaganda sheets for my opponent." Taft then devoted several pages to characteristically mathematical breakdowns of crucial delegations, to the Texas question (a bogus issue trumped up by self-righteous opponents), to the Brown amendment ("probably a mistake because it showed that the combined forces against us controlled the convention"), and to what he called the "key vote" on the Georgia delegation. He concluded by admitting that he could have tried to throw his support to MacArthur (or to "some other candidate holding my general views") after the first ballot, "if it became clear that I could not be nominated and that he would have been stronger on the second ballot than I." But throughout his analysis he stressed his lack of votes in uncommitted states like Pennsylvania, California, and Michigan, and he reiterated that a "tremendous publicity blitz" had frightened John Fine, Arthur Summerfield, and their followers. As Richard Nixon was to do publicly in the aftermath of his defeat for the governorship of California in 1962, Taft ended — privately — by placing much of the blame on the press.[6]

In many ways the document revealed the man. It showed his preoccupation with statistics, his dogged loyalty to his advisers, his coolly professional understanding that last-minute tactical maneuvers seldom determine nominating conventions. It also exposed his instinctive distrust of eastern financiers. This emotion may have seemed strange in a man who was often dismissed as a spokesman for business, but it flared in the thinking of many midwestern

Americans, and it had pulsed deeply in the family tradition since Alphonso had complained in 1838 that in New York "money is the all and all." Above all, Taft's analysis proved that the media had frayed his nerves, and that beneath the efficiently mathematical analyst of voting trends lay a vulnerable human being.

Careful readers could detect this undertone of bitterness. Yet the document, like the man, muted his emotions, for he had written it partly to stop the recriminations that were threatening to divide his advisers. "I have toned this way down," he explained privately, "because of my fear that it might easily be published and create . . . dissension . . . Perhaps after the whole thing is over I might talk with you regarding it." [7]

His covering letters came a little closer to expressing the true extent of his unhappiness, particularly with the role played by specific individuals. Thus he confessed that Thomas Coleman had made a mistake in relying on Summerfield's impartiality — "in fact," Taft admitted, "I understand he [Summerfield] definitely agreed to be for Eisenhower on June 28th." Taft also hit sharply at Harold Stassen and Earl Warren. "The truth is," he told Ingalls, . . . "we needed about fifty more delegates in the various contests in order to be on safe ground; or else we needed a Warren and a Stassen who had some intelligence." Of Pennsylvania's kingmaker, Taft was contemptuous. "The less said about our friend, Governor Fine," he wrote, "the better." And he complained repeatedly of the "Eastern businessmen and the editorials and the radio people." The "New Deal," he concluded, "has wined and dined and flattered the editors so that they have been pretty much converted to the New Deal point of view, particularly on foreign policy." [8] Considering the defeat he had suffered, most of his letters showed considerable restraint. But they also proved that the cool breezes of Murray Bay had failed to blow away all traces of hard feeling.

The Eisenhower camp sensed Taft's attitude and quickly grew concerned. Indeed, Eisenhower himself had wired Taft on July 17, "I would be happy to plan for a meeting to suit your convenience after your holiday is over." Henry Cabot Lodge, Sherman Adams, General Lucius Clay, and other Eisenhower men adopted their nominee's posture, and the French Canadian telephone operators at Murray Bay soon had to handle frequent calls from luminaries throughout the United States. One caller, financier Winthrop Aldrich of New York, even offered to send up his private plane to take Taft to a meeting with Eisenhower.[9]

But Taft's friends were demanding a hard line. The Dewey crowd, Jack Martin wrote, just want to "use your good name to give the impression that all has been forgotten." If Eisenhower won, Martin added, "Dewey and his crowd will come out of the wall and try to accomplish their one objective — your political demise." At Murray Bay Taft was getting similar advice, especially from Darrah Wunder. "I love taking their calls," she recorded in her diary, "and telling them sweetly that Bob is fishing and cannot be reached . . . I'm pleasant but firm." Two weeks later she added: "they have all been urging him to see Ike, that is Summerfield, . . . Adams, Aldrich, etc. *I have encouraged him to take his time.*" Whenever Taft seemed to bend, Mrs. Wunder persisted. "I guess you are right, Darrah," he acquiesced, and went fishing.[10]

Besides, he had not forgotten the slurs on his name. "The tactics used by our opponents," he wrote, "are difficult indeed to forgive." The Texas business, he added, was "the most complete theft . . . that I have ever seen take place in my time." He also relished the attention his enemies were lavishing on him. Thus he told Eisenhower he would see him, but put off the meeting until September. He also urged his friends to "hold off any cooperation" until then and to "stall off" requests to help raise money. "I am going to stay here and say nothing until September 8," he told Lou Guylay. "Perhaps by that time they may be scared enough to really want advice and assistance and not merely the appearance of it for publicity purposes." [11]

Having agreed to meet Eisenhower in September, he quickly recognized a maze of unattractive courses to follow. On the one hand, he recoiled from the thought of supporting Governor Adlai Stevenson of Illinois, the Democratic nominee. "Stevenson," he explained, "would give us a complete continuation of what Truman has supplied, although perhaps with a more cultivated accent." On the other hand, he truly wondered about Eisenhower. "The candidate," he told his friend Walter Trohan of the Chicago *Tribune,* "doesn't understand what the issues are." And he feared

the Deweyites. Eisenhower, he wrote, "is inclined to be conservative; but I certainly do not trust four-fifths of his supporters, and it
would be more difficult to combat a Republican New Deal than a
Democratic one." Senator Alexander Smith observed in his diary
that Taft was "in doubt about going all out . . . he wants to
know if it is to be a 'me-too' campaign and a 'me-too' administration." [12]

In this frame of mind in early August, Taft sat down to write a
lengthy "Memorandum on General Eisenhower." He began by
observing that he had spent a year calling for "certain principles,"
and that he had "built up a tremendous following because of that
campaign." Thus, "I cannot do anything to indicate that I am
giving up those principles." Second, he could not ignore his supporters, who were "angry enough at the tactics used at the convention to form a third party today if it were practical, which of course
it is not." And third, Eisenhower's course suggested that the election would "put into power a New Deal Republican administration, perhaps dominated by Dewey." This crowd of "editorial and
financial backers are extremely vindictive . . . I cannot let down
my supporters and let them be purged . . . I should only cooperate and forgive and forget if General Eisenhower and his supporters are willing to do some forgiving and forgetting themselves." [13]

Taft followed these arguments to their logical conclusions. If a
meeting was to be held, he wrote, Eisenhower must agree to "certain assurances" in advance. He must promise no discrimination
against Taft people, either during the campaign or later when patronage was handed out. He must let Taft state his own views.
These included reducing spending by the 1954–1955 fiscal year to
$60 billion (the total for fiscal 1952–1953 was to be $74.2 billion);
cutting taxes to $60 billion, also by 1955; defending the Taft-
Hartley law "except as to various minor changes on which most
people today can agree"; adhering to a "reasonably conservative
farm policy"; and "attacking Truman and Acheson and the whole
foreign policy of the Administration on the basis of Yalta, Tehran,
Potsdam, and Manchuria." Eisenhower must also give assurances
about "the general character of the Cabinet and the foreign policy,
the including of Governor Dewey in the Cabinet, etc." Taft conceded that such commitments would be hard to make, but unless

they were made he would feel obliged to state that "while I would support the ticket, I could not ask others to do so." Because "that would not be very agreeable to me," perhaps it would be "better to avoid any meeting and simply let me go out and make my own speeches as I see fit to make them." [14]

Once Taft had marshaled his arguments, he wasted no time, and on August 6 he asked Everett Dirksen to contact Senator Frank Carlson of Kansas, who could transmit the terms to Eisenhower. And these terms, while following the outline in his memorandum, sounded even more explicit in his letter to Dirksen. Eisenhower should agree that "no spender like Paul Hoffman [a liberal Republican who had directed the Marshall Plan in Europe] be appointed Secretary of State and that Dewey not be appointed Secretary of State." He should also consent to "representation on approximately equal terms in the Cabinet of Taft supporters." If Eisenhower agreed, he should repeat these assurances to congressional leaders and Taft advisers. Under such conditions (which Taft added were "of course open to discussion") Taft said he would gladly meet the general "as soon as possible" and that he would "campaign vigorously for the ticket." [15]

If Taft expected such medicine to heal the wounds within the party — and he appears at least to have hoped so — he was mistaken, for days passed without assurances from the enemy. A little miffed, he busied himself explaining his position to friends, grumbling anew about the "disgraceful" methods of Eisenhower's managers, and complaining about the likelihood of a "Republican New Deal administration." A third party now, he explained to one angry supporter, was "absolutely impossible" for organizational reasons. But "if Eisenhower is elected and things go badly, it might be well to build up such a party during the next four years." [16] Taft, "Mr. Republican," never suggested such a move again. But in mentioning it at all he showed his acute unhappiness.

By the end of August Taft's attitude was attracting nationwide attention, and it began to appear as though the rivals would never meet. Edwin Lahey, who went to Murray Bay, found Taft "still burning with indignation at what had happened at the convention," and demanding concessions before agreeing to talk. "Do you think anybody'll be interested in paying the price?" Lahey asked. "He gave me one of those big toothy grins," Lahey recalled, "and he said, 'I don't think so.'" A few days later, still awaiting word from Carlson, Taft abruptly canceled a meeting tentatively scheduled for New York. Eisenhower, he complained, "seems to be prone to give assurances in such general terms that they don't mean anything." [17]

But events finally conspired to bring the two men together. Because Horace was to be married September 9 in Washington, the Tafts flew off from Murray Bay September 7. Arriving in the capital, he and Martha checked into the Mayflower Hotel, where the family gathered for a series of celebrations — his sixty-third birthday September 8, a gala party for the wedding guests that evening, the wedding itself September 9. But Taft was also thinking politics, and reporters, eagerly following every move, noticed that he took time to confer with Carlson and Summerfield at the hotel.[18]

Eisenhower, meanwhile, was giving signs of capitulation. His campaign had been moving sluggishly, and the Scripps-Howard papers had run page one headlines, "IKE, WHEN DO WE START?" His campaign, these papers added, was "running like a dry creek." Visiting Cleveland on September 8, he suffered through a series of local squabbles and found only the slightest ripples of enthusiasm on the streets. To newsmen the contrast was glaringly obvious: Taft celebrating in Washington, and Eisenhower staggering through the rounds with half the party sitting on its hands. Unless the candidate proved willing to deal, he might stumble to defeat in November.[19]

The ensuing pace of events surprised even the most diligent reporters. According to a schedule worked out with Carlson at the Mayflower, Taft flew on September 11 from Cincinnati to New York City, where Carlson greeted him at the airport. Reporters, spying them there, discovered that a meeting had been set for the next morning at Eisenhower's headquarters on Morningside Heights. Taft gave Carlson a statement, admonishing him to present it to Eisenhower and to discuss it with no one. And the next morning Taft appeared at 7:30 for breakfast with his rival. When photographers were finally asked in at 9:30, they found both men talking easily about fishing. Taft then said goodbye, strode across the street to a hotel, and endorsed his rival. The meeting, so long awaited, was over at last.[20]

The statement that Taft gave to reporters at the hotel outlined the agreement the two men had reached. In some ways it was more moderate than the terms he had originally spelled out to Dirksen. It said nothing about Eisenhower's repeating assurances to Taft advisers and congressional leaders, neglected to call for equal representation of Taft men in the cabinet, and made no mention of barring Dewey, Hoffman, or anyone else from office — when reporters pressed him Taft insisted that he had not even raised this matter. Taft also explained that he had asked for no written assurances. And he admitted that Eisenhower continued to hold differing views on foreign policy. To those who had been privy to the negotiations it was clear that Taft was not disposed to drive too hard a bargain.

Yet Taft had gained immeasurably more than he had conceded. The statement proclaimed that Eisenhower agreed with what Taft called the fundamental issue of the campaign: "liberty against the creeping socialism in every domestic field." It committed the nominee to aim at a budget of $60 billion in 1954–1955, to cut taxes to the same level, and to support the major features of the Taft-Hartley law. Astonishingly, it described their disagreements over foreign policy — conflicts basic enough to form one of Eisenhower's chief reasons for running — merely as "differences of degree." And it committed Eisenhower to a policy of "no discrimination against anyone because he or she has supported" Taft.[21]

The circumstances surrounding the statement must have pleased Taft even more than the substance. Here he, the defeated rival, not Eisenhower, was proclaiming the agreement. Taft explained to reporters that he had drafted most of the statement himself and that the general had merely offered a few minor suggestions. Reporters also learned that Eisenhower had not even seen the statement before breakfast. Why this was so was not entirely clear — probably because he must have been apprised by aides of the general thrust of it — but the fact remained that Eisenhower had approved an important position paper without giving it much thought. What kind of a President would such a careless operator make? Walter Lippmann wondered a few days later. Liberal Republicans angrily dubbed the occasion the "Surrender at Morningside Heights," and Wayne Morse of Oregon publicly dissociated himself from the party.[22]

Eisenhower's administration was to reveal that he really surrendered rather little. On the contrary, he believed almost as fervently as Taft in governmental economy, and on issues such as public housing and aid to education he stood to the right of his rival. Even on foreign policy the differences seemed small, for during the campaign Eisenhower denounced Truman's China policy and called for a policy of liberation in eastern Europe. In agreeing to the statement Eisenhower also showed a political astuteness hardly expected of him. Whether he had to do so to win the election could never be settled — in light of his extraordinary appeal at the polls, perhaps not. But the Morningside Heights meeting represented a grand step toward unifying the party. For him, as for Taft, the conference at Morningside Heights had been satisfying indeed.

.

In the ensuing election campaign Taft occasionally complained privately about the candidate. He doubted the wisdom of Eisenhower's call for the liberation of eastern Europe. "I agree that liberation should be our goal," Taft wrote a friend, "but I can't see us starting a war for that purpose." He grumbled about the language of one of Eisenhower's speeches on Taft-Hartley. And when Nixon, whom Taft liked, was criticized for accepting a personal campaign fund from constituents, Taft publicly defended him, then complained privately when Eisenhower hesitated before backing his running mate. Without such special funds, Taft explained to friends, politics would be strictly a rich man's pastime. "Eisenhower," he added, "showed the quality which he is accused of having, an inability to make up his mind." [23]

But Taft otherwise proclaimed his admiration for Eisenhower and appeared in twenty states of the West and Midwest in the six weeks remaining before election day. Everywhere he rallied his sullen supporters and praised his former rival. He also labored behind the scenes — unsuccessfully as it turned out — to get Douglas MacArthur to endorse the ticket, and in Ohio he supported Char-

All American teamwork. *L. D. Warren, Cincinnati* Enquirer

lie's futile campaign to become governor. He also outdid himself
in damning the Democrats. "Stevenson's policy," he proclaimed,
"is a surrender to Communist policy." His election "would mean
a continuation of the wavering, unstable, pro-Communist philosophy that has almost brought this country to destruction." Midway

through his travels Taft caught a bad cold, and in Illinois he was shaken up when a faulty elevator plunged three floors to the basement of a building. Still, he carried on as if he were the nominee.[24]

The election justified such efforts. Eisenhower polled almost 34,000,000 votes — 6,500,000 more than Stevenson — won an impressive 55 per cent of the vote, took all but nine states, and carried the electoral college, 442 to 89. Republicans even won control of both houses of Congress, 48 to 47 in the Senate (Morse had become an Independent) and 221 to 211 in the House. For only the second time since entering the Senate in 1939 Taft was to be a member of the majority, and for the first time since 1921, his freshman term in the Ohio legislature, he would be working with a chief executive of his own party.

These results caused people to wonder: What if Taft, not Eisenhower, had headed the ticket? Taft composed an analysis arguing that he, too, would have won. The standard bearer was popular, Taft wrote, but he could not have triumphed without the party vote or the "negative enthusiasm against what had been going on in Washington." Taft also complained that Eisenhower had not worked hard enough to reelect conservative Republican senators like Harry Cain of Washington, Zales Ecton of Montana, and James Kem of Missouri.[25]

Most scholars agreed that widespread dissatisfaction with Truman had assisted Eisenhower. But analysts also pointed to polls showing that Taft remained weak in the key urban states of the northeast. And they took issue with Taft's belief that the independent vote would have gone — as he argued it had in 1950 — to an aggressive and partisan campaigner like himself. On the contrary, they argued, most so-called independents tended to be apathetic citizens who voted Democratic if they bothered to vote at all. The consensus of analysts suggested that Taft would have won, but on nothing like the scale amassed by the beloved Ike.[26]

One "if" question suggested another. What kind of a President would Taft have made in 1953? Taft, pretending no false modesty, thought he knew. "I am confident," he wrote Lou Guylay in December, "that my administration would have given the people what they want much more than the General's will." [27] His many admirers naturally tended to agree. They knew he was orderly, dedicated, honest, hard-working, and intelligent. Much more than Eisenhower — indeed more than anyone in public life in 1952 — he knew the details of domestic legislation, and he had an unparalleled grasp of the workings of the federal government. The son of a President, senator for fourteen years, Taft had much more political experience than Eisenhower, and he knew what he wanted. He was well acquainted with key congressmen, he had shown an ability to grow, and he surely possessed the capacity for decision. He would also have responded more creatively than Eisenhower did to some of the pressing domestic issues of the 1950's. Under his guidance Congress might have appropriated more money for public housing, and the nation might not have had to wait until 1965 for generous federal aid to education.[28]

Even on foreign policy issues, where he had often been less well-informed, it seemed as though he stood shoulder to shoulder with Eisenhower. The general expediently embraced Senator William Jenner of Indiana, deleted a passage praising General Marshall to please the McCarthyites in Wisconsin, and proclaimed that America "must avoid the kind of bungling that led us into Korea." Besides, some of Taft's bluntly partisan remarks about foreign policy had come from a man who had spent a lifetime in opposition; perhaps the responsibilities of office would have broadened him.

Still, doubts remain. What sort of President would a man make who had allowed himself to be surrounded by plodding party regulars all his life? Would he have been able — would he have tried — to widen his circle of advisers and to bring fresh ideas into policy making? Could he have cut the budget without inflicting drastic blows on the economy? Subsequent experience suggested that America needed expansionary fiscal policies to alleviate the social and economic problems which were allowed to fester in the 1950's.

It is also questionable whether Taft could have provided the nation with the pause from partisan warfare that the people apparently expected Eisenhower to bring. Americans, it seemed, regarded the general as the veritable personification of national unity, who could heal the wounds of postwar American society. Taft, who had symbolized partisanship, might have found it more difficult than Eisenhower did to disengage the country from the bitterly divisive Korean War, and he surely could not have captured the popular imagination as the general did in going to Korea after the election. For these reasons he might have been trapped in the same quarreling which had damaged Truman during his last three years in office.[29] Taft, had he lived long enough, might have joined his father and Herbert Hoover as the third twentieth century American President to be voted out of office after one term.

Yet any judgment of Taft as President must remain speculative. Few people in 1932 predicted that Roosevelt would press for the New Deal programs he did in 1933. Fewer still could have recognized in 1945 the Truman who emerged by 1948. How many political pundits in 1964 knew that Lyndon Johnson would engage the nation so deeply in Viet Nam? And what knowledgeable observers in 1968 thought that Richard Nixon would pay a visit to Peking or establish price and wage controls on the economy? Though more consistent and principled than many politicians, Taft was flexible, and he, like all Presidents, would have been prisoner as well as manipulator of events. It is impossible to say whether the pressures of the White House would have overwhelmed him, left him unchanged, or lifted him to pinnacles of vision and greatness.

.

Two more hurdles threatened amicable Taft-Eisenhower relations in late 1952. The first involved appointments, especially to the cabinet. The second concerned Taft's own place in the Congress.

In the aftermath of the election Taft hoped for the best on appointments. "Up to this time," he wrote on November 13, "the General has shown a disposition to ask advice from myself and others, and I hope that he may sometimes take it." Encouraged, Taft talked frequently by phone with Herbert Brownell and the other Eisenhower leaders in New York.[30] And he freely suggested a number of names. On lower levels these included his old friend Lewis Strauss for undersecretary of defense; his supporter Walter J. Hickel for governor of the Alaska territory; Samuel W. King, an old acquaintance, for governor of Hawaii; and James Selvage, his occasional publicity man, for assistant secretary of commerce. For more important posts he recommended Vernon Romney of Utah, his mountain states coordinator, as secretary of the interior; Harry Byrd, his conservative Democratic colleague from Virginia, as secretary of the treasury; Carlson as secretary of agriculture; B. E. Hutchinson, a Chrysler Corporation executive, as secretary of defense; and either the moderate John Danaher, a former Senate colleague from Connecticut, or the very conservative Clarence Manion, dean of the law school at Notre Dame, as secretary of labor. Some of these men, like Carlson, Romney, and Hutchinson, Taft did not recommend very vigorously; probably he simply felt obliged to put forward their names. But he strongly supported Byrd for the treasury, and he expected to be consulted on the others.[31]

Eisenhower was able to satisfy Taft on a few major appointments. For secretary of state he picked John Foster Dulles, an international lawyer with wide experience in foreign affairs. Earlier in the year Taft had worried that Dulles was "likely to let himself be pushed around by those who are with him," but by December he admitted that Dulles was "probably the best appointment that could be made." Indeed, he even wrote Dulles to intimate that he might help by taking — at long last — a place on the Senate Foreign Relations Committee.[32] Taft acquiesced also in the appointments of Arthur Summerfield as postmaster general and Douglas McKay, a conservative from Oregon, as interior secretary. And he welcomed the selection of Ezra Taft Benson of Utah as secretary of agriculture. "You will be the only member of the Cabinet," Taft wrote him in early December, "who openly supported me before the Convention." [33]

But three other appointments distressed Taft. One of these was the selection of Charles E. Wilson, the head of General Motors, as secretary of defense. "The way things have come out," Taft sniped to Hutchinson, "it looks to me as if the government cars hereafter will be Chevrolets." "I don't like the fact," he added later in December, "that we have so many big businessmen in the Cabinet." A second disappointment was the choice of George Humphrey, a steel company executive from Cleveland, as secretary of the treasury. Taft knew Humphrey and recognized him as a fiscal conservative. But he had favored Byrd as a means of constructing an alliance of Republicans and conservative Democrats in Congress.

Courtesy, The Washington (D.C.) Star

Eisenhower, he grumbled to friends, had named an Ohioan without even asking his opinion.[34]

The crowning insult came when Eisenhower named Martin Durkin, a plumbers' union president who had supported Stevenson, as secretary of labor. "The appointment of Mr. Durkin," Taft announced publicly, "is an incredible appointment . . . it was never even suggested that a man would be appointed who has always been a partisan Truman Democrat, who fought General Eisenhower's election, and advocated the repeal of the Taft-Hartley law." Taft's objection was not personal. It stemmed instead from Durkin's attitude toward Taft-Hartley. The appointment, he explained privately, was "exactly as if he had appointed

Acheson secretary of state, or even perhaps Senator [Pat] McCarran [of Nevada], or Senator Jenner, or Senator McCarthy." It was "the first repudiation by the General of the position he took in the campaign and in my conference with him. I don't know whether he realizes that, but if he doesn't he is very stupid indeed." [35]

As a group, Eisenhower's cabinet reflected a rather conservative color — eight millionaires and a plumber, Democrats sniped. Yet Taft emerged so unhappy from the process that he journeyed to New York to insist that senators be consulted at least on the names of people from their own state. He also complained to Summerfield of the "indecent haste with which all the Eisenhower supporters seem to be demanding and obtaining jobs." And like some of the President-elect's critics, he wondered anew about Eisenhower's intelligence. "The trouble seems to be," Taft wrote, "that he doesn't read anything." [36]

The friction that developed over appointments also sent consternation through the ranks of Republicans who were hoping for a harmonious congressional session in January. Until then many of them had assumed that Taft would take the post of majority leader. Indeed, Eisenhower seemed to be operating on that assumption when he telephoned Taft the day after the election to set up a meeting to plan for the coming session. Taft had also spoken out confidently on tasks he wished undertaken in the session — surveys of military policy and of welfare programs, a study of federal-state relations, and — most important — what he told friends would be a "big housecleaning party in Washington." He had also begun to figure out ways of placing Morse on committees where he could do the least damage. And Taft had asked Darrah Wunder to stay on and serve as his hostess for twice-a-week dinner parties " 'until we get the administration running smoothly.' " [37]

But Taft had held mixed feelings from the start about becoming majority leader, a job which would have forced him to stay on the floor for hours listening to his colleagues and which might have required him to surrender his chairmanship of the Labor Committee. The Durkin appointment thus gave him pause, and he told friends he was beginning to think twice about becoming majority leader. "I have a good deal of doubt," he wrote a friend, "largely because I don't know whether I can agree with the Eisenhower administration, and if I can't perhaps I'd better have a more independent position." [38]

Eisenhower's friends also worried about having Taft as their congressional leader. "If Senator Taft wants to squabble with General Eisenhower," one anonymous senator exclaimed, "that is his business, but the party can't afford to have him do that as majority leader." Casting about for an alternative, they seized on Styles Bridges of New Hampshire, a veteran who had held the title of minority leader since Kenneth Wherry had died in the fall of 1951. Bridges, it appeared, preferred to become chairman of the powerful Appropriations Committee and to enjoy the honor, bestowed on the senior Republican senator, of sitting in the chair as president pro tem. But rumors emanated from Bridges' friends that he might take the job. And if he did not, William Knowland was known to be waiting in the wings.[39]

At this point Taft took charge. Calling up Knowland, Taft secured his support by promising him the chairmanship of the GOP policy committee. He then phoned Carlson and asked him to come quietly to the Hill on Sunday morning, December 14. There he confessed that he did wish to become majority leader. Would Carlson discover Eisenhower's opinion? Gladly assenting, Carlson went to New York on December 16, talked with Eisenhower, staged a press conference, and endorsed Taft for the job. The implication, as other senators immediately understood, was that Eisenhower did, too. Taft then contacted Bridges and three days later ended speculation by announcing that he would run for the post. When the session opened, Knowland got what he had been promised, and Taft was unanimously elected leader.[40]

As at Morningside Heights, Taft had profited from Eisenhower's sensible refusal to stand in his way. But Taft, too, showed realism and responsibility in angling for the job. Despite his disappointments, he still felt he could work with Eisenhower, and he recognized that no figurehead like Bridges could do so any better. "You can't have a lot of fellows running down to the White House and then coming back to the Senate to speak for the President," he said. "That voice has got to be one voice." He also remained indelibly partisan; after waiting twenty years for a Republican administration, he knew that December 1952 was no time to let pettiness fritter away chances for success. Finally, he truly wanted Eisenhower to succeed; otherwise, he believed, not only the party but the nation would suffer. As majority leader Taft would not be President — that dream had vanished forever. But he could be — he would be? — the President's adviser.[41]

Despite the vicissitudes in Taft-Eisenhower relations following the events at Chicago, both men had kept their poise under circumstances almost as threatening as those which had driven more revengeful Americans like John Calhoun and Theodore Roosevelt to provoke lasting splits in their parties. Eisenhower had possessed the good sense to give ground at Morningside Heights, and Taft, the party loyalist, had slowly but surely come forward to meet him near the center. As the new year opened Taft prepared to sustain his chief.[42]

CHAPTER 37

First Mate

THE CONGRESSIONAL SESSION of 1953, divided 48 to 47 for the GOP, promised to place heavy demands on Taft and the other Republican senators who yearned to show that they could run the country. In Korea, blood continued to flow. In the Soviet Union, Joseph Stalin still ruled, his grasp on the helm of state apparently more firm than ever. In Indochina, the French were wasting millions of American dollars in an ineffectual attempt to slaughter the followers of Ho Chi Minh. And at home, Senator Joseph McCarthy carried on as noisily as before. Americans had rejected the Democrats, but for what? The tensions of midcentury were still rending American society.

Never one to philosophize for long about such sweeping events, Taft busied himself with organizing the Congress before inauguration day, January 20. He took a front row seat, immediately struck up an easy relationship with Lyndon Johnson, his Democratic counterpart across the center aisle, and worked out an agreement with Southern Democrats that defeated an effort to liberalize the Senate filibuster rule. He saw to it that colleagues from his wing of the party received the vacant spots on the GOP policy committee, acquiesced in a move that stripped Wayne Morse of his assignments on the Armed Services and Labor Committees, and even left his own number two position on the Finance Committee to take a slot on Foreign Relations. With William Langer of North Dakota, Homer Ferguson of Michigan, and William Knowland taking three other vacancies on that committee, he expected to moderate the internationalist tendencies of Alexander Wiley of Wisconsin, the committee's new chairman. With Eisenhower men like James Duff of Pennsylvania and Leverett Saltonstall of Massachusetts neatly relegated to lesser positions, with Henry Cabot Lodge already sent to the sidelines by John F. Kennedy in November, Taft had quietly returned his friends to power in the Senate.[1]

He then worked at bridging some of the chasms that divided the party. He traveled to New York with Knowland and Eugene Millikin to see Eisenhower for what the press called a "showdown" over the handling of patronage. Taft labored hard to get all the Cabinet nominees confirmed before inauguration day. And he tried to control Joseph McCarthy by handing the communist issue to William Jenner of Indiana, the new chairman of the internal security subcommittee, and by establishing a guideline that all investigations be cleared through the party leadership. As Richard Rovere remembered it, Taft was so pleased with this maneuver that "he did not just grin like a Cheshire cat — he purred, too, and in time his whole face was suffused by the grin." "We've got McCarthy where he can't do any harm," he chortled.[2]

Taft did not entirely succeed in these ventures. Senators still grumbled that Eisenhower ignored them in matters of patronage. Morse filibustered so long against Charles Wilson, defense secretary-designate, that confirmation of the cabinet had to be put off until after the inauguration. And McCarthy simply used his chairmanship of the Committee on Government Operations as the forum for his accusations. But Taft had done the best he could and had succeeded in sending Eisenhower off to a reasonably auspicious beginning.

The mood on inauguration day seemed to promise further successes. A record throng of 750,000 people crowded into the city to watch a festive parade under sunny skies. Eisenhower, relaxed and smiling, gave a short inaugural address stressing his hope for peace. Taft did not reveal his feelings on this momentous day, except to worry about the new President. Eisenhower, he wrote, was "a man of good will, but I doubt whether he has the mental capacity to analyze clearly the problems that come before him." But Taft also confessed that "so far everything has gone well in the Senate, with an amount of harmony which is almost unprecedented." Amid such good cheer it seemed that the enmities that had hardened during the postwar years were beginning to thaw.[3]

Most new presidential administrations are given a period of grace during which doubters keep quiet and enemies sharpen their weapons. For several reasons Eisenhower's honeymoon lasted longer than most. Lyndon Johnson ably led the Democrats toward cooperation and compromise, and columnists, recognizing the new President's inexperience, generously gave him time.[4] Eisenhower himself seemed so well meaning that few people chose to attack him at the start. Even right-wing Republicans, some of whom were soon to emerge as the President's most dangerous enemies, seemed content to have Taft work out proper communications with the White House. When Eisenhower followed Taft's advice by ending price and wage controls early in February, they rejoiced.[5]

Taft, while pleased with these developments, continued to harbor some doubts. The administration let him press for mild changes in Taft-Hartley, but it proved unable to force Secretary of Labor Martin Durkin and Secretary of Commerce Sinclair Weeks to cooperate with one another. For the next few months Taft had to take charge himself of ultimately fruitless negotiations over labor amendments between the two departments while White House liaison men helplessly wrung their hands.[6]

He worried, too, about government spending. Truman had submitted a $78 billion budget for 1953–1954, which Taft was determined to reduce by $8 billion. But Defense Secretary Wilson seemed reluctant to cut military spending, and by late February Taft was already beginning to despair. The government, he wrote, "must make drastic economies forthwith . . . I give them until about May first to make the recommendations which will bring about a substantial reduction."[7] Unlike some of his economy-conscious Republican colleagues, he recognized that prior commitments destroyed chances for a balanced budget in 1953, he rejected demands for a tax cut before 1954, and he took a more progressive stand than Eisenhower over public housing and aid to education. But cutting federal expenditures, especially for defense, had been the essence of his demands at Morningside Heights, and in 1953 it remained his highest priority. He fumed especially over the lavishness of the military establishment, and at one White House meeting when the President seemed ready to name a general to head the Veterans Administration, Taft exploded. "No, no!" he snapped to Eisenhower. "No more generals! No more generals!" Stunned by such monumental tactlessness, Eisenhower and his advisers backed off, and Taft won the skirmish. But he was still miffed. "The trouble was," he explained later to his family, "*nobody laughed.*" [8]

Differences over foreign policy also kept him at arm's length from the internationalist wing of the party. Taft demanded cuts in foreign aid, criticized the Point Four program of technical assistance, pressed hard — ultimately with success — for air- and seapower champions as new chiefs of staff, and continued to insist that the Europeans contribute a greater share to their own defense. He offered qualified support to the Bricker amendment, a complicated proposal opposed by the administration and aimed at restricting presidential discretion in foreign policy. And he called publicly for the bombing of Manchuria. "The complete success and recognition of the Chinese Communists," he explained to a soldier in February, "would lead to the steady spread of communism down through Indo-China, Burma, and Thailand, to Singapore." This "domino theory" regarding Korea did not seem to worry the President. Indeed, Eisenhower was even then quietly threatening the enemy with military escalation if it did not agree to peace terms. Nonetheless, Taft's stance on foreign policy early in 1953 did little to reassure the eastern internationalists. [9]

Finally, the tricky problems of patronage continued to plague relations between Taft and the White House. With his party returning to power at last, Taft found himself swamped with requests for jobs, with complaints by his supporters about discrimination, and with demands by fellow senators that he educate the administration about practical politics. Because he cared more about policy than patronage, he grumbled about the situation. "I don't know of anything that gives me as much trouble as the problems of patronage," he wrote. "I never had to worry about it before in twenty-three years of legislative experience." But he felt an obligation to his friends and toiled hard to make the White House accommodate their demands. Nothing, not even the tedious negotiations over Taft-Hartley, consumed more of his time in early 1953. [10]

Eisenhower steadfastly refused to let these irritants get below his skin. On the contrary, he arranged to meet at least once a week with congressional leaders, and he told Taft to come to the White House at any time, even without securing an appointment in advance. Eisenhower phoned Taft several times to arrange golf games, began addressing him as "Bob," and in March made a point of coming to a large reception at Taft's Georgetown home.[11] The President also named Taft's son Bill as Ambassador to Ireland. Bill, an Irish scholar who had spent three years in Ireland with the foreign aid mission, was qualified, and Republican Senator Prescott Bush of Connecticut had assisted him in actively seeking the post. But many others also coveted the job, and though Taft himself kept out of the matter, Jack Martin let it be known (apparently without Taft's knowledge) that the senator was hurt at the delay in the appointment. It was certain that Bill's lineage had done him no harm.[12]

Eisenhower's conciliatory posture stemmed partly from political considerations. But he was also beginning to form a genuine personal admiration for his gracious rival, who seemed ready to restrain the party's right-wingers in Congress. Some of these Republicans, Eisenhower ruefully concluded, seemed to care little for the party. But Taft, he recalled, "was a shining exception. I quickly learned that I could count on his staunch support." As early as February 7, Eisenhower noted in his diary that "Senator Taft has been the model of cheerful and effective cooperation," and by April 1, after several golf games and innumerable private conferences, he recorded that "Senator Taft and I are becoming right good friends." [13]

Taft was a little more restrained. Wary of easy familiarity, he carefully referred to Eisenhower as "Mr. President." Respectful of the office that his father had held, he also insisted on securing appointments at the White House in advance, even after Eisenhower chided him for such formality. Taft had always been slow to form personal friendships with fellow officeholders, and he was careful about unbending with Eisenhower as well.

Yet the President had not labored in vain. By mid-February, Taft was telling friends that Eisenhower seemed to be casting aside the "Dewey organization." He added that "he has treated me very kindly in asking for advice." A month later he complained that

Eisenhower's inexperience meant that "there really is no administration policy as yet." But he excused his chief on the grounds that it took time to get organized, and he even began to warm to Eisenhower personally. After one conference in March Taft surprised a friend by suddenly exclaiming, "You know, that man is a man of good will." [14]

Thus it was that Taft seemed indispensable to the administration early in 1953. In order to concentrate on the time-consuming tasks of the leadership he turned down practically all invitations to speak outside the city, and his attendance record, always good, was better from January through April (a total of four absences in four months) than it had been since the Republicans had controlled the Senate in 1947. He also seemed adept at his job, for he kept his word, played fair with Lyndon Johnson, used his old contacts with southern Democrats, and proved a master of parliamentary procedures. As one reporter observed admiringly, he had lost none of his remarkable capacity for work, and he proved able to hold down the leadership while serving conscientiously on both Labor and Foreign Relations. The same reporter also marveled at Taft's ability to do many things at once — to read his mail while at work on the floor, to lean across the aisle to chat with Johnson, to whisper animatedly with colleagues during debate, suddenly to interpose an objection to the chair, then to resume talking as if nothing had happened.[15] Republican senators showed more unity on key roll-call votes in 1953 than at any time in years, and if the desire for a good showing in the first year of a new administration was primarily responsible for such solidarity, Taft's loyalty to the White House contributed to it.[16]

Taft swallowed his doubts on a number of occasions in order to help the administration handle its most delicate task: preventing the two wings of the party from breaking apart over foreign policy. The first of these confrontations arose in February when Eisenhower and Dulles sponsored a resolution damning secret agreements that had been "perverted" to place free peoples under Soviet influence. The resolution attempted to give lip service to the party platform that had attacked the Yalta and Potsdam accords, and to offer meaningless support to Republican talk about "liberation" of eastern Europe. But Republican partisans in the Senate nonetheless blanched when they saw the resolution, for instead of repudiating these accords per se, it merely accused the Soviets of perverting them. Dulles explained patiently that any official rejection of the agreements would enable the Soviets to repudiate them also. But the party's right wing, anxious to embarrass the Democrats, insisted that nothing short of explicit repudiation would do.

Taft sympathized with his angry colleagues. He, too, had regularly and passionately denounced these agreements for years. When he heard John Foster Dulles' plan at a White House meeting, he was careful to say that he would not support it. Then he joind six other Republicans and one Democrat on the Foreign Relations Committee in rewording the resolution so that it did not constitute any approval of the accords. Infuriated, the Democrats accused the GOP of trying to sabotage bipartisanship in foreign affairs. Equally irate, Republicans refused to budge. The stage was set for the first test of will of the new administration.

At this point fate — the death of Stalin on March 5, 1953 — intervened to save the party from a row. Despite Taft's distaste for the Yalta agreements, he had not relished the thought of a party split. Now, with Stalin dead, he accepted Dulles' argument that any resolution concerning Yalta might unsettle Soviet-American relations at an uncertain phase, and he acquiesced in steps keeping the whole issue in committee. Taft and some of his Republican colleagues had let a provocative platform plank threaten presidential-legislative harmony, to say nothing of Soviet-American relations. But had Taft persisted in his course he could have made the issue considerably more troublesome than he did. His ultimate forbearance suggested that he would not harm the administration if he could avoid it.[17]

Taft also surprised some of his Republican colleagues by his attitude toward McCarthy and other Red-hunters. On the one hand, he praised McCarthy's probe of the Voice of America as "very helpful and constructive." "I'd have fired the whole Voice of America setup," he added. But behind the scenes he gave his rambunctious colleague no encouragement, and when congressional committees began searching for communists in the universities, Taft was quick to protest. "I see no reason why the government should continue to employ people with Communist sympathies,"

he proclaimed in Chicago, heartland of the pro-McCarthy *Tribune*. "On the other hand . . . as a member of the board of trus-
tees of a university, I would not favor firing anyone for simply
being a Communist unless I was certain that he was teaching communism or having some effect on the development of the thoughts
of the students in that field." [18]

Taft's stand was not precise enough to satisfy all civil libertarians, and it did not stop a few frightened college administrators
from harassing leftist professors. It also had little immediate effect
on the Red-hunters in Congress, who carried on until McCarthy
overreached himself and was censured by the Senate in 1954. But
Taft's statement showed him at his libertarian best. When friends
wrote to complain, Taft explained that as a trustee he had objected
to the political views of prospective professorial appointees in the
past, but that he did not believe in bothering them once they had
been appointed.

> I don't feel that a man should be dismissed simply because of his
> thoughts. I think the essential freedom of this country includes the
> right to think your own thoughts, and have your own opinions
> . . . Private universities have always been the protector of free
> thinking of all kinds, and I don't like to see them lose that status.[19]

Taft's most important service to the administration in these
early months involved Eisenhower's nomination of Charles E.
("Chip") Bohlen as ambassador to the Soviet Union. A career
diplomat, Bohlen was widely recognized as one of America's top
experts on the Soviet Union. But he had been at Yalta as an inter-
preter, and to many Republicans he symbolized what they called
the "Truman-Acheson policy of appeasement." Styles Bridges, Mc-
Carthy, and others publicly attacked the nomination in early
March, and Pat McCarran, a vehemently anticommunist Democrat from Nevada, accused Dulles of concealing damaging FBI
evidence about Bohlen. McCarthy then applied the final touch by
demanding that Bohlen submit to a lie-detector test. By mid-March
the controversial nomination threatened to destroy Bohlen's subsequent usefulness as ambassador and to challenge the administration's control of foreign policy.

Taft responded to the Bohlen nomination much as he had to

the Yalta resolution a month earlier. Like his right-wing colleagues, he had often attacked the State Department, and he had
frequently demanded the resignation of Dean Acheson. But Taft
again shrank from letting such an issue divide the party, and he
turned red with anger when McCarthy demanded that Dulles tes-
tify under oath about the contents of the FBI files. Dulles' "statement not under oath," he bellowed on the floor of the Senate, "is
just as good as Mr. Dulles' statement under oath as far as I am
concerned." Furthermore, Taft added, FBI chief J. Edgar Hoover
himself opposed lie-detector tests. Again taking a civil libertarian
position, Taft opposed making the FBI files public — or even
available to the Senate. This strong stand, the first he had ever
taken publicly against McCarthy on an important Senate issue,
startled his friends.[20]

But McCarthy kept up the attack, and Taft felt forced to compromise. Why not let two senators, one from each party, look at
summaries of the files? he suggested. His colleagues, anxious to
escape the impasse, eagerly seized on this proposal, and Taft and
John Sparkman of Alabama were dispatched to do the job. For
three hours the next day they did so, only to find nothing to suggest that Bohlen was not devoted to American interests. Both senators then said as much, and the outcome was foreordained. On
March 27 Bohlen was confirmed, 74 to 13. Among the opponents
were Bridges, McCarthy, Bricker, Dirksen, newcomer Barry Goldwater of Arizona, and six other Republicans, most of them Taft
supporters in 1952.[21]

The battle over, Taft moved quickly to prevent such a confrontation again. "No more Bohlens," he told the White House. He
also did his best to pacify his angry friends. The opposition to
Bohlen, he confessed privately, was "perfectly reasonable . . .
and I would have joined it myself except that I did not think the
position of Ambassador to Russia was any sufficiently important
position to make an issue of." To another correspondent he even
defended McCarthy. "I think McCarthy joined the opposition a
little too vociferously," he wrote, "but that was principally because
the newspapers insist on playing up everything he says or does."
When reporters asked him if the Bohlen affair signified a break
with McCarthy, Taft was quick to reply, "No, no, no, no." [22]

Still, Taft had placed loyalty to the administration before strong personal preference. In so doing he helped prevent his Republican colleagues from dealing a blow to the President's prestige. Nothing that he did during his tenure as majority leader better revealed the absence of spitefulness in his spirit. The party might throw mud in his face in 1952, but now that he had the responsibility of the leadership, he would wipe it off and move on as best he could.

.

By April some people were speculating uneasily about Taft's role. They noted that he possessed astonishing power — more, perhaps, than such titans as John Calhoun and Daniel Webster in their day, and as much as the President himself. But what if he decided to swing his prestige against the administration — as some of his colleagues pressed him to do? And was it wise in midcentury America for a President to take such a restricted interpretation of his role as legislative leader? The fact that these questions were asked suggested the beginnings of disenchantment with Eisenhower's low-key leadership. It also revealed concern about Taft's enormous role in the administration.[23]

Yet to Eisenhower, who very much needed experienced men to help him, Taft's cooperative attitude was a boon. "During those days when I needed him most," he said later, "he was there, with all his vast knowledge of government — all his wisdom and experience." Neutral observers also sighed gratefully at Taft's assistance to the President, for it appeared essential to a nation long locked in partisan battles. Columnists, including many who had criticized Taft for years, competed with one another in praising him, and one cartoonist drew a confident Taft with a crown shaped like the Capitol dome on his head. "Mr. Congress," read the caption. As Richard Rovere observed in March, Taft had risen above defeat to work unselfishly with the White House and to become a major barrier to the ambitions and expectations of the Republican right.[24]

Rovere also noted a personal change in Taft, whom he called "thoroughly overhauled, remodeled, and Simonized." Taft, he wrote, was "relaxed and genial. He moves about the floor wreathed in smiles, a friend of all men, almost a gladhander. He uncomplainingly endures hours on end of Senate ritual and almost unendurable Senate oratory." Always a "true lover of ideas," always a defender of academic freedom, Taft was now stating his views openly and unashamedly. What had happened, Rovere concluded, was that "the private Taft has become the public Taft. There was always a striking difference between the mulish, doctrinaire figure of the public image and the reflective, open-minded man one encountered as an individual among individuals."

Rovere also offered an interpretation of why this change had occurred. "The pressures are off," he wrote, "the political suspense is broken, and Taft's private judgments and political aims are no longer in conflict with each other." Taft, in short, was at last a majority-party senator under a Republican President. He was the official leader of his party in the Senate, and he had to act responsibly because what he said and did really mattered. Most important, he was freed at last from his heritage. Trained to serve, he had entered public life. Raised to excel, he had aimed for the top. Now, at the age of sixty-three, he knew he could do no more than he was doing; he had found his station in life, perhaps his place in history.

CHAPTER 38

The Sudden Ending

ON APRIL 19, 1953 Taft boarded the presidential plane to fly to Augusta, Georgia, for a weekend of golf with Eisenhower. He remembered the area, for his parents had vacationed there with him before they entered the White House in 1909. Young Bob, then a junior at Yale, had driven about the countryside and played golf with his father during his Christmas vacation. Now, years later at the age of sixty-three, he might have pondered the twists of fate that brought him back again.

The weekend brought little but disappointment and pain. Eisenhower, playing his best golf of the year, scored an 86, while Taft shot erratically and lost by several strokes. It then turned cold, and they teed off the second morning in forty-degree weather. This time Taft played what he called "rather ragged golf," and Eisenhower beat him again. By the time Taft returned to Washington, he was feeling weak, and his left hip ached. Darrah Wunder, alarmed, wrote, "Bob seems tired out." [1]

Back at the Capitol, he resumed a work schedule as exhausting as any of his career. Besides the time-consuming tasks of the leadership, the haggling over patronage, and the endless negotiations over revisions in Taft-Hartley, he had to combat a filibuster against an administration bill giving states their claims to oil in the tidelands off their shores. Angered by the filibuster, he kept the Senate in continuous session in order to break the endurance of his opponents. They finally surrendered, but not until Wayne Morse set a record by talking nonstop for 22.5 hours. When the bill finally passed early in May, Taft was worn with fatigue. [2]

At the same time he was growing so impatient to cut military spending that on April 30 he finally exploded during a White House conference. "With a program like this," he shouted to Eisenhower and various congressional leaders and budget officials, "we'll never elect a Republican Congress in 1954." Pounding the table, he cried that "you're taking us down the same road Truman traveled. It's a repudiation of everything we promised in the campaign." Taft's outburst stunned the assembled potentates, and Eisenhower flushed. Fortunately for party harmony, others intervened with small talk, and the next week Taft apologized for his display of temper. But he still complained about spending, and when Treasury Secretary George Humphrey delayed turning in budget estimates, Taft testily announced that the "administration is going to have to decide what they want. I haven't been able to get even a hint of what they will recommend." [3]

Taft did not say so, but his outburst at the White House may have tumbled from a body increasingly racked with pain. In the ten days after his return from Augusta on April 20, the ache in his hip had spread to his thighs, then to most of his joints. He tired easily. And the trek up three flights of stairs in his home left him breathless and exhausted. Thinking he had caught cold, he determined to play golf again to dispel the stiffness. But when he tried to play the weekend after Augusta, he found his knees too weak to take the strain. By April 26 Darrah Wunder was noticing that he limped. "He isn't well," she confided to her diary, "and I fear it is serious." [4]

At first Taft refused to complain. Unlike his father, who regaled friends with gruesomely detailed accounts of his various ailments, Taft paid little attention to his health. Besides, he had little cause for concern before his trip to Augusta.[5] Though he had suffered from a brief attack of influenza in January, he had bounced back as if nothing had happened. In late March the columnist Marquis Childs wondered at the ease with which he was running the Senate, and added: "Taft looks like a man who eats well and sleeps well; his complexion is like that of a contented baby." Taft naturally hoped for the best.[6] He refused to interrupt his work, to move down from the third floor of his house, or to let on that he was hurting.

But by the end of April he knew he had to do something,

and after consulting Dr. Bretney Miller, Martha's physician, he
began a series of tests as an outpatient at Walter Reed Hospital.
By then he was running a fever, and the doctors concluded he was
anemic. But they were baffled by the other symptoms, and they
tried to get him to enter the hospital. Like many busy men, Taft
at first resisted, but the pain gave him no rest, and on May 20 he
checked into Walter Reed. It was a month to the day after his golf
in Augusta.

He spent four days and three nights at Walter Reed, and he
used some of his free time to reassure his worried friends. "I have
acquired a most unpleasant disease," he wrote a Yale classmate,
"and I am doing my best to try to find out how to cure it. Primarily, it is an anemic condition and a lack of red corpuscles." But
otherwise he chafed under the hospital routine. The doctors punc-
tured him with needles, gave him blood transfusions, and took
countless x-rays. Once, he complained later to Mrs. Wunder, he
felt as if he was going to strangle after being sprayed in the throat
with Xylocain. When they released him on May 23, he arrived
home pale, limping badly, and weak with pain. And all for nothing, for the doctors failed to diagnose his problem. Taft had Jack
Martin give the press a reassuring statement. Then he left for Cincinnati, where he was due to deliver a speech May 26. Once in his
native town, he checked immediately into Holmes Hospital under
the care of Dr. Johnson McGuire, long his personal physician.[7]

The speech, given before the National Conference of Christians
and Jews, had to be delivered instead by his son, Bob. But the
ideas were authentically his own, and they caused a minor sensa-
tion. The administration was then trying to get a truce in Korea
that would divide the peninsula near the Thirty-Eighth Parallel. Most senators, tired of the war, had been offering at least
tacit support to such negotiations, and the end of the war seemed
within reach. Yet Taft demurred. "I think we should do our best
now to negotiate this truce," he said, "and if we fail, then let England and our other allies know that we are withdrawing from all
further peace negotiations in Korea." America, he continued,
should have insisted on a "general peace negotiation with China,
including a unification of Korea under free Koreans, and a pledge
[by China] against further expansion in Southeast Asia." Taft

then conceded that the United States should stop communist aggression "where it occurs and where it is within our means to stop it." But Asia (including Indochina) was no such place, for Americans were outnumbered. "I believe we might as well abandon any idea of working with the United Nations in the East," he proclaimed, "and reserve to ourselves a completely free hand."

He explained that his words would shock partisans of the UN, which he conceded was useful as an agency of discussion. But he insisted that it had failed as a means of preventing aggression. (Indeed, Truman himself had bypassed it for the Truman Doctrine in 1947 and for NATO in 1949.) Taft then criticized NATO, called for a greater defense effort by the Europeans, and proposed a conference to work out a new UN charter. Concluding, he asked whether "uniting the free world against communism" was a "practical long term policy," and his answer, in view of the unreliability of America's allies, was obviously no. America, he was saying, could not rely on its friends.[8]

Taft had said many of these things before, and his remarks about the UN repeated passages in speeches delivered almost ten years earlier. "I don't think I really said anything different from what Dulles believes," he added to a friend, "if only he had the determination to carry it out." Taft also explained two weeks later that he did not favor the abolition of all American alliances abroad. On the contrary, he would sustain agreements with Australia, New Zealand, Japan, and the Philippines, and recognize America's "very definite understanding [calling for financial support] with the French in Indochina." The United States should have a "free hand to form a [military] alliance with the British [on] Far Eastern affairs . . . but not one in which they possess any final veto against our policies."[9]

Yet Taft still preferred to keep some distance from England and other American allies. "I never said we should 'go it alone,'" he wrote Hoover, "But I certainly want a freer hand than we have and don't want to have the British able to bring a lot of pro-communist nations . . . against our freedom of action." To another old friend he added: "I think the British are the best propagandists and the most unprincipled people . . . I think the real criticism of Acheson's policy was that he did whatever the British asked him

"Mind moving over just a little more?"
Copyright 1953 by Herblock in the Washington Post

to do." And to Bill in Ireland he observed laconically that the Egyptians were throwing eggs at Dulles. "Sometimes I think the Irish are the only people who love us." [10]

Reporters were not privy to such private comments, but they did not have to be, for they recognized that the tone and substance of his speech, particularly the phrase calling for a "completely free hand" in Asia, was challenging the consensus which two administrations had worked hard to build up and threatening the success of the delicate armistice negotiations at Panmunjom. Even Eisenhower felt obliged to disagree mildly with his hospital. ed friend. It testified to Taft's extraordinary power and prestige that one speech, delivered by his son, could so disturb the columnists and unsettle the administration. And it showed that he still rebelled against the binding alliances worked out under bipartisan leadership during the previous years. As in the debates over lend-lease and NATO, he preferred the policy of the "free hand" and the protection of American liberty to all else. As he lay on his back in Cincinnati he saw no reason to change his mind.

•

If Taft worried much about the consternation he had triggered, he gave little sign of it in the hospital. Indeed, he struck Dr. McGuire as amazingly composed under the series of tests that kept him there for nine days. Perhaps it was because he had accustomed himself to the need for thorough testing. Or perhaps it was because x-ray therapy and cortisone stopped the fever and reduced the intense pain in his joints. At any rate, he seemed cheerful and optimistic.[11]

But the doctors worried, for he had a low grade fever and an anemia, and because his weight, which had hovered around 200 pounds for most of his mature years, had dropped to 183 in the five weeks since Augusta. They also discovered nodules in the skin of his abdomen and forehead. When these were removed for biopsies, they provided a diagnosis at last. Taft, it seemed all but certain, had developed a malignancy. Dr. McGuire then broke the news: cancer, with the site of the primary tumor still unknown. The outlook, he told Taft, was very grim. He recommended that Taft continue getting treatments and confirm the diagnosis elsewhere.[12]

Taft's calm reaction to the news of cancer amazed the specialists whom Dr. McGuire had brought into the case. He took the verdict, Dr. Charles M. Barrett recalled, "with no display of emotion," and spent the next few days, while receiving radiation treatments, quizzing the doctors for more information. Soon, Dr. Barrett remembered, "he commanded such respect because of his total ability to understand that we spoke to him in terms of a colleague rather than patient." It was clear that the Taft who might die of cancer was as self-controlled and as demanding of the facts as was the senator on the floor or in committee.

Because there was little more Dr. McGuire could do, he let Bob, Jr., accompany his father on a plane back to Washington. There Taft concealed the diagnosis from the world. The x-ray therapy, he wrote Horace, was "very successful, and I feel 100 per cent better." He also showed up briefly on crutches at the Senate. But Mrs. Wunder, seeing him for the first time on crutches, noted that he looked "thinner, frail, a pale green color," and Taft had to tell her the truth about his condition. He then hobbled upstairs to the second floor sitting room to break the news to Martha. "Oh, nonsense," she replied, "they said that about father, and it wasn't true." Confined to a wheelchair and bitter about her fate, Martha steadfastly refused to believe what her husband was telling her, and in the next few weeks she complained that Dr. Miller spent more time with Bob than with her. To the end Taft had to contend with and worry about the sorry condition of his wife.[13]

He also knew that he could not wait long for confirmation of Dr. McGuire's diagnosis, and he turned to Dr. Stanhope Bayne-Jones, a Yale classmate, fellow member of Skull and Bones, and old friend. Dr. Bayne-Jones, then president of the New York Hospital-Cornell Medical Center, phoned Dr. McGuire, consulted with other doctors, and then came to Washington. The obvious place to go, he told Taft, was New York's Memorial Hospital for Cancer and Allied Diseases. But Taft resisted; he did not want it to leak that he might have cancer. Dr. Bayne-Jones then suggested the New York Hospital. It adjoined the cancer hospital, he explained, and Taft could register under an assumed name. The patient agreed, and on June 7, 1953, four days after his return from Cincinnati, he entered the hospital as Howard Roberts, Jr. It was his third hospital in less than three weeks.[14]

The ruse fooled the press, for he rested in a private room off in a wing. But the doctors, after concurring in the diagnosis of cancer, still wondered about the location of the primary tumor. Indeed, eleven eminent physicians and specialists, including the Surgeon General of the United States, gathered at one point to figure out what to do. Some thought the primary tumor originated in the stomach, some in the kidney, some in the lung, some in the pancreas, and some in the genitourinary tract. Some, arguing that the source must be found to stop the malignancy from spreading, advised an exploratory abdominal operation. But others, including Dr. McGuire, thought the tumors had already spread too far, that the answer was continued x-ray therapy to keep the patient comfortable. Taft listened carefully to the conflicting opinions and then insisted on returning to Washington for a day or two.[15]

So it was that on June 10 reporters watched Taft swing heavily down the aisle of the Senate a few minutes before the bell was due to sound the start of the day's business. Pale and drawn, his collar hanging loosely about his neck, he sat down next to William Knowland, propped his crutches against the desk, and whispered something in his ear. A few minutes later, at noon, a statement from Jack Martin told the press what was happening. Taft, it explained, was suffering from a serious illness and was turning over the floor leadership to Knowland for the remaining few weeks of the session. Stunned, for Taft had kept them fooled, the reporters rushed down for further details. He obliged them by heaving himself out of the chamber for a brief press conference. But he still withheld the truth. Doctors in New York, he explained, said he had a "hip lesion." That, Taft concluded, was "all I got out of them." He then compounded the deception by sitting in on a Labor Committee hearing that afternoon and by taking Martha to a party that night.[16]

The confirmation that he was seriously ill shook the Capitol. And his choice of Knowland took his colleagues by surprise. Taft had consulted Eugene Millikin, and the day before at the hospital he had telephoned Knowland his plans, but he had asked advice of no one else, and his failure to consult Leverett Saltonstall of Massachusetts, who held the title of whip, miffed some of the eastern wing of the party. His choice was also mildly controversial, for Knowland was an aggressive, somewhat humorless man for whom Taft had no special personal affection and who later proved too independent to work harmoniously with Eisenhower.

But Knowland also struck Taft as courageous enough to resist the eastern internationalists. (One reporter wrote later that Taft had said, "I'm going away and I've asked Bill to carry on for me. Nobody can push him around.") The choice revealed also that Taft had lost none of his political shrewdness, for in presenting his colleagues with a fait accompli he prevented a potentially divisive struggle for the post. Besides, as Taft made clear, Knowland was to be an *acting* leader. Despite the gloomy pronouncements from his doctors, he refused to concede that he was through, and he told no one, Knowland included, of the nature of his illness.[17]

His duty to the Senate disposed of, he returned to his office. There he called in Jack Martin and Blanche O'Berg, his personal secretary since 1945, to be witnesses as he settled the will which Bob, Jr., had prepared for him. Unlike William Howard Taft, who had left small sums to Yale, to Taft School, to the Unitarian Church, and to long-time personal employees, he left everything to his family. Martha was to inherit his tangibles, his personal effects, and a trust for 49 per cent of his estate. She was also to receive a trust for the remaining 51 per cent, to be divided among the four sons after her death. His estate, it was revealed later, was worth $447,880, including $160,310 in *Times-Star* stock; $84,808 in the Gruen Watch Co. of Cincinnati; $74,100 in shares of the Central Trust Co., also of Cincinnati; and $65,000, the value attached to the Georgetown home. Like his father, who had left his wife $475,000, Bob made a financial success of his life. But he had not grown rich in public service.[18]

On June 12 Taft returned to New York Hospital, registering this time under his own name. There he underwent x-ray treatments, received a few visitors (including Herbert Hoover and, to his surprise, Tom Dewey), and consulted with Dr. Frank Glenn, chief of surgery at the hospital. Dr. Glenn explained that the origin of the cancer remained unclear and recommended an exploratory operation. He advised Taft to clean up affairs in Washington, then (because the disease might be terminal) to go to Cincinnati for the operation. As if mapping out a political campaign or preparing a statistical report, Taft asked detailed questions, then said he would think things over.[19]

When he returned to Washington June 17, he found the administration beset with problems. In South Korea, President Syngman Rhee threw the peace negotiations into turmoil by suddenly freeing some 25,000 anticommunist North Korean prisoners. In East Berlin mobs rioted against their government. On Capitol Hill senators angrily debated a controversial military aid bill and struggled to finish their business in order to escape to cooler climes. Outside the White House pickets marched solemnly back and forth urging Eisenhower to prevent the execution for espionage of Julius and Ethel Rosenberg. The Rosenbergs went to the electric chair on June 19. Washington was hardly the place to seek a cool respite from controversy.

Taft had lost none of his passion for public affairs, and he wrote pessimistic letters about some of these events. "The President," he wrote one supporter, "is being pulled in two directions, and usually when it is toward socialism I find it comes from what you might call the Dewey camp." To Homer Bone, a former colleague from Washington who had opposed the drift to war in 1940, he bemoaned the state of the world. "I don't suppose we could be in a bigger mess in foreign policy than we are. The general attitude that you and I took was right when we took it and, while times have changed and we have to make a good many concessions today, fundamentally it is the right policy now." And to party wheelhorse Katharine Kennedy Brown of Ohio he promised to help the Taft partisans find jobs. "The question of patronage is still a very troublesome one," he wrote, "and I am particularly concerned about our southern friends. I am going to have to make a special effort to see if I can't straighten out the matter with Len Hall [GOP National Chairman], and the President himself." [20] Despite his illness, Taft showed no signs of forgetting about the plight of his friends and no sense of pique at being bothered by mundane matters at so critical a time.

Yet these expressions of discontent with Eisenhower were rare during the last two weeks of June. Instead, Taft spent most of his time reassuring old friends about his health. "I feel certain that the treatments now agreed upon," he wrote on June 19, "are going to be very beneficial and bring about a complete cure." "Please don't be troubled too much about my problems," he added the same day to another friend. "Many people are doing their level best to solve them." To another correspondent he joked mildly about his unexpected visitor in New York. "As you probably heard, I had a half hour call from Tom Dewey, in which he seemed to endeavor to be extremely agreeable, and we did not mention controversial subjects." And ten days later he even kept his old friend Stanley Rowe in the dark. "During the past week," he wrote, "I have gained back six pounds and generally feel infinitely better than I did . . . We do hope to move to Cincinnati about Labor Day for the balance of the year." [21]

Some of this optimism stemmed from his habitual desire to keep his troubles to himself; there was no point in telling people he was going to die. But Taft did in fact hold out a little hope. X-ray therapy and blood transfusions were making him feel better, and he was regaining a little of his lost weight. Despite tiring daily treatments at Walter Reed, he felt strong enough to attend afternoon sessions on the Hill, to participate in continuing negotiations over revision of Taft-Hartley, to attend luncheons and conferences at the White House, and even to speak on the Senate floor. On July 1 he arose without his crutches to call for the full authorization scheduled for foreign aid. Though he then hedged his position by indicating he might later vote to cut the appropriation, his speech reflected his continuing loyalty to the President. To the end he was prepared to soften some of his objections to foreign spending.[22]

Taft seemed mellow, light-hearted, even jocular. Secretaries in his office, long accustomed to brusque greetings from their boss, now found him pausing to chat, calling them by their first names, asking gently for little favors. At a White House meeting someone grumbled about being held to a diet, whereupon Taft joked that *his* doctors were telling him to eat as much as he wanted. When Eisenhower sent him a book on golf entitled *The Laws of the Links,* Taft had a snappy reply: "glancing through the book, I am afraid that a lot of our friends don't follow the rules as they are written, but that seems to be true in politics also." [23] When doctors gave him a new drug called ACTH, he quipped, "After cortisone, try Hadacol." And even at home, where Martha's misery cast a pall on his last days, he seemed content. He dictated letters, chatted with Darrah Wunder, joked about the assortment of pills he was required to take, and sat up well into the evening reading spy stories or doing crossword puzzles. Whether his mellowness stemmed from renewed hope or from resignation, there was no doubting his courage under stress. "He laugh and joke all the time around the house so as not to worry Mrs. Taft or Mrs. Wunder," Mack Gray marveled later. "God, how could that man *laugh* at a time like that?" But Darrah Wunder was not fooled. "He looks more ill every day," she lamented, "and my heart is a cold grey stone . . . It is heartbreaking to see him come down the long stairs so painfully, trying to smile." [24]

Meanwhile, the doctors were continuing to watch and worry. Almost daily, in fact, they had been taking samples of his skin, injecting it into hamsters, and trying out new antitumor drugs on the hamsters. Taft had agreed to this painful process because he was ready to try anything to find a cure, but he wondered about it, and he even wrote Horace, his physicist son, to ask if such treatment was worthwhile. (It was not, and doctors later told him all the hamsters had died.) Keeping faithfully in touch with Dr. Glenn (who opposed such treatment), Taft explained that he was willing to undergo an operation. "In fact," he explained with characteristic precision, "I am in favor of it, 1.) if the other treatment brings disappointing [results] or 2.) even encouraging results which only promise a lifetime of medicine." Five days later, after a conference with doctors on June 30, he told Darrah Wunder that he was going to return to New York. The doctors had let him make the decision himself, and though he knew an operation could prove fatal, he chose that dangerous course rather than live on — perhaps a few more months — under a regimen of unpleasant treatments.[25]

Having done so, he prepared a form letter, which he had his office send even to such old antagonists as Herbert Brownell. "I will probably have to go back to the New York Hospital next week for another checkup," he wrote. "I do feel very much better, however, and believe that steady improvement is being made." As if to prove his point, Taft kept up the façade of good health, and on July 2 he stood, supported by his crutches, to watch his old friend Lewis Strauss sworn in at the White House as head of the Atomic Energy Commission. As he must have known, it was to be his last visit to the house he had lived in as a young man and to which he had aspired to return. But he was cheerful. "I had a transfusion this morning," he told Strauss, "so I'd be sure to make it." [26] That afternoon he conferred again over Taft-Hartley amendments. The next morning he talked briefly with reporters, then kept the last appointment of his life — with Harold Stassen, then Eisenhower's foreign aid administrator. Taft then departed for his home. On his desk he left behind a miscellany of letters, memos, and scribblings, on NATO, the budget, the excess profits tax, patronage in Arkansas, tidelands oil, and Russian interference with salmon fishing in the Bering Sea. One, undated and unexplained, was intriguing: "No Indo China — Except in case of emergency invasion by the Chinese." [27]

•

The next day, July 4, Taft was back in the New York Hospital. Four days later Dr. Glenn led a team of surgeons who cut into his abdomen in search of the primary tumor. But the operation did not take long, for the doctors quickly discovered cancer everywhere. Unable to detect the source, the surgeons closed him up. Taft recovered easily, and the next day he was eating cereals and broth. But there was no longer any doubt.[28]

For the next two weeks he kept his feelings under control. "He was calm. I don't recall his ever showing any fear," Dr. Bayne-Jones recalled. Confined to his bed, he worked on puzzles and watched the boats churn through the East River below. He called Martha every night and had Bob, Jr., and Jack Martin issue encouraging reports about his progress. (One such release, sent out by AP July 20, indicated he would be out of the hospital in ten days.) But doctors observed his deepening depression, and when he started vomiting on July 25, they worried that the cancer had reached the brain. By July 27, when he grew drowsy, confused, slow in speech, they knew it.[29] On July 28 his sister Helen, his son Lloyd, Jack Martin, and Mrs. Wunder brought Martha, still only dimly aware of her husband's sickness, to his side. Half-conscious, Taft propped himself up, smiled, kissed her, and talked softly with her for fifteen minutes. When she left — to be taken back to Washington — he drifted off again, and the rest of the family, including Bill from Ireland, assembled for the end. After a coma lasting thirteen hours death came at last of a brain hemorrhage at 11:30 on the morning of July 31.[30]

.

Taft's sudden passing stunned his friends and colleagues. As soon as Eisenhower heard the news, he and his wife hurried to Taft's Georgetown home to pay their respects to Martha. "He didn't know how he would get along without Bob," Mrs. Wunder noted. "He grasped both my hands and had tears in his eyes." [31] Senators, who had been frantically trying to adjourn for the year, cut short debate and proceeded instead to devote their time to eulogies. Two days later his body, like his father's twenty-three years before, was placed in the Capitol rotunda, where thousands of people paused to pay their last respects, and at noon on August 3, Eisenhower, the cabinet, the diplomatic corps, the black-robed justices of the supreme court, and his congressional colleagues, filed into the rotunda to join Martha and the family for a brief memorial service. Fittingly secular, the ceremony featured a eulogy by John Bricker, and its only gestures to religion were an invocation and benediction. Dignified, it excluded television, radio, and newsreel cameras.[32] After the service the casket was flown to Cincinnati, where more thousands viewed it that night at a downtown funeral home. The next day, after private services at the Indian Hill Episcopal Presbyterian Church, professional pall bearers laid him to rest in a gentle slope behind the church. Only a small marker, inscribed "Robert A. Taft: United States Senator, 1889–1953," identified his grave, but in a grove of trees a few yards away a bronze medallion of him was set into a stone. It quoted him: "The consideration which ought to determine every decision is the necessity of preserving, maintaining, and increasing the liberty of the people of our country." [33]

.

Taft's death set people wondering. Why had the doctors taken so long to diagnose his illness? And why had they been unable to discover the source of the cancer? Others asked quietly why he had faded so quickly. Had he been feeling poorly in 1952, when he set

The fallen pillar. *Cyrus C. Hungerford, Pittsburgh* Post Gazette

out to capture the nomination? And Republicans worried about the future. With Taft gone, the Senate would be divided 47 to 47 (plus Morse), and Lausche was certain to replace Taft with a Democrat. Could Knowland — could anyone? — do for Eisenhower what Taft had done in 1953? And how would his party, indeed the nation at large, fare without the man whom Herbert Hoover, still vigorous and active on the day of Taft's death, called "more nearly the irreplaceable man in American life than we have seen in three generations."

Answers to the medical questions ultimately came from an autopsy requested by the doctors. This confirmed the hospital's earlier diagnosis of "widespread, highly malignant, rapidly growing tumors." The cancer, it concluded, was so extensive that its source was hard to establish, but it had "almost certainly" started in one of the bronchial tubes. If this tumor had expanded there, doctors surmised later, x-rays would have established the diagnosis of primary lung cancer. He also probably would have coughed or hemorrhaged, providing symptoms that might have led them to the source. Instead, the tumor had remained as a tiny area in the bronchus and spread cells instead to other parts of the body, including the hip, where he first felt the pain. Considering the lack of symptoms, it was not surprising that it took a few weeks to diagnose cancer. And given the speed with which the tumors had raced through his body, doctors doubted that an accurate diagnosis three weeks earlier would have helped much. Taft, a nonsmoker, had been at the peak of his powers when he fell suddenly to a dread disease that doctors had not even suspected in April 1953, let alone in 1952. Feeling fine, he had had no reason whatsoever to pull out of the race for the presidency.[34]

The deeper questions about his political legacy seemed, superficially at least, simple to answer. Long after his death he was repeatedly honored, eulogized, and memorialized. Senator John Kennedy not only devoted a chapter to him in his *Profiles in Courage* (stressing the speech against the Nuremberg trials) but later headed a bipartisan Senate committee that elected Taft, with John C. Calhoun, Daniel Webster, Henry Clay, and Robert La Follette, Sr., to a Senate Hall of Fame. These five men, the committee said in 1957, transcended party and state lines and "left a permanent mark on our nation's history and brought distinction to the Senate." Crowning the tributes paid to him was the dedication next to the Capitol in 1959 of a hundred-foot tower housing a twenty-seven-bell carillon. Though private subscription paid for building the tower, the gift of choice public land for a memorial to a senator would almost certainly have been denounced by Taft had he been alive. But such was the power of his name that when the project was discussed in 1955, it passed both houses unanimously.[35]

In the 1950's it became clear, too, that his loss hurt the administration. Knowland, who succeeded him as leader and held the post until 1959, proved far less cooperative with the White House and far less influential with his colleagues. With Taft gone no one remained with force enough to restrain the right wing of the party, and Democrats like Lyndon Johnson in the Senate and Sam Rayburn in the House had to stay the impetuous thrusts of men like Barry Goldwater and to make possible even the limited legislative accomplishments of Eisenhower's presidency.[36]

Yet this rampant Republican "conservatism" of the 1950's and 1960's showed that many members of his party had rather quickly forgotten him. Senators like Goldwater claimed to wear Taft's mantle, but they stood well to his right on domestic matters and sounded much more warlike on international affairs. Taft, who had recognized his differences with the Right, would probably have smiled grimly had he been present at a meeting of a Senate housing subcommittee on July 31, 1959, six years to the day after his death. On that day the Democratic members of the committee played a recording of one of his speeches in favor of public housing, in the hope of persuading Republicans to back a liberal bill that Eisenhower had vetoed. Of course, the Democratic maneuver failed. The voice of Taft often echoed but faintly in the deliberations of congressional Republicans after 1953.[37]

All of his ideas did not die with him. Supporters of aid to education and public housing kept bringing forward his name. Advocates of welfare reform admiringly cited his demands for a "floor" under income — or what they called "income maintenance." Critics of American involvement in Viet Nam seized on his opposition to the draft, his demands for greater congressional influence in the making of foreign policy, and his criticisms of American overinvolvement and imperialism. And libertarians frequently revived his critique of excessive presidential activity, his appeals for decentralization, and his demands for a rule of law not men. But to be seriously considered, Taft's beliefs in aid to education, public housing, and a floor under income had to await the return of Democrats to power in the 1960's. Others of his crusades, for decentralization and for restraint abroad, were largely ignored by both parties in the decade and a half after his death.[38]

This limited legacy did not result from a lack of intelligence, industry, or forcefulness, qualities in which he was matched by few politicians of his time, but from his dogged adherence to ideas that were becoming unfashionable even while he lived. The depression shattered his party, weakened the ideology of states rights, and elevated the presidency to a preeminent role. World War II drove all but a few Americans to a faith in wide-ranging internationalism. And the Cold War froze the nation into these ways of thought long after his death. Though Taft was more flexible than either his admirers or his critics recognized, he remained too suspicious of federal power to reassure New Dealers, too partisan to satisfy independents, and too critical of American adventurism abroad to win over a majority of his own party in national nominating conventions.

In many ways Taft's career resembled that of one of the other five in the Senate Hall of Fame, John C. Calhoun of South Carolina. Both men were ambitious, competitive, dedicated, and more devoted to ideological principles than most American politicians. Both became enormously powerful in the Senate. But each proved unable, and often unwilling, to restrain his more extreme followers — fire-eaters in the 1840's and McCarthyites and superpatriots a century later. Each man also displayed a zealousness for his cause, and occasionally a frustration that erupted in rhetorical excesses, that alarmed more pragmatic contemporaries. Neither man bent far enough to stay always abreast of his times, and neither succeeded in receiving his party's presidential nomination. Denied the White House pulpit, both senators died as strong spokesmen for sectional and ideological factions instead of as the national leaders they had earnestly worked to be.

Still, Taft's personal triumphs far outnumbered his disappointments. He dominated a sizable wing of his party for fifteen years; he enjoyed power in the Senate matched by few men; and he ordinarily wielded it responsibly. Above all his stature depended on personal qualities: honesty, conscientiousness, courage, dignity, and intelligence. These attributes were counter-balanced by a partisan combativeness which made him as feared as he was respected, and by a refusal — usually — to depart from principles, leaving him vulnerable to the charge that he was stubborn and reactionary. But they also gave him the strength to rise above personal defeats and to maintain his commitment to serve. It was given to him as it is to few men: to embark on a career he had been trained to follow and to pursue it effectively until the day he died.

Bibliographical Note
Notes

Bibliographical Note

MANUSCRIPTS

CHIEF IN IMPORTANCE among the many revealing manuscript sources used in this biography is the huge Robert A. Taft collection at the Manuscripts Division of the Library of Congress. Consisting of nearly 1400 manuscript boxes, this collection of letters, speeches, and documents was closed to most scholars prior to the writing of this book, but the family intends to make it open to qualified researchers. It contains numerous personal letters, much political correspondence, a speech file for his Senate years, carbons of his outgoing letters during the Senate years, many newspaper clippings, revealing tax records, huge quantities of constituent mail, and carefully compiled tables of his votes on all the issues. During the course of writing this book I also used several suitcases and trunks full of personal correspondence, newsreels, and recordings sent to me from the Taft family home in Indian Hill, Ohio. These I looked at in Indiana, then forwarded to the Library of Congress for incorporation in the larger collection. Though Taft was a reticent man who did not bare his soul in his letters and speeches, his papers enabled me to follow his opinions on a host of subjects throughout his career. I know of no larger or more useful collection belonging to any twentieth century senator or congressman.

Second in importance were the papers of his father, President and Chief Justice William Howard Taft. This voluminous collection, also in the Library of Congress (smaller collections of papers are at Yale University and at the Cincinnati Historical Society), contains hundreds of personal letters to, from, and concerning Robert Taft, especially in the years prior to 1930. Without this source I would not have presumed to try to deal at any length with his years of childhood or early adulthood. Few biographers are fortunate enough to write about a family which saves so much or has such a sense of history.

The papers of Charles P. Taft, 2nd, Robert's brother, were also essential for my purposes. These are in Mr. Taft's possession in Cincinnati, and contain a large number of family letters, especially for the period before 1935. Also essential for these years were the papers of the law firm, Taft, Stettinius, and Hollister, in which both brothers served from 1924 through 1937. These remain in the firm's offices in Cincinnati and contain much correspondence and information concerning Taft's legal and political activities in Cincinnati and Ohio. Mrs. Helen Taft Manning, Taft's sister, granted me access to a few letters in her possession in Haverford, Pennsylvania.

Several of Taft's friends and associates let me examine personal papers which proved of considerable importance. These included John Hollister of Cincinnati, Mrs. Lillian Dykstra of South Yarmouth, Massachusetts, Mrs. Darrah Wunder of Cincinnati, Mrs. I. Jack Martin of Kensington, Maryland, and Dr. Frank Glenn of New York, who made available to me Taft's medical records. The notes reveal my special debt to Mrs. Wunder, whose diary for the years 1952 and 1953 was an invaluable source, and to Mrs. Martin, whose husband's papers include much material not available elsewhere. All these collections remain with their owners.

Other especially useful collections were the Thomas E. Dewey papers at the University of Rochester, the Richard Scandrett papers at Cornell University, the Herbert Hoover papers at the Hoover Library in West Branch, Iowa, the Paul Walter papers at the Western Reserve Historical Society in Cleveland, and the Thomas Coleman papers at the State Historical Society of Wisconsin. Scandrett, a New Yorker who tried to advise Taft on foreign policy over the years, kept numerous informative letters. Coleman, Taft's floor manager in 1952, saved several revealing memoranda and letters concerning the 1952 campaign. And Walter, who also dictated many lengthy memoranda concerning Taft (which remain in my possession), kept a wide variety of political material from all Taft's campaigns for the Senate and the presidency.

The following archives also contained some useful materials: the Hoover Library at Stanford University (papers of the American Relief Administration; of Joseph C. Green, an associate of Taft in the 1920 Hoover campaign; and of the United States Food Administration); the National Archives, Suitland, Maryland branch (Food Administration papers); the Zionist Archives in Cleveland; the Douglas MacArthur Memorial Bureau of Archives, Norfolk, Virginia (correspondence between Taft and MacArthur); the Taft School Archives in Watertown, Connecticut (an indispensable source for his school years which also includes some letters and papers of his uncle, Horace D. Taft); and the Yale University Archives in New Haven, which has a host of materials relating to Taft's college years, as well as some papers of his father, and the papers of such friends or acquaintances as Thomas L. Riggs, Edward Ingraham, Carl Lohmann, Charles Seymour, Charles D. Hilles, Irving Fisher, Sumner Keller, Sherman Kent, Henry Stimson, George H. E. Smith (his top aide on the Senate GOP policy committee for most of the years between 1944 and 1953), and some miscellaneous materials from constituents relating to Taft's 1940 campaign. Yale University also granted me access to the minutes of the Yale Corporation. At Harvard University's law school archives I found some interesting materials in the papers of Zechariah Chafee, one of Taft's classmates, and of Ezra R. Thayer and Roscoe Pound, law school professors in Taft's time. The library has also preserved some of Taft's own class notes.

The presidential libraries contain some pertinent items. The Franklin D. Roosevelt Library at Hyde Park, New York, has a few letters about Taft, especially in the voluminous diaries of Treasury Secretary Henry Morgenthau, Jr. The Harry Truman Library in Independence, Missouri, contains many collections, the most useful of which for me were the papers of Frank McNaughton, a reporter, and of the Democratic National Committee, which kept a clipping file on Taft. Less useful there were the papers of Clark Clifford, Paul M. Herzog, and the Ohio CIO-PAC. Oral history transcripts consulted at the Truman Library included those by Joseph G. Feeney, Samuel C. Brightman, John Franklin Carter, and James L. Sundquist. The Dwight D. Eisenhower Library at Abilene, Kansas, contains a clipping file on Taft, plus materials on Taft-Hartley, patronage, and legislative conferences. I also read oral history transcripts by Edward Thye, George Aiken, General Lucius Clay, Jacob Javits, Prescott Bush, Richard Rovere, Leverett Saltonstall, and Charles Halleck.

I am indebted also to the following individuals for sending me a few letters by and concerning Taft: Julius Klein of Chicago; Mrs. Frances Ricker of Lima, Ohio; Miss Blanche O'Berg of Washington, D.C. (Taft's personal secretary from 1945 through 1953); L. Richard Guylay of New York City (his publicity director in 1948, 1950, and 1952); Vincent Starzinger of Des Moines (a law school friend and political supporter); Stanley and Dorothy Rowe of Cincinnati (perhaps the Tafts' closest friends); Gordon Grayson of Washington, D.C. (stepson of George Harrison, Taft's college friend); Taft's sons, William, Robert, Jr., Lloyd, and Horace; and William B. Shaffer, Jr., of Cincinnati, who supplied me with the minutes of the Cincinnati Yale Club for 1916—1917.

The Ohio Historical Society in Columbus has the papers of John Bricker, Walter F. Brown, Myers Cooper, Simeon Fess, John Vorys, George White, and Clarence Brown, one of Taft's top campaign managers in 1948 and 1952. Most of these collections are thin, but the Clarence and Walter Brown papers contain some useful items. At the State Historical Society of Wisconsin in Madison I found revealing materials in the papers of Bruce Barton, John W. Hill, and Roger Faherty. The Dorothy Thompson papers at Syracuse University contained one interesting letter regarding Taft in 1940. The papers of Karl Butler, one of Taft's advisers on agricultural matters, also have some relevant material; they are at Cornell University. At Princeton I found the papers of Arthur Krock useful, and the collection of H. Alexander Smith, Taft's Senate colleague from New Jersey, particularly revealing in places. The papers of George Harrison, Taft's close friend in college, are at Columbia University, but included little of value for my purposes. Senator Arthur Vandenberg's papers at the University of Michigan include considerable important material.

The Library of Congress houses innumerable manuscript collections relevant to this study. Those which helped me were the NAACP papers, and the papers of John C. O.'Loughlin, Felix Frankfurter, Mabel T. Boardman, George von Meyer, Henry F. Pringle, Helen Taft Manning, Harold H. Burton, and especially Raymond Clapper. Disappointing were the papers of Thomas Connally, Theodore Green, Wallace White, Charles L. McNary, William Borah, George Norris, and Robert La Follette, Jr., all senators during Taft's tenure. I also found little of value in the papers of Elihu Root, Amos Pinchot, William Allen White, Frank Knox, and Ogden Mills.

I visited or used Xeroxed materials from the following collections, but found little of value in most of them: the Charles Tobey papers at Dartmouth College; the Robert Bulkley and John Clarke papers at the Western Reserve Historical Society; the Charles Halleck papers at Lilly Library, Indiana University; the John Marshall papers at Bethany College, Bethany, West Virginia; the Robert C. Hendrickson and Ralph Flanders papers at Syracuse University; the Hiram Johnson papers at the University of California, Berkeley; the Joseph Martin, Jr., papers at Stonehill College in North Easton, Massachusetts; and the Ansellary Smith, Owen Cleary, and Blair Moody papers at the Michigan Historical Collections at Ann Arbor. Also the Francis B. Loomis papers at Stanford University; the Thomas V. Smith papers at the University of Chicago library; the Wilbur Matson papers at Marietta College; the Henry Bentley papers at the Cincinnati Historical Society; the Walter Hallanan papers at the University of West Virginia, Morgantown; and the Irving Ives papers and Frank Gannett papers at Cornell University.

INTERVIEWS

I SPENT considerable time interviewing people who knew Taft. These interviews helped me understand his personal side, and provided anecdotes to support impressions gained through letters and other written sources. They were not used to establish facts. Those interviewed included the following friends from his youth: Dr. Stanhope Bayne-Jones of Washington (Yale classmate); John M. Ewen of Washington (Yale classmate); Frederick Exton of Paris and Murray Bay (childhood friend); Carroll Glover of Washington (classmate and friend in D.C.); Walter Logan of Washington, Connecticut (Yale classmate); and Stephen Philbin of New York (Yale classmate). Cincinnati friends interviewed were Robert P. Goldman (a lawyer); Willis Gradison (stockbroker, legislative colleague, and political associate); Joseph C. Green (co-worker for Hoover, 1920, now of Chevy Chase, Maryland); John Hollister (childhood friend and law partner); John W. Hudson (partner in Taft's law firm); Harry L. Linch (businessman and aide to Taft's Uncle Charley); Dr. Johnson McGuire (Taft's personal physician); Dr. Charles M. Barrett of Cincinnati; John Herron More (cousin and partner in firm); Justin Rollman (businessman); Stanley and Dorothy Rowe (personal friends, from Indian Hill); Mrs. Robert Black (personal friend); Mrs. Russell Wilson (personal friend); and Mrs. Darrah Wunder (personal friend, companion of Mrs. Taft, 1950, 1952–1958).

I also interviewed the following people who knew Taft in his senatorial years: Senator George Aiken of Vermont; Hal Alderson of Washington, Taft's stenographer in political tours, 1947–1948; Jack Bell of the Associated Press's Washington Bureau; Fred Berquist of Washington, a top aide on the Joint Congressional Committee on the Economic Report; former Governor and Senator John Bricker of Ohio; Herbert Brownell of New York, a top aide of Thomas E. Dewey; Thomas I. Emerson, professor of law at Yale; former Senator Homer Ferguson of Michigan; Dr. Frank Glenn of New York, his surgeon in 1953; L. Richard Guylay of New York, his publicity man; Miss Marie Hein of Washington, secretary to I. Jack Martin, his administrative assistant in the Senate; Charles A. Halleck of Rensselaer, former congressman from

Indiana; Ralph Holsinger, professor of journalism at Indiana University and former reporter in Dayton; David S. Ingalls of Cleveland, Taft's cousin, political aide, and campaign manager in 1940 and 1952; Mrs. Muriel Kirk, friend and political worker from Oklahoma; and William Knowland of Oakland, former senator from California.

Also Frank Lausche of Washington, former governor and senator from Ohio; Mrs. I. Jack Martin of Kensington, Maryland, widow of his administrative assistant from 1944 through 1953; Gerald Morgan, a Washington attorney; Miss Blanche O'Berg of Washington, Taft's personal secretary from 1945 through 1953; Floyd Riddick, Senate parliamentarian; Thomas Shroyer of Washington, attorney, draftsman for Taft-Hartley, and occasional Taft aide; Admiral Lewis Strauss of Washington, personal friend and former chairman of the Atomic Energy Commission; Ben Tate, Jr. of Cincinnati, son of Taft's chief fundraiser; Glenn Thompson of Dayton, former Washington reporter for the Cincinnati *Enquirer;* Walter Trohan of Washington, Chicago *Tribune* correspondent; Paul Walter of Cleveland, a top Taft aide in all his campaigns; and Earl Warren, former Chief Justice of the United States.

Others interviewed included Professor Austin Scott of the Harvard Law School, who taught there in Taft's time; and the following members of the Taft family: his sons, William, Robert, Jr., Lloyd, and Horace; his daughters-in-law Barbara (Mrs. William H. Taft III) and Blanca (the late Mrs. Robert Taft, Jr.); his sister Helen Taft Manning of Haverford, Pennsylvania; his brother Charles P. Taft 2nd of Cincinnati; and his nephew, Seth Taft, of Cleveland.

Before I began work on this biography the Taft Institute of Government had funded a Taft Oral History project at the Oral History Research Office of Columbia University. I used interviews conducted for this project by Harry Jeffrey, Jr., and John T. Mason, Jr., with Harvey Bundy, Katharine Kennedy Brown, William H. Davis, John P. Frey, George Fuller, Richard Hawes, Bourke Hickenlooper, Clarence B. Kelland, Edwin Lahey, Alfred M. Landon, Helen Taft Manning, L. Randolph Mason, Benjamin Reese, Vernon Romney, Sr., Stanley Rowe, Dorothy Rowe, Mrs. Robert Black, H. Alexander Smith, Mrs. Barbara Taft, Fred C. Tanner, Ludwig Teller, and Howard Young. Columbia also houses a Dwight D. Eisenhower project, including transcripts of interviews with George Aiken, Prescott Bush, Ralph Flanders, Charles Halleck, Edward McCabe, Richard Rovere, Leverett Saltonstall, and Edward Thye. I have forwarded to Columbia many of the transcripts of my interviews.

Finally, I consulted the following transcripts at the John Foster Dulles Oral History Project at Princeton University: Sherman Adams, Charles Bohlen, Herbert Brownell, Mrs. Preston Davie, Dwight D. Eisenhower, Joseph C. Green, James Hagerty, John Hollister, George Humphrey, Arthur Krock, Henry Cabot Lodge, Jr., Henry Luce, and H. Alexander Smith. See also the list of transcripts read at the presidential libraries, listed under Manuscripts above.

CORRESPONDENTS

I BENEFITED by exchanging letters with the following personal friends of Taft: Ernest Angell of New York, Monte Appel of Washington, Norman Armour of New York, Hildreth Benner of South Yarmouth, Massachusetts, Lloyd Bowers of Chicago, Mrs. Louise Bowers of New York, Charles W. Briggs of St. Paul, Paul Cruikshank of Watertown, Connecticut, Mrs. Robert French of North Haven, Connecticut, George Gregg Fuller of Washington, Perrin Galpin of Pelham Manor, New York, Richard Hawes of Fall River, Massachusetts, Maurice Hirsch of Houston, Edward Ingraham of Bristol, Connecticut, Lyndon King of Minneapolis, Henry Hall Lyman of Portland, Connecticut, L. Randolph Mason of New York, Dr. R. Bretney Miller of Washington, Frank T. Nelson of Grosse Pointe, Michigan, Robert W. Perkins of Harrison, New York, Edward L. Ryerson of Chicago, Vincent Starzinger of Des Moines, and Clare M. Torrey of New York.

Also the following writers, editors, and journalists: Lee Barker of Doubleday, Inc., Brady Black of the Cincinnati *Enquirer,* Turner Catledge of the New York *Times,* John Fox of Boston, Nathaniel Howard of Cleveland, John S. Knight of the Akron *Beacon-Journal,* Felix Morley of Gibson Island, Maryland, J. B. Mullaney of the Cleveland *Plain Dealer,* Philip Porter of Cleveland, Eric Sevareid of Washington, Reed Smith of Columbus, Robert Stopher of the Akron *Beacon-Journal,* and Alden Todd of Leonia, New Jersey.

Also the following members of the Yale Corporation: Dean Acheson, Rev. Arthur Bradford, Wilmarth Lewis, James Lee Loomis, Rt. Rev. Henry Knox Sherrill, and George van Santvoord. And the following, who worked in Taft's office or supported him politically: Malcolm Baldridge of Watertown, Connecticut, Samuel King of Honolulu, Harry J. Maginnis of Bethesda, Maryland, James P. Selvage of Coral Gables, Florida, and Mrs. Dennis Sherman of Clearwater, Florida.

The following who knew him in Ohio in the 1920's or 1930's also sent useful letters: Thomas E. Bateman of Columbus, Kyle F. Brooks of

Cincinnati, Esther L. Carman of Cleveland, John A. Hadden of Cleveland, Paul M. Herbert of Columbus, Jack Kroll of Cincinnati, Miles Kuhns of Dayton, Clarence D. Laylin of Columbus, Vera Norcross of Lakewood, and Webb I. Vorys of Columbus. The following Ohio rabbis offered helpful insights into his support of Zionism: Daniel Silver of Cleveland, Saul Spiro of Dayton, and Leon Feuer of Toledo.

And finally the following national political figures: former Connecticut senators William Benton, Raymond Baldwin, and Prescott Bush; former Connecticut governor and head of OPA Chester Bowles; Rep. Jonathan Bingham of New York; Rep. Clarence Brown, Jr., of Ohio; Chief Justice Warren Burger; former Kansas Senator Frank Carlson; the late Thomas E. Dewey of New York; Senator Barry Goldwater of Arizona; Marshall Plan administrator Paul Hoffman; General Wilton Persons of Ft. Lauderdale, a top aide for Eisenhower; Bernard Shanley of Newark, another Eisenhower aide; Harold Stassen of Philadelphia; John Swomley of Kansas City, of the National Council Against Conscription; and former Senator Burton K. Wheeler of Montana. The following were too ill or for other reasons could not answer questions: former GOP national chairman John D. M. Hamilton and Ray Bliss, former senators Joseph Ball of Minnesota, Wayne Morse of Oregon, and Richard Russell of Georgia; senators Allen Ellender of Louisiana, Hubert Humphrey of Minnesota, Mike Mansfield of Montana, Karl Mundt of South Dakota, and Margaret Chase Smith of Maine; former Presidents Harry S Truman and Lyndon B. Johnson; Alfred M. Landon, the GOP's 1936 presidential nominee; and President Richard M. Nixon.

PRINTED DOCUMENTS

AMONG THE MOST USEFUL printed documents and official sources for Taft's career to 1920 are William Clinton Mullendore, *History of the United States Food Administration* (The Hoover Library on War, Revolution, and Peace Publication No. 18, Stanford, 1941); Suda Lorena Bane and Ralph Haswell Lutz, eds., *The Blockade of Germany After the Armistice, 1918–1919: Selected Documents of the Supreme Economic Council, Superior Blockade Council, American Relief Administration, and Other Wartime Organizations* (Hoover Library Publication No. 16, Stanford, 1942); and Bane and Lutz, eds., *Organization of American Relief in Europe, 1918–1919, Including Negotiations Leading Up to the Establishment of the Office of Director General of Relief at Paris by the Allied and Associate Powers* (Stanford, 1943).

For his activities in Ohio politics in the 1920's relevant sources are City Survey Committee, Lent D. Upson, director, *The Government of Cincinnati and Hamilton County* (Cincinnati, 1924); *Report of the Joint Legislative Committee on Economics and Taxation of the 86th General Assembly of Ohio* (Columbus, 1926); James Mercer, *Ohio Legislative History*, Vols. 4–6 (Columbus, 1921–1926), especially Robert Taft, "Record of the 86th General Assembly," pp. 594–602 in Vol. 6; *Report of the Legislative Agent of the Ohio State Federation of Labor* (published by Thomas J. Donnelly, 1921, 1923, 1925, 1931); *Journal of the House of Representatives of the 84th General Assembly of the State of Ohio*, Vol. 109 (Columbus, 1921), and Vols. 110 (1923) and Vol. 111 (1925) for the 85th and 86th sessions; and *Ohio Senate Journal*, Vol. 114 (Columbus, 1931). The journals, unfortunately, do not carry verbatim debates. The important documents in the gold cases, 1935–1937, are *Dixie Terminal v. U.S.* (302 US 329), and *Records and Briefs of Cases Decided by the Supreme Court of the United States*, Vol. 8, Part I, U.S. 302, pp. 329–378.

The documents available for his later career are too numerous to mention here, but aside from the *Congressional Record,* some of the most relevant are U.S. Congress, Senate, Hearings Before the Subcommittee on Privileges and Elections of the Committee on Rules and Administration, *Investigation into the 1950 Senatorial Campaign,* 82 Congress, 1st and 2d Sessions (Washington D.C., 1952); U.S. Congress, Senate, Committee on Banking and Currency, *Hearings on Bretton Woods Agreements,* 79 Congress, 1st Session (Washington, 1945); U.S. Congress, Senate, Committee on Labor and Public Welfare, *Federal Labor Relations Act of 1947,* Senate Report No. 105, 80 Congress, 1st Session (Washington 1947); and *Memorial Services . . . together with Remarks Presented in Eulogy of Robert Alphonso Taft, Late a Senator from Ohio,* 83 Congress, 2d Session (Washington 1954). Also essential for this study are the Official Reports for 1936, 1940, 1944, 1948, and 1952 of the *Proceedings of the Republican National Convention,* published by the GOP National Committee.

MASTERS' THESES AND DOCTORAL DISSERTATIONS

RELEVANT DOCTORAL DISSERTATIONS include John Paul Armstrong, "Senator Taft and American Foreign Policy: The Period of Opposition," Chicago, 1953; Frank A. Burd, "Robert A. Taft and the American Understanding of Politics," Chicago, 1969; Pauline Helen Isaacson,

"Robert Alphonso Taft: An Assessment of a Persuader," Minnesota, 1956; and Noel G. Rapp, "The Political Speaking of Robert A. Taft, 1939 to 1953," Purdue, 1955. Armstrong is very critical, Burd generally sympathetic. The Isaacson and Rapp theses contain many letters to the authors from associates of Taft who had died by the time I started my work.

Doctoral theses relating to his Senate career include Alonzo Lee Hamby, "Harry S Truman and American Liberalism, 1945–1948," Missouri, 1965; Susan M. Hartmann, "President Truman and the 80th Congress," Missouri, 1966; Walter Sloan Poole, "The Quest for a Republican Foreign Policy, 1941–1951," Pennsylvania, 1968; and Bernard Weiner, "The Truman Doctrine: Background and Presentation," Claremont, 1966.

I consulted the following among the many masters' theses dealing with Taft: Allen Gardner Pease, "Senator Robert Taft's Concept of the Presidential Powers," Ohio State, 1952; Richard Leroy Custer, "Robert A. Taft and the 1952 Republican Presidential Nomination," Ohio State, 1965; Anne W. Buck, "Robert A. Taft: The Emergence of a Statesman," Kent State, 1960; Shirley Schlafman, "An Isolationist Faces War: A Historical Review of the Foreign Policy Views of Senator Robert A. Taft Between 1939 and 1945," Ohio State, 1967; and Haskell Penn Short, "Robert Alphonso Taft: His Eight Years in the Ohio General Assembly," Ohio State, 1951. This last work, unfortunately, is too confusingly written to be of much help.

An unpublished manuscript, which I found in the files of Charles P. Taft, 2nd, of Cincinnati, also proved very helpful concerning Alphonso Taft, Robert's grandfather. It is Martha Willard, "Notes for a Biographer," Swarthmore College, 1935. Stephen J. Mack's honors thesis (Princeton, 1958), "The Makings of Greatness: Robert Alphonso Taft, His Early Life and Pre-Senatorial Career," also contains interesting material gathered with some cooperation from the family.

NEWSPAPERS AND MAGAZINES

THE MOST IMPORTANT NEWSPAPERS for this study were the Cincinnati *Enquirer,* Cincinnati *Times-Star,* Cincinnati *Post,* Columbus *Evening Dispatch,* and the *Ohio State Journal,* all of which I read for the years 1920 through 1938, and the New York *Times,* which I used extensively from 1900 to 1953. I also turned frequently to the Cleveland *Plain Dealer,* Akron *Beacon Journal,* Dayton *Journal-Herald,* Washington *Post,* and New York *Herald Tribune.* The notes indicate my use for special purposes of the New Haven *Evening Register*, Baltimore *Sun*, Columbus *Citizen*, Toledo *Blade*, Youngstown *Vindicator*, Washington *Star*, Chicago *Tribune*, San Francisco *Chronicle*, and Houston *Post*. Other papers cited stem from my use of clippings in various manuscript collections. Indices for several of these Ohio papers exist for selected periods of the 1930's in the Library of Congress.

The following magazines proved most useful: *Time, Newsweek, New Republic, The Nation, Saturday Evening Post, Collier's, National Municipal Review, American Political Science Review, Look, Harper's, Atlantic, Life, Congressional Digest,* and *Vital Speeches.*

The most important articles were the following:

BY TAFT:

"Let's Mind Our Own Business," *Current History,* Vol. 50 (June 1939), pp. 32–33; "The Issues in 1940," ibid., Vol. 51 (May 1940), p. 23; "A 1944 Program for Republicans," *Saturday Evening Post,* Vol. 216 (Dec. 11, 1943), p. 17; "Senator Taft's Peace Program," New York *Times Magazine,* Feb. 6, 1944, p. 8; (with Senator Claude Pepper), "Two Senators State the Campaign Issues," ibid., Sept. 3, 1944, p. 12; (as told to James C. Derieux). "No Substitute for Freedom," *Collier's,* Vol. 119 (Feb. 1, 1947), p. 13; "My Advice to the Republican Party," *Pageant,* Vol. 3 (May 1947), p. 4; "What Is Liberalism?", New York *Times Magazine,* April 18, 1948, p. 10; "The Case Against President Truman," *Saturday Evening Post,* Vol. 221 (Sept. 25, 1948), p. 18; "Why We're Fighting Truman," *Look,* Vol. 13 (May 10, 1949), p. 23; "How Much Government Can Free Enterprise Stand?" *Collier's,* Vol. 124 (Oct. 22, 1949), p. 16; "The Dangerous Decline of Political Morality," *Reader's Digest,* Vol. 58 (Nov. 1950), pp. 153–156; "The Taft-Hartley Act," *Annals of the American Academy of Political and Social Science,* Vol. 274 (March 1951), pp. 195–200; "Why I Oppose Truman's Foreign Policy," *Look,* Vol. 15 (Nov. 6, 1951), p. 96; "What I Believe," *Collier's,* Vol. 129 (April 12, 1952), p. 15; and "What the G.O.P. Must Do to Win in 1954," ibid., Vol. 131 (April 21, 1953), p. 42.

ABOUT TAFT (GENERAL):

Beverly Smith, "Bob and Martha Take the Stump," *American Magazine,* Vol. 128 (Sept. 1939), p. 40; Joseph Alsop and Robert Kintner, "Taft and Taft," *Life,* Vol. 8 (March 18, 1940), p. 90; Walter Davenport, "Bashful Buckeye," *Collier's,* Vol. 105 (April 16, 1940), p. 11; Alice Longworth, "What's the Matter with Bob Taft?" *Saturday Evening Post,* Vol. 212 (May 4, 1940), p. 29; Joseph and Stewart Alsop, "Taft and Vandenberg," *Life,* Vol. 21 (Oct. 7, 1946), p. 102; Arthur

M. Schlesinger, Jr., "His Eyes Have Seen the Glory," *Collier's,* Vol. 119 (Feb. 22, 1947), p. 12; "The Republicans: Honeymoon Is Over," *Fortune,* Vol. 35 (April 1947), p. 77; Edward B. Lockett, "Big Two on Capitol Hill," New York *Times Magazine,* June 1, 1947, p. 9; Fred Rodell, "Taft: Model T-Candidate," *'47 — The Magazine of the Year,* Vol. 1 (Nov. 1947), pp. 2–13; Henry Wallace, "Taft as a Candidate for President," *New Republic,* Vol. 117 (Dec. 29, 1947), pp. 11–13; Roger Butterfield, "Possible Presidents: Robert A. Taft," *Ladies' Home Journal,* Vol. 65 (Feb. 1948), p. 36; and Richard H. Rovere, "Taft: Is This the Best We've Got?" *Harper's,* Vol. 196 (April 1948), pp. 289–299.

Also William S. White, "How to Win Influence, If Not Friends," New York *Times Magazine,* May 1, 1949, p. 10; Felix Morley, "The Case for Taft," *Life,* Vol. 24 (Feb. 9, 1948), pp. 50–66; Beverly Smith, "Can Senator Taft Win His Biggest Fight?" *Saturday Evening Post,* Vol. 222 (June 3, 1950), p. 26; Benjamin Stolberg, "Robert A. Taft: American Liberal," *American Mercury,* Vol. 71 (Oct. 1950), pp. 387–399; William S. White, "Almost Equal to Being President," New York *Times Magazine,* Jan. 14, 1951, p. 10; Samuel Lubell, "How Taft Did It," *Saturday Evening Post,* Vol. 223 (Feb. 10, 1951), p. 32; and D. W. Brogan, "Mr. Republican," *Spectator,* Vol. 187 (Dec. 7, 1951), p. 763.

Also Cabell Phillips, "With Candidate Taft on the Road," New York *Times Magazine,* Nov. 12, 1951, p. 12; Zora Neale Hurston, "A Negro Voter Sizes Up Taft," *Saturday Evening Post,* Vol. 224 (Dec. 8, 1951), p. 29; Helen Taft Manning, "My Brother Bob Taft," *American Magazine,* Vol. 153 (Jan. 1952), p. 14; "Consecrated Tory: Robert A. Taft," *New Republic,* Vol. 126 (Series, March 17–May 5, 1952); Richard H. Rovere, "What's Happened to Taft?" *Harper's,* Vol. 204 (April 1952), pp. 38–44; William V. Shannon, "Last of the Old Breed," *Progressive,* Vol. 16 (June 1952), pp. 5–8; Willard Shelton, "The Retrogression of Senator Taft," *The Nation,* Vol. 174 (May 17, 1952), pp. 473–475; "Tafts of Cincinnati," *Life,* Vol. 32 (May 26, 1952), pp. 105–113; Rovere, "Letter from Chicago," *New Yorker,* Vol. 28 (July 19, 1952), p. 72; Rovere, "What Course for the Powerful Mr. Taft?" New York *Times Magazine,* March 22, 1953, p. 9; and Duncan Norton-Taylor, "Robert Taft's Congress," *Fortune,* Vol. 48 (August 1953), pp. 136–138. In my view, the most perceptive articles about Taft were those by White and Rovere.

Among the many posthumous articles about him are Jhan and June Robbins, "Heroic Last Days of Robert Taft," *Reader's Digest,* Vol. 64 (April 1954), pp. 10–14; Darrah Dunham Wunder, "My Most Unforgettable Character," *Reader's Digest,* Vol. 80 (June 1962), pp. 83–88;

and Russell Kirk, "Keeping Taft's Memory Alive," *National Review*, Vol. 18 (Dec. 13, 1966), p. 1276.

ABOUT TAFT'S FOREIGN POLICY:

Vernon van Dyke and Edward Lane Davis, "Senator Taft and American Security," *Journal of Politics*, Vol. 14 (May 1952), pp. 177–202; W. R. West, "Senator Taft's Foreign Policy," *Atlantic Monthly*, Vol. 189 (June 1952), pp. 50–52; "Minimum Foreign Policy," *Fortune*, Vol. 46 (July 1952), p. 65; John P. Armstrong, "The Enigma of Senator Taft and American Foreign Policy," *Review of Politics*, Vol. 17 (April 1955), pp. 206–231; Henry W. Berger, "A Conservative Critique of Containment: Senator Taft on the Early Cold War Program," in David Horowitz, ed., *Containment and Revolution* (Boston, 1967), pp. 125–139; and Berger, "Senator Robert A. Taft Dissents from Military Escalation," in Thomas G. Paterson, ed., *Cold War Critics: Alternatives to American Foreign Policy in the Truman Years* (Chicago, 1971), pp. 167–204.

ABOUT HIS DOMESTIC POLICY:

Richard O. Davies, " 'Mr. Republican' Turns 'Socialist': Robert A. Taft and Public Housing," *Ohio History*, Vol. 73 (Summer 1964), pp. 135–143; and Charles C. Brown, "Robert A. Taft: Champion of Public Housing and National Aid to Schools," *Bulletin of the Cincinnati Historical Society*, Vol. 26 (July 1968), pp. 225–253.

ABOUT TAFT-HARTLEY:

Sumner Slichter, "The Taft-Hartley Act," *Quarterly Journal of Economics*, Vol. 63 (Feb. 1949), pp. 1–31; Daniel Bell, "Taft-Hartley, Five Years After," *Fortune*, Vol. 46 (July 1952), p. 69; "Mr. Taft Proposes His Taft-Hartley Amendments," *Fortune*, Vol. 48 (Jan. 1953), p. 63; Slichter, "Revision of the Taft-Hartley Act," *Quarterly Journal of Economics*, Vol. 67 (May 1953), pp. 149–180; Fred Witney, "Taft-Hartley and the Eighty-Third Congress," *Labor Law Journal*, Vol. 5 (Jan. 1954), p. 3; Seymour Z. Mann, "Policy Formation in the Executive Branch: The Taft-Hartley Experience," *Western Political Quarterly*, Vol. 13 (Sept. 1960), pp. 597–608; Gerard D. Reilly, "The Legislative History of the Taft-Hartley Act," *George Washington Law Review*, Vol. 29 (Dec. 1960), pp. 285–300; and Gerald Pomper, "Labor and Congress: The Repeal of Taft-Hartley," *Labor History*, Vol. 2 (Fall 1961), pp. 323–343. The April 1958 issue of *Industrial and Labor Relations Review* is devoted to exceptionally useful articles concerning Taft-Hartley ten years after passage.

ABOUT CONGRESS (GENERAL):

"Truman versus Taft," *Congressional Quarterly Almanac,* Vol. 7 (1951), pp. 780–793; Richard E. Neustadt, "Congress and the Fair Deal: A Legislative Balance Sheet," *Public Policy,* Vol. 5 (1954), pp. 349–382; Donald R. McCoy, "Republican Opposition During Wartime, 1941–1945," *Mid-America,* Vol. 49 (July 1967), pp. 174–189; John Robert Moore, "The Conservative Coalition in the United States Senate, 1942–1945," *Journal of Southern History,* Vol. 32 (Aug. 1967), pp. 368–376; R. Alton Lee, "The Truman–80th Congress Struggle over Tax Policy," *Historian,* Vol. 33 (Nov. 1970), pp. 68–82; and John E. Jackson, "Statistical Models of Senate Roll Call Voting," *American Political Science Review,* Vol. 65 (June 1971), pp. 451–470. The articles by Floyd Riddick summarizing each congressional session for the 1940's are also useful; they appeared regularly in the *American Political Science Review* shortly after the sessions closed.

ON CONSERVATISM:

Samuel P. Huntington, "Conservatism as an Ideology," *American Political Science Review,* Vol. 51 (June 1957), pp. 454–473; Herbert McCloskey, "Conservatism and Personality," ibid., Vol. 52 (March 1958), pp. 27–45; and Ronald Lora, "Twentieth Century Conservatives and their Critique of Mass Society," unpubl. ms. 1971.

ABOUT TAFT AND OHIO, 1920's:

George E. Stevens, "The Cincinnati *Post* and Municipal Reform, 1914–1941," *Ohio History,* Vol. 79 (Summer–Autumn 1970), pp. 231–242; Henry Bentley, "Why Cincinnati Voted for P.R. and a City Manager," *National Municipal Review,* Vol. 14 (Feb. 1925), pp. 69–74; Robert A. Taft, "The Present Tax Situation in Ohio," ibid., Vol. 15 (May 1926), pp. 262–265; Bentley, "Cincinnati's Right About Face in Government," ibid., Vol. 15 (Aug. 1926), pp. 465–471; Russell Wilson, "Our American Mayors — Murray Seasongood of Cincinnati," ibid., Vol. 18 (Feb. 1929), pp. 68–75; and Robert P. Goldman, "An Analysis of Cincinnati's Proportional Representation Elections," *American Political Science Review,* Vol. 24 (Aug. 1930), pp. 699–710.

ABOUT TAFT, 1930's:

Carl L. Bumiller, "Constitutionality of the Distributive Sections of the Ohio Intangible Tax Act," *University of Cincinnati Law Revew,* Vol. 6 (Nov. 1932), pp. 373–403; "Gold Challenge," *Literary Digest,* Vol. 119 (March 23, 1935), p. 8; "Taft to Fore," ibid., Vol. 121 (May 23, 1936), pp. 5–6; Henry Bentley, "Three Cincinnati Elections," *National Municipal Review,* Vol. 26 (Jan. 1937), pp. 16–22; and Edward First,

"The Gold Clause in the Supreme Court," *Georgetown Law Review*, Vol. 26 (March 1938), pp. 732–739.

ABOUT HIS WIFE, MARTHA, AND HIS BROTHER, CHARLIE:

Dewey L. Fleming, "Mrs. Robert Taft, A Helpmate Indeed," *Current History*, Vol. 51 (April 1940), p. 52; Frank Gervasi, "Bob Taft's Martha," *Collier's*, Vol. 121 (April 3, 1948), pp. 62–64; "Charlie Taft's Big Chance," *Fortune*, Vol. 36 (Aug. 1947), p. 84, and William H. Hessler, "The Brothers Taft," *Reporter*, Vol. 6 (Jan. 8, 1952), p. 6.

SECONDARY WORKS

ROBERT TAFT:

The starting point toward understanding Taft is William S. White, *The Taft Story* (New York, 1954), a brief but perceptive account by a New York *Times* reporter who knew Taft well. It deals primarily with his senatorial career. A straightforward and sympathetic treatment of Taft's ideas is Russell Kirk and James McClellan, *The Political Principles of Robert A. Taft* (New York, 1967). Largely laudatory brief biographies are Caroline T. Harnsberger, *A Man of Courage* (New York, 1952), and Phyllis Robbins, *Robert A. Taft: Boy and Man* (Cambridge, 1963). Gerald Schomp's, *The Political Assassination of Robert A. Taft* (Plantation, Florida, 1967), is a more balanced account of Taft's campaign for the presidency in 1952 than the title suggests. Briefer accounts are Holmes Alexander, *The Famous Five* (New York, 1958), which contains a very sympathetic chapter on him; Elmo Roper, *You and Your Leaders: Their Actions and Your Reactions, 1936–1956* (New York, 1957); and Marvin C. Harrison, *Robert A. Taft: Our Illustrious Dunderhead* (Cleveland, 1944), a 64-page pamphlet by an Ohio Democrat. *The Speaker's Handbook* (1950) by the United Labor League of Ohio, a 218-page study of Taft's voting record, and "The Robert Alphonso Taft Story," a 16-page comic book also done by his labor opponents in the 1950 election, are very hostile accounts which may be found in the Taft papers. Taft's own writings in book form consist only of *A Foreign Policy for Americans* (Garden City, 1951), and (with Congressman T. V. Smith of Illinois), *Foundations of Democracy: A Series of Debates* (New York, 1939). Between them, they provide handy and reliable guides to his thinking. Jhan and June Robbins, *Eight Weeks to Live: The Last Chapter in the Life of Senator Robert A. Taft* (Garden City, 1954), is a careful if syrupy account of his battle against cancer; and Dorothy Snowden Rowe, "Tribute to a Friend" (privately printed, Christmas 1964), is an appreciative brief account by a personal friend.

GLIMPSES OF TAFT:

Many memoirs and biographies include pointed references to Taft. Among those which are critical of him are Dean Acheson, *Sketches from Life of Men I Have Known* (New York, 1959); Tom Connally, as told to Alfred Steinberg, *My Name Is Tom Connally* (New York, 1954); Dwight D. Eisenhower, *Stories I Tell My Friends* (Garden City, 1967); Elting Morison, *Turmoil and Tradition: A Study of the Life and Times of Henry L. Stimson* (Boston, 1960); Sydney Hyman, *The Lives of William Benton* (Chicago, 1969); Wilmarth S. Lewis, *One Man's Education* (New York, 1967); and C. L. Sulzberger, *A Long Row of Candles: Memoirs and Diaries, 1934–1954* (New York, 1969). Accounts by newsmen are Jack Bell, *The Splendid Misery: The Story of the Presidency and Power Politics at Close Range* (Garden City, 1960); and Arthur Krock, *Memoirs: 60 Years on the Firing Line* (New York, 1968). Anecdotes and stories which are more friendly to Taft include Turner Catledge, *My Life and Times* (New York, 1971); Eisenhower, *Mandate for Change, 1953–1956* (Garden City, 1963); Ralph E. Flanders, *Senator from Vermont* (Boston, 1961); John F. Kennedy, *Profiles in Courage* (New York, 1955); and Donald R. Richberg, *My Hero: The Indiscreet Memoirs of an Eventful but Unheroic Life* (New York, 1954). *A Senate Journal, 1943–1945,* by the journalist and novelist Allen Drury, is an exceptionally rich source sympathetic to Taft. These are but a few of the many books which pay some attention to him; notes identify the rest.

WILLIAM HOWARD TAFT:

By far the most reliable account is Henry F. Pringle's, *The Life and Times of William Howard Taft,* 2 vols. (New York, 1939). This was the biography which Robert Taft himself authorized. Another important source is the account by President Taft's aide, Archie Butt, *Taft and Roosevelt: The Intimate Letters of Archie Butt,* 2 vols. (Garden City, 1930). Less useful are Herbert S. Duffy, *William Howard Taft* (New York, 1930); and Robert Lee Dunn, *William Howard Taft: American* (Boston, 1908), which is interesting only for some of the informal photographs printed therein. William Manners, *TR and Will: A Friendship that Split the Republican Party* (New York, 1969) is rather breathless popular history; and Lillian Rogers Parks, in collaboration with Frances Spatz Leighton, *My Thirty Years Backstage at the White House* (New York, 1961), and Irwin Hood ("Ike") Hoover, *42 Years in the White House* (Boston, 1934) are two of many "inside" accounts of family life in the White House which include Taft's time. Alpheus T. Mason, *William Howard Taft: Chief Justice* (New York, 1965) focuses on Taft's career after 1920, but tells rather more about his personal activities than his judicial philosophy. Perhaps the best way to note the often striking similarities in the thinking of William Howard Taft and Robert is to read the ex-President's own words. Among his many collections of speeches and essays are *Popular Government: Its Essence, Its Permanence, and Its Perils* (New Haven, 1913); *Our Chief Magistrate and His Powers* (New York, 1916); and *Liberty Under Law* (New Haven, 1922). Theodore Marburg and Horace E. Flack, eds., collected many of his ideas on foreign policy in *Taft Papers on the League of Nations* (New York, 1920).

TAFT FAMILY:

The basic source is Ishbel Ross, *An American Family: The Tafts, 1678 to 1964,* 2d ed. (Cleveland, 1964). Ross is uncritical and much too discursive, but her work is based on considerable research in archival sources. Stephen Hess, *America's Political Dynasties from Adams to Kennedy* (Garden City, 1966) contains an interesting — and occasionally critical — chapter on the Tafts. It, too, is well researched. Bella Kornitzer, *American Fathers and Sons* (no place of publication, 1952) also includes a brief chapter on Robert Taft and his father. Lewis Alexander Leonard, *Life of Alphonso Taft* (New York, 1920) is a pedestrian but useful account of President Taft's father. Robert's mother, Helen Herron Taft, recounted (with the aid of her daughter and a magazine writer) some episodes of her life in *Recollections of Full Years* (New York, 1914). This book unfortunately is reticent about her personal life. Other books by Tafts which provide bits of insight are Henry W. Taft (Robert's uncle), *Opinions, Literary and Otherwise* (New York, 1930); Charles P. Taft, *You and I — and Roosevelt* (New York, 1936) and *Democracy in Politics and Economics* (New York, 1950). Earlier generations of Tafts receive some attention in *The Taft Family Gathering: Proceedings of the Meeting of the Taft Family, at Uxbridge, Mass., Aug. 12, 1874* (Uxbridge, 1874); and James H. Phelps, *Collections Relating to the History and Inhabitants of the Town of Townshend, Vermont,* parts I and II (Brattleboro, 1877, 1884).

EARLY LIFE:

Some of the more useful books dealing with Cincinnati in Taft's youth are Clara Longworth de Chambrun, *Cincinnati: Story of the Queen City* (New York, 1939); Zane L. Miller, *Boss Cox's Cincinnati: Urban Politics in the Progressive Era* (New York, 1968); William C. Smith, *Queen City Yesterdays: Sketches of Cincinnati in the Eighties*

(Crawfordsville, Indiana, 1959); and Louis L. Tucker, *Cincinnati: A Student's Guide to Localized History* (New York, 1969). Two informative books on the Philippines by members of William Howard Taft's party are Edith Moses, *Unofficial Letters of an Official's Wife* (New York, 1908); and James A. Le Roy, *Philippine Life in Town and Country* (New York, 1912). Helen Herron Taft's *Recollections*, cited above, also describes the Taft family's activities there.

SCHOOLING:

Horace D. Taft, Robert's uncle and the headmaster of Taft School, left a highly readable account of his life and educational philosophy, *Memories and Opinions* (New York, 1942). The key source for Yale is George Wilson Pierson, *Yale: College and University, 1871–1937*, Vol. I (1871–1921) (New Haven, 1952). This is an unusually fine university history. Also useful for glimpses of life at Yale during Taft's time are William Lyon Phelps, *Autobiography with Letters* (New York, 1939); Henry Seidel Canby, *Alma Mater: The Gothic Age of the American Colleges* (New York, 1936); William C. De Vane, *Higher Education in Twentieth Century America* (Cambridge, 1965); and Owen Johnson's light-hearted but revealing novel, *Stover at Yale* (Boston, 1911). Arthur E. Sutherland's, *The Law at Harvard: A History of Ideas and Men, 1817–1967* (Cambridge, 1967) is the very informative basic source for Taft's years in Cambridge.

CINCINNATI, WASHINGTON, PARIS, 1913–1919:

Besides the books cited above concerning Cincinnati, I relied on Earl D. Babst and Lewis G. Vander Velde, *Michigan and the Cleveland Era: Sketches of University of Michigan Staff Members and Alumni Who Served the Cleveland Administrations, 1885–1889, 1893–1897* (Ann Arbor, 1948). This includes a chapter on Lawrence Maxwell, Taft's boss from 1913 through 1917. Books dealing with the Food Administration in World War I include Maxcy Robson Dickson, *The Food Front in World War I* (Washington, 1944); Herbert Hoover, *The Memoirs of Herbert Hoover: Years of Adventure, 1874–1920* (New York, 1951); Frank M. Surface and Raymond L. Bland, *American Food in the World War and Reconstruction Period: Operations of the Organizations Under the Direction of Herbert Hoover, 1914 to 1924* (Stanford, 1931); Edgar Eugene Robinson and Paul Carroll Edwards, eds., *The Memoirs of Ray Lyman Wilbur, 1875–1949* (Stanford, 1960); and Lewis L. Strauss, *Men and Decisions* (Garden City, 1962). Constance McLaughlin Green, *Washington: Capitol City, 1879–1950* (Princeton, 1963) is an excellent urban history which proved helpful in setting the atmosphere of Taft's Washington years. The most informative sources regarding Taft's activities in Paris include Hoover, *An American Epic: Famine in 45 Nations: Organization Behind the Front, 1914–1922* (Chicago, 1960), and *The Battle on the Front Line, 1914–1923* (Chicago, 1961); Hoover, *America's First Crusade* (New York, 1941); Warren F. Kuehl, *Seeking World Order: The United States and International Organization to 1920* (Nashville, 1969); Arno J. Mayer, *Politics and Diplomacy of Peacemaking: Containment and Counterrevolution at Versailles, 1918–1919* (New York, 1967); and Charles Seymour, *Letters from the Paris Peace Conference* (New Haven, 1965). Because Taft's views on foreign policy often bore a striking resemblance to Hoover's, the Hoover books are especially important sources.

CINCINNATI YEARS, 1920'S AND 1930'S:

The basic work on Cincinnati's urban reformers is Louis Leonard Tucker, *Cincinnati's Citizen Crusaders: A History of the Cincinnatus Association, 1920–1965* (Cincinnati, 1967). Accounts highly partial to the reformers include Murray Seasongood, *Local Government in the United States: A Challenge and an Opportunity* (Cambridge, 1933); Charles P. Taft, *City Management: The Cincinnati Experiment* (New York, 1933); Murray Seasongood, "Robert Heuck, and the Citizen's Movement in Hamilton County, Ohio," in J. T. Salter, *The American Politician* (Chapel Hill, 1938); and Silas Bent, *Strange Bedfellows: A Review of Politics, Personalities, and the Press* (New York, 1926). Eleanor Gholson Taft, *Hither and Yon on Indian Hill* (Cincinnati, Indian Hill Garden Club, 1962), offers a brief but useful view of life in Indian Hill, Taft's home. The literature on Ohio politics is very thin, but Hoyt Landon Warner, *Progressivism in Ohio, 1897–1917* (Columbus, 1964), is a solid monograph. Other works include Harlow Lindley, compiler, *Ohio in the 20th Century, 1900–1938* (Columbus, 1942); Eugene H. Roseboom and Francis P. Weisenburger, *A History of Ohio*, 2d ed. (Columbus, 1967); and Harvey Walker, *Constructive Government in Ohio: The Story of the Administration of Governor Myers Cooper of Ohio, 1929–1930* (Columbus, 1948). Occasionally interesting memoirs by Ohio Democrats are Charles Sawyer, *Concerns of a Conservative Democrat* (Carbondale, 1968); and Stephen M. Young, *Tales Out of Congress* (Philadelphia, 1964). Scholars working on twentieth century Ohio politics since 1917, however, must really rely very heavily on newspapers and on the documents cited above.

GENERAL WORKS ON POLITICS AND CONGRESS:

Four books which I found helpful on voting behavior are Lee Bogart,

Age of Television: A Study of Viewing Habits and the Impact of Television on American Life (New York, 1956); Eugene Burdick and Arthur J. Brodbeck, eds., *American Voting Behavior* (New York, 1959); Angus Campbell, et al., *The American Voter* (New York, 1960); and Campbell, et al., *Elections and the Political Order* (New York, 1966). Works dealing with the GOP are Donald R. McCoy, *Landon of Kansas* (Lincoln, 1966); George H. Mayer, *The Republican Party, 1854–1966*, 2d ed. (New York, 1967); and Malcolm Moos, *The Republicans: A History of Their Party* (New York, 1956). Books on Congress include Stephen K. Bailey and Howard D. Samuel, *Congress at Work* (New York, 1965), which has an excellent chapter on Taft-Hartley; Robert Dahl, *Congress and Foreign Policy* (New York, 1950); Randall Ripley, *Power in the Senate* (New York, 1969); David Truman, *The Congressional Party, a Case Study* (New York, 1959), which deals with the Eighty-First Congress of 1949–50; and William S. White, *The Citadel: The Story of the United States Senate* (New York, 1956). Particularly useful works are Donald R. Matthews, *United States Senators and Their World* (Chapel Hill, 1960); *Congressional Quarterly Almanac, 1945——;* and Congressional Quarterly Service, *Congress and the Nation, 1945–1964: A Review of Government and Politics in the Postwar Years* (Washington, 1965). A sketchy account of the war years is Roland Young, *Congressional Politics in the Second World War* (New York, 1956).

CONSERVATISM AND POLITICAL IDEOLOGY:

Perhaps the most relevant book in this genre is Thomas Hewes, *Decentralize for Liberty* (New York, 1945), which Taft read and recommended to colleagues, including Senator Robert Wagner of New York. Morton Keller's *In Defense of Yesterday: James M. Beck and the Politics of Conservatism, 1861–1936* (New York, 1958) is an able biography of a conservative of the generation before Taft. Two surveys are Russell Kirk, *The Conservative Mind from Burke to Santayana* (Chicago, 1953); and Gordon Harrison, *The Road to the Right: The Tradition and Hope of American Conservatism* (New York, 1954). William F. Buckley, Jr., ed., *American Conservative Thought in the 20th Century* (Indianapolis, 1970) interestingly enough does not mention Taft.

DOMESTIC POLICIES, 1938–1945:

The most important books for this period are Jerold S. Auerbach, *Labor and Liberty: The La Follette Committee and the New Deal* (Indianapolis, 1966); James MacGregor Burns, *Franklin D. Roosevelt: The Lion and the Fox* (New York, 1956); and *Soldier of Freedom* (New York, 1970); Hadley Cantril, *Public Opinion, 1935–1946* (Princeton,

1951); Hoover, *The Memoirs of Herbert Hoover: The Great Depression, 1929–1941* (New York, 1952); J. Joseph Huthmacher, *Senator Robert F. Wagner and the Rise of Urban Liberalism* (New York, 1968); Eliot Janeway, *The Struggle for Survival: A Chronicle of Economic Mobilization in World War II* (New Haven, 1951); William E. Leuchtenburg, *Franklin D. Roosevelt and the New Deal, 1932–1940* (New York, 1963); Richard R. Lingeman, *Don't You Know There's a War On? The American Home Front, 1941–1945* (New York, 1970); Randolph Paul, *Taxation in the United States* (Boston, 1954); and Maximilian St. George and Lawrence Dennis, *A Trial on Trial: The Great Sedition Trial of 1944* (no place of publication, 1946). An enormous amount of work remains to be done on the domestic politics of this period.

1940 CAMPAIGN:
This election has attracted much more than its share of attention. Among the more useful books are Ellsworth Barnard, *Wendell Willkie: Fighter for Freedom* (Marquette, Michigan, 1966); Joseph Barnes, *Willkie* (New York, 1952); Marcia Davenport, *Too Strong for Fantasy* (New York, 1967); Mary Earhart Dillon, *Wendell Willkie, 1892–1944* (Philadelphia, 1952); Bernard F. Donahoe, *Private Plans and Public Dangers: The Story of FDR's Third Nomination* (South Bend, 1965); Rupert Hughes, *Attorney for the People: The Story of Thomas E. Dewey* (Boston, 1940); Donald B. Johnson, *The Republican Party and Wendell Willkie* (Urbana, 1960); and Herbert S. Parmet and Marie B. Hecht, *Never Again: A President Runs for a Third Term* (New York, 1968).

FOREIGN POLICY, 1938–1945:
This area, too, has attracted many able historians. Among the better studies of the pre-Pearl Harbor period are Selig Adler, *The Isolationist Impulse: Its Twentieth Century Reaction* (New York, 1957); Wayne S. Cole, *America First: The Battle Against Intervention, 1940–1941* (Madison, 1953); Cole, *Senator Gerald P. Nye and American Foreign Relations* (Minneapolis, 1962); James V. Compton, *The Swastika and the Sword: Hitler, the United States, and the Origins of World War II* (Boston, 1967); Raymond H. Dawson, *The Decision to Aid Russia: Foreign Policy and Domestic Politics* (Chapel Hill, 1959); Robert A. Divine, *The Illusion of Neutrality: Franklin D. Roosevelt and the Struggle over the Arms Embargo* (Chicago, 1962); T. R. Fehrenbach, *F.D.R.'s Undeclared War, 1939 to 1941* (New York, 1967); Alton Frye, *Nazi Germany and the American Hemisphere, 1933–1941* (New Haven, 1967); Walter Johnson, *The Battle Against Isolation* (Chicago, 1944);

Manfred Jonas, *Isolationism in America, 1935–1941* (Ithaca, 1966); Warren F. Kimball, *The Most Unsordid Act: Lend Lease, 1939–1941* (Baltimore, 1969); William L. Langer and S. Everett Gleason, *The Challenge to Isolation: The World Crisis of 1937–1940 and American Foreign Policy* (New York, 1952), and *The Undeclared War, 1940–1941* (New York, 1953); Robert James Maddox, *William E. Borah and American Foreign Policy* (Baton Rouge, 1969); and Henry L. Stimson and McGeorge Bundy, *On Active Service in Peace and War* (New York, 1947). The huge majority of these books takes an anti-isolationist point of view.

Studies dealing with the war period are David A. Baldwin, *Economic Development and American Foreign Policy, 1943–1962* (Chicago, 1966); John Morton Blum, ed., *From the Morgenthau Diaries,* vols. 2 and 3 (Boston, 1959–1967); Divine, *Roosevelt and World War II* (Baltimore, 1969); Divine, *Second Chance: The Triumph of Internationalism in America During World War II* (New York, 1967); Richard N. Gardner, *Sterling-Dollar Diplomacy: Anglo-American Collaboration in the Reconstruction of Multilateral Trade* (New York, 1956); Hoover and Hugh Gibson, *The Problems of Lasting Peace* (New York, 1942); Gabriel Kolko, *The Politics of War: The World and United States Foreign Policy, 1943–1945* (New York, 1968); Richard P. Stevens, *American Zionism and United State Foreign Policy, 1942–1947* (New York, 1962); Christopher Sykes, *Crossroads to Israel* (London, 1965); and H. Bradford Westerfield, *Foreign Policy and Party Politics: Pearl Harbor to Korea* (New Haven, 1955).

DOMESTIC AFFAIRS, TRUMAN ERA:

An important memoir is Chester Bowles, *Promises to Keep: My Years in Public Life, 1941–1969* (New York, 1971). Also essential for understanding the struggles over OPA are Harvey C. Mansfield, et al., *A Short History of OPA* (Washington, 1947); and Lester V. Chandler, *Inflation in the United States, 1940–1948* (New York, 1951). Other key books dealing with economic policies are Edmund S. Flash, Jr., *Economic Advice and Presidential Leadership: The Council of Economic Advisers* (New York, 1965); Herbert Stein, *The Fiscal Revolution in America* (Chicago, 1969); and especially the thoughtful book, *United States Fiscal Policy, 1945–1959, Its Contribution to Economic Stability* (London, 1961), by A. E. Holmans. Important monographs are Stephen Kemp Bailey, *Congress Makes a Law: The Story Behind the Employment Act of 1946* (New York, 1950); William C. Berman, *The Politics of Civil Rights in the Truman Administration* (Columbus, 1970); William J. Bosch, *Judgment on Nuremberg: American Attitudes Toward the*

Major German War-Crime Trials (Chapel Hill, 1970); Robert Divine, *American Immigration Policy, 1924–1952* (New Haven, 1957); Richard O. Davies, *Housing Reform During the Truman Administration* (Columbia, Missouri, 1966); and, for farm policies, Reo M. Christenson, *The Brannan Plan: Farm Politics and Policy* (Ann Arbor, 1959); and Allen J. Matusow, *Farm Policies and Politics in the Truman Years* (Cambridge, 1967).

Studies dealing with education policy are Frank J. Munger and Richard F. Fenno, *National Politics and Federal Aid to Education* (Syracuse, 1962); and Fenno, "The House of Representatives and Federal Aid to Education," in Robert L. Peabody and Nelson W. Polsby, eds., *New Perspectives on the House of Representatives* (Chicago, 1963), pp. 195–235. Cabell Phillips', *The Truman Presidency: The History of a Triumphant Succession* (New York, 1966), while essentially uncritical, remains the most comprehensive survey of the period, and Truman's *Memoirs*, 2 vols. (Garden City, 1955); and Rowland Evans and Robert Novak, *Lyndon B. Johnson: The Exercise of Power* (New York, 1968) are helpful in places. Barton J. Bernstein, ed., *Politics and Policies of the Truman Administration* (Chicago, 1970); and Richard S. Kirkendall, ed., *The Truman Period as a Research Field* (Columbia, Missouri, 1967), are two excellent collections of critical essays.

Among the many works dealing with labor policy are Fred Hartley, Jr., *Our New National Labor Policy* (New York, 1948); R. Alton Lee, *Truman and Taft-Hartley: A Question of Mandate* (Lexington, 1966); Arthur F. McClure, *The Truman Administration and the Problems of Postwar Labor, 1945–1948* (Rutherford, New Jersey, 1969); Harry A. Millis and Emily Clark Brown, *From the Wagner Act to Taft-Hartley: A Study of National Labor Policy and Labor Relations* (Chicago, 1950); Joel Seidman, *American Labor from Defense to Reconversion* (Chicago, 1953); and Fred Witney, *Government and Collective Bargaining* (Philadelphia, 1951). I found the careful monograph by Lee and the encyclopedic study by Millis and Brown particularly relevant.

Books on communism and McCarthy include Robert Griffith, *The Politics of Fear: Joseph R. McCarthy and the Senate* (Lexington, 1970); Alan D. Harper, *The Politics of Loyalty: The White House and the Communist Issue, 1946–1952* (Westport, Connecticut, 1969); Earl Latham, *The Communist Controversy in Washington: From the New Deal to McCarthy* (Cambridge, 1966); and the still important *Senator Joe McCarthy* (New York, 1959) by Richard Rovere.

ELECTIONS, 1948, 1950, 1952:

For 1948, the books to consult include Curtis D. MacDougall, *Gid-*

eon's Army, 3 vols. (New York, 1965); Jules Abels, *Out of the Jaws of Victory* (New York, 1959); and especially Irwin Ross, *The Loneliest Campaign: The Truman Victory of 1948* (New York, 1968). There exists no careful biography of Dewey. For 1950, books which deal in part with Taft's senatorial victory are Fay Calkins, *The C.I.O. and the Democratic Party* (Chicago, 1952); James Cannon, ed., *Politics U.S.A.* (New York, 1960); and especially Samuel Lubell, *The Future of American Politics,* 3d ed. (New York, 1965). For 1952, Courtney Whitney, *MacArthur: His Rendezvous with History* (New York, 1964); and Earl Mazo, *Richard Nixon: A Political and Personal Portrait* (New York, 1959) help in places. Essential are Richard C. Bain, *Convention Decisions and Voting Records* (Washington, 1960); Paul M. David, et al., *The Politics of National Party Conventions* (Menasha, Wisconsin, 1960); and especially the five volume study edited by David, *Presidential Nominating Politics in 1952* (Baltimore, 1954).

POSTWAR FOREIGN POLICY:

Relevant memoirs and diaries include Dean Acheson, *Present at the Creation* (New York, 1969); Arthur Vandenberg, Jr., ed., *The Private Papers of Senator Vandenberg* (Boston, 1952); and especially George Kennan, *Memoirs, 1925–1950* (Boston, 1967). Polemical pieces include Bonner Fellers, *Wings for Peace: A Primer for a New Defense* (Chicago, 1953); and Henry Hazlitt, *Will Dollars Save the World?* (Irvington on Hudson, 1948). Taft corresponded with General Fellers, and recommended Hazlitt's book to friends. Useful general surveys are Herbert Feis, *From Trust to Terror: The Onset of the Cold War, 1945–1950* (New York, 1970); Walter La Feber, *America, Russia, and the Cold War, 1945–1966* (New York, 1968); and especially Stephen Ambrose, *Rise to Globalism* (New York, 1971).

More specialized works are Ronald J. Caridi, *The Korean War and American Politics: The Republican Party as a Case Study* (Philadelphia, 1968); Lloyd C. Gardner, *Architects of Illusion: Men and Ideas in American Foreign Policy, 1941–1949* (Chicago, 1970); Harry Bayard Price, *The Marshall Plan and Its Meaning* (Ithaca, 1955); John W. Spanier, *The Truman-MacArthur Controversy and the Korean War* (New York, 1959); Athan G. Theoharis, *The Yalta Myths, An Issue in U.S. Politics, 1945–1955* (Columbia, Missouri, 1970); Tang Tsou, *America's Failure in China, 1941–1950* (Chicago, 1963); and Adam B. Ulam, *Expansion and Coexistence: The History of Soviet Foreign Policy* (New York, 1968). C. David Tompkins, *Senator Arthur H. Vandenberg: The Evolution of a Modern Republican, 1884–1945* (East Lansing, 1970) takes his subject, uncritically, to the start of the postwar era.

Three rather partisan books are Norman Graebner, *The New Isolationism: A Study in Politics and Foreign Policy Since 1950* (New York, 1956); Richard Rovere and Arthur M. Schlesinger, Jr., *The MacArthur Controversy and American Foreign Policy* (New York, 1965); and John M. Swomley, Jr., *The Military Establishment* (Boston, 1964).

Two exceptionally important books are Roland N. Stromberg, *Collective Security and American Foreign Policy: From the League of Nations to NATO* (New York, 1963); and Thomas G. Paterson, ed., *Cold War Critics: Alternatives to American Foreign Policy in the Truman Years* (Chicago, 1971). Stromberg's book is a highly critical survey of ideas, while Paterson's includes essays of a high quality from a revisionist perspective.

EISENHOWER:

Historians have been very slow to study the Eisenhower years, and accounts by journalists or members of the administration remain the major sources. These include Sherman Adams, *First Hand Report: The Story of the Eisenhower Administration* (New York, 1961); Marquis Childs, *Eisenhower: Captive Hero: A Critical Study of the General and the President* (New York, 1958); Robert J. Donovan, *Eisenhower: The Inside Story* (New York, 1956); Arthur Larson, *Eisenhower: The President Nobody Knew* (New York, 1968); Emmet John Hughes, *Ordeal of Power: A Political Memoir of the Eisenhower Years* (New York, 1963); Merlo Pusey, *Eisenhower the President* (New York, 1956); and Richard Rovere, *Affairs of State: The Eisenhower Years* (New York, 1956). More scholarly studies are James N. Rosenau, *The Nomination of "Chip" Bohlen* (New York, 1960); and David A. Frier, *Conflict of Interest in the Eisenhower Administration* (Baltimore, 1969).

GENERAL WORKS, PSYCHOLOGY:

The following works offered psychological insights: Bernard Berelson and Gary A. Steiner, *Human Behavior: An Inventory of Scientific Findings* (New York, 1964); Erik Erikson, *Childhood and Society*, 2d ed. (New York, 1963); Erikson, *Identity and the Life Cycle: Selected Papers* (New York, 1959); Sigmund Freud, *The Psychopathology of Everyday Life* (London, 1914); John Garraty, *The Nature of Biography* (New York, 1957); Calvin S. Hall and Gardner Lindzey, *Theories of Personality* (New York, 1957); Karen Horney, *The Neurotic Personality of Our Time* (New York, 1937); C. G. Jung, "Psychological Types," in C. M. Campbell, *Problems of Personality* (New York, 1925); Clyde Kluckhohn and Henry A. Murray, eds., *Personality in Nature, Society, and Culture* (New York, 1949); Harold D. Lasswell, *Power and*

Personality (New York, 1948); A. H. Maslow, *Motivation and Personality* (New York, 1954); and Theodor Reik, *A Psychologist Looks at Love* (New York, 1944). A relevant article is Frank E. Manuel, "The Use and Abuse of Psychology in History," *Daedalus* (Winter 1971), 187–210. Careful readers will note my indebtedness to Erikson in dealing with Taft's life from 1913 to 1917, to Reik in handling his marriage, to Horney in placing Taft in American culture, and to Kluckhohn and Murray, whose model of tension → reduction of tension helped me understand Taft's great drive to excel.

Notes

THE FOLLOWING ABBREVIATIONS will appear in the notes: COHP — Taft project, Columbia University Oral History Project; CR — Congressional Record; LC — Library of Congress, Division of Manuscripts; RT — Robert A. Taft; RTP — Robert A. Taft Papers; WHT — William Howard Taft; WHTP — William Howard Taft Papers; TSHP — Taft, Stettinius, and Hollister Papers.

CHAPTER 1: A STRIVING BOY

1. WHT to Alphonso, Sept. 10, 1889, series 1, box 28, WHTP, LC.
2. William C. Smith, *Queen City Yesterdays: Sketches of Cincinnati in the Eighties* (Crawfordsville, Ind., 1959), p. 38; Louis L. Tucker, *Cincinnati: A Student's Guide to Localized History* (New York, 1969), p. 23; Zane L. Miller, *Boss Cox's Cincinnati: Urban Politics in the Progressive Era* (New York, 1968), p. 18.
3. Henry F. Pringle, *The Life and Times of William Howard Taft,* Vol. 1 (New York, 1939), pp. 128–129.
4. Ibid., p. 143.
5. *Williams' Cincinnati Directory* (annual vols., Cincinnati, 1886–1902); Files, Recorder's Office, Cincinnati.
6. Interviews, Helen Taft Manning, John Hollister, Mrs. Russell Wilson, Frederick Exton (COHP). Pringle, Vol. 1, pp. 121–122; Mrs. William Howard Taft, *Recollections of Full Years* (New York, 1914), pp. 23–30.
7. Pringle, Vol. 1, p. 123; Interviews, Exton (COHP), Manning, Mrs. Robert Black (COHP), p. 24; Mrs. Taft, *Recollections*, pp. 308–309; Robert Lee Dunn, *William Howard Taft: American* (Boston, 1908), p. 30.
8. *The Taft Family Gathering: Proceedings of the Meeting of the Taft Family, at Uxbridge, Mass., Aug. 12, 1874* (Uxbridge, 1874); Horace D. Taft, *Memories and Opinions* (New York, 1942), pp. 1, 11.
9. Martha Willard, "Notes for a Biographer," Unpublished ms., Swarthmore College, 1935 (in papers of Charles P. Taft, 2nd, Cincinnati).
10. Willard, p. 10.
11. Pringle, Vol. 1, p. 22.
12. Willard, p. 3.
13. Lewis Alexander Leonard, *Life of Alphonso Taft* (New York, 1920), passim; Ishbel Ross, *An American Family: The Tafts, 1678 to 1964,* 2d ed. (Cleveland, 1964), pp. 3–110; Horace Taft, *Memories*, Chs. 1, 2.

14. RT to Horace D. Taft, Jan. 11, 1934, Horace Taft papers, Taft School, Watertown, Conn.

15. Pringle, Vol. 1, p. 236.

16. Ibid., Vol. 2, p. 962.

17. Archie Butt, *Taft and Roosevelt: The Intimate Letters of Archie Butt* (Garden City, 1930), Vol. 1, p. 21; Stephen Hess, "Big Bill Taft," *American Heritage*, Vol. 17 (Oct. 1966), pp. 32–37; Hess, *America's Political Dynasties from Adams to Kennedy* (Garden City, 1966), p. 309; Horace Taft, *Memories*, p. 112.

18. WHT to Alphonso, Sept. 15, 1889, Nov. 20, 1890, Feb. 14, 1891, April 18, 1891, series 1, box 28, WHTP.

19. WHT to Mrs. WHT, May 10, 1891, Charles P. Taft, 2nd, papers.

20. WHT to his mother, Jan. 5, 1893, series 1, box 30, WHTP.

21. WHT to Mrs. WHT, March 19, 1892, Charles P. Taft, 2nd, papers; Pringle, Vol. 1, p. 149. Maurice Hirsch, a classmate of Bob's at law school, recalled visiting at the White House while Taft was President. Hirsch said, "The President and Bob unabashedly greeted each other with a hug and a kiss." Hirsch to author, August 1971.

22. Pringle, Vol. 2, p. 906.

23. WHT, "The College Slouch," *Ladies' Home Journal,* Vol. 31 (May 1914), p. 13.

24. Charles A. Selden, "Six White House Wives and Widows," *Ladies' Home Journal,* Vol. 44 (June 1927), p. 18; Mrs. WHT, *Recollections,* passim; Pringle, Vol. 1, p. 69; Interviews, Helen Manning, Charles P. Taft, 2nd; miscellaneous letters from Mrs. WHT to RT in suitcases and trunks found in Taft home in Indian Hill and subsequently forwarded to LC for inclusion in RTP. Citations to RTP will ordinarily carry the box number; references without box numbers will be to this material in the suitcases.

25. Butt, Vol. 1, p. 64; Mrs. WHT, *Recollections,* pp. 327, 393.

26. Pringle, Vol. 1, p. 69; George G. Hill, "The Wife of the New President," *Ladies' Home Journal,* Vol. 26 (March 1909), p. 13.

27. WHT to Mrs. WHT, July 8, 1895, and July 14, 1896, Mrs. WHT to WHT, June 9, 1890, WHTP; Pringle, Vol. 1, p. 442.

28. Mrs. WHT to WHT, June 9, 1890, Aug. 15, 1890, Aug. 21, 1890, June 10, 1891, Sept. ?, 1891, March 17, 1892, series 2, box 41, WHTP. These are but a few of the many letters concerning Bobbie in the papers.

29. Mrs. WHT to WHT, Feb. 13, 1894, series 2, box 42, WHTP.

30. Mrs. WHT to WHT, Dec. 6, 1899, series 2, box 44; March 23, 1896, series 2, box 43; WHTP; Helen Manning to author, Feb. 1970; Exton interview (COHP).

31. Ross, p. 122.

CHAPTER 2: THE STRUGGLE FOR SELF-CONTROL

1. San Francisco *Chronicle,* April 18, 1900, p. 5.

2. Ibid., April 17, 1900, p. 1.

3. RT to Mama, n.d. 1900, series 1, box 32, WHTP, LC.

4. Mrs. WHT, *Recollections of Full Years* (New York, 1914), p. 48; Henry

F. Pringle, *The Life and Times of William Howard Taft,* Vol. 1 (New York, 1939), p. 166; Alice Roosevelt Longworth, *Crowded Hours: Reminiscences of Alice Roosevelt Longworth* (New York, 1933), pp. 66–92; WHT to Charles P. Taft, May 8, 1900, May 12, 1900, series 1, box 31, WHTP; Interview, Helen Taft Manning (COHP) is a key source for these early years.

5. Edith Moses, *Unofficial Letters of an Official's Wife* (New York, 1908), pp. 1–32; Pringle, Vol. 1, p. 206.

6. WHT to Charles P. Taft, Aug. 31, 1900, Sept. 21, 1900, series 1, box 32, WHTP.

7. WHT to C. P. Taft, Oct. 15, 1900; to Mother, Nov. 30, 1900; to Mrs. Herron, Jan. 19, 1901, ibid.

8. WHT to Mother, Dec. 20, 1900, to Charles P. Taft, March 17, 1901, box 33, to Mother, July ?, 1901 and Oct. 21, 1901, WHTP; Mrs. WHT, *Recollections,* pp. 138, 157, 217.

9. Mrs. WHT, *Recollections,* p. 229; Pringle, Vol. 1, pp. 212–215.

10. Mrs. WHT to WHT, Feb. 1, 1902, series 2, box 45, Maria Herron to WHT, April 22, 1902, series 1, box 34, WHTP; Interview, John Hollister, pp. 2–3 (COHP); Pringle, Vol. 1, p. 215.

11. Mrs. WHT, *Recollections,* pp. 247–248; WHT to Charles P. Taft, July 20, 1902, series 1, box 34, WHTP; Caroline T. Harnsburger, *A Man of Courage* (New York, 1952), p. 65.

12. Mrs. Alphonso Taft to WHT, July 28, 1902, cited in Phyllis Robbins, *Robert A. Taft: Boy and Man* (Cambridge, 1963), pp. 84–85; *Time,* Jan. 29, 1940, p. 21; WHT to Mrs. WHT, Aug. 5, 1902, cited in Ishbel Ross, *An American Family: The Tafts, 1678 to 1964,* 2d ed. (Cleveland, 1964), p. 147; WHT to Aunt Delia, July 14, 1902, series 1, box 34, Mrs. WHT to WHT, July 25, 1902, July 6, 1902, Aug. 17, 1902, series 2, box 45, WHTP.

13. WHT to Mother, Nov. 23, 1902, March 7, 1903, series 1, box 34, WHTP.

14. "Pilot Chart of the N. Pacific Ocean," 1902, RTP, LC; San Francisco *Chronicle,* Sept. 18, 1903.

15. WHT to H. C. Hollister, July 12, 1902, Cincinnati Historical Society; Mrs. Alphonso Taft to WHT, July 28, 1902, in Robbins, pp. 84–85.

16. Mrs. WHT to WHT, Aug. 24, 1902, series 2, box 45, WHT to Mother, April 7, 1902, and to Horace D. Taft, July 20, 1902, series 1, box 34, WHTP; Mrs. WHT, *Recollections,* p. 248.

17. Manning (COHP), p. 72.

18. WHT to Horace D. Taft, Aug. 19, 1903, series 1, box 35, WHTP.

19. Miscellaneous material and photographs, Taft School Archives, Watertown, Conn.

20. Horace D. Taft, *Memories and Opinions* (New York, 1942), pp. 245–249.

21. *Taft: 75 Years in Pictures,* school archives; *Catalogue*(s), 1903–1906 (quote is, 1903, p. 25); Interviews, John More, Robert Taft, Jr., Horace Dwight Taft; Henry Hall Lyman to Noel G. Rapp, July 29, 1953, cited in Rapp, "The Political Speaking of Robert A. Taft, 1939 to 1953," doctoral thesis, Purdue, 1955, p. 48.

22. Horace D. Taft to WHT, Sept. 30, 1903, Oct 17, 1903, Oct. 24, 1903, Nov. 2, 1903, series 1, box 35, WHTP.

23. RT to Mama, Nov 15, 1903, Nov. 22, 1903, Feb. 21, 1904, Horace D. Taft

to WHT, Feb. 25, 1904, all series 1, box 35, WHTP; *Papyrus* (school paper), May 6, 1904, p. 3, Taft School archives.

24. RT to Mama, Feb. 12, 1905, Feb. 19, 1905, Oct. 8, 1905, RT to Helen Taft, Oct. 15, 1905, series 1, boxes 35–36, WHTP; Taft *Annual* (yearbook), 1906, pp. 55, 65; *Annual,* 1905, pp. lx, 43; *Annual,* 1904, p. xii.

25. RT to Mama, Jan. 10, 1904, Jan. 16, 1904, RT to WHT, Jan. 27, 1904, Oct. 5, 1905, Horace D. Taft to WHT, Oct. 5, 1905, May 15, 1905, May 27, 1905, June 21, 1905, series 1, box 36, WHTP. Quotes are RT to Mama, June 21, 1905, and WHT to RT, Oct. 11, 1905, series 8, letterbook 5, WHTP.

26. WHT to Mrs. WHT, March 3, 22, 28, 29, 30, and 31, 1904; April 2, 3, 1904, series 2, box 46, WHTP.

27. RT to Mama, April 10, 1904, May 1, 1904, series 1, box 35, WHTP.

28. WHT to RT, Oct. 27, 1903, series 1, box 35, Feb. 6, 1904, series 8, letterbook 1, WHT to Horace D. Taft, April 25, 1904, series 8, letterbook 4, all WHTP.

29. RT to Mama, Oct. 8, 1904, April 23, 1905, Horace D. Taft to WHT, Nov. 29, 1904, series 1, box 35, WHTP; New York *Times,* Oct. 7, 1906, p. 1; *Annual,* 1904, p. xii.

30. *Annual,* 1906, p. 65.

31. *Papyrus,* Feb. 5, 1906, Feb. 9, Feb. 23, March 21, May 18, 1905, Jan. 20, March 8, April 19, 1906; RT to Mama, Feb. 19, 1905, series 1, box 35, WHTP.

32. Horace D. Taft to WHT, Jan. 25, 1905, March 1, 1906, series 1, box 36, WHTP.

33. Andrew D. McIntosh to Pauline Isaacson, Oct. 23, 1954, school archives. Isaacson cites several other letters from people who knew him in school, in her doctoral thesis, "Robert Alphonso Taft: An Assessment of a Persuader," Minnesota, 1956, p. 63.

CHAPTER 3: AVOIDING THE LIMELIGHT

1. Henry F. Pringle, *The Life and Times of William Howard Taft,* Vol. 1 (New York, 1939), p. 31.

2. WHT to RT, Oct. 26, 1905, series 8, letterbook 5, WHTP, LC.

3. Henry Seidel Canby, *Alma Mater: The Gothic Age of the American Colleges* (New York, 1936), pp. 34–38, 53, 91–93; William C. De Vane, *Higher Education in Twentieth Century America* (Cambridge, 1965), p. 16; *Yale Daily News,* and *Banner and Pot-Pourri,* Yale University Archives.

4. New York *Times,* Sept. 22, 1908.

5. Interviews, Walter Logan, Carroll Glover, Jack Ewen (COHP); Richard K. Hawes to author, Nov. 5, 1969; New York *Times,* March 23, 1909, p. 3; RT to Mama, May 12, 1908, May 24, 1908, series 1, box 38, and Feb. 19, 1907, box 37, WHTP; RT to Charlie, summer 1916, Charles P. Taft, 2nd, papers, Cincinnati.

6. RT to Mama, Oct. 13, 1907, series 1, box 37, May ?, 1909, series 7, RT to Martha Bowers, March 12, 1914, to Robert Taft, Jr., May 16, 1938, RTP, LC; Harvey Bundy (COHP), pp. 22.

7. RT, "Volunteer Watching in New York," 1910, RTP; New York *Times*, April 6, 1910, p. 10.

8. RT to Mama, May 19, 1909, series 7, WHTP; Yale *Daily News*, May 10, 1910, p. 1; RT, "Non Scholae sed Vitae Discimus," RTP.

9. Yale *Daily News*, April 24, 1909; *Banner and Pot-Pourri, 1909–1910*, p. 79; RT, "The 15th Amendment," April 23, 1909, RTP.

10. New York *Times*, Sept. 22, 1908; "Yale College — Scholarship Record," Registrar's Office, Yale; WHT to RT, Oct. 28, 1909, series 9, letterbook 8, WHTP; *History of the Class of 1910*, Vol. 1 (New Haven, 1910), p. 316; letters to Pauline Isaacson, in her doctoral thesis, "Robert Alphonso Taft: An Assessment of a Persuader," Minnesota, 1956, pp. 71–74.

11. Class notes, Bakewell lectures, RTP; Notes, Fisher course, RTP.

12. Robert Taft, Jr., to Mother, March 1, 1937, RTP.

13. *History of the Class of 1910*, Vol. 1, p. 117ff.; Yale University *Catalogue, 1908–1909*, p. 59; *The Course of Study in Yale College, 1907–1908* (New Haven, 1907); ibid., 1908–1909, 1909–1910; George Wilson Pierson, *Yale: College and University, 1871–1937*, Vol. 1 (1871–1921) (New Haven, 1952), pp. 200, 309, 346; William Lyon Phelps, *Autobiography with Letters* (New York, 1939), p. 287; Owen Johnson, *Stover at Yale* (Boston, 1911).

14. Harvey Bundy (COHP), 19; RT to Charlie, March 1, 1914, Charles P. Taft, 2nd, papers.

15. Quoted in preface by Austin W. Scott, in Arthur E. Sutherland, *The Law at Harvard: A History of Ideas and Men, 1817–1967* (Cambridge, 1967), p. vii.

16. New York *Times*, Oct. 2, 1910.

17. Sutherland, p. 215; Interviews, Austin Scott, Robert P. Goldman; Vincent Starzinger to author, Feb. 24, 1970; Robert W. Perkins to author, March 4, 1970; *Harvard Law Review*, Vol. 15 (Dec. 1911), p. 169; ibid., Vol. 16 (Dec. 1912), p. 161.

18. Donald Gallagher to Mother, June 19, 1911, series 7, WHTP.

19. RT to Martha Bowers, Dec. 5, 1912, RTP; Frank E. Tyler, "Bob Taft: An Appreciation," *Harvard Law School Bulletin*, Vol. 4 (Oct. 1953), pp. 10–11; Roscoe Pound to Thomas R. McManus, Sept. 14, 1959, Pound papers, Harvard Law School; RT notebooks, Harvard Law School; notebooks of Zechariah Chafee, Harvard Law School.

20. Dean Ezra R. Thayer to WHT, Aug. 24, 1911, series 8, letterbook 29, WHTP; Helen Taft to RT, Sept. 7, 1911, RTP; Richard K. Hawes to author, Nov. 5, 1969; Harvard Law School *Catalogue of Courses*, 1910–1913; Taft transcript, Harvard Law School registrar's office; WHT to Mabel Boardman, June 19, 1913, box 6, Boardman papers, LC.

21. Interviews, Austin Scott, Walter Logan; Ernest Angell to author, Feb. 26, 1970; Norman Armour to author, Feb. 26, 1970; Francis M. Burdick, "Is Law the Expression of Class Selfishness?" *Harvard Law Review*, Vol. 25 (Feb. 1912), p. 371.

22. Pound, "Sociological Jurisprudence, Scope and Purpose of," *Harvard Law Review*, Vols. 24 and 25 (June 1911–April 1912), quote on p. 516; Chafee to law school, n.d., Chafee papers. Of Taft, Chafee commented later, "The contrast between his shyness at that time and his subsequent success in getting along with people is very marked. One would have expected

while he was in law school that he gain fame by the mastery of ideas rather than by mastery of men, which was not then apparent" (to Pauline Isaacson, Oct. 27, 1955, Chafee papers). See also Robert Stevens, "Two Cheers for 1870: The American Law School," in *Perspectives in American History,* Vol. 5 (1971), esp. pp. 424–441.

23. RT to WHT, Nov. 13, 1912, John C. Gray to WHT, Nov. 19, 1912, WHT to RT, Nov. 19, 1912, all series 7, WHTP.

24. Maurice Hirsch to author, Aug. 1971; Rev. Morgan Phelps Noyes to author, Oct. 17, 1969; Charles W. Briggs to author, March 2, 1970.

25. Pringle, Vol. 2, pp. 782–783; WHT to Dean Wright, June 10, 1910, Yale University. WHT also wrote Dean Thayer, Sept. 6, 1911, "Your letter about Bob has braced me up and made me indifferent to the slings and arrows of outrageous fortune, or the quips and gibes of men who believe in judicial recall" (series 8, letterbook 29), WHTP.

26. For WHT as a politician, Pringle, Vol. 1, p. 455; Horace Taft, *Memories and Opinions* (New York, 1942), pp. 116–120.

27. Pringle, Vol. 1, pp. 290, 311–313.

28. Quote is Dr. Stanhope Bayne-Jones (COHP). For "Die-Nasty," see Ross, p. 218; also interview with Helen Taft Manning; Manning, "Debut in the White House," unpub. speech, 1969, author's possession.

29. Major sources for his social activities are RT to Helen Taft, July 23, 1911, series 7, WHTP; Butt, Vol. 1, passim; Lillian Rogers Parks, in collaboration with Frances Spatz Leighton, *My Thirty Years Backstage at the White House* (New York, 1961), p. 111; Helen Taft to RT, March 11, 1913, RTP; and the New York *Times,* Dec. 16–30, 1908, Jan. 1, March 20, April 11, April 15, Dec. 25–30, 1909; Dec. 27–31, 1910; Jan. 1, June 18, 1911. The RTP (no box numbers) contain scores of letters to him from friends in these years.

30. RT to Mama, June 3, 1908, RT to WHT, Oct. 16, 1908, series 1, box 38, RT to Delia Torrey, Jan. 8, 1909, WHTP; Archie Butt, *Taft and Roosevelt: The Intimate Letters of Archie Butt,* Vol. 1 (Garden City, 1930), passim.

31. Mrs. WHT to RT, June 10, 1908, RTP.

32. Frances to RT, Feb. 17, 1913, Kim Townsend to RT, March 22, 1911, Helen Taft to RT, Dec. 15, 1911, all RTP; Interviews, Stephen Philbin, Charles P. Taft, 2nd; letters to author by Edward Ingraham, Sept. 24, 1969, Frank T. Nelson, March 26, 1969, Maurice Hirsch, Aug. 1971.

33. WHT to RT, Aug. 27, 1911, RTP.

34. Chicago *Tribune,* June 14, 17, 19, 1908; New York *Times,* June 18, 1908, March 3, 5, 1909, June 23, 1912; Washington *Post,* March 5, 6, 8, 1909; RT to Mama, June 28, 1908, RT to WHT, Oct. 16, 1908, series 1, box 36, WHTP; William Manners, *TR and Will: A Friendship that Split the Republican Party* (New York, 1969), pp. 48, 54, 61.

35. RT spelled out his philosophical kinship with WHT in a letter to Henry F. Pringle, Aug. 31, 1939, box 6, RTP. For WHT's views, see esp. his *Popular Government: Its Essence, Its Permanence, and Its Perils* (New Haven, 1913), which RT read at the time and called "very interesting." RT to Martha Bowers, n.d. [1914], RTP.

36. RT to Pringle, May 30, 1938, box 6, RTP.

37. RT to Isobel Smith Lawton, Jan. 6, 1945, I. Jack Martin papers, Kensington, Md.; RT to John Temple Graves, Jan. 20, 1947, ibid.; memo to publicity department, *Reporter,* Jan. 1, 1952, box 405, RTP.
38. In 1926 WHT wrote, "the danger to this country is in the enlargement of the power of Congress," cited in Alpheus T. Mason, *William Howard Taft: Chief Justice* (New York, 1965), pp. 90–91. See also p. 93.
39. RT to Martha Bowers, Sept. 29, 1913, RTP.
40. *Time,* Aug. 10, 1953, p. 19; Helen Taft Manning, "My Brother Bob Taft," *American Magazine,* Vol. 153 (Jan. 1952), p. 14.
41. RT to Martha Bowers, Sept. 10, Sept. 24, 1912, April ?, April 14, 1913, RTP.
42. Manning, "My Brother"; Manning to author, Feb. 1970. An unidentified clipping, RTP, quotes WHT as saying after a speech at Yale (in 1907 or early 1908) that it was the first time Bob had been in the audience to hear him speak. On Oct. 25, 1943, RT thanked a friend for sending him WHT's *Liberty Under Law* (New Haven, 1922), which RT said he had never read. (RT to John Bankhead, RTP). The "Crown Prince" reference is from *History of Class of 1910, Yale College,* Vol. 2 (New Haven, 1917), p. 16; and New Haven *Register,* June 20, 1910, p. 10.
43. RT to Martha Bowers, Nov. 16, 1912, RTP; Interviews, Walter Logan, Horace Taft.
44. Johnson, p. 28; New Haven *Register,* Feb. 10, 1910; Lorraine Thomas, "Young Man with a Tongue," undated clipping, RTP.
45. Tyler, "Bob Taft," pp. 10–11. Ross, p. 234, tells of RT going to the railroad station to meet his father during the presidential years, only to be ordered by a guard to stand back. RT did so "without a word of protest" and stayed there until recognized by his father.
46. RT to Martha Bowers, May 25, 1913, RTP.

CHAPTER 4: DAYS OF DRIFT AND DEFERENCE

1. RT to Martha Bowers, Nov. 16, 1912, April 20, 1913, RTP, LC; RT to Mabel Boardman, Dec. 29, 1912, box 6, Boardman papers, LC; RT to WHT, March 2, 1913, series 3, box 251, WHTP, LC.
2. RT to Martha Bowers, March 29, 1913, RTP.
3. Mrs. WHT to RT, April 13, 1913, RT to Martha Bowers, April 20, 1913, RTP; WHT to James B. Reynolds, Dec. 26, 1910, series 8, letterbook 21, WHTP.
4. WHT to Maxwell, Nov. 27, 1912, series 7, file 407, WHTP (original in RTP).
5. WHT to RT, Dec. 12, 1912, RT to Martha Bowers, Dec. 5, 1912, RTP; Interview, Robert Goldman; For Maxwell, Earl D. Babst and Lewis G. Vander Velde, *Michigan and the Cleveland Era . . .* (Ann Arbor, 1948), pp. 139–160.
6. RT to Martha Bowers, Nov. 30, Oct. 19, 1913, RTP.
7. RT to Mama, Oct. ?, 1913, series 3, box 262, WHTP; RT to Martha Bowers, Nov. 30, Oct. 19, 1913, Feb. 4, Sept. 24, 1914, RTP; Mrs. Robert Black (COHP), p. 9.

8. RT to Martha Bowers, early 1914, Feb. 18, 1914, RTP.

9. RT to Martha Bowers, Sept. 7, Nov. 30, 1913, RTP; Babst and Vander Velde, pp. 139–160.

10. New York *Times,* Dec. 16, 1913, p. 1; RT to Martha Bowers, Dec. 16, 1913, Jan. 5, March 22, July 21, 23, 27, 1914, RTP.

11. RT to WHT, Sept. 7, 28, 1913, May 29, 1914, series 3, boxes 259, 260, 281, WHTP; RT to Martha Bowers, Oct. 19, 1913, RTP; Interviews, Robert Goldman, John Hollister. For Charles P. Taft see Stephen Hess, *America's Political Dynasties from Adams to Kennedy* (Garden City, 1966), p. 307; and Ishbel Ross, *An American Family: The Tafts, 1678 to 1964,* 2d ed. (Cleveland, 1964).

12. RT to Martha Bowers, March 28, 1914, RTP.

13. RT to Martha Bowers, Feb. 28, July 16, 1914, Sept. 6, 1916, RTP; WHT to RT, May 14, 31, 1914, series 8, letterbooks 17, 18, RT to WHT, Feb. 25, 1916, Jan. 8, 1917, series 3, boxes 338, 365, WHTP.

14. He was also practical. In 1945, when his son, Bob, Jr., balked at working in his father's firm, Taft reminded him of the benefits of starting where he had contacts. "I had the same advantage of family background and material assistance from Mr. Charles P. Taft, who had extensive interests and certainly made it possible for me to get a much better start than I would have obtained elsewhere." RT to Mrs. RT, Jr., Oct. 16, 1945, RTP.

15. Interview, Stanley Rowe.

16. "Lloyd W. Bowers," *Dictionary of American Biography,* Vol. 1, p. 508; Dance Card, May 9, 1908, Rosemary Hall, RTP; John Chamberlain, "Martha Taft," Richard Scandrett papers, Cornell University; Interview, Carroll Glover.

17. *National Cyclopedia of Biography,* Vol. 22 (1922), p. 148; in 1902 WHT recommended Bowers for the Supreme Court, WHT to Theodore Roosevelt, Nov. 9, 1902, Charles P. Taft, 2nd, papers, Cincinnati.

18. RT's friend, George Harrison, who also sought Martha's hand, later congratulated him: "There's one big objection I have to the match, and that is that it's an outrage to have so much brains in one family, but try as hard as I may I can't see how I can make the Sherman law apply." Jan. 19, 1914, RTP. Other recollections of Martha were provided the author by letters from and telephone conversations with her classmates, Mrs. Walter O. Wilson, Mrs. Newton K. Hartford, Mrs. Jeannette Michael, Mrs. Josiah Lasell, Mrs. Bradley Dewey, and Mrs. Walter Clem; and from Mrs. Charles Marshall and Mrs. E. B. Ozdemir of Rosemary Hall; Also *Answer Book,* 1908 (school yearbook).

19. RT to Martha Bowers, Sept. 7, 1913, RTP.

20. Harrison to RT, Nov. 13, 1913, RTP.

21. RT to Martha, Jan. 3, 12, ?, 1914, RTP.

22. RT to Martha, Jan. 23, 27, Feb. 1, March 10, 1914, RTP. Martha's letters are also in RTP.

23. RT to Martha, March 28, 1914, RTP.

24. RT to WHT, April ?, 1914, series 3, box 278, WHTP; WHT to Mabel Boardman, April 1 and Aug. 23, 1914, boxes 6 and 7, Boardman papers; RT to Martha, May 25, 1914, WHT to Martha, April 1, 1914, RTP.

25. Martha to RT, Oct. 14, 1914, RTP; New York *World,* Sept. 19, 1914;

New York *Times,* Oct. 17, 1914; *Williams' Cincinnati City Directory, 1914;* Mrs. Russell Wilson interview.

26. *Time,* Oct. 13, 1958, p. 20; Martha to RT, June 28, 1916, RTP; Interviews, William H. Taft III, Barbara Taft, Lloyd Taft, Horace Taft, Robert Taft, Jr.; Theodor Reik, *A Psychologist Looks at Love* (New York, 1944), esp. p. 177ff.

27. WHT to Horace D. Taft, March 2, 1915, series 8, vol. 28, WHTP.

28. RT to Martha, June 29, July 18, 1916, RTP; RT to WHT, Dec. 2, 1914, April 9, July 11, 1916, series 3, boxes 292 and 342, WHTP; RT to Charlie (Taft), summer 1916, Charles P. Taft, 2nd, papers.

29. RT to Martha, Sept. 29, Oct. 19, 1913, Sept. 2, 1916, RTP; RT to WHT, series 3, box 358, WHTP.

30. RT to Martha, Jan. ?, Feb. 28, 1914, Sept. 29, 1913, RTP; John Hollister (COHP), p. 6.

31. RT to WHT, Jan. 8, 1917, series 3, box 365, WHTP; Cincinnati *Times-Star,* March 31, 1917, p. 2; Cincinnati *Post,* April 18, 1917, p. 3; RT, "A Charter for Cincinnati," March, 1917, TSHP, Cincinnati.

32. RT to Dr. M. L. Bates, Dec. 18, 1916, to M. Linley Bates, Jan. 1, 1917, TSHP; RT to WHT, May 5, 1917, series 3, box 376, WHTP.

33. RT to Martha, June 28, 30, July 23, 1916, RTP.

34. RT to Aunt Delia, Aug. 11, 1915, series 3, box 318, WHTP.

CHAPTER 5: FINDING HIMSELF

1. RT to Martha, July 25, 1915, Sept. 3, 1914, June 24, 1916, RTP, LC.

2. Minutes, Cincinnati Yale Club, March 10, 1917, Cincinnati; *Yale Alumni Weekly,* Vol. 26 (March 23, 1917), p. 74; Herbert F. Koch, *Centennial History of the Cincinnati Yale Club, 1864–1964* (privately printed, 1964).

3. File No. 499.4, TSHP, Cincinnati; Application for service, May 14, 1917, Hoover papers, Hoover Library, Stanford, Calif.: WHT to RT, May 5 and May 15, 1917, series 8, letterbook 61, and RT to WHT, series 3, box 376, WHTP, LC.

4. Hoover to RT, June 28, 1917, RT to Hoover, Oct. 18, 1918, Hoover to RT, Oct. 30, 1918, Hoover papers, Stanford; RT to WHT, Sept. ?, 1918, series 3, box 423, WHTP; WHT to Mabel Boardman, July 27, 1917, box 8, Boardman papers, LC; WHT to Charles P. Taft, July 4, 9, Aug. 2, 1917, Charles P. Taft, 2nd, papers, Cincinnati; Charlie Taft to Helen Taft, July 8, 1917, and to Mrs. WHT, Aug. 9, 1918, Helen Taft Manning papers, Haverford, Pa.

5. Constance McLaughlin Green, *Washington: Capitol City, 1879–1950* (Princeton, 1963), p. 236; WHT to Charles P. Taft, Sept. 15, 1917, Charles P. Taft, 2nd, papers; WHT to RT, July 18, 1917, File No. 499.86, TSHP, Cincinnati; Harvey Bundy (COHP), pp. 71, 251; Interviews, Walter Logan, Lewis L. Strauss.

6. William C. Mullendore, *History of the United States Food Administration* (Stanford, 1941), passim; Herbert Hoover, *The Memoirs of Herbert Hoover: Years of Adventure, 1874–1920* (New York, 1951), p. 240; Maxcy Robson Dickson, *The Food Front in World War I* (Washington, 1944), p. 43; Lewis L. Strauss, *Men and Decisions* (Garden City, 1962), p. 8; Edgar Eugene Robinson and Paul Carroll Edwards, eds., *The Memoirs*

of Ray Lyman Wilbur, 1875–1949 (Stanford, 1960), pp. 253–277; Food Administration Records, Record Group 4, National Archives (Suitland, Md.), boxes 593–605; Hoover, *An American Epic: Famine in 45 Nations: Organization Behind the Front* (Chicago, 1960), pp. 36, 91.

7. For Taft's activities, RT to Mrs. WHT, July 29, 1917, series 3, box 382, WHTP; RT to Hoover, Aug. 30, 1917, box 1, Food Administration papers; RT to Hoover, Sept. 17, Nov. 7, 1917, March 5, 1918, Hoover papers, Stanford; WHT to Mabel Boardman, Oct. 30, 1917, box 8, Boardman papers; WHT to Charles P. Taft, 2nd, Sept. 5, 1917, March 11, 1918, Charles P. Taft, 2nd, papers; RT to Charles P. Taft, 2nd, March 11, 1918, ibid.; W. C. Mullendore to author, Sept. 1971; and Mullendore, "Powers of the Food Administration," box 1303, RTP.

8. Judge Curtis H. Lindley to Hoover, Sept. 7, 1917, Hoover papers, Stanford.

9. New York *Times,* Nov. 17, 1918, p. 9; Hoover, *An American Epic: Organization,* pp. 261–262.

10. New York *Times,* Nov. 24, 1918, p. 20; RT to Martha, Nov. 21, 1918, series 3, box 429, WHTP.

11. Charles Seymour, *Letters from the Peace Conference* (New Haven, 1965), passim.

12. Ibid., pp. 51–52; WHT to RT, Feb. 10, 1919, series 8, letterbook 83, WHTP; WHT to Charles P. Taft, 2nd, July 22, 1919, Charles P. Taft, 2nd, papers.

13. Hoover, *Memoirs,* Vol. 1, pp. 280, 295, 428; Rental Agreement, n.d., File No. 499.38, TSHP; RT to Hoover, March 13, 1919, and to Joseph C. Green, April 2, 1919, Hoover papers, Stanford; RT to Green, March 13, 1939, Green papers, Hoover Library, Stanford; Hoover, *An American Epic: The Battle on the Front Line, 1914–1922* (Chicago, 1961), pp. 130, 146, 264, 325; *Ohio State Journal,* June 13, 1931, p. 2; Suda Lorena Bane and Ralph Haswell Lutz, *Organization of American Relief in Europe . . .* (Stanford, 1943), p. 722; Interviews, Joseph C. Green and Lewis Strauss; letters to author from Clare M. Torrey, Sept. 29, 1969, Frederick Exton, Aug. 24, 1968.

14. Hoover report to Woodrow Wilson, n.d. (1919), box 1303, RTP; Arno J. Mayer, *Politics and Diplomacy of Peacemaking: Containment and Counterrevolution at Versailles, 1918–1919* (New York, 1967), p. 274; Bane and Lutz, *The Blockade of Germany After the Armistice . . .* (Stanford, (1942), pp. 629–804.

15. Hoover, *An American Epic: Organization,* pp. 284–296, 318; Strauss, p. 42; Hoover, *Memoirs,* Vol. 1, p. 329; Hoover, *America's First Crusade* (New York, 1941), pp. 42–47, 51–52, 76.

16. RT to Charlie (Taft), March 31, 1918, Charles P. Taft, 2nd, papers.

17. RT to WHT, Dec. 4, 1918, series 3, box 430, WHTP.

18. RT to WHT, Dec. 14, 1918, Jan. 5, 1919, series 3, boxes 431 and 434, WHTP.

19. RT to WHT, March 30, 1919, series 3, box 442, WHTP.

20. RT, draft of speech, n.d. (fall, 1919), box 1303, RTP.

21. RT, "The Failure of the Paris Peace Conference" (draft), n.d. (early 1920), box 1303, RTP.

22. RT to Hoover, Jan. 3, 1942, box l–k/135, Hoover papers, Hoover Library, West Branch, Iowa; Interview, Helen Taft Manning; For WHT's views, Theodore Marburg and Horace E. Flack, eds., *Taft Papers on the League of Nations* (New York, 1920), esp. pp. 28–52, 79–81, 172–173.
23. RT to WHT, Jan. 5, 1919, series 3, box 434, WHTP; RT to Hoover, Aug. 3, 1941, box l–k/135, Hoover papers, Iowa; New York *Times,* April 11, 1920, section 2, p. 1; Harvey Bundy (COHP), p. 76.
24. For Taft's activities late 1919–early 1920, File No. 499.2, TSHP

CHAPTER 6: NEOPHYTE POLITICIAN

1. File No. 499.85, TSHP, Cincinnati.
2. RT, "Summary of Arguments in Favor of Mr. Hoover's Nomination," n.d. (1920), Joseph Green papers, Hoover Library, Stanford; RT to John W. Hallowell, May 10, 1920, box 1179, RTP, LC.
3. Franklin D. Roosevelt to Hugh Gibson, Jan. 1, 1920, cited in Barry Karl, "Presidential Planning and Social Science Research: Mr. Hoover's Experts," *Perspectives in American History,* Vol. 3 (1969), p. 353; RT to Editor of Tiffin *Tribune,* April 22, 1920, and RT to J. W. Hallowell, April 14, 1920, box 1179, RTP; RT to WHT, Feb. 3, 1920, series 3, box 478, WHTP, LC.
4. RT to WHT, RT to Herbert Hoover, both March 26, 1920, series 3, box 468, WHTP; New York *Times,* March 31, 1920, p. 1.
5. Cincinnati *Enquirer,* March 13, 1920, p. 5; New York *Times,* March 16, 1920, p. 17; RT to George B. Baker, Feb. 13, 1920, RT to James Bell, March 16, 1920, box 1179, RTP; Interview, Joseph Green.
6. New York *Times,* April 19, 1920, section 2, p. 1; RT to Marion *Star,* May 4, 1920; RT to Gus Karger, April 3, 1920, and May 3, 1920, box 1179, RTP; RT to WHT, April 13, 20, June 1, 1920, series 3, boxes 469 and 471, WHTP; *Official Report of the Proceedings of the 17th Republican National Convention* (New York, 1920), passim; New York *Times,* June 12, 1920, p. 21; Interview, Joseph Green.
7. RT to WHT, June 1, 1920, series 3, box 471, WHTP.
8. Cincinnati *Enquirer,* May 25, 1920, p. 10; May 26, 1920, p. 19; May 27, 1920, p. 16.
9. Charles P. Taft 2nd to Henry L. Stimson, Aug. 17, 1920, Stimson papers, Yale University; File No. 499.69, TSHP.
10. RT to Charles P. Taft, 2nd, Aug. 10, 1920, Charles P. Taft, 2nd, papers, Cincinnati; Cincinnati *Enquirer,* Aug. 12, 1920, p. 4; RT to Edmund W. Pugh, Aug. 16, 1920, box 6, RTP; Board of Elections, Hamilton County, Ohio, Xeroxed statistics, 1920.
11. RT, "The Federal Government," 1920, box 1303, RTP; Cincinnati *Enquirer,* July 1, 1920, p. 8.
12. Board of Elections, Hamilton County, statistics, 1920; Cincinnati *Enquirer,* Nov. 3, 1920, p. 13.
13. New York *Times,* Jan. 4, 1921, p. 23.
14. *Report of the Legislative Agent of the Ohio State Federation of Labor* (Thomas J. Donnelly, 1921), pp. 7–8; Haskell Penn Short, "Robert Alphonso Taft: His Eight Years in the Ohio General Assembly," masters

thesis, Ohio State University, 1951, passim; RT to Cincinnati *Times-Star*, June 9, 1921, box 1303, RTP.

15. Louis Taber (COHP), p. 367; Walter Rogers to Pauline Isaacson, May 15, 1956, in Isaacson, "Robert Alphonso Taft: An Assessment of a Persuader," doctoral thesis, Minnesota, 1956, p. 130; Miles Kuhn to author, March 22, 1970.

16. Interview, Monte Appel, quoted in Isaacson, p. 130.

17. Columbus *Citizen*, April 27, 1921, p. 8; Short, p. 16; New York *Times*, April 9, 1921, p. 10; Cincinnati *Enquirer*, Feb. 3, March 9, May 12, 15, 16, 27, 29, 1921, all p. 1; *Ohio State Journal*, March 17, 18, 1921, p. 1; *Report of Legislative Agent*, 1921; "Senator Robert A. Taft Expresses His Views on Labor," brochure, 1944, Paul Walter papers, Western Reserve Historical Society, Cleveland; Columbus *Evening Dispatch*, Feb. 3, 1921, p. 1; *Journal of the House of Representatives of the 84th General Assembly of the State of Ohio*, Vol. 109 (Columbus, 1921), pp. 121–123.

18. Hoyt Landon Warner, *Progressivism in Ohio, 1897–1917* (Columbus, 1964), pp. 280–281, 333, 396; Harlow Lindley, compiler, *Ohio in the 20th Century, 1900–1938* (Columbus, 1942), pp. 49–50; Short, p. 4.

19. Cincinnati *Enquirer*, Nov. 4, 1920, p. 10.

20. RT, speech draft, n.d. (probably early 1921), and Saul Zielonka to RT, Dec. 11, 1920, box 1303, RTP; RT memo, File No. 499.78, 1921, TSHP.

21. RT, draft, "A Bill to Authorize the Taxing Authorities of Municipal Corporations to Fund Deficiencies in Operating Revenue for the Year 1921, Issue Bonds, and to Levy Taxes for Such Purpose," 1921, box 1303, RTP; James Mercer, *Ohio Legislative History*, Vol. 4 (Columbus, 1921), p. 453; Cincinnati *Enquirer*, Jan. 5, 21, 30, 1921, all p. 1; Columbus *Evening Dispatch*, Jan. 5, 1921, p. 2; *House Journal*, 1921, pp. 37, 63, 114–115.

22. Columbus *Evening Dispatch*, Feb. 17, 1921, p. 3; Short, pp. 12–13; Cincinnati *Enquirer*, Feb. 9, 10, 12, 17, 20, March 17, 20, 31, 1921, all p. 1; *Ohio State Journal*, Feb. 17, March 30, 31, 1921, p. 9; *House Journal*, 1921, pp. 202–203, 747.

23. RT to WHT, Oct. 21, 1922, series 3, box 526, WHTP.

24. Cincinnati *Post*, Nov. 9, 1922, p. 1; Cincinnati *Enquirer*, Aug. 8, 1922, p. 20, Nov. 1, 3, 9, 1922, all p. 1; Board of Elections, Hamilton County, statistics, 1922.

25. *Literary Digest*, Vol. 78 (Aug. 25, 1923), pp. 40–48; Charles Merz, "Vic Donahey of Ohio," *Independent*, Vol. 120 (Jan. 28, 1928), pp. 78–80; Oswald Garrison Villard, "Presidential Possibilities: A. Victor Donahey," *The Nation*, Vol. 126 (April 18, 1928), pp. 426–428; Charles P. Sweeney, "An Interview with Governor Donahey of Ohio," *Collier's*, Vol. 77 (Sept. 1, 1923), p. 22; Columbus *Evening Dispatch*, Feb. 5, 1923, p. 2; Cincinnati *Enquirer*, April 8, 1923, p. 33; John A. Hadden to author, June 4, 1970; RT to WHT, Oct. 21, 1922, series 3, box 526, WHTP.

26. *Report of Legislative Agent*, 1923, passim; Columbus *Evening Dispatch*, Feb. 22, 1923, p. 2.

27. New York *Times*, Nov. 8, 1923, p. 1; David M. Chalmers, *Hooded Americanism: The History of the Ku Klux Klan* (Chicago, 1968), pp. 175–183.

28. Cincinnati *Enquirer*, Feb. 7, 1923, p. 1; Columbus *Evening Dispatch*, Feb. 7, 1923, p. 3.

29. RT, "A Proposed Revision of the Smith Law," 1922, File No. 499.73, TSHP; RT to Horace D. Taft, box 1, RTP.

30. Columbus *Evening Dispatch*, Jan. 24, 28, March 1, 5, 1923, all p. 1; Cincinnati *Enquirer*, Feb. 28, March 1, 1923, p. 3.

31. Columbus *Evening Dispatch*, March 8, 27, 1923, p. 1; Cincinnati *Enquirer*, March 8, 1923, p. 5; WHT to RT, April 4, 1923, File No. 499.86, TSHP.

32. Columbus *Evening Dispatch*, March 29, April 18, 19, 27, 1923, all p. 1; Cincinnati *Enquirer*, March 26, 1923, p. 3, March 29, 1923, p. 2; *House Journal*, 1923, pp. 996, 1039–1044; Mercer, 1923, pp. 14–19, 47–50.

33. *Journal of the Ohio State Teachers Association*, Vol. 1 (March, 1923), p. 14; Columbus *Evening Dispatch*, Nov. 1, 1923, p. 10, Nov. 2, 1923, p. 6, Nov. 4, 1923, p. 3; Cincinnati *Enquirer*, Oct. 11, 1923, p. 7, Oct. 12, 1923, p. 3, Oct. 21, 1923, p. 11, Nov. 6, 1923, p. 4; WHT to Helen Taft Manning, Oct. 7, 1923, Manning papers, LC; RT to WHT, Oct. 4, 18, 1923, series 3, box 545, WHTP.

34. Cincinnati *Enquirer*, Nov. 7, 1923, p. 1; Columbus *Evening Dispatch*, Nov. 7, 1923, p. 1; Board of Elections, Hamilton County, 1924; Cincinnati *Enquirer*, Nov. 5, 1924, p. 26, Nov. 6, 1924, p. 13.

35. Columbus *Evening Dispatch*, Dec. 17, 1924, p. 6, Dec. 18, 1924, p. 8; Cincinnati *Enquirer*, Dec. 17, 1924, p. 3; Dec. 18, 1924, p. 1.

36. RT to James K. Pollack, Jr., April 29, 1925, File No. 499.30, to Louis H. Brush, Nov. 15, 1926, File No. 499.55, TSHP; Columbus *Evening Dispatch*, March 11, 1925, p. 1.

37. "Legislative Record of Robert A. Taft," box 49, RTP; *Report of Legislative Agent*, 1925; RT to Cincinnati Planer Co., Nov. 13, 1924, File No. 499.49, TSHP; Columbus *Evening Dispatch*, Jan. 28, 1925, p. 1; WHT to RT, Dec. 22, 1924, File No. 499.86, TSHP.

38. RT to Milo J. Warner, May 15, 1925, File No. 499.4, TSHP.

39. Columbus *Evening Dispatch*, March 20, 1925, p. 1.

40. Ibid., Feb. 27, 1925, pp. 2, 11; Short, pp. 61–65, 73–74.

41. Columbus *Evening Dispatch*, March 28, April 30, 1925, both p. 1; Cincinnati *Enquirer*, April 17, 1925, p. 1; New York *Times*, May 1, 1925, p. 3.

42. Cincinnati *Enquirer*, Aug. 13, 1924, p. 1; RT to WHT, June 30, 1924, series 3, box 561, WHTP; RT to Fred W. Warren, Jan. 9, 1925, File No. 499.49, TSHP; Cincinnati *Enquirer*, Dec. 16, 1924, p. 2.

43. RT to Henry Bentley, Feb. 20, 1925, Bentley papers, Cincinnati Historical Society; Columbus *Evening Dispatch*, Jan. 22, 1925, p. 1, Jan. 23, p. 6, Jan. 27, p. 2, March 29, p. 1; RT to WHT, Feb. 14, 1925, File No. 499.86, and to Clarence J. Neal, Oct. 10, 1924, File No. 499.49, TSHP.

44. Columbus *Evening Dispatch*, Feb. 12–26, 1925; Lindley, p. 44.

45. RT, "The Present Tax Situation in Ohio," *National Municipal Review*, Vol. 15 (May 1926), pp. 262–265; RT to Dr. G. W. Grant, March 15, 1926, File No. 499.30, TSHP; *Report of the Joint Legislative Committee on Economics and Taxation of the 86th General Assembly of Ohio* (Columbus, 1926).

46. Columbus *Evening Dispatch*, March 24, 28, 1925, both p. 1.

47. Ibid., March 29, 1925, Jan. 16, 1926, both p. 1; RT to WHT, April 29, 1922, April 29, 1925, File No. 499.86, TSHP; *House Journal*, 1925, passim; Lindley, p. 45; T. Howard Winters, "Recent School Legislation," *Journal*

of the Ohio State Teachers Association. Vol. 3 (July 1925), pp. 22–23; Clarence Laylin to author, Dec. 23, 1969.

48. For relations with the Cincinnati organization, File No. 499.30, TSHP.
49. For retrospective accounts praising his work in the legislature, Short, p. 51, and Anne W. Buck, "Robert A. Taft, the Emergence of a Statesman," masters thesis, Kent State, 1960, pp. 25, 31; for the campaign of friends to make him governor, see WHT to RT, May 17, 1926, series 3, box 600, WHTP; WHT to Charles P. Taft, 2nd, May 17, June 12, 1926, Charles P. Taft, 2nd, papers, Cincinnati; WHT to RT, April 5, 1925, File No. 499.86, RT to Charles L. Knight, May 8, 1926, File No. 499.53, TSHP.

CHAPTER 7: LIFE IN CINCINNATI

1. Louis L. Tucker, *Cincinnati: A Student's Guide to Localized History* (New York, 1969), p. 24.
2. Interviews, John Hollister, Lloyd Taft, Robert Goldman; Charles P. Taft, 2nd, to author, March 27, 1970.
3. Interview, Harry Linch; "The Dixie Terminal Co.: Financial History, June 20, 1916 to Dec. 31, 1942" (Cincinnati, 1943), box 1342, RTP, LC; RT to Charles P. Taft, 2nd, May 19, 1921, Charles P. Taft, 2nd, papers, Cincinnati.
4. Interview, Robert Taft, Jr.; RT to WHT, Oct. 12, 1919, series 3, box 458, and July 13, 24, 1922, box 519, WHTP, LC.
5. Louis L. Tucker, *Cincinnati's Citizen Crusaders: A History of the Cincinnatus Association, 1920–1965* (Cincinnati, 1967), p. 68; Interviews, John More, John Hollister (COHP), p. 9, Robert Goldman.
6. Dr. Stanhope Bayne-Jones (COHP), p. 17; Arthur Schlesinger, Jr., "His Eyes Have Seen the Glory," *Collier's,* Vol. 19 (Feb. 22, 1947), p. 12; William S. White, "How to Win Influence, If Not Friends," *New York Times Magazine,* May 1, 1949, p. 10.
7. Interview, Willis Gradison; Richard H. Rovere, "Taft, Is This the Best We've Got?" *Harper's,* Vol. 196 (April 1948), pp. 289–299.
8. RT to WHT, May 4, 1924, series 3, box 558, WHTP; WHT to RT, Feb. 13, 1927, box 3, RTP; Charles P. Taft 2nd to WHT, Feb. 11, 1924, Charles P. Taft, 2nd, papers.
9. RT to Mrs. WHT, June 9, 1921, series 3, box 489, to WHT, July 3, 1921, April 7, 12, May 4, Dec. 1, 1924, boxes 493, 556, 558, 570, WHT to RT, Sept. 13, 1925, box 585, WHTP; WHT to Helen Manning, Nov. 29, 1925, Manning papers, LC; Henry Bentley to A. R. Hatton, Jan. 20, 1925, Bentley papers, Cincinnati Historical Society; Cincinnati *Enquirer,* June 10, 1924, p. 16, Dec. 16, 1924, p. 1, Oct. 20, 1925, p. 12; Interview, John Hudson; Charles P. Taft, *City Management: The Cincinnati Experience* (New York, 1933), pp. 112–114.
10. *National Observer,* Oct. 23, 1971, p. 1; Interviews, Lloyd Taft, Harry Linch.
11. Charles P. Taft, 2nd, to WHT, July 17, 1923, Charles P. Taft, 2nd, papers.
12. Cincinnati *Enquirer,* Nov. 6, 1927, p. 1, Feb. 20, 1931, p. 12; "Preliminary Agreement," 1924, File No. 133.1, TSHP, LC; RT to WHT, March 25, 1929, series 3, box 663, WHTP; Charles P. Taft, 2nd, to Mrs. WHT,

April 9, 1931, Charles P. Taft, 2nd, papers; Interview, Lewis Strauss; Strauss, *Men and Decisions* (Garden City, 1962), p. 84.

13. File Nos. 499.84, 499.85, TSHP; box 1362, RTP.

14. RT to Harry P. Bingham, July 24, 1923, box 1, also boxes 1, 3, 12, 1336, Lucien Wulsin, "The Conception and Birth of the Cincinnati Institute of Fine Arts," n.d., RT to Horace D. Taft, June 3, 1927, box 1, RTP.

15. Frank J. Jones to RT, June 12, 1923, RT to Jones, June 15, 1923, box 1344, RTP; RT to WHT, April 2, 1921, Oct. 21, 1922, June 20, 1924, boxes 485, 526 and 561, WHT to RT, June 3, 1923, box 539, RT to Mrs. WHT, April 28, 1920, box 469, all series 3, WHTP; RT to Pliny Johnston, Oct. 1, 1920, File No. 499.36, TSHP; Interviews, Horace Taft, Robert Taft, Jr., Mrs. Robert Black (COHP), p. 11, Stanley and Dorothy Rowe (COHP), p. 4.

16. Eleanor Gholson Taft, *Hither and Yon on Indian Hill* (Cincinnati, 1962); "Indian Hill Acres," RT to Rowe, April 6, 1939, Rowe to RT, June 5, 1953, RTP; Interview, Rowe.

17. Interviews, Lloyd Taft (COHP); Horace Taft (COHP); William H. Taft III; RT to Aunt Maria, Aug. 22, 1915 (in possession of Mrs. William H. Taft III, Washington, D.C.); RT to WHT, April 14, 1925, File No. 499.86, TSHP; RT to RT, Jr., Jan. 1, 1939, RTP.

18. Ledgers for Sky Farm, RT to F. J. Salter, Dec. 20, 1930, box 14, RTP; RT to Charles P. Taft, 2nd, May 19, 1921, Charles P. Taft, 2nd, papers; Interviews, Horace D., Robert, Jr., William H. Taft III.

19. New York *Times*, July 16, 1920, p. 11, Sept. 16, 1927, p. 1; RT to Charles P. Taft, 2nd, March 9, 1953, box 1246, RTP; personal observations.

20. Interviews, Mrs. Russell Wilson, Mrs. Robert Black, Stanley and Dorothy Rowe, William H. Taft III, Horace Taft (COHP).

21. Dorothy Rowe, "Tribute to a Friend" (privately printed, Christmas 1964).

22. *Newsweek*, Aug. 5, 1946, pp. 2–3.

23. Cincinnati *Post*, March 13, 1933, p. 9; Cincinnati *Enquirer*, Oct. 18, 1933; Theodor Reik, *A Psychologist Looks at Love* (New York, 1944), passim.

24. Charles P. Taft, 2nd, to Mrs. WHT, Dec. 28, 1932, Charles P. Taft, 2nd, papers; Rovere, p. 290.

CHAPTER 8: THE GOSPEL OF PARTY REGULARITY

1. Key sources on Cincinnati politics are Zane L. Miller, *Boss Cox's Cincinnati: Urban Politics in the Progressive Era* (New York, 1968); and Louis L. Tucker, *Cincinnati's Citizen Crusaders: A History of the Cincinnatus Association, 1920–1965* (Cincinnati, 1967). Other accounts, by reformers, are Murray Seasongood, *Local Government in the United States: A Challenge and an Opportunity* (Cambridge, 1933); Charles P. Taft, *City Management: The Cincinnati Experiment* (New York, 1933); and Seasongood, "Robert Heuck and the Citizen's Movement in Hamilton County, Ohio," in J. T. Salter, ed., *The American Politician* (Chapel Hill, 1938).

2. Lent D. Upson, director, *The Government of Cincinnati and Hamilton County* (Cincinnati, 1924), esp. pp. 36–38.

3. Henry Bentley, "Why Cincinnati Voted for P.R. and a City Manager," *National Municipal Review*, Vol. 14 (Feb. 1925), pp. 69–74. Other relevant articles, also by reformers, are Bentley, "Cincinnati's Right About Face in Government," ibid., Vol. 15 (Aug. 1926), pp. 465–471; and Russell Wilson, "Our American Mayors — Murray Seasongood of Cincinnati," ibid., Vol. 18 (Feb. 1929), pp. 68–75. Scholarly articles are George E. Stevens, "The Cincinnati *Post* and Municipal Reform, 1914–1941," *Ohio History*, Vol. 79 (Summer–Autumn, 1970), pp. 231–242; and Robert P. Goldman, "An Analysis of Cincinnati's Proportional Representation Elections," *American Political Science Review*, Vol. 24 (Aug. 1930), pp. 699–710.

4. Upson, pp. 38, 42, 183; Cincinnati *Enquirer*, July 29, 1924, entire issue.

5. Tucker, pp. 59, 80, 105; Cincinnati *Enquirer*, Oct. 19, 1923, p. 4, Oct. 10–12, 1923, "The Cincinnatus Association, 1938" (handbook, n.d.), box 1324, RTP, LC.

6. Tucker, p. 130; Taft, p. 50; Bentley articles; Goldman, "An Analysis"; Cincinnati *Enquirer* and *Times-Star*, Nov. 2–5, 1924; Seasongood, *Local Government*, p. 24; Silas Bent, *Strange Bedfellows: A Review of Politics, Personalities, and the Press* (New York, 1926), p. 96.

7. Report of Committee on Organization [of Cincinnatus Organization], Feb. 1920, File No. 499.15, TSHP, Cincinnati; Tucker, p. 69; Interviews, John Hollister (COHP), pp. 19–20, Mrs. Russell Wilson, Robert Goldman.

8. RT to Mayor John Galvin, May 13, 1920, RT to C. Lawson Reed, July 27, 1921, File No. 499.15, TSHP; RT to WHT, Jan. 1, 1923 and July 26, 1924, series 3, boxes 532 and 563, WHTP, LC; RT to WHT, Oct. 10, 1924, File No. 499.86, and RT to W. L. Tobey, Dec. 22, 1925, File No. 499.30, TSHP; RT to Horace D. Taft, Sept. 29, 1925, box 1, RTP.

9. Charles P. Taft, 2nd, to WHT, Oct. 14, 20, 24, 1924, Charles P. Taft, 2nd, papers, Cincinnati; Robert N. Gorman to Henry Bentley, Oct. 16, 1924, Bentley papers, Cincinnati Historical Society; Murray Seasongood to Newbold Morris, Dec. 1, 1955, Seasongood papers (in possession of William Baughin, Cincinnati); Cincinnati *Enquirer*, Oct. 22, 1924; Cincinnati *Post*, June 11, July 1, 1924, both p. 1; RT memo to publicity department, *Reporter*, Jan. 1, 1952, box 405, RTP.

10. Cincinnati *Commercial-Tribune*, Nov. 1, 1924, p. 1; RT to Charles L. Knight, Nov. 13, 1924, File No. 499.49, TSHP.

11. WHT, *Liberty Under Law* (New Haven, 1922), p. 32; WHT to RT, March 15, 1925, File No. 499.86, TSHP; Interviews, Charles P. Taft, 2nd, John Hollister, Mrs. Darrah Wunder, Mr. and Mrs. Stanley Rowe.

12. Cincinnati *Enquirer*, July 8, Oct. 10, 12, Nov. 4, 1926, p. 1, p. 18, p. 11, p. 8; "Report of Charter Amendment Commission," 1926, File No. 499.13, TSHP.

13. RT to Alden D. Kumler, Dec. 23, 1927, File No. 499.35, TSHP.

14. Quotes from RT to Horace D. Taft, Aug. 30, 1928, box 1, and RT to W. C. Procter, April 13, 1929, box 32, RTP; Similar letters are RT to WHT, Feb. 25, May 11, Aug. 30, boxes 3 and 649, RT to Herbert Hoover, April 25, 1928, box 1179, RTP.

15. RT to Thomas R. White, Feb. 9, 1929, box 13, RTP.

16. Charlie's letter is April 13, 1927, Charles P. Taft, 2nd, papers. Also Charlie Taft to Arthur Kimball, Sept. 24, 1926, and to WHT, March 22, 1927, and March 6, 1928, ibid.; Tucker, p. 144; Charles P. Taft, 2nd, interview.

17. Quotes from "Charlie Taft's Big Chance," *Fortune*, Vol. 36 (Aug. 1947), p. 86. Also J. Beatty, "The Other Taft," *American Magazine*, Vol. 144 (July 1947), p. 24; William H. Hessler, "The Brothers Taft," *Reporter*, Vol. 6 (Jan. 8, 1952), p. 6; Stephen Hess, *America's Politcal Dynasties from Adams to Kennedy* (Garden City, 1966), p. 326.

18. WHT to RT, Nov. 17, 1928, box 3, and Horace D. Taft to Martha, Oct. 27, 1930, RTP.

19. Interviews, Seth Taft, Mrs. Russell Wilson, William H. Taft III, Lloyd Taft, Charles P. Taft, 2nd, Horace D. Taft; Diary, Mrs. Wunder, Jan. 1, 1952 (possession of Mrs. Wunder, Cincinnati).

20. RT to Horace D. Taft, Aug. 24, 1928, box 1, RTP; Taft, *City Management*, p. 145.

21. Goldman, "An Analysis"; Seasongood, *Local Government;* Tucker.

22. Stevens, p. 241; Cincinnati *Enquirer,* Nov. 8, 1932, p. 10.

23. Cincinnati *Post,* March 18, 1940; Seasongood to C. L. Miller, Nov. 15, 1959, Seasongood papers.

24. RT to Stephen D. Paddock, March 1, 1939, box 23, RTP.

CHAPTER 9: YEARS OF FRUSTRATION, 1930–1937

1. WHT to Helen Taft Manning, Jan. 13, 1929, Manning papers, LC.

2. Last Will and Testament of William Howard Taft, March 13, 1930, Probate Court, D.C.: Cincinnati *Enquirer,* March 13, 22, 1930, both p. 1.

3. RT to A. E. Anderson, April 24, RT to George Heitzler, May 20, 1930, box 33, and RT to David Ingalls, Feb. 21, RT to Governor Myers Cooper, April 10, 1929, box 463, RTP, LC; Cincinnati *Enquirer,* May 28, Aug. 10, 13, 1930, all p. 1; Board of Elections, Hamilton County, statistics for 1930 primaries.

4. Cincinnati *Enquirer,* Nov. 6, 1930, p. 1; Board of Elections data.

5. Columbus *Evening Dispatch,* Jan. 5, 28, Feb. 19, April 11, 12, May 27, all p. 1, 1931; Cincinnati *Times-Star,* March 24, 31, 1931, all p. 1; *Ohio Senate Journal,* Vol. 114 (Columbus, 1931), pp. 64, 74, 156, 350, 359, 411, 598, 617, 669, 698; RT to Leonard S. Smith, Jr., Feb. 28, 1931, box 463, "Proposed County and Regional Zoning Bill: History," box 464, RTP.

6. RT to Charles S. Riley, Feb. 21, 1931, box 463, RT to Arthur H. Fix, April 25, 1929, RT to Walter Millard, April 14, 1931, RTP; *Ohio Senate Journal,* 1931, passim.

7. RT to Governor George White, July 7, 1931, box 463, RT to Harry Worcester, July 3, 1931, RTP. His relations with Governor White were excellent; see boxes 463, 466, 978, RTP, for their correspondence.

8. *Report of the Legislative Agent of the Ohio State Federation of Labor* (Thomas J. Donnelly, 1931); Cincinnati *Enquirer,* April 12, 1931, p. 17; Columbus *Evening Dispatch,* April 10, 11, May 2, 1931, all p. 1; Robert S. Allen, "Men Who Would Be President: Taft for Safety," *The Nation,* Vol. 150 (May 25, 1940), pp. 649–652; George White, "Ohio Lives within

Its Income," *Review of Reviews,* Vol. 84 (Oct. 1932), p. 27; quote is RT to White, March 15, 1932, box 464, RTP.

9. Columbus *Evening Dispatch,* April 1, 3, May 16, Sept. 27, Sept. 30, Oct. 1, 1932, all p. 1; Cincinnati *Enquirer,* Oct. 1, 1932, p. 1.

10. Based on much material, boxes 463, 464, 470, RTP, esp. RT to Governor Myers Cooper, Nov. 9, 1929, box 470, and RT, "The Effect of the New Tax Program on Real Estate Taxation," 1931, box 463; and Cincinnati *Enquirer,* Oct. 24, 1929, pp. 10, 20, Oct. 26, 1929, p. 8.

11. Quote is RT to Fred B. Creamer, Jan. 14, 1931, box 470, RTP; RT, "Address on Taxation," Feb. 5, 1932, RT to Oscar Bigler, April 27, 1932, box 467, RT to Governor White, Dec. 7, 1934, box 18, RTP; Columbus *Evening Dispatch,* Feb. 15, March 8, 17, 26, 29, April 7, 1931, all p. 1.

12. Quote is in Columbus *Evening Dispatch,* March 26, 1931, p. 6.

13. Columbus *Evening Dispatch,* May 10, 1931, p. 1; RT, "The New Intangibles Tax Law" (Cincinnati, 1931), in box 465, RT, "The Effect of the New Tax Program," box 463, RTP; New York *Times,* July 17, 1932, section 10.

14. Columbus *Evening Dispatch,* May 12, 26, 1931, pp. 6, 7.

15. Cleveland *Plain Dealer,* May 28, 1931; *Ohio State Journal,* March 25, May 24, 1931, pp. 4, 1; Columbus *Evening Dispatch,* May 28, June 2, 3, 10, pp. 3, 1; RT, "Final Report of Joint Taxation Committee of the 89th General Assembly," 1932, box 461, RTP.

16. Cincinnati *Enquirer,* Oct. 1, 4, 1933, p. 10, and Dec. 7, 1934, p. 1; Clarence Laylin to author, Dec. 23, 1969; RT to George F. Huit, July 30, 1936, box 18, material in boxes 464, 466, RTP.

17. Day speeches, July 28, Aug. 1, 1938, Paul Walter papers, Western Reserve Historical Society; Columbus *Evening Dispatch,* July 29, 30, Aug. 2, 1938, all p. 1.

18. Tax returns, RT and Martha Taft, boxes 1349, 1358, RT to Fred G. Reiners, March 3, 1941, box 1349, RT to John More, Feb. 10, 1941, RTP; Columbus *Evening Dispatch,* Feb. 5, 1931, p. 1.

19. Brief filed [by RT] by Special Joint Taxation Committee of the 89th General Assembly, to Supreme Court, Nov. 1932, box 462, RTP; Carl L. Bumiller, "Constitutionality of the Distributive Features of the Ohio Intangibles Tax Act," *University of Cincinnati Law Review,* Vol. 6 (Nov. 1932), pp. 373–403; Cincinnati *Enquirer,* June 9, 1932, p. 6, June 11, 1932, p. 10; Charles P. Taft, *City Management: The Cincinnati Experiment* (New York, 1933), p. 216; RT to Martha, Sept. 12, 1932, box 1358, RT to George R. Balch, June 27, 1932, box 467, RTP.

20. Martha Taft to RT, Jr., Nov. 3, 1932, RTP.

21. Cincinnati *Enquirer,* May 10, 11, 12, Nov. 10, 1932; Board of Elections, Hamilton County, statistics; Interview, Willis Gradison; RT to W. A. Greenlund, Nov. 15, 1932, box 466, RTP; Charles P. Taft, 2nd, to Mrs. WHT, Oct. 18, Nov. 16, 1932, Charles P. Taft, 2nd, papers, Cincinnati.

22. RT to Herman L. Vail, Dec. 2, 1932, RT to RT, Jr., Nov. 16, 1932, box 16, RTP. This box, and boxes 15, 34, 462, and 1362 contain many letters concerning his defeat.

23. New York *Times,* Feb. 13, 1928, p. 40; Mrs. RT to RT, Jr., Oct. 2, 1933, RTP; miscellaneous papers boxes 14, 1179, RTP.

24. Cincinnati *Enquirer,* Feb. 8, 1928, p. 1; New York *Times,* Feb. 8, 12, 1928, both p. 7; April 25, 26, 1928, both p. 1; Cincinnati *Times-Star,* June 13, 16, 1932; quote is RT to WHT, Nov. 9, 1928, series 3, box 654, WHTP; Mrs. RT to RT, Jr., Nov. 3, 1932, Mrs. Herbert Hoover to RT and Mrs. RT, March ?, 1930, box 4, RTP; RT-Hoover correspondence, box 1-D/ 250, Hoover papers, Hoover Library, Iowa. RT also played an active role in the 1932 Republican national convention — see boxes 12, 1358, and esp. 16, 34, 1179, RTP.

25. "Ohio Anti-Tax Amendment League," 1933 material, box 460, RT to H. S. Hicks, Oct. 18, RT to Richard Forster, Oct. 2, RT to R. E. Miles, Sept. 26, 1933, box 467, RTP; letters re taxes, 1933–1934, boxes 17, 18, 464, and re state politics, boxes 17, 18, 34, 35, 37, RTP.

26. Charles P. Taft, 2nd, to WHT, April 23, 1928, Charles P. Taft, 2nd, papers; RT to R. C. Bassett, April 4, 1928, box 18, RTP.

27. RT to Julius B. Cohn, April 14, 1931, box 33, RTP; Interview, Hollister; Cincinnati *Enquirer,* May 18, 1931, p. 8.

28. Rumors placing RT in the Cabinet include, Cincinnati *Enquirer,* Jan. 17, 1929, p. 2; New York *Times,* Jan. 18, 27, 1929, pp. 4, 1; Washington *Post,* Feb. 27, March 1, 1929; New York *Times,* Feb. 5, 6, 31, 1930, pp. 2, 12, 4; Cincinnati *Enquirer,* Feb. 5, 1930, p. 2. Those who knew both RT and Hoover well do not recall that Hoover seriously considered Taft for a post prior to 1930 — probably because WHT remained Chief Justice. And thereafter, perhaps, Hoover feared being charged with playing on the name of WHT. Interviews, Lewis Strauss, John Hollister, David Ingalls.

29. RT to Walter Albaugh, Feb. 2, 1932, box 34, RT to C. E. Knapp, Feb. 5, 1936, box 38, RTP; Cincinnati *Post,* Oct. 15, 1935.

30. RT to James A. Dixon, April 2, 1934, box 35, RTP; also Simeon Fess to Lehr Fess, April 28, 1934, Fess papers, Ohio Historical Society, and Hollister to RT, Jan. 16, 1934, Hollister papers (in his possession, Cincinnati); Columbus *Evening Dispatch,* April 19, 1931, p. 3, May 22, 1932, p. 5. Rumors also had RT running for governor in 1932 (Cincinnati *Enquirer,* April 14, 1931, p. 8), for Vice-President, 1932 (Cincinnati *Times-Star,* June 16, 1932, p. 1), and for senator, to fill a vacancy, 1929 (New York *Times,* Nov. 2, 1929, p. 16, Cincinnati *Enquirer,* Oct. 29, 1929, p. 2). Active on his behalf for higher office were his father (WHT to Helen Manning, Oct. 30, 1927, Nov. 3, 1929, Manning papers), and Hollister (COHP), pp. 27–28.

31. Cincinnati *Enquirer,* Oct. 14, 1930, p. 24; RT to Henry C. Segal, Nov. 1, 1930, box 32, RTP; miscellaneous material, box 33, RTP.

32. RT to Governor Myers Cooper, Nov. 10, 1930, RTP; RT, "The Republican Party Asks Support on the Record of National, State, and City Administrations," speech Oct. 6, 1930, box 465, RTP; Charles Taft, *City Management,* p. 195; miscellaneous material, boxes, 6, 18, 19, RTP.

33. Quote is from RT radio address, Nov. 2, 1935, box 35, RTP. For some of the key newspaper accounts of local politics, see the Cincinati *Enquirer, Times-Star,* and *Post,* Nov. 5, 1930, May 9, 11, 13, 17, 19, 25, June 6, Nov. 1, 4, 1931, Oct. 29, 1932, Oct. 23, 28, Nov. 7, 1934, Nov. 6, 1935, March 1, June 24, Aug. 1, 1936, Nov. 10, 1937. Also boxes 34, 36, 38, RTP; and Charles P. Taft, 2nd, to Mrs. WHT, Nov. 8, 1934, Nov. 1935, Charles P. Taft, 2nd, papers.

34. Cincinnati *Enquirer,* Aug. 21, 1930, p. 10, Sept. 20, 23, 1930, pp. 1, 26; Cincinnati *Times-Star,* Sept. 20, 1930, pp. 1, 6; Charles P. Taft, 2nd, to Mrs. WHT, Oct. 2, 1930, Charles P. Taft, 2nd, papers.
35. Cincinnati *Enquirer,* May 11, 17, 24, June 5, 11, 1932; Columbus *Evening Dispatch,* May 22, 1932, p. 3; Cincinnati *Post,* May 17, 1932, p. 13; Charles P. Taft, 2nd, to Mrs. WHT, May 19, 1932, Charles P. Taft, 2nd, papers; Interview, Gradison.
36. Cincinnati *Enquirer,* June 6, 7, 8, 22, 28, Nov. 1, 1933; Cincinnati *Times-Star,* June 6, 27, 1933.
37. Charles P. Taft, 2nd, to Mrs. WHT, June 6, 1933, Charles P. Taft, 2nd, papers.
38. Cincinnati *Enquirer,* May 5 ,22, July 14, 17, 18, Sept. 12, 21, Oct. 17, 1934; Cincinnati *Post,* July 16, 17, 25, 1934; New York *Times,* June 24, 1934, section 2, p. 6; RT to L. M. King, Sept. 27, 1934, box 17, RTP.
39. RT to Horace Taft, Oct. 13, 1933, box 1, RTP; Kyle Brooks to author, March 17, 1969; Interview, Robert Goldman.

CHAPTER 10: A PHILOSOPHY FOR HARD TIMES

1. Louis L. Tucker, *Cincinnati: A Student's Guide to Localized History* (New York, 1969), p. 33; "Statement of Unemployment Relief Expenditures and Needs in Hamilton County, prepared for Senator Robert A. Taft," 1932, box 468, RTP, LC; Cincinnati *Enquirer,* June 9, 1932, p. 12, Dec. 4, 1934, p. 14; Charles P. Taft, *City Management: The Cincinnati Experience* (New York, 1933), pp. 227–230; Charles P. Taft, *You and I — and Roosevelt* (New York, 1936), p. 65.
2. RT to Harrison, Nov. 21, Harrison to RT, Dec. 3, 1929, box 13, RT to Hollister, Feb. 2, 12, April 6, 1932, boxes 16, 32, RT to Franklin Fort, Sept. 15, 1932, box 16, RTP.
3. RT, "Notes for Speech," Aug. 25, 1933, box 1249, RT to Horace D. Taft, April 11, 1933, box 1, RTP.
4. RT speech, May 3, 1940, Paul Walter papers, Western Reserve Historical Society, Cleveland; RT, "Notes for Speech," RTP.
5. For RT finances in 1930's, boxes 1, 17, 1357, 1358, 1360, 1362, 1363, RTP; "Estate of Anna Sinton Taft, Auditors Report,"RTP; Last Will and Testament of Charles P. Taft, July 1, 1925, Oct. 11, 1927, Probate Court, Hamilton County; Henry P. Stearns to author, Dec. 7, 1970.
6. Charles P. Taft, 2nd, to Horace Taft, Sept. 15, 1932, to Mrs. WHT, Aug. 12, 1932, Charles P. Taft, 2nd, papers, Cincinnati; Interviews, Lloyd Taft (COHP), p. 52; Horace Taft (COHP), pp. 46–47; Martha Taft-Lillian Dykstra correspondence (in possession of Mrs. Dykstra, S. Yarmouth, Mass.); RT to Martha, Feb. 2, 1933, Aug. 27, 1934, June 6, July 23, 1936, RTP.
7. Boxes 1314–1319, RTP.
8. RT to Harrison, April 25, 1933, box 17, RT to Fess, Aug. 22, 1934, box 35, to George B. Chandler, Nov. 20, 1935, and to L. Randolph Mason, Jan. 21, 1936, box 20, RTP.
9. RT speech, Warren, Ohio, box 253, RT speech, Jan. 18, 1936, box 1249, RT to Eustace Seligman, Nov. 14, 1934, box 18, RTP.

10. RT to Mrs. WHT, Sept. 26, 1932, box 1362, RTP; Cincinnati *Enquirer,* Nov. 5, 1932, p. 10.
11. RT to Robert H. Lucas, May 17, 1933, box 17, RT to Mrs. WHT, Oct. 21, 1933, box 1362, RT to Arthur Morgan, Oct. 23, 1933, box 34, RTP.
12. RT to K. K. Brown, Dec. 14, 1933, box 34, RT to William C. Proctor, Feb. 16, 1934, box 35, RTP.
13. RT to Isabella Hopkins, Feb. 2, 1934, box 35, RT to Thomas H. Darby, March 14, 1934, RT to J. H. Sears, April 11, 1934, box 18, RTP.
14. RT to Edmund W. Pugh, Oct. 1, 1934, box 17, RT to Herbert Hoover, Dec. 24, 1934, RT to Lewis Strauss, July 22, 1935, box 19, RT speech, Warren, Ohio, RT speech, "Something for Nothing," Jan. 1936, RTP.
15. Edward First, "The Gold Clause in the Supreme Court," *Georgetown Law Review,* Vol. 26 (March 1938), pp. 732–739; *Records and Briefs of Cases Decided by the Supreme Court of the U.S.,* Vol. 8, Pt. I, U.S. 302, pp. 329–378; *Dixie Terminal v. U.S.* (302 U.S. 329); New York *Times,* Oct. 12, 1933, March 12, 17, April 2, 13, 26, May 9, June 28, Dec. 24, 1935, Feb. 26, 29, March 10, April 21, 1936, May 8, June 2, Nov. 19, Dec. 14–15, 1937; RT to Irving Fisher, May 8, 1936, Fisher papers, Yale University; Franklin Fort to Hoover and to Chandler Hovey, March 13, 1935, Hoover papers, Hoover Library, Iowa; and esp. RT letters in File Nos. 187.77 and 187.77a, TSHP, Cincinnati.
16. Walter Brown to Herbert Hoover, Dec. 6, 1935, Walter Brown papers, Ohio Historical Society; Hollister to RT, Jan. 10, and to Ed Schorr, Feb. 20, 1936, Hollister papers (in possession of Hollister, Cincinnati); RT to Hollister, Feb. 8, and to Hulbert Taft, Feb. 19, 1936, box 39, Martha to RT, Jr., Feb. 14, 1936, RTP; Cincinnati *Enquirer,* Jan. 1, Feb. 27, 28, p. 1.
17. Bert Buckley to Carl Bachmann, March 8, April 26, 1936, box 399, Borah papers, LC; RT to E. Kendall Gilbert, April 13, box 39, and RT to Horace D. Taft, March 3, 1936, box 20, RTP.
18. RT, Jr., to Martha, March 31, 1936, RTP; Walter Brown to Hoover, Feb. 2, 28, April 18, Brown papers; Cincinnati *Enquirer,* May 14, 16, 1936, pp. 1, 26; New York *Times,* May 14, 16, 1936, pp. 1, 6; RT to Martha, Jan. 19, 1936, to Samuel M. Rinakur, July 25, box 20, to Frank Ransbottom, May 19, and David Ingalls, May 18, 1936, box 39, RTP.
19. Cincinnati *Enquirer,* June 4, 5, 7–12, 1936; New York *Times,* June 9–12, 1936; RT to René de Bonand, May 21, 1936, box 39, RTP; *Proceedings of the Republican National Convention, 1936* (New York, 1936), p. 176.
20. Cincinnati *Post,* Feb. 28, 1936, p. 1; Martha to RT, Jr., May 8, 1936, RTP; New York *Times,* June 12, 19, 1936, pp. 16, 12; Cincinnati *Enquirer,* May 20, June 13, 1936, both p. 1; Hollister to RT, May 27, 1936, and Hollister diary, June 23, 1936, Hollister papers; Interview, Hollister; Landon (COHP), p. 26; Charles P. Taft, 2nd; and Malcolm Baldridge (by phone) to author, May 25, 1970, June 1970.
21. RT to Mrs. Albert S. Ingalls, June 22, 1936, box 20, and to Martha, June 30, July 4, 1936, RTP.
22. RT to Martha, July 8, 1936, RTP.
23. RT, "Liberalism — Real or New Deal," *Young Republican* (May 1936), pp. 6–7; New York *Times,* July 5, 1936, p. 12; RT to Fisher, May 8, 1936, box 39, RT to Robert French, Feb. 11, 1936, box 20, RTP.

24. Cincinnati *Enquirer,* April 2, 1936, p. 1; RT speech, April 4, 1936, box 1249, RTP; *Ohio State Journal,* April 15, 1936, p. 1; RT to Albert D. Cash, Sept. 30, box 40, RT to Charles P. Taft, 2nd, July 25, 1936, box 20, RTP.
25. RT to Paul Cruikshank, Nov. 27, 1936, box 1, to Horace D. Taft, June 11, 1937, box 6, RTP.
26. RT to Horace D. Taft, Sept. 26, box 1, RT to RT, Jr., Oct. 29, RT to William Taft, Oct. 19, 1936, box 20, RTP.
27. Cincinnati *Enquirer,* Nov. 4, 1936; Secretary of State, 1957–1958, *Ohio Election Statistics* (1958), pp. 378–380; RT to John G. Buchanan, Nov. 4, box 20, RT to Horace D. Taft, Nov. 14, 1936, box 1, RTP.

CHAPTER 11: THE PATH TO THE SENATE

1. Rowe to Pauline Isaacson, Feb. 7, 1956, quoted in Isaacson, "Robert Alphonso Taft: An Assessment of a Persuader," doctoral thesis, Minnesota, 1956, p. 449; Dorothy Rowe, "Tribute to a Friend" (privately printed, Christmas 1964); Dorothy and Stanley Rowe (COHP), pp. 11–12.
2. RT to Hulbert Taft, Feb. 11, 1937, box 21, RTP, LC; Martha to RT, Jr., Feb. 1, 1938, RTP; Interviews, John Hollister (COHP), p. 23, RT, Jr., William H. Taft III; Cincinnati *Enquirer,* Nov. 17, 1935, p. 26; RT to Horace, April 6, 1937, box 21, RTP.
3. *Ohio State Journal,* March 27, July 29, Oct. 30, 1937, all p. 2; RT to Walter Brown, May 5, 1937, Walter Brown papers, Ohio Historical Society; Cincinnati *Enquirer,* June 4, 6, 13, 16, 29, 1937; RT to Helen Manning, Aug. 8, 1937, Helen Manning papers, LC.
4. "Memorandum on Organization," box 50, RT to Paul Walter, Jan. 10, 1938, box 49, RTP.
5. Norcross to author, June 26, 1971; Ingalls to author, June 11, 1971.
6. Box 43, RTP; box 21, Paul Walter papers, Western Reserve Historical Society, Cleveland; RT to Rowe, June 19, 1938, Rowe papers (in Rowe's possession, Cincinnati); RT to Ingalls, June 11, 1938, box 49, RTP; Columbus *Evening Dispatch,* Nov. 3, 1938, p. 6A.
7. RT to Lewis Strauss, May 31, June 6, 1938, boxes 54, 49, RT to Hoover, Aug. 15, 1938, box 49, RT to Horace Taft, Aug. 15, 1938, box 22, RT to Paul Block, Aug. 23, 1938, box 53, RTP.
8. Columbus *Evening Dispatch,* Aug. 10, 1938, p. 1; *Time,* Jan. 29, Feb. 26, 1940; Martha to Jack Kennon, March 2, 1940, Martha to RT, Jr., May 16, 1938, and RT to RT, Jr., May 16, 1938, RTP.
9. Columbus *Evening Dispatch,* July 10, 22, 1938, p. C3, 5; Cincinnati *Enquirer,* Aug. 1, 1937, p. 24; Raymond Clapper dispatch, Feb. 5, 1938, Clapper papers, LC.
10. RT to Ingalls, April 4, 1938, box 49, RTP; Interviews, Ingalls, Walter (COHP), p. 19.
11. S. J. Woolf, "Robert Taft Sets a Mark for the Minority," *New York Times Magazine,* Nov. 27, 1938; Report on RT measurements, by I. Jack Martin, 1951, box 438, RTP; Holmes Alexander, *The Famous Five* (New York, 1958), p. 166; photographs, box 1324, RTP.
12. Walter (COHP), p. 23.
13. Phonograph records, RTP.

14. Noel G. Rapp, "The Political Speaking of Robert A. Taft, 1939 to 1953," doctoral thesis, Purdue, 1955, passim; Isaacson, passim.

15. Morris Edwards, Memoir on Taft, p. 15, RTP.

16. RT to Horace, Dec. 12, 1937, box 21, RTP; Horace to Fannie Taft, Oct. 9, 1937, Charles P. Taft, 2nd, papers, Cincinnati.

17. RT to Martha, Sept. 7, 1937, RT to Fred Manning, Oct. 14, 1936, box 1, RTP.

18. RT to Horace Taft, Nov. 14, 1936, box 1, RTP.

19. Seth Taft (COHP), p. 22; Ishbel Ross, *An American Family* (Cleveland, 1964), p. 378.

20. Clarence Laylin to author, Dec. 23, 1969; Columbus *Citizen,* Feb. 9, 1938, p. B1; Walter Davenport, "Bashful Buckeye," *Collier's,* Vol. 105 (April 16, 1940), p. 11.

21. Carman to author, April 1971; Forrest Davis to Grove Patterson, May 25, 1940, RTP.

22. RT Senate Campaign Committee, "Two Men and a Job," RTP; esp. campaign literature, Paul Walter papers.

23. RT to John T. Flynn, April 4, to George Sokolsky, May 9, 1938, boxes 53, 54, RTP; Walter (COHP).

24. RT to Seymour, May 12, 1938, box 1327; RT to Robert French, May 12, 1938, to Pringle, March 4, May 30, 1938, box 6, letters from Lloyd Taft to RT and Mrs. RT, 1937–1938, RT to RT, Jr., May 16, 1938, RTP.

25. RT to Walter, April 6, 1938, Walter papers.

26. Horace to Martha, Aug. 5, 1938; RT to Edwin Davis, Aug. 2, 1938, box 43, and to George Sokolsky, Aug. 2, 1938, box 49, RTP. For Day's assaults, boxes 45, 46, RTP, and Walter papers; Columbus *Evening Dispatch,* July 22–Aug. 7, 1938.

27. "Taft-Day Vote by Wards," Walter to N. R. Howard, Aug. 31, 1938, Walter papers; Columbus *Evening Dispatch,* Aug. 11, 1938, p. 11; Board of Elections, Hamilton County, statistics, 1938.

28. RT to Henry Taft, Aug. 24, 1938, box 49, RTP.

29. *Ohio State Journal,* Aug. 11, 1938, p. 1.

30. Walter (COHP), p. 5.

31. RT to Frank O. Lowden, Aug. 15, 1938, box 54, RTP.

32. New York *Times,* Jan. 4, 1939, p. 11; box 43, RTP.

33. RT to John Hamilton, Aug. 21, 1938, box 53, RT to Edward M. Baker, Nov. 1, 1938, box 22, RT to Walter White, Oct. 31, 1938, box 54, RTP.

34. Campaign Material, "Statement on Issues," 1938, RTP.

35. RT to Vandenberg, Oct. 14, 1938, box 49; "Statement on Issues," RTP; Akron *Beacon-Journal,* Nov. 7, 1938, p. 19.

36. Akron *Beacon-Journal,* Nov. 2, 7, 1938, pp. 7, 6; RT speech, Marietta, box 49, RTP.

37. Speech to Slovenes, speech to Czechs, box 49, RTP.

38. RT to Walter, Oct. 31, 1938, Walter papers.

39. Harold L. Ickes, *The Secret Diary of Harold L. Ickes: The Inside Struggle, 1936–1939,* Vol. 2 (New York, 1954), p. 499; "How Will the Election Come Out?" *New Republic,* Vol. 96 (Nov. 2, 1938), pp. 351–353; Akron *Beacon-Journal,* Nov. 10, 1938, p. 4.

40. Columbus *Evening Dispatch,* Oct. 9, 15, 22, 26, 28, 30, Nov. 1, 1938; copies of RT speeches, Walter papers, box 49, RTP.
41. W. A. Deely to M. H. McIntyre, Oct. 12, 1938, 300-Ohio B, Franklin D. Roosevelt papers, Hyde Park; Martha to RT, Jr., Oct. 30, 1938, RTP.
42. Akron *Beacon-Journal,* Columbus *Evening Dispatch,* Nov. 3–9, 1938.

CHAPTER 12: THE YOUNG SENATOR

1. Constance McLaughlin Green, *Washington: Capitol City, 1879–1950* (Princeton, 1963), passim.
2. New York *Times,* Jan. 22, 1939, section 2, p. 4; Cincinnati *Post,* Jan. 7, 1939, p. 3; Martha to RT, Jr., Jan. 20, 1939; RT, Jr., to Martha, Jan. 9, 1939, RTP, LC.
3. Cleveland *Press,* Jan. 4, 1939; Washington *Star,* Jan. 17, 1939; RT to Dorothy Rowe, Jan. 8, 1939, Rowe papers (possession of Rowes, Cincinnati).
4. RT to Dorothy Rowe, Jan. 8, 1939, Rowe papers; Washington *Post,* Feb. 1, 1939; New York *Times,* Feb. 12, 1939, section 9, p. 12; Norman Cousins, "What I Learned about Congress," *Saturday Review of Literature,* Vol. 28 (June 24, 1944), p. 7.
5. Taft and Smith, *Foundations of Democracy: A Series of Debates* (New York, 1939); speeches, early 1939, box 1251, RTP; RT to Paul Walter, March 2, 1939, Walter papers, Western Reserve Historical Society, Cleveland; *New Republic,* Vol. 98 (March 1939), pp. 100–101; Hadley Cantril, *Public Opinion, 1935–1946* (Princeton, 1951).
6. Copy of speech, April 15, 1939, box 1251, RTP; box 30, Raymond Clapper papers, LC.
7. "Roosevelt–Garner Gridiron Dinner," April 15, 1939, box 1, Clapper papers; Turner Catledge, *My Life and Times* (New York, 1971), p. 119; *PM,* Oct. 4, 1942; John C. O'Loughlin to Herbert Hoover, April 17, 24, 1939, box 45, O'Loughlin papers, LC; Sam Clyde to Clapper, May 24, 1939, box 31, Clapper papers; *Time,* April 24, 1939, p. 18.
8. Cleveland *Plain Dealer,* June 1, 1939; boxes 24, 751–758, RTP; Interview, Marjorie Hein; Harry Maginnis (COHP); Mildred Reeves Sherman to author, Nov. 1971.
9. *CR Index,* passim, 1939; Noel G. Rapp, "The Political Speaking of Robert A. Taft, 1939 to 1953," doctoral thesis, Purdue, 1955, pp. 182, 195.
10. *CR,* 1939, p. 1275; Housing amendment, Feb. 9, 1939, Voting Record, 1939, box 1250; RT to Richard D. Downing, Nov. 6, 1939 and to John Ihdler, March 15, 1939, boxes 1184, 476, Statement re Housing bill, June 6, 1939, box 1252, Charles P. Taft, 2nd, to Mrs. WHT, April 14, 1939, box 1355, RTP.
11. Hiram Johnson to Hiram Johnson, Jr., Jan. 14, 1939, Johnson papers, Berkeley, Cal.
12. RT to McNary, Dec. 16, 1938, box 1345, RTP; New York *Times,* Jan. 11, 1939, p. 7.
13. Taft and Smith, p. 262.
14. RT to Hoover, Feb. 23, 1939, box 490, RTP, Taft and Smith, p. 224.
15. RT, "Statement on Farm Policy," 1939, box 473, RTP; speech, March 18,

1939, Walter papers; speeches, 1939, box 1251, RTP; Taft and Smith, passim; New York *Times,* Feb. 2, 1937, p. 27.

16. Jonathan Mitchell, "Taft; Unreconstructed Puritan," *New Republic,* Vol. 102 (June 1940), pp. 755–757; "Record of Robert A. Taft," box 688, RT speeches, boxes 1250–1252, voting record, box 760, RTP; New York *Times,* July 26, 27, Aug. 1, Dec. 13, 1939, Jan. 6, 1940; *Time,* Jan. 15, 1940, p. 15; RT to Horace Taft, Jan. 11, 1940, Taft School archives.

17. Taft and Smith, p. 27.

18. RT to Henry Pringle, Aug. 31, 1939, box 3, Pringle papers, LC; Taft and Smith, pp. 174–183.

19. RT speech, March 2, 1939, Walter papers.

20. Taft and Smith, p. 19; RT to Harvey L. Williams, Dec. 26, 1939, box 71, RTP; speech, May 4, 1940, Walter papers.

21. Taft and Smith, pp. 103–104.

22. Ibid., pp. 62–63, 108, 139, 14–15.

23. *CR,* 1939, pp. 8614, 8934; New York *Times,* Feb. 9, April 2, 5, 1940; RT to Harold Jones, Feb. 13, RT to Horace Taft, Jan. 22, RT to Vincent Starzinger, March 29, 1940, boxes 63, 25, 69, speeches, boxes 1254, 1255, RTP.

24. New York *Times,* May 28, 1940, p. 1; *CR,* 1940, pp. 6904–6906; Jerold S. Auerbach, *Labor and Liberty: The La Follette Committee and the New Deal* (Indianapolis, 1966), pp. 198–203.

25. RT to Monte Appel, March 4, April 6, RT to Howard Jones, Feb. 13, RT to Ralph Gifford, boxes 72, 63, 70, RTP; New York *Times,* March 21, 1940, p. 1; *CR,* 1940, pp. 3140–3144, 3200.

26. Re Pringle, RT to Frederick J. Manning, June 21, 1939, RT to Pringle, May 30, 1938, RT to William R. Pringle, Jan. 1, 1940, RT to Horace D. Taft, Dec. 21, 1938, box 6; re Yale Corp., letters, box 1329; re law school, RT to Charles Seymour, May 12, 1938, box 1327, RTP. In this letter he also recommended his brother Charlie for dean of the law school. "He is certainly in no way reactionary. He has taken the lead in a complete reformation of local government in Cincinnati . . . I think he represents a medium position between the extremists like Thurman Arnold and the stand-pat conservatives."

CHAPTER 13: FOREIGN POLICY INTRUDES

1. Key works are Robert A. Divine, *The Illusion of Neutrality: Franklin D. Roosevelt and the Struggle over the Arms Embargo* (Chicago, 1962); Divine, *Roosevelt and World War II* (Baltimore, 1969); William L. Langer and S. Everett Gleason, *The Challenge to Isolation: The World Crisis of 1937–1940 and American Foreign Policy* (New York, 1952); Langer and Gleason, *The Undeclared War, 1940–1941* (New York, 1953); Selig Adler, *The Isolationist Impulse: Its Twentieth Century Reaction* (New York, 1957); and Manfred Jonas, *Isolationism in America, 1935–1941* (Ithaca, 1966).

2. "Record of Robert A. Taft," box 688, RTP, LC.

3. RT, "Statement on Issues," 1938, RTP.

4. RT statement, Jan. 4, 1939, box 1251, RTP; New York *Times,* Feb. 15, 1939, p. 27.

5. New York *Times,* April 21, 1939; RT to David Ingalls, June 21, 1939, box 78, RTP; New York *Herald Tribune,* April 22, 26, 29, 1939.
6. RT to Mrs. Wyman Graham, Nov. 10, 1939, box 63, RTP.
7. *CR,* April 24, 1939, p. A1698, Sept. 30, 1939, p. A77.
8. "The Republicans, Honeymoon Is Over," *Fortune,* Vol. 35 (April 1947), pp. 77–85; *CR,* March 2, 1940, p. A1218; speech, Oct. 13, 1939, Paul Walter papers, Cleveland.
9. *CR,* Jan. 22, 1939, p. A253; box 1251, RTP.
10. Ingalls to author, May 11, 1971; RT to Ingalls, April 12, 1939, box 23, RTP; *CR,* March 2, 1940, p. A1218.
11. RT to Iley T. Yates, April 17, 1939, box 62, RTP; *CR,* Jan. 22, 1939, p. A253.
12. *CR,* May 20, 1940, p. A3178, May 28, 1941, pp. A2557–2559; box 1250, RTP.
13. *CR,* May 20, 1940, pp. 3177–3178.
14. Chicago *Tribune,* Jan. 16, 1944; Interview, Horace D. Taft; Martha to Lillian Dykstra, Oct. 3, 1938, Dec. 5, 1940, Dykstra papers (her possession, S. Yarmouth, Mass.); L. F. Worley to Martha, Oct. 31, and William S. Foulis to Martha, Dec. 19, 1941, RTP.
15. Henry F. Pringle, *The Life and Times of William Howard Taft,* Vol. 2 (New York, 1939), p. 737; WHT, "Why We Entered the Great War," *Current History Magazine,* New York *Times,* section 6, Part 2 (Aug. 1917), pp. 317–320.
16. *CR,* Jan. 22, 1939, p. A253.
17. RT to Ingalls, April 12, 1939, box 23, RTP. Critiques of RT's thinking are Richard H. Rovere, "Taft, Is This the Best We've Got?" *Harper's,* Vol. 196 (April 1948), pp. 289–299; John P. Armstrong, "The Enigma of Senator Taft and American Foreign Policy," *Review of Politics,* Vol. 17 (April 1955), pp. 206–231; Vernon van Dyke and Edward Lane Davis, "Senator Taft and American Security," *Journal of Politics,* Vol. 14 (May 1952), pp. 177–202; Russell Kirk and James McClellan, *The Political Principles of Robert A. Taft* (New York, 1967), Ch. 8; Armstrong, "Senator Taft and American Foreign Policy: The Period of Opposition," doctoral thesis, Chicago, 1953; and Shirley Schlafman, "An Isolationist Faces War: A Historical Review of the Foreign Policy Views of Senator Robert A. Taft Between 1939 and 1945," masters thesis, Ohio State, 1967.
18. *CR,* April 25, 1939, p. A1698, copy in Walter papers; New York *Times,* Sept. 5, Oct. 1, 4, 7, 25, 27, 1939.
19. RT statements, Sept. 11, 29, 1939, box 1250, RTP, and Oct. 2, 1939, Walter papers; RT, "Should Congress Amend the Neutrality Law?" *Congressional Digest,* Vol. 18 (Oct. 1939), pp. 244–246, copy in box 639, RTP; RT to Frank Gunter, Oct. 4 and to Sam Rinakur, Oct. 24, 1939, boxes 63, 66, RTP; *CR,* March 2, 1940, p. A1218.
20. RT to General Charles G. Dawes, Oct. 24, 1939, box 67, RTP.
21. Harold L. Ickes, *The Secret Diary of Harold L. Ickes: The Inside Struggle, 1936–1939,* Vol. 2 (New York, 1954), p. 595.
22. *CR,* Feb. 20, 1939, p. 1596; Cincinnati *Post,* Feb. 21, 1939, p. 18.
23. Tom Connally, *My Name Is Tom Connally* (New York, 1954), p. 311.
24. Pauline Isaacson, "Robert Alphonso Taft: An Assessment of a Persuader,"

doctoral thesis, Minnesota, 1956, pp. 474–475; RT to Robert McDougal, June 13, 1939, box 6, RTP.

25. Richard Scandrett to Russel Wiggins, April 30, 1940, Vol. 10B, Scandrett papers, Cornell University; Forrest Davis to Damon Runyon, March 20, 1940, RTP.

CHAPTER 14: SEEKING THE TOP

1. Gridiron Club speech, 1948, RTP, LC.
2. Dorothy Rowe (COHP), pp. 11–12; Boston *Globe,* Dec. 7, 1938; RT to William J. Reardon, Feb. 15, RT to James T. Begg, March 11, RT to Jack Kennon, May 27, RT to Charles D. Hilles, June 21, 1939, boxes 83, 80, 78, RTP; James Selvage to author, Oct. 18, 1969; Cincinnati *Post,* April 18, 1939, p. 5.
3. Buffalo *Courier,* Dec. 6, 1938. Also Interviews, RT, Jr.; Mrs. Robert Black (COHP), p. 30; Paul Walter; Edwin Lahey (COHP), p. 53.
4. RT to Paul Walter, Feb. 2, RT to David Ingalls, April 29, 1939, box 23, RTP; New York *Times,* April 19, 1939, p. 46; Cincinnati *Post,* May 16, 1939, p. 9.
5. RT to Martha, July 22, 1939, RTP; box 78, RTP is full of letters revealing RT's views of Bricker.
6. Columbus *Citizen,* July 6, 1953; Cincinnati *Post,* July 27, 1939, p. 9; Ingalls to Hollister, July 27, 1939, box 97, RTP; New York *Times,* Aug. 3, 1939, p. 1; RT to Ingalls, July 28 and RT to Henry W. Taft, Aug. 7, 1939, box 78, RTP; New York *Times,* Aug. 3, 1939, p. 1; RT to Walter, Aug. 5, 1939, Walter papers, Cleveland; Hollister memo, "Summary of Part in Taft Nomination Campaign," Oct. 22, 1940, box 99, RTP; Walter Interview. An aide, Richard Scandrett of New York, did think a deal had been concluded: Scandrett to Jesse Barrett, June 23, 1943, Vol. 18B, Scandrett papers, Cornell University.
7. RT to Ingalls, July 28, RT to Bricker, Aug. 7, 1939, box 78, RTP. This box contains much other inside information.
8. Box 78, RTP; RT to Charles W. Montgomery, May 30, box 82, RT to George H. Moses, March 29, box 74, RT to Vincent Starzinger, May 31, 1940, box 69, RTP; Hollister to Lester Bradshaw, Dec. 22, 1939, Hollister papers, Cincinnati.
9. RT to Herbert Hoover, Aug. 23, 1939, box l–k/135 file, Hoover papers, Hoover Library, Iowa; to Ben Katz, Aug. 5, 1939, box 46, RTP.
10. Interviews, David Ingalls, Paul Walter; Ray Tucker, "Washington Letter," *Living Age,* Vol. 358 (Feb. 1940), pp. 581–583; Scandrett, "Notes on the Convention," 1940, Vol. 10A, Scandrett papers; RT to Bernard Kilgore, June 13, 1940, RTP; miscellaneous reports, Hollister, in Hollister papers; and Ingalls to Horace D. Taft, Feb. 14, 1940, Horace D. Taft papers, Taft School.
11. New York *Times,* Dec. 12, 1939, p. 32; speeches, Jan.–March, 1940, box 1254, RTP; "Taft Stumps Florida for the Presidential Nomination," *Life,* Vol. 8, (Feb. 19, 1940), pp. 17–21.
12. Boxes 79, 99, RTP contain many letters concerning Ohio problems at this time. Quote is from RT to Walter, March 19, 1940, box 79, RTP.

13. RT to Walter, March 12, RT to Alexander Jackson, April 8, RT to King Swope, June 13, 1940, boxes 84, 100, 84, RTP.

14. New York *Times*, Feb. 24, April 18, 1940, pp. 7, 18; *Wall Street Journal*, May 21, 1940; Baltimore *Sun*, April 14, 1940; Hollister to James Lowell, Nov. 13, 1939, Hollister papers; RT to Sam Rinakur, Jan. 10, RT to Colonel R. R. McCormick, Feb. 8, 1940, boxes 66, 67, Lee Nixon to Ingalls, Dec. 12, 1939, box 62, RTP.

15. New York *Times*, April 8, 1940, p. 4; Milton Mackaye, "Gallery for 1940," *Ladies' Home Journal*, Vol. 56 (Dec. 1939), p. 22; John O'Loughlin to Herbert Hoover, Feb. 24, 1940, box 45, O'Loughlin papers, LC; White, "Candidates in the Spring," *Yale Review*, Vol. 29 (March 1940), pp. 433–443.

16. RT speech, March 28, 1940, Walter papers; RT to Paul Grischy, Feb. 29, 1940, box 81, RTP.

17. Raymond Clapper memo, June 29, 1939, box 1, Clapper papers, LC; George H. Mayer, *The Republican Party, 1854–1966*, 2d ed. (New York, 1967), p. 454; Raymond Moley, *Twenty-Seven Masters of Politics* (New York, 1949), pp. 56–65; Forrest Davis to A. J. Martin, April 5, 1940, RTP; Scandrett to Jouett Ross Todd, March 8, 1940, Vol. 10A, Scandrett papers; RT to Mac Baldridge, March 15, 1940, box 74, RTP; O'Loughlin to Herbert Hoover, May 4, 1940, box 45, O'Loughlin papers.

18. Hollister to Lester Bradshaw, Dec. 30, 1939, Hollister papers; Hollister to William R. Eaton, May 17, 1940, box 99, RTP; Scandrett to William Allen White, March 15, 1940, Vol. 10B, Scandrett papers; Hollister, "Summary of Part in Taft Nomination Campaign," Oct. 22, 1940, box 99, RTP; Clapper to Alfred Landon, March 4, 1940, box 49, Clapper papers.

19. Miller Davis to Ingalls, Jan. 10, 1940, box 99, RTP; Edwin B. Bartlett to Hollister, Jan. 30, 1940, Hollister papers. Also Jouett Todd to Scandrett, March 23, 1940, Vol. 10A, Scandrett papers.

20. New York *Times*, Aug. 4, 1939, March 3, 1940, pp. 12, 1; *Time*, Jan. 29, 1940, p. 22; Alice Longworth, "What's the Matter with Bob Taft?" *Saturday Evening Post*, Vol. 212 (May 4, 1940), p. 29; clippings, Walter papers; New York *Herald Tribune*, Feb. 13, 1940.

21. Sinclair Weeks to Hollister, Dec. 15, 1939, Hollister papers; Miller Davis to Hollister, Oct. 2, 1939, box 97, RTP; Carl Kiger to Vincent Starzinger, Feb. 28, 1940, Starzinger papers (his possession, Des Moines).

22. Forrest Davis to Arthur Krock, March 15, 1940, RTP; Hollister to Ingalls, Aug. 14, 1939, box 97, RTP; Ingalls Interview.

23. New York *Times*, March 12, 1940, p. 8; "Taft, The Record and the Views of United States Senator Robert A. Taft of Ohio," pamphlet, 1940, RTP; Davis to Grove Patterson, June 3, 1940, RTP.

24. Horace Taft to Martha, Aug. 28, 1939, RT to Cyrus Smith, Jan. 9, 1940, box 74, movie reels, RTP; Barton to Scandrett, June 20, 1940, Vol. 10A, Scandrett papers.

25. *Christian Science Monitor*, Jan. 14, 1940, p. 15; Joseph Alsop and Robert Kintner, "Taft and Taft," *Life*, Vol. 8 (March 18, 1940), p. 90; Beverly Smith, "Bob and Martha Take the Stump," *American Magazine*, Vol. 228 (Sept. 1939), p. 40.

26. *Time,* Jan. 29, 1940, p. 20; Arthur Schlesinger, Jr., "His Eyes Have Seen the Glory," *Collier's,* Vol. 119 (Feb. 22, 1947), p. 12.
27. *Time,* Dec. 18, 1939, pp. 13–14, Jan. 15, 1940, p. 15, Feb. 12, 1940, p. 18, April 15, 1940, p. 20; *Life,* Vol. 8 (Feb. 19, 1940), pp. 17–21.
28. *Current History,* Vol. 51 (April 1948), pp. 46–48; Hadley Cantril, *American Public Opinion, 1935–1946* (Princeton, 1951), pp. 577–578; New York *Times,* May 31, 1939, p. 8.
29. C. Vivian Anderson to Hollister, March 14, 1940, Hollister papers; Walter Davenport, "Bashful Buckeye," *Collier's,* Vol. 105 (April 16, 1940), p. 11.
30. RT to A. D. Kirk, April 10, RT to Mary Truesdale, April 30, 1940, box 70, 73, RTP.
31. RT to Hoover, Jan. 25, 1940, box 1-k/135, Hoover papers; *CR,* March 2, 1940, p. A1219; New York *Times,* Jan. 20, April 8, 1940, pp. 2, 1.
32. RT to Martha, May 16, 1940, RTP; Landon (COHP), p. 9; New York *Herald Tribune,* May 19, 1940.
33. *CR,* May 20, 1940, p. A3178; New York *Times,* May 21, 1940, p. 16; Herbert S. Parmet and Marie B. Hecht, *Never Again: A President Runs for a Third Term* (New York, 1968), p. 111.
34. Horace D. Taft to Fannie Taft, March 2, 1940, Horace D. Taft papers; William H. Hessler, "The Brothers Taft," *Reporter,* Vol. 6 (Jan. 8, 1952), p. 6; Hollister to Ingalls, June 7, 1940, box 99, RTP; Davis to Scandrett, June 6, 1940, and Marshall to Scandrett, June 13, 1940, Vol. 10B, Scandrett papers.
35. Turner Catledge, *My Life and Times* (New York, 1971), pp. 118–119.
36. New York *Times,* May 23, 1940, p. 15; RT radio speech, May 29, 1940, box 633, RT to Charles Goodspeed, June 3, 1940, box 67, RTP.
37. RT to Newbold Noyes, June 3, 6, RT to Mrs. Lloyd Bowers, June 13, 1940, box 25, RTP.
38. Martha to Lillian Dykstra, July 1940, Dykstra papers (her possession, S. Yarmouth, Mass.); Reporter unidentified.
39. Thompson to Paul Block, June 7, 1940, Thompson papers, Syracuse University. See also Donald B. Johnson, *The Republican Party and Wendell Willkie* (Urbana, 1960), pp. 105–106; Interview, Lloyd Taft (COHP), p. 86; RT to Donald B. Johnson, June 25, 1951, box 1193, RTP.
40. Scandrett to Bryant Smith, Oct. 29, 1940, Vol. 16, Scandrett papers.
41. Catledge, p. 118.

CHAPTER 15: A CERTAIN GRACE IN DEFEAT

1. Marcia Davenport, *Too Strong for Fantasy* (New York, 1967), p. 270; Ellsworth Barnard, *Wendell Willkie: Fighter for Freedom* (Marquette, Michigan, 1966), pp. 172–173.
2. New York *Times,* June 3, 1940. Taft also worried at this time about a special session Bricker called in Ohio to separate the state and national ballots in the election. See boxes 7, 80, 83, 98, RTP, LC; Cincinnati *Times-Star,* June 18, 20, 1940, pp. 1, 13.
3. Hadley Cantril, *American Public Opinion, 1935–1946* (Princeton, 1951), passim; New York *Herald Tribune,* June 25, 1940.

4. RT to Richard B. Scandrett, June 19, 1940, box 76; also many letters, boxes 62, 66, 67, 69, 74, 79, RTP; New York *Times,* June 26, 27, 1940, p. 1; Forrest Davis to James A. Hagerty, June 3, 1940, RTP; RT to Wilbur D. Matson, June 15, 1940, Matson papers, Marietta College; Harold L. Ickes, *The Secret Diary of Harold L. Ickes: The Inside Struggle, 1936–1939,* Vol. 2 (New York, 1954), pp. 201, 211, 219.

5. Scandrett, "First Ballot Forecast," June 22, 1940, Vol. 10A, Scandrett papers, Cornell University; RT tally sheet of delegates, May 18, 1940, John Hollister papers, Cincinnati; Donald Johnson, *The Republican Party and Wendell Willkie* (Urbana, 1960), pp. 72–88.

6. *Official Report of the Proceedings of the Republican National Convention, 1940* (D.C., 1940), passim; Herbert S. Parmet and Marie B. Hecht, *Never Again: A President Runs for a Third Term* (New York, 1968), pp. 147–150; Barnard, p. 181.

7. *Official Report,* pp. 279–287; Scandrett to Walter Brown, July 2, 1940, and "Notes on the Convention," Vol. 10A, Scandrett papers.

8. *Official Report,* pp. 288–301; Parmet and Hecht, p. 153.

9. Hollister (COHP), p. 55.

10. *Official Report,* p. 302; Joseph Barnes, *Willkie* (New York, 1952), p. 184; Donald McCoy, *Landon of Kansas* (Lincoln, 1966), pp. 430, 445–446; Donald Johnson to author, Nov. 21, 1969; Johnson, p. 98.

11. *Official Report,* pp. 306–307; Joseph Martin Jr., *My First Fifty Years in Politics* (New York, 1950), p. 153.

12. C. David Tompkins, *Senator Arthur H. Vandenberg; The Evolution of a Modern Republican, 1884–1945* (E. Lansing, 1970); Johnson, p. 100; Arthur Vandenberg, Jr., ed., *The Private Papers of Senator Vandenberg* (Boston, 1952), pp. 6–7; Mary Earhart Dillon, *Wendell Willkie, 1892–1944* (Philadelphia, 1952), p. 166; Scandrett memo, 1940, Vol. 16, Scandrett papers.

13. *Official Report,* p. 307; Hugh Ross, "Was the Nomination of Wendell Willkie a Political Mistake?" *Indiana Magazine of History,* Vol. 58 (June 1962), pp. 79–100.

14. Des Moines *Register,* Aug. 1, 1953.

15. New York *Times,* June 29, 1940, p. 3; Davenport, pp. 273–274; Mildred Reeves to Charles Sweeney, July 17, 1940, box 86, RT to Robert Ramaze, July 9, 1940, box 83, RTP; Scandrett to Paul Windels, July 9, 1940, Vol. 10B, Scandrett papers.

16. Martha to Lillian Dykstra, July, 1940, Dykstra papers (her possession, S. Yarmouth, Mass.).

17. John Hollister, "Summary of Part in Taft Nominating Campaign," Oct. 22, 1940, Hollister papers, Cincinnati; Charles P. Taft, 2nd, to Horace D. Taft, July 17, 1940, Horace D. Taft papers, Taft School; Charles P. Taft, 2nd, to Mrs. WHT, July 9, 1940, Charles P. Taft, 2nd, papers, Cincinnati; Scandrett, "Notes on the Convention," 1940, Vol. 10A, Scandrett papers; Thomas Dewey to author, Oct. 20, 1969; Warren Moscow, *Roosevelt and Willkie* (Englewood Cliffs, N.J., 1968), p. 55; Johnson, pp. 103–108; Interview, Walter.

18. RT to Michael Gallagher, July 6, RT to Lida Frost, July 9, RT to Samuel Kupferman, July 15, RT to Scandrett, July 19, RT to Longworth, July 31, RT to Walter F. Brown, July 31, 1940, boxes 81, 76, 82, RTP.

19. RT to Scandrett, July 5, RT to Lewis B. Rock, July 10, 1940, RT to Horace Taft, RT to Walter, boxes 76, 83, 25, 84, also RT to R. B. Creager, July 9, RT to Thomas R. White, July 10, 19, RT to General Hugh Johnson, Nov. 5, 1940, boxes, 87, 86, 90, RTP.
20. George H. Mayer, *The Republican Party, 1854–1966*, 2d ed. (New York, 1967), pp. 456–457; Parmet and Hecht, pp. 130–131. Barnard, p. 187, disagrees.
21. Raymond Clapper thought Pew turned from Taft after the Gridiron dinner in 1939. Clapper memo, Oct. 28, 1939, box 2, Clapper papers, LC.
22. RT to Charles L. Horn, July 29, 1940, RT to Bricker, Feb. 27, 1943, boxes 72, 487, RTP; Arthur Schlesinger, Jr., "His Eyes Have Seen the Glory," *Collier's,* Vol. 119 (Feb. 22, 1947), p. 12.
23. Martha to Lillian Dykstra, July 1940, Dykstra papers; RT to Mrs. Henry Lippitt, July 6, 1940, box 25, RTP.

CHAPTER 16: THE ROAD TO PEARL HARBOR

1. Martha to Lillian Dykstra, Jan. 1940, Dykstra papers (her possession, S. Yarmouth, Mass.); Rachel La Follette to Jane, Aug. 1953, box C–26, Robert La Follette, Jr., papers, LC; Senator Burton Wheeler to author, Sept. 1971.
2. Martha to Lillian Dykstra, Jan. 17, Dec. 5, 1940, Dykstra papers.
3. RT to Martha, Aug. 4, 12, 1940, RTP, LC.
4. RT to Horace, July 6, 1940, Horace D. Taft papers, Taft School; RT to Martha, Aug. 7, RT to Stephen Philbin, July 9, 1940, box 76, RT to Dewey, box 96, RTP. Other letters re Willkie, boxes 25, 64, 69.
5. RT to I. H. Burnett, July 9, to Burton, July 5, 1940, boxes 74, 13, RTP.
6. RT speeches, boxes 770, 1255, RTP; for Martha's activities, Rockford, Ill., *Morning Star*, Oct. 15, Tuscarawas County *Daily Reporter*, Oct. 13, 1940.
7. RT to Paul Walter, Sept. 11, 1940, Walter papers, Cleveland; RT to Walter Newton, Nov. 5, RT to Emma A. Miller, Nov. 12, RT to W. A. Bartlett, Nov. 20, 1940, boxes 90, 82, 105, RTP. Also letters, boxes 68, 86, 107.
8. Bernard F. Donahoe, *Private Plans and Public Dangers: The Story of FDR's Third Nomination* (South Bend, 1965), p. 188; Hadley Cantril, *Public Opinion, 1935–1946* (Princeton, 1951), p. 617; Herbert S. Parmet and Marie B. Hecht, *Never Again: A President Runs for a Third Term* (New York, 1968), p. 273.
9. New York *Times,* Sept. 29, 1940, Jan. 4, 1941, pp. 38, 5; RT speeches, 1940–1941, boxes 1256–1257; RT, "Considerations for Thought in December, 1940," box 694, RTP.
10. New York *Times,* June 30, 1941, p. 15; original in box 1257, RTP.
11. RT to Martha, Aug. 22, 1941, RTP; New York *Times,* April 4, 1941, p. 18; speeches, boxes 1256–1257, speech, Cincinnati, March 27, 1941, box 596, RTP.
12. *CR*, Sept. 19, 1940, p. 12304; New York *Times,* Sept. 27, 1941, p. 6; New York *Journal of Commerce,* Dec. 13, 1940; Randolph Paul, *Taxation in the United States* (Boston, 1954), p. 260; speeches, boxes 1256–1257, RTP.
13. RT, "Bureaucratic Confusion in War," *Vital Speeches,* Vol. 7 (May 1, 1941), pp. 503–505, original in box 1256, RTP; New York *Times,* April 19,

Oct. 31, 1941, pp. 8, 40; RT, "Memorandum Opinion," June 28, 1941, box 263, RTP.

14. RT radio talk, Oct. 30, 1941, box 1258, RTP; New York *Times,* Oct. 31, Dec. 11, 1941, Jan. 6, 10, 11, 1942; Michael Straight, "The Republicans Betray Defense," *New Republic,* Vol. 105 (Nov. 17, 1941), pp. 641–642; RT-Herbert Hoover correspondence, 1941–1942, box l–k/135, Hoover papers, Hoover Library, Iowa; RT to Hulbert Taft, Jan. 10, 1942, Cincinnati Historical Society.

15. U. S. Congress, U. S. Senate, Hearings before the Committee on Military Affairs, 76 Cong., 3d Sess., *on Nomination of Henry L. Stimson to be Secretary of War;* copy of RT statement, July 9, 1940, box 1255, RTP.

16. Elting E. Morison, *Turmoil and Tradition: A Study of the Life and Times of Henry L. Stimson* (Boston, 1960), p. 484; Frankfurter to Erwin Griswold, July 31, 1952, box 14, Frankfurter papers, LC.

17. RT to Frances Ricker, July 8, 1940, Ricker papers (her possession, Lima, Ohio), to Helen Manning, Aug. 3, 1940, box 25, RTP.

18. William S. White, *The Taft Story* (New York, 1954), p. 154; *CR,* Aug. 14, 1940, p. 10308, original in box 1255, RTP.

19. *CR,* ibid.; New York *Times,* Aug. 28, 29, 1940, both p. 1; RT to Martha, Aug. 26, 1940, RTP.

20. RT to Richard K. Hawes, Sept. 11, 1940 (compliments, of Hawes, Fall River, Mass.), RT to George F. Stanley, Sept. 8, 1944, box 31, RTP; John M. Swomley, Jr., *The Military Establishment* (Boston, 1964), pp. 18–20; Swomley to author, April 22, 1971.

21. RT to Captain Melvin Brown, Aug. 29, RT to Horace Taft, Dec. 28, 1940, boxes 85, 25, RTP; RT to Paul Walter, Dec. 20, 1940, Walter papers; Martha to R. Douglas Stuart, Jr., Aug. 7, 1940, box 1358, RT speech, "Roosevelt's Defense Record," E. Liverpool, Ohio, Oct. 30, 1940, box 770, RTP; New York *Times,* Aug. 7, Sept. 11, 12, Nov. 22, 1940; *CR,* Sept. 10, 1940, p. 11846–11847; Wayne S. Cole, *America First: The Battle Against Intervention, 1940–1941* (Madison, 1953), pp. 12, 167.

22. Hiram Johnson to Hiram Johnson, Jr., Jan. 26, 1941, Johnson papers, University of Calif., Berkeley.

23. New York *Herald Tribune,* Dec. 12, 1940; RT to Mrs. Monte Appel, Dec. 26, 1940, box 106, RTP; *CR,* Jan. 23, 1941, p. 258, Feb. 22, 1941, p. 1276.

24. New York *Times,* Jan. 13, 15, 24, 26, 1941, all p. 1; RT to Jane Ingalls, March 3, 1941, box 108, RTP.

25. RT statement, Feb. 26, 1941, box 618, RTP; RT to Sumner Keller, Feb. 18, 1941, Keller papers, Yale University.

26. RT to Hoover, Feb. 25, 1941, and "Summary of Proposed Senate Amendments to H.R. 1776," box l–k/135, Hoover papers; Statement, Feb. 10, 1941, box 1256, RTP; *CR,* Feb. 22, 1941, p. 1277.

27. New York *Times,* Feb. 10, 11, March 8, 25, 1941; RT to Charles Paddock, Feb. 6, RT to Albert White, March 3, 1941, box 103, RTP. Secondary sources on lend-lease include Warren F. Kimball, *The Most Unsordid Act: Lend Lease, 1939–1941* (Baltimore, 1969); William L. Langer and S. Everett Gleason, *The Undeclared War, 1940–1941* (New York, 1953); Selig Adler, *The Isolationist Impulse: Its Twentieth Century Reaction* (New

York, 1957); also, on Taft, Vernon Van Dyke and Edward Lane Davis, "Senator Taft and American Security," *Journal of Politics,* Vol. 14 (May 1952), pp. 177–202; and John P. Armstrong, "The Enigma of Senator Taft and American Foreign Policy," *Review of Politics,* Vol. 17 (April 1955), pp. 206–231.

28. Martha to Darrah Wunder, April 14, 1941, Wunder papers (her possession, Cincinnati); RT to George Stanley, Sept. 8, 1944, box 31, RTP.

29. RT speeches, May 12, 17, 1941, box 1256, RTP; *CR,* May 28, 1941, p. A2559; New York *Times,* April 2, 1941, p. 9; RT to Hulbert Taft, April 10, RT to Henry Fletcher, June 2, RT to Monte Appel, June 7, 1941, boxes 26, 106, RTP.

30. New York *Times,* July 11, 1941, p. 1; RT to Martha, Aug. 5, 1941, RTP, RT to Hoover, July 16, RT to Frank Lowden, July 30, boxes 1179, 107, RTP; RT to Paul Walter, July 31, 1941, Walter papers; RT to Hollister, July 14, 1941, Hollister papers, Cincinnati.

31. *CR,* June 26, 1941, p. A3077, original in box 768, RTP; New York *Times,* June 26, 1941, p. 7; RT to Wilbur Matson, June 24, 1941, Matson papers, Marietta College; RT to Hoover, June 26, 1941, box l–k/135, Hoover papers. Raymond H. Dawson, *The Decision to Aid Russia: Foreign Policy and Domestic Politics* (Chapel Hill, 1959), pp. 35–36.

32. New York *Times,* July 22, 23, 29, 31, Aug. 6, Sept. 26, Oct. 9, 24, 29, Nov. 8, 1941; RT speeches, late 1941, boxes 767, 1257–1258; letters to Martha, Aug. 14, RT to Hulbert Taft, Aug. 26, box 26, RT to Colonel Julius Klein, Sept. 26, box 103, RT to Harry Sandager, Nov. 25, box 110, RT to John E. Jackson, Nov. 26, 1941, box 106, RTP.

33. Cleveland *Plain Dealer,* Feb. 16, 1941; speech, Feb. 10, 1941, box 634, RT to editor, Dayton *Daily News,* Sept. 17, 1945, box 31, RTP; RT to D. M. Crowley, May 31, 1951, I. Jack Martin papers, Kensington, Md.

34. Horace to R. L. DeWilton, Sept. 8, 1941, Horace D. Taft papers; RT to Martha, Aug. 12, 1941, RTP.

35. RT to Martha, Aug. 14, 1941; RT to Harry Sandager, Nov. 25, 1941, box 110, RTP.

36. RT to Scandrett, Jan. 29, 1941, box 107, RTP; Scandrett to John Marshall, March 10, 1942, Vol. 13, Scandrett papers, Cornell University; RT to Louise Thompson, Sept. 30, 1941, box 768, RT speech, Sept. 22, 1941, box 767, RTP.

37. Scandrett to Wallace Townsend, Nov. 6, 1941, Vol. 12A, Scandrett papers; Mrs. Robert French to author, Oct. 15, 1969.

38. RT speech, Dec. 19, 1941, box 1258, RT to Chase S. Osborn, April 23, 1942, box 104, radio speech, July 5, 1942, box 1259, RTP; RT to John C. Taylor, June 16, 1944, Martin papers; RT to Mrs. C. A. Dykstra, March 1, 1951, RTP.

39. Relevant studies are James V. Compton, *The Swastika and the Sword: Hitler, the United States, and the Origins of World War II* (Boston, 1967), p. 251; Alton Frye, *Nazi Germany and the American Hemisphere, 1933–1941* (New Haven, 1967), pp. vii, 194.

CHAPTER 17: ADVANCING IN THE SENATE, 1942–1944

1. Richard R. Lingeman, *Don't You Know There's a War On? The American Home Front, 1941–1945* (New York, 1970); Richard Polenberg, *War and Society: The United States, 1941–1945* (Philadelphia, 1972).

2. RT to Aunt Fannie, March 19, June 10, July 1, 1943; Mrs. RT to RT, Aug. 18, 23, 1942, RTP, LC.

3. RT to Aunt Fannie, June 10, 1943, RTP.

4. RT to Melvin Harrison, June 24, 1943, TSHP, Cincinnati; Diary, Mrs. Darrah Wunder, March 11, 1952, Wunder papers (her possession, Cincinnati): Interviews, William H. Taft III, Horace D. Taft, Barbara Taft, Dr. Standhope Bayne-Jones (COHP), p. 25; personal observation (compliments Mrs. David Ginsburg).

5. RT, "The United States at War," *Vital Speeches*, Vol. 8 (Dec. 19, 1941), pp. 169–173, original in box 1258, RTP; RT to Hulbert Taft, Feb. 25, 1942, RTP.

6. RT to Hoover, Jan. 24, 1942, box l–k/135, Hoover papers, Hoover Library, Iowa; RT to Romney Vaughn, Jan. 27, 1942, RT to Luigi Criscuolo, Dec. 27, 1941, boxes 103, 667, RTP; RT to Richard Scandrett, Feb. 4, 1942, Vol. 13, Scandrett papers, Cornell University; RT to Semple, April 27, 1942, box 1350, RTP.

7. New York *Times*, Jan. 27, 29, Feb. 5, 13, April 8, 24, 1942; RT to George Harrison, Feb. 1, RT to Robert Patterson, April 9, Patterson to RT, April 11, RT to Hoover, May 15, 1942, boxes 769, 672, 1179, RTP.

8. New York *Times*, May 3, 6, June 26, 1942; RT to Marrs McLean, Aug. 6, 1942, box 110, RTP. For the sedition trial, New York *Journal American*, Aug. 16, 1942; *CR*, Aug. 10, 1942, pp. 6790–6791; Cincinnati *Post*, Jan. 15, 1943; *New Republic*, Vol. 108 (Jan. 4, 1943), p. 21; Maximilian St. George and Lawrence Dennis, *A Trial on Trial: The Great Sedition Trial of 1944* (1946).

9. Randolph Paul, *Taxation in the United States* (Boston, 1954), p. 280; Joel Seidman, *American Labor from Defense to Reconversion* (Chicago, 1953), pp. 278–281; RT speeches, early 1942, boxes 607, 1259, RTP; New York *Times*, March 8, May 3, July 25, Aug. 12, 17, 1942; RT to Matt Formato, April 11, 1942, Paul Walter papers, Cleveland.

10. RT to William Taft, July 28, 1942, RTP; Morgenthau Diary, Vol. 337, Roosevelt Library, Hyde Park; RT to Hoover, Sept. 1, 1942, box l–k/135, Hoover papers; RT to Hollister, Sept. 15, 1942, Hollister papers, Cincinnati; RT to Roy Finch, Aug. 19, 1942, box 1349, RTP.

11. Paul, pp. 294, 317; New York *Times*, Oct. 22, 1942, p. 22.

12. Harvey C. Mansfield, et al., *A Short History of the OPA* (Washington, 1947), p. 40; Chester Bowles, *Promises to Keep: My Years in Public Life, 1941–1949* (New York, 1971), pp. 30, 107–108, RT to David Ginsburg, April 6, 17, 1942, RT to Leon Henderson, April 9, 15, July 3, Henderson to RT, April 27, 28, box 669, RTP; Henderson to Edgar Rickard, June 11, 1942, box l–k/135, Hoover papers; RT speeches, boxes 543, 607, 1259, RTP.

13. RT speech, Sept. 7, 1942, box 665; speech Sept. 18, 1942, box 263; Mrs. RT to RT, Sept. 14; RT to Jack Kennon, Oct. 1, box 108; RT to Paul

Walter, Oct. 7, box 109; RT to Martha, Sept. 28, 1942, RTP; New York *Times,* Sept. 23, Oct. 1, 3, 1942, all p. 1.

14. Mansfield, passim; Bowles, p. 33.
15. New York *Times,* Feb. 20, 1943, p. 5; Charles C. Brown, "Robert A. Taft: Champion of Public Housing and National Aid to Schools," *Bulletin of the Cincinnati Historical Society,* Vol. 26 (July 1968), pp. 225–253.
16. John Robert Moore, "The Conservative Coalition in the United States Senate, 1942–1945," *Journal of Southern History,* Vol. 32 (Aug. 1967), pp. 368–376; Donald R. McCoy, "Republican Opposition During Wartime, 1941–1945," *Mid-America,* Vol. 49 (July 1967), pp. 174–189; articles on congressional sessions by Floyd Riddick, *American Political Science Review,* 1942–1945.
17. New York *Times,* May 28, June 9, 14, 17, 19, 24, 26–30, July 1–9, Nov. 28, Dec. 5, 16, 17, 24, 1943; *CR,* June 30, 1943, p. 6819; Paul, p. 327; RT to Wilbur Matson, Feb. 11, 1943, Matson papers, Marietta College; RT to Aunt Fannie, July 22, 1943, RTP.
18. New York *Times,* Oct. 13, 21, 1943, pp. 20, 1; RT to J. H. Bankhead, Oct. 25, RT to Aunt Fannie, Oct. 22, RT to Charles N. King, Nov. 9, 1943, box 528, RTP; *CR,* Oct. 14, 1943, p. 8307.
19. Paul, p. 359; Bernard DeVoto, "Easy Chair: G.O.P. Candidates and Policies," *Harper's,* Vol. 189 (June 1944), pp. 44–47.
20. Quote is RT speech, "Sound Financing or Spending in the Postwar Era," Feb. 29, 1944, box 119, RTP; also New York *Times,* Feb. 18, March 28, Sept. 28, 1944; speeches, Jan. 14, 18, Walter papers; RT, "A 1944 Program for Republicans, *Saturday Evening Post,* Vol. 216 (Dec. 11, 1943), p. 17; "Steering Committee Meeting" minutes, May 19, 1944, box 721, RTP; RT to Horace D. Taft, Jan. 1, March 8, May 3, 1944, Horace D. Taft papers (his possession, New Haven); RT to Chester Bowles, June 10, 1944, I. Jack Martin papers, Kensington, Md.; RT to Harold Prescott, July 13, 1944, box 121, RTP.
21. New York *Times,* Jan. 25, 27, Feb. 2–9, 1944; *CR,* Jan. 26, 1944, pp. 710–722; RT to Norman Cousins, Aug. 8, 1944, box 31, RTP. Quote is RT to J. B. Doan, Feb. 24, 1944, box 119, RTP.
22. Jay Hayden, Washington *Times-Herald,* Feb. 7, 1944; Allen Drury, *A Senate Journal, 1943–1945* (New York, 1963), p. 57.
23. *CR,* Feb. 9, 1944, p. 1478, Feb. 11, 1944, p. 1624; New York *Times,* Feb. 10–12, 24, May 6, 26, June 6, 17, 1944.
24. Drury, pp. 10, 30, 155.
25. Ibid., pp. 254, 150, 19; William S. White, *The Taft Story* (New York, 1954), pp. 61, 24–27; Interview, George Aiken; Marriner Eccles, *Beckoning Frontiers: Public and Personal Recollections* (New York, 1951), p. 431; For a particularly unflattering anecdote, which I cannot get fully confirmed, see Sydney Hyman, *The Lives of William Benton* (New York, 1969), p. 271.
26. Interview, Floyd Riddick; Thomas Stokes, New York *World Telegram,* Aug. 2, 1943.
27. Drury, pp. 40, 43, 102, 114; New York *Times,* March 16, 1944, pp. 36, 19, April 22, 1944; Smith to "Senators," April 29, 1944, and miscellaneous papers, George H. E. Smith papers, Yale University.

CHAPTER 18: ALMOST DEFEATED, 1944

1. RT to Monte Appel, Dec. 26, 1941, RT to Marrs McLean, June 23, 1942, boxes 106, 110, RTP, LC; Interview, John Bricker.

2. Harold H. Burton Diary, Nov. 21, 25, box 1, Burton papers, LC; RT to Bert Long, Dec. 4, 1942, box 1260, RTP; Cincinnati *Post*, Dec. 9, 1942; RT to Hulbert Taft, Nov. 27, 1942, Cincinnati Historical Society.

3. RT to James P. Selvage, Nov. 12, RT to Marrs McLean, Nov. 30, 1942, boxes 27, 110, RTP.

4. RT to Ingalls, May 14, RT to Richard Scandrett, June 8, RT to Jack Kennon, July 27, RT to Walter, Nov. 24, boxes 28, 107, 28, 118, RTP.

5. RT to Hollister, March 8, 1944, Hollister papers, Cincinnati; RT to Hollister, April 20, box 1364, RT to Bricker, March 16, April 7, June 10, 1944, boxes 771, 113, 488, RTP; RT to Bricker, Jan. 25, 1944, box 64, Bricker papers, Ohio Historical Society; Bricker to Taft, June 10, 1944, box 488, RTP.

6. RT to Louis Bromfield, Jan. 26, RT to Roger Faherty, April 6, 1944, boxes 108, 113, RTP.

7. RT to Thomas E. Dewey, July 27, 1942, box 107, Dewey to RT, Sept. 16, 1943, RT to Dewey, Sept. 21, 1943, box 115, RTP; Dewey to William Knowland, June 22, 1942, personal files, Thomas E. Dewey papers, University of Rochester.

8. RT to Hulbert Taft, Dec. 18, 1942, Cincinnati Historical Society; RT to Burrell Wright, Sept. 16, 1943, box 105, RT to RT, Jr., May 5, RT to Aunt Fannie, March 8, RT to Hulbert Taft, April 12, RT to Lester Bradshaw, May 30, 1944, box 1212, RTP.

9. Taft headed the platform committee at the convention. See New York *Times*, June 28, 1944, p. 11; Donald Johnson, *The Republican Party and Wendell Willkie* (Urbana, 1960), p. 290; RT letters, box 121, RTP; Arthur Vandenberg to John Foster Dulles, June 14, 1944, Vandenberg papers, Ann Arbor.

10. Dewey to RT, July 14, Aug. 11, RT to Dewey, July 5, 27, 1944, I. Jack Martin papers, Kensington, Md.

11. RT to Colonel Lester Abele, July 18, box 117, RT to Martha, Aug. 16, RT to Alfred M. Landon, Aug. 11, box 121, RT to Bricker, July 5, 1944, box 488, RTP; RT to Horace D. Taft, Aug. 29, 1944, Horace D. Taft papers (his possession, New Haven).

12. RT to Taft, Stettinius, and Hollister, Dec. 31, 1940, Hollister papers, Cincinnati; RT to Vincent Starzinger, Nov. 8, 1943, Starzinger papers (his possession, Des Moines).

13. George H. E. Smith memo re Taft, 1959, Smith papers, Yale University; Interviews, Mrs. I. Jack Martin, Blanche O'Berg.

14. RT to Hollister, March 8, 1944, Hollister papers; RT to Hulbert Taft, March 20, RT to RT, Jr., May 5, to James T. Begg, April 22, 1944, box 114, RTP.

15. Allen Drury, *A Senate Journal, 1943–1945* (New York, 1963), p. 229; RT to Horace, Aug. 29, 1944, Horace D. Taft papers; Cincinnati *Enquirer*, Aug. 18, 1944, p. 10; RT to Robert Beightler, Aug. 22, RT to Martha, Aug. 29, 1944, RTP.

16. Cincinnati *Enquirer,* July 21, 1944, p. 5; Akron *Beacon-Journal,* Oct. 29, 1944, p. 2; Pickrel campaign literature, Paul Walter papers, Cleveland; Pickrel speech, Oct. 21, 1944, box 1262, RTP; Cleveland *Plain Dealer,* Oct. 22, 1944, p. 2.
17. Akron *Beacon-Journal,* Oct. 27, p. 13; Columbus *Evening Dispatch,* Oct. 22, p. 3; Cincinnati *Enquirer,* Oct. 28, 1944, p. 2; Cleveland *Plain Dealer,* Oct. 28, 1944, p. 1.
18. "Dunderhead," RTP.
19. Box 258, RTP; also Cincinnati Historical Society. Opponents also circulated an eight-page pornographic comic that showed Taft's incredible sexual prowess delivering him such affection among strikers' wives that they pressed their husbands to return to work. (Institute for Sex Research, Indiana University.)
20. Columbus *Evening Dispatch,* Oct. 7, 1944, p. 1; Martha speech notes, RTP.
21. RT speech, Oct. 21, 1944, box 1262, RTP; Cleveland *Plain Dealer,* Oct. 22, 1944, p. 2; Cincinnati *Times-Star,* Oct. 31, 1944; Dayton *Journal,* Nov. 5, 1944, p. 12.
22. RT to Martha, Sept. 8, 1944, RTP.
23. Mullaney to author, April 24, 1971.
24. RT "Statement to Negro Press of Ohio," April 14, 1944, Walter papers; press release to Ohio editors, Sept. 1944, box 1262, RTP; speeches, ibid.
25. RT speech, Cleveland, Oct. 21, 1944, box 117, RTP.
26. RT speeches, Sept. 14, Oct. 4, Oct. 21, 1944, box 117, RTP; RT, "The Republican Platform, 1944," box 121, RTP; Dewey quoted in James MacGregor Burns, *Roosevelt: Soldier of Freedom* (New York, 1970), p. 529.
27. Cincinnati *Enquirer,* Nov. 6, 1944, p. 15; Akron *Beacon-Journal,* Nov. 12, 1944, p. 3; Interview, Horace D. Taft.
28. Secretary of State's office, Ohio, *Election Statistics for 1944,* p. 200; *Statistics of the Presidential and Congressional Election of Nov. 7, 1944* (William Graf, compiler) (D.C., 1945); Columbus *Evening Dispatch,* Akron *Beacon-Journal,* Nov. 8–10, 1944.
29. Cincinnati *Enquirer,* Nov. 9, 12, 19; Akron *Beacon-Journal,* Nov. 9, 1944, p. 13; Interviews, Paul Walter, Frank Lausche; New York *Post,* March 26, 1952.
30. U. S. Congress, Senate, Hearings Before the Subcommittee on Privileges and Elections of the Committee on Rules and Administration, Eighty-second Congress, First and Second Sessions, *Investigation into the 1950 Senatorial Campaign* (Washington, 1952), original, box 282, RTP; RT to Ingalls, Nov. 10, 1944, RT to George Eyrich, March 7, 1945, box 31, Paul Walter to Carl D. Sheppard, Feb. 21, 1945, RTP.
31. RT to Ingalls, Nov. 10, RT to Aunt Fannie, Nov. 17, RT to J. R. Neuger, Nov. 11, 1944, box 646, RTP.
32. Robert Sherwood, *Roosevelt and Hopkins: An Intimate History* (New York, 1948), p. 828.
33. RT to Cruikshank, June 26, 1937, box 1, RTP; "They Fought for Our Cause: The Influential Taft Family and their Attitude to Jewry," as told by Rabbi El. Silver, ed. by Z. H. Wachsman, RTP; RT speech, March 21, 1944, box 1262, RTP. Cruikshank (letter to author, July 1971) argued

that Taft School "never limited Jewish boys to a specific number. However, the school did feel that — in general terms — it should not have 'too
many Jewish boys.' On the other hand it also felt that it shouldn't have
too many Christian Scientists or too many N.Y. City — or Waterbury boys.
If Taft had a quota for Jews in the thirties it also had a quota for all other
categories, too."

34. Silver memoirs, unpublished, p. 6, Zionist archives, Cleveland; Silver to
RT, June 26, RT to Silver, Oct. 12, 1944, Zionist archives; RT to Henry
Stimson, Sept. 12, 1944, Martin papers; Paul Walter memorandum to au-
thor, Sept. 10, 1970; Selig Adler to author, July 9, 1971; Richard P. Stevens,
American Zionism and American Foreign Policy, 1942–1947 (New York,
1962), passim; Rabbis Leon Feuer and Daniel Jeremy Silver to author,
Dec. 23, 1970, Jan. 13, 1971, Dec. 29, 1970.

35. Taft speeches, box 1262, RTP; New York *Times,* Feb. 2, March 22, 1944.

36. Cleveland *Plain Dealer,* Oct. 23, 1944, p. 12; RT to Silver, Oct. 23, 1944,
and RT release, late Oct. 1944, Zionist archives; Walter (COHP), p. 13.

37. RT to Walter, Nov. 21, 1944, Walter papers; Edwin Lahey (COHP), p. 31.

38. RT to Horace D. Taft, Nov. 13, 1944, Horace D. Taft papers; RT to
Ingalls, Nov. 10, 1944, RTP.

39. RT to Ingalls, Dec. 26, 1944, RTP; RT to Hollister, Dec. 8, 1944, Hollister
papers, Cincinnati; RT to Jack Kennon, Feb. 26, 1945, box 31, RTP.

CHAPTER 19: PLANNING FOR THE POSTWAR WORLD

1. Herbert Hoover to RT, Dec. 8, 1941, RT to Hoover, Jan. 3, 1942, box
l–k/135, Hoover papers, Iowa; RT to Hulbert Taft, Jan. 22, 1942, RTP,
LC.

2. To Hulbert Taft, April 27, 1942, box 695, RTP. Letters re Willkie and
GOP are RT to Wilbur Matson, Nov. 27, 1941, Matson papers, Marietta
College, and boxes 27, 103, RTP. Also Arthur Vandenberg, Jr., ed., *The
Private Papers of Senator Vandenberg* (Boston, 1952), p. 30; and Donald
Johnson, *Wendell Willkie and the Republican Party* (Urbana, 1960), pp.
204–208.

3. RT to Marrs McLean, June 23, 1942, box 110, RTP. Letters critical of the
administration in early 1942 are RT to Arthur Krock, Feb. 2, 1942, Krock
papers, Princeton University, RT to Mrs. Lloyd Bowers, Feb. 6, RT to
Charles Seymour, April 9, RT to Stanley Pearce, May 7, 1942, boxes 27,
1329, 103, RTP.

4. RT radio speech, July 5, 1942, box 1259, RT to M. S. Sherman, May 6,
box 103, RT to Carl Lohmann, June 16, box 1329, RT to Hoover, July
14, 1942, box 1179, RTP.

5. New York *Times,* March 22, 1943, p. 16; RT speech, Commonwealth Club,
March 26, 1943, and "Statement on the Ball Resolution," March 23, 1943,
boxes 1261, 555, RTP. Secondary sources are Robert Divine, *Second
Chance; The Triumph of Internationalism in America During World
War II* (New York, 1967), p. 109; C. David Tompkins, *Senator Arthur
H. Vandenberg: The Evolution of a Modern Republican, 1884–1945* (East
Lansing, 1970), p. 211. Thinking remarkably similar to Taft's is Herbert

Hoover and Hugh Gibson, *The Problems of Lasting Peace* (New York, 1942).

6. RT radio speeches, April 7, 19, box 1261, RTP.

7. New York *Times,* May 26, 1943, p. 20; RT, Grove City speech, May 22, 1943, box 546, RT to Roger Faherty, June 10, 1943, box 105, RTP.

8. RT speech, American Bar Association, Aug. 26, 1943, box 207, RT to Mrs. Agnes Scandrett, April 14, 1943, box 104, RTP.

9. New York *Herald Tribune,* Sept. 6, 1943, p. 1; RT to Arthur Krock, Sept. 16, 1943, box 115, RTP; Johnson, p. 245; Vandenberg, pp. 53–54, 62–65; Divine, p. 130.

10. New York *Times,* Nov. 6, 1943, p. 1; *CR,* Nov. 4, 1943, pp. 9095–9102; RT radio speech, Nov. 16, 1943, box 1261, RT to Richard Scandrett, Oct. 11, 1943, box 107, RTP; Divine, p. 152.

11. Hoover and Gibson; RT to Mrs. Agnes Scandrett, April 14, 1943, box 104, RTP.

12. Robert Divine, *Roosevelt and World War II* (Baltimore, 1969), pp. 63–64; RT to Mrs. Helen Bragdon, April 11, 1944, RTP.

13. The following section relies heavily on Richard N. Gardner, *Sterling-Dollar Diplomacy: Anglo–American Collaboration in the Reconstruction of Multilateral Trade* (New York, 1956); John Morton Blum, ed., *From the Morgenthau Diaries: Years of War, 1941–1945* (Boston, 1967); and David Baldwin, *Economic Development and American Foreign Policy, 1943–1962* (Chicago, 1966).

14. RT speeches, March 20, April 9, 1945, boxes 1264, 490, RTP; RT, *Vital Speeches,* Vol. 11 (Aug. 1, 1945), pp. 643–648, and ibid., Vol. 12 (June 1, 1946), pp. 500–508; RT to John S. Plummer, April 26, 1945, I. Jack Martin papers, Kensington, Md.; RT to Tom L. Gibson, Sept. 19, 1945, RTP; U.S. Congress, Senate, Banking and Currency Committee, *Bretton Woods Trade Agreements Act,* Seventy-ninth Congress, First Session; *CR,* July 12, 19, 20, pp. 7439–7443, 7771–7774, 7828.

15. New York *Times,* July 12, 1944, p. 1; RT to Flora R. Harlow, Aug. 3, 1945. Martin papers; RT to Roger Faherty, Aug. 2, 1945, box 1, Faherty papers, State Historical Society of Wisconsin; RT to Horace D. Taft, July 30, 1945, Horace D. Taft papers (his possession, New Haven); Hearings, *Bretton Woods,* p. 98.

16. Blum, p. 429.

17. RT to Thomas E. Dewey, Feb. 26, 1945, box 31, RT speech, May 5, box 546, April 22, 1945, box 1264, "Why the U.S. Should Join a League of Nations" (release, n.d. early 1945), box 546, "Notes on the Dumbarton Oaks Proposals," (n.d., spring 1945), box 546, RTP; New York *Times,* May 21, 1945, p. 5.

18. *CR,* July 28, 1945, p. 8152; RT to Hulbert Taft, Aug. 2, RT to Roger Ferger, Aug. 7, 1945, box 31, RTP; RT to Roscoe McCullough, Aug. 6, 1945, Martin papers; RT speech, July 28, 1945, RTP.

19. New York *Times,* Nov. 30, 1945; *CR,* Dec. 4, 1945, pp. 11401–11409; RT to Edwin Borchard, Nov. 13, 1945, box 748, RT to Dick Nielsen, Jan. 30, 1946, box 784, RT to K. A. Frast, May 5, 1952, box 294, RTP; Divine, *Second Chance,* p. 313.

20. RT speech, Cleveland, May 6, 1944, box 546 (frequently repeated, 1945–

1953), RTP; RT to John C. Taylor, June 16, 1944, Martin papers; RT to Horace D. Taft, Feb. 7, 1945, Horace D. Taft papers.

21. For critiques of RT's ideas, John Paul Armstrong, "Senator Taft and American Foreign Policy: The Period of Opposition," doctoral thesis, Chicago, 1953, pp. 227, 240; "Consecrated Tory — Robert A. Taft," *New Republic,* Vol. 126 (March 31, 1952), p. 11. A thoughtful book about ideas prior to 1920 is Warren Kuehl, *Seeking World Order: The United States and International Organization to 1920* (Nashville, 1969), pp. 190–192, 301, 340. Roland N. Stromberg, *Collective Security and American Foreign Policy: From the League of Nations to NATO* (New York, 1963), esp. pp. 230–247, argues very persuasively for a balance of power approach.

CHAPTER 20: THE PARTISAN DIMENSION, 1945–1946

1. For RT's very hostile view of FDR in late 1944 and early 1945, RT to Edwin Borchard, Dec. 23, RT to H. J. Hamlin, Dec. 29, 1944, I. Jack Martin papers, Kensington, Md.; RT to Alta Gilbert, Jan. 15, 1945, box 31, RTP, LC. For efforts to goad the GOP to partisan efforts, RT to Thomas E. Dewey, Dec. 13, box 31, RT to Harrison Spangler, Dec. 28, 1944, box 31, RT to Joseph Pew, Jan. 2, box 1321, RT to James Selvage, Jan. 11, box 31, RT to Dewey, Jan. 30, 1945, box 722, RTP; RT to Herbert Hoover, Dec. 14, 1944, box l–k/136, Hoover papers, Hoover Library, Iowa; New York *Times,* Feb. 2, 6, March 29, 1945; *CR,* March 7, p. 1833, March 8, pp. 1918–1920, March 29, pp. 2956–2957. For RT complaints re Army policy, Martha to RT, Jr., March 4, and RT to George Toe Water, March 20, 1945, box 702, RTP.

2. RT to L'Engle Hartridge, April 17, 1945, RTP; Allen Drury, *A Senate Journal, 1943–1945* (New York, 1963), pp. 417–418. RT elaborated on policy toward Japan in, RT to George R. Landon, May 23, to Griscom Morgan, June 6, 1945, Martin papers.

3. RT to Henry E. T. Herman, May 12, RT to Lunsford Yandell, April 26, 1945, Martin papers; RT to R. I. Ingalls, May 12, 1945, RTP; New York *Times,* April 19, May 11, 18, 1945; Truman, *Memoirs, Year of Decision,* Vol. 1 (New York, 1955), pp. 57–58.

4. On price control, RT to Bertha Weber, April 18, 1945, Martin papers; RT to Hoover, May 23, box 31, RT to Charles S. Davis, June 26, 1945, box 644, RTP; RT speech, May 10, 1945, box 1264, RTP; New York *Times,* May 30, June 5, 7, 9, 12, 1945; *CR,* June 11, 1945, pp. 5885–5886. Re Truman, RT to Henry W. Taft, May 25, 1945, RTP.

5. RT to William F. Maag, Jr., Aug. 8, box 31, RT to Hulbert Taft, June 2, 1945, RTP; RT to George E. Stringfellow, June 21, 1945, Martin papers; Henry F. Pringle, *The Life and Times of William Howard Taft,* Vol. 1 (New York, 1939), p. 421.

6. He was vigorous in demanding a tough line regarding lend-lease to the Soviet Union. See New York *Times,* May 21, 1945, p. 6.

7. RT to A. D. Seawright, Sept. 26, to Nadine Stewart, Sept. 1, 1945, Martin papers; to David Ingalls, Aug. 6, 1945, RTP.

8. RT speech, Aug. 5, box 1265, Oct. 19, 1945, box 528, RTP; to J. S. Halsted, Oct. 25, to Henry Stoner, Oct. 29, 1945, Martin papers; New York

Times, Oct. 28, Dec. 20, 1945, pp. 26, 1; Randolph Paul, *Taxation in the United States* (Boston, 1954), p. 420.

9. New York *Times,* Sept. 8, 20, 28, 29, 1945; Stephen Kemp Bailey, *Congress Makes a Law: The Story Behind the Employment Act of 1946* (New York, 1950); RT to James S. Kemper, Aug. 4, box 31, RT to Martha, Sept. 9, 13, 1945, RTP. RT re Truman is RT to Horace D. Taft, Jan. 7, 1946, Horace D. Taft papers (his possession, New Haven); and RT to Louis E. Kline, Nov. 1, 1945, box 31, RTP.

10. RT to Charles D. Hilles, May 21, 1945, box 696, RT to Joe Martin, May 4, 1946, box 537, RTP; RT to Harry E. Davis, March 8, 1946, Martin papers; New York *Times,* Feb. 10, 1946, p. 1; *CR,* Feb. 9, 1946, p. 1219.

11. RT also spent considerable time, early 1946, trying to cut a proposed loan to Great Britain. See RT to Irvin Westheimer, Sept. 6, RT to W. J. Galvin, Dec. 26, 1945, Martin papers; RT to Dr. H. H. Beneke, Feb. 20, 1946, box 776, RT speech, April 24, 1946, box 548, RTP; New York *Times,* March 14, April 11, 25, May 10, 11, 1946.

12. New York *Times,* Feb. 8, March 21, April 10, May 26, 1946; RT speeches, May 25, June 8, 1946, boxes 613, 1266, RTP; Harry A. Millis and Emily Clark Brown, *From the Wagner Act to Taft-Hartley: A Study of National Labor Policy and Labor Relations* (Chicago, 1950), p. 360.

13. New York *Times,* May 25, 26, 29, June 1, 1946, all p. 1; *CR,* May 25, 1946, p. 5714; RT speech, May 31, 1946, box 1266, RTP.

14. RT speech, June 21, 1946, box 1266, RTP; RT to R. I. Ingalls, June 12, 1946, Martin papers; RT to Hulbert Taft, May 30, 1946, RTP.

15. Basic sources are Harvey C. Mansfield et al., *A Short History of OPA* (Washington, 1947), p. 99; Chester Bowles, *Promises to Keep: My Years in Public Life, 1941–1969* (New York, 1971), pp. 51, 108, 127; Lester V. Chandler, *Inflation in the United States, 1940–1948* (New York, 1951), pp. 3, 386; Cabell Phillips, *The Truman Presidency: The History of a Triumphant Succession* (New York, 1966), p. 109. Also RT speech, Dec. 6, 1945, box 1265, RTP.

16. For RT-Bowles, New York *Times,* Dec. 7, 1945, April 13, 17, 23, 1946; RT to C. C. Dibert, March 9, RT to T. A. Kendall, July 2, 1946, Martin papers.

17. New York *Times,* June 13, 14, 26, 28, 29, 30, July 5, 6, 10–13, 20–27, 1947; *CR,* June 27, 1946, p. 7805; RT speeches, July 1, 26, 1946, boxes 668, 1266, RTP; Herbert Stein, *The Fiscal Revolution in America* (Chicago, 1969), p. 217; Allen J. Matusow, *Farm Policies and Politics in the Truman Years* (Cambridge, 1967), p. 53.

18. Some of RT's letters are to E. J. Falkenstein, July 3, to Merrill Atkinson, July 30, 1946, both box 782, to H. M. Baldridge, July 30, 1946, RTP; to Quentin Reynolds, Aug. 3, to Clarence R. Huston, Aug. 6, 1946, Martin papers.

19. RT to Dorothy Rowe, Aug. 2, 1946, Rowe papers (her possession, Cincinnati).

20. *U. S. News & World Report,* May 17, 1946; *Newsweek,* July 15, 1946; *Time,* June 10, 1946; Alsops, Washington *Post,* March 11, 1946, p. 9; Leverett Saltonstall to author, Oct. 6, 1969.

21. RT to Dewey, n.d. (c. Sept. 15, 1946), personal correspondence, Thomas

Dewey papers, University of Rochester; New York *Times,* Sept. 12, 21, Oct. 12, 17, 21, 24, 30, 31, Nov. 4, 1946; RT speeches, box 1267, RTP.
22. Martha to Darrah Wunder, Jan. 2, 1947, Wunder papers (her possession, Cincinnati).
23. *Time,* March 5, 1935, pp. 17–18.

CHAPTER 21: THE TAFT PHILOSOPHY

1. Richard O. Davies, *Housing Reform During the Truman Administration* (Columbia, Mo., 1966); Charles C. Brown, "Robert A. Taft, Champion of Public Housing and National Aid to Schools," *Bulletin of the Cincinnati Historical Society,* Vol. 26 (July 1968), pp. 225–253; letters to President Truman, 1946, boxes 294–296, OF-63, Truman papers, Truman Library, Independence, Mo.
2. Interview, Stanley Rowe (COHP), p. 51; Cincinnati *Post,* Jan. 31, 1946, p. 20; Brown article; RT to Mayor James Stewart, Nov. 25, 1938, box 22, RTP, LC.
3. RT to Robert Moses, Jan. 23, box 594, RT to Ernest J. Bohn, April 19, 1945, box 594, RT speech, Jan. 20, 1945, box 1264, RTP; Brown article; Davies, pp. 25–27; Davies, " 'Mr. Republican' Turns 'Socialist': Robert A. Taft and Public Housing," *Ohio History,* Vol. 73 (Summer 1964), pp. 135–143.
4. RT, subcommittee report, Aug. 1, 1945, box 1265, RTP; Brown article, p. 238.
5. Robert Wagner to RT, July 23, 30, 31, RT to Wagner, July 31, 1945, box 594, RTP; William H. Davis (COHP), pp. 170–171; RT to Robert Moses, June 21, 1945, I. Jack Martin papers, Kensington, Md.
6. Davies, *Housing Reform,* p. 139; J. Joseph Huthmacher, *Senator Robert F. Wagner and the Rise of Urban Liberalism* (New York, 1968), p. 300; New York *Times,* Aug. 2, 1945, p. 21; RT to Rowe, Aug. 4, 1945, RTP.
7. Wagner to Taft, Sept. 29, Oct. 9, 15, 1945, box 595, RTP; New York *Times,* Nov. 15, 1945, p. 38.
8. RT speech to home-builders, Dec. 14, 1945, box 582, RTP.
9. Davies article; Huthmacher, pp. 322–323; "What They Say About the W-E-T Bill," *Architectural Record,* Vol. 100 (Sept. 1946), p. 14.
10. Lee F. Johnson, "How They Licked the TEW Bill," *Survey Graphic,* Vol. 38 (Nov. 1948), pp. 445–449; Brown article; Davies, *Housing Reform.*
11. Robert Bendiner, "Retrogression in Ohio," *The Nation,* Vol. 163 (Nov. 2, 1946), pp. 493–494; Davies, *Housing Reform,* p. 49.
12. RT to Walter L. Tarr, Aug. 25, 1944, box 528, RTP; to Kenneth Ivins, Jan. 23, 1945, Martin papers.
13. New York *Times,* Feb. 9, 27, 1945; RT to A. Graves Williams, Aug. 8, 1945, Martin papers; Brown article.
14. RT to Most Rev. Edward F. Hoban, Nov. 5, 1945, to editor of *Catholic Telegraph-Register,* Jan. 30, 1946, both box 232, RTP.
15. RT speech, March 27, 1946, box 1266, RTP; New York *Times,* May 18, 1946, p. 32.
16. For RT health plan, see RT speeches, Feb. 11, April 18, 1947, May 3, 1946, boxes 1268, 1266, RTP; Cincinnati *Enquirer,* April 3, 1946, p. 1;

Cleveland *Plain Dealer*, May 3, 1946, p. 1; *Time*, April 15, 1946, p. 20; "Taft as a Liberal," *New Republic*, Vol. 114 (May 27, 1946), p. 751; Michael M. Davies, "You Can Get It If You Go for It," *Survey Graphic*, Vol. 35 (Sept. 1946), pp. 317–318.

17. Quoted in Joseph and Stewart Alsop, "Taft and Vandenberg," *Life*, Vol. 21 (Oct. 7, 1946), p. 103.

18. Fletcher Knebel, Des Moines *Register*, Aug. 1, 1953; Gordon Harrison, *The Road to the Right: The Tradition and Hope of American Conservatism* (New York, 1954), p. 297; Interview, L. Richard Guylay; George Smith comment, in Frank McNaughton papers, Truman Library.

19. Richard Rovere, "Taft: Is This the Best We've Got?" *Harper's*, Vol. 196 (April 1948), pp. 289–299; Smith memo re RT, 1959, Smith papers, Yale University; Rovere, *Affairs of State: The Eisenhower Years* (New York, 1956), pp. 101–111; Stewart Alsop, Toledo *Blade*, May 20, 1950; Interviews, Thomas Shroyer, Joseph C. Green.

20. Schlesinger, "His Eyes Have Seen the Glory," *Collier's*, Vol. 119 (Feb. 22, 1947), p. 12; Felix Morley, "The Case for Taft," *Life*, Vol. 24 (Feb. 9, 1948), pp. 50–66; Rovere, "Taft"; Interview, Barbara Taft.

21. Dallas speech, Feb. 14, 1946, reprinted in *CR*, pp. A1051–1052; also speeches, New York, May 16, 1946, Columbus, Sept. 11, 1946, boxes 1266, 1267, RTP.

22. "The Heritage of the English-Speaking Peoples and Their Responsibility," Oct. 5, 1946, box 210, RTP; New York *Times*, Oct. 6, 1946, p. 1.

23. Interview, Barbara Taft; Martha, on "Meet the Press," Feb. 27, 1948, transcript in RTP.

24. New York *Times*, Oct. 6–11, 1946; John F. Kennedy, *Profiles in Courage* (New York, 1955), p. 221; *CIO News*, Oct. 14, 1946, box 277, RTP.

25. New York *Times*, Oct. 8, 10, 1946; William J. Bosch, *Judgment on Nuremberg: American Attitudes Toward the Major German War-Crime Trials* (Chapel Hill, 1970), pp. 30–31, 74, 97.

26. RT to Richard Scandrett, Nov. 4, 1946, box 784, Jack Martin to Taft, Oct. 17, 1946, box 561, RTP.

27. RT to Westbrook Pegler, Oct. 14, 1946, box 780, RTP; *CR*, 1946, pp. A1051–1052.

28. Rovere, "Taft"; Bosch, p. 7; Kennedy, pp. 215–224.

29. RT to LaMotte T. Cohu, Oct. 30, 1945, box 31, RTP; Rovere, *Affairs of State*, p. 111; William S. White, "Almost Equal to Being President," *New York Times Magazine*, Jan. 14, 1951, p. 10; RT notation, 1951, box 972, RTP. In 1948 he wrote Walter Trohan, a Chicago *Tribune* reporter, "I hear you got the Colonel off safely to Europe, where I trust he will not start a war with the British." (July 1, 1948, Trohan papers, Hoover Library, Iowa).

30. Hewes, *Decentralize for Liberty* (New York, 1945); RT to Hewes, Feb. 28, 1945, RT speech, May 1, 1950, box 1278, RTP; Duncan Norton-Taylor, "Robert Taft's Congress," *Fortune*, Vol. 48 (August 1953), pp. 136–138.

31. Among the many attempts to define "conservatism," are Herbert McCloskey, "Conservatism and Personality," *American Political Science Review*, Vol. 52 (March 1958), pp. 27–45; Samuel P. Huntington, "Conservatism as an Ideology," ibid., Vol. 51 (June 1957), pp. 454–473; Ronald Lora,

"Twentieth Century Conservatives and their Critique of Mass Society," unpublished manuscript, 1971; Russell Kirk, *The Conservative Mind from Burke to Santayana* (Chicago, 1953); and Peter Vierick, *Conservatism: From John Adams to Churchill* (New York, 1956).

32. RT to Richard S. Wilcox, Dec. 27, 1952, box 404, RTP.
33. RT to Dr. L. H. Foster, March 18, 1947, Martin papers.
34. Helen Manning to author, Oct. 5, 1971; Norton-Taylor, p. 145.
35. RT, "My Political Credo," pamphlet, 1948, RTP; Russell Kirk and James McClellan, *The Political Principles of Robert A. Taft* (New York, 1967), p. 67.
36. RT speech, "The Future of the Republican Party," Jan. 28, 1949, box 275, RTP; RT, "No Substitute for Freedom," *Collier's,* Vol. 119 (Feb. 1, 1947), p. 13.
37. RT to Ben S. McGiveran, June 20, 1951, Martin papers.
38. Critiques of Taft are Fred Rodell, "Taft — Model T Candidate," '47 — *The Magazine of the Year,* Vol. 1 (Nov. 1947), pp. 2–13; Henry Steele Commager, *Reporter,* July 22, 1952, pp. 11–13. More favorable are William S. White, *The Taft Story* (New York, 1954), and Frank A. Burd, "Robert A. Taft and the American Understanding of Politics," doctoral thesis, Chicago, 1969.

CHAPTER 22: THE QUALITIES OF LEADERSHIP, 1947

1. New York *Times,* Jan. 4, 1947; Richard E. Neustadt, "Congress and the Fair Deal; A Legislative Balance Sheet," *Public Policy,* Vol. 5 (1954), pp. 349–382; Susan M. Hartmann, "President Truman and the 80th Congress," doctoral thesis, Missouri, 1966.
2. "Old Guard Supreme," *New Republic,* Vol. 116 (Jan. 13, 1947), p. 116.
3. Edward B. Lockett, "Big Two on Capitol Hill," *New York Times Magazine,* June 1, 1947, p. 9; "Bob Taft — Workhorse of the Senate," *Chicago Tribune,* June 1, 1947; Frank McNaughton report, Jan. 9, 1947, McNaughton papers, Truman Library, Independence, Mo. In 1948 Taft finally bought a new car — a Plymouth. (RT to B. E. Hutchinson, April 14, 1948, RTP, LC.)
4. New York *Times,* Jan. 24, 25, 1947, p. 1; RT to John E. Jackson, Feb. 19, 1947, I. Jack Martin papers, Kensington, Md.; Randall Ripley, *Power in the Senate* (New York, 1969), p. 5; McNaughton report, Jan. 9, 1947, McNaughton papers; TRB, *New Republic,* Vol. 116 (May 3, 1947), p. 11.
5. RT to Mrs. Stanley Rowe, Dec. 29, 1946, Rowe papers (her possession, Cincinnati).
6. Hugh Butler to RT, Nov. 16, 1946, box 502, RTP; New York *Times,* Dec. 24, 29, 31, 1946.
7. RT to George Aiken, Nov. 19, 1946, box 501, RTP; Interview, Hollister; New York *Times,* Nov. 25, 1946, p. 4; RT to Alfred M. Landon, May 17, 1947, box 792, RTP.
8. New York *Times,* Nov. 15, 16, 19, 21, 23, 1946, follow RT's negotiations. Also RT to Republican senators, Nov. 19, 1946, box 1267, and speech on GOP program, Jan. 9, 1947, box 1268, RTP.

9. Frank McNaughton report, April 14, 1947, McNaughton papers; *Time,* March 17, 1947, p. 23; *New Republic,* Vol. 116 (March 17, 1947), p. 10.

10. McNaughton report, Jan. 9, 1947, McNaughton papers.

11. Vandenberg to RT, April 23, RT to Vandenberg, Oct. 20, Vandenberg to RT, Oct. 29, 1946, boxes 780, 778, RTP.

12. Arthur Vandenberg, Jr., *The Private Papers of Senator Vandenberg* (Boston, 1952), pp. 93, 319; H. Alexander Smith (COHP), pp. 105–106, 127, 138; RT to Vandenberg, Oct. 6, 1947, box 649, RTP; New York *Times,* Feb. 12, 1947, p. 22; H. Bradford Westerfield, *Foreign Policy and Party Politics: Pearl Harbor to Korea* (New Haven, 1955); McNaughton report, Feb. 15, 1947, McNaughton papers.

13. Martha to RT, Jr., July 29, 1945, RTP.

14. Interview, Frederick Berquist; Blanche O'Berg to author, June 24, 1971.

15. James Lee Loomis to author, Sept. 1969.

16. Interview, Barbara Taft; William S. White, *The Taft Story* (New York, 1954), p. 11.

17. White, pp. 62, 201–202; McNaughton report, Feb. 15, 1947, McNaughton papers.

18. Mrs. Harold Stevens (sic) to Pauline Isaacson, Feb. 22, 1956, cited in Isaacson, "Robert Alphonso Taft: An Assessment of a Persuader," doctoral thesis, Minnesota, 1956, pp. 461–462; White, p. 26.

19. Wilmarth S. Lewis, *One Man's Education* (New York, 1967), p. 322; Charles S. Dickey to author, Sept. 24, 1969.

20. "The Republican Honeymoon Is Over," *Fortune,* Vol. 35 (April 1947), p. 77; Helen Manning to author, May 30, 1968; Interviews, William H. Taft III, Horace D. Taft. In late 1945 RT alarmed several Yale Corporation members by trying to block the appointment to the law school faculty of Harold Lasswell, a renowned political scientist, and Thomas I. Emerson, a lawyer who had served the NLRB and the OPA. For this issue, see memos and opinions, box 1331, RTP; Yale Corporation minutes, Nov. 8, 1945, Jan. 12, 1946; James Loomis to author, Sept. 1969; and Henry Knox Sherrill to author, Oct. 4, 1969.

21. RT speeches, Feb. 22, April 2, 1947, box 1268, RTP; New York *Times,* April 2, 3, 4, 10, 1947; *Time,* April 14, 1947, p. 23; RT to Robert F. Goldman, April 9, 1947, box 787, Helen Manning memo to RT, Feb. 17, 1947, RTP; Interview, Lewis Strauss; Lilienthal, *The Journals of David E. Lilienthal: The Atomic Energy Years, 1945–1950* (New York, (1964), p. 150. Quote is in "The Honeymoon Is Over," *Fortune,* p. 77.

22. L. Richard Guylay (COHP), p. 44; *Time,* Jan. 20, 1947, p. 26; Ishbel Ross, *An American Family: The Tafts, 1678 to 1964* (Cleveland, 1964), pp. 378–382; Interview, Horace D. Taft; William S. White, "How to Win Influence, If Not Friends," *New York Times Magazine,* May 1, 1949, p. 10.

23. Interview, Horace D. Taft; RT to Andrew McIntosh, Jan. 16, 1950, RTP.

24. Miscellaneous letters, Stanley and Dorothy Rowe papers; and Gordon Grayson papers, Washington, D.C.; Ross, pp. 378–379; White, *Taft Story,* p. 33; Isaacson, pp. 468–489.

25. Dr. Charles M. Barrett to author, Feb. 22, 1972; Reston, New York *Times,* Nov. 14, 1950; Richard Rovere, *Affairs of State: The Eisenhower Years* (New York, 1956), pp. 150–151; White, *Taft Story;* Lahey (COHP), p. 129.

Also John F. Kennedy, *Profiles in Courage* (New York, 1955), p. 214. Taft, Kennedy said, had a "surprising and unusual personal charm, and a disarming simplicity of manner."

26. White, *Taft Story*, p. 11; Arthur Schlesinger, Jr., "His Eyes Have Seen the Glory," *Collier's*, Vol. 119 (Feb. 22, 1947), p. 12; Darrah Wunder, "My Most Unforgettable Character," *Reader's Digest*, Vol. 80 (June 1962), pp. 83–88; Duncan Norton-Taylor, "Robert Taft's Congress," *Fortune*, Vol. 48 (August 1953), pp. 136–138; Interviews, Barbara Taft, Darrah Wunder, Muriel Kirk; L. Randolph Mason to author, Sept. 23, 1969.

27. Interview, Fred E. Berquist; Rovere, "Taft: Is This the Best We've Got?" *Harper's*, Vol. 196 (April 1948), pp. 289–299; George Smith memo re Taft, 1959, Smith papers, Yale University.

28. Interviews, Berquist, Paul Walter; White, *Taft Story*, pp. 200–201.

29. Miscellaneous memos re Minority Committee payroll, July 1951 and April 30, 1952, Smith papers; William L. Neumann to author, June 3, 1971.

30. Frank McNaughton report, July 25, 1947, McNaughton papers; Interview, Floyd Riddick; William S. White, *The Citadel: The Story of the United States Senate* (New York, 1956), p. 105.

31. Roscoe Drummond, *Christian Science Monitor*, Aug. 3, 1953; Lippmann quote in Malcolm Moos, *The Republicans: A History of Their Party* (New York, 1956), p. 430.

32. RT voting record, *New Republic*, Vol. 119 (Sept. 27, 1948), pp. 12–13; *Congressional Quarterly Almanac*, 1952, p. 67; RT voting records, RTP; Donald R. Matthews, *United States Senators and Their World* (Chapel Hill, 1960), p. 130; "Truman vs. Taft," *Congressional Quarterly Almanac*, Vol. 7 (1951), pp. 780–793.

33. Horace D. Taft (COHP), p. 78; Horace D. Taft to author, Jan. 25, 1971.

CHAPTER 23: TAFT-HARTLEY

1. New York *Times*, June 29, 1947, pp. 33, 46; *Life*, Feb. 9, 1948, p. 58; Interview, Lloyd Taft; Stephen Hess, *America's Political Dynasties from Adams to Kennedy* (Garden City, 1966), p. 328.

2. A key source for this entire chapter is Harry A. Millis and Emily Clark Brown, *From the Wagner Act to Taft-Hartley: A Study of National Labor Policy and Labor Relations* (Chicago, 1950). For this paragraph, see pp. 237, 260, 301, 311, 363. Also Fred Witney, *Government and Collective Bargaining* (Philadelphia, 1951), pp. 257–271; J. Joseph Huthmacher, *Senator Robert F. Wagner and the Rise of Urban Liberalism* (New York, 1968), p. 328; and Gerard D. Reilly, "The Legislative History of the Taft-Hartley Act," *George Washington Law Review*, Vol. 29 (Dec. 1960), pp. 285–300.

3. R. Alton Lee, *Truman and Taft-Hartley: A Question of Mandate* (Lexington, 1966), p. 53; Fred Hartley, Jr., *Our New National Labor Policy* (New York, 1948), pp. 51–52; New York *Times*, Feb. 13, April 18, 1947, both p. 1; Millis and Brown, p. 365; Interview, Charles A. Halleck.

4. RT to Bruce Kirk, Jan. 21, 1952, box 1010, RTP, LC; H. Alexander Smith

to Everett L. Crawford, Jan. 28, 1947, box 130, Smith papers, Princeton University.

5. Alexander Smith to RT, April 22, 1947, box 130, Smith papers.

6. RT to Prescott Cookingham, Aug. 8, 1945, box 31, RTP.

7. New York *Times,* April 30, 1947, p. 18.

8. Thomas Shroyer to Kenneth Colegrove, May 23, 1952, box 1012, RTP; Interview, George Aiken; Millis and Brown, p. 365.

9. William S. White, *The Taft Story* (New York, 1954), p. 68; New York *Times,* April 8, 1947, p. 1.

10. RT to Cole J. Younger, Jan. 21, 1947, box 793, RTP; RT to Leland J. Gordon, April 25, 1947, I. Jack Martin papers, Kensington, Md.; RT foreword to Hartley book, copy of draft, box 614, RTP. On the anticommunist oath, *CR,* May 9, 1947, p. 4880, and RT speech, Sept. 28, 1947, box 1269, RTP.

11. Quote is RT to Willis B. York, March 12, 1947, Martin papers. Also Ludwig Teller (COHP), p. 68.

12. Huthmacher, p. 336; *CR,* April 17, 1947, p. 3614.

13. Millis and Brown, p. 377; Reilly; RT release, April 22, 1947, box 1268, RTP; New York *Times,* May 4, 1947, section 4, p. 2.

14. Stephen K. Bailey and Howard D. Samuel, *Congress at Work* (New York, 1965), p. 422; Lee, pp. 69–74; New York *Times,* May 1, 1947, p. 1.

15. New York *Times,* April 27, 30, 1947, both p. 1; RT to DeWitt Emery, June 10, 1947, box 791, RTP.

16. RT to Emery, ibid.; RT to Robert R. Kennedy, May 19, 1952, box 1013, RTP.

17. New York *Times,* May 8, 9, 10, 1947, all p. 1.

18. Ibid., May 13, 14, 1947.

19. Millis and Brown, pp. 380–384; New York *Times,* June 15, 1947.

20. RT to R. B. Creager, May 23, 1947, box 791, RTP.

21. New York *Times,* May 16, 21, 27, 30, 1947; Millis and Brown, p. 387; Witney, p. 269; Hartley, p. 76; Bailey and Samuel, p. 432; Lee p. 74; U.S. Congress, Senate Report No. 105, *Federal Labor Relations Act of 1947,* Eightieth Congress, First Session.

22. New York *Times,* June 5, 7, 21, 22, 24, 1947; Lee, p. 80; Paul Herzog to President Truman, June ?, 1947, Sumner H. Slichter to John Steelman, June 10, 1947, and Truman to Charles Murphy, June 18, 1947, all box 1114, OF-407, Truman papers, Truman Library.

23. RT, "The Taft-Hartley Act — What It Does Do. What It Does Not Do," 1947, Paul Walter papers, Cleveland; RT remarks, Sept. 9, 1947, box 604, RTP; Interview, Thomas Shroyer (COHP), p. 15.

24. George Eyrich to RT, March 12, 1947, RTP; Murray and Green cited in Joseph G. Rayback, *A History of American Labor* (New York, 1959), p. 400.

25. Sumner H. Slichter, "The Taft-Hartley Act," *Quarterly Journal of Economics,* Vol. 63 (Feb. 1949), pp. 1–31; Philip Taft, "Internal Affairs of Unions and the Taft-Hartley Act," *Industrial and Labor Relations Review,* Vol. 11 (April 1958), pp. 352–360. (This key issue hereafter cited as *ILRR.*)

26. Mack Swigert, "Did Taft Favor Change in Taft-Hartley?" *U.S. News &
    World Report,* Vol. 47 (Nov. 16, 1959), pp. 93–94; Slichter, "Taft-Hartley";
    Lee, p. 183; Ida Klaus, "The Taft-Hartley Experiment in Separation of
    NLRB Functions," *ILRR,* pp. 371–391; Clyde W. Summers, "A Sum-
    mary Evaluation of the Taft-Hartley Act," *ILRR,* pp. 405–413; Edwin
    E. Witte, "An Appraisal of the Taft-Hartley Act," *American Economic
    Review,* Vol. 38 (May 1948), pp. 368–382; Joseph Shister, "The Impact of
    the Taft-Hartley Act in Union Strength and Collective Bargaining,"
    ILRR, pp. 339–351; Millis and Brown, p. 659.
27. Philip Taft, *ILRR;* Summers, *ILRR.*
28. Fred Witney, "Taft-Hartley and the 83d Congress," *Labor Law Journal,*
    Vol. 5 (Jan. 1954), pp. 3–6, 76–79; Daniel Bell, "Taft-Hartley, Five Years
    After," *Fortune,* Vol. 46 (July 1952), p. 69; Slichter, "Revision of the
    Taft-Hartley Act," *Quarterly Journal of Economics,* Vol. 67 (May 1953),
    pp. 149–180.
29. *Life,* Vol. 23 (Sept. 1947), p. 40. See also Chapter 28.
30. Articles, supra, by Bell, Swigert, Shister, Witte. Quote is Slichter, "Taft-
    Hartley Act" (1949). See also New York *Times* evaluations, June 26, 1950,
    Sept. 7, 1952.
31. Claude Robinson, "The Strange Case of the Taft-Hartley Law, *Look,* Sept.
    30, 1947; Lee, pp. 145–154; RT to John W. Baird, May 27, 1948, box 173,
    RTP. Angus Campbell, *The American Voter* (New York, 1960), p. 172;
    Elmo Roper, *You and Your Leaders: Their Actions and Your Reactions,
    1936–1956* (New York, 1957), pp. 196, 200–201; Washington *Post* poll,
    Feb. 18, 1948.
32. Ludwig Teller (COHP), p. 67; Benjamin Aaron, "Amending the Taft-
    Hartley Act: A Decade of Frustration," *ILRR,* pp. 327–338.

CHAPTER 24: THE PERILS OF PROMINENCE, 1947

1. Key essays dealing with the Truman Doctrine may be found in Thomas G.
   Paterson, ed., *Cold War Critics: Alternatives to American Foreign Policy
   in the Truman Years* (Chicago, 1971); and Barton J. Bernstein, ed., *Politics
   and Policies of the Truman Administration* (Chicago, 1970). For RT's
   anticommunism, see his speech, *CR,* May 20, 1945, p. A2412. For RT-
   Truman relations, Truman, *Memoirs: Years of Trial and Hope* (New York,
   1955), p. 105; and RT comment, *CR,* April 27, 1951, p. 4466; A persuasive
   doctoral thesis is Bernard Weiner, "The Truman Doctrine: Background
   and Presentation," Claremont, 1966.
2. New York *Times,* March 13, 16, 1947, pp. 3, 1.
3. RT to Arthur Vandenberg, March 18, 1947, I. Jack Martin papers, Kensington, Md.; RT's questions — and those of others — are summarized in
   Department of State, *Bulletin,* Supplement, Vol. 16, No. 409A (May 4,
   1947), pp. 827–909.
4. RT to Fiorello La Guardia, April 18, RT to Joseph R. O'Connell, April
   5, 1947, box 790, RTP, LC; New York *Times,* April 11, 1947, p. 13, original, box 548, RTP.
5. A relevant article is Henry W. Berger, "A Conservative Critique of Containment: Senator Taft on the Early Cold War Program," in David

Horowitz, ed., *Containment and Revolution* (Boston, 1967), pp. 125–139. Also Weiner, Bernstein, "American Foreign Policy and the Origins of the Cold War," in Bernstein, ed., pp. 15–77; and George Kennan, *Memoirs, 1925–1950* (Boston, 1967), Ch. 13. For the vote, New York *Times*, April 23, 1947, p. 1.

6. RT to Herbert Hoover, Jan. ? 1945, RTP.

7. RT "speech material," 1947–1948, box 205, press release, April 28, 1947, box 263, RTP.

8. RT to L. K. Shaver, June 17, 1947, box 791, RTP.

9. RT to Walter Hallanan, March 12, 1947, Martin papers; New York *Times*, Jan. 1, March 19, 1947.

10. RT speech material, box 205, RT speeches, May 25, June 13, 1947, boxes 491, 1268, RTP.

11. R. Alton Lee, "The Truman-80th Congress Struggle over Tax Policy," *Historian*, Vol. 33 (Nov. 1970), pp. 68–82; RT to Robert E. Jones, Jan. 23, 1947, Martin papers; New York *Times*, Feb. 3, March 28, May 29, June 4, 1947; Irving Ives to Thomas E. Dewey, April 19, 1947, personal file, Dewey papers, University of Rochester.

12. New York *Times*, June 17, 18, July 19, 1947.

13. RT to Charles D. Hilles, July 11, 1947, Hilles papers, Yale University; Susan M. Hartmann, "President Truman and the 80th Congress," doctoral thesis, Missouri, 1966, p. 113.

14. Edwin Lahey (COHP), p. 16.

15. An excellent work on fiscal policy is A. E. Holmans, *United States Fiscal Policy, 1945–1959, Its Contribution to Economic Stability* (London, 1961); also Herbert Stein, *The Fiscal Revolution in America* (Chicago, 1969), p. 214.

16. Memo, John Hollister, April 2, 1947, Hollister papers, Cincinnati; descriptions of various RT aides, from interviews, Ralph Holsinger, Ben Tate, Jr., Paul Walter.

17. John Marshall to Roger Faherty, Dec. 26, 1946, box 1, Faherty papers, State Historical Society of Wisconsin; Joseph Mears to Walter, May 1, Walter to Carroll Reece, May 15, 1947, Walter papers, Cleveland; miscellaneous memos, Clarence Brown papers, Ohio Historical Society, Columbus; Brown to RT, Aug. 22, 1947, box 194, RTP.

18. RT to Noah Mason, Nov. 19, 1945, RT to Arthur E. Carr, Jan. 18, 1946, boxes 31, 783, RTP; RT to Hollister, Aug. 17, 1946, Hollister papers.

19. RT to Hollister, ibid.; Columbus *Evening Dispatch*, Dec. 24, 1946; RT to Hollister, Jan. 7, 1947, RTP.

20. RT to John M. Henry, Sept. 21, RT to Hulbert Taft, Jan. 26, 1946, box 779, RTP; RT to Col. R. B. Creager, April 15, 1946, Martin papers; RT to David Ingalls, Feb. 11 and April 25, 1946, RTP.

21. RT to Dewey, Sept. 15, Thomas E. Dewey to RT, Sept. 17, 1946, box 782, RT to George Sokolsky, Sept. 18, 1946, box 784, RT to H. Hayes Landon, Sept. 14, 1945, box 31, RTP. FDR quoted in James MacGregor Burns, *Roosevelt: Soldier of Freedom* (New York, 1970), p. 502.

22. Hollister to Wade T. Childress, Aug. 4, 1947, Hollister papers; RT to Clarence Brown, Aug. 13, 1947, Walter papers; Baltimore *Sun*, Oct. 12, 1947, p. Al; *Newsweek*, Oct. 20, 1947, p. 30.

23. New York *Times*, Sept. 12, 17, 27, 1947; *Newsweek*, Sept. 29, 1947, p. 23.
24. New York *Times*, Sept. 13, 14, 1947.
25. Reported in *Time*, Oct. 27, 1947, p. 74; Democratic National Committee files, Truman Library, Independence, Mo.
26. *Newsweek*, Sept. 29, 1947, p. 23; *Time*, Oct. 1, 1947, pp. 24–25.
27. *Time*, Oct. 6, 1947, pp. 24–25. At a press conference in Los Angeles on Sept. 15, reporters asked RT to provide his next releases in time for a "flat PM release." Taft replied, "Frankly, I do not know about this AM and PM release business." His comment symbolized his lack of understanding of the mechanics of newspaper reporting (transcript, box 1269, RTP).
28. RT speech, Tacoma, Sept. 25, 1947, box 1269, RTP. Other speeches, ibid.
29. *Newsweek*, Oct. 6, 1947, p. 17; Frank Gervasi, "Bob Taft's Martha," *Collier's*, Vol. 121 (April 3, 1948), pp. 62–64.
30. Hadley Cantril, *Public Opinion, 1935–1946* (Princeton, 1951), p. 643; RT to Kyle Palmer, Oct. 9, box 129, RT to Richard Scandrett, Oct. 20, 1947, box 170, RTP.

CHAPTER 25: PYRRHIC VICTORIES IN THE SENATE, 1947–1948

1. New York *Times*, Nov. 18, 1947, p. 1; original, box 263, RTP, LC.
2. New York *Times*, Nov. 22, Dec. 2, 19, 1947, pp. 4, 28, 1; RT to Sinclair Weeks, Nov. 15, box 153, RT to Marion Bennett, Nov. 29, box 158, RT to Joe R. Hanley, Dec. 30, 1947, box 167, RTP; RT, "Police State Methods Are Wrong," *Vital Speeches*, Vol. 14 (Dec. 1, 1947), pp. 104–107.
3. RT to Herbert Hoover, July 11, Aug. 13, 1947, box 1-k/136, Hoover papers, Hoover Library, Iowa; RT to Felix Hebert, Dec. 7, 1947, box 184, RTP; WHT, "Why We Entered the Great War," *Current History Magazine*, New York *Times*, section 6, part 2 (Aug. 1917), pp. 317–320.
4. RT to Ferdinand Mayer, Nov. 19, box 189, RT to Grier Bartol, Nov. 19, 1947, box 189, RTP.
5. RT to Fred W. Kinley, Oct. 20, 1947, box 175, RTP; New York *Times*, Nov. 12, 1947, p. 1.
6. For RT speeches, New York *Times*, Oct. 29, Nov. 11, 12, 27, 29, 1947; RT, "Memorandum of Remarks on Interim Aid to Europe," Nov. 28, 1947, box 1295, RTP; also RT to Carl E. Curtis, Oct. 15, 1947, box 135, RTP.
7. New York *Times*, Dec. 2, 20, 1947.
8. Thomas G. Paterson, "The Quest for Peace and Prosperity: International Trade, Communism, and the Marshall Plan," in Barton J. Bernstein, ed., *Policies and Politics of the Truman Administration* (Chicago, 1970), pp. 78–112; Cabell Phillips, *The Truman Presidency: The History of a Triumphant Succession* (New York, 1966), p. 190; Harry Bayard Price, *The Marshall Plan and Its Meaning* (Ithaca, 1955), pp. 110, 399; Curtis D. MacDougall, *Gideon's Army* (New York, 1965), p. 239.
9. RT quote, in New York *Times*, Sept. 26, 1947, p. 16. Criticisms of his stand are New York *Herald Tribune*, Jan. 5, 1948; *Time*, Dec. 8, 1947, p. 24; Richard Rovere, "Taft: Is This the Best We've Got?" *Harper's*, Vol. 196 (April 1948), pp. 289–299; J. L. Benvenisti, "Mr. Taft and American Aid," *Commonweal*, Vol. 47 (Dec. 12, 1947), pp. 222–224; Fred Rodell,

"Taft — Model T Candidate," *'47 — The Magazine of the Year*, Vol. 1 (Nov. 1947), pp. 2–13. Vandenberg remarked privately that "I was seriously disturbed by backstage efforts which were made against my point of view when I was leading the battle for the Marshall Plan." Vandenberg to E. Howell King, Nov. 13, 1950, Vandenberg papers, University of Michigan.

10. "Payroll, Taft HQ, 1947–1948," Clarence Brown papers, Ohio Historical Society, Columbus; Brown to Katharine Kennedy Brown, April 2, 6, 1948, box 173, miscellaneous RT letters, boxes 194, 196, 197; speeches early 1948, box 1271, RTP. For the plane crash, New York *Times*, March 16, 1948, p. 1; RT to Horace Hildreth, March 24, 1948, box 797, RTP. ("I was not concerned at the time, perhaps because the snow looked smoother than it turned out to be.")

11. RT to Henry E. T. Herman, Dec. 31, 1947, box 190, RT to John McFaul, Jan. 3, box 151, RT to B. L. Noojin, Feb. 20, box 124, RT to John A. Wagner, Feb. 27, 1948, box 155, RTP; Irwin Ross, *The Loneliest Campaign: The Truman Victory of 1948* (New York, 1968), p. 72; RT, Gridiron speech, 1948, Blanche O'Berg papers (her possession, D.C., copy with author also).

12. RT letters, late 1947–early 1948, boxes 153, 180, 533, esp. 795, RTP; New York *Times*, March 13, 14, 1948, pp. 1, 53; H. Bradford Westerfield, *Foreign Policy and Party Politics: Pearl Harbor to Korea* (New Haven, 1955), p. 285.

13. Susan M. Hartmann, "President Truman and the 80th Congress," doctoral thesis, Missouri, 1966, pp. 86, 199–203, 207–226; New York *Times*, June 18, 1948, p. 1; A. E. Holmans, *United States Fiscal Policy, 1945–1959, Its Contribution to Economic Stability* (London, 1961), p. 91; on civil rights, RT to Grant Reynolds, Dec. 31, 1947, box 170, RT to Josiah Rose, Feb. 5, 1948, box 139, RT statement re FEPC, 1948, box 195, RTP; and Roy Wilkins to William Walker, July 20, 1950, box 408 (2), NAACP papers, LC. On taxes, RT to E. Kendall Gilbert, Jan. 27, box 167, RT to William E. Clow, Jr., March 26, 1948, box 141, RTP.

14. Richard P. Stevens, *American Zionism and United States Foreign Policy, 1942–1947* (New York, 1962); RT to Secretary of State George Marshall, Feb. 17, 1947, box 648, RT to Julius Klein, April 3, 1948, RT releases, Feb. 21, March 25, May 16, 1948, box 1271, RTP; New York *Times*, Feb. 22, March 20, May 2, 1948.

15. RT speech, Feb. 13, 1948, box 474, RTP; New York *Times*, Feb. 14, 1948, p. 7.

16. New York *Times*, April 6, 1948, p. 2; RT to Oarke Kerbaugh, March 5, 1948, box 142, RT release, 1948, box 205, RTP; Allen J. Matusow, *Farm Policies and Politics in the Truman Years* (Cambridge, 1967), p. 141; Reo M. Christenson, *The Brannan Plan: Farm Politics and Policy* (Ann Arbor, 1959), p. 15.

17. Cincinnati *Times-Star*, Oct. 21, 1947, p. 1; Cleveland *Press*, March 11, 1947; Richard O. Davies, *Housing Reform During the Truman Administration* Columbia, Mo., 1966), p. 77; *Newsweek*, May 24, 1948, p. 16; RT to B. L. Noojin, Nov. 29, 1947, box 124, RT to Frank E. Tyler, May 27, 1948, box 148, RTP.

18. RT speeches, Feb. 21, March 24, boxes 1271, 233, RTP; New York *Times*, March 25, April 2, 1948, pp. 38, 1; Charles C. Brown, "Robert A. Taft: Champion of Public Housing and National Aid to Schools," *Bulletin of the Cincinnati Historical Society*, Vol. 26 (July 1968), pp. 225–253; Frank J. Munger and Richard F. Fenno, *National Politics and Federal Aid to Education* (Syracuse, 1962), pp. 138–144; *The Nation*, Vol. 166 (April 10, 1948), p. 388; *Newsweek*, April 12, 1948, p. 27.

19. New York *Times*, June 19, 20, 1948; *Newsweek*, June 21, 1948, p. 27; *CR*, June 15, 1948, pp. 8310, 8322; Westerfield, pp. 289–297; Robert Dahl, *Congress and Foreign Policy* (New York, 1950), p. 231; Raymond Baldwin to author, Oct. 10, 1969.

20. John M. Swomley, Jr., *The Military Establishment* (Boston, 1964), p. 77; *CR*, June 10, 1948, p. 7681; New York *Times*, June 11, 19, 20, 21, 1948; RT to Alva Swain, March 26, box 133, RT to Roy D. Moore, March 26, box 185, RT to R. G. Cooney, July 1, box 185, RT to Frederick Ware, July 1, 1948, box 796, RTP. For RT on air power, see Bonner Fellers, *Wings for Peace: A Primer for a New Defense* (Chicago, 1953); and RT to Herbert Hoover, Oct. 11, 1947, box 136, RTP. (Here RT said he "entirely agreed" with an article by Fellers on air power.)

21. New York *Times*, June 20–22, 1947.

22. "Truman versus Taft," *Congressional Quarterly Almanac*, Vol. 7 (1951), pp. 780–783.

CHAPTER 26: CAN TAFT WIN?

1. For Dewey and Stassen, Jules Abels, *Out of the Jaws of Victory* (New York, 1959), p. 50; Irwin Ross, *The Loneliest Campaign: The Truman Victory of 1948* (New York, 1968), p. 29.

2. Richard Rovere, "Taft: Is This the Best We've Got?" *Harper's*, Vol. 196 (April 1948), pp. 289–299. Other relevant articles are Kenneth Crawford, "Taft, The Presidential Candidate," *American Mercury*, Vol. 66 (June 1948), pp. 647–653; and Roger Butterfield, "Possible Presidents: Robert A. Taft," *Ladies' Home Journal*, Vol. 65 (Feb. 1948), p. 36.

3. Edwin Lahey (COHP), p. 29.

4. RT speeches, 1948, esp. box 1272, Walter Trohan to RT, April 1, 1948, RTP, LC.

5. RT to Harry H. Hansen, May 24, 1946, box 780, Bill McAdams, "Outline of Publicity Program," box 1274, RTP; John W. Hill to McAdams, Jan. 22, McAdams to RT, Jan. 15, Hill to Edwin F. Dakin, Feb. 24, 1948, boxes 37, 38, John W. Hill papers, State Historical Society of Wisconsin.

6. Richard Scandrett to John Marshall, Jan. 5, 1948, Vol. 21A, Scandrett papers, Cornell University; Guylay material, 1948, boxes 1272, 1274, RTP; Interviews, L. Richard Guylay (COHP), p. 10, Jack Bell, Hal Alderson; James Selvage to author, Oct. 18, 1969.

7. "My Political Credo," and radio spots in box 205, RTP; Guylay interview.

8. Release by Clarence Brown (n.d.), L. Richard Guylay papers (his possession, New York).

9. The RTP contain many films of RT.

10. "The Story of Bob Taft," box 205, RTP.

11. G. J. Grieshaber to Martha, April 21, 1948, RTP.

12. "G.O.P. Prepares to Name a President," *Life*, Vol. 24 (June 21, 1948), pp. 27–35; John Hollister to Preston Hotchkiss, July 26, 1948, Hollister papers, Cincinnati: RT to G. M. Humphrey, April 1, 1948, box 175, quote by RT is RT to Hollister, Feb. 8, 1936, box 39, RTP. Also interviews, Charles P. Taft, 2nd (COHP), p. 9, Alderson, Walter Trohan (COHP), p. 5. For Walter-Brown feuds, Brown to Walter, Aug. 15, Walter to RT, Aug. 29, 1947, and Walter memo, July 12, 1948, Paul Walter papers, Cleveland; and Walter-Brown-RT correspondence, 1947–1948, box 207, RTP.

13. John W. Hill to Bill McAdams, Feb. 5, Edwin Dakin to RT, Feb. 15, Hill to RT, Feb. 24, Brown to Hill, Feb. 26, 1948, box 37, Hill papers; for Brown, *Current Biography, 1947*, pp. 66–68; interviews, Glenn Thompson, Paul Walter. Also Abels, p. 64, William S. White, *The Taft Story* (New York, 1954), p. 118.

14. Brown to RT, Aug. 15, 1947, box 207, RTP; White, *The Citadel: The Story of the United States Senate* (New York, 1956), p. 171; Richard Scandrett to Howard C. Rowe, June 10, 1948, Vol. 21B, Scandrett papers; Walter interview; James Selvage to author, Oct. 18, 1969.

15. Ben Katz to Mildred Reeves, Oct. 14, 1947, box 175, RTP; *Newsweek*, April 5, 1948, p. 23; Lahey (COHP), p. 65; Clarence Brown to Noel G. Rapp, Aug. 4, 1954, Brown papers, Ohio Historical Society; RT to Stanley Grothaus, March 3, 1950, box 223, RTP. ("I have never been successful in permitting other people to write my speeches — in fact, I think I have written every speech that I have ever made.")

16. Goodwin to Bolton, Sept. 22, 1947, box 30, Walter papers.

17. Interview, Darrah Wunder; Confidential interview.

18. RT to Hulbert Taft, March 13, RT to Howard Buffett, Dec. 4, 1947, box 787, RTP.

19. Jack Redding, *Inside the Democratic Party* (New York, 1956), pp. 61–62; William L. Batt, Jr., to J. Howard McGrath, April 20, 1948, Clark Clifford papers, Truman Library, Independence.

20. *Life* cover story, Feb. 9, 1948.

21. Truman cited in Leonard Liggio and Ronald Radosh, "Henry A. Wallace and the Open Door," in Thomas G. Paterson, ed., *Cold War Critics: Alternatives to American Foreign Policy in the Truman Years* (New York, 1971), p. 90; FDR in James MacGregor Burns, *Roosevelt: Soldier of Freedom* (New York, 1970), pp. 453, 509.

22. RT radio broadcast, Sept. 20, 1943, transcript, box 1261, RTP; Interview, Thompson; Lahey column, Chicago *Daily News*, Feb. 5, 1949; Lahey (COHP), pp. 35–36.

23. Bruce Barton to Thomas E. Dewey, Sept. 30, 1947, personal file, Dewey papers, University of Rochester. Interestingly, WHT also distrusted the press. "Being a member of the newspaper craft," he wrote a reporter in 1911, "you know what infernal liars your profession can produce." (WHT to James C. Hemphill, Nov. 13, 1911, cited in Willard B. Gatewood, "The President and the 'Deacon' in the Campaign of 1912: The Correspondence of William Howard Taft and James C. Hemphill," *Ohio History*, Vol. 74 [Winter 1965], pp. 35–55.)

24. DeWitt Sage to RT, March 19, RT to Thomas B. Curtis, April 9, 1948, box 200, RTP; RT to Walter Tooze, March 23, 1948, Brown papers.

25. Hollister to RT, Jan. 23, 1948, box 175, polls, box 799, RTP; William E. Johnson to Herbert Brownell, March 7, 1948, presidential campaign file, Dewey papers; Ross, p. 44.

26. RT to Howard A. Coffin, April 20, 1948, box 154, RTP; *Newsweek,* April 24, 1948, p. 25; Washington *Daily News,* April 14, 1948; William Lemke to Frances Bolton, Oct. 8, 1947, Walter papers. ("I feel that he cannot be elected even if he is nominated . . . the 1948 election is the crucial test of whether we are going to continue the America we know, or accept the international America we know nothing about . . . Therefore I feel we should choose a candidate with care . . . We must have one that can be elected.")

27. RT to George B. Harris, Dec. 31, 1947, box 200, RTP; RT to Paul Walter, Nov. 29, 1947, Walter papers; Clarence Brown to Roy Irons, Jan. 30, 1948, box 175, RTP; *Time,* Feb. 9, 1948, p. 20; Frank McNaughton report, Feb. 27, 1947, McNaughton papers, Truman Library; Abels, p. 55; New York *Times,* Jan. 27, 1948, p. 10.

28. RT to Dudley White, Jan. 25, RT to Genevieve Seger, Feb. 2, 1948, boxes 200, 179, RTP; Lahey (COHP), p. 17.

29. RT to William A. Mason, Feb. 9, RT to Vincent Starzinger, Feb. 2, RT to Willis Gradison, May 19, 1948, boxes 176, 175, 147; Akron *Beacon–Journal,* May 2, 1948.

30. RT to J. Howard Pew, May 29, 1948, box 197, RT speeches, box 1272, RTP; Michael Straight, "Battle for Ohio," *New Republic,* Vol. 118 (May 3, 1948), pp. 9–10; *Newsweek,* May 3, 1948, pp. 19–20; New York *Times,* May, 1, 1948, p. 9; Brown to Ruth Giles, May 1, 1948, box 141, RTP.

31. *Newsweek,* May 17, 1948, p. 28; RT to Mars Mitchell, May 18, RT to Vincent Starzinger, June 1, 1948, boxes 176, 147, RTP.

32. Reston quoted in Ross, pp. 46–47; RT to Fred Atterbury, June 1, 1948, box 161, RTP.

33. RT to Thomas B. Curtis, May 27, RT to Joseph Scott, June 1, 1948, boxes 160, 127, RTP; RT to delegates, June 1, 1948, Brown papers.

34. RT to Peter Wynne, May 29, 1948, box 171, RTP; to Hinton Jones, June 1, 1948, Brown papers.

CHAPTER 27: A SECOND DEFEAT AT PHILADELPHIA

1. New York *Herald Tribune,* June 24, 1948, p. 3.

2. Clarence Brown to John J. McDonald, June 4, 1948, box 198, RTP, LC; List of "Distinguished People and Where Located," Clarence Brown papers, Ohio Historical Society; Organization Chart, box 198, RT to RT, Jr., May 31, 1948, RTP; Interviews, Lloyd Taft (COHP), p. 78, Horace D. Taft (COHP), p. 49.

3. New York *Herald Tribune,* New York *Times,* June 21, 1948, p. 1; William S. White, "The Meaning of Taft — Then and Now," *Taft Alumni Bulletin,* June 1954, p. 2.

4. New York *Times,* June 19, 1948, p. 7; New York *Herald Tribune,* June

20, 1948, p. 3; *Life*, Vol. 25 (July 5, 1948), pp. 17–29; William S. White, *The Taft Story* (New York, 1954), p. 118.

5. News clipping, Carlton Matson, box 199, RTP; John Hollister to RT, Feb. 8, 1952, Hollister papers, Cincinnati.

6. New York *Times*, June 22, 1948, p. 4; New York *Herald Tribune*, June 17, 1948, p. 5; Jules Abels, *Out of the Jaws of Victory* (New York, 1959), p. 61; Interview, Paul Walter; Richard Scandrett, "Memorandum Re Republican Convention, Philadelphia," June 28, 1948, box 204, RTP (also Scandrett papers, Vol. 21A, Cornell University).

7. Rumors of a deal proliferated. Some may be found in New York *Times*, June 19, 21, 1948, pp. 6, 2; New York *Herald Tribune*, June 16, 20, 22, 1948. Also H. Bradford Westerfield, *Foreign Policy and Party Politics: Pearl Harbor to Korea* (New Haven, 1955), p. 297; Scandrett, "Memorandum for Governor Stassen," 1948, Vol. 21A, Scandrett papers.

8. New York *Times*, June 22, 23, 1948, pp. 6, 1; Scandrett, "Memo Re Republican Convention."

9. New York *Times*, *Tribune*, June 24, 25, 1948.

10. New York *Herald Tribune*, June 24, 1948, p. 3; *Newsweek*, July 5, 1948, pp. 14–15.

11. *Official Report of the Proceedings of the Republican National Convention* (Washington, 1948).

12. New York *Herald Tribune*, June 25, 1948, p. 3.

13. For Connecticut, see Connecticut folder, 1948 presidential campaign, Thomas E. Dewey papers, University of Rochester; New York *Times*, June 25, 1948, p. 3; Raymond Baldwin to author, Feb. 26, 1971. For dealings with Harold Stassen, Arthur Krock, *Memoirs: 60 Years on the Firing Line* (New York, 1968), p. 246; "Stassen Background Memo," Arthur Krock papers, Princeton; Des Moines *Register*, June 26, 1948; RT to Gladys Williams, July 2, 1948, box 136, RTP. For RT activities, William S. White, "How to Win Influence, If Not Friends," *New York Times Magazine*, May 1, 1949, p. 10.

14. New York *Herald Tribune*, June 25, 1948, p. 3; RT handwritten statement, Blanche O'Berg papers (her possession, D.C.); *Official Report*, pp. 272–273.

15. Willard Shelton, "Portrait of a Conservative," *New Republic*, Vol. 120 (April 4, 1949), pp. 18–20; New York *Herald Tribune*, June 25, 1948, p. 3; Scandrett, "Memo Re Republican Convention."

16. New York *Times*, June 25, 1948, p. 1.

17. A post-mortem stressing Taft's inability to deal with Stassen is Willard Shelton, "The Retrogression of Senator Taft," *The Nation*, Vol. 174 (May 17, 1952), p. 473. See also RT to Colonel R. R. McCormick, June 29, 1948, box 1183, RTP, and Arthur Vandenberg to J. W. Kane, July 1, 1948, Vandenberg papers, University of Michigan. Also Joseph Martin, Jr. (as told to Robert J. Donovan), *My First Fifty Years in Politics* (New York, 1960), p. 165, and Donald R. McCoy, *Landon of Kansas* (Lincoln, 1966), p. 539.

18. White, *Taft Story*, p. 126; Hollister to Preston Hotchkiss, July 28, 1948, Hollister papers; Scandrett, "Memo Re Peter Wynne, the Bronx," Vol. 21A, Scandrett papers; New York *Herald Tribune*, June 26, 27, 1948, p. 13,

section 2, p. 1; Ernest L. Klein to Julius Klein, June 28, 1948, box 142, RTP.

19. Re Charles A. Halleck, see Halleck Interview (Indiana University); RT to A. Lewis Oswald, June 30, RT to Kurt F. Pantzer, July 9, 1948, boxes 148, 146, RTP; re Pennsylvania, White, *Taft Story,* p. 122. Dewey said later, "I never promised a Cabinet position to anybody in my life" (oral history transcript, p. 12, Dewey papers). Selvage to author, Oct. 18, 1969. James Reston reported in 1952 that Taft had asked Vandenberg in 1948 to become his secretary of state ("Inquiry into Four Political Assumptions," *New York Times Magazine,* Feb. 17, 1952, p. 7), but Reston cannot recall his source, and I can find no confirmation.

20. Jouett Ross Todd to Scandrett, May 27, Clarence Brown to Scandrett, July 14, 1948, Vol. 21B, Scandrett papers.

21. RT comments, box 204, RTP.

22. RT to Hugh Butler, June 29, box 161, RT to Sam Pryor, July 10, box 134, RT to General Oscar Solbert, June 30, box 1183, RT to Alfred A. Dustin, Dec. 29, 1948, box 799, RT to Josiah T. Rose, July 1, box 1183, RT to Vincent Starzinger, July 1, box 147, RT to Ernest Klein, June 28, 1948, box 142, RTP.

23. RT to Sinclair Weeks, July 1, box 153, RT to Rupert Warburton, July 1, box 796, RTP.

24. RT to John W. Haussermann, July 12, 1948, RT to Solbert, July 10, 1948, box 170, RTP.

25. New York *Herald Tribune,* June 26, 1948, p. 13.

CHAPTER 28: SURMOUNTING DISAPPOINTMENTS, 1948–1949

1. New York *Times,* June 27, July 13, 1948, pp. 30, 11; RT to H. H. Selseth, July 9, 1948, box 177, RTP, LC.

2. Cabell Phillips, *The Truman Presidency: The History of a Triumphant Succession* (New York, 1966), pp. 226–228; Truman, *Memoirs: Years of Trial and Hope* (New York, 1955), pp. 206–208; Robert A. Divine, *American Immigration Policy, 1924–1952* (New Haven, 1957), p. 123.

3. Richard O. Davies, *Housing Reform During the Truman Administration* (Columbia, Mo., 1966), pp. 94, 97.

4. RT to John D. Hartigan, July 1, 1948, to Governor Green, June 29, 1948, box 141, RT to Katharine Kennedy Brown, June 29, 1948, box 173, RTP.

5. RT notes, July 13, 1948, box 204, RTP; *Newsweek,* July 26, 1948, p. 27.

6. Thomas E. Dewey to E. Grace Dewey, July 27, 1948, personal correspondence, Dewey papers, University of Rochester. ("Mr. Truman's special session is a nuisance, but I do not believe it will have much effect on the election.")

7. Herbert Brownell and Hugh Scott version in Irwin Ross, *The Loneliest Campaign: The Truman Victory of 1948* (New York, 1968), pp. 136–137, and Brownell interview. Also Dewey to author, Oct. 20, 1969.

8. RT speeches, box 1274, RTP; Jules Abels, *Out of the Jaws of Victory* (New York, 1959), pp. 169–170, 193–194; RT to Governor Theodore McKeldin, Feb. 1, 1952, box 333, RT to Alfred A. Dustin, Oct. 2, 1948, box 799, RTP.

9. Cleveland *Plain Dealer*, Oct. 28, 1948, p. 10; Washington *Post*, Oct. 31, 1948, section 2, p. 1; Edwin Lahey (COHP), pp. 47–48.

10. Martha to Lillian Dykstra, March 1949, Dykstra papers, her possession, S. Yarmouth, Mass.; comment re Dewey is RT to John Marshall, Sept. 16, 1948, Marshall papers, Bethany College (W. Va.) Library.

11. William S. White, *The Taft Story* (New York, 1954), p. 83; RT to Dewey, Nov. 3, 1948, Blanche O'Berg papers, her possession, D.C.

12. RT to Charles W. Vursell, Jan. 2, box 809, RT to B. L. Noojin, Jan. 17, RT to Arthur Betts, Jan. 15, 1949, box 233, RTP. RT repeated such statements in many letters during the next four years. See boxes 199, 809, RTP.

13. Louisville *Courier-Journal*, Nov. 18, 1948; Harold Ickes, "Taft Minus Hartley," *New Republic*, Vol. 121 (July 18, 1949), p. 16.

14. George H. Mayer, *The Republican Party, 1854–1966* (New York, 1967), p. 469; Abels, p. 302.

15. Robert E. Lane, *Political Life: Why People Get Involved in Politics* (Glencoe, 1959), pp. 25–26; Richard O. Davies, "Whistle-Stopping Through Ohio," *Ohio History*, Vol. 71 (July 1962), pp. 113–123.

16. Abels, p. 307; Ross, ch. 11; Angus Campbell, et al., *The American Voter* (New York, 1960), pp. 208–209, 522; Bernard Berelson, Paul Lazarsfeld, and William N. McPhee, "Political Perception," in Eleanor E. Maccoby, et al., *Readings in Social Psychology*, 3d. ed. (New York, 1958), p. 85; Samuel Lubell, *The Future of American Politics* (New York, 1952).

17. New York *Times*, Nov. 4, Dec. 2, 18, 19, 1948.

18. RT to Tom L. Gibson, Dec. 28, 1948, box 1321, RTP. ("We are about to start a session which I do not look forward to with any pleasure.")

19. Chicago *Tribune*, Jan. 2, 1949, p. 16; New York *Times*, Nov. 16, 1948, Jan. 2, 1949; Stephen K. Bailey and Howard K. Samuel, *Congress at Work* (New York, 1965), pp. 71–72; William J. Miller, *Henry Cabot Lodge: A Biography* (New York, 1967), pp. 201–202; Sydney Hyman, *The Lives of William Benton* (New York, 1969), pp. 406–408; Raymond Baldwin to author, Oct. 10, 1969.

20. "Taft the Liberal," *New Republic*, Vol. 120 (Jan. 17, 1949), p. 9; New York *Times*, *Herald Tribune*, Jan. 3, 4, 1949; White, *Taft Story*, p. 84; RT to Basil Brewer, Dec. 23, 1948, box 199, RT to Albert W. Hawkes, Jan. 5, 1949, box 809, RTP; Lodge to Eugene Millikin, Nov. 20, 1948, Lodge to Vandenberg, Dec. 23, 1948, Vandenberg papers, University of Michigan.

21. Comments about Lodge and Hugh Scott of Pennsylvania suggested his feelings. See RT to Basil Brewer, Jan. 22, 1949, box 199, and to Carroll Reece, June 2, 1950, box 819, RTP. ("Hugh Scott is and always has been a complete screwball.") In 1949 RT was periodically involved in battles to remove Scott as chairman of the GOP National Committee. He failed in Jan. 1949, but succeeded that summer. "Blood in nostrils" is White, *Taft Story*, pp. 84–85.

22. Roscoe Drummond, *Christian Science Monitor*, Feb. 2, 1949; RT release re FEPC, Sept. 23, 1949, box 270, RTP; New York *Times*, March 12, 17, 18, 31, 1949; *Congressional Quarterly Almanac*, 1949, p. 583; RT to Stanley Caldwell, March 24, box 809, RT to Henry C. Bucher, June 16, box 802,

RT to Raymond Baldwin, Oct. 16, box 1184, RT to Fred Mourey, Dec. 24, 1949, box 802, RTP; *CR,* April 5, 1950, p. 4799; Robert A. Divine, *American Immigration Policy, 1924–1952* (New Haven, 1957), p. 137; David B. Truman, *The Congressional Party: A Case Study* (New York, 1949), pp. 25–27; "81st Congress: A Progress Report," *New Republic,* Vol. 121 (Nov. 14, 1949), pp. 17–32.

23. RT to Charles M. White, June 15, 1949, box 802, RTP; New York *Times,* May 3, 22, 26, 1949, pp. 18, 1, 25; RT radio debate with J. K. Galbraith, Jan. 30, 1949, box 1275, RTP. Quote re army is from radio interview, Aug. 31, 1949, box 1276, RTP. For Brannan Plan, Allen Matusow, *Farm Policies and Politics in the Truman Years* (Cambridge, 1967), p. 196; Reo M. Christenson, *The Brannan Plan: Farm Politics and Policy* (Ann Arbor, 1959), pp. 3, 34; RT to Roy B. Smith, Oct. 3, box 225, RT to John T. Brown, Nov. 6, 1949, box 1184, RTP; *CR,* Oct. 12, 1949, pp. 14310–14312.

24. RT to Prescott Bush, June 27, RT to James H. Duff, May 24, RT to Harold Burton, Dec. 14, 1950, box 817, RT speech, May 4, 1949, box 1275, RTP; New York *Times,* May 5, 17, 19, 1949; "Memo on Status of Taft-Hartley Repeal," May 6, 1949, box 1114, OF-407, Truman papers, Truman Library; R. Alton Lee, *Truman and Taft-Hartley: A Question of Mandate* (Lexington, 1966), p. 162; Ludwig Teller (COHP), p. 268; Gerald Pomper, "Labor and Congress: The Repeal of Taft-Hartley," *Labor History,* Vol. 2 (Fall 1961), pp. 323–343.

25. Quote in Lee, p. 177; New York *Times,* June 29, 30, July 1, 1949, all p. 1.

26. Benjamin Aaron, "Amending the Taft-Hartley Act: A Decade of Frustration," *Industrial and Labor Relations Review,* Vol. 11 (April 1958), pp. 327–338; Ives to Thomas E. Dewey, July 5, 1949, personal correspondence, Thomas Dewey papers, University of Rochester. Morse quoted in Willard Shelton, "Portrait of a Conservative," *New Republic,* Vol. 120 (April 4, 1949), pp. 18–20; Alsop, New York *Herald Tribune,* July 4, 1949.

27. RT to Willis Gradison, May 10, 1949, box 257, on health insurance, RT to Bromwell Ault, Feb. 20, 1948, box 165, RT to George M. Monahan, Sept. 25, 1949, box 211, RT release, April 14, 1949, box 1275, RTP.

28. *CR,* May 2, 1949, p. 5489; RT to Mrs. H. B. Diefenbach, May 31, box 802, RT to Victor Emanuel, June 20, box 256, RT to Joseph Gelin, July 13, 1949, box 232, RTP; RT, "Education in the Congress," *Educational Record,* July 1949, pp. 337–356.

29. New York *Times,* May 3, 4, 6, 1949, pp. 18, 22, 1; Richard F. Fenno, "The House of Representatives and Federal Aid to Education," in Robert L. Peabody and Nelson W. Polsby, eds., *New Perspectives on the House of Representatives* (Chicago, 1963), pp. 195–235; Charles C. Brown, "Robert A. Taft: Champion of Public Housing and National Aid to Schools," *Bulletin of the Cincinnati Historical Society,* Vol. 26 (July 1968), pp. 225–253. Richard M. Nixon of California also voted against the bill in House committee.

30. New York *Times,* Jan. 6, 7, 26, 1949.

31. RT to Harold D. Comey, March 9, box 805, RT to Willis Gradison, April 14, 1949, box 257, RTP. Also *Newsweek,* April 25, 1949, p. 26; Brown, passim; Richard O. Davies, *Housing Reform During the Truman Administration* (Columbia, Mo., 1966), p. 101. John T. Flynn complained that Taft,

in backing housing and education bills, was turning the country on a "march toward Socialism on the Fabian model." Flynn to RT, Feb. 3, 1949, Flynn papers, University of Oregon (compliments of Justus Doenecke).

32. *The Nation,* Vol. 167 (April 30, 1949), p. 486; Davies, passim; Brown, passim; Truman to RT, July 16, 1949, box 285, RTP.

33. RT release, Dec. 23, 1948, box 1274, RT to F. L. Daily, Feb, 14, box 801, RT to Henry Hazlitt, box 801, RT to W. L. Weber, June 20, 1949, RTP; New York *Times,* May 24, 30, 31, 1949.

34. Arthur Vandenberg, Jr., ed., *The Private Papers of Senator Vandenberg* (Boston, 1952), p. 501.

35. New York *Times,* Feb. 21, 26, 29, 1949; RT speech March 31, 1949, box 550, RTP.

36. RT, "Shall the United States Undertake to Arm the Nations of Western Europe?" July 11, 1949, box 255, RTP; New York *Times,* July 10, 12, 13, 22, 1949; RT to Lewis H. Brown, July 26, 1949, box 241, RTP; Vandenberg, p. 498.

37. *CR,* Sept. 22, 1949, pp. 13165–13168; New York *Times,* Sept. 23, 1949, p. 1.

38. RT, "The Future of the Republican Party," Jan. 28, 1949, box 275, RTP.

39. Isaac Deutscher, "Myths of the Cold War," in David Horowitz, ed., *Containment and Revolution* (Boston, 1967), p. 14; Walter La Feber, *America, Russia, and the Cold War, 1945–1966* (New York, 1968), p. 128; Henry W. Berger, "Senator Robert A. Taft Dissents from Military Escalation," in Thomas G. Paterson, ed., *Cold War Critics: Alternatives to American Foreign Policy in the Truman Years* (Chicago, 1971), pp. 167–204; George Kennan, *Memoirs, 1925–1950* (Boston, 1967), p. 407.

40. Critiques of Taft are John Paul Armstrong, "Senator Taft and American Foreign Policy: The Period of Opposition," doctoral thesis, Chicago, 1953; Armstrong, "The Enigma of Senator Taft and American Foreign Policy," *Review of Politics,* Vol. 18 (April 1955), pp. 206–231; C. L. Sulzberger, *A Long Row of Candles: Memoirs and Diaries, 1934–1954* (New York, 1969), p. 616. RT on Asia, in New York *Times,* Feb. 24, 1948, p. 12; RT speech material, box 205, RT to H. Alexander Smith, Dec. 19, 1949, box 811, RTP. (Here he said re Asia, "There is no subject which puzzles me so much. I know we should not be in the mess we are in, but it is difficult to see how we can get out of it.")

41. New York *Times,* July 13, 1949; William S. White, "Almost Equal to Being President," *New York Times Magazine,* Jan. 14, 1951, p. 10.

42. Vandenberg to Charles P. Taft, 2nd, Nov. 11, 1949, Charles P. Taft, 2nd, to Vandenberg, Nov. 15, 1949, Vandenberg papers.

43. Willard Shelton, "Portrait of a Conservative," *New Republic,* Vol. 120 (April 4, 1949), pp. 18–20; Youngstown *Vindicator,* April 29, 1949; Cincinnati *Post,* Sept. 2, 1949, p. 1.

CHAPTER 29: A TROUBLED, PARTISAN TAFT, 1950

1. L. Richard Guylay to RT, April 12, 27, 1949, Guylay papers (his possession, New York); Interview, Guylay; *Time,* Sept. 12, 1949, p. 21, Dec. 19, 1949, p. 14; *Newsweek,* Sept. 19, 1949, pp. 18–20; Cincinnati *Enquirer,* Dec. 4,

1949, section 3, p. 3; RT to Margaret Baker, March 14, box 213, RT to T. Emerson Smith, May 27, box 214, RT to Clarence Ehrhart, June 21, box 218, RT to William E. Halley, Nov. 14, 1949, box 220, RTP, LC; RT to Dorothy Rowe, June 19, 1949, Rowe papers (her possession, Cincinnati).

2. *Newsweek,* Jan. 16, 1950, p. 40: New York *Times,* Jan. 3, 5, 1950.

3. New York *Times,* Jan. 11, 1950, p. 1; *Time,* Jan. 23, 1950, p. 23; RT speech, Jan. 12, 1950, box 1300, RTP.

4. New York *Times,* Jan. 12, 1950, p. 1; Richard Scandrett to Bruce Barton, Jan. 12, 1950, box 62, Barton papers, State Historical Society of Wisconsin; Arthur Vandenberg to RT, Jan. 19, 1950, Vandenberg papers, University of Michigan.

5. New York *Times,* Jan. 19, April 9, June 15, 1950; RT to Paul Walter, May 2, box 273, RT to Sister Maurine Sullivan, July 19, 1950, box 816, RT speech, April 22, 1950, box 1278, RTP; RT on Brannan Plan, *CR,* May 19, 1950, pp. 7299–7300; RT to Charles M. White, May 12, box 257, RT to Paul A. Sihler, June 15, box 813, RT to Jack Kroll, Aug. 10, 1950, box 257, RTP; on FEPC, RT to Walter, May 8, 1950, Paul Walter papers, Cleveland; on rent control, RT to Mrs. John M. Logan, May 15, 1950, box 216, RTP.

6. RT, "Is President Truman Taking Us Down the British Road?" *Collier's,* April 8, 1950, p. 13; Cleveland *Plain Dealer,* April 25, 1950.

7. New York *Times,* Jan. 6, April 22, May 6, 24, 26, 1950; *Newsweek,* June 5, 1950, p. 21; *Time,* May 15, 1950, p. 20.

8. Robert Griffith, *The Politics of Fear: Joseph R. McCarthy and the Senate* (Lexington, 1970), p. 49.

9. RT to Lester Bradshaw, April 11, 1946, RT to Paul Walter, June 4, 1947, Walter papers; RT to McCarthy, Oct. 29, 1946, box 782, McCarthy to RT, Jan. 7, 1949, box 502, RTP.

10. RT to editor, Cleveland *News,* May 4, RT to Alfred Segal, May 24, 1950, box 813, RTP; RT to Benjamin S. Hubbell, Aug. 17, 1951, I. Jack Martin papers, Kensington, Md.

11. RT to Zechariah Chafee, Sept. 3, 1949, box 802, RTP.

12. Richard Rovere, *Senator Joe McCarthy* (New York, 1959), p. 135; Baltimore *Sun,* March 23, 1950, p. 4; Rovere, "What's Happened to Taft?" *Harper's,* Vol. 204 (April 1952), pp. 38–44; RT speech, March 23, 1950, box 1300, RTP.

13. RT to B. L. Noojin, April 7, 1950, RTP; New York *Times,* March 23, 26, 28, April 2, 13, 1950; RT statement, March 31, 1950, box 815, RTP.

14. RT to Joseph Sagmaster, Feb. 26, 1945, RT speech, Oct. 26, 1946, box 1267, RTP.

15. RT comments, Oct. 21, 1947, box 174, RT to Marrs McLean, Jan. 7, 1948, box 187, RTP.

16. RT radio speech, May 18, 1948, box 1273, RT form letter re Mundt-Ferguson bill, 1950, box 270, RT to William Grossman, Dec. 31, 1947, box 152, RT to B. E. Hutchinson, Feb. 4, 1950, box 814, RTP.

17. RT to Ernest M. Ach, April 8, box 270, RT to Art Barrie, May 2, 1950, box 234, RTP; New York *Times,* May 2, 1950, p. 1; Stewart Alsop, Toledo *Blade,* May 20, 1950.

18. Rovere, "What Course for the Powerful Mr. Taft?" *New York Times Magazine,* March 22, 1953, p. 9; William G. Carlton, "Kennedy in History: An Early Appraisal," *Antioch Review,* Vol. 24 (Feb. 1964), pp. 277–300; New York *Times,* June 2, 1950, p. 1.

19. New York *Times,* Nov. 13, 1948, p. 2, Feb. 5, July 21, 1949, pp. 8, 2.

20. Re labor, RT to Clinton S. Posten, May 23, 1950, box 212, RT to Cole J. Younger, Sept. 25, 1949, box 811, RTP; re NAACP, Walter White to William Walker, July 19, Roy Wilkins to Walker, July 20, RT to White, July 25, White to RT, July 26, Wilkins to Henry Lee Moon, Aug. 8, White to NAACP branches, Aug. 10, 1950, box 408 (2), NAACP papers, LC; re Catholics, RT to Ben Tate, March 29, 1949, Martin papers; RT to Raoul Desvernine, Oct. 4, 16, 1950, box 284, RTP.

21. William S. White, *The Taft Story* (New York, 1954), p. 86.

22. Dr. Stanhope Bayne-Jones (COHP), p. 17.

23. RT to Walter E. Batterson, Aug. 28, 1951, Martin papers; Interview, George Aiken.

24. Darrah Wunder to author, Dec. 5, 31, 1970; Interview, Mrs. Wunder; *Time,* Oct. 13, 1958, p. 20, has a romanticized version.

25. RT to F. L. D. Goodrich, July 3, 1950, box 1359, RTP; Wunder to RT, Jr., Feb. 6, 1954, TSHP; Interviews, Helen Manning, Barbara Taft; Dr. Bretney Miller to author, March 16, 1971.

26. Horace D. Taft (COHP), p. 58; *CR,* May 15, p. 7000, May 16, p. 7064, May 17, pp. 7135, 7173, May 18, pp. 7190, 7217, 7226, May 19, 1950, pp. 7292, 7305, 7320, 7360; New York *Times,* May 18, 19, 23, pp. 5, 12, 2; RT to Horace, July 6, 1950, Horace D. Taft papers (his possession, New Haven).

27. Interviews, Horace D. Taft, Robert Taft, Jr.; Helen Manning to author, Feb. 24, 1970.

28. RT to William G. Bray, July 3, 1947, Martin papers; *CR,* Oct. 12, 1949, p. 14337, May 25, 1950, pp. 7688–7725.

29. RT speech, June 28, 1950, box 258, RTP.

30. RT speech, June 29, 1950, box 1300, radio broadcast, July 2, box 1278, RTP; Eric Goldman, *The Crucial Decade: America 1945–1955* (New York, 1959), p. 164.

31. *Newsweek,* July 10, 1950, p. 25; RT speech, June 28, 1950, box 258, RTP.

32. RT speech, June 28, 1950, RT and Joe Martin release, July 18, 1950, boxes 258, 1278; RT to D. R. Gosney, July 24, RT to Harry Stapler, July 18, 1950, boxes 214, 822, RTP. In 1938 he had written Martha, "Dean Acheson was there [at a Yale Corporation meeting], and made a more pleasant impression on me than he does in society." Nov. 11, 1938, RTP.

33. New York *Times,* July 24, 27, Aug. 1, 11, 12, 15, 18, 22, Sept. 1, 2, 23, 1950; RT speeches, July 24, Aug. 11, box 270, RTP; Herbert Hoover to RT, Aug. 13, 1950, box l–k/136, Hoover papers, Hoover Library, Iowa; A. E. Holmans, *United States Fiscal Policy, 1945–1959, Its Contribution to Economic Stability* (London, 1961), p. 132; Edmund S. Flash, Jr., *Economic Advice and Presidential Leadership: The Council of Economic Advisers* (New York, 1965), pp. 60–61, 68–69.

34. New York *Times,* July 22, 1950, p. 32; RT to Dorothy Thompson, July 25, 1950, box 819, RTP.

35. *CR,* Sept. 15, 1950, pp. 14929–14930, 15182; RT to Harold Henderson, July 25, 1950, box 223, RTP.

CHAPTER 30: A MAGNIFICENT TRIUMPH

1. Joseph T. Ferguson brochures, box 278, RTP, LC; Dayton *Journal Herald,* Nov. 11, 1950, p. 4; Beverly Smith, "Can Senator Taft Win His Biggest Fight?" *Saturday Evening Post,* Vol. 222 (June 3, 1950), p. 26; New York *Times,* Nov. 8, 1950.
2. RT to Victor Emanuel, July 6, 1949, box 256, RTP; Jack Kroll, "Reflections of a Union Organizer," author's files; Interview, Frank Lausche.
3. Bruce Biossat column, Ashtabula *Star-Beacon,* Oct. 24, 1950; Stewart Alsop column, Cleveland *Plain Dealer,* Oct. 27, 1950.
4. Wooster *Daily-Record,* May 4, 1950; Cleveland *Plain Dealer,* clipping, 1950, RTP.
5. Tiffin *Advertiser-Tribune,* Aug. 17, 1950.
6. "Speaker's Handbook," box 282, RTP; Fay Calkins, *The CIO and the Democratic Party* (Chicago, 1952), p. 16; U.S. Congress, Senate, Hearings before the Subcommittee on Privileges and Elections of the Committee on Rules and Administration, *Investigation into the 1950 Senatorial Campaign,* Eighty-second Congress, First and Second Sessions (Washington, D.C., 1952; (henceforth noted as *Hearings*).
7. "The Robert Alphonso Taft Story," RTP; "Findings, Observations and Recommendations of the Subcommittee on Privileges and Elections," 1952, I. Jack Martin papers, Kensington, Md.
8. *Newsweek,* Oct. 30, 1950, p. 16; Samuel Lubell, "How Taft Did It," *Saturday Evening Post,* Vol. 223 (Feb. 10, 1951), p. 32.
9. RT to Harry Harriman, July 21, 1950, box 237, RT marked copies of "Handbook," box 282, RT reply to "Handbook," box 258, Charles P. Taft, 2nd, to Jack Kroll, June 1, 1950, box 281, RTP.
10. New York *Times,* Nov. 13, 1949, section 4, p. 7; Memo, Paul Walter, "Massachusetts Ballot Story," (author's possession); Lloyd Taft (COHP), p. 101; Walter to RT, Nov. 19, 1948, box 273, RT to Albina Cermak, Sept. 8, 1949, box 215, RTP.
11. RT to Margaret Baker, March 14, 1949, box 213, Ray Bliss to Paul Walter, March 16, 1950, box 273, RTP. For Taft's dealings, 1944–1949, with the Ohio GOP, see box 25, Harold Burton papers, LC; RT to John S. Knight, Sept. 29, 1944, box 113, RT to Margaret Baker, Sept. 14, 1945, box 662, RTP.
12. RT to Paul Walter, Sept. 4, 1951, Walter papers, Cleveland; RT letters seeking money, boxes 245, 1191, RTP; Interview, Walter; Donald R. Matthews, *United States Senators and Their World* (Chapel Hill, 1960), p. 72; Paul M. David, ed., *Presidential Nominating Politics in 1952,* Vol. 4 (Baltimore, 1954), p. 10; RT to Gradison, Feb. 26, 1949, box 257, RTP.
13. Calkins, p. 28; *Time,* Oct. 30, 1950, pp. 22–25; *Newsweek,* Sept. 19, 1949, pp. 18–20, Oct. 30, 1950, pp. 19–20; RT, "How Much Government Can Free Enterprise Stand?" *Collier's,* Vol. 124 (Oct. 22, 1949), p. 16; Interview, Willis Gradison; *Reporter,* Vol. 3 (Nov. 12, 1950), pp. 36–37.
14. Interviews, Guylay (COHP); Robert Taft, Jr.; recordings, RTP.
15. Recordings, RT weekly columns (Capitol Report), box 1300, RTP.

16. RT to Carl F. Routzahn, Feb. 3, 1950, box 234, RTP.
17. Mark Gilstrap, "Taft's Battle in Ohio," *Christian Science Monitor Magazine,* Sept. 30, 1950, p. 3; Brady Black to author, Dec. 11, 1970; William S. White, *The Taft Story* (New York, 1954), p. 95.
18. James Cannon, ed., *Politics, U.S.A.* (New York, 1960), p. 276; RT to key people, May 25, RT to William Vodrey, Jr., July 19, 1950, both box 214, RTP; *Hearings;* Jack Martin to RT, Oct. 17, 1950, box 258, RTP; *Newsweek,* Oct. 30, 1950, pp. 19–20; Akron *Beacon-Journal,* Nov. 4, 1950, p. 1.
19. RT speech, Dayton, Sept. 13, 1950, box 1279, RTP; New York *Times,* Sept. 3, 1940, section 4, p. 10, Nov. 6, 1950, p. 19; RT to William Edward Hale, July 27, 1950, box 218, RT, "Washington Report," Nov. 1, 1950, box 279, RTP.
20. RT speech, Oct. 1, 1950, box 1279, RTP; Washington *Star,* Oct. 13, 1950; *The Nation,* Vol. 171 (Oct. 28, 1950), p. 373; *Hearings.*
21. United Auto Workers flier, box 258, RTP.
22. New York *Times,* Oct. 31, 1950; *Hearings.*
23. Mt. Vernon (Ohio) *News,* Aug. 10, 1950; Cleveland *Plain Dealer,* Aug. 30, Oct. 21, 1950; Lorain *Journal,* Oct. 18, 1950.
24. Cincinnati *Times-Star,* Sept. 29, 1950, p. 30; *Hearings.*
25. Youngstown *Vindicator,* Aug. 29, 30, 1950; New York *Times,* Aug. 30, 31, 1950, pp. 1, 23; Walter (COHP), pp. 23–24.
26. Akron *Beacon-Journal,* Nov. 5, 1950, p. 3B; *Newsweek,* Oct. 30, 1950, p. 20; New York *Times,* Nov. 6, 1950, p. 18.
27. Polls, box 272, RTP.
28. RT telegram to Arthur Vandenberg, Nov. 4, 1950, Vandenberg papers, University of Michigan; Dayton *Journal,* Nov. 6, 1950, p. 3.
29. Akron *Beacon-Journal,* Nov. 7, 1950, p. 1; Cincinnati *Times-Star,* Nov. 8, 9, 1950; Interviews, Barbara Taft, Horace D. Taft; New York *Times,* Nov. 8, 1950, p. 1.
30. Secretary of State, Ohio, 1950, Official election statistics; Cincinnati *Enquirer,* Nov. 9, 1950; New York *Times,* Nov. 9, 1950, p. 1; Comparative analyses of Taft elections, by counties, Walter papers; RT to Don H. Enbright, Nov. 11, 1950, box 220, RTP.
31. Akron *Beacon-Journal,* Nov. 5, 1950, p. 1.
32. RT to Paul F. Schenck, Nov. 16, 1950, box 231, RT to Clyde Mann, Dec. 14, 1950, box 237, RT to Richard Childs, Dec. 6, 1950, box 819, RTP; David, Vol. 4, p. 15.
33. RT to Gordon Renner, Nov. 20, 1950, box 265, RT to Hugh Morton, Dec. 31, 1951, box 1197, RT to Ed Schorr, Nov. 21, 1950, box 269, RTP; Akron *Beacon-Journal,* Nov. 8, 1950, p. 2; Bruce Biossat column for NEA papers, Nov. 27–30, 1950, in box 241, RTP.
34. Samuel Lubell, *The Future of American Politics* (New York, 1952), p. 101; Lubell, "How Taft Did It," p. 32; "The Taft Vote in Ohio's Industrial Counties," No. A64–10, box 4, James Mitchell papers, Dwight D. Eisenhower Library, Abilene; RT to Russell Campbell, Nov. 16, 1950, box 219, RT to Fred Broda, Dec. 11, 1950, box 236, RTP; Calkins, pp. 31–36; Akron *Beacon-Journal,* Nov. 12, 1950, p. 8B; Jack Kroll to author, n.d.; *Newsweek,* Nov. 20, 1950, p. 25; RT to Herbert Hoover, Nov. 21, 1950, box l–k/136, Hoover papers, Hoover Library, Iowa.

35. RT to Vandenberg, Nov. 11, 1950, Vandenberg papers.
36. Akron *Beacon-Journal*, Nov. 12, 1950, p. 2; Dayton *Journal Herald*, Nov. 11, 1950, p. 4; Washington *Post*, New York *Times*, Nov. 14, 1950.
37. RT to Mrs. Florence Morrison, Dec. 6, 1950, Walter papers.

CHAPTER 31: FOREIGN POLICY MOVES IN, 1951

1. RT to Frederick Exton, Nov. 29, 1950, RTP, LC; speech, April 30, 1951, box 1281, RTP.
2. William S. White, *The Taft Story* (New York, 1954), p. 148; RT to Forrest Davis, Jan. 18, 1951, box 848, RTP; RT to Robert Harriss, Jan. 8, 1951, I. Jack Martin papers, Kensington, Md.
3. William L. Neumann to author, June 3, 1971; White, p. 154; New York *Times*, Jan. 8, 1951.
4. RT to Robert J. Havighurst, Jan. 23, 1951, Martin papers; RT press conference, Jan. 9, 1951, box 134, H. Alexander Smith papers, Princeton University; RT to Ralph Bard, Dec. 13, 1950, box 874, RTP.
5. RT to Muste, March 8, 1951, Martin papers; Muste, "The Global Picture," *Fellowship*, Vol. 17 (Feb. 1951), pp. 1–7.
6. RT to Thomas, March 13, 1951, Martin papers. Also RT to Charles P. Taft, 2nd, May 24, 1951, box 1204, RTP. ("I have a real admiration for Norman Thomas, and he is much more of a Republican than a New Dealer.")
7. RT to Mrs. Drew Pearson, Jan. 9, 1951, RT to Benjamin Katz, Nov. 29, 1950, RTP.
8. *CR*, March 9, 1951, pp. 2186–2207, June 1, 1951, p. 6029; RT to Muste, March 8, 1951, Martin papers.
9. RT to Arthur Vandenberg, Nov. 11, 1950, box 820, RTP.
10. *Time*, Nov. 20, 27, 1950, pp. 20, 16; State Department *Bulletin*, Vol. 23 (Nov. 27, 1950), p. 839; RT to Titus Crasto, Nov. 24, box 815, RT to John Foster Dulles, Nov. 16, 1950, box 821, RTP.
11. New York *Times*, Jan. 6, 1951, p. 1, original in box 554, RTP; also *CR*, Jan. 5, 1951, p. 61.
12. New York *Times*, Jan. 6, 1951, pp. 4, 5; *Time*, Jan. 22, 1951, pp. 15–16; *CR*, Jan. 5, 1951, p. 61.
13. New York *Times*, Jan. 8, 12, 1951, pp. 6, 11.
14. Ibid., Jan. 12, 1951, p. 1.
15. Ibid., Jan. 8, 1951, p. 1; "Meet the Press," Jan. 7, 1951, transcript, box 1280, RTP; RT to Horace D. Taft, Jan. 18, 1951, Horace D. Taft papers (his possession, New Haven); RT to Barbara Taft, Jan. 18, 1951, box 1204, RTP; RT to Ethan Shepley, Jan. 8, RT to William Maag, Jan. 13, 1951, Martin papers.
16. New York *Times*, Jan. 10, 11, 1951; National Press Club speech, transcript, box 134, Smith papers; Washington *Post*, Jan. 10, 1951 (Drew Pearson).
17. RT to Bruce Barton, Jan. 15, 1951, box 67, Barton papers, State Historical Society of Wisconsin; RT to George P. Day, Feb. 23, 1951, box 906, RTP.
18. New York *Times*, Jan. 16, 1951, pp. 1, 11; Jan. 9, 1951, p. 1.
19. For a few of RT's many comments during this period, see speeches, Jan. 26, box 1280, Feb. 8, box 1280, testimony to Foreign Relations Committee,

Feb. 26, boxes 749, 559, speech, March 29, 1951, box 554, RTP. Also New York *Times*, Feb. 18, 27, April 8, 1951; *Congressional Quarterly Almanac, 1951*, p. 63; *Newsweek*, April 16, 1951, pp. 27–28; Willard Shelton, "Vote of No Confidence," *Nation*, Vol. 172 (April 14, 1951), pp. 341–342; and Ronald J. Caridi, *The Korean War and American Politics: The Republican Party as a Case Study* (Philadelphia, 1968), pp. 136–138. Some of RT's letters are to John S. Wood, Jan. 23, box 1193, to Eugene Millikin, Feb. 24, box 829, to Joseph R. Grundy, March 8, box 837, to Vandenberg, March 26, box 944, to Robert E. Dent, box 923, RTP.

20. RT quote, in testimony to Foreign Relations Committee, box 749, RTP. Evaluations of the debate include Herbert Feis, *From Trust to Terror: The Onset of the Cold War, 1945–1950* (New York, 1968), pp. 285, 380; Edward S. Corwin, "The President's Power," *New Republic*, Vol. 124 (Jan. 29, 1951), pp. 15–16; Henry W. Berger, "Senator Robert A. Taft Dissents from Military Escalation," in Thomas G. Paterson, *Cold War Critics: Alternatives to American Foreign Policy in the Truman Years* (Chicago, 1971), pp. 167–204.

21. *CR*, Jan. 5, 1951, pp. 58–64; Lawrence Dennis, *Appeal to Reason*, Nos. 198, 250, 266; A. J. Muste, "The Global Picture," *Fellowship*, Vol. 17 (Feb. 1951), pp. 1–7.

22. New York *Times*, Feb. 18, 1951, Vol. 4, p. 3; *The Nation*, Vol. 171 (Jan. 13, 20, 1951), p. 21, 54; *New Republic*, Vol. 124 (Jan. 15, 1951), pp. 3–4; John P. Armstrong, "The Enigma of Senator Taft and American Foreign Policy," *Review of Politics*, Vol. 17 (April 1955), pp. 206–231.

23. John T. Greene to Harry S Truman, Jan. 7, 1951, Gene Chapman to Truman, Feb. 15, 1951, PPF 2950, Truman papers, Truman Library, Independence.

24. Dwight D. Eisenhower, *Stories I Tell My Friends* (Garden City, 1967), pp. 371–372; General Wilton Persons to author, Aug. 27, 1970; Arthur Larson, *Eisenhower: The President Nobody Knew* (New York, 1968), pp. 68–69; Roscoe Drummond, *Christian Science Monitor*, April 9, 1969; Eisenhower, *Mandate for Change, 1953–1956* (New York, 1963), pp. 13, 14, 21; Interview, Paul Walter (COHP), p. 89. For a view of RT-Eisenhower relations in 1947, Arthur Krock, *Memoirs: 60 Years on the Firing Line* (New York, 1968), p. 268.

25. RT to John B. Chapple, Jan. 10, 1951, Martin papers.

26. RT to Horace D. Taft, Dec. 6, 1950, Horace D. Taft papers.

27. "Meet the Press," Jan. 7, 1951, transcript, box 1280, RTP; New York *Times*, Jan. 8, 1951, p. 1; RT speech, Chicago, Jan. 26, 1951, box 1280, RT to L. H. McCamic, Jan. 17, 1951, box 1196, RTP.

28. New York *Times*, April 12, 1951, p. 8; RT to Clarence O. Sherrill, March 20, 1945, Douglas MacArthur archives, Norfolk, Va.; RT to Julius Klein, Sept. 5, 1945, RTP; MacArthur to RT, June 14, 1946, MacArthur archives; Cincinnati *Enquirer*, Oct. 21, 1953.

29. RT, "Korean War and MacArthur Dismissal," *Vital Speeches*, Vol. 17 (May 11, 1951), pp. 420–422 (speech given, April 12, 1951); New York *Times*, April 13, 1951, p. 4.

30. RT to Elmer Bruss, April 19, 1951, box 456, RTP; Joseph Martin (as told to Robert J. Donovan), *My First Fifty Years in Politics* (New York, 1960),

p. 208; *Newsweek,* May 7, 1951, p. 25; *CR,* April 27, 1951, p. 4462 (original in box 554, RTP); New York *Times,* April 27, 28, 1951; RT to J. B. Walter, April 30, 1951, Martin papers. (Taft said he had received 3500 telegrams and 12,000 letters, "of which not more than one per cent supports the President.")

31. RT to Earl Jones, June 22, box 898, RT to E. L. Chandler, June 25, box 874, RT to J. C. Argetsinger, July 10, 1951, box 1186, RTP; RT to MacArthur, Aug. 9, 1951, MacArthur archives ("I suppose a stalemate peace at the 38th parallel is better than a stalemate war, but in the end it can only mean our failure in all of the noble purposes which we are constantly proclaiming."); for Wherry, *Reporter,* Vol. 4 (April 17, 1951), pp. 10–11.

32. RT release, May 27, 1951, box 1281, RTP; RT to Charles J. Turck, June 1, 1951, Martin papers; RT to George W. Curtis, July 13, 1951, box 874, speech, Indianapolis, June 23, 1951, box 874, RTP; New York *Times,* July 22, Aug. 19, Oct. 9, 1951; radio interview, July 3, 1951, box 1281, RTP.

33. Critiques of Taft are "Aid and Comfort," *Commonweal,* Vol. 54 (Aug. 3, 1951), p. 397; Tom Connally, (as told to Alfred Steinberg), *My Name Is Tom Connally* (New York, 1954), pp. 353, 355; Armstrong, "Enigma"; "Meet the Press," Jan. 24, 1952, box 1284, RTP. RT on Mao is letter to Mrs. Alexandra de Goguel, Aug. 8, 1951, box 848, RTP; RT on Asia, *CR,* Feb. 24, 1948, p. A1072.

34. Other critiques are John W. Spanier, *The Truman-MacArthur Controversy and the Korean War* (New York, 1959), p. 161; Richard Rovere and Arthur Schlesinger, Jr., *The MacArthur Controversy and American Foreign Policy* (New York, 1965), pp. 228–229; Rovere, *New Yorker,* April 21, 1951, p. 111; Caridi, passim. Quote is RT to Hugh W. Sanford, Jr., May 22, 1951, Martin papers.

35. John Franklin Carter to Dewey, May 24, 1951, personal correspondence, Dewey papers, University of Rochester.

36. RT to J. Thomas Baldwin, July 31, 1951, box 1187, RTP.

37. Lee Barker to author, April 27, 1971; Blanche O'Berg to author, July 14, 1971; Horace D. Taft (COHP), p. 73.

38. RT, *A Foreign Policy for Americans* (Garden City, 1951), Ch. 8; *CR,* Jan. 5, 1951, p. 61. See also the pamphlet by his friend, General Bonner Fellers, " 'Thought War' Against the Kremlin," Human Affairs Pamphlet #46, 1949.

39. RT, *Foreign Policy,* Ch. 6.

40. Ibid., pp. 110–112, 73.

41. Ibid., pp. 1–8, Ch. 1.

42. RT to Gardner Cowles, Nov. 21, 1951, Lou Guylay to RT, Nov. 15, Dec. 5, box 841, and RT to Helen Manning, Dec. 29, 1951, RTP. Also *Publisher's Weekly,* Vol. 160 (Dec. 1, 1951), pp. 2114–2115; Lee Barker to author, Dec. 29, 1970, Lee Barker to RT, Aug. 6, 1952, box 1320, RTP.

43. Chicago *Tribune,* Nov. 18, 1951, p. 3; MacArthur to RT, Nov. 19, 1951, MacArthur archives; John Hamilton to Roy Dunn, Dec. 10, 1951, box 422, RTP.

44. James Reston, New York *Times,* Nov. 15, 1951, p. 22; "But Senator, They

Don't Fit," *Collier's,* Vol. 129 (Jan. 19, 1952), p. 70; Louisville *Courier Journal,* Nov. 26, 1951; Richard Strout, *Christian Science Monitor,* Nov. 16, 1951; Joseph Evans, *Wall Street Journal,* Nov. 15, 1951; Lewis Galantière, *Saturday Review of Literature,* Nov. 17, 1951, p. 13; *Newsweek,* Nov. 19, 1951, pp. 28–29; New York *Herald Tribune,* Nov. 16, 1951, p. 18; *Time,* Nov. 26, 1951, pp. 23–24; *Life,* Dec. 3, 1951, p. 44; Lindsay Rogers, *New York Times Book Review,* Nov. 18, 1951, p. 3; Bundy, *Reporter,* Dec. 11, 1951, p. 37.

45. Dayton *News,* Nov. 18, 1951. Other reviews, box 841, RTP.
46. RT speech, Nov. 27, 1951, box 1283, RTP. For the view of a thorough-going noninterventionist see "Bob Taft's Foreign Policy," *The Freeman,* Dec. 17, 1951, pp. 165–166.

CHAPTER 32: THE LAST, BEST CHANCE

1. New York *Times,* Oct. 17, 1951, pp. 1, 26.
2. RT to Colonel Robert McCormick, May 29, 1950, box 260, RTP, LC.
3. Ibid., Nov. 11, 1950, box 819, John Marshall to RT, March 12, 1951, box 310, RTP; Richard Scandrett, Marshall letters, box 1, Roger Faherty papers, State Historical Society of Wisconsin.
4. Dr. R. Bretney Miller to Dr. E. R. Henderson, June 27, July 24, 1951, RTP; Dr. Miller explained that in 1950 Martha had suffered a "cerebral vascular accident," which resulted in "left hemiplegia from which she made a reasonably good recovery" prior to her decline in 1951; RT to Barbara Taft, Jan. 18, RT to Mrs. Hulbert Taft, Feb. 5, 1951, both box 1204, RTP.
5. RT to Horace D. Taft, Jan. 18, 1951, Horace D. Taft papers, his possession, New Haven; Stanley Rowe (COHP), p. 33.
6. RT to Horace D. Taft, Jan. 18, 1951, Horace D. Taft papers; Dorothy Rowe, "Tribute to a Friend" (privately printed, 1964); Interview, Horace D. Taft.
7. RT debate with Paul Douglas, July 22, 1951, box 1281, RTP.
8. R. Alton Lee, *Truman and Taft-Hartley: A Question of Mandate* (Lexington, 1966), p. 179; RT to B. E. Hutchinson, Nov. 29, 1950, box 817, RT to Richard J. Gray, July 24, box 1188, RT to W. A. R. Bruehl, Sept. 11, box 1188, RT to Sinclair Weeks, Oct. 25, 1951, box 1206, RTP.
9. RT to Will A. Foster, April 20, RT to Charles R. Hook, Dec. 28, box 1186, RT to Marrs McLean, Oct. 6, 1951, box 390, RTP; RT to Eugene Carr, Sept. 26, 1951, I. Jack Martin papers, Kensington, Md.
10. William V. Shannon, "Last of the Old Breed," *Progressive,* Vol. 16 (June 1952), pp. 5–8; George H. Hall, "The Sinister Alliance Between McCarthy and Taft," St. Louis *Post-Dispatch,* Feb. 18, 1951; Benjamin H. Reese (COHP), pp. 98–101.
11. New York *Times,* June 15, Oct. 23, 1951, pp. 3, 14; *Newsweek,* Nov. 5, 1951, p. 28; RT to George Chaplin, July 10, 1951, box 874, Aug. 17, 1951, box 944, RT speech, June 23, 1951, box 874, RTP.
12. RT to Gordon Scherer, March 29, 1951, Martin papers; RT to Tom Power, Sept. 17, 1951, box 953, RTP.
13. RT to General Albert Wedemeyer, Nov. 22, 1950, box 814, RT to J. W.

Moore, July 25, 1951, box 912, RT to Ben Tate, Jan. 2, 1952, box 321, RTP; New York *Times,* Feb. 3, July 1, Aug. 13, Oct. 12, 17, 19, 20, 1951; A. E. Holmans, *United States Fiscal Policy, Its Contribution to Economic Stability, 1945–1959* (London, 1961), pp. 157, 179.

14. RT to Blanche G. Schwartz, Dec. 27, 1950, box 216, RT to Frank P. Doherty, March 20, RT to Zach Cobb, March 26, 1951, both box 296, RTP.

15. RT to David Ingalls, Jan. 20, box 1193, RT to John Marshall, March 21, box 310, RT to Don Ebright, Feb. 19, box 456, Ingalls to Ned Creighton, March 26, May 22, 1951, box 294, RTP. Also miscellaneous correspondence re Ingalls in Tom Coleman papers, State Historical Society of Wisconsin.

16. *Life,* Aug. 6, 1951, p. 94; Guylay to RT, July 31, 1951, box 415, RTP.

17. RT to Mrs. David Childs, May 10, 1951, RTP; William H. Taft to Roger Faherty, March 26, 1951, box 1, Faherty papers, State Historical Society of Wisconsin; Ingalls to Robert W. Kellough, Sept. 1, 1951, box 376, RTP.

18. *U.S. News & World Report,* Aug. 24, 1951, pp. 28–29; RT handwritten thoughts, box 415, RTP.

19. Ingalls to Claude G. Baughman, Oct. 11, 1951, box 341; L. Richard Guylay to RT, Sept. 25, 1951, Martin papers.

20. *Life,* Oct. 15, 1951, p. 82.

21. Harry S Truman to RT, Oct. 17, box 954, RT to Truman, Oct. 29, box 405, Thomas E. Dewey to RT, Nov. 1, 1951, box 954, RTP.

22. New York *Times,* Nov. 27, 28, 1951, pp. 26, 28; *Newsweek,* Dec. 10, 1951, p. 24; "Findings, Observations, and Recommendations of the Subcommittee on Privileges and Elections," 1952, Martin papers; U.S. Congress, Senate, Hearings Before the Subcommittee on Privileges and Elections of the Committee on Rules and Administration, *Investigation into the 1950 Senatorial Campaign,* Eighty-second Congress, First and Second Sessions (Washington, D.C., 1952).

23. "The Charles Taft Story," 1952, Charles P. Taft, 2nd, papers, Cincinnati; C. P. Taft, *You and I — and Roosevelt* (New York, 1936), p. 4; C. P. Taft, *Democracy in Politics and Education* (New York, 1950); RT to Horace D. Taft, July 6, 1937, box 21, Hollister to RT, Jan. 27, 1939, RT to Dr. H. H. Beneka, Feb. 20, 1946, box 776, RTP; Interview, Charles P. Taft, 2nd, Cincinnati *Enquirer,* Oct. 21, 1951, section 3, p. 3.

24. RT to Martha, Aug. 10, 1941, Charles P. Taft to RT, July 18, 1944, RTP; William H. Hessler, "The Brothers Taft," *Reporter,* Vol. 6 (Jan. 8, 1952), p. 6.

25. RT to Roy E. Fry, Sept. 7, 1951, RT to Charles P. Taft, 2nd, Oct. 20, 1951, Aug. 24, 1952, RTP.

26. Cabell Phillips, "With Candidate Taft on the Road," *New York Times Magazine,* Nov. 12, 1951, p. 12; RT speeches, schedules, box 1283, RTP.

27. Quote is RT to Jack Martin, Dec. 1, 1951, box 405, RTP. See also letters to Mrs. John W. Herron, Jr., July 10, Louise Laws, Nov. 20, John Martin, Oct. 17, box 405, and Karl Mundt, Dec. 27, 31, 1951, box 385, RTP. Also Zora Neale Hurston, "A Negro Voter Sizes Up Taft," *Saturday Evening Post,* Vol. 224 (Dec. 8, 1951), p. 29.

28. New York *Herald Tribune,* Dec. 3, 1951, Washington *Post,* Dec. 9, 1951, section 2, p. 1b; "Taft's Campaigners," *U.S. News & World Report,*

Vol. 32 (June 13, 1952), p. 40; *Time,* Jan. 21, June 2, 1952, p. 18; Coleman to RT, June 28, 1949, Coleman to Barry Goldwater, Sept. 10, 1963, boxes 5, 15, Coleman papers.

29. M. McMillin, "How Taft Was Saved," *New Republic,* Vol. 126 (April 14, 1952), pp. 16–17; Interviews, Earl Warren, Darrah Wunder, Edwin Lahey (COHP), p. 18, Lou Guylay, Lloyd Taft, Justin Rollman.

30. Hugh Scott, *Come to the Party* (Englewood Cliffs, N.J., 1968), p. 74; Paul David, ed., *Presidential Nominating Politics in 1952,* Vol. 1 (Baltimore, 1954), p. 25; Thomas E. Dewey to Dwight D. Eisenhower, Sept. 1, 1948, personal correspondence, Thomas Dewey papers, University of Rochester; Arthur Vandenberg to Eisenhower, Sept. 8, 1949, Vandenberg papers, University of Michigan.

31. H. Alexander Smith (COHP), pp. 259, 271; Howard Pyle press conference, 1951, box 294, RTP.

32. Washington *Post,* Aug. 26, 1951; *Newsweek,* Dec. 31, 1951, p. 20, Feb. 18, 1952, p. 27; Elmo Roper, *You and Your Leaders: Their Actions and Your Reactions, 1936–1956* (New York, 1957), pp. 202–203.

33. RT to Major General Robert S. Beightler, Nov. 24, 1950, Blanche O'Berg papers, her possession, D.C.; RT to Guylay, Dec. 11, 1950, box 814, RTP; RT to K. K. Brown, March 9, 1951, Martin papers.

34. Ingalls to Paul Sexson, Aug. 10, box 294, Ingalls to Robert Leach, Oct. 27, box 341; RT to Charles M. White, Oct. 29, box 405, RT to Fellers, Dec. 31, box 1190; Jack Martin to Marrs McLean, Dec. 28, 1951, box 1190; Ingalls to Ralph Perkins, Nov. 14, 1951, box 329, RTP. Also RT, "Meet the Press," Jan. 20, 1952, RTP ("I think it would be perfectly possible to reconcile my policies with General Eisenhower's. The questions . . . are not questions of principle; they're rather questions of degree").

35. RT to Albert J. Bell, Oct. 28, RT to Billie Noojin, Nov. 20, box 1199, RT to Tom Coleman, Dec. 1, 1951, box 1188, RTP.

36. RT to Sen. Hugh Butler, Dec. ?, 1951, box 405, RTP.

37. RT to Dr. McGuire, May 17, box 1196, RT to Alvin Weichel, Dec. 31, box 1206, RT to Eugene Pulliam, Dec. 1, 1951, box 1055, RT to X. North, Jan. 3, 1952, box 1224, RT to John E. Jackson, Jan. 1, 1952, box 405, RTP.

CHAPTER 33: THE TENSIONS OF CAMPAIGNING

1. Henry F. Pringle, *The Life and Times of William Howard Taft,* Vol. 1, (New York, 1939), p. 264.

2. *U.S. News & World Report,* Feb. 15, 1952, pp. 20, 22; RT speeches and schedule, Jan.–Feb., 1952, box 1284, RTP, LC; *Congressional Quarterly Almanac, 1952,* p. 75; Noel G. Rapp, "The Political Speaking of Robert A. Taft, 1939 to 1953," doctoral thesis, Purdue, 1955, p. 456; New York *Times,* Feb. 24, section 4, p. 7, May 11, 1952, section 4, p. 1; "1952 Schedule," box 13, Thomas Coleman papers, State Historical Society of Wisconsin.

3. RT letters, boxes 437–447, RTP; Clarence B. Kelland (COHP), p. 103; RT office to Jean, Jan. 30, 1952, box 1227, RTP.

4. RT to Jack Schmetterer, Feb. 27, 1952, I. Jack Martin papers, Kensington, Md.; RT to A. G. Spieker, Feb. 8, box 371, RT to Robert Hoffman, April

22, box 1044, RTP; *Christian Science Monitor,* Feb. 23, 1952; Ferguson-Taft constitutional amendment, May 16, 1952, box 1286, RTP.

5. New York *Times,* Feb. 22, 1952, p. 13; Douglass Cater, "Bob Taft in Dixieland," *Reporter,* Vol. 6 (Jan. 22, 1952), pp. 27–29; RT to Clarence Manion, Feb. 26, 1952, box 323, RT speech, Tampa, Jan. 28, 1952, box 1284, RTP.

6. RT to General Albert Wedemeyer, Dec. 12, 1951, box 301, to Thomas Werdel, Jan. 3, 1952, box 307, RTP; Earl Mazo, *Richard Nixon, A Political and Personal Portrait* (New York, 1959), pp. 88–89; miscellaneous memos and letters, box 18, Coleman papers; Paul David, ed., *Presidential Nominating Politics in 1952* (Baltimore, 1954), Vol. 3, p. 293, Vol. 4, p. 198; Fred Maytag, Jr. to Walter Rogers, April 7, 1952, RT to Ottis Reynolds, Jan. 14, 1952, box 366, RTP.

7. Press endorsements of Dwight D. Eisenhower, collected in box 2, Roger Faherty papers, State Historical Society of Wisconsin; New York *Times,* Feb. 28, 1952, p. 17.

8. RT to General Albert Wedemeyer, Feb. 25, box 361, RT to William Loeb, Jan. 17, box 349, RT to Russell B. Stearns, Jan. 19, 1952, box 336, RTP; Diary, Darrah Wunder, Jan. 22, 1952, her possession, Cincinnati; New York *Times,* Feb. 10, 1952, p. 1.

9. Richard Rovere, *New Yorker,* Jan. 19, 1952, p. 65. (Eisenhower, Rovere said, defined "security" as "a man serving a life time sentence in a federal prison.") John W. Hill to L. Richard Guylay, Feb. 11, 1952, Hill papers, State Historical Society of Wisconsin; *Newsweek,* Jan. 28, 1952, p. 19; "Anti-Eisenhower material," box 16, Coleman papers.

10. Wunder diary, Jan. 19, 1952; RT to Kyle Palmer, Jan. 19, 1952, box 967, RT to Guylay, Jan. 20, 1952, box 1217, RTP.

11. Wunder diary, Feb. 17, 1952; Marquis Childs, *Memphis Commercial Appeal,* Feb. 12, 1952, p. 6; *U.S. News & World Report,* Feb. 15, 1952, p. 21; Wunder diary, Feb. 27, 1952.

12. *Time,* Feb. 25, 1952, p. 24; New York *Daily News,* Feb. 18, 1952; Childs, Memphis *Commercial Appeal,* Feb. 12, 1952.

13. St. Louis *Post Dispatch,* Jan. 27, 1952; New York *Times,* Jan. 26, 1952, p. 7; Interview, Guylay; Wunder diary, Feb. 29, 1952.

14. Wunder diary, Feb. 11, 24, March 2, 13, 1952.

15. Ibid., Feb. 18, 1952.

16. Ibid., March 3, Feb. 21, 1952.

17. Washington *Star,* March 9, 1952, p. C1; New York *Times,* March 7, 1952, p. 14; *Newsweek,* Feb. 25, 1952, p. 26; RT speeches, box 1285, RTP.

18. New York *Times,* March 2, 8, 11, 1952; Wunder diary, March 9, 1952.

19. David, Vol. 2, p. 33; Wunder diary, March 12, 1952.

20. RT releases, March 12, 13, 1952, box 1285, RTP.

21. Rovere, *Affairs of State: The Eisenhower Years* (New York, 1956), Jan. 25, 1953, pp. 84–85; Washington *Post,* March 8, 1952; and Jack Martin to Charles M. White, March 9, 1952, box 1226, RTP, reveal preprimary comments concerning "attacks" on Eisenhower. Post-mortems are *Time,* March 24, 1952, p. 19; New York *Times,* March 12, 13, 16, 1952; Charlotte *Observer,* Aug. 3, 1953; Hollister to RT, March 28, 1952, Hollister papers, Cincinnati.

22. RT to Joseph Grundy, March 20, box 382, RT to F. E. Johnston, March 22, box 349, April 11, box 1219, RTP.
23. Minutes of meeting of Taft staff, Nov. 16, 1951, box 13, Coleman papers; Wunder diary, Jan. 8, Feb. 3, 1952; Hollister memo to RT, Jan. 19, 1952, box 350, RTP; New York *Times*, Jan. 3, March 2, 1952, p. 1, section 4, p. 7; *Newsweek*, Feb. 11, 1952, pp. 24–25; Memo, Paul Walter, "New Hampshire Primary," author's files.
24. RT to Richard Jordan, Feb. 5, 1952, box 349, RTP.
25. Ibid.; to Arch N. Bobbitt, Feb. 25, 1952, box 332, RTP.
26. David, Vol. 4, p. 164; New York *Times*, March 20, 21, 1952.
27. C. L. Sulzberger, *A Low Row of Candles: Memoirs and Diaries, 1934–1954* (New York, 1969), pp. 616, 693, 702, 736; New York *Times*, March 21, 1952, p. 1.
28. New York *Times*, March 19, 21, 1952, pp. 17, 1; *Time*, March 31, 1952, p. 20; David, Vol. 2, p. 190; RT release, March 20, 1952, box 1285, RTP.
29. New York *Times*, April 16, 17, 1952, pp. 1, 16; RT to David Baird, April 24, 1952, box 351, RTP.
30. *Newsweek*, March 24, 31, 1952, pp. 35, 20.
31. RT schedule, March–April, 1952, boxes 1285–1286, RTP; Rapp, p. 448; Democratic National Committee files, clippings re Taft, Truman Library, Independence; New York *Times*, March 18, 19, 30, April 2, 3, 1952; Coleman memo to Barry Goldwater, Sept. 10, 1963, box 13, Coleman papers; David, Vol. 4, p. 133.
32. New York *Times*, April 3, 1952, p. 1; RT press conference, April 2, 1952, box 1286, RT to Woodrow Hedge, April 15, 1952, box 1218, RTP; David, Vol. 4, p. 138.
33. David, Vol. 4, p. 287; New York *Times*, April 3, 1952, p. 1.
34. New York *Times*, April 10, 27, May 1, 2, 11, 18, 1952; David (chapters on Ill., Pa., Mass., Ore., R.I., Vt.); RT to Lowell Paget, March 1, RT to Prescott Cookingham, April 11, 1952, box 1213, RTP.
35. RT to James E. Schaal, April 26, 1952, box 1011, RTP; *CR*, April 2, 1952, p. 3419; Washington *Post*, April 19, 1952.
36. Milwaukee *Journal*, March 3, 1952; RT to Herbert Hoover, Feb. 5, 1952, box 995, RTP; New York *Times*, Jan. 20, 1952, p. 41; speeches re Indo-China, Feb., 1952, box 1284, RTP.
37. *Newsweek*, May 19, June 2, 1952, pp. 27, 21; RT to Charles Kutill, May 16, RT to Clara M. Payette, April 25, 1952, box 996, RTP; New York *Times*, Feb. 7, 8, March 12, May 25, 29, 1952; Milwaukee *Journal*, March 31, 1952.
38. RT to M. J. Moss, May 6, 1952, box 1223, RT to C. D. Walker, June 25, 1952, box 996, Coleman memo to Ingalls and others, May 24, 1952, RT radio interview, June 5, 1952, box 1286, RTP.
39. RT to Hoover, Dec. 27, box 405, RT to Harvey Higley, Dec. 29, 1951, box 1192, RTP; St. Louis *Post-Dispatch*, March 24, 1952.
40. Memo, J.H. to RT, Dec. 19, 1951, box 14, Coleman papers; Ben Tate to RT, Dec. 26, 1951, box 949, RTP; Wunder diary, Feb. 1, 1952. ("As Bob says, Joe gets excited and swings a little wide, but there were fellow travellers in the State Department and Communists.")
41. "Consecrated Tory: Robert A. Taft," *New Republic*, Vol. 126 (March 17–

May 5, 1952); "Senator Taft's Remedy for Asian Problems," *Christian Century*, Vol. 69 (Feb. 27, 1952), p. 235; Arthur Schlesinger, Jr., "The New Isolationism," *Atlantic*, May 1952, p. 36; Richard Rovere, "What's Happened to Taft?" *Harper's*, Vol. 204 (April 1952), pp. 38–44.

42. RT to Helen Manning, Dec. 29, 1951, RTP; Wunder diary, April 11, 1952. Martha and Mrs. Manning did read and correct Mrs. Harnsberger's draft. (RT to Mrs. Harnsberger, Nov. 24, 1951, box 840, RTP).

43. RT to Harold Heminger, Jan. 20, box 1191, RT to Curtis Dozier, Dec. 28, 1951, box 1189, RT to friends, April 30, 1952, box 424, RTP.

44. RT to Morris Shawkey, Jan. 3, box 927, RT to Gervais Reed, May 15, box 329, RT to Willis Sweetland, April 14, 1952, box 342, RTP; New York *Times*, May 14, 1952, p. 1. Re W. Va. Taft must have seen an early edition; the city edition headlined, "TAFT WINS EASILY IN WEST VIRGINIA."

45. RT to B. E. Hutchinson, April 11, 1952, box 1218, RTP.

46. RT to Frank Gannett, Feb. 20, 1952, box 1216, RTP; Chicago *Tribune* polls, Dec. 24, 1951, Feb. 10, 1952; Interview, Lou Guylay.

47. Angus Campbell, et al., *The American Voter* (New York, 1960), pp. 110–113, 142–145; Robert E. Lane, *Political Life: Why People Get Involved in Politics* (Glencoe, 1959), pp. 286–288; Lee Bogart, *Age of Television: A Study of Viewing Habits and the Impact of Television on American Life* (New York, 1956), pp. 210, 221; Bernard Berelson and Gary A. Steiner, *Human Behavior: An Inventory of Scientific Findings* (New York, 1964), p. 529.

48. New York *Post*, March 26, 1952; Lahey (COHP), p. 11; "Consecrated Tory," *New Republic*, March 17, 1952, p. 9.

49. Wunder diary, April 19, 1952.

50. Tate (for Adolph Menjou), Nov. 19, 1951, box 949, John Hamilton to RT, Feb. 24, 1952, box 456, RTP; John Hollister to RT, March 28, 1952, Hollister papers; "Thoughts Expressed by Mr. Samuel Pryor and His Friends to General Julius Klein in Regard to Taft Campaign," 1952, RTP; Eric Sevareid to author, Sept. 23, 1969.

51. Interviews, Ingalls, Clarence Kelland (COHP), p. 103; Les Arends (COHP), pp. 5–6; Richard Rovere, "Letter from Chicago," *New Yorker*, Vol. 28 (July 19, 1952), p. 72; Wunder diary, May 4, 1952.

CHAPTER 34: "STEALING" DELEGATES

1. Optimistic reports are Clarence Brown to Omar Hurst, June 13, 1952, Clarence Brown papers, Ohio Historical Society; RT delegate count, "States Already Voting," May 6, 1952, box 1287, RTP, LC; RT to James F. Dewey, May 16, box 393, RT to Mrs. F. H. Cabot, May 20, RT to Horace Taft, May 21, RT to James Clark, June 9, box 990, RT to Victor Emanuel, June 17, box 990, RT to E. B. Keeton (returning money), Nov. 28, 1952, box 979, RTP. In RT to John Hamilton, June 28, 1952, box 1217, RTP, he asked Hamilton to stay on during the campaign and suggested Everett Dirksen of Illinois as the "most vigorous campaign chairman."

2. Paul M. David, *Presidential Nominating Politics in 1952*, Vol. 4 (Baltimore, 1954), p. 261; *Newsweek*, June 16, 1952, p. 27; New York *Times*, June 5, 1952, p. 17.

3. New York *Times*, June 1–5, 1952, p. 1; David F. Schoenbrun, "The Ordeal of General Eisenhower," *Harper's*, Vol. 205 (Oct. 1952), pp. 25–34; Carroll Reece in New York *Times*, June 5, 1952, p. 17; prairie fire, ibid., June 15, 1952, section 4, p. 1.

4. Willard Shelton, "The Retrogression of Senator Taft," *The Nation*, Vol. 174 (May 17, 1952), pp. 473–475; William V. Shannon, "Last of the Old Breed," *Progressive*, Vol. 16 (June 1952), pp. 5–8.

5. "The 1912 Overture to 1952," *Life*, June 23, 1952; also July 7, 1952.

6. RT also got some TV time. See TV script, June 19, 1952, box 1286, RTP. For a typical RT complaint re media, RT to Governor John Fine, June 26, 1952, box 382, RTP.

7. David, Vol. 3, p. 315, is a key source for the following pages. For background, see also "Texas Confidential," box 188, and box 187, RTP.

8. David Ingalls to RT, Jan. 31, box 414, Marrs McLean to RT, Aug. 11, box 390, Ingalls to H. J. Porter, Sept. 18, and Ingalls to Henry Zweifel, Sept. 4, 1951, box 389, RTP; Thomas Coleman to Ingalls, Sept. 25, Ingalls to Coleman, Sept. 27, 1951, box 13, Coleman papers, State Historical Society of Wisconsin.

9. Ben Tate to Webster Atwell, Jan. 29, 1952, box 20, Coleman papers; RT to Carroll Reece, Feb. 25, box 1226, RT to John Jackson, March 11, box 1219, Coleman memo of meeting, March 17, 1952, box 388, RTP.

10. Houston *Post*, New York *Times*, May 2–6, 1952; David, Vol. 3, p. 315.

11. Houston *Post*, May 7, 1952, p. 1.

12. Houston *Post*, New York *Times*, May 22–28, 1952; David, Vol. 3, p. 320.

13. RT, handwritten, "What Really Happened in Texas," 1952, Blanche O'Berg papers, her possession, D.C.; Clarence Kelland (COHP), p. 90; John Hamilton to RT, June 18, 1952, box 1217, RTP.

14. RT to McLean, May 6, box 390, May 19, box 1231, RTP.

15. Zweifel to Jack Martin, May 13, M. W. Webb to RT, May 10, McLean to RT, May 1 and to Ingalls, May 7, 1952, box 390, RTP; McClean to RT, May 14, 1952, box 20, Coleman papers; letters from Texas, box 14, Coleman papers.

16. Joseph Alsop, *Houston Post*, May 29, 1952, p. 1; Moley, *Newsweek*, June 9, 1952, p. 100; New York *Times*, June 15, 1952, section 4, p. 3.

17. New York *Times*, June 22, 1952, p. 1; Eisenhower literature re Texas, in Texas file, Paul Walter papers, Cleveland; Jack Bell, *The Splendid Misery: The Story of the Presidency and Power Politics at Close Range* (Garden City, 1960), p. 201.

18. John Hamilton memo to RT, June 18, 1952, box 1177, RTP; John Hollister to RT, June 21, 1952, Hollister papers, Cincinnati; Walter (COHP), pp. 91–92.

19. RT to Steven B. Wilson, June 3, box 384, RT interview, June 5, box 1286, RT to Jesse Jones, June 25, 1952, box 389, RTP. Pauline Isaacson, "Robert Alphonso Taft: An Assessment of a Persuader," doctoral thesis, Minnesota, 1956, p. 300, quotes several interviews and letters from Taft supporters about Texas.

20. RT to John Jackson, June 23, box 331, RT to Guy Gabrielson, July 3, 1952, box 389, RTP.
21. David, Vol. 3, p. 326.
22. New York *Times*, July 1–5, 1952, p. 1.
23. Ibid., July 3, 1952, p. 14; Interviews, Paul Walter, Frank Lausche.
24. *Newsweek*, June 30, 1952, p. 27; polls, New York *Times*, July 5–7, 1952.
25. Dykstra to Franz R. Dykstra, July 4, 1952, Dykstra papers (her possession, S. Yarmouth, Mass.). On June 3 RT had written, "As far as Stassen is concerned, I don't think he has any more influence today, and I doubt if anybody on any side is going to give him a job" (to R. G. Martin, box 370, RTP).
26. David, Vol. 1, p. 382; New York *Times*, July 1–3, 1952.
27. David Caldwell to RT, July 4, box 388, Edward F. Clark, Jr. to RT, July 4, 1952, RTP. The RT papers contain many such letters and telegrams — some of them, no doubt, the result of a campaign by Eisenhower people.

CHAPTER 35: DEFEAT AT CHICAGO

1. Henry F. Pringle, *The Life and Times of William Howard Taft*, Vol. 2 (New York, 1939), pp. 801–803.
2. New York *Times*, July 7, 1952, p. 1; Paul M. David, *Presidential Nominating Politics in 1952* (Baltimore, 1954), Vol. 2, p. 155; Lillian Dykstra to Franz Dykstra, July 8, 1952, Dykstra papers (her possession, S. Yarmouth, Mass.).
3. St. Louis *Post Dispatch*, July 31, 1953; *Newsweek*, July 7, 1952, p. 18.
4. Dykstra to Franz Dykstra, July 5, 1952, Dykstra papers; diary, Mrs. Darrah Wunder, June 29–30, 1952 (her possession, Cincinnati); Interview, Blanche O'Berg; Des Moines *Register*, New York *Times*, July 6, 1952, p. 1.
5. Dykstra to Franz Dykstra, July 5, 1952, Dykstra papers; Wunder diary, July 5, 6, 1952; *Life*, July 7, 1952, p. 11; RT release, July 1, 1952, RTP, LC.
6. David, Vol. 1, p. 189; lists of "key men," box 308, RTP; organization charts and notebooks, box 16, Thomas Coleman papers, State Historical Society of Wisconsin; statistics re delegates, boxes 435–436, RTP, and in Paul Walter papers, Cleveland.
7. New York *Times*, June 30, July 5, 1952, p. 1; Clarence Kelland (COHP), pp. 103–104; Wunder diary, March 9, 1952; Courtney Whitney, *MacArthur: His Rendezvous with History* (New York, 1964), p. 523; *Life*, Sept. 5, 1955, p. 81; New York *Times*, Aug. 1, 1953. John Bricker told the author flatly that Taft would have chosen MacArthur as his running mate. But David Ingalls and Paul Walter, two of Taft's closest friends, insisted in interviews that Taft had not made up his mind. Basil Brewer, a Massachusetts publisher who ardently supported Taft, said at the time that Taft had told him that Representative Joseph Martin, Jr., of Mass. was his "choice as a running mate" (undated memo, 1952, Martin papers, North Easton, Mass.) No one else, however, thought Taft would pick Martin. It seems unlikely that he had definitely committed himself to anyone.

8. Chicago *Tribune*, New York *Times*, July 6–8, 1952; Rovere, *Affairs of State: The Eisenhower Years* (New York, 1956), p. 25.

9. David, Vol. 5, p. 225; Earl Mazo, *Richard Nixon: A Political and Personal Portrait* (New York, 1959), pp. 92–93; Interviews, Earl Warren, William Knowland; Ben Tate memo re Calif., June 9, 1952, box 300, RT to Norman Chandler, July 18, 1952, box 296, RTP.

10. Walter memo to author, "Background on the Wilson Nomination for Secretary of Defense," 1970; Coleman memo, Dec. 29, Arthur Summerfield to Coleman, Nov. 26, 1951, box 18, Coleman papers; Coleman to Jack Martin, April 10, 1952, RTP; David, Vol. 4, p. 44.

11. David, Vol. 2, p. 267; RT to Governor John Fine, June 19, 26, 1952, box 382, RTP; New York *Times*, June 12, July 10, 1952, pp. 22, 20; *Time*, July 7, 1952, p. 12; Wunder diary, April 28, 1952.

12. Re Louisiana, David, Vol. 3, p. 265; Richard Lewis, "How Taft Stole the South," *New Republic*, Vol. 128 (July 7, 1952), pp. 11–12; RT to John E. Jackson, Jan. 1, March 3, 1952, boxes 331, 332, RTP.

13. *Official Report of the Proceedings of the 25th Republican National Convention . . . 1952* (D.C., 1952), pp. 7–29.

14. Coleman to Brown, July 14, 1952, box 15, Coleman papers; William J. Miller, *Henry Cabot Lodge: A Biography* (New York, 1967), p. 246; New York *Times*, July 8, 1952, p. 1; David, Vol. 1, p. 68.

15. David, Vol. 1, p. 68; *Proceedings*, pp. 26–30; Interview, Paul Walter.

16. *Time*, July 21, 1952, p. 13; Walter memo to author, Feb. 27, 1970; Pauline Isaacson, "Robert Alphonso Taft, An Assessment of a Persuader," doctoral thesis, Minnesota, 1956, pp. 324–327.

17. *Proceedings*, pp. 30–52.

18. Post-mortems are *Time*, July 21, 1952, pp. 12–13; *Newsweek*, July 14, 1952, p. 23; Hugh Scott, *Come to the Party* (Englewood Cliffs, N.J., 1968), p. 100; David, Vol. 1, p. 381, Vol. 2, p. 267, Vol. 4, pp. 56–57; Coleman to James W. Irwin, July 16, Coleman to RT, July 14, 1952, box 15, Coleman papers; Diary, H. Alexander Smith, July 8, 1952, Smith papers, Princeton University; Interviews, Vernon Romney (COHP), p. 17, Paul Walter (COHP), p. 94, Edwin Lahey (COHP), p. 18, Charles P. Taft, 2nd (COHP), p. 10, William Knowland.

19. RT press conference, July 8, 1952, RTP; Hoover statement, July 9, 1952, box 1–1/136, Hoover papers, Hoover Library, Iowa; Dykstra to Franz Dykstra, July 8, 1952.

20. Re Fine and Summerfield, Dwight D. Eisenhower, *Mandate for Change, 1953–1956* (New York, 1963), p. 40; Interview, Charles Halleck.

21. Background on Georgia is David Ingalls memo, Sept. 1, box 312, Ingalls to Mrs. Margaret Rockwell, Sept. 4, box 294, Ingalls to A. C. Mattei, Sept. 24, box 299, Harry Sommers to RT, Sept. 24, box 1004, Loren Berry to Ben Tate, Nov. 26, 1951, box 312, Sommers to Ingalls, Jan. 16, box 312, Jack Martin to Sommers, Jan. 19, box 312, Ingalls to W. D. Malone, March 31, 1952, box 292, RTP; Atlanta *Constitution*, Feb. 15, 1952, p. 18; *Time*, July 14, 1952, pp. 18–19; David, Vol. 3, p. 85.

22. *Proceedings*, pp. 175–178.

23. *Proceedings*, pp. 179–195.

24. David, Vol. 1, p. 75; New York *Times*, July 9–10, 1952; *Proceedings*, pp. 196–215.

25. Dykstra to Franz Dykstra, July 9, 1952, Dykstra papers; Rovere, *Affairs of State*, pp. 27–28; Clarence Kelland (COHP), p. 92; Lodge oral account, Princeton University, pp. 7–8; Isaacson, pp. 331–332.

26. Chicago *Tribune*, July 12, 1952, p. 7; Interview, Paul Walter (COHP), pp. 29, 90; Jack Bell, *The Splendid Misery: The Story of the Presidency and Power Politics at Close Range* (Garden City, 1960), p. 217.

27. Bell, p. 217; *Proceedings*, pp. 388–407.

28. Clarence Kelland (COHP), p. 92; New York *Times*, July 12, 1952, p. 9; *Newsweek*, July 21, 1952, p. 22; Interview, Earl Warren; *Time*, July 21, 1952, pp. 12, 18; Smith diary, July 19, 1952; Alexander R. Abrahams to Ingalls, Aug. 4, 1952, box 306, RTP; Coleman to Ingalls, July 24, 1952, Coleman to Robert Taft, Jr., Oct. 14, 1963, boxes 15, 7, Coleman papers.

29. New York *Times*, July 16, 1952, p. 15.

30. David, Vol. 1, pp. 286–287; "The Taft Defeat," *Christian Century*, Vol. 69 (July 23, 1952), pp. 926–927; *Reporter*, Vol. 7 (Aug. 5, 1952), p. 5. Both these articles blamed Taft's ambition.

31. David, Vol. 1, pp. 68–100, passim; Coleman to Charles S. Thomas, July 21, 1952, Coleman to Barry Goldwater, Sept. 10, 1963, boxes 15, 13, Coleman papers; RT tabulations, scribbled at convention, box 422, RTP.

32. William S. White, *The Taft Story* (New York, 1954), pp. 182–183; John Franklin Carter to Thomas E. Dewey, March 1, 1952, personal correspondence, Dewey papers, University of Rochester.

33. David, Vol. 1, pp. 323–324; Rovere interview, pp. 7–8, Lucius Clay interview, pp. 19–20 (both at Eisenhower Library, Abilene); Raymond Moley, *Newsweek*, July 21, 1952, p. 29; *Time*, Aug. 10, 1953, p. 15; New York *Times*, July 13, 1952, Section 4, p. 3.

34. New York *Times*, Chicago *Tribune*, July 12, 1952; Eisenhower, pp. 44–46.

35. Interviews, Lloyd Taft (COHP), p. 89; Horace D. Taft (COHP), pp. 70–71; Robert Taft, Jr., to author, March 1970; New York *Times*, July 12, 1952, p. 6. A more dramatic account by Mrs. Lillian Dykstra was sent to her son, Franz, on July 19, 1952. "I don't suppose you know what happened during the minutes after he went into Bob's office after the ballotting and until he came out with Bob. Bobby and Lloyd were trying to keep him [Eisenhower] from fainting. Bob was hunting for some whiskey for him. He [Eisenhower] was hysterical, crying and wringing his hands saying, 'I can't do it, Senator, you've got to stand by me. This is awful.' You can understand some of it — but not from the man who made the Normandy landings . . . Bob kept reassuring him and saying, 'come on, General, we've got to see the press. I'll help you.' Then more fainting and crying. Bobby said that he was afraid that Eisenhower would pass out completely. But I suppose there's hope he will grow up and be able to take it." (Dykstra papers.) All accounts agree that Eisenhower was in fact highly agitated at the time, and C. L. Sulzberger, the *Times* reporter who was with him at the time he was nominated, wrote that Eisenhower was "pale and stunned with his thoughts obviously far, far away." (*A Long Row of Candles: Memoirs and Diaries, 1934–1954* (New York, 1969), p. 772. But

Mrs. Dykstra was not with Taft at these moments, and neither Lloyd nor Robert Taft, Jr., recall a scene as dramatic as the one she described.

36. New York *Times,* Chicago *Tribune,* New York *Herald Tribune,* July 12, 1952; *Time,* July 21, 1952, pp. 18–19.

37. New York *Herald Tribune,* July 12, 1952; Interview, Ben Tate, Jr.

38. Des Moines *Register,* Aug. 1, 1953; Wunder diary, July 12, 1952; Edwin Lahey (COHP), p. 18. For a contrary view, not well supported, see Sulzberger, p. 774.

39. New York *Times,* July 15, 1952.

40. Smith diary, July 10, 11, 1952; Sherman Adams, *First Hand Report: The Story of the Eisenhower Administration* (New York, 1961), pp. 34–36; David, Vol. 1, p. 99; Malcolm Moos, *The Republicans: A History of Their Party* (New York, 1956), p. 483.

41. Smith diary, July 12, 1952; Mazo, pp. 89, 96; Adams, pp. 34–36.

42. Smith diary, July 12, 1952; Smith (COHP), p. 281; Bell, p. 438; Dewey to author, Oct. 20, 1969. RT emphatically said he would not have taken the vice-presidency if it had been offered, RT to Cole Younger, Sept. 18, 1952, box 362, RTP; Washington *Times-Herald,* July 12, 1952.

43. Smith diary, July 12, 1952; Interview, Lloyd Taft (COHP), p. 89; Dykstra to Franz Dykstra, July 12, 19, 1952, Dykstra papers.

44. *Time,* July 21, 1952, p. 60; New York *Times,* July 13, 1952, p. 1.

45. Lloyd Bowers to author, June 29, 1970; Dorothy Rowe, "A Tribute to a Friend," (privately printed, 1964); Interviews, Stanley and Dorothy Rowe, Mrs. Robert Black; Darrah Wunder to author, Feb. 8, 1971; Mrs. I. Jack Martin to author, March 21, 1971. Mrs. Martin was in the car with the Tafts.

CHAPTER 36: FENCING WITH EISENHOWER

1. Interviews, the Robert Blacks, the Stanley Rowes (COHP), p. 63; Diary, Darrah Wunder, July 16, 17, 22, 1952, her possession, Cincinnati.

2. Wunder diary, July 14, 1952; Helen Manning, "A Moose in Canadian Politics," author's possession.

3. Interview, Barbara Taft.

4. Interviews, Horace D. Taft (COHP), pp. 61–62, Lloyd Taft (COHP), p. 42; Richard Rovere, *Affairs of State: The Eisenhower Years* (New York, 1956), pp. 101–111; RT to Elsie Asbury, Aug. 6, 1952, box 1209, RTP, LC.

5. James R. Clark to RT, Aug. 19, Ben Tate to RT, July 22, Hulbert Taft to RT, July 24, 1952, RTP; Karl Butler to J. W. Butler, July 16, 1952, Butler papers, Cornell University; Alexander Smith (COHP), p. 285; *CR,* July 31, 1953, p. 10641.

6. Printed in New York *Times,* Nov. 25, 1959, p. 1; RT drafts, box 422, RTP.

7. RT to Glenn Thompson, Aug. 4, 1952, box 969, RT to Harold Jones, Aug. 1, 1952, box 298, RT to Richard Scandrett, Aug. 29, 1952, box 360, RTP.

8. RT to Homer Ferguson, July 18, box 1215, RT to David Ingalls, July 18, box 456, RT to Edward Martin, Aug. 13, box 1054, RT to Harold Jones, Aug. 1, box 298, RT to Myers Cooper, Sept. 1. box 368, RT to Bernard McCabe, Aug. 22, 1952, box 336, RTP.

9. Dwight D. Eisenhower to RT, July 17, 1952, box 990, RTP; Interviews, John Hollister, Lloyd Taft.

10. Martin to RT, July 25, Aug. 14, 1952, Martin papers, Kensington, Md.; Wunder diary, Aug. 2, 12, 14, 20, 24, 1952.

11. RT to Edmund Turner, Aug. 5, RT to Alexander Abrahams, Aug. 21, box 305, RT to Cole Younger, Aug. 7, 1952, box 1231, RTP; RT to L. Richard Guylay, July 29, 1952, Guylay papers, his possession, New York.

12. RT to Walter Trohan, Sept. 3, box 308, RT to Ray Anderson, Aug. 8, 1952, RTP; Smith diary, Aug. 4, 1952, Princeton University.

13. RT, "Confidential — Memorandum on General Eisenhower," attached to letter from Frank Carlson to RT, Aug. 5, 1952, box 1178, RTP.

14. Ibid.

15. RT to Dirksen, Aug. 6, 1952, Martin papers; RT to Hugh Butler, Aug. 13, box 1054, RT to Wallace Townsend, Aug. 11, 1952, box 294, RTP.

16. RT to Charles H. Anthony, Aug. 25, box 305, RT to General Albert Wedemeyer, Aug. 22, RT to Paul Walter, Sept. 1, 1952, box 1230, RTP.

17. Edwin Lahey (COHP), pp. 5, 129; RT to Henry Fletcher, Sept. 1, box 384, RT to Carroll Reece, Sept. 3, box 387, RT to Frank P. Doherty, Sept. 4, 1952, box 296; Wunder diary, Aug. 28, 1952.

18. RT to Paul Walter, Sept. 1, 1952, box 1230, RTP; Wunder diary, Sept. 8, 9, 10, 1952; New York *Times,* Sept. 8, 1952, p. 1.

19. *Time,* Sept. 8, 1952, p. 21; New York *Times,* Sept. 9, 10, 1952.

20. New York *Times,* Sept. 11, 12, 1952; Interview, John Hollister; Frank Carlson to author, Aug. 4, 1970; Paul Walter memo to author, "Background on the Eisenhower campaign," 1970.

21. New York *Times,* Sept. 13, 1952, p. 1; transcript of press conference, Sept. 12, 1952, box 412, RTP; RT statement, Sept. 12, 1952, Martin papers.

22. Lippmann, Washington *Post,* Sept. 16, 1952; William S. White, *The Taft Story* (New York, 1954), pp. 186–194; New York *Times,* Sept. 14, 1952, p. 1.

23. RT to Ferdinand Mayer, Sept. 3, box 1222, RTP; RT to Sherman Adams, Sept. 19, 1952, box 640, OF 124-E, Eisenhower papers, Eisenhower Library, Abilene; David A. Frier, *Conflict of Interest in the Eisenhower Administration* (Baltimore, 1969), Ch. 3; RT to John Hamilton, Sept. 28, 1952, box 404, RT to Frank P. Doherty, Sept. 27, 1952, box 296, RTP.

24. RT schedule, box 991, RTP; Wunder diary, Oct. 17, Nov. 4, 1952; RT speeches, box 1286–1287, Eisenhower to RT, Oct. 29, box 989, RT to Eisenhower, Oct. 31, box 1214, RT to Harold Jones, Sept. 29, box 298, RT to General Albert Wedemeyer, Oct. 24, 1952, box 364, RTP; New York *Times,* Oct. 1, 14, 16, 1952; *Newsweek,* Oct. 20, 1952, p. 57.

25. RT article, Cincinnati *Times-Star,* Nov. 11, 1952; RT, "Results of Election," box 428, RT to Edward W. Allen, Nov. 13, 1952, box 404, RTP.

26. Angus Campbell, et al. *The American Voter* (New York, 1960), pp. 217, 537–538; Samuel Lubell, *Revolt of the Moderates* (New York, 1956), pp. 288–289; *U. S. News & World Report,* Nov. 14, 1952, pp. 66–67; Richard Rovere, "What Course for the Powerful Mr. Taft?" *New York Times Magazine,* March 22, 1953, p. 9.

27. RT to Guylay, Dec. 1, 1952, box 978, RTP.

28. Richard Rovere, "Taft: Is This the Best We've Got?" *Harper's,* Vol. 196 (April 1948), pp. 289–299.

29. Rovere, "Eisenhower Revisited — A Political Genius? A Brilliant Man?" *New York Times Magazine,* Feb. 7, 1971, p. 14.
30. RT to Kurt P. Pantzer, Nov. 13, 1952, box 323, RTP; Sherman Adams, *First Hand Report: The Story of the Eisenhower Administration* (New York, 1961), p. 45; Interview, Lucius Clay, pp. 50, 78, Eisenhower Library.
31. RT letters to Arthur Summerfield, Dec., 1952, box 1229, RT to Charles E. Wilson, Dec. 23, box 404, RT to J. Bates Gerald, Nov. 28, box 404, RT to Julius Klein, Jan. 1, box 650, RT to Herbert Brownell, Dec. 17, box 404, RT to M. W. Thatcher, Nov. 16, 1952, box 404, RT Cabinet choices, box 428, RTP.
32. RT to Ferdinand Mayer, May 20, 1952, box 1222, RTP; John Hollister, interview, pp. 2–3, Princeton University; RT to George O. Coughlin, Dec. 1, RT to Stephen Debalta, Nov. 13, RT to John Foster Dulles, Dec. 3, 1952, all box 404, RTP. For Dulles on RT, see C. L. Sulzberger, *A Long Row of Candles: Memoirs and Diaries, 1934–1954* (New York, 1969), pp. 746–747.
33. RT to Vernon Romney, Nov. 28, Dec. 2, RT to Ezra Taft Benson, Dec. 3, 1952, all box 404, RTP.
34. RT to Hutchinson, Nov. 28, box 338, RT to Richard S. Wilcox, Dec. 27, box 404, RT to E. Kendall Gilbert, Jan. 27, box 1126, RT to Wallace D. Malone, Dec. 6, 1952, box 404, RTP; Paul Walter memo to author, "The George Humphrey Story," 1970. General Albert Wedemeyer later claimed that Taft in July 1953 said he would have named him secretary of defense. (Wedemeyer to Walter Trohan, Sept. 10, 1953, Walter Trohan papers, Hoover Library, Iowa.)
35. New York *Times,* Dec. 3, 1952; RT statement on Martin Durkin, Dec. 2, 1952, box 1088, RT to Kurt Panzer, Dec. 6, box 323, RT to James P. Selvage, Dec. 23, RT to Walter Hallanan, Dec. 5, RT to Richard Scandrett, Dec. 3, 1952, all box 404, RTP; RT to Paul Stockhammer, Dec. 10, 1952, Blanche O'Berg papers (her possession, D.C.).
36. RT to General Wedemeyer, Dec. 6, RT to Arthur Summerfield, Dec. 2, RT to James Selvage, Dec. 23, 1952, all box 404, RTP.
37. New York *Times,* Nov. 20, 1952, p. 1; RT to John Hartigan, Dec. 6, RT to Francis Case, Dec. 6, 1952, box 404, RTP; Wunder diary, Dec. 4, 1952.
38. RT to Eleanora Sears, Dec. 6, RT to Cecil Highland, Dec. 5, 1952, box 404, RT to General Douglas MacArthur, Jan. 16, 1953, box 1114, RTP.
39. *Time,* Dec. 15, 1952, p. 17; New York *Times,* Dec. 13, 16, 1952, pp. 21, 22.
40. New York *Times,* Dec. 20, 21, 1952, p. 1, section 4, p. 3; *Newsweek,* Dec. 29, 1952, p. 14; Carlson to author, Aug. 4, 1970; Interview, William Knowland; Adams, pp. 23–24.
41. White, p. 216; RT to J. E. Broyhill, Jan. 16, 1953, box 1234, RTP.
42. RT to Mrs. James Shattuck, Dec. 30, 1952, RTP; New York *Times,* Dec. 31, 1952, Jan. 1, 1953, p. 1, p. 40; Wunder diary, Dec. 21, 1952. ("He seems to be anticipating it [the coming session] with delight.").

CHAPTER 37: FIRST MATE

1. New York *Times,* Jan. 4–14, 1953; *Newsweek,* Jan. 19, 26, 1953, pp. 24–25, p. 29.

2. RT to Norman Thomas, Dec. 1, 1952, box 404, RTP, LC; Richard Rovere, *Senator Joe McCarthy* (New York, 1959), p. 188.

3. New York *Times,* Jan. 21, 1953; RT to W. T. Semple, Jan. 15, RT to C. Wayland Brooks, Jan. 17, 1953, box 1234, RTP.

4. On June 12, 1953, two days after stepping down as leader, RT wrote Lyndon Johnson, "It has been the greatest pleasure to serve with you. I do not see how any Majority and Minority leaders could cooperate better than we have done, and it is due very largely to your thoughtfulness, and consideration and good judgment in advance about the people who may be interested or make trouble."

5. On controls, RT to Dwight D. Eisenhower, Jan. 8, Eisenhower to RT, Jan. 9, both box 1083, RTP; RT to Hoey Hennessy, Jan. 24, 1953, I. Jack Martin papers, Kensington, Md.

6. R. Alton Lee, *Truman and Taft-Hartley: A Question of Mandate* (Lexington, 1966), p. 210; New York *Times,* Jan. 27, Feb. 10, March 15, 1953, p. 1; General Wilton Persons to Sherman Adams, Feb. 12, 1953, box 34, Gerald Morgan papers, Eisenhower Library, Abilene; "Mr. Taft Proposes His Taft-Hartley Amendments," *Fortune,* Vol. 47 (Jan. 1953), pp. 63–64; boxes 640–641, OF 124-E, Eisenhower papers, Eisenhower Library; RT to Robert Scott, Dec. 16, 1952, box 404, RT to Theodore Gray, April 7, 1953, RTP.

7. Quote RT to Edmund E. Lincoln, Feb. 26, box 1145, RTP. Also RT to B. E. Hutchinson, March 11, RT to Walter Harnischfeger, Jan. 17, box 1078, RT to Victor E. Spittler, March 13, 1953, box 1078, Joseph Dodge to RT, Feb. 9, 1953, box 519, RTP; RT, "What the GOP Must Do to Win in 1954," *Look,* Vol. 131 (April 21, 1953), p. 42; A. E. Holmans, *United States Fiscal Policy, 1945–1959, Its Contribution to Economic Stability* (London, 1961), p. 202.

8. "Agenda for Conference with Congressional Leaders," March 23, 1953, RT to William Knowland, March 10, 1953, box 1240, RTP; Eisenhower to Clarence Brown, June 12, 1957, OF 99-Z, Eisenhower papers. (Here the President, in talking of an aid to education bill, said "the bill that Senator Taft advocated was far more 'liberal and radical' than anything to which I could ever agree."); William S. White, *The Taft Story* (New York, 1954), pp. 221–222; Sherman Adams, *First Hand Report: The Story of the Eisenhower Administration* (New York, 1961), p. 79; Interview, Lloyd Taft.

9. Quote is RT to Robert L. Byrne, Feb. 26, 1953, Martin papers. Also RT to Bruce Barton, Feb. 26, box 1093, RT to Ernest Palmer, Jr., April 24, box 1136, RT to Samuel Guidiei, May 13, 1953, box 1101, RTP; New York *Times,* Feb. 10, May 12, 1953; Diary, Darrah Wunder, May 15, 1953 (her possession, Cincinnati).

10. Charlie Willis to Sherman Adams, Feb. 17, 1953, GF 121, Eisenhower papers; RT to James R. Clark, April 9, box 1090, RT to George Humphrey, May 23, box 1128, RT to Sherman Adams, June 6, 1953, box 1232, RTP.

11. Adams, pp. 23–24; RT appointment book, 1953, box 1304, RTP; Office of Staff Secretary's files, agenda for White House meetings, Eisenhower

papers; Eisenhower to RT, March 6, 1953, box 1178, RTP; White, pp. 220–221; Wunder diary, March 25, 1953.

12. Prescott Bush, interview, Eisenhower Library, p. 70; Bush to author, Oct. 1, 1969; William H. Taft III to author, March 1971.

13. Eisenhower, *Mandate for Change, 1953–1956* (New York, 1963), pp. 194–195; New York *Times*, Oct. 30, 1954, May 18, 1957.

14. Quotes are RT to Colonel Cecil Highland, Feb. 12, RT to Vernon Romney, March 18, 1953, Martin papers, and Cleveland *Plain Dealer,* March 22, 1953. Also RT to Willis Sargent, Feb. 28, RT to French Jenkins, April 8, 1953, Martin papers; General Wilton Persons to author, Aug. 27, 1970.

15. White, p. 29; Duncan Norton-Taylor, "Robert Taft's Congress," *Fortune,* Vol. 48 (Aug. 1953), p. 136; Noel G. Rapp, "The Political Speaking of Robert A. Taft, 1939 to 1953," doctoral thesis, Purdue, 1955, p. 454; RT to W. Manly Sheppard, April 17, 1953, box 1103, RTP ("I have taken on one speech a month, and I find that even that is too much.").

16. *Congressional Quarterly Almanac,* 1953, p. 92.

17. New York *Times,* Feb. 2, 4, 17, 22, 25, March 1, 4, 5, 8, 1953; *Newsweek,* Feb. 16, March 2, p. 37, pp. 21–23; Adams, pp. 92–93; RT to Vernon Romney, March 18, 1953, Martin papers.

18. For RT on academic freedom pre-1953, RT to Ellsworth B. Foote, June 16, 1951, Martin papers, RT to Francis Klauder, Jan. 4, 1952, box 1335, RTP. For RT in 1953, *Newsweek,* March 23, 1953, p. 29; New York *Times,* March 8, 16, 1953, pp. 44, 1; Richard Rovere, *New Yorker,* Jan. 31, 1953, p. 58; RT Chicago speech, Feb. 25, 1953, box 505, RTP.

19. RT to Victor Emanuel, March 6, 1953, box 1082, RTP. Also to Ethan W. Judd, April 22, 1953, Martin papers.

20. James N. Rosenau, *The Nomination of "Chip" Bohlen* (New York, 1960); New York *Times,* March 16, 22, 24, 1953. General files, GF 9-B, boxes 201–202, Eisenhower papers; Interview, Bohlen, Princeton University, p. 1546; Interview, Lloyd Taft.

21. New York *Times,* March 25, 26, 28, 1953.

22. Adams, p. 95; RT to Don Rowley, April 15, 1953, Blanche O'Berg papers, her possession, D.C.; RT to Glenn O. Young, April 7, 1953, box 1112, RTP; New York *Times,* March 28, 1953, p. 1.

23. New York *Times,* April 5, 26, 1953; Walter Lippmann, Cincinnati *Enquirer,* Aug. 7, 1953, p. 4.

24. Doris Fleeson, Washington *Star,* Feb. 27, Marquis Childs, Washington *Post,* March 20, New York *Herald Tribune,* Feb. 25, 1953; *Time,* April 20, 1953, p. 24; Eisenhower quote, New York *Times,* April 5, 1959; Rovere, "What Course for the Powerful Mr. Taft?" *New York Times Magazine,* March 22, 1953, p. 9.

CHAPTER 38: THE SUDDEN ENDING

1. New York *Times,* April 20, 21, 1953, pp. 14, 1; Robert J. Donovan, *Eisenhower: The Inside Story* (New York, 1956), p. 108; Diary, Darrah Wunder, April 21, 1953 (her possession, Cincinnati), RT to Doris Fleeson, June 6, 1953, box 1120, RTP, LC. ("The hip trouble did develop somewhere

around the time I was in Augusta, although I can't trace any direct connection.")

2. RT to GOP senators, April 16, 1953, box 745, RTP; New York *Times,* April 19, 26, 29, May 6, 1953; Eisenhower to RT, April 24, 1953, box 745, RTP.

3. Sherman Adams, *First Hand Report: The Story of the Eisenhower Administration* (New York, 1961), pp. 20–25; Donovan, pp. 102–108; Dwight D. Eisenhower, *Mandate for Change, 1953–1956* (New York, 1963), pp. 130, 219; Jack Bell, *The Spendid Misery: The Story of the Presidency and Power Politics at Close Range* (Garden City, 1960), p. 20; New York *Times,* May 13, 1953, p. 1.

4. Wunder diary, April 21, 23, 26, 28, 1953; RT medical history file, provided by Dr. Frank Glenn, New York Hospital. (Hereafter noted as RT medical history.)

5. Dr. Johnson McGuire to RT, April 23, 1951, McGuire to Dr. George Calver, April 23, 1951, RTP. (Dr. McGuire told RT, after a general physical, "practically all of your tests were splendid. By practically all, the sedimentation rate suggests a focus of infection, and there is and has been a trace of albumin with occasional casts in the urine for some time." It was then that Dr. McGuire urged Taft to have his tonsils taken out, to eliminate a "background of bursitis and the episode of laryngitis.").

6. For WHT, Henry F. Pringle, *The Life and Times of William Howard Taft* (New York, 1939), Vol. 2, p. 1072; Childs, Washington *Post,* March 20, 1953.

7. RT to Carl Lohmann, May 23, box 1114, RT to Bernard Baruch, May 22, 1953, box 1114, RTP; Wunder diary, May 23, 1953; New York *Times,* May 21, 26, 1953, pp. 33, 31; RT medical history.

8. RT speech, May 26, 1953, box 1288, RTP; William S. White, *The Taft Story* (New York, 1954), pp. 139–142.

9. RT to William Loeb, June 8, 1953, box 1148, RTP; New York *Times,* June 6, 1953, p. 3; *Time,* June 15, 1953, p. 21.

10. RT to Herbert Hoover, June 5, 1953, box l–k/136, Hoover Library, Iowa; RT to Ray Henle, June 6, 1953, box 1093, RT to William H. Taft, June 5, 1953, RTP.

11. Dr. McGuire to author, June 1970; William R. Dickens to Dr. Frank Glenn, June 15, 1953, Glenn papers (his possession, New York); RT to William H. Taft, June 5, 1953, RTP.

12. RT medical history; Dr. McGuire to Pauline Isaacson, in Isaacson, "Robert Alphonso Taft: An Assessment of a Persuader," doctoral thesis, Minnesota, 1956, p. 506; "Post-mortem record," Dept. of Pathology, New York Hospital, by Dr. John G. Kidd, Autopsy #15147; Jhan and June Robbins, "The Great Untold Story of Senator Taft's Eight Weeks to Live," *This Week* (Jan. 17, 1954), p. 12.

13. Dr. Charles M. Barrett to author, Feb. 1972; RT to Horace D. Taft, June 5, 1953, Horace D. Taft papers (his possession, New Haven); Wunder diary, May 28, June 3, 1953.

14. Wunder diary, June 5–10, 1953; Interview, Dr. Stanhope Bayne-Jones (COHP), p. 41; New York *Times,* June 4, 5, 1953, pp. 7, 1.

15. Dr. Glenn memo, June 10, 1953, Glenn papers.

16. New York *Times,* June 11, 1953, p. 1; RT scribbled statement, Blanche O'Berg papers (her possession, D.C.); White, pp. 258–261; *Time,* June 22, 1953, p. 18.
17. Interview, William Knowland; Eugene Millikin to Pauline Isaacson, April 7, 1955, in Isaacson, p. 508; Leverett Saltonstall to author, Oct. 6, 1969; Bell, p. 32.
18. New York *Times,* Aug. 6, 1953, p. 13, Jan. 23, 1954, p. 15; Last Will and Testament of Robert A. Taft, June 12, 1953, Probate Court, Hamilton County, Ohio.
19. Dr. Glenn memos, June 12–16, 1953, Glenn papers; Interview, Dr. Glenn; New York *Times,* June 14, 1953, p. 44; Hoover memo, June 16, 1953, box l-k/136, Hoover papers; RT to William Chadbourne, June 27, 1953, box 1120, RTP. Thomas E. Dewey was informed by John Franklin Carter on June 25 that Taft had cancer and would "die within two or three months." Carter to Dewey, personal correspondence, Thomas Dewey papers, University of Rochester.
20. RT to Kurt F. Pantzer, July 1, 1953, Martin papers; RT to Homer Bone, July 1, RT to Katharine Kennedy Brown, July 1, 1953, both box 1142, RTP.
21. RT to Eleanora Sears, June 19, 1953, RTP; RT to Victor Emanuel, June 19, 1953, Glenn papers; RT to Mrs. Preston Davie, June 29, box 1120, RT to Stanley Rowe, June 29, 1953, RTP.
22. General Leonard D. Heaton to Victor Emanuel, June 23, 1953, Glenn papers; New York *Times,* June 26, July 2, 1953, pp. 3, 1; RT to James Selvage, July 1, 1953, box 1142, RTP.
23. General Wilton Persons to author, Aug. 27, 1970; RT to Eisenhower, July 3, 1953, RTP; Interview, Marjorie Hein; Alexander Smith to Charles P. Taft, 2nd, Aug. 24, 1953, box 136, Smith papers, Princeton.
24. Wunder diary, June 23, 27, 1953; White, p. 11.
25. Interview, Horace D. Taft; RT to Dr. Glenn, June 25, 1953, Glenn papers. Wunder diary, June 30, 1953.
26. RT to Herbert Brownell, July 3, 1953, Martin papers; Interview, Lewis Strauss; RT appointment book, box 1304, RTP.
27. RT appointment book, 1953, box 1304, RTP; New York *Times,* July 5, 1953, p. 1; folder, "From Senator's Desk," RTP.
28. Dr. Glenn memo, July 8, 1953, Glenn papers; Interview, Dr. Glenn.
29. Chronology, Dr. Glenn, Glenn papers; Dr. Bayne-Jones (COHP), p. 46; Interview, John Hollister; Dr. John L. McClenehan to author, Nov. 3, 1969; Wunder diary, July 18, 25, 1953; Eisenhower, p. 221.
30. Wunder diary, July 27–31, 1953; Interview, Dr. McGuire; Robbins; Dr. Glenn to author, April 14, 1971; New York *Times,* July 31, Aug. 1, 1953, both p. 1.
31. Wunder diary, July 31, 1953.
32. Alexander Smith diary, Aug. 5, 1953, Smith papers; New York *Times,* Aug. 2–5, 1953, p. 1; *CR,* Aug 3, 1953, pp. 10638–10646, 10984–10989.
33. Personal observation.
34. "Post-Mortem Record," Department of Pathology, New York Hospital, by Dr. John G. Kidd, Autopsy #15147, Glenn papers; Department of Health, New York City, Certificate of Death, Nov. 5, 1953, copy in TSHP; Inter-

view, Dr. Glenn; Dr. Claude Forkner to RT, Jr., Oct. 9, 1953, Glenn papers; New York *Times*, Oct. 3, 1953, p. 25; for Hoover's comment, Cleveland *Plain Dealer*, Aug. 1, 1953.

35. John F. Kennedy, *Profiles in Courage* (New York, 1955); New York *Times*, May 1, 1957. Taft, Kennedy said, was the top choice for the Hall of Fame by the forty-five senators who sent in nominations — and among the top ten in a poll of 150 scholars. Arthur Krock said he had urged Kennedy to include Taft in his profiles in courage, only to be told during the 1960 campaign, "one of the things I wish you had not persuaded me to do was to put Taft in the *Profiles*." (Krock, *Memoirs: 60 Years on the Firing Line* [New York, 1968], p. 355.) For the memorial, see New York *Times*, April 15, 1959, p. 1.

36. Hugh Scott, *Come to the Party* (Englewood Cliffs, N.J., 1968), pp. 133–134; William V. Shannon, "Vacuum in the Senate," New Republic, Vol. 129 (Aug. 10, 1953), pp. 9–10; "Nation Loses in Death of Taft," *Christian Century*, Vol. 70 (Aug. 12, 1953), p. 70; New York *Times*, July 19, 1953, section 4, p. 3; *Congressional Quarterly Almanac*, 1953, p. 87, 1954, pp. 37–39.

37. Cincinnati *Enquirer*, Aug. 1, 1959; Interview, Ralph Holsinger.

38. A few of many articles dealing with Taft are Allan C. Brownfield, "A Volunteer Army," *Roll Call: The Newspaper of Capitol Hill*, April 17, 1969; Stewart Alsop, *Newsweek*, May 31, 1971, p. 88; Richard Rovere, *New Yorker*, July 10, 1970, p. 72; Nicholas von Hoffman, Washington *Post*, May 19, 1971; Richard Strout, *Christian Science Monitor*, May ?, 1971; Murray Rothbard, New York *Times*, Feb. 9, 1971; William V. Shannon, Louisville *Courier Journal*, April 6, 1971; Emmet John Hughes, *Saturday Review*, Oct. 17, 1970, p. 26; and Russell Kirk, "Keeping Taft's Memory Alive," *National Review*, Vol. 18, (Dec. 13, 1966), p. 1276. See also the many reviews of William S. White's, *The Taft Story* (New York, 1954), April–June, 1954; the comments about Taft and Martha at the time of her death in October 1958; and the statements re RT at the dedication of the bell tower, April 15, 1959.

Index

Index